FREQUENTLY USED SYMBOLS AND ABBREVIATIONS (CONTINUED)

N_n	Net Proceeds from the Sale of New Common Stock
N_p	Net Proceeds from the Sale of the Preferred Stock
NAFTA	North American Free Trade Agreement
NCAI	Net Current Asset Investment
NFAI	Net Fixed Asset Investment
NOPAT	Net operating profits after taxes
NPV	Net Present Value
O	Order Cost Per Order
OC	Operating Cycle
OCF	Operating Cash Flow
P	Price (value) of asset
P_0	Value of Common Stock
$PBDT_t$	Profits Before Depreciation and Taxes in year t
PD	Preferred Stock Dividend
P/E	Price/Earnings Ratio
PI	Profitability Index
PMT	Amount of Payment
Pr	Probability
PV	Present Value
Q	• Order Quantity in Units • Sales Quantity in Units
r	• Actual, Expected ($\bar{r}$), or Required Rate of Return • Annual Rate of Interest • Cost of Capital
r^*	Real Rate of Interest
r_a	Weighted Average Cost of Capital
r_d	• Required Return on Bond • Before-Tax Cost of Debt
r_i	After-Tax Cost of Debt
r_j	Required Return on Asset j
r_m	• Market Return • Return on the Market Portfolio of Assets
r_p	• Cost of Preferred Stock • Portfolio Return
r_r	Cost of Retained Earnings
r_s	• Required Return on Common Stock • Cost of Common Stock Equity
R_F	Risk-Free Rate of Interest
RADR	Risk-Adjusted Discount Rate
RE	Ratio of Exchange
ROA	Return on Total Assets
ROE	Return on Common Equity
S	• Usage in Units per Period • Sales in Dollars
SML	Security Market Line
t	Time
T	Firm's Marginal Tax Rate
TVW	Theoretical Value of a Warrant
V	• Value of an Asset or Firm • Venture Capital
V_C	Value of Entire Company
V_D	Value of All Debt
V_P	Value of Preferred Stock
V_S	Value of Common Stock
VC	Variable Operating Cost per Unit
w_j	• Proportion of the Portfolio's Total Dollar Value Represented by Asset j • Proportion of a Specific Source of Financing j in the Firm's Capital Structure
WACC	Weighted Average Cost of Capital
WTO	World Trade Organization
YTM	Yield to Maturity
ZBA	Zero Balance Account
σ	Standard Deviation
Σ	Summation Sign

Principles of

Managerial Finance

The Prentice Hall Series in Finance

Adelman/Marks
Entrepreneurial Finance

Andersen
Global Derivatives: A Strategic Risk Management Perspective

Bekaert/Hodrick
International Financial Management

Berk/DeMarzo
*Corporate Finance**

Berk/DeMarzo
*Corporate Finance: The Core**

Berk/DeMarzo/Harford
*Fundamentals of Corporate Finance**

Boakes
Reading and Understanding the Financial Times

Brooks
*Financial Management: Core Concepts**

Copeland/Weston/Shastri
Financial Theory and Corporate Policy

Dorfman/Cather
Introduction to Risk Management and Insurance

Eiteman/Stonehill/Moffett
Multinational Business Finance

Fabozzi
Bond Markets: Analysis and Strategies

Fabozzi/Modigliani
Capital Markets: Institutions and Instruments

Fabozzi/Modigliani/Jones/Ferri
Foundations of Financial Markets and Institutions

Finkler
Financial Management for Public, Health, and Not-for-Profit Organizations

Frasca
Personal Finance

Gitman/Joehnk/Smart
*Fundamentals of Investing**

Gitman/Zutter
*Principles of Managerial Finance**

Gitman/Zutter
*Principles of Managerial Finance—Brief Edition**

Goldsmith
Consumer Economics: Issues and Behaviors

Haugen
The Inefficient Stock Market: What Pays Off and Why

Haugen
The New Finance: Overreaction, Complexity, and Uniqueness

Holden
Excel Modeling and Estimation in Corporate Finance

Holden
Excel Modeling and Estimation in Investments

Hughes/MacDonald
International Banking: Text and Cases

Hull
Fundamentals of Futures and Options Markets

Hull
Options, Futures, and Other Derivatives

Hull
Risk Management and Financial Institutions

Keown
*Personal Finance: Turning Money into Wealth**

Keown/Martin/Petty
*Foundations of Finance: The Logic and Practice of Financial Management**

Kim/Nofsinger
Corporate Governance

Madura
*Personal Finance**

Marthinsen
Risk Takers: Uses and Abuses of Financial Derivatives

McDonald
Derivatives Markets

McDonald
Fundamentals of Derivatives Markets

Mishkin/Eakins
Financial Markets and Institutions

Moffett/Stonehill/Eiteman
Fundamentals of Multinational Finance

Nofsinger
Psychology of Investing

Ormiston/Fraser
Understanding Financial Statements

Pennacchi
Theory of Asset Pricing

Rejda
Principles of Risk Management and Insurance

Seiler
Performing Financial Studies: A Methodological Cookbook

Shapiro
Capital Budgeting and Investment Analysis

Sharpe/Alexander/Bailey
Investments

Solnik/McLeavey
Global Investments

Stretcher/Michael
Cases in Financial Management

Titman/Keown/Martin
*Financial Management: Principles and Applications**

Titman/Martin
Valuation: The Art and Science of Corporate Investment Decisions

Van Horne
Financial Management and Policy

Van Horne/Wachowicz
Fundamentals of Financial Management

Weston/Mitchel/Mulherin
Takeovers, Restructuring, and Corporate Governance

PEARSON ALWAYS LEARNING

Lawrence J. Gitman • Chad J. Zutter

Principles of Managerial Finance

Thirteenth Edition

Custom Edition for Portland State University

Taken from:
Principles of Managerial Finance, Thirteenth Edition
by Lawrence J. Gitman and Chad J. Zutter

Cover Art: Courtesy of Photodisc, EyeWire/Getty Images, brandXpictures

Taken from:

Principles of Managerial Finance, Thirteenth Edition
by Lawrence J. Gitman and Chad J. Zutter

Published by Prentice Hall
Upper Saddle River, New Jersey 07458

This special edition published in cooperation with Pearson Learning Solutions.

Pearson Learning Solutions, 501 Boylston Street, Suite 900, Boston, MA 02116
A Pearson Education Company
www.pearsoned.com

Printed in the United States of America

2 3 4 5 6 7 8 9 10 V092 16 15 14 13 12

000200010271292726

CT

ISBN 10: 1-256-51576-0
ISBN 13: 978-1-256-51576-0

Dedicated to the memory
of my mother, Dr. Edith Gitman,
who instilled in me the importance
of education and hard work.

LJG

Dedicated to my wonderful wife,
Heidi Zutter, who unconditionally
supports my every endeavor.

CJZ

Our Proven Teaching and Learning System

Users of *Principles of Managerial Finance* have praised the effectiveness of the book's Teaching and Learning System, which they hail as one of its hallmarks. The system, driven by a set of carefully developed learning goals, has been retained and polished in this thirteenth edition. The "walkthrough" on the pages that follow illustrates and describes the key elements of the Teaching and Learning System. We encourage both students and instructors to acquaint themselves at the start of the semester with the many useful features the book offers.

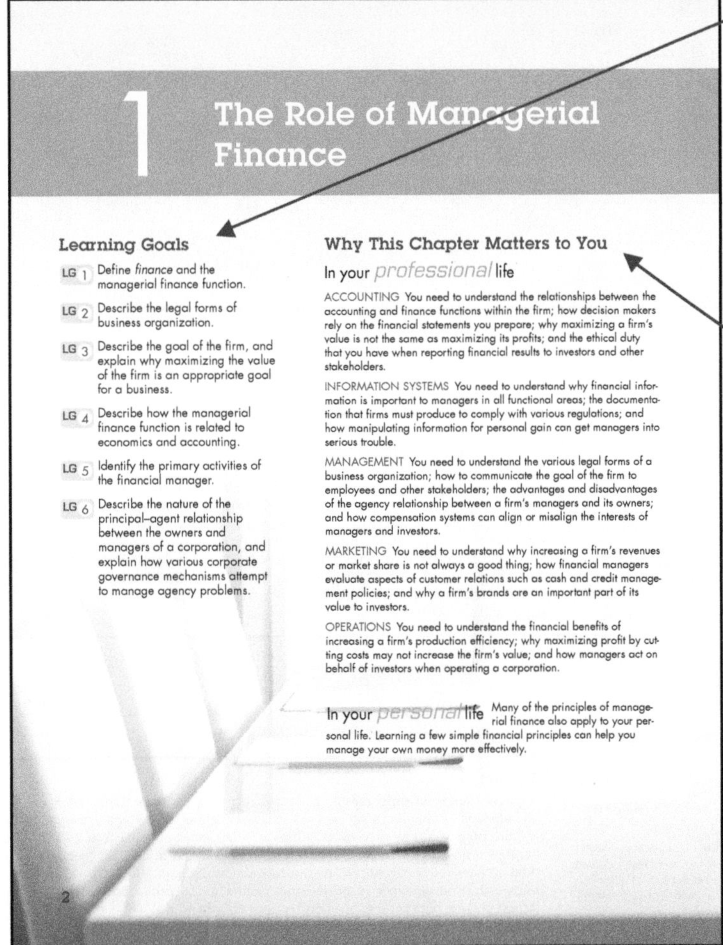

1 The Role of Managerial Finance

Learning Goals

LG 1 Define *finance* and the managerial finance function.

LG 2 Describe the legal forms of business organization.

LG 3 Describe the goal of the firm, and explain why maximizing the value of the firm is an appropriate goal for a business.

LG 4 Describe how the managerial finance function is related to economics and accounting.

LG 5 Identify the primary activities of the financial manager.

LG 6 Describe the nature of the principal–agent relationship between the owners and managers of a corporation, and explain how various corporate governance mechanisms attempt to manage agency problems.

Why This Chapter Matters to You

In your *professional* life

ACCOUNTING You need to understand the relationships between the accounting and finance functions within the firm; how decision makers rely on the financial statements you prepare; why maximizing a firm's value is not the same as maximizing its profits; and the ethical duty that you have when reporting financial results to investors and other stakeholders.

INFORMATION SYSTEMS You need to understand why financial information is important to managers in all functional areas; the documentation that firms must produce to comply with various regulations; and how manipulating information for personal gain can get managers into serious trouble.

MANAGEMENT You need to understand the various legal forms of a business organization; how to communicate the goal of the firm to employees and other stakeholders; the advantages and disadvantages of the agency relationship between a firm's managers and its owners; and how compensation systems can align or misalign the interests of managers and investors.

MARKETING You need to understand why increasing a firm's revenues or market share is not always a good thing; how financial managers evaluate aspects of customer relations such as cash and credit management policies; and why a firm's brands are an important part of its value to investors.

OPERATIONS You need to understand the financial benefits of increasing a firm's production efficiency; why maximizing profit by cutting costs may not increase the firm's value; and how managers act on behalf of investors when operating a corporation.

In your *personal* life Many of the principles of managerial finance also apply to your personal life. Learning a few simple financial principles can help you manage your own money more effectively.

2

Six **Learning Goals** at the start of the chapter highlight the most important concepts and techniques in the chapter. Students are reminded to think about the learning goals while working through the chapter by strategically placed **learning goal icons.**

Every chapter opens with a feature, titled **Why This Chapter Matters to You**, that helps motivate student interest by highlighting both professional and personal benefits from achieving the chapter learning goals.

Its first part, **In Your Professional Life,** discusses the intersection of the finance topics covered in the chapter with the concerns of other major business disciplines. It encourages students majoring in accounting, information systems, management, marketing, and operations to appreciate how financial acumen will help them achieve their professional goals.

The second part, **In Your Personal Life,** identifies topics in the chapter that will have particular application to personal finance. This feature also helps students appreciate the tasks performed in a business setting by pointing out that the tasks are not necessarily different from those that are relevant in their personal lives.

Each chapter begins with a short **opening vignette** that describes a recent real-company event related to the chapter topic. These stories raise interest in the chapter by demonstrating its relevance in the business world.

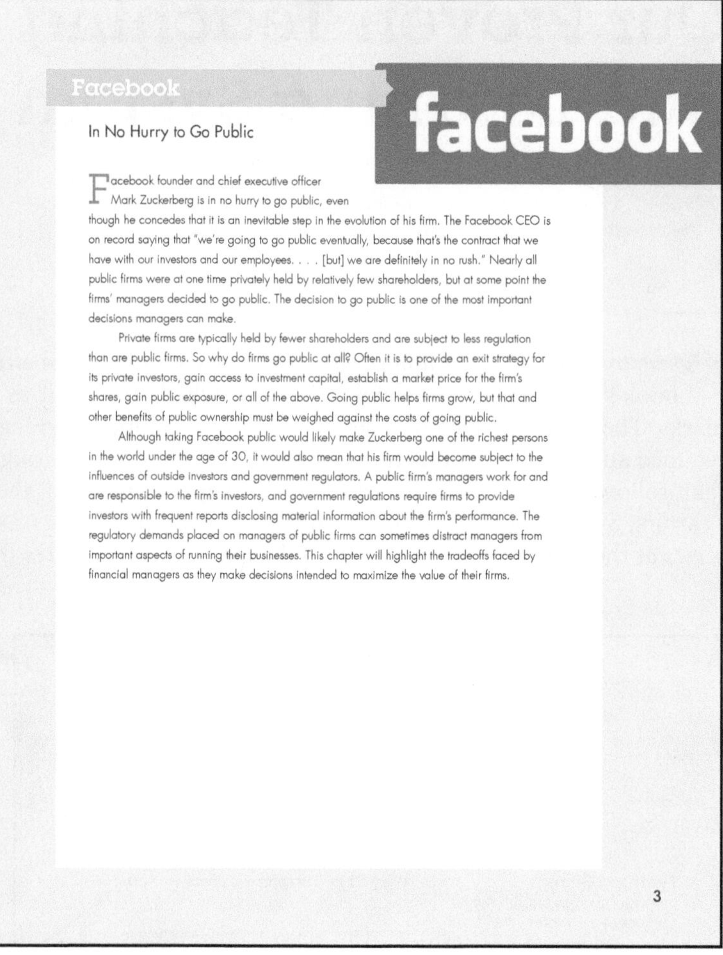

Facebook

facebook

In No Hurry to Go Public

Facebook founder and chief executive officer Mark Zuckerberg is in no hurry to go public, even though he concedes that it is an inevitable step in the evolution of his firm. The Facebook CEO is on record saying that "we're going to go public eventually, because that's the contract that we have with our investors and our employees. . . . [but] we are definitely in no rush." Nearly all public firms were at one time privately held by relatively few shareholders, but at some point the firms' managers decided to go public. The decision to go public is one of the most important decisions managers can make.

Private firms are typically held by fewer shareholders and are subject to less regulation than are public firms. So why do firms go public at all? Often it is to provide an exit strategy for its private investors, gain access to investment capital, establish a market price for the firm's shares, gain public exposure, or all of the above. Going public helps firms grow, but that and other benefits of public ownership must be weighed against the costs of going public.

Although taking Facebook public would likely make Zuckerberg one of the richest persons in the world under the age of 30, it would also mean that his firm would become subject to the influences of outside investors and government regulators. A public firm's managers work for and are responsible to the firm's investors, and government regulations require firms to provide investors with frequent reports disclosing material information about the firm's performance. The regulatory demands placed on managers of public firms can sometimes distract managers from important aspects of running their businesses. This chapter will highlight the tradeoffs faced by financial managers as they make decisions intended to maximize the value of their firms.

3

Learning goal icons tie chapter content to the learning goals and appear next to related text sections and again in the chapter-end summary, end-of-chapter homework materials, and supplements such as the *Study Guide, Test Item File,* and MyFinanceLab.

LG 1 LG 2 **1.1 Finance and Business**

The field of finance is broad and dynamic. Finance influences everything that firms do, from hiring personnel to building factories to launching new advertising campaigns. Because there are important financial dimensions to almost any aspect of business, there are many financially oriented career opportunities for those who understand the basic principles of finance described in this textbook. Even if you do not see yourself pursuing a career in finance, you'll find that an understanding of a few key ideas in finance will help make you a smarter consumer and a wiser investor with your own money.

For help in study and review, boldfaced **key terms** and their definitions appear in the margin where they are first introduced. These terms are also boldfaced in the book's index and appear in the end-of-book glossary.

Corporations

corporation
An entity created by law.

stockholders
The owners of a corporation, whose ownership, or *equity,* takes the form of either common stock or preferred stock.

A **corporation** is an entity created by law. A corporation has the legal powers of an individual in that it can sue and be sued, make and be party to contracts, and acquire property in its own name. Although only about 20 percent of all U.S. businesses are incorporated, the largest businesses nearly always are; corporations account for nearly 90 percent of total business revenues. Although corporations engage in all types of businesses, manufacturing firms account for the largest portion of corporate business receipts and net profits. Table 1.1 lists the key strengths and weaknesses of corporations.

Matter of fact

Problems with P/E Valuation

The P/E multiple approach is a fast and easy way to estimate a stock's value. However, P/E ratios vary widely over time. In 1980, the average stock had a P/E ratio below 9, but by the year 2000, the ratio had risen above 40. Therefore, analysts using the P/E approach in the 1980s would have come up with much lower estimates of value than analysts using the model 20 years later. In other words, when using this approach to estimate stock values, the estimate will depend more on whether stock market valuations generally are high or low rather than on whether the particular company is doing well or not.

Matter of Fact boxes provide interesting empirical facts that add background and depth to the material covered in the chapter.

In more depth

To read about *Deriving the Constant-Growth Model*, go to www.myfinancelab.com

myfinancelab

$$P_0 = \frac{D_0 \times (1+g)^1}{(1+r_s)^1} + \frac{D_0 \times (1+g)^2}{(1+r_s)^2} + \cdots + \frac{D_0 \times (1+g)^\infty}{(1+r_s)^\infty} \quad (7.3)$$

If we simplify Equation 7.3, it can be rewritten as:

In More Depth boxes point students to additional material, available on MyFinanceLab, intended to further highlight a particular topic for students who want to explore a topic in greater detail.

Example 6.3 ▸ The nominal interest rates on a number of classes of long-term securities in May 2010 were as follows:

Security	Nominal interest rate
U.S. Treasury bonds (average)	3.30%
Corporate bonds (by risk ratings):	
High quality (Aaa–Aa)	3.95
Medium quality (A–Baa)	4.98
Speculative (Ba–C)	8.97

Because the U.S. Treasury bond would represent the risk-free, long-term security, we can calculate the risk premium of the other securities by subtracting the risk-free rate, 3.30%, from each nominal rate (yield):

Security	Risk premium
Corporate bonds (by ratings):	
High quality (Aaa–Aa)	3.95% − 3.30% = 0.65%
Medium quality (A–Baa)	4.98 − 3.30 = 1.68
Speculative (Ba–C)	8.97 − 3.30 = 5.67

Examples are an important component of the books learning system. Numbered and clearly set off from the text, they provide an immediate and concrete demonstration of how to apply financial concepts, tools, and techniques.

Some Examples demonstrate time-value-of-money techniques. These examples often show the use of time lines, equations, financial calculators, and spreadsheets (with cell formulas).

Personal Finance Example 5.7 ▸ Fran Abrams wishes to determine how much money she will have at the end of 5 years if she chooses annuity A, the ordinary annuity. She will deposit $1,000 annually, at the *end of each* of the next 5 years, into a savings account paying 7% annual interest. This situation is depicted on the following time line:

Time line for future value of an ordinary annuity ($1,000 end-of-year deposit, earning 7%, at the end of 5 years)

Personal Finance Examples demonstrate how students can apply managerial finance concepts, tools, and techniques to their personal financial decisions.

The Equation for Present Value

The present value of a future amount can be found mathematically by solving Equation 5.4 for PV. In other words, the present value, PV, of some future amount, FV_n, to be received n periods from now, assuming an interest rate (or opportunity cost) of r, is calculated as follows:

$$PV = \frac{FV_n}{(1+r)^n} \quad (5.7)$$

Note the similarity between this general equation for present value and the equation in the preceding example (Equation 5.6). Let's use this equation in an example.

Key equations appear in green boxes throughout the text to help readers identify the most important mathematical relationships. The variables used in these equations are, for convenience, printed on the *front endpapers* of the book.

Review Questions appear at the end of each major text section. These questions challenge readers to stop and test their understanding of key concepts, tools, techniques, and practices before moving on to the next section.

→ **REVIEW QUESTIONS**

5–14 What effect does compounding interest more frequently than annually have on (**a**) future value and (**b**) the *effective annual rate (EAR)?* Why?

5–15 How does the future value of a deposit subject to continuous compounding compare to the value obtained by annual compounding?

5–16 Differentiate between a *nominal annual rate* and an *effective annual rate (EAR)*. Define *annual percentage rate (APR)* and *annual percentage yield (APY)*.

In Practice boxes offer insights into important topics in managerial finance through the experiences of real companies, both large and small. There are three categories of In Practice boxes:

Focus on Ethics boxes in every chapter help readers understand and appreciate important ethical issues and problems related to managerial finance.

Focus on Practice boxes take a corporate focus that relates a business event or situation to a specific financial concept or technique.

Global Focus boxes look specifically at the managerial finance experiences of international companies.

All three types of In Practice boxes end with one or more *critical thinking questions* to help readers broaden the lesson from the content of the box.

focus on ETHICS

If It Seems Too Good to Be True Then It Probably Is

in practice For many years, investors around the world clamored to invest with Bernard Madoff. Those fortunate enough to invest with "Bernie" might not have understood his secret trading system, but they were happy with the double-digit returns that they earned. Madoff was well connected, having been the chairman of the board of directors of fraud. Madoff's hedge fund, Ascot Partners, turned out to be a giant Ponzi scheme.

Over the years, suspicions were raised about Madoff. Madoff generated high returns year after year, seemingly with very little risk. Madoff credited his complex trading strategy for his investment performance, but other investors employed similar strate- Madoff's arrest indicated that investors' accounts contained over $64 billion, in aggregate. Many investors pursued claims based on the balance reported in these statements. However, a recent court ruling permits claims up to the difference between the amount an investor deposited with Madoff and the amount they withdrew. The judge also ruled that investors who managed to with-

focus on PRACTICE

Limits on Payback Analysis

in practice In tough economic times, the standard for a payback period is often reduced. Chief information officers (CIOs) are apt to reject projects with payback periods of more than 2 years. "We start with payback period," says Ron Fijalkowski, CIO at Strategic Distribution, Inc., in Bensalem, Pennsylvania. "For sure, if the payback period is over 36 months, it's not going to get approved. But our rule of thumb is we'd like to see 24 months. And if it's close to 12, it's probably a no-brainer."

While easy to compute and easy to understand, the payback periods simplicity brings with it some drawbacks. "Payback gives you an answer that tells you a bit about the beginning stage of a project, but it doesn't tell you much about the full lifetime of the project," says Chris Gardner, a cofounder of in Barrington, Illinois. "The simplicity of computing payback may encourage sloppiness, especially the failure to include all costs associated with an investment, such as training, maintenance, and hardware upgrade costs," says Douglas Emond, senior vice president and chief technology officer at Eastern Bank in Lynn, Massachusetts. For example, he says, "you may be bringing in a hot new technology, but uh-oh, after implementation you realize that you need a dot-net guru in-house, and you don't have one."

But the payback method's emphasis on the short term has a special appeal for IT managers. "That's because the history of IT projects that take longer than 3 years is disastrous," says Gardner. Indeed, Ian Campbell, chief research officer at Nucleus Research, Inc., in Wellesley, Massachusetts, says payback period is an absolutely essen- even more important than discounted cash flow (NPV and IRR)—because it spotlights the risks inherent in lengthy IT projects. "It should be a hard and fast rule to never take an IT project with a payback period greater than 3 years, unless it's an infrastructure project you can't do without," Campbell says.

Whatever the weaknesses of the payback period method of evaluating capital projects, the simplicity of the method does allow it to be used in conjunction with other, more sophisticated measures. It can be used to screen potential projects and winnow them down to the few that merit more careful scrutiny with, for example, net present value (NPV).

► ***In your view, if the payback period method is used in conjunction with the NPV method, should it be used before or after the NPV evaluation?***

GLOBAL focus

An International Flavor to Risk Reduction

in practice Earlier in this chapter (see Table 8.5 on page 318), we learned that from 1900 through 2009 the U.S. stock market produced an average annual nominal return of 9.3 percent, but that return was associated with a relatively high standard deviation: 20.4 percent per year. Could U.S. investors have done better by diversifying globally? The answer is a qualified yes. Elroy Dimson, Paul Marsh, and Mike Staunton calculated the historical returns on a portfolio that included U.S. stocks as well as stocks from 18 other countries. This diversified portfolio produced returns that were not quite as high as the U.S. average, just 8.6 percent per year. However, the globally diversified portfolio was also less volatile, with an annual standard deviation of 17.8 percent. Dividing the standard deviation by the annual return produces a coefficient of variation for the globally diversified portfolio of 2.07, slightly lower than the 2.10 coefficient of variation reported for U.S. stocks in Table 8.5.

► ***International mutual funds do not include any domestic assets whereas global mutual funds include both foreign and domestic assets. How might this difference affect their correlation with U.S. equity mutual funds?***

Source: Elroy Dimson, Paul Marsh, and Mike Staunton, *Triumph of the Optimists: 101 Years of Global Investment Returns* (Princeton University Press, 2002).

Summary

FOCUS ON VALUE

Time value of money is an important tool that financial managers and other market participants use to assess the effects of proposed actions. Because firms have long lives and some decisions affect their long-term cash flows, the effective application of time-value-of-money techniques is extremely important. These techniques enable financial managers to evaluate cash flows occurring at different times so as to combine, compare, and evaluate them and link them to the firm's **overall goal of share price maximization.** It will become clear in Chapters 6 and 7 that the application of time value techniques is a key part of the value determination process needed to make intelligent value-creating decisions.

REVIEW OF LEARNING GOALS

LG 1 **Discuss the role of time value in finance, the use of computational tools, and the basic patterns of cash flow.** Financial managers and investors use time-value-of-money techniques when assessing the value of expected cash flow streams. Alternatives can be assessed by either compounding to find future value or discounting to find present value. Financial managers rely primarily on present value techniques. Financial calculators, electronic spreadsheets, and financial tables can streamline the application of time value techniques. The cash flow of a firm can be described by its pattern—single amount, annuity, or mixed stream.

The end-of-chapter **Summary** consists of two sections. The first section, **Focus on Value**, explains how the chapter's content relates to the firm's goal of maximizing owner wealth. The feature helps reinforce understanding of the link between the financial manager's actions and share value.

The second part of the Summary, the **Review of Learning Goals**, restates each learning goal and summarizes the key material that was presented to support mastery of the goal. This review provides students with an opportunity to reconcile what they have learned with the learning goal and to confirm their understanding before moving forward.

Opener-in-Review

In the chapter opener you learned that it costs Eli Lilly close to $1 billion to bring a new drug to market, and by the time all of the R&D and clinical trials are completed, Lilly may have fewer than 10 years left to sell the drug under patent protection.

Assume that the $1 billion cost of bringing a new drug to market is spread out evenly over 10 years, and then 10 years remain for Lilly to recover their investment. How much cash would a new drug have to generate in the last 10 years to justify the $1 billion spent in the first 10 years? Assume that Lilly uses a required rate of return of 10%.

Self-Test Problems (Solutions in Appendix)

LG 2 LG 5 **ST5–1** **Future values for various compounding frequencies** Delia Martin has $10,000 that she can deposit in any of three savings accounts for a 3-year period. Bank A compounds interest on an annual basis, bank B compounds interest twice each year, and bank C compounds interest each quarter. All three banks have a stated annual interest rate of 4%.

a. What amount would Ms. Martin have at the end of the third year, leaving all interest paid on deposit, in each bank?

b. What *effective annual rate (EAR)* would she earn in each of the banks?

c. On the basis of your findings in parts **a** and **b**, which bank should Ms. Martin deal with? Why?

d. If a fourth bank (bank D), also with a 4% stated interest rate, compounds interest continuously, how much would Ms. Martin have at the end of the third year? Does this alternative change your recommendation in part **c**? Explain why or why not.

An **Opener-in-Review** question at the end of each chapter revisits the opening vignette and asks students to apply a lesson from the chapter to that business situation.

Self-Test Problems, keyed to the learning goals, give readers an opportunity to strengthen their understanding of topics by doing a sample problem. For reinforcement, solutions to the Self-Test Problems appear in the appendix at the back of the book.

Warm-Up Exercises All problems are available in myfinancelab.

LG 2 **E5–1** Assume a firm makes a $2,500 deposit into its money market account. If this account is currently paying 0.7% (yes, that's right, less than 1%!), what will the account balance be after 1 year?

LG 2 LG 5 **E5–2** If Bob and Judy combine their savings of $1,260 and $975, respectively, and deposit this amount into an account that pays 2% annual interest, compounded monthly, what will the account balance be after 4 years?

Warm-Up Exercises follow the Self-Test Problems. These short, numerical exercises give students practice in applying tools and techniques presented in the chapter.

Problems All problems are available in MyFinanceLab.

LG 1 P5-1 **Using a time line** The financial manager at Starbuck Industries is considering an investment that requires an initial outlay of $25,000 and is expected to result in cash inflows of $3,000 at the end of year 1, $6,000 at the end of years 2 and 3, $10,000 at the end of year 4, $8,000 at the end of year 5, and $7,000 at the end of year 6.

a. Draw and label a time line depicting the cash flows associated with Starbuck Industries' proposed investment.

b. Use arrows to demonstrate, on the time line in part **a,** how compounding to find future value can be used to measure all cash flows at the end of year 6.

LG 5 P4-19 **Integrative—Pro forma statements** Red Queen Restaurants wishes to prepare financial plans. Use the financial statements on page 155 and the other information provided below to prepare the financial plans.

Comprehensive **Problems**, keyed to the learning goals, are longer and more complex than the Warm-Up Exercises. In this section, instructors will find multiple problems that address the important concepts, tools, and techniques in the chapter.

A short descriptor identifies the essential concept or technique of the problem. Problems labeled as **Integrative** tie together related topics.

Personal Finance Problem

LG 2 P5-7 **Time value** You can deposit $10,000 into an account paying 9% annual interest either today or exactly 10 years from today. How much better off will you be at the end of 40 years if you decide to make the initial deposit today rather than 10 years from today?

LG 6 P5-62 **ETHICS PROBLEM** A manager at a "Check Into Cash" business (see *Focus on Ethics* box on page 192) defends his business practice as simply "charging what the market will bear." "After all," says the manager, "we don't force people to come in the door." How would you respond to this ethical defense of the payday-advance business?

Personal Finance Problems specifically relate to personal finance situations and Personal Finance Examples in each chapter. These problems will help students see how they can apply the tools and techniques of managerial finance in managing their own finances.

The last item in the chapter Problems is an **Ethics Problem.** The ethics problem gives students another opportunity to think about and apply ethics principles to managerial financial situations.

All exercises and problems are available in MyFinanceLab.

Spreadsheet Exercise

You are interested in purchasing the common stock of Azure Corporation. The firm recently paid a dividend of $3 per share. It expects its earnings—and hence its dividends—to grow at a rate of 7% for the foreseeable future. Currently, similar-risk stocks have required returns of 10%.

Every chapter includes a **Spreadsheet Exercise.** This exercise gives students an opportunity to use Excel® software to create one or more spreadsheets with which to analyze a financial problem. The spreadsheet to be created often is modeled on a table or Excel screenshot located in the chapter. Students can access working versions of the Excel screenshots in MyFinanceLab.

Integrative Case 1

Merit Enterprise Corp.

Sara Lehn, chief financial officer of Merit Enterprise Corp., was reviewing her presentation one last time before her upcoming meeting with the board of directors. Merit's business had been brisk for the last two years, and the company's CEO was pushing for a dramatic expansion of Merit's production capacity. Executing the CEO's plans would require $4 billion in capital in addition to $2 billion in excess cash that the firm had built up. Sara's immediate task was to brief the board on options for raising the needed $4 billion.

Unlike most companies its size, Merit had maintained its status as a private company, financing its growth by reinvesting profits and, when necessary, borrowing from banks. Whether Merit could follow that same strategy to raise the $4 billion necessary to expand at the pace envisioned by the firm's CEO was uncertain, though it seemed unlikely to Sara. She had identified two options for the board to consider:

An **Integrative Case** at the end of each part of the book challenges students to use what they have learned over the course of several chapters.

Additional chapter resources, such as Chapter Cases, Group Exercises, Critical Thinking Problems, and numerous online resources, intended to provide further means for student learning and assessment are available in MyFinanceLab at www.myfinancelab.com.

Brief Contents

Contents

Part 2 Financial Tools 55

4 Cash Flow and Financial Planning
page 113

Apple—Investors Want Apple to Take a Bite Out of its Cash Hoard page 114

5 Time Value of Money
page 159

Part 3 Valuation of Securities 219

Part 4 Risk and the Required Rate of Return 307

Part 5 Long-Term Investment Decisions 387

12
Risk and Refinements in Capital Budgeting

About the Authors

Lawrence J. Gitman is an emeritus professor of finance at San Diego State University. Dr. Gitman has published more than 50 articles in scholarly journals as well as textbooks covering undergraduate- and graduate-level corporate finance, investments, personal finance, and introduction to business. Dr. Gitman is past president of the Academy of Financial Services, the San Diego Chapter of the Financial Executives Institute, the Midwest Finance Association, and the FMA National Honor Society. Dr. Gitman served as Vice-President of Financial Education of the Financial Management Association, as a director of the San Diego MIT Enterprise Forum, and on the CFP® Board of Standards. He received his B.S.I.M. from Purdue University, his M.B.A. from the University of Dayton, and his Ph.D. from the University of Cincinnati. He and his wife have two children and live in La Jolla, California, where he is an avid bicyclist, having twice competed in the coast-to-coast Race Across America.

Chad J. Zutter is an associate professor of finance at the University of Pittsburgh. Dr. Zutter recently won the Jensen Prize for the best paper published in the *Journal of Financial Economics* and has also won a best paper award from the *Journal of Corporate Finance*. His research has a practical, applied focus and has been the subject of feature stories in, among other prominent outlets, *The Economist* and *CFO Magazine*. His papers have been cited in arguments before the U.S. Supreme Court and in consultation with companies such as Google and Intel. Dr. Zutter has also won teaching awards at Indiana University and the University of Pittsburgh. He received his B.B.A. from the University of Texas at Arlington and his Ph.D. from Indiana University. He and his wife have four children and live in Pittsburgh, Pennsylvania. Prior to his career in academics, Dr. Zutter was a submariner in the U.S. Navy.

Preface

The desire to write *Principles of Managerial Finance* came from the experience of teaching the introductory managerial finance course. Those who have taught the introductory course many times can appreciate the difficulties that some students have absorbing and applying financial concepts. Students want a book that speaks to them in plain English and a book that ties concepts to reality. These students want more than just description—they also want demonstration of concepts, tools, and techniques. This book is written with the needs of students in mind, and it effectively delivers the resources that students need to succeed in the introductory finance course.

Courses and students have changed since the first edition of this book, but the goals of the text have not changed. The conversational tone and wide use of examples set off in the text still characterize *Principles of Managerial Finance.* Building on those strengths, 13 editions, numerous translations, and well over half a million U.S. users, *Principles* has evolved based on feedback from both instructors and students, from adopters, nonadopters, and practitioners.

In this edition, Chad Zutter of the University of Pittsburgh joins the author team. A recent recipient of the Jensen Prize for the best paper published in the *Journal of Financial Economics*, Chad brings a fresh perspective to *Principles.* Larry and Chad have worked together to incorporate contemporary thinking and pedagogy with the classic topics that Gitman users have come to expect.

NEW TO THE THIRTEENTH EDITION

As we made plans to publish the thirteenth edition, we carefully assessed market feedback about content changes that would better meet the needs of instructors teaching the course.

The chapter sequence is similar to the prior edition, but there are some noteworthy changes. The thirteenth edition contains 19 chapters divided into eight parts. Each part is introduced by a brief overview, which is intended to give students an advance sense for the collective value of the chapters included in the part.

In Part 1, a new Chapter 2 expands coverage of financial markets and institutions, with particular emphasis on the recent financial crisis and recession. This chapter not only explores the root causes and consequences of the financial crisis, but it also discusses the changing regulatory landscape within which financial institutions and markets function.

Part 2 contains three chapters in the same order in which they appeared in the twelfth edition. These chapters focus on basic financial skills such as financial statement analysis, cash flow analysis, and time-value-of-money calculations.

Part 3 focuses on bond and stock valuation. We moved these two chapters forward in this edition, just ahead of the risk and return chapter, to provide students with exposure to basic material on bonds and stocks that is easier to grasp than some of the more theoretical concepts in the next part.

Part 4 contains the risk and return chapter as well as the chapter on the cost of capital, which we have moved forward to lead into Part 5 on capital budgeting. We also moved up the chapter on the cost of capital so that it follows directly on the heels of the risk and return material. We believe that this makes the subsequent discussion of capital budgeting topics more meaningful because students will already have an idea of where a project "hurdle rate" comes from.

Part 5 contains three chapters on various capital budgeting topics. A change from the last edition here is that we present capital budgeting methods before the chapter on capital budgeting cash flows.

Parts 6, 7, and 8 contain the same seven chapters in the same order that appeared in the latter part of the twelfth edition. These chapters cover topics such as capital structure, payout policy, working capital management, derivatives, mergers, and international finance. Details about the revisions made to these chapters appear below.

Although the text content is sequential, instructors can assign almost any chapter as a self-contained unit, enabling instructors to customize the text to various teaching strategies and course lengths.

A number of new topics have been added at appropriate places, and new features appear in each chapter. The Matter of Fact feature provides additional detail and interesting empirical facts that help students understand the practical implications of financial concepts. For students who want to explore particular topics more deeply on their own, the In More Depth feature, available on MyFinanceLab, offers a guide for further study. In addition, as the detailed list shows, the chapter-opening vignettes and In Practice boxes have been replaced or heavily revised: For example, three-quarters of the chapter-opening vignettes are new, focusing on companies such as Facebook, Abercrombie & Fitch, and Best Buy that have student appeal, and more than half of the Focus on Ethics boxes are new. Also new to this edition are Opener-in-Review questions, which appear at the end of each chapter.

The following chapter-by-chapter list details several of the notable content changes in the thirteenth edition.

Chapter 1 The Role of Managerial Finance

- Revised opening vignette discusses Facebook's possible IPO.
- New Focus on Practice box discusses professional certifications in finance.
- New Matter of Fact feature provides statistics on the number of businesses and the revenues they generate by legal form of organization.
- Sections on financial markets and business taxes have been moved to a new, expanded Chapter 2.
- Coverage of the difference between cash flow and profit as part of the discussion surrounding the goal of the firm has been revised.
- New Focus on Ethics box highlights the ethical issues that Google faced during its expansion to China.
- Coverage of agency issues has been substantially revised, and a new Matter of Fact feature provides data on the link between pay and performance for several prominent firms.

Chapter 2 The Financial Market Environment

- This new chapter focuses on financial markets and institutions as well as the recent financial crisis.
- New opening vignette traces JP Morgan's performance during the crisis.

- New section provides coverage of commercial banks, investment banks, and the shadow banking system.
- New Focus on Ethics box is related to the Martha Stewart insider trading scandal.
- New section has been added on causes and consequences of financial crisis.
- Coverage of regulatory issues has been updated.

Chapter 3 Financial Statements and Ratio Analysis

- New opening vignette has been added (financial results, Abercrombie & Fitch).
- New Global Focus box covers International Financial Reporting Standards (IFRS).
- New Focus on Ethics box describes ethical issues related to corporate earnings reports.
- New table shows values of key ratios for several prominent firms and the related industry averages. Five related Matter of Fact features explain why certain ratio values vary systematically across industries.

Chapter 4 Cash Flow and Financial Planning

- New opening vignette highlights Apple's huge cash hoard.
- New Matter of Fact box illustrates where Apple's cash flow comes from.
- New Focus on Practice box dissects a recent earnings report by Cisco Systems to explore the firm's underlying cash generation.
- Discussion of alternative cash flow measures has been revised.
- New In More Depth feature (on MyFinanceLab) discusses the value of using regression analysis to estimate fixed costs.

Chapter 5 Time Value of Money

- New In More Depth feature (on MyFinanceLab) shows how the firm Royalty Pharma makes lump-sum payments to acquire royalty streams from other firms.
- References to financial tables and interest rate factors have been eliminated.
- Coverage of calculations using Excel has been expanded.
- New Matter of Fact feature describes a Kansas truck driver's choice to take a lump-sum payment rather than an annuity due after winning the lottery.
- The Focus on Ethics box on subprime loans has been revised.

Chapter 6 Interest Rates and Bond Valuation

- Opening vignette (U.S. Treasury, public debt) has been updated.
- New Matter of Fact feature highlights a 2008 U.S. Treasury auction in which bill returns briefly turned negative.
- Discussion of factors that influence interest rates, particularly inflation, has been substantially revised.
- New In More Depth feature (on MyFinanceLab) points students to an animation on the Web that illustrates historical yield curve behavior.
- Major revisions have been made to coverage of the term structure of interest rates.
- Focus on Ethics box on the performance of rating agencies during the financial crisis has been revised.

Chapter 7 Stock Valuation

- New opening vignette has been added about A123 Systems Inc., a company that uses nanotechnology to make more powerful batteries for electric cars.
- New In More Depth feature (on MyFinanceLab) discusses the U.S. bankruptcy process.
- New Matter of Fact box describes how assets are divided in bankruptcy.
- New In More Depth feature (on MyFinanceLab) discusses the hierarchy of the efficient market hypothesis.
- New In More Depth feature (on MyFinanceLab) illustrates the derivation of the constant-growth model.
- New Matter of Fact box describes how P/E ratios fluctuate over time.

Chapter 8 Risk and Return

- New opening vignette has been added about a mutual fund that ranked near the bottom and then at the top of all mutual funds in consecutive years.
- New Focus on Ethics box features Bernie Madoff.
- New numerical examples have data drawn from the real world.
- Historical returns on U.S. stocks, bonds, and bills have been updated.
- Discussion of investor risk preferences has been substantially revised.
- New Matter of Fact feature discusses Nicholas Taleb's *Black Swan*.
- New Matter of Fact box compares historical returns on large stocks versus small stocks.
- New Global Focus box features data on international diversification.

Chapter 9 The Cost of Capital

- New opening vignette focuses on General Electric.
- New Focus on Ethics box deals with Merck's handling of Vioxx.
- New In More Depth feature (on MyFinanceLab) discusses changes in the weighted average cost of capital.
- New Matter of Fact box presents a more comprehensive cost of retained earnings.
- New Focus on Practice feature focuses on WACC's susceptibility to the 2008 financial crisis and the 2009 great recession.
- New integrative case for Part 4 has been added.

Chapter 10 Capital Budgeting Techniques

- New opening vignette describes techniques used by Genco Resources to evaluate a proposal to expand its mining operations.
- New In More Depth feature (on MyFinanceLab) discusses the Accounting Rate of Return method.
- Substantially revised opening section discusses the capital budgeting process.
- Coverage of profitability index approach has been expanded.
- Coverage of economic value added has been expanded.
- New Matter of Fact box provides evidence on the extent to which firms use different capital budgeting methods.

Chapter 11 Capital Budgeting Cash Flows

- Opening vignette (project costs at ExxonMobil) has been updated.
- New Matter of Fact box provides statistics on foreign direct investment in the United States.
- Global Focus box (foreign direct investment in China) has been updated.
- Focus on Ethics box (accuracy of cash flow estimates) has been updated.
- Two new Integrative Problems have been added.

Chapter 12 Risk and Refinements in Capital Budgeting

- New opening vignette discusses BP oil spill.
- New In More Depth feature (on MyFinanceLab) directs students to a Crystal Ball simulation of a mining investment on the Internet.
- New Matter of Fact box provides evidence on the frequency with which firms make adjustments to their investment analysis to account for currency risk.
- New Focus on Ethics box discusses the implications of the BP oil spill on the firm's cost of capital.

THE THIRTEENTH EDITION

Like the previous editions, the thirteenth edition incorporates a proven learning system, which integrates pedagogy with concepts and practical applications. It concentrates on the knowledge that is needed to make keen financial decisions in an increasingly competitive business environment. The strong pedagogy and generous use of examples—including personal finance examples—make the text an easily accessible resource for in-class learning or out-of-class learning, such as online courses and self-study programs.

ORGANIZATION

The text's organization conceptually links the firm's actions and its value, as determined in the financial market. Each major decision area is presented in terms of both risk and return factors and their potential impact on owners' wealth. A Focus on Value element at the end of each chapter helps reinforce the student's understanding of the link between the financial manager's actions and the firm's share value.

In organizing each chapter, we have adhered to a managerial decision-making perspective, relating decisions to the firm's overall goal of wealth maximization. Once a particular concept has been developed, its application is illustrated by an example—a hallmark feature of this book. These examples demonstrate, and solidify in the student's thought, financial decision-making considerations and their consequences.

INTERNATIONAL CONSIDERATIONS

We live in a world where international considerations cannot be divorced from the study of business in general and finance in particular. As in prior editions, discussions of international dimensions of chapter topics are integrated throughout the book. International material is integrated into learning goals and end-of-chapter materials. In addition, for those who want to spend more time addressing the topic, a separate chapter on international managerial finance concludes the book.

PERSONAL FINANCE LINKAGES

The thirteenth edition contains several features designed to help students see the value of applying financial principles and techniques in their personal lives. At the start of each chapter, the feature titled *Why This Chapter Matters to You* helps motivate student interest by discussing how the topic of the chapter relates to the concerns of other major business disciplines and to personal finance. Within the chapter, Personal Finance Examples explicitly link the concepts, tools, and techniques of each chapter to personal finance applications. Throughout the homework material, the book provides numerous personal finance problems. The purpose of these personal finance materials is to demonstrate to students the usefulness of managerial finance knowledge in both business and personal financial dealings.

ETHICAL ISSUES

The need for ethics in business remains as important as ever. Students need to understand the ethical issues that financial managers face as they attempt to maximize shareholder value and to solve business problems. Thus, every chapter includes an In Practice box that focuses on current ethical issues.

HOMEWORK OPPORTUNITIES

Of course, practice is essential for students' learning of managerial finance concepts, tools, and techniques. To meet that need, the book offers a rich and varied menu of homework assignments: short, numerical Warm-Up Exercises; a comprehensive set of Problems, including more than one problem for each important concept or technique and personal finance problems; an Ethics Problem for each chapter; a Spreadsheet Exercise; and, at the end of each part of the book, an Integrative Case. In addition, the end-of-chapter problems are available in algorithmic form in myfinancelab. These materials (see pages xi through xii for detailed descriptions) offer students solid learning opportunities, and they offer instructors opportunities to expand and enrich the classroom environment.

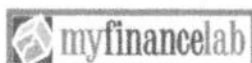

MyFinanceLab

This fully integrated online homework system gives students the hands-on practice and tutorial help they need to learn finance efficiently. There are ample opportunities for online practice and assessment that is automatically graded in MyFinanceLab (www.myfinancelab.com).

Chapter Cases with automatically graded assessment are also provided in MyFinanceLab. These cases have students apply the concepts they have learned to a more complex and realistic situation. These cases help strengthen practical application of financial tools and techniques.

MyFinanceLab also has **Group Exercises** where students can work together in the context of an ongoing company. Each group creates a company and follows it through the various managerial finance topics and business activities presented in the textbook.

MyFinanceLab provides **Critical Thinking Problems**, which require students to apply the various finance concepts and managerial techniques presented in the textbook. These are rigorous problems that are designed to test a student's ability to understand the financial management situation, apply the necessary managerial finance concepts, and find the value-maximizing solution.

An online glossary, digital flashcards, financial calculator tutorials, videos, Spreadsheet Use examples from the text in Excel, and numerous other premium resources are available in MyFinanceLab.

From classroom to boardroom, the thirteenth edition of *Principles of Managerial Finance* can help users get to where they want to be. We believe that it is the best edition yet—more relevant, more accurate, and more effective than ever. We hope you agree that *Principles of Managerial Finance,* Thirteenth Edition, is the most effective introductory managerial finance text for your students.

Lawrence J. Gitman
La Jolla, California

Chad J. Zutter
Pittsburgh, Pennsylvania

Supplements to the Thirteenth Edition

The *Principles of Managerial Finance* Teaching and Learning System includes a variety of useful supplements for teachers and for students.

TEACHING TOOLS FOR INSTRUCTORS

The key teaching tools available to instructors are the *Instructor's Manual,* testing materials, and *PowerPoint Lecture Presentations.*

Instructor's Manual *Revised by Thomas Krueger, Texas A&M University–Kingsville and accuracy-checked by Gordon Stringer, University of Colorado, Colorado Springs.* This comprehensive resource pulls together the teaching tools so that instructors can use the textbook easily and effectively in the classroom. Each chapter provides an overview of key topics and detailed answers and solutions to all review questions, Opener-in-Review questions, Warm-Up Exercises, end-of-chapter problems, and chapter cases, plus suggested answers to all critical thinking questions in chapter boxes, Ethics Problems, and Group Exercises. At the end of the manual are practice quizzes and solutions. The complete *Instructor's Manual,* including Spreadsheet Exercises, is available online at the Instructor's Resource Center (www.pearsonhighered.com/irc).

Test Item File *Revised by Shannon Donovan, Bridgewater State University.* Thoroughly revised to accommodate changes in the text, the *Test Item File* consists of a mix of true/false, multiple-choice, and essay questions. Each test question includes identifiers for type of question, skill tested by learning goal, and key topic tested plus, where appropriate, the formula(s) or equation(s) used in deriving the answer.

The *Test Item File* is also available in *Test Generator Software (TestGen)* for either Windows or Macintosh. The *Test Item File* and *TestGen* are available online at the Instructor's Resource Center (www.pearsonhighered.com/irc).

PowerPoint Lecture Presentation *Revised by Thomas Boulton, Miami University.* This presentation combines lecture notes with all of the art from the textbook. The *PowerPoint Lecture Presentation* is available online at the Instructor's Resource Center (www.pearsonhighered.com/irc).

LEARNING TOOLS FOR STUDENTS

Beyond the book itself, students have access to valuable resources, such as MyFinanceLab and the *Study Guide,* that if taken advantage of can help ensure their success.

myfinancelab

MyFinanceLab MyFinanceLab opens the door to a powerful Web-based diagnostic testing and tutorial system designed specifically for the Gitman/Zutter, *Principles of Managerial Finance* textbooks. With MyFinanceLab, instructors can create, edit, and assign online homework and test and track all student work in the online gradebook. MyFinanceLab allows students to take practice tests correlated to the textbook and receive a customized study plan based on the test results.

Most end-of-chapter problems are available in MyFinanceLab, and because the problems have algorithmically generated values, no student will have the same homework as another; there is an unlimited opportunity for practice and testing. Students get the help they need, when they need it, from the robust tutorial options, including "View an Example" and "Help Me Solve This," which breaks the problem into its steps and links to the relevant textbook page.

This fully integrated online homework system gives students the hands-on practice and tutorial help they need to learn finance efficiently. There are ample opportunities for online practice and assessment that is automatically graded in MyFinanceLab (www.myfinancelab.com).

Advanced reporting features in MyFinanceLab also allow you to easily report on AACSB accreditation and assessment in just a few clicks.

Chapter Cases with automatically graded assessment are also provided in MyFinanceLab. These cases have students apply the concepts they have learned to a more complex and realistic situation. These cases help strengthen practical application of financial tools and techniques.

MyFinanceLab also has Group Exercises where students can work together in the context of an ongoing company. Each group creates a company and follows it through the various managerial finance topics and business activities presented in the textbook.

MyFinanceLab provides Critical Thinking Problems, which require students to apply the various finance concepts and managerial techniques presented in the textbook. These are rigorous problems that are designed to test a student's ability to understand the financial management situation, apply the necessary managerial finance concepts, and find the value-maximizing solution.

An online glossary, digital flashcards, financial calculator tutorials, videos, Spreadsheet Use examples from the text in Excel, and numerous other premium resources are available in MyFinanceLab.

Students can use MyFinanceLab with no instructor intervention. However, to take advantage of the full capabilities of MyFinanceLab, including assigning homework and tracking student progress in the automated gradebook, instructors will want to set up their class. To view a demo of MyFinanceLab or to request instructor access go to www.myfinancelab.com.

Study Guide *Revised by Shannon Donovan, Bridgewater State University.* The *Study Guide* is an integral component of the *Principles of Managerial Finance* Teaching and Learning System. It offers many tools for studying finance. Each chapter contains the following features: chapter summary enumerated by learning goals; topical chapter outline, also broken down by learning goals for quick review; sample problem solutions; study tips and a full sample exam with the answers at the end of the chapter. A financial dictionary of key terms is located at the end of the *Study Guide,* along with an appendix with tips on using financial calculators.

Acknowledgments

TO OUR COLLEAGUES, FRIENDS, AND FAMILY

Prentice Hall sought the advice of a great many excellent reviewers, all of whom influenced the revisions of this book. The following individuals provided extremely thoughtful and useful comments for the preparation of the thirteenth edition:

Johnny C. Chan, *Western Kentucky University*
Kent Cofoid, *Seminole Community College*
Shannon Donovan, *Bridgewater State University*
Suk Hun Lee, *Loyola University Chicago*
Hao Lin, *California State University–Sacramento*
Larry Lynch, *Roanoke College*
Alvin Nishimoto, *Hawaii Pacific University*
William Sawatski, *Southwestern College*
Steven R. Scheff, *Florida Gulf Coast University*
Michael Schellenger, *University of Wisconsin, Oshkosh*
Gordon M. Stringer, *University of Colorado–Colorado Springs*
Barry Uze, *University of Southwestern Louisiana*
Sam Veraldi, *Duke University*
John Zietlow, *Malone University*

Our special thanks go to the following individuals who analyzed the manuscript in previous editions:

Saul W. Adelman
M. Fall Ainina
Gary A. Anderson
Ronald F. Anderson
James M. Andre
Gene L. Andrusco
Antonio Apap
David A. Arbeit
Allen Arkins
Saul H. Auslander
Peter W. Bacon
Richard E. Ball
Thomas Bankston
Alexander Barges
Charles Barngrover
Michael Becker
Omar Benkato
Scott Besley
Douglas S. Bible
Charles W. Blackwell
Russell L. Block
Calvin M. Boardman
Paul Bolster
Robert J. Bondi
Jeffrey A. Born
Jerry D. Boswell
Denis O. Boudreaux
Kenneth J. Boudreaux
Wayne Boyet
Ron Braswell
Christopher Brown
William Brunsen
Samuel B. Bulmash
Francis E. Canda
Omer Carey
Patrick A. Casabona
Robert Chatfield
K. C. Chen
Roger G. Clarke
Terrence M. Clauretie
Mark Cockalingam
Boyd D. Collier
Thomas Cook
Maurice P. Corrigan
Mike Cudd
Donnie L. Daniel
Prabir Datta
Joel J. Dauten
Lee E. Davis
Irv DeGraw
Richard F. DeMong
Peter A. DeVito
James P. D'Mello
R. Gordon Dippel
Carleton Donchess
Thomas W. Donohue
Vincent R. Driscoll
Betty A. Driver
Lorna Dotts
David R. Durst
Dwayne O. Eberhardt
Ronald L. Ehresman
Ted Ellis
F. Barney English
Greg Filbeck
Ross A. Flaherty
Rich Fortin
Timothy J. Gallagher
George W. Gallinger
Sharon Garrison
Gerald D. Gay
Deborah Giarusso

R. H. Gilmer
Anthony J. Giovino
Michael Giuliano
Philip W. Glasgo
Jeffrey W. Glazer
Joel Gold
Ron B. Goldfarb
Dennis W. Goodwin
David A. Gordon
J. Charles Granicz
C. Ramon Griffin
Reynolds Griffith
Arthur Guarino
Lewell F. Gunter
Melvin W. Harju
John E. Harper
Phil Harrington
George F. Harris
George T. Harris
John D. Harris
Mary Hartman
R. Stevenson Hawkey
Roger G. Hehman
Harvey Heinowitz
Glenn Henderson
Russell H. Hereth
Kathleen T. Hevert
J. Lawrence Hexter
Douglas A. Hibbert
Roger P. Hill
Linda C. Hittle
James Hoban
Hugh A. Hobson
Keith Howe
Kenneth M. Huggins
Jerry G. Hunt
Mahmood Islam
James F. Jackson
Stanley Jacobs
Dale W. Janowsky
Jeannette R. Jesinger
Nalina Jeypalan
Timothy E. Johnson
Roger Juchau
Ashok K. Kapoor
Daniel J. Kaufman Jr.
Joseph K. Kiely
Terrance E. Kingston
Raj K. Kohli
Thomas M. Krueger
Lawrence Kryzanowski
Harry R. Kuniansky
Richard E. La Near
William R. Lane
James Larsen
Rick LeCompte
B. E. Lee
Scott Lee
Michael A. Lenarcic
A. Joseph Lerro
Thomas J. Liesz
Alan Lines
Christopher K. Ma
James C. Ma
Dilip B. Madan
Judy Maese
James Mallet
Inayat Mangla
Bala Maniam
Timothy A. Manuel
Brian Maris
Daniel S. Marrone
William H. Marsh
John F. Marshall
Linda J. Martin
Stanley A. Martin
Charles E. Maxwell
Timothy Hoyt McCaughey
Lee McClain
Jay Meiselman
Vincent A. Mercurio
Joseph Messina
John B. Mitchell
Daniel F. Mohan
Charles Mohundro
Gene P. Morris
Edward A. Moses
Tarun K. Mukherjee
William T. Murphy
Randy Myers
Lance Nail
Donald A. Nast
Vivian F. Nazar
G. Newbould
Charles Ngassam
Gary Noreiko
Dennis T. Officer
Kathleen J. Oldfather
Kathleen F. Oppenheimer
Richard M. Osborne
Jerome S. Osteryoung
Prasad Padmanabahn
Roger R. Palmer
Don B. Panton
John Park
Ronda S. Paul
Bruce C. Payne
Gerald W. Perritt
Gladys E. Perry
Stanley Piascik
Gregory Pierce
Mary L. Piotrowski
D. Anthony Plath
Jerry B. Poe
Gerald A. Pogue
Suzanne Polley
Ronald S. Pretekin
Fran Quinn
Rich Ravichandran
David Rayone
Walter J. Reinhart
Jack H. Reubens
Benedicte Reyes
William B. Riley Jr.
Ron Rizzuto
Gayle A. Russell
Patricia A. Ryan
Murray Sabrin
Kanwal S. Sachedeva
R. Daniel Sadlier
Hadi Salavitabar
Gary Sanger
Mukunthan Santhanakrishnan
William L. Sartoris
Michael Schinski
Tom Schmidt
Carl J. Schwendiman
Carl Schweser
Jim Scott
John W. Settle
Richard A. Shick
A. M. Sibley
Sandeep Singh
Surendra S. Singhvi
Stacy Sirmans
Barry D. Smith
Gerald Smolen
Ira Smolowitz
Jean Snavely
Joseph V. Stanford
John A. Stocker
Lester B. Strickler
Elizabeth Strock
Donald H. Stuhlman
Sankar Sundarrajan
Philip R. Swensen
S. Tabriztchi
John C. Talbott
Gary Tallman
Harry Tamule
Richard W. Taylor

Rolf K. Tedefalk
Richard Teweles
Kenneth J. Thygerson
Robert D. Tollen
Emery A. Trahan
Pieter A. Vandenberg
Nikhil P. Varaiya
Oscar Varela
Kenneth J. Venuto
James A. Verbrugge
Ronald P. Volpe
John M. Wachowicz Jr.
Faye (Hefei) Wang
William H. Weber III
Herbert Weinraub
Jonathan B. Welch
Grant J. Wells
Larry R. White
Peter Wichert
C. Don Wiggins
Howard A. Williams
Richard E. Williams
Glenn A. Wilt Jr.
Bernard J. Winger
Tony R. Wingler
I. R. Woods
John C. Woods
Robert J. Wright
Richard H. Yanow
Seung J. Yoon
Charles W. Young
Philip J. Young
Joe W. Zeman
J. Kenton Zumwalt
Tom Zwirlein

A special thanks goes to Thomas J. Boulton of Miami University for his work on the Focus on Ethics boxes and to Alan Wolk of the University of Georgia for accuracy checking the quantitative content in the textbook. We are pleased by and proud of all their efforts.

No textbook would be complete, let alone usable, if not for the accompanying instructor and student supplements. We are grateful to the following individuals for their work creating, revising, and accuracy checking all of the valuable instructor and student resources that support the use of *Principles:* Thomas Krueger of Texas A&M University–Kingsville for updating the *Instructor's Manual,* Gordon Stringer of University of Colorado–Colorado Springs for accuracy checking the *Instructor's Manual*, Thomas J. Boulton of Miami University for revising the *PowerPoint Lecture Presentation*, and Shannon Donovan of Bridgewater State University for revising the *Test Item File* and the *Study Guide.*

A hearty round of applause also goes to the publishing team assembled by Prentice Hall—including Donna Battista, Tessa O'Brien, Kerri McQueen, Melissa Pellerano, Nancy Freihofer, Alison Eusden, Nicole Sackin, Miguel Leonarte, and others who worked on the book—for the inspiration and the perspiration that define teamwork. Also, special thanks to the formidable Prentice Hall sales force in finance, whose ongoing efforts keep the business fun!

Finally, and most important, many thanks to our families for patiently providing support, understanding, and good humor throughout the revision process. To them we will be forever grateful.

Lawrence J. Gitman
La Jolla, California

Chad J. Zutter
Pittsburgh, Pennsylvania

To the Student

Because you have a good many options for getting your assigned reading materials we appreciate your choosing this textbook as the best means for learning in your managerial finance course. You should not be disappointed. In writing this edition, we have been mindful of students and careful to maintain a student focus.

The learning system in this book has been used by many of your predecessors in the course and has been proven effective. It integrates various learning tools with the concepts, tools, techniques, and practical applications you will need to learn about managerial finance. We have worked hard to present in a clear and interesting way the information you will need. This book is loaded with features designed to motivate your study of finance and to help you learn the course material. Go to pages vii–xii ("Our Proven Teaching and Learning System") for an overview and walkthrough of those features. Notice that the book includes Personal Finance Examples (and related end-of-chapter problems) that show how to apply managerial finance concepts and tools to your personal financial life.

About some of the specific features: First, pay attention to the learning goals, which will help you focus on what material you need to learn, where you can find it in the chapter, and whether you've mastered it by the end of the chapter.

Second, avoid the temptation to rush past the Review Questions at the end of each major text section. Pausing briefly to test your understanding of the section content will help you cement your understanding. Give yourself an honest assessment. If some details are fuzzy, go back (even briefly) and review anything that still seems unclear.

Third, look for (or make) opportunities to talk with classmates or friends about what you are reading and learning in the course. Talking about the concepts and techniques of finance demonstrates how much you've learned, uncovers things you haven't yet understood fully, and gives you valuable practice for class and (eventually) the business world. While you're talking, don't neglect to discuss the issues raised in the Focus on Ethics boxes, which look at some of the opportunities to do right (or not) that business people face.

MyFinanceLab opens the door to a powerful Web-based diagnostic testing and tutorial system designed for this text. MyFinanceLab allows you to take practice exams correlated to the textbook and receive a customized study plan based on your results. The assignment Problems in MyFinanceLab, based on the even-numbered end-of-chapter Problems in the book, have algorithmically generated values. Thus, the numbers in your homework will differ from those of your classmates, and there is an unlimited opportunity for practice and testing. You can get the help you need, when you need it, from the robust tutorial options, including "View an Example" and "Help Me Solve This," which breaks the problem into steps and links to the relevant textbook page.

Given today's rapidly changing technology, who knows what might be available next? We are striving to keep pace with your needs and interests, and would like to hear your ideas for improving the teaching and learning of finance.

We wish you all the best in this course and in your academic and professional careers.

Lawrence J. Gitman
La Jolla, California

Chad J. Zutter
Pittsburgh, Pennsylvania

Part 1 Introduction to Managerial Finance

Chapters in This Part

Part 1 of *Principles of Managerial Finance* discusses the role that financial managers play in businesses and the financial market environment in which firms operate. We argue that the goal of managers should be to maximize the value of the firm and by doing so maximize the wealth of its owners. Financial managers act on behalf of the firm's owners by making operating and investment decisions whose benefits exceed their costs. These decisions create wealth for shareholders. Maximizing shareholder wealth is important because firms operate in a highly competitive financial market environment that offers shareholders many alternatives for investing their funds. To raise the financial resources necessary to fund the firm's ongoing operations and future investment opportunities, managers have to deliver value to the firm's investors. Without smart financial managers and access to financial markets, firms are unlikely to survive, let alone achieve the long-term goal of maximizing the value of the firm.

1 The Role of Managerial Finance

Learning Goals

LG 1 Define *finance* and the managerial finance function.

LG 2 Describe the legal forms of business organization.

LG 3 Describe the goal of the firm, and explain why maximizing the value of the firm is an appropriate goal for a business.

LG 4 Describe how the managerial finance function is related to economics and accounting.

LG 5 Identify the primary activities of the financial manager.

LG 6 Describe the nature of the principal–agent relationship between the owners and managers of a corporation, and explain how various corporate governance mechanisms attempt to manage agency problems.

Why This Chapter Matters to You

In your *professional* life

ACCOUNTING You need to understand the relationships between the accounting and finance functions within the firm; how decision makers rely on the financial statements you prepare; why maximizing a firm's value is not the same as maximizing its profits; and the ethical duty that you have when reporting financial results to investors and other stakeholders.

INFORMATION SYSTEMS You need to understand why financial information is important to managers in all functional areas; the documentation that firms must produce to comply with various regulations; and how manipulating information for personal gain can get managers into serious trouble.

MANAGEMENT You need to understand the various legal forms of a business organization; how to communicate the goal of the firm to employees and other stakeholders; the advantages and disadvantages of the agency relationship between a firm's managers and its owners; and how compensation systems can align or misalign the interests of managers and investors.

MARKETING You need to understand why increasing a firm's revenues or market share is not always a good thing; how financial managers evaluate aspects of customer relations such as cash and credit management policies; and why a firm's brands are an important part of its value to investors.

OPERATIONS You need to understand the financial benefits of increasing a firm's production efficiency; why maximizing profit by cutting costs may not increase the firm's value; and how managers act on behalf of investors when operating a corporation.

In your *personal* life

Many of the principles of managerial finance also apply to your personal life. Learning a few simple financial principles can help you manage your own money more effectively.

Facebook

facebook

In No Hurry to Go Public

Facebook founder and chief executive officer Mark Zuckerberg is in no hurry to go public, even though he concedes that it is an inevitable step in the evolution of his firm. The Facebook CEO is on record saying that "we're going to go public eventually, because that's the contract that we have with our investors and our employees. . . . [but] we are definitely in no rush." Nearly all public firms were at one time privately held by relatively few shareholders, but at some point the firms' managers decided to go public. The decision to go public is one of the most important decisions managers can make.

Private firms are typically held by fewer shareholders and are subject to less regulation than are public firms. So why do firms go public at all? Often it is to provide an exit strategy for its private investors, gain access to investment capital, establish a market price for the firm's shares, gain public exposure, or all of the above. Going public helps firms grow, but that and other benefits of public ownership must be weighed against the costs of going public.

Although taking Facebook public would likely make Zuckerberg one of the richest persons in the world under the age of 30, it would also mean that his firm would become subject to the influences of outside investors and government regulators. A public firm's managers work for and are responsible to the firm's investors, and government regulations require firms to provide investors with frequent reports disclosing material information about the firm's performance. The regulatory demands placed on managers of public firms can sometimes distract managers from important aspects of running their businesses. This chapter will highlight the tradeoffs faced by financial managers as they make decisions intended to maximize the value of their firms.

LG 1 LG 2

1.1 Finance and Business

The field of finance is broad and dynamic. Finance influences everything that firms do, from hiring personnel to building factories to launching new advertising campaigns. Because there are important financial dimensions to almost any aspect of business, there are many financially oriented career opportunities for those who understand the basic principles of finance described in this textbook. Even if you do not see yourself pursuing a career in finance, you'll find that an understanding of a few key ideas in finance will help make you a smarter consumer and a wiser investor with your own money.

WHAT IS FINANCE?

finance
The science and art of managing money.

Finance can be defined as the science and art of managing money. At the personal level, finance is concerned with individuals' decisions about how much of their earnings they spend, how much they save, and how they invest their savings. In a business context, finance involves the same types of decisions: how firms raise money from investors, how firms invest money in an attempt to earn a profit, and how they decide whether to reinvest profits in the business or distribute them back to investors. The keys to good financial decisions are much the same for businesses and individuals, which is why most students will benefit from an understanding of finance regardless of the career path they plan to follow. Learning the techniques of good financial analysis will not only help you make better financial decisions as a consumer, but it will also help you understand the financial consequences of the important business decisions you will face no matter what career path you follow.

CAREER OPPORTUNITIES IN FINANCE

Careers in finance typically fall into one of two broad categories: (1) financial services and (2) managerial finance. Workers in both areas rely on a common analytical "tool kit," but the types of problems to which that tool kit is applied vary a great deal from one career path to the other.

financial services
The area of finance concerned with the design and delivery of advice and financial products to individuals, businesses, and governments.

Financial Services

Financial services is the area of finance concerned with the design and delivery of advice and financial products to individuals, businesses, and governments. It involves a variety of interesting career opportunities within the areas of banking, personal financial planning, investments, real estate, and insurance.

managerial finance
Concerns the duties of the *financial manager* in a business.

Managerial Finance

Managerial finance is concerned with the duties of the *financial manager* working in a business. **Financial managers** administer the financial affairs of all types of businesses—private and public, large and small, profit seeking and not for profit. They perform such varied tasks as developing a financial plan or budget, extending credit to customers, evaluating proposed large expenditures, and raising money to fund the firm's operations. In recent years, a number of factors have increased the importance and complexity of the financial manager's duties. These factors include the recent global financial crisis and subsequent responses

financial manager
Actively manages the financial affairs of all types of businesses, whether private or public, large or small, profit seeking or not for profit.

by regulators, increased competition, and technological change. For example, globalization has led U.S. corporations to increase their transactions in other countries, and foreign corporations have done likewise in the United States. These changes increase demand for financial experts who can manage cash flows in different currencies and protect against the risks that arise from international transactions. These changes increase the finance function's complexity, but they also create opportunities for a more rewarding career. The increasing complexity of the financial manager's duties has increased the popularity of a variety of professional certification programs outlined in the *Focus on Practice* box below. Financial managers today actively develop and implement corporate strategies aimed at helping the firm grow and improving its competitive position. As a result, many corporate presidents and chief executive officers (CEOs) rose to the top of their organizations by first demonstrating excellence in the finance function.

LEGAL FORMS OF BUSINESS ORGANIZATION

One of the most basic decisions that all businesses confront is how to choose a legal form of organization. This decision has very important financial implications because how a business is organized legally influences the risks that the

focus on PRACTICE

Professional Certifications in Finance

in practice To be successful in finance and just about any other field, you need to continue your education beyond your undergraduate degree. For some people that means getting an MBA, but there are many other ways to advance your education and enhance your credentials without getting a graduate degree. In finance, there are a variety of professional certification programs that are widely recognized in the field.

Chartered Financial Analyst (CFA)—Offered by the CFA Institute, the CFA program is a graduate-level course of study focused primarily on the investments side of finance. To earn the CFA Charter, students must pass a series of three exams, usually over a 3-year period, and have 48 months of professional experience. Although this program appeals primarily to those who work in the investments field, the skills developed in the CFA program are useful in a variety of corporate finance jobs as well.

Certified Treasury Professional (CTP)—The CTP program requires students to pass a single exam that is focused on the knowledge and skills needed for those working in a corporate treasury department. The program emphasizes topics such as liquidity and working capital management, payment transfer systems, capital structure, managing relationships with financial service providers, and monitoring and controlling financial risks.

Certified Financial Planner (CFP)—To obtain CFP status, students must pass a 10-hour exam covering a wide range of topics related to personal financial planning. The CFP program also requires 3 years of full-time relevant experience. The program focuses primarily on skills relevant for advising individuals in developing their personal financial plans.

American Academy of Financial Management (AAFM)—The AAFM administers a host of certification programs for financial professionals in a wide range of fields. Their certifications include the Chartered Portfolio Manager, Chartered Asset Manager, Certified Risk Analyst, Certified Cost Accountant, Certified Credit Analyst, and many other programs. See the AAFM website for complete details on all of the AAFM educational programs.

Professional Certifications in Accounting—Most professionals in the field of managerial finance need to know a great deal about accounting to succeed in their jobs. Professional certifications in accounting include the Certified Public Accountant (CPA), Certified Management Accountant (CMA), Certified Internal Auditor (CIA), and many other programs.

► ***Why do employers value having employees with professional certifications?***

firm's owners must bear, how the firm can raise money, and how the firm's profits will be taxed. The three most common legal forms of business organization are the *sole proprietorship,* the *partnership,* and the *corporation.* More businesses are organized as sole proprietorships than any other legal form. However, the largest businesses are almost always organized as corporations. Even so, each type of organization has its advantages and disadvantages.

Sole Proprietorships

sole proprietorship
A business owned by one person and operated for his or her own profit.

A **sole proprietorship** is a business owned by one person who operates it for his or her own profit. About 73 percent of all businesses are sole proprietorships. The typical sole proprietorship is small, such as a bike shop, personal trainer, or plumber. The majority of sole proprietorships operate in the wholesale, retail, service, and construction industries.

Typically, the owner (proprietor), along with a few employees, operates the proprietorship. The proprietor raises capital from personal resources or by borrowing, and he or she is responsible for all business decisions. As a result, this form of organization appeals to entrepreneurs who enjoy working independently.

unlimited liability
The condition of a sole proprietorship (or general partnership), giving creditors the right to make claims against the owner's personal assets to recover debts owed by the business.

A major drawback to the sole proprietorship is **unlimited liability,** which means that liabilities of the business are the entrepreneur's responsibility, and creditors can make claims against the entrepreneur's personal assets if the business fails to pay its debts. The key strengths and weaknesses of sole proprietorships are summarized in Table 1.1.

Partnerships

partnership
A business owned by two or more people and operated for profit.

A **partnership** consists of two or more owners doing business together for profit. Partnerships account for about 7 percent of all businesses, and they are typically larger than sole proprietorships. Partnerships are common in the finance, insurance, and real estate industries. Public accounting and law partnerships often have large numbers of partners.

articles of partnership
The written contract used to formally establish a business partnership.

Most partnerships are established by a written contract known as **articles of partnership.** In a *general* (or *regular*) *partnership,* all partners have unlimited liability, and each partner is legally liable for *all* of the debts of the partnership. Table 1.1 summarizes the strengths and weaknesses of partnerships.

Matter of fact

BizStats.com Total Receipts by Type of U.S. Firm

Although there are vastly more sole proprietorships than there are partnerships and corporations combined, they generate the lowest level of receipts. In total, sole proprietorships generated more than $969 billion in receipts, but this number hardly compares to the more than $17 trillion in receipts generated by corporations.

BizStats.com Total Receipts by Type of U.S. Firm

	Sole proprietorships	Partnerships	Corporations
Number of firms (millions)	17.6	1.8	4.8
Percentage of all firms	73%	7%	20%
Total receipts ($ billions)	969	1,142	17,324
Percentage of all receipts	5%	6%	89%

TABLE 1.1 Strengths and Weaknesses of the Common Legal Forms of Business Organization

	Sole proprietorship	Partnership	Corporation
Strengths	• Owner receives all profits (and sustains all losses) • Low organizational costs • Income included and taxed on proprietor's personal tax return • Independence • Secrecy • Ease of dissolution	• Can raise more funds than sole proprietorships • Borrowing power enhanced by more owners • More available brain power and managerial skill • Income included and taxed on partner's personal tax return	• Owners have *limited liability,* which guarantees that they cannot lose more than they invested • Can achieve large size via sale of ownership (stock) • Ownership (stock) is readily transferable • Long life of firm • Can hire professional managers • Has better access to financing
Weaknesses	• Owner has *unlimited liability*—total wealth can be taken to satisfy debts • Limited fund-raising power tends to inhibit growth • Proprietor must be jack-of-all-trades • Difficult to give employees long-run career opportunities • Lacks continuity when proprietor dies	• Owners have *unlimited liability* and may have to cover debts of other partners • Partnership is dissolved when a partner dies • Difficult to liquidate or transfer partnership	• Taxes generally higher because corporate income is taxed, and dividends paid to owners are also taxed at a maximum 15% rate • More expensive to organize than other business forms • Subject to greater government regulation • Lacks secrecy because regulations require firms to disclose financial results

Corporations

corporation
An entity created by law.

stockholders
The owners of a corporation, whose ownership, or *equity,* takes the form of either common stock or preferred stock.

limited liability
A legal provision that limits stockholders' liability for a corporation's debt to the amount they initially invested in the firm by purchasing stock.

common stock
The purest and most basic form of corporate ownership.

A **corporation** is an entity created by law. A corporation has the legal powers of an individual in that it can sue and be sued, make and be party to contracts, and acquire property in its own name. Although only about 20 percent of all U.S. businesses are incorporated, the largest businesses nearly always are; corporations account for nearly 90 percent of total business revenues. Although corporations engage in all types of businesses, manufacturing firms account for the largest portion of corporate business receipts and net profits. Table 1.1 lists the key strengths and weaknesses of corporations.

The owners of a corporation are its **stockholders,** whose ownership, or *equity,* takes the form of either common stock or preferred stock. Unlike the owners of sole proprietorships or partnerships, stockholders of a corporation enjoy **limited liability,** meaning that they are not personally liable for the firm's debts. Their losses are limited to the amount they invested in the firm when they purchased shares of stock. In Chapter 7 you will learn more about common and preferred stock, but for now it is enough to say that **common stock** is the purest and most basic form of corporate ownership. Stockholders expect to earn a

dividends
Periodic distributions of cash to the stockholders of a firm.

return by receiving **dividends**—periodic distributions of cash—or by realizing gains through increases in share price. Because the money to pay dividends generally comes from the profits that a firm earns, stockholders are sometimes referred to as *residual claimants,* meaning that stockholders are paid last—after employees, suppliers, tax authorities, and lenders receive what they are owed. If the firm does not generate enough cash to pay everyone else, there is nothing available for stockholders.

board of directors
Group elected by the firm's stockholders and typically responsible for approving strategic goals and plans, setting general policy, guiding corporate affairs, and approving major expenditures.

As noted in the upper portion of Figure 1.1, control of the corporation functions a little like a democracy. The stockholders (owners) vote periodically to elect members of the *board of directors* and to decide other issues such as amending the corporate charter. The **board of directors** is typically responsible for approving strategic goals and plans, setting general policy, guiding corporate affairs, and approving major expenditures. Most importantly, the board decides when to hire or fire top managers and establishes compensation packages for the most senior executives. The board consists of "inside" directors, such as key corporate executives, and "outside" or "independent" directors, such as executives from other companies, major shareholders, and national or community leaders. Outside directors for major corporations receive compensation in the form of cash, stock, and stock options. This compensation often totals $100,000 per year or more.

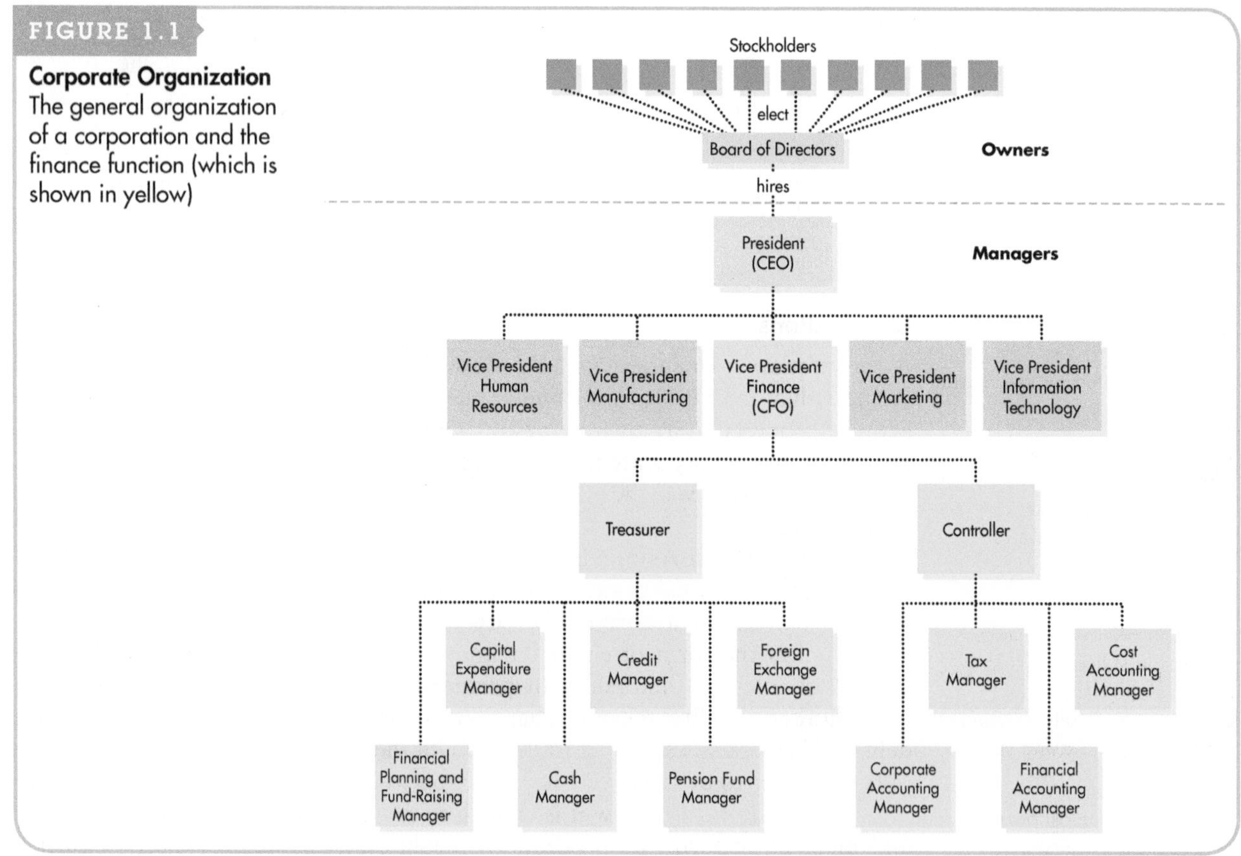

FIGURE 1.1
Corporate Organization
The general organization of a corporation and the finance function (which is shown in yellow)

president or chief executive officer (CEO)
Corporate official responsible for managing the firm's day-to-day operations and carrying out the policies established by the board of directors.

limited partnership (LP)

S corporation (S corp)

limited liability company (LLC)

limited liability partnership (LLP)
See "In More Depth" feature.

In more depth

To read about *Other Limited Liability Organizations*, go to www.myfinancelab.com

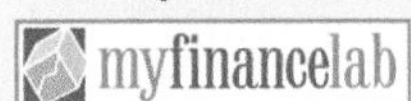

The **president or chief executive officer (CEO)** is responsible for managing day-to-day operations and carrying out the policies established by the board of directors. The CEO reports periodically to the firm's directors.

It is important to note the division between owners and managers in a large corporation, as shown by the dashed horizontal line in Figure 1.1. This separation and some of the issues surrounding it will be addressed in the discussion of *the agency issue* later in this chapter.

Other Limited Liability Organizations

A number of other organizational forms provide owners with limited liability. The most popular are **limited partnership (LP), S corporation (S corp), limited liability company (LLC),** and **limited liability partnership (LLP)**. Each represents a specialized form or blending of the characteristics of the organizational forms described previously. What they have in common is that their owners enjoy limited liability, and they typically have fewer than 100 owners.

WHY STUDY MANAGERIAL FINANCE?

An understanding of the concepts, techniques, and practices presented throughout this text will fully acquaint you with the financial manager's activities and decisions. Because the consequences of most business decisions are measured in financial terms, the financial manager plays a key operational role. People in all areas of responsibility—accounting, information systems, management, marketing, operations, and so forth—need a basic awareness of finance so they will understand how to quantify the consequences of their actions.

OK, so you're not planning to major in finance! You still will need to understand how financial managers think to improve your chance of success in your chosen business career. Managers in the firm, regardless of their job descriptions, usually have to provide financial justification for the resources they need to do their job. Whether you are hiring new workers, negotiating an advertising budget, or upgrading the technology used in a manufacturing process, understanding the financial aspects of your actions will help you gain the resources you need to be successful. The "Why This Chapter Matters to You" section that appears on each chapter opening page should help you understand the importance of each chapter in both your professional and personal life.

As you study this text, you will learn about the career opportunities in managerial finance, which are briefly described in Table 1.2 on page 10. Although this text focuses on publicly held profit-seeking firms, the principles presented here are equally applicable to private and not-for-profit organizations. The decision-making principles developed in this text can also be applied to personal financial decisions. We hope that this first exposure to the exciting field of finance will provide the foundation and initiative for further study and possibly even a future career.

→ REVIEW QUESTIONS

1–1 What is *finance?* Explain how this field affects all of the activities in which businesses engage.

1–2 What is the *financial services* area of finance? Describe the field of *managerial finance.*

TABLE 1.2 Career Opportunities in Managerial Finance

Position	Description
Financial analyst	Prepares the firm's financial plans and budgets. Other duties include financial forecasting, performing financial comparisons, and working closely with accounting.
Capital expenditures manager	Evaluates and recommends proposed long-term investments. May be involved in the financial aspects of implementing approved investments.
Project finance manager	Arranges financing for approved long-term investments. Coordinates consultants, investment bankers, and legal counsel.
Cash manager	Maintains and controls the firm's daily cash balances. Frequently manages the firm's cash collection and disbursement activities and short-term investments and coordinates short-term borrowing and banking relationships.
Credit analyst/manager	Administers the firm's credit policy by evaluating credit applications, extending credit, and monitoring and collecting accounts receivable.
Pension fund manager	Oversees or manages the assets and liabilities of the employees' pension fund.
Foreign exchange manager	Manages specific foreign operations and the firm's exposure to fluctuations in exchange rates.

1–3 Which legal form of business organization is most common? Which form is dominant in terms of business revenues?

1–4 Describe the roles and the basic relationships among the major parties in a corporation—stockholders, board of directors, and managers. How are corporate owners rewarded for the risks they take?

1–5 Briefly name and describe some organizational forms other than corporations that provide owners with limited liability.

1–6 Why is the study of managerial finance important to your professional life regardless of the specific area of responsibility you may have within the business firm? Why is it important to your personal life?

LG 3

1.2 Goal of the Firm

What goal should managers pursue? There is no shortage of possible answers to this question. Some might argue that managers should focus entirely on satisfying customers. Progress toward this goal could be measured by the market share attained by each of the firm's products. Others suggest that managers must first inspire and motivate employees; in that case, employee turnover might be the key success metric to watch. Clearly the goal that managers select will affect many of the decisions that they make, so choosing an objective is a critical determinant of how businesses operate.

MAXIMIZE SHAREHOLDER WEALTH

Finance teaches that managers' primary goal should be to maximize the wealth of the firm's owners—the stockholders. The simplest and best measure of stockholder wealth is the firm's share price, so most textbooks (ours included) instruct managers to take actions that increase the firm's share price. A common misconception is that when firms strive to make their shareholders happy, they do so at the expense of other constituencies such as customers, employees, or suppliers. This line of thinking ignores the fact that in most cases, to enrich shareholders, managers must first satisfy the demands of these other interest groups. Recall that dividends that stockholders receive ultimately come from the firm's profits. It is unlikely that a firm whose customers are unhappy with its products, whose employees are looking for jobs at other firms, or whose suppliers are reluctant to ship raw materials will make shareholders rich because such a firm will likely be less profitable in the long run than one that better manages its relations with these stakeholder groups.

Therefore, we argue that the goal of the firm, and also of managers, should be *to maximize the wealth of the owners for whom it is being operated*, or equivalently, to maximize the stock price. This goal translates into a straightforward decision rule for managers—*only take actions that are expected to increase the share price*. Although that goal sounds simple, implementing it is not always easy. To determine whether a particular course of action will increase or decrease a firm's share price, managers have to assess what return (that is, cash inflows net of cash outflows) the action will bring and how risky that return might be. Figure 1.2 depicts this process. In fact, we can say that *the key variables that managers must consider when making business decisions are return (cash flows) and risk*.

earnings per share (EPS)
The amount earned during the period on behalf of each outstanding share of common stock, calculated by dividing the period's total earnings available for the firm's common stockholders by the number of shares of common stock outstanding.

MAXIMIZE PROFIT?

It might seem intuitive that maximizing a firm's share price is equivalent to maximizing its profits, but that is not always correct.

Corporations commonly measure profits in terms of **earnings per share (EPS),** which represent the amount earned during the period on behalf of each outstanding share of common stock. EPS are calculated by dividing the period's total earnings available for the firm's common stockholders by the number of shares of common stock outstanding.

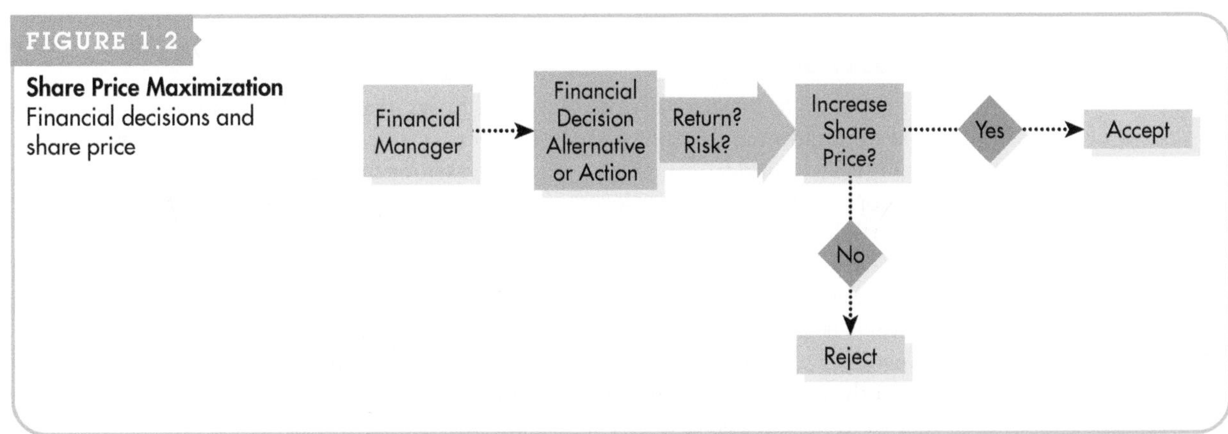

FIGURE 1.2
Share Price Maximization
Financial decisions and share price

Example 1.1 ▸ Nick Dukakis, the financial manager of Neptune Manufacturing, a producer of marine engine components, is choosing between two investments, Rotor and Valve. The following table shows the EPS that each investment is expected to have over its 3-year life.

	Earnings per share (EPS)			
Investment	**Year 1**	**Year 2**	**Year 3**	**Total for years 1, 2, and 3**
Rotor	$1.40	$1.00	$0.40	$2.80
Valve	0.60	1.00	1.40	3.00

In terms of the profit maximization goal, Valve would be preferred over Rotor because it results in higher total earnings per share over the 3-year period ($3.00 EPS compared with $2.80 EPS).

But does profit maximization lead to the highest possible share price? For at least three reasons the answer is often no. First, timing is important. An investment that provides a lower profit in the short run may be preferable to one that earns a higher profit in the long run. Second, profits and cash flows are not identical. The profit that a firm reports is simply an estimate of how it is doing, an estimate that is influenced by many different accounting choices that firms make when assembling their financial reports. Cash flow is a more straightforward measure of the money flowing into and out of the company. Companies have to pay their bills with cash, not earnings, so cash flow is what matters most to financial managers. Third, risk matters a great deal. A firm that earns a low but reliable profit might be more valuable than another firm with profits that fluctuate a great deal (and therefore can be very high or very low at different times).

Timing

Because the firm can earn a return on funds it receives, *the receipt of funds sooner rather than later is preferred.* In our example, in spite of the fact that the total earnings from Rotor are smaller than those from Valve, Rotor provides much greater earnings per share in the first year. The larger returns in year 1 could be reinvested to provide greater future earnings.

Cash Flows

Profits do *not* necessarily result in cash flows available to the stockholders. There is no guarantee that the board of directors will increase dividends when profits increase. In addition, the accounting assumptions and techniques that a firm adopts can sometimes allow a firm to show a positive profit even when its cash outflows exceed its cash inflows.

Furthermore, higher earnings do not necessarily translate into a higher stock price. Only when earnings increases are accompanied by increased future cash flows is a higher stock price expected. For example, a firm with a high-quality product sold in a very competitive market could increase its earnings by significantly reducing its equipment maintenance expenditures. The firm's expenses would be reduced, thereby increasing its profits. But if the reduced maintenance results in lower product quality, the firm may impair its competitive position, and its stock price could drop as many well-informed investors sell the stock in anticipation of lower future cash flows. In this case, the earnings increase was accompanied by lower future cash flows and therefore a lower stock price.

Risk

risk
The chance that actual outcomes may differ from those expected.

Profit maximization also fails to account for **risk**—the chance that actual outcomes may differ from those expected. A basic premise in managerial finance is that a trade-off exists between return (cash flow) and risk. *Return and risk are, in fact, the key determinants of share price, which represents the wealth of the owners in the firm.*

Cash flow and risk affect share price differently: Holding risk fixed, higher cash flow is generally associated with a higher share price. In contrast, holding cash flow fixed, higher risk tends to result in a lower share price because the stockholders do not like risk. For example, Apple's CEO, Steve Jobs, took a leave of absence to battle a serious health issue, and the firm's stock suffered as a result. This occurred not because of any near-term cash flow reduction but in response to the firm's increased risk—there's a chance that the firm's lack of near-term leadership could result in reduced future cash flows. Simply put, the increased risk reduced the firm's share price. In general, stockholders are **risk averse**—that is, they must be compensated for bearing risk. In other words, investors expect to earn higher returns on riskier investments, and they will accept lower returns on relatively safe investments. The key point, which will be fully developed in Chapter 5, is that differences in risk can significantly affect the value of different investments.

risk averse
Requiring compensation to bear risk.

WHAT ABOUT STAKEHOLDERS?

Although maximization of shareholder wealth is the primary goal, many firms broaden their focus to include the interests of *stakeholders* as well as shareholders. **Stakeholders** are groups such as employees, customers, suppliers, creditors, owners, and others who have a direct economic link to the firm. A firm with a *stakeholder focus* consciously avoids actions that would prove detrimental to stakeholders. The goal is not to maximize stakeholder well-being but to preserve it.

stakeholders
Groups such as employees, customers, suppliers, creditors, owners, and others who have a direct economic link to the firm.

The stakeholder view does not alter the goal of maximizing shareholder wealth. Such a view is often considered part of the firm's "social responsibility." It is expected to provide long-run benefit to shareholders by maintaining positive relationships with stakeholders. Such relationships should minimize stakeholder turnover, conflicts, and litigation. Clearly, the firm can better achieve its goal of shareholder wealth maximization by fostering cooperation with its other stakeholders, rather than conflict with them.

THE ROLE OF BUSINESS ETHICS

business ethics
Standards of conduct or moral judgment that apply to persons engaged in commerce.

Business ethics are the standards of conduct or moral judgment that apply to persons engaged in commerce. Violations of these standards in finance involve a variety of actions: "creative accounting," earnings management, misleading financial forecasts, insider trading, fraud, excessive executive compensation, options backdating, bribery, and kickbacks. The financial press has reported many such violations in recent years, involving such well-known companies as

Apple and Bank of America. As a result, the financial community is developing and enforcing ethical standards. The goal of these ethical standards is to motivate business and market participants to adhere to both the letter and the spirit of laws and regulations concerned with business and professional practice. Most business leaders believe businesses actually strengthen their competitive positions by maintaining high ethical standards.

Considering Ethics

Robert A. Cooke, a noted ethicist, suggests that the following questions be used to assess the ethical viability of a proposed action.[1]

1. Is the action arbitrary or capricious? Does it unfairly single out an individual or group?
2. Does the action violate the moral or legal rights of any individual or group?
3. Does the action conform to accepted moral standards?
4. Are there alternative courses of action that are less likely to cause actual or potential harm?

Clearly, considering such questions before taking an action can help to ensure its ethical viability.

Today, many firms are addressing the issue of ethics by establishing corporate ethics policies. The *Focus on Ethics* box provides an example of ethics policies at Google. A major impetus toward the development of ethics policies has been the Sarbanes-Oxley Act of 2002. Frequently, employees are required to sign a formal pledge to uphold the firm's ethics policies. Such policies typically apply to employee actions in dealing with all corporate stakeholders, including the public.

Ethics and Share Price

An effective ethics program can enhance corporate value by producing a number of positive benefits. It can reduce potential litigation and judgment costs, maintain a positive corporate image, build shareholder confidence, and gain the loyalty, commitment, and respect of the firm's stakeholders. Such actions, by maintaining and enhancing cash flow and reducing perceived risk, can positively affect the firm's share price. *Ethical behavior is therefore viewed as necessary for achieving the firm's goal of owner wealth maximization.*

→ REVIEW QUESTIONS

1–7 What is the goal of the firm and, therefore, of all managers and employees? Discuss how one measures achievement of this goal.

1–8 For what three basic reasons is profit maximization inconsistent with wealth maximization?

1. Robert A. Cooke, "Business Ethics: A Perspective," in *Arthur Andersen Cases on Business Ethics* (Chicago: Arthur Andersen, September 1991), pp. 2 and 5.

focus on **ETHICS**

Will Google Live Up to Its Motto?

in practice Google offers an interesting case study on value maximization and corporate ethics. In 2004, Google's founders provided "An Owner's Manual" for shareholders, which stated that "Google is not a conventional company" and that the company's ultimate goal "is to develop services that significantly improve the lives of as many people as possible." The founders stressed that it was not enough for Google to run a successful business but that they want to use the company to make the world a better place. The "Owner's Manual" also unveiled Google's corporate motto, "Don't Be Evil." The motto is intended to convey Google's willingness to do the right thing even when doing so requires the firm to sacrifice in the short run. Google's approach does not appear to be limiting its ability to maximize value—the company's share price increased from $100 to approximately $500 in 6 years.

Google's business goal is "instantly delivering relevant information on any topic" to the world. However, when the company launched its search engine in China in early 2006, it agreed to the Chinese government's request to censor search results. Some observers felt that the opportunity to gain access to the vast Chinese market led Google to compromise its principles.

In January 2010, Google announced that the Gmail accounts of Chinese human-rights activists and a number of technology, financial, and defense companies had been hacked. The company threatened to pull out of China unless an agreement on uncensored search results could be reached. Two months later, Google began routing Chinese web searches to their uncensored servers in Hong Kong, a move that was cheered by activists and human-rights groups, but criticized by the Chinese government. In the short term, Google's shareholders suffered. During the first quarter of 2010, Google's share price declined by 8.5 percent, compared to an increase of 45.2 percent for Google's main rival in China, Baidu.com.

Google's founders seemed to anticipate the current situation in the firm's "Owner's Manual." According to the firm, "If opportunities arise that might cause us to sacrifice short-term results but are in the best long-term interest of our shareholders, we will take those opportunities. We have the fortitude to do this. We would request that our shareholders take the long-term view." It remains to be seen whether Google's short-term sacrifice will benefit shareholders in the long run.

▶ ***Is the goal of maximization of shareholder wealth necessarily ethical or unethical?***

▶ ***How can Google justify its actions in the short run to its long-run investors?***

Source: 2004 Founders' IPO Letter, **http://investor.google.com/corporate/2004/ipo-founders-letter.html**

1–9 What is *risk?* Why must risk as well as return be considered by the financial manager who is evaluating a decision alternative or action?

1–10 Describe the role of corporate ethics policies and guidelines, and discuss the relationship that is believed to exist between ethics and share price.

LG 4 LG 5

1.3 Managerial Finance Function

People in all areas of responsibility within the firm must interact with finance personnel and procedures to get their jobs done. For financial personnel to make useful forecasts and decisions, they must be willing and able to talk to individuals in other areas of the firm. For example, when considering a new product, the financial manager needs to obtain sales forecasts, pricing guidelines, and advertising and promotion budget estimates from marketing personnel. The managerial finance function can be broadly described by considering its role within the organization, its relationship to economics and accounting, and the primary activities of the financial manager.

ORGANIZATION OF THE FINANCE FUNCTION

The size and importance of the managerial finance function depend on the size of the firm. In small firms, the finance function is generally performed by the accounting department. As a firm grows, the finance function typically evolves into a separate department linked directly to the company president or CEO through the chief financial officer (CFO). The lower portion of the organizational chart in Figure 1.1 on page 8 shows the structure of the finance function in a typical medium- to large-size firm.

treasurer
The firm's chief financial manager, who manages the firm's cash, oversees its pension plans, and manages key risks.

controller
The firm's chief accountant, who is responsible for the firm's accounting activities, such as corporate accounting, tax management, financial accounting, and cost accounting.

foreign exchange manager
The manager responsible for managing and monitoring the firm's exposure to loss from currency fluctuations.

Reporting to the CFO are the treasurer and the controller. The **treasurer** (the chief financial manager) typically manages the firm's cash, investing surplus funds when available and securing outside financing when needed. The treasurer also oversees a firm's pension plans and manages critical risks related to movements in foreign currency values, interest rates, and commodity prices. The **controller** (the chief accountant) typically handles the accounting activities, such as corporate accounting, tax management, financial accounting, and cost accounting. The treasurer's focus tends to be more external, whereas the controller's focus is more internal.

If international sales or purchases are important to a firm, it may well employ one or more finance professionals whose job is to monitor and manage the firm's exposure to loss from currency fluctuations. A trained financial manager can "hedge," or protect against such a loss, at a reasonable cost by using a variety of financial instruments. These **foreign exchange managers** typically report to the firm's treasurer.

RELATIONSHIP TO ECONOMICS

marginal cost–benefit analysis
Economic principle that states that financial decisions should be made and actions taken only when the added benefits exceed the added costs.

The field of finance is closely related to economics. Financial managers must understand the economic framework and be alert to the consequences of varying levels of economic activity and changes in economic policy. They must also be able to use economic theories as guidelines for efficient business operation. Examples include supply-and-demand analysis, profit-maximizing strategies, and price theory. The primary economic principle used in managerial finance is **marginal cost–benefit analysis,** the principle that financial decisions should be made and actions taken only when the added benefits exceed the added costs. Nearly all financial decisions ultimately come down to an assessment of their marginal benefits and marginal costs.

Example 1.2 ▸ Jamie Teng is a financial manager for Nord Department Stores, a large chain of upscale department stores operating primarily in the western United States. She is currently trying to decide whether to replace one of the firm's computer servers with a new, more sophisticated one that would both speed processing and handle a larger volume of transactions. The new computer would require a cash outlay of $8,000, and the old computer could be sold to net $2,000. The total benefits from the new server (measured in today's dollars) would be $10,000. The benefits over a similar time period from the old computer (measured in today's dollars) would be $3,000. Applying marginal cost–benefit analysis, Jamie organizes the data as follows:

Benefits with new computer	$10,000
Less: Benefits with old computer	3,000
(1) Marginal (added) benefits	$ 7,000
Cost of new computer	$ 8,000
Less: Proceeds from sale of old computer	2,000
(2) Marginal (added) costs	$ 6,000
Net benefit [(1) − (2)]	$ 1,000

Because the marginal (added) benefits of $7,000 exceed the marginal (added) costs of $6,000, Jamie recommends that the firm purchase the new computer to replace the old one. The firm will experience a net benefit of $1,000 as a result of this action.

RELATIONSHIP TO ACCOUNTING

The firm's finance and accounting activities are closely related and generally overlap. In small firms accountants often carry out the finance function, and in large firms financial analysts often help compile accounting information. However, there are two basic differences between finance and accounting; one is related to the emphasis on cash flows and the other to decision making.

Emphasis on Cash Flows

accrual basis
In preparation of financial statements, recognizes revenue at the time of sale and recognizes expenses when they are incurred.

cash basis
Recognizes revenues and expenses only with respect to actual inflows and outflows of cash.

The accountant's primary function is to develop and report data for measuring the performance of the firm, assess its financial position, comply with and file reports required by securities regulators, and file and pay taxes. Using generally accepted accounting principles, the accountant prepares financial statements that recognize revenue at the time of sale (whether payment has been received or not) and recognize expenses when they are incurred. This approach is referred to as the **accrual basis.**

The financial manager, on the other hand, places primary emphasis on *cash flows*, the intake and outgo of cash. He or she maintains the firm's solvency by planning the cash flows necessary to satisfy its obligations and to acquire assets needed to achieve the firm's goals. The financial manager uses this **cash basis** to recognize the revenues and expenses only with respect to actual inflows and outflows of cash. Whether a firm earns a profit or experiences a loss, *it must have a sufficient flow of cash to meet its obligations as they come due.*

Example 1.3 ▸ Nassau Corporation, a small yacht dealer, sold one yacht for $100,000 in the calendar year just ended. Nassau originally purchased the yacht for $80,000. Although the firm paid in full for the yacht during the year, at year-end it has yet to collect the $100,000 from the customer. The accounting view and the financial view of the firm's performance during the year are given by the following income and cash flow statements, respectively.

Accounting view (accrual basis)	
Nassau Corporation income statement for the year ended 12/31	
Sales revenue	$100,000
Less: Costs	80,000
Net profit	$ 20,000

Financial view (cash basis)	
Nassau Corporation cash flow statement for the year ended 12/31	
Cash inflow	$ 0
Less: Cash outflow	80,000
Net cash flow	($80,000)

In an accounting sense, Nassau Corporation is profitable, but in terms of actual cash flow it is a financial failure. Its lack of cash flow resulted from the uncollected accounts receivable of $100,000. Without adequate cash inflows to meet its obligations, the firm will not survive, regardless of its level of profits.

As the example shows, accrual accounting data do not fully describe the circumstances of a firm. Thus the financial manager must look beyond financial statements to obtain insight into existing or developing problems. Of course, accountants are well aware of the importance of cash flows, and financial managers use and understand accrual-based financial statements. Nevertheless, the financial manager, by concentrating on cash flows, should be able to avoid insolvency and achieve the firm's financial goals.

Personal Finance Example 1.4 ▸ Individuals do not use accrual concepts. Rather, they rely solely on cash flows to measure their financial outcomes. Generally, individuals plan, monitor, and assess their financial activities using cash flows over a given period, typically a month or a year. Ann Bach projects her cash flows during October 2012 as follows:

	Amount	
Item	**Inflow**	**Outflow**
Net pay received	$4,400	
Rent		$1,200
Car payment		450
Utilities		300
Groceries		800
Clothes		750
Dining out		650
Gasoline		260
Interest income	220	
Misc. expense		425
Totals	$4,620	$4,835

Ann subtracts her total outflows of $4,835 from her total inflows of $4,620 and finds that her *net cash flow* for October will be –$215. To cover the $215 shortfall, Ann will have to either borrow $215 (putting it on a credit card is a form of borrowing) or withdraw $215 from her savings. Or she may decide to reduce her outflows in areas of discretionary spending—for example, clothing purchases, dining out, or areas that make up the $425 of miscellaneous expense.

Decision Making

The second major difference between finance and accounting has to do with decision making. Accountants devote most of their attention to the *collection and presentation of financial data.* Financial managers evaluate the accounting statements, develop additional data, and *make decisions* on the basis of their assessment of the associated returns and risks. Of course, this does not mean that accountants never make decisions or that financial managers never gather data but rather that the primary focuses of accounting and finance are distinctly different.

PRIMARY ACTIVITIES OF THE FINANCIAL MANAGER

In addition to ongoing involvement in financial analysis and planning, the financial manager's primary activities are making investment and financing decisions. Investment decisions determine what types of assets the firm holds. Financing decisions determine how the firm raises money to pay for the assets in which it invests. One way to visualize the difference between a firm's investment and financing decisions is to refer to the balance sheet shown in Figure 1.3. Investment decisions generally refer to the items that appear on the left-hand side of the balance sheet, and financing decisions relate to the items on the right-hand side. Keep in mind, though, that financial managers make these decisions based on their impact on the value of the firm, not on the accounting principles used to construct a balance sheet.

→ REVIEW QUESTIONS

1–11 In what financial activities does a corporate treasurer engage?

1–12 What is the primary economic principle used in managerial finance?

1–13 What are the major differences between accounting and finance with respect to emphasis on cash flows and decision making?

1–14 What are the two primary activities of the financial manager that are related to the firm's balance sheet?

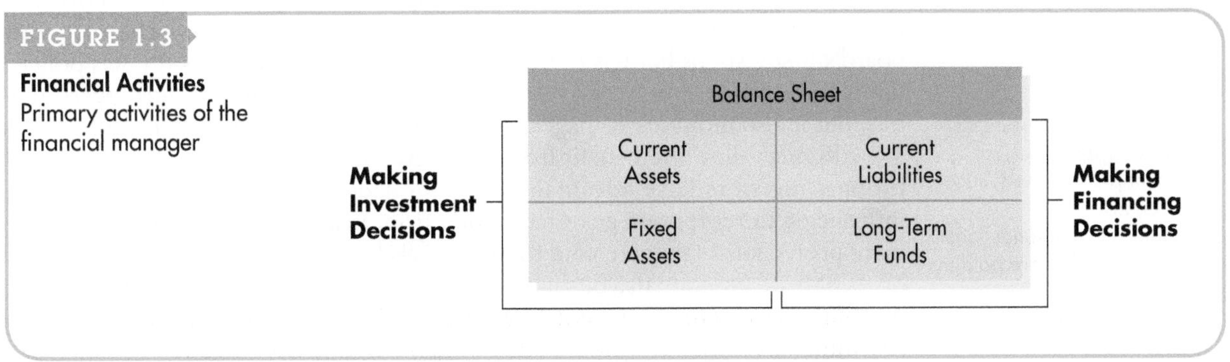

FIGURE 1.3

Financial Activities
Primary activities of the financial manager

LG 6

1.4 Governance and Agency

As noted earlier, the majority of owners of a corporation are normally distinct from its managers. Nevertheless, managers are entrusted to only take actions or make decisions that are in the best interests of the firm's owners, its shareholders. In most cases, if managers fail to act on the behalf of the shareholders, they will also fail to achieve the goal of maximizing shareholder wealth. To help ensure that managers act in ways that are consistent with the interests of shareholders and mindful of obligations to other stakeholders, firms aim to establish sound corporate governance practices.

CORPORATE GOVERNANCE

corporate governance
The rules, processes, and laws by which companies are operated, controlled, and regulated.

Corporate governance refers to the rules, processes, and laws by which companies are operated, controlled, and regulated. It defines the rights and responsibilities of the corporate participants such as the shareholders, board of directors, officers and managers, and other stakeholders, as well as the rules and procedures for making corporate decisions. A well-defined corporate governance structure is intended to benefit all corporate stakeholders by ensuring that the firm is run in a lawful and ethical fashion, in accordance with best practices, and subject to all corporate regulations.

A firm's corporate governance is influenced by both internal factors such as the shareholders, board of directors, and officers as well as external forces such as clients, creditors, suppliers, competitors, and government regulations. The corporate organization, depicted in Figure 1.1 on page 8, helps to shape a firm's corporate governance structure. In particular, the stockholders elect a board of directors, who in turn hire officers or managers to operate the firm in a manner consistent with the goals, plans, and policies established and monitored by the board on behalf of the shareholders.

Individual versus Institutional Investors

individual investors
Investors who own relatively small quantities of shares so as to meet personal investment goals.

To better understand the role that shareholders play in shaping a firm's corporate governance, it is helpful to differentiate between the two broad classes of owners—individuals and institutions. Generally, **individual investors** own relatively small quantities of shares and as a result do not typically have sufficient means to directly influence a firm's corporate governance. In order to influence the firm, individual investors often find it necessary to act as a group by voting collectively on corporate matters. The most important corporate matter individual investors vote on is the election of the firm's board of directors. The corporate board's first responsibility is to the shareholders. The board not only sets policies that specify ethical practices and provide for the protection of stakeholder interests, but it also monitors managerial decision making on behalf of investors.

institutional investors
Investment professionals, such as banks, insurance companies, mutual funds, and pension funds, that are paid to manage and hold large quantities of securities on behalf of others.

Although they also benefit from the presence of the board of directors, institutional investors have advantages over individual investors when it comes to influencing the corporate governance of a firm. **Institutional investors** are investment professionals that are paid to manage and hold large quantities of securities on behalf of individuals, businesses, and governments. Institutional investors include banks, insurance companies, mutual funds, and pension funds. Unlike individual investors, institutional investors often monitor and directly influence a firm's corporate governance by exerting pressure on management to perform or communicating their concerns to the firm's board. These large investors can also threaten to exercise their voting rights or liquidate their holdings if the board does not respond positively to their concerns. Because individual and institutional investors share the same goal, individual investors benefit from the shareholder activism of institutional investors.

Government Regulation

Unlike the impact that clients, creditors, suppliers, or competitors can have on a particular firm's corporate governance, government regulation generally shapes the corporate governance of all firms. During the past decade, corporate governance has received increased attention due to several high-profile corporate scandals involving abuse of corporate power and, in some cases, alleged criminal activity by corporate officers. The misdeeds derived from two main types of issues: (1) false disclosures in financial reporting and other material information releases and (2) undisclosed conflicts of interest between corporations and their analysts, auditors, and attorneys and between corporate directors, officers, and shareholders. Asserting that an integral part of an effective corporate governance regime is provisions for civil or criminal prosecution of individuals who conduct unethical or illegal acts in the name of the firm, in July 2002 the U.S. Congress passed the **Sarbanes-Oxley Act of 2002** (commonly called **SOX**).

Sarbanes-Oxley Act of 2002 (SOX)
An act aimed at eliminating corporate disclosure and conflict of interest problems. Contains provisions about corporate financial disclosures and the relationships among corporations, analysts, auditors, attorneys, directors, officers, and shareholders.

Sarbanes-Oxley is intended to eliminate many of the disclosure and conflict of interest problems that can arise when corporate managers are not held personally accountable for their firm's financial decisions and disclosures. SOX accomplished the following: established an oversight board to monitor the accounting industry; tightened audit regulations and controls; toughened penalties against executives who commit corporate fraud; strengthened accounting disclosure requirements and ethical guidelines for corporate officers; established corporate board structure and membership guidelines; established guidelines with regard to analyst conflicts of interest; mandated instant disclosure of stock sales by corporate executives; and increased securities regulation authority and budgets for auditors and investigators.

THE AGENCY ISSUE

We know that the duty of the financial manager is to maximize the wealth of the firm's owners. Shareholders give managers decision-making authority over the firm; thus managers can be viewed as the *agents* of the firm's shareholders. Technically, any manager who owns less than 100 percent of the firm is an agent acting on behalf of other owners. This separation of owners and managers is shown by the dashed horizontal line in Figure 1.1 on page 8, and it is representative of the classic **principal–agent relationship,** where the shareholders are the principals. In general, a contract is used to specify the terms of a principal–agent relationship. This arrangement works well when the agent makes decisions that are in the principal's best interest but doesn't work well when the interests of the principal and agent differ.

principal–agent relationship
An arrangement in which an agent acts on the behalf of a principal. For example, shareholders of a company (principals) elect management (agents) to act on their behalf.

In theory, most financial managers would agree with the goal of shareholder wealth maximization. In reality, however, managers are also concerned with their personal wealth, job security, and fringe benefits. Such concerns may cause managers to make decisions that are not consistent with shareholder wealth maximization. For example, financial managers may be reluctant or unwilling to take more than moderate risk if they perceive that taking too much risk might jeopardize their job or reduce their personal wealth.

In more depth

To read about *Agency Problems*, go to www.myfinancelab.com

agency problems
Problems that arise when managers place personal goals ahead of the goals of shareholders.

agency costs
Costs arising from agency problems that are borne by shareholders and represent a loss of shareholder wealth.

incentive plans
Management compensation plans that tie management compensation to share price; one example involves the granting of *stock options*.

stock options
Options extended by the firm that allow management to benefit from increases in stock prices over time.

performance plans
Plans that tie management compensation to measures such as EPS or growth in EPS. *Performance shares* and/or *cash bonuses* are used as compensation under these plans.

performance shares
Shares of stock given to management for meeting stated performance goals.

cash bonuses
Cash paid to management for achieving certain performance goals.

The Agency Problem

An important theme of corporate governance is to ensure the accountability of managers in an organization through mechanisms that try to reduce or eliminate the principal–agent problem; however, when these mechanisms fail agency problems arise. **Agency problems** arise when managers deviate from the goal of maximization of shareholder wealth by placing their personal goals ahead of the goals of shareholders. These problems in turn give rise to agency costs. **Agency costs** are costs borne by shareholders due to the presence or avoidance of agency problems, and in either case represent a loss of shareholder wealth. For example, shareholders incur agency costs when managers fail to make the best investment decision or when managers have to be monitored to ensure that the best investment decision is made, because either situation is likely to result in a lower stock price.

Management Compensation Plans

In addition to the roles played by corporate boards, institutional investors, and government regulations, corporate governance can be strengthened by ensuring that managers' interests are aligned with those of shareholders. A common approach is to *structure management compensation* to correspond with firm performance. In addition to combating agency problems, the resulting performance-based compensation packages allow firms to compete for and hire the best managers available. The two key types of managerial compensation plans are incentive plans and performance plans.

Incentive plans tie management compensation to share price. One incentive plan grants **stock options** to management. If the firm's stock price rises over time, managers will be rewarded by being able to purchase stock at the market price in effect at the time of the grant and then to resell the shares at the prevailing higher market price.

Many firms also offer **performance plans** that tie management compensation to performance measures such as earnings per share (EPS) or growth in EPS. Compensation under these plans is often in the form of performance shares or cash bonuses. **Performance shares** are shares of stock given to management as a result of meeting the stated performance goals, whereas **cash bonuses** are cash payments tied to the achievement of certain performance goals.

The execution of many compensation plans has been closely scrutinized in light of the past decade's corporate scandals and financial woes. Both individual and institutional stockholders, as well as the Securities and Exchange Commission (SEC) and other government entities, continue to publicly question the appropriateness of the multimillion-dollar compensation packages that many corporate executives receive. The total compensation in 2009 for the chief executive officers of the 500 biggest U.S. companies is considerable. For example, the three highest-paid CEOs in 2009 were (1) H. Lawrence Culp Jr. of Danaher Corp., who earned \$141.36 million; (2) Lawrence J. Ellison of Oracle Corp., who earned \$130.23 million; and (3) Aubrey K. McClendon of Chesapeake Energy Corp., who earned

Matter of fact

Forbes.com CEO Performance versus Pay

A quick check of the most recent Forbes.com reporting of CEO performance versus pay for the top 500 U.S. companies reveals that the highest-paid CEOs are not necessarily the best-performing CEOs. In fact, the total compensation of the top three performing CEOs is less than 4 percent of the total compensation for the top-paid CEOs, all of whom have performances ranked 82nd or worse.

Forbes.com CEO Performance vs. Pay

Efficiency ranking	Chief executive officer	Company	Compensation	Compensation rank
1st	Jeffery H. Boyd	Priceline.com	$7.49 mil.	135th
2nd	Jeffrey P. Bezos	Amazon.com	$1.28 mil.	463rd
3rd	Leonard Bell	Alexion Pharmaceuticals	$4.26 mil.	286th
90th	H. Lawrence Culp Jr.	Danaher Corp.	$141.36 mil.	1st
82nd	Lawrence J. Ellison	Oracle Corp.	$130.23 mil.	2nd
163rd	Aubrey K. McClendon	Chesapeake Energy Corp.	$114.29 mil.	3rd

$114.29 million. Tenth on the same list is Jen-Hsun Huang of NVIDIA Corp., who earned $31.40 million.

Most studies have failed to find a strong relationship between the performance that companies achieve and the compensation that CEOs receive. During the past few years, publicity surrounding these large compensation packages (without corresponding performance) has driven down executive compensation. Contributing to this publicity is the SEC requirement that publicly traded companies disclose to shareholders and others the amount of compensation to their CEO, CFO, three other highest-paid executives, and directors; the method used to determine it; and a narrative discussion regarding the underlying compensation policies. At the same time, new compensation plans that better link managers' performance to their compensation are being developed and implemented. As evidence of this trend, consider that the average total compensation for the top three CEOs in 2009 was down slightly more than 69 percent from the average for the top three CEOs in 2006. The average in 2006 was $421.13 million versus an average of $128.63 million in 2009.

The Threat of Takeover

When a firm's internal corporate governance structure is unable to keep agency problems in check, it is likely that rival managers will try to gain control of the firm. Because agency problems represent a misuse of the firm's resources and impose agency costs on the firm's shareholders, the firm's stock is generally depressed, making the firm an attractive takeover target. The *threat of takeover* by another firm that believes it can enhance the troubled firm's value by restructuring its management, operations, and financing can provide a strong source of external corporate governance. The constant threat of a takeover tends to motivate management to act in the best interests of the firm's owners.

Unconstrained, managers may have other goals in addition to share price maximization, but much of the evidence suggests that share price maximization—the focus of this book—is the primary goal of most firms.

→ REVIEW QUESTIONS

1–15 What is *corporate governance*? How has the Sarbanes-Oxley Act of 2002 affected it? Explain.

1–16 Define *agency problems*, and describe how they give rise to *agency costs*. Explain how a firm's *corporate governance structure* can help avoid agency problems.

1–17 How can the firm *structure management compensation* to minimize agency problems? What is the current view with regard to the execution of many compensation plans?

1–18 How do market forces—both shareholder activism and the threat of takeover—act to prevent or minimize the *agency problem*? What role do *institutional investors* play in shareholder activism?

Summary

FOCUS ON VALUE

Chapter 1 established the primary goal of the firm—**to maximize the wealth of the owners for whom the firm is being operated.** For public companies, value at any time is reflected in the stock price. Therefore, management should act only on those opportunities that are expected to create value for owners by increasing the stock price. Doing this requires management to consider the returns (magnitude and timing of cash flows), the risk of each proposed action, and their combined effect on value.

REVIEW OF LEARNING GOALS

LG 1 **Define *finance* and the managerial finance function.** Finance is the science and art of managing money. It affects virtually all aspects of business. Managerial finance is concerned with the duties of the *financial manager* working in a business. Financial managers administer the financial affairs of all types of businesses—private and public, large and small, profit seeking and not for profit. They perform such varied tasks as developing a financial plan or budget, extending credit to customers, evaluating proposed large expenditures, and raising money to fund the firm's operations.

LG 2 **Describe the legal forms of business organization.** The legal forms of business organization are the sole proprietorship, the partnership, and the corporation. The corporation is dominant in terms of business receipts, and its owners are its common and preferred stockholders. Stockholders expect to earn a return by receiving dividends or by realizing gains through increases in share price.

LG 3 **Describe the goal of the firm, and explain why maximizing the value of the firm is an appropriate goal for a business.** The goal of the firm is to maximize its value and therefore the wealth of its shareholders. Maximizing the value of the firm means running the business in the interest of those who own it—the shareholders. Because shareholders are paid after other stakeholders, it is generally necessary to satisfy the interests of other stakeholders to enrich shareholders.

LG 4 **Describe how the managerial finance function is related to economics and accounting.** All areas of responsibility within a firm interact with finance personnel and procedures. The financial manager must understand the economic environment and rely heavily on the economic principle of marginal cost–benefit analysis to make financial decisions. Financial managers use accounting but concentrate on cash flows and decision making.

LG 5 **Identify the primary activities of the financial manager.** The primary activities of the financial manager, in addition to ongoing involvement in financial analysis and planning, are making investment decisions and making financing decisions.

LG 6 **Describe the nature of the principal–agent relationship between the owners and managers of a corporation, and explain how various corporate governance mechanisms attempt to manage agency problems.** This separation of owners and managers of the typical firm is representative of the classic principal–agent relationship, where the shareholders are the principals and managers are the agents. This arrangement works well when the agent makes decisions that are in the principal's best interest but can lead to agency problems when the interests of the principal and agent differ. A firm's corporate governance structure is intended to help ensure that managers act in the best interests of the firm's shareholders, and other stakeholders, and it is usually influenced by both internal and external factors.

Opener-in-Review

In the chapter opener you read about Facebook and its founder's reluctance to go public. If Zuckerberg is expected to remain the CEO of Facebook after the IPO, why would he be worried about going public?

Self-Test Problem (Solution in Appendix)

LG 4 **ST1–1** **Emphasis on Cash Flows** Worldwide Rugs is a rug importer located in the United States that resells its import products to local retailers. Last year Worldwide Rugs imported $2.5 million worth of rugs from around the world, all of which were paid for prior to shipping. On receipt of the rugs, the importer immediately resold them to local retailers for $3 million. To allow its retail clients time to resell the rugs, Worldwide Rugs sells to retailers on credit. Prior to the end of its business year, Worldwide Rugs collected 85% of its outstanding accounts receivable.

a. What is the accounting profit that Worldwide Rugs generated for the year?
b. Did Worldwide Rugs have a successful year from an accounting perspective?
c. What is the financial cash flow that Worldwide Rugs generated for the year?
d. Did Worldwide Rugs have a successful year from a financial perspective?
e. If the current pattern persists, what is your expectation for the future success of Worldwide Rugs?

Warm-Up Exercises

All problems are available in myfinancelab.

LG 2 **E1–1** Ann and Jack have been partners for several years. Their firm, A & J Tax Preparation, has been very successful, as the pair agree on most business-related questions. One disagreement, however, concerns the legal form of their business. Ann has tried for the past 2 years to get Jack to agree to incorporate. She believes that there is no downside to incorporating and sees only benefits. Jack strongly disagrees; he thinks that the business should remain a partnership forever.

First, take Ann's side, and explain the positive side to incorporating the business. Next, take Jack's side, and state the advantages to remaining a partnership. Lastly, what information would you want if you were asked to make the decision for Ann and Jack?

LG 4 **E1–2** The end-of-year parties at Yearling, Inc., are known for their extravagance. Management provides the best food and entertainment to thank the employees for their hard work. During the planning for this year's bash, a disagreement broke out between the treasurer's staff and the controller's staff. The treasurer's staff contended that the firm was running low on cash and might have trouble paying its bills over the coming months; they requested that cuts be made to the budget for the party. The controller's staff felt that any cuts were unwarranted as the firm continued to be very profitable.

Can both sides be right? Explain your answer.

LG 5 **E1–3** You have been made treasurer for a day at AIMCO, Inc. AIMCO develops technology for video conferencing. A manager of the satellite division has asked you to authorize a capital expenditure in the amount of $10,000. The manager states that this expenditure is necessary to continue a long-running project designed to use satellites to allow video conferencing anywhere on the planet. The manager admits that the satellite concept has been surpassed by recent technological advances in telephony, but he feels that AIMCO should continue the project. His reasoning is based on the fact that $2.5 million has already been spent over the past 15 years on this project. Although the project has little chance to be viable, the manager believes it would be a shame to waste the money and time already spent.

Use *marginal cost–benefit analysis* to make your decision regarding whether you should authorize the $10,000 expenditure to continue the project.

LG 6 **E1–4** Recently, some branches of Donut Shop, Inc., have dropped the practice of allowing employees to accept tips. Customers who once said, "Keep the change," now have to get used to waiting for their nickels. Management even instituted a policy of requiring that the change be thrown out if a customer drives off without it. As a frequent customer who gets coffee and doughnuts for the office, you notice that the lines are longer and that more mistakes are being made in your order.

Explain why tips could be viewed as similar to stock options and why the delays and incorrect orders could represent a case of *agency costs*. If tips are gone forever, how could Donut Shop reduce these agency costs?

Problems

All problems are available in myfinancelab.

LG 2 **P1–1** **Liability comparisons** Merideth Harper has invested $25,000 in Southwest Development Company. The firm has recently declared bankruptcy and has $60,000 in unpaid debts. Explain the nature of payments, if any, by Ms. Harper in each of the following situations.

a. Southwest Development Company is a *sole proprietorship* owned by Ms. Harper.
b. Southwest Development Company is a 50–50 *partnership* of Ms. Harper and Christopher Black.
c. Southwest Development Company is a *corporation*.

LG 4 **P1–2** **Accrual income versus cash flow for a period** Thomas Book Sales, Inc., supplies textbooks to college and university bookstores. The books are shipped with a proviso that they must be paid for within 30 days but can be returned for a full refund credit within 90 days. In 2009, Thomas shipped and billed book titles totaling $760,000. Collections, net of return credits, during the year totaled $690,000. The company spent $300,000 acquiring the books that it shipped.

a. Using accrual accounting and the preceding values, show the firm's net profit for the past year.
b. Using cash accounting and the preceding values, show the firm's net cash flow for the past year.
c. Which of these statements is more useful to the financial manager? Why?

Personal Finance Problem

LG 4 **P1–3** **Cash flows** It is typical for Jane to plan, monitor, and assess her financial position using cash flows over a given period, typically a month. Jane has a savings account, and her bank loans money at 6% per year while it offers short-term investment rates of 5%. Jane's cash flows during August were as follows:

Item	Cash inflow	Cash outflow
Clothes		$1,000
Interest received	$ 450	
Dining out		500
Groceries		800
Salary	4,500	
Auto payment		355
Utilities		280
Mortgage		1,200
Gas		222

a. Determine Jane's total cash inflows and cash outflows.
b. Determine the *net cash flow* for the month of August.
c. If there is a shortage, what are a few options open to Jane?
d. If there is a surplus, what would be a prudent strategy for her to follow?

LG 3 LG 5

P1–4 Marginal cost–benefit analysis and the goal of the firm Ken Allen, capital budgeting analyst for Bally Gears, Inc., has been asked to evaluate a proposal. The manager of the automotive division believes that replacing the robotics used on the heavy truck gear line will produce total benefits of $560,000 (in today's dollars) over the next 5 years. The existing robotics would produce benefits of $400,000 (also in today's dollars) over that same time period. An initial cash investment of $220,000 would be required to install the new equipment. The manager estimates that the existing robotics can be sold for $70,000. Show how Ken will apply *marginal cost–benefit analysis* techniques to determine the following:
a. The marginal (added) benefits of the proposed new robotics.
b. The marginal (added) cost of the proposed new robotics.
c. The net benefit of the proposed new robotics.
d. What should Ken Allen recommend that the company do? Why?
e. What factors besides the costs and benefits should be considered before the final decision is made?

LG 6

P1–5 Identifying agency problems, costs, and resolutions Explain why each of the following situations is an agency problem and what costs to the firm might result from it. Suggest how the problem might be dealt with short of firing the individual(s) involved.
a. The front desk receptionist routinely takes an extra 20 minutes of lunch time to run personal errands.
b. Division managers are padding cost estimates so as to show short-term efficiency gains when the costs come in lower than the estimates.
c. The firm's chief executive officer has had secret talks with a competitor about the possibility of a merger in which she would become the CEO of the combined firms.
d. A branch manager lays off experienced full-time employees and staffs customer service positions with part-time or temporary workers to lower employment costs and raise this year's branch profit. The manager's bonus is based on profitability.

LG 3

P1–6 ETHICS PROBLEM What does it mean to say that managers should maximize shareholder wealth "subject to ethical constraints"? What ethical considerations might enter into decisions that result in cash flow and stock price effects that are less than they might otherwise have been?

Spreadsheet Exercise

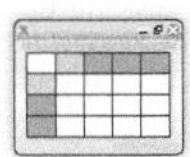

Assume that Monsanto Corporation is considering the renovation and/or replacement of some of its older and outdated carpet-manufacturing equipment. Its objective is to improve the efficiency of operations in terms of both speed and reduction in the number of defects. The company's finance department has compiled pertinent data that will allow it to conduct a *marginal cost–benefit analysis* for the proposed equipment replacement.

The cash outlay for new equipment would be approximately $600,000. The net book value of the old equipment and its potential net selling price add up to $250,000. The total benefits from the new equipment (measured in today's dollars) would be $900,000. The benefits of the old equipment over a similar period of time (measured in today's dollars) would be $300,000.

TO DO

Create a spreadsheet to conduct a *marginal cost–benefit analysis* for Monsanto Corporation, and determine the following:

a. The marginal (added) benefits of the proposed new equipment.
b. The marginal (added) cost of the proposed new equipment.
c. The net benefit of the proposed new equipment.
d. What would you recommend that the firm do? Why?

Visit www.myfinancelab.com for **Chapter Case: *Assessing the Goal of Sports Products, Inc.,*** Group Exercises, and numerous online resources.

2 The Financial Market Environment

Learning Goals

LG 1 Understand the role that financial institutions play in managerial finance.

LG 2 Contrast the functions of financial institutions and financial markets.

LG 3 Describe the differences between the capital markets and the money markets.

LG 4 Explain the root causes of the 2008 financial crisis and recession.

LG 5 Understand the major regulations and regulatory bodies that affect financial institutions and markets.

LG 6 Discuss business taxes and their importance in financial decisions.

Why This Chapter Matters to You

In your *professional* life

ACCOUNTING You need to understand how business income is taxed and the difference between average and marginal tax rates.

INFORMATION SYSTEMS You need to understand how information flows between the firm and financial markets.

MANAGEMENT You need to understand why healthy financial institutions are an integral part of a healthy economy and how a crisis in the financial sector can spread and affect almost any type of business.

MARKETING You need to understand why it is important for firms to communicate about their operating results with external investors and how regulations constrain the types of communication that occur.

OPERATIONS You need to understand why external financing is, for most firms, an essential aspect of ongoing operations.

In your *personal* life

Making financial transactions will be a regular occurrence throughout your entire life. These transactions may be as simple as depositing your paycheck in a bank or as complex as deciding how to allocate the money you save for retirement among different investment options. Many of these transactions have important tax consequences, which vary over time and from one type of transaction to another. The content in this chapter will help you make better decisions when you engage in any of these transactions.

JPMorgan Chase & Co.

Cut to the Chase

Since the recession of the early 1990s, business had been booming for JPMorgan Chase, one of the leading investment banking firms on Wall Street. After hitting a low of roughly $2 per share in October 1990, Chase stock went on a tear, rising at a rate of about 21 percent per year and hitting the $50 range by April 2007. The bank's investors enjoyed increasing dividend payments along with the rising stock price. JPMorgan Chase increased its dividend payout from $0.0833 per share in December 1990 to $0.38 per share in July 2007, an increase of more than 350 percent.

Trouble was brewing, however. In the summer of 2007, data began to emerge that prices of single-family homes were falling in many U.S. cities and homeowners were starting to default on their mortgages. Rumors swirled that JPMorgan and other banks held large investments in securities tied to residential mortgages. On September 15, 2008, the venerable investment banking firm, Lehman Brothers, filed for bankruptcy, and JPMorgan shares fell 10 percent in a single day. Bad news about the economy and the financial sector continued through the fall, and Chase's stock hit a low point on November 21 near $20, losing more than half its value in roughly 18 months.

All of this prompted JPMorgan management to make two difficult decisions. The first was to accept a $25 billion "investment" (some referred to it as a bailout) from the U.S. Treasury on October 28, 2008. The second was to cut its quarterly dividend by almost 87 percent, from $0.38 to $0.05 per share. These decisions, combined with a slowly improving economy, helped JPMorgan survive the 2008 financial crisis and the subsequent recession. By the summer of 2009, JPMorgan Chase repaid the $25 billion (with interest) that it had received from the government, and the bank's stock had recovered most of the value that it had lost.

LG 1 LG 2 LG 3

2.1 Financial Institutions and Markets

Most successful firms have ongoing needs for funds. They can obtain funds from external sources in three ways. The first source is through a *financial institution* that accepts savings and transfers them to those that need funds. A second source is through *financial markets,* organized forums in which the suppliers and demanders of various types of funds can make transactions. A third source is through *private placement.* Because of the unstructured nature of private placements, here we focus primarily on the role of financial institutions and financial markets in facilitating business financing.

FINANCIAL INSTITUTIONS

financial institution
An intermediary that channels the savings of individuals, businesses, and governments into loans or investments.

Financial institutions serve as intermediaries by channeling the savings of individuals, businesses, and governments into loans or investments. Many financial institutions directly or indirectly pay savers interest on deposited funds; others provide services for a fee (for example, checking accounts for which customers pay service charges). Some financial institutions accept customers' savings deposits and lend this money to other customers or to firms; others invest customers' savings in earning assets such as real estate or stocks and bonds; and some do both. Financial institutions are required by the government to operate within established regulatory guidelines.

Key Customers of Financial Institutions

For financial institutions, the key suppliers of funds and the key demanders of funds are individuals, businesses, and governments. The savings that individual consumers place in financial institutions provide these institutions with a large portion of their funds. Individuals not only supply funds to financial institutions but also demand funds from them in the form of loans. However, individuals as a group are the *net suppliers* for financial institutions: They save more money than they borrow.

Business firms also deposit some of their funds in financial institutions, primarily in checking accounts with various commercial banks. Like individuals, firms borrow funds from these institutions, but firms are *net demanders* of funds: They borrow more money than they save.

Governments maintain deposits of temporarily idle funds, certain tax payments, and Social Security payments in commercial banks. They do not borrow funds *directly* from financial institutions, although by selling their debt securities to various institutions, governments indirectly borrow from them. The government, like business firms, is typically a *net demander* of funds: It typically borrows more than it saves. We've all heard about the federal budget deficit.

Major Financial Institutions

The major financial institutions in the U.S. economy are commercial banks, savings and loans, credit unions, savings banks, insurance companies, mutual funds, and pension funds. These institutions attract funds from individuals, businesses, and governments, combine them, and make loans available to individuals and businesses.

COMMERCIAL BANKS, INVESTMENT BANKS, AND THE SHADOW BANKING SYSTEM

commercial banks
Institutions that provide savers with a secure place to invest their funds and that offer loans to individual and business borrowers.

investment banks
Institutions that assist companies in raising capital, advise firms on major transactions such as mergers or financial restructurings, and engage in trading and market making activities.

Glass-Steagall Act
An act of Congress in 1933 that created the federal deposit insurance program and separated the activities of commercial and investment banks.

shadow banking system
A group of institutions that engage in lending activities, much like traditional banks, but do not accept deposits and therefore are not subject to the same regulations as traditional banks.

Commercial banks are among the most important financial institutions in the economy because they provide savers with a secure place to invest funds and they offer both individuals and companies loans to finance investments, such as the purchase of a new home or the expansion of a business. **Investment banks** are institutions that (1) assist companies in raising capital, (2) advise firms on major transactions such as mergers or financial restructurings, and (3) engage in trading and market making activities.

The traditional business model of a commercial bank—taking in and paying interest on deposits and investing or lending those funds back out at higher interest rates—works to the extent that depositors believe that their investments are secure. Since the 1930s, the U.S. government has given some assurance to depositors that their money is safe by providing deposit insurance (currently up to $250,000 per depositor). Deposit insurance was put in place in response to the banking runs or panics that were part of the Great Depression. The same act of Congress that introduced deposit insurance, the **Glass-Steagall Act,** also created a separation between commercial banks and investment banks, meaning that an institution engaged in taking in deposits could not also engage in the somewhat riskier activities of securities underwriting and trading.

Commercial and investment banks remained essentially separate for more than 50 years, but in the late 1990s Glass-Steagall was repealed. Companies that had formerly engaged only in the traditional activities of a commercial bank began competing with investment banks for underwriting and other services. In addition, the 1990s witnessed tremendous growth in what has come to be known as the shadow banking system. The **shadow banking system** describes a group of institutions that engage in lending activities, much like traditional banks, but these institutions do not accept deposits and are therefore not subject to the same regulations as traditional banks.[1] For example, an institution such as a pension fund might have excess cash to invest, and a large corporation might need short-term financing to cover seasonal cash flow needs. A business like Lehman Brothers acted as an intermediary between these two parties, helping to facilitate a loan, and thereby became part of the shadow banking system. In March 2010, Treasury Secretary Timothy Geithner noted that at its peak the shadow banking system financed roughly $8 trillion in assets and was roughly as large as the traditional banking system.

Matter of fact

Consolidation in the U.S. Banking Industry

The U.S. banking industry has been going through a long period of consolidation. According to the FDIC, the number of commercial banks in the United States declined from 11,463 in 1992 to 8,012 at the end of 2009, a decline of 30 percent. The decline is concentrated among small community banks, which larger institutions have been acquiring at a rapid pace.

1. The Dodd-Frank Wall Street Reform and Consumer Protection Act was passed in 2010 in response to the financial crisis and recession of 2008–2009. This legislation will likely have a dramatic impact on the regulation of both traditional and shadow banking institutions, but it is too early to tell exactly what the new law's effects will be. In the wake of the law's passage, many commentators suggested that the law did not exercise enough oversight of the shadow banking system to prevent a financial meltdown similar to the one that motivated the law's enactment.

FINANCIAL MARKETS

financial markets
Forums in which suppliers of funds and demanders of funds can transact business directly.

Financial markets are forums in which suppliers of funds and demanders of funds can transact business directly. Whereas the loans made by financial institutions are granted without the direct knowledge of the suppliers of funds (savers), suppliers in the financial markets know where their funds are being lent or invested. The two key financial markets are the money market and the capital market. Transactions in short-term debt instruments, or marketable securities, take place in the *money market*. Long-term securities—bonds and stocks—are traded in the *capital market*.

private placement
The sale of a new security directly to an investor or group of investors.

public offering
The sale of either bonds or stocks to the general public.

primary market
Financial market in which securities are initially issued; the only market in which the issuer is directly involved in the transaction.

secondary market
Financial market in which preowned securities (those that are not new issues) are traded.

To raise money, firms can use either private placements or public offerings. A **private placement** involves the sale of a new security directly to an investor or group of investors, such as an insurance company or pension fund. Most firms, however, raise money through a **public offering** of securities, which is the sale of either bonds or stocks to the general public.

When a company or government entity sells stocks or bonds to investors and receives cash in return, it is said to have sold securities in the **primary market.** After the primary market transaction occurs, any further trading in the security does not involve the issuer directly, and the issuer receives no additional money from these subsequent transactions. Once the securities begin to trade between investors, they become part of the **secondary market.** On large stock exchanges, billions of shares may trade between buyers and sellers on a single day, and these are all secondary market transactions. Money flows from the investors buying stocks to the investors selling them, and the company whose stock is being traded is largely unaffected by the transactions. The primary market is the one in which "new" securities are sold. The secondary market can be viewed as a "preowned" securities market.

THE RELATIONSHIP BETWEEN INSTITUTIONS AND MARKETS

Financial institutions actively participate in the financial markets as both suppliers and demanders of funds. Figure 2.1 depicts the general flow of funds through and between financial institutions and financial markets as well as the

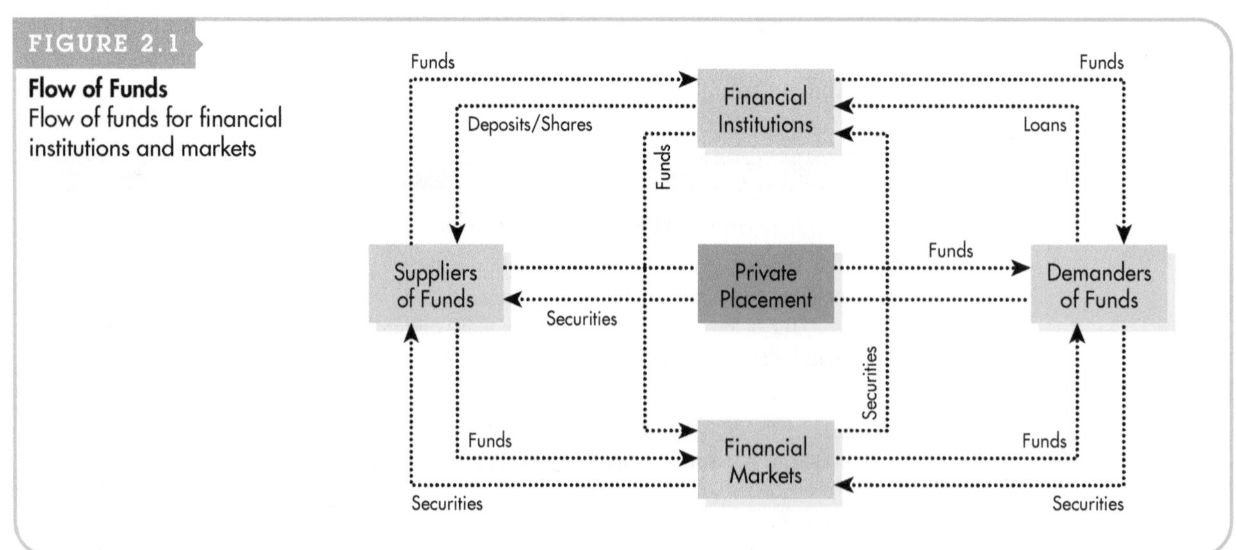

FIGURE 2.1
Flow of Funds
Flow of funds for financial institutions and markets

mechanics of private placement transactions. Domestic or foreign individuals, businesses, and governments may supply and demand funds. We next briefly discuss the money market, including its international equivalent—the *Eurocurrency market.* We then end this section with a discussion of the capital market, which is of key importance to the firm.

THE MONEY MARKET

money market
A financial relationship created between suppliers and demanders of *short-term funds.*

The **money market** is created by a financial relationship between suppliers and demanders of *short-term funds* (funds with maturities of one year or less). The money market exists because some individuals, businesses, governments, and financial institutions have temporarily idle funds that they wish to invest in a relatively safe, interest-bearing asset. At the same time, other individuals, businesses, governments, and financial institutions find themselves in need of seasonal or temporary financing. The money market brings together these suppliers and demanders of short-term funds.

marketable securities
Short-term debt instruments, such as U.S. Treasury bills, commercial paper, and negotiable certificates of deposit issued by government, business, and financial institutions, respectively.

Most money market transactions are made in **marketable securities**—short-term debt instruments, such as U.S. Treasury bills, commercial paper, and negotiable certificates of deposit issued by government, business, and financial institutions, respectively. Investors generally consider marketable securities to be among the least risky investments available. Marketable securities are described in Chapter 15.

Eurocurrency market
International equivalent of the domestic money market.

The international equivalent of the domestic money market is called the **Eurocurrency market.** This is a market for short-term bank deposits denominated in U.S. dollars or other major currencies. Eurocurrency deposits arise when a corporation or individual makes a bank deposit in a currency other than the local currency of the country where the bank is located. If, for example, a multinational corporation were to deposit U.S. dollars in a London bank, this would create a Eurodollar deposit (a dollar deposit at a bank in Europe). Nearly all Eurodollar deposits are *time deposits.* This means that the bank would promise to repay the deposit, with interest, at a fixed date in the future—say, in 6 months. During the interim, the bank is free to lend this dollar deposit to creditworthy corporate or government borrowers. If the bank cannot find a borrower on its own, it may lend the deposit to another international bank.

THE CAPITAL MARKET

capital market
A market that enables suppliers and demanders of *long-term funds* to make transactions.

The **capital market** is a market that enables suppliers and demanders of *long-term funds* to make transactions. Included are securities issues of business and government. The backbone of the capital market is formed by the broker and dealer markets that provide a forum for bond and stock transactions. International capital markets also exist.

Key Securities Traded: Bonds and Stocks

The key capital market securities are *bonds* (long-term debt) and both *common stock* and *preferred stock* (equity, or ownership).

bond
Long-term debt instrument used by business and government to raise large sums of money, generally from a diverse group of lenders.

Bonds are long-term debt instruments used by business and government to raise large sums of money, generally from a diverse group of lenders. *Corporate bonds* typically pay interest *semiannually* (every 6 months) at a stated *coupon interest rate.* They have an initial *maturity* of from 10 to 30 years, and a *par,* or *face, value* of $1,000 that must be repaid at maturity. Bonds are described in detail in Chapter 7.

Example 2.1 ▶ Lakeview Industries, a major microprocessor manufacturer, has issued a 9% coupon interest rate, 20-year bond with a $1,000 par value that pays interest semiannually. Investors who buy this bond receive the contractual right to $90 annual interest (9% coupon interest rate × $1,000 par value) distributed as $45 at the end of each 6 months (1/2 × $90) for 20 years, plus the $1,000 par value at the end of year 20.

preferred stock
A special form of ownership having a fixed periodic dividend that must be paid prior to payment of any dividends to common stockholders.

broker market
The securities exchanges on which the two sides of a transaction, the buyer and seller, are brought together to trade securities.

securities exchanges
Organizations that provide the marketplace in which firms can raise funds through the sale of new securities and purchasers can resell securities.

dealer market
The market in which the buyer and seller are not brought together directly but instead have their orders executed by securities dealers that "make markets" in the given security.

market makers
Securities dealers who "make markets" by offering to buy or sell certain securities at stated prices.

Nasdaq market
An all-electronic trading platform used to execute securities trades.

over-the-counter (OTC) market
Market where smaller, unlisted securities are traded.

As noted earlier, shares of *common stock* are units of ownership, or equity, in a corporation. Common stockholders earn a return by receiving dividends—periodic distributions of cash—or by realizing increases in share price. **Preferred stock** is a special form of ownership that has features of both a bond and common stock. Preferred stockholders are promised a fixed periodic dividend that must be paid prior to payment of any dividends to common stockholders. In other words, preferred stock has "preference" over common stock. Preferred stock and common stock are described in detail in Chapter 8. See the *Focus on Practice* box for the story of one legendary stock price and the equally legendary man who brought it about.

Broker Markets and Dealer Markets

By far the vast majority of trades made by individual investors take place in the secondary market. When you look at the secondary market *on the basis of how securities are traded,* you will find you can essentially divide the market into two segments: broker markets and dealer markets.

The key difference between broker and dealer markets is a technical point dealing with the way trades are executed. That is, when a trade occurs in a **broker market,** the two sides to the transaction, the buyer and the seller, are brought together and the trade takes place at that point: Party A sells his or her securities directly to the buyer, Party B. In a sense, with the help of a *broker,* the securities effectively change hands on the floor of the exchange. The broker market consists of national and regional **securities exchanges,** which are organizations that provide a marketplace in which firms can raise funds through the sale of new securities and purchasers can resell securities.

In contrast, when trades are made in a **dealer market,** the buyer and the seller are never brought together directly. Instead, **market makers** execute the buy/sell orders. Market makers are *securities dealers* who "make markets" by offering to buy or sell certain securities at stated prices. Essentially, two separate trades are made: Party A sells his or her securities (in, say, Dell) to a dealer, and Party B buys his or her securities (in Dell) from another, or possibly even the same, dealer. Thus, there is always a dealer (*market maker*) on one side of a dealer–market transaction. The dealer market is made up of both the **Nasdaq market,** an all-electronic trading platform used to execute securities trades, and the **over-the-counter (OTC) market,** where smaller, unlisted securities are traded.

Broker Markets If you are like most people, when you think of the "stock market" the first name to come to mind is the New York Stock Exchange, known currently as the NYSE Euronext after a series of mergers that expanded the

focus on PRACTICE

Berkshire Hathaway—Can Buffett Be Replaced?

in practice In early 1980, investors could buy one share of Berkshire Hathaway Class A common stock (stock symbol: BRKA) for $285. That may have seemed expensive at the time, but by September 2010 the price of just one share had climbed to $125,000. The wizard behind such phenomenal growth in shareholder value is the chairman of Berkshire Hathaway, Warren Buffett, nicknamed the Oracle of Omaha.

With his partner, Vice-Chairman Charlie Munger, Buffett runs a large conglomerate of dozens of subsidiaries with 222,000 employees and more than $112 billion in annual revenues. He makes it look easy. In his words, "I've taken the easy route, just sitting back and working through great managers who run their own shows. My only tasks are to cheer them on, sculpt and harden our corporate culture, and make major capital-allocation decisions. Our managers have returned this trust by working hard and effectively."[a]

Buffett's style of corporate leadership seems rather laid back, but behind that "aw-shucks" manner is one of the best analytical minds in business. He believes in aligning managerial incentives with performance. Berkshire employs many different incentive arrangements, with their terms depending on such elements as the economic potential or capital intensity of a CEO's business. Whatever the compensation arrangement, Buffett tries to keep it both simple and fair. Buffett himself receives an annual salary of $100,000—not much in this age of supersized CEO compensation packages. Listed for many years among the world's wealthiest people, Buffett has donated most of his Berkshire stock to the Bill and Melinda Gates Foundation.

Berkshire's annual report is a must-read for many investors due to the popularity of Buffett's annual letter to shareholders with his homespun take on such topics as investing, corporate governance, and corporate leadership. Shareholder meetings in Omaha, Nebraska, have turned into cultlike gatherings, with thousands traveling to listen to Buffett answer questions from shareholders. One question that has been firmly answered is the question of Mr. Buffett's ability to create shareholder value.

The next question that needs to be answered is whether Berkshire Hathaway can successfully replace Buffett (age 80) and Munger (age 86). In October 2010, Berkshire hired hedge fund manager Todd Combs to handle a significant portion of the firm's investments. Berkshire shareholders hope that Buffett's special wisdom applies as well to identifying new managerial talent as it does to making strategic investment decisions.

► ***The share price of BRKA has never been split. Why might the company refuse to split its shares to make them more affordable to average investors?***

[a]Berkshire Hathaway, Inc., "Letter to Shareholders of Berkshire Hathaway, Inc.," *2006 Annual Report*, p. 4.

exchange's global reach. In point of fact, the NYSE Euronext is the dominant broker market. The American Stock Exchange (AMEX), which is another *national exchange,* and several so-called *regional exchanges* are also broker markets. These exchanges account for about 60 percent of *the total dollar volume* of all shares traded in the U.S. stock market. In broker markets all the trading takes place on centralized trading floors.

Most exchanges are modeled after the New York Stock Exchange. For a firm's securities to be listed for trading on a stock exchange, a firm must file an application for listing and meet a number of requirements. For example, to be eligible for listing on the NYSE, a firm must have at least 400 stockholders owning 100 or more shares; a minimum of 1.1 million shares of publicly held stock outstanding; pretax earnings of at least $10 million over the previous 3 years, with at least $2 million in the previous 2 years; and a minimum market value of public shares of $100 million. Clearly, only large, widely held firms are candidates for NYSE listing.

Once placed, an order to buy or sell on the NYSE can be executed in minutes, thanks to sophisticated telecommunication devices. New Internet-based brokerage systems enable investors to place their buy and sell orders electronically.

Information on publicly traded securities is reported in various media, both print, such as the *Wall Street Journal,* and electronic, such as MSN Money (www.moneycentral.msn.com).

Dealer Markets One of the key features of the *dealer market* is that it has no centralized trading floors. Instead, it is made up of a large number of *market makers* who are linked together via a mass-telecommunications network.

bid price
The highest price offered to purchase a security.

ask price
The lowest price at which a security is offered for sale.

Each market maker is actually a securities dealer who makes a market in one or more securities by offering to buy or sell them at stated bid/ask prices. The **bid price** and **ask price** represent, respectively, the highest price offered to purchase a given security and the lowest price at which the security is offered for sale. In effect, an investor pays the ask price when buying securities and receives the bid price when selling them.

As described earlier, the dealer market is made up of both the *Nasdaq market* and the *over-the-counter (OTC) market,* which together account for about 40 percent of all shares traded in the U.S. market—with the Nasdaq accounting for the overwhelming majority of those trades. (As an aside, the *primary market* is also a dealer market because all new issues are sold to the investing public by securities dealers, acting on behalf of the investment banker.)

The largest dealer market consists of a select group of stocks that are listed and traded on the *National Association of Securities Dealers Automated Quotation System,* typically referred to as *Nasdaq*. Founded in 1971, Nasdaq had its origins in the OTC market but is today considered *a totally separate entity that's no longer a part of the OTC market.* In fact, in 2006 Nasdaq was formally recognized by the SEC as a "listed exchange," essentially giving it the same stature and prestige as the NYSE.

International Capital Markets

Eurobond market
The market in which corporations and governments typically issue bonds denominated in dollars and sell them to investors located outside the United States.

Although U.S. capital markets are by far the world's largest, there are important debt and equity markets outside the United States. In the **Eurobond market,** corporations and governments typically issue bonds denominated in dollars and sell them to investors located outside the United States. A U.S. corporation might, for example, issue dollar-denominated bonds that would be purchased by investors in Belgium, Germany, or Switzerland. Through the Eurobond market, issuing firms and governments can tap a much larger pool of investors than would be generally available in the local market.

Matter of fact

NYSE Euronext is the World's Largest Stock Exchange

According to the World Federation of Exchanges, the largest stock market in the world, as measured by the total market value of securities listed on that market, is the NYSE Euronext, with listed securities worth more than \$11.8 trillion in the United States and \$2.9 trillion in Europe. Next largest is the London Stock Exchange, with securities valued at £1.7 trillion, which is equivalent to \$2.8 trillion given the exchange rate between pounds and dollars prevailing at the end of 2009.

foreign bond
A bond that is issued by a foreign corporation or government and is denominated in the investor's home currency and sold in the investor's home market.

The *foreign bond market* is an international market for long-term debt securities. A **foreign bond** is a bond issued by a foreign corporation or government that is denominated in the investor's home currency and sold in the investor's home market. A bond issued by a U.S. company that is denominated in Swiss francs and sold in Switzerland is a foreign bond. Although the foreign bond market is smaller than the Eurobond market, many issuers have found it to be an attractive way of tapping debt markets around the world.

international equity market
A market that allows corporations to sell blocks of shares to investors in a number of different countries simultaneously.

Finally, the **international equity market** allows corporations to sell blocks of shares to investors in a number of different countries simultaneously. This market enables corporations to raise far larger amounts of capital than they could in any single market. International equity sales have been indispensable to governments that have sold state-owned companies to private investors.

The Role of Capital Markets

efficient market
A market that allocates funds to their most productive uses as a result of competition among wealth-maximizing investors and that determines and publicizes prices that are believed to be close to their true value.

From a firm's perspective, the role of a capital market is to be a liquid market where firms can interact with investors to obtain valuable external financing resources. From investors' perspectives, the role of a capital market is to be an **efficient market** that allocates funds to their most productive uses. This is especially true for securities that are actively traded in broker or dealer markets, where the competition among wealth-maximizing investors determines and publicizes prices that are believed to be close to their true value.

The price of an individual security is determined by the interaction between buyers and sellers in the market. If the market is efficient, the price of a stock is an unbiased estimate of its true value, and changes in the price reflect new information that investors learn about and act on. For example, suppose a certain stock currently trades at $40 per share. If this company announces that sales of a new product have been higher than expected, investors will raise their estimate of what the stock is truly worth. At $40, the stock is a relative bargain, so there will temporarily be more buyers than sellers wanting to trade the stock, and its price will have to rise to restore equilibrium in the market. The more efficient the market is, the more rapidly this whole process works. In theory, even information known only to insiders may become incorporated in stock prices as the *Focus on Ethics* box on page 40 explains.

Not everyone agrees that prices in financial markets are as efficient as described in the preceding paragraph. Advocates of *behavioral finance*, an emerging field that blends ideas from finance and psychology, argue that stock prices and prices of other securities can deviate from their true values for extended periods. These people point to episodes such as the huge run-up and subsequent collapse of the prices of Internet stocks in the late 1990s and the failure of markets to accurately assess the risk of mortgage-backed securities in the more recent financial crisis as examples of the principle that stock prices sometimes can be wildly inaccurate measures of value.

In more depth

To read about *The Efficient Markets Hypothesis*, go to www.myfinancelab.com

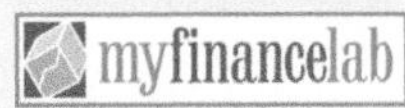

Just how efficient are the prices in financial markets? That is a question that will be debated for a long time. It is clear that prices do move in response to new information, and for most investors and corporate managers the best advice is probably to be cautious when betting against the market. Identifying securities that the market has over- or undervalued is extremely difficult, and very few people have demonstrated an ability to bet against the market correctly for an extended time.

focus on ETHICS

The Ethics of Insider Trading

in practice On December 27, 2001, Martha Stewart sold nearly 4,000 shares in ImClone Systems stock. The following day, the Food and Drug Administration delivered some bad news regarding ImClone's cancer drug, Erbitux, and ImClone's stock price dropped substantially. It appeared that Martha Stewart had picked the right time to sell.

Martha Stewart was not the only ImClone shareholder who was selling. The company's founder, Sam Waksal, also tried to sell his stock (brokers refused to execute the sales), as did his daughter. The U.S. Securities and Exchange Commission and the Federal Bureau of Investigation were soon looking into the transactions. Sam Waksal ultimately received an 87-month prison sentence and $3 million in fines for insider trading and tax evasion. Martha Stewart was convicted of conspiracy, obstruction, and making false statements to federal investigators and served 5 months in jail, 5 months of home confinement, and 2 years of probation and paid a $30,000 fine. In addition, she was forced to resign as chairman and CEO of the company she had founded, Martha Stewart Living Omnimedia. On the day of her conviction, the company's shares lost 23 percent of their value.

Laws prohibiting insider trading were established in the United States in the 1930s. These laws are designed to ensure that all investors have access to relevant information on the same terms. However, many market participants believe that insider trading should be permitted. Their argument is rooted in the efficient-market hypothesis (EMH). According to the EMH, stock prices fully reflect all publicly available information. Of course, a significant amount of information about every company is not publicly available. Thus, stock prices may not accurately reflect all that is known about a company.

Those who argue for allowing insider trading believe that market prices influence the allocation of resources among companies. Firms with higher stock prices find it easier to raise capital, for example. Therefore, it is important that market prices reflect as much information as possible. Advocates of allowing insider trading argue that investors would quickly convert inside information into publicly available information if insider trading were permitted. If, for example, Sam Waksal had been permitted to sell his stock after learning of the FDA's decision, market participants might view his actions and come to the judgment that ImClone's prospects had dimmed. Of course, the other necessary condition is that outsiders can observe the stock market transactions of insiders.

Interestingly, Eugene Fama, who is viewed by many as the father of the efficient-market hypothesis, does not believe that insider trading should be permitted.[a] Fama believes that allowing insider trading creates a moral hazard problem. For example, if insiders are allowed to trade on proprietary information, they may have the incentive to hold back information for their personal gain.

▶ ***If efficiency is the goal of financial markets, is allowing or disallowing insider trading more unethical?***

▶ ***Does allowing insider trading create an ethical dilemma for insiders?***

[a] www.dimensional.com/famafrench/2010/04/qa-is-insider-trading-beneficial.html

→ REVIEW QUESTIONS

2–1 Who are the key participants in the transactions of financial institutions? Who are *net suppliers*, and who are *net demanders?*

2–2 What role do *financial markets* play in our economy? What are *primary* and *secondary* markets? What relationship exists between financial institutions and financial markets?

2–3 What is the *money market?* What is the *Eurocurrency market?*

2–4 What is the *capital market?* What are the primary securities traded in it?

2–5 What are *broker markets?* What are *dealer markets?* How do they differ?

2–6 Briefly describe the international capital markets, particularly the *Eurobond market* and the *international equity market.*

2–7 What are *efficient markets?* What determines the price of an individual security in such a market?

LG 4 2.2 The Financial Crisis

In the summer and fall of 2008, the U.S. financial system, and financial systems around the world, appeared to be on the verge of collapse. Troubles in the financial sector spread to other industries, and a severe global recession ensued. In this section, we outline some of the main causes and consequences of that crisis.

FINANCIAL INSTITUTIONS AND REAL ESTATE FINANCE

In the classic film *It's a Wonderful Life,* the central character is George Bailey, who runs a financial institution called the Bailey Building and Loan Association. In a key scene in that movie, a bank run is about to occur and depositors demand that George return the money that they invested in the Building and Loan. George pleads with one man to keep his funds at the bank, saying:

> You're thinking of this place all wrong, as if I have the money back in a safe. The money's not here. Your money is in Joe's house. That's right next to yours—and then the Kennedy house, and Mrs. Maklin's house, and a hundred others. You're lending them the money to build, and then they're going to pay it back to you as best they can. What are you going to do, foreclose on them?

This scene offers a relatively realistic portrayal of the role that financial institutions played in allocating credit for investments in residential real estate for many years. Local banks took deposits and made loans to local borrowers. However, since the 1970s, a process called securitization has changed the way that mortgage finance works. **Securitization** refers to the process of pooling mortgages or other types of loans and then selling claims or securities against that pool in a secondary market. These securities, called **mortgage-backed securities,** can be purchased by individual investors, pension funds, mutual funds, or virtually any other investor. As homeowners repay their loans, those payments eventually make their way into the hands of investors who hold the mortgage-backed securities. Therefore, a primary risk associated with mortgage-backed securities is that homeowners may not be able to, or may choose not to, repay their loans. Banks today still lend money to individuals who want to build or purchase new homes, but they typically bundle those loans together and sell them to organizations that securitize them and pass them on to investors all over the world.

securitization
The process of pooling mortgages or other types of loans and then selling claims or securities against that pool in the secondary market.

mortgage-backed securities
Securities that represent claims on the cash flows generated by a pool of mortgages.

FALLING HOME PRICES AND DELINQUENT MORTGAGES

Prior to the 2008 financial crisis, most investors viewed mortgage-backed securities as relatively safe investments. Figure 2.2 on page 42 illustrates one of the main reasons for this view. The figure shows the behavior of the Standard & Poor's Case-Shiller Index, a barometer of home prices in ten major U.S. cities, in each month from January 1987 to February 2010. Historically, declines in the index were relatively infrequent, and between July 1995 and April 2006 the index rose continuously without posting even a single monthly decline. When house prices are rising, the gap between what a borrower owes on a home and what the home is worth widens. Lenders will allow borrowers who have difficulty making payments on their mortgages to tap this built-up home equity to refinance their loans and lower their payments. Therefore, rising home prices helped keep mortgage default rates low from the mid-1990s through 2006. Investing in real estate and mortgage-backed securities seemed to involve very little risk during this period.

FIGURE 2.2

Housing Values
Standard & Poor's Case-Shiller Home Price Index, January 1987 through February 2010

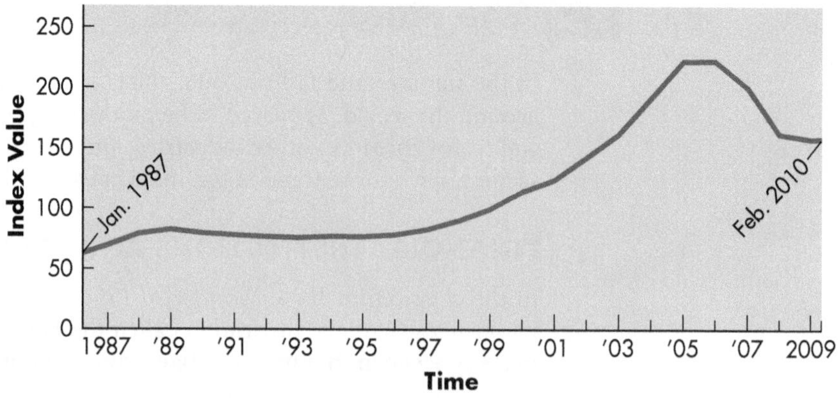

In part because real estate investments appeared to be relatively safe, lenders began relaxing their standards for borrowers. This led to tremendous growth in a category of loans called subprime mortgages. Subprime mortgages are mortgage loans made to borrowers with lower incomes and poorer credit histories as compared to "prime" borrowers. Often, loans granted to subprime borrowers have adjustable, rather than fixed, interest rates. This makes subprime borrowers particularly vulnerable if interest rates rise, and many of these borrowers (and lenders) assumed that rising home prices would allow borrowers to refinance their loans if they had difficulties making payments. Partly through the growth of subprime mortgages, banks and other financial institutions gradually increased their investments in real estate loans. In the year 2000, real estate loans accounted for less than 40 percent of the total loan portfolios of large banks. By 2007, real estate loans grew to more than half of all loans made by large banks, and the fraction of these loans in the subprime category increased as well.

Unfortunately, as Figure 2.2 shows, home prices fell almost without interruption from May 2006 through May 2009. Over that three-year period, home prices fell on average by more than 30 percent. Not surprisingly, when homeowners had difficulty making their mortgage payments, refinancing was no longer an option, and delinquency rates and foreclosures began to climb. By 2009, nearly 25 percent of subprime borrowers were behind schedule on their mortgage payments. Some borrowers, recognizing that the value of their homes was far less than the amount they owed on their mortgages, simply walked away from their homes and let lenders repossess them.

CRISIS OF CONFIDENCE IN BANKS

With delinquency rates rising, the value of mortgage-backed securities began to fall, and so too did the fortunes of financial institutions that had invested heavily in real estate assets. In March 2008, the Federal Reserve provided financing for the acquisition (that is, the rescue) of Bear Stearns by JPMorgan Chase. Later that year, Lehman Brothers filed for bankruptcy. Throughout 2008 and 2009, the Federal Reserve, the Bush administration, and finally the Obama administration took unprecedented steps to try to shore up the banking sector and stimulate the economy, but these measures could not completely avert the crisis.

FIGURE 2.3

Bank Stock Values
Standard & Poor's Banking Index, January 1, 2008 through May 17, 2010

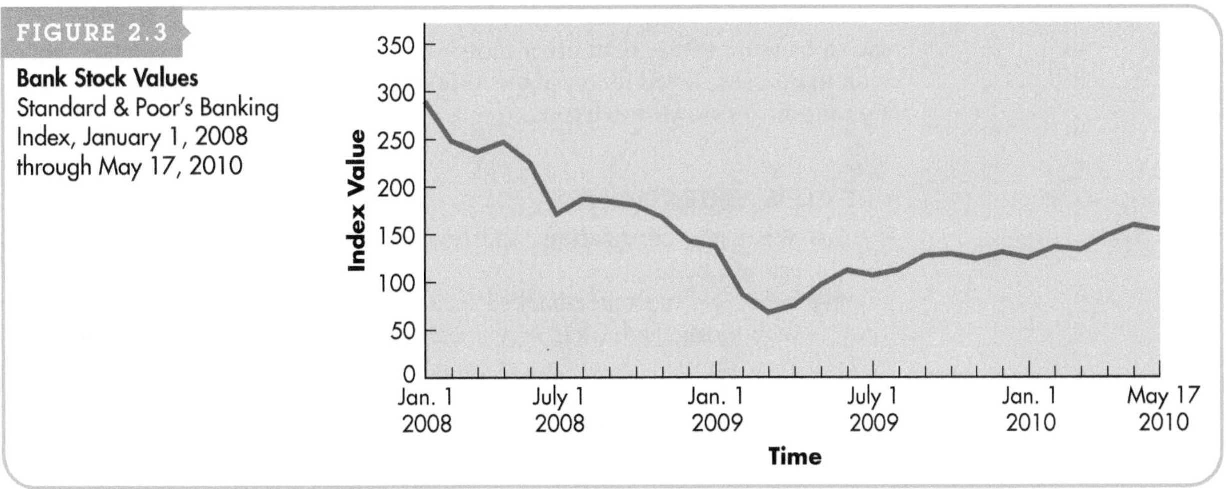

Figure 2.3 shows the behavior of the Standard & Poor's Banking Index, an index that tracks bank stocks. Bank stocks fell 81 percent between January 2008 and March 2009, and the number of bank failures skyrocketed. According to the Federal Deposit Insurance Corporation (FDIC), only three banks failed in 2007. In 2008 that number rose by a factor of eight to 25 failed banks, and the number increased nearly six times to 140 failures in 2009. While the economy began to recover in 2010, bank failures continued at a rapid pace, with 139 institutions failing in the first 10 months of that year.

SPILLOVER EFFECTS AND THE GREAT RECESSION

As banks came under intense financial pressure in 2008, they began to tighten their lending standards and dramatically reduced the quantity of loans they made. In the aftermath of the Lehman Brothers bankruptcy, lending in the money market contracted very sharply. Corporations who had relied on the money market as a source of short-term funding found that they could no longer raise money in this market or could do so only at extraordinarily high rates.

As a consequence, businesses began to hoard cash and cut back on expenditures, and economic activity contracted. Gross domestic product (GDP) declined in five out of six quarters starting in the first quarter of 2008, and the economy shed more than 8 million jobs in 2008–2009 as the unemployment rate reached 10 percent. Congress passed an $862 billion stimulus package to try to revive the economy, and the Federal Reserve pushed short-term interest rates close to 0 percent. By late 2009 and early 2010, there were signs that a gradual economic recovery had begun, but the job market remained stagnant, and most forecasts called for anemic economic growth.

Perhaps the most important lesson from this episode is how important financial institutions are to a modern economy. By some measures, the 2008–2009 recession was the worst experienced in the United States since the Great Depression. Indeed, there many parallels between those two economic contractions. Both were preceded by a period of rapid economic growth, rising stock prices, and movements by banks into new lines of business, and both involved a major crisis in the financial sector. Recessions associated with a banking crisis tend to be more severe than other recessions because so many businesses rely on credit to operate. When financial institutions contract borrowing, activity in most other industries slows down too.

→ REVIEW QUESTIONS

2–8 What is securitization, and how does it facilitate investment in real estate assets?

2–9 What is a mortgage-backed security? What is the basic risk associated with mortgage-backed securities?

2–10 How do rising home prices contribute to low mortgage delinquencies?

2–11 Why do falling home prices create an incentive for homeowners to default on their mortgages even if they can afford to make the monthly payments?

2–12 Why does a crisis in the financial sector spill over into other industries?

LG 5

2.3 Regulation of Financial Institutions and Markets

The previous section discussed just how vulnerable modern economies are when financial institutions are in a state of crisis. Partly to avoid these types of problems, governments typically regulate financial institutions and markets as much or more than almost any other sector in the economy. This section provides an overview of the financial regulatory landscape in the United States.

REGULATIONS GOVERNING FINANCIAL INSTITUTIONS

As mentioned in the previous section, Congress passed the Glass-Steagall Act in 1933 during the depths of the Great Depression. The early 1930s witnessed a series of banking panics that caused almost one-third of the nation's banks to fail. Troubles within the banking sector and other factors contributed to the worst economic contraction in U.S. history, in which industrial production fell by more than 50 percent, the unemployment rate peaked at almost 25 percent, and stock prices dropped roughly 86 percent. The Glass-Steagall Act attempted to calm the public's fears about the banking industry by establishing the **Federal Deposit Insurance Corporation (FDIC),** which provided deposit insurance, effectively guaranteeing that individuals would not lose their money if they held it in a bank that failed. The FDIC was also charged with examining banks on a regular basis to ensure that they were "safe and sound." The Glass-Steagall Act also prohibited institutions that took deposits from engaging in activities such as securities underwriting and trading, thereby effectively separating commercial banks from investment banks.

Federal Deposit Insurance Corporation (FDIC)
An agency created by the Glass-Steagall Act that provides insurance for deposits at banks and monitors banks to ensure their safety and soundness.

Over time, U.S. financial institutions faced competitive pressures from both domestic and foreign businesses that engaged in facilitating loans or making loans directly. Because these competitors either did not accept deposits or were located outside the United States, they were not subject to the same regulations as domestic banks. As a result, domestic banks began to lose market share in their core businesses. Pressure mounted to repeal the Glass-Steagall Act to enable U.S. banks to compete more effectively, and in 1999 Congress enacted and President Clinton signed the **Gramm-Leach-Bliley Act,** which allows commercial banks, investment banks, and insurance companies to consolidate and compete for business in a wider range of activities.

Gramm-Leach-Bliley Act
An act that allows business combinations (that is, mergers) between commercial banks, investment banks, and insurance companies, and thus permits these institutions to compete in markets that prior regulations prohibited them from entering.

In the aftermath of the recent financial crisis and recession, Congress passed the Dodd-Frank Wall Street Reform and Consumer Protection Act in July 2010. In print, the new law runs for hundreds of pages and calls for the creation of several new agencies including the Financial Stability Oversight Council, the Office of Financial Research, and the Bureau of Consumer Financial Protection. The act also realigns the duties of several existing agencies and requires existing and new agencies to report to Congress regularly. As this book was going to press, the various agencies affected or created by the new law were writing rules specifying how the new law's provisions would be implemented, so exactly how the new legislation will affect financial institutions and markets remains unclear.

REGULATIONS GOVERNING FINANCIAL MARKETS

Two other pieces of legislation were passed during the Great Depression that had an enormous impact on the regulation of financial markets. The **Securities Act of 1933** imposed new regulations governing the sale of new securities. That is, the 1933 act was intended to regulate activity in the primary market in which securities are initially issued to the public. The act was designed to insure that the sellers of new securities provided extensive disclosures to the potential buyers of those securities.

Securities Act of 1933
An act that regulates the sale of securities to the public via the primary market.

The **Securities Exchange Act of 1934** regulates the secondary trading of securities such as stocks and bonds. The Securities Exchange Act of 1934 also created the **Securities and Exchange Commission (SEC),** which is the primary agency responsible for enforcing federal securities laws. In addition to the one-time disclosures required of security issuers by the Securities Act of 1933, the Securities Exchange Act of 1934 requires ongoing disclosure by companies whose securities trade in secondary markets. Companies must make a 10-Q filing every quarter and a 10-K filing annually. The 10-Q and 10-K forms contain detailed information about the financial performance of the firm during the relevant period. Today, these forms are available online through the SEC's website known as EDGAR (Electronic Data Gathering, Analysis, and Retrieval). The 1934 act also imposes limits on the extent to which corporate "insiders," such as senior managers, can trade in their firm's securities.

Securities Exchange Act of 1934
An act that regulates the trading of securities such as stocks and bonds in the secondary market.

Securities and Exchange Commission (SEC)
The primary government agency responsible for enforcing federal securities laws.

→ REVIEW QUESTIONS

2–13 Why do you think so many pieces of important legislation related to financial markets and institutions were passed during the Great Depression?

2–14 What different aspects of financial markets do the Securities Act of 1933 and the Securities Exchange Act of 1934 regulate?

LG 6

2.4 Business Taxes

Taxes are a fact of life, and businesses, like individuals, must pay taxes on income. The income of sole proprietorships and partnerships is taxed as the income of the individual owners; corporate income is subject to corporate taxes.

Regardless of their legal form, all businesses can earn two types of income, ordinary and capital gains. Under current law, these two types of income are treated differently in the taxation of individuals; they are not treated differently for entities subject to corporate taxes. However, frequent amendments are made to the tax code, particularly as economic conditions change and when party control of the legislative and executive branches of government shifts.

ORDINARY INCOME

ordinary income
Income earned through the sale of a firm's goods or services.

The **ordinary income** of a corporation is income earned through the sale of goods or services. Ordinary income in 2010 was taxed subject to the rates depicted in the corporate tax rate schedule in Table 2.1.

Example 2.2 ▸

Webster Manufacturing, Inc., a small manufacturer of kitchen knives, has before-tax earnings of \$250,000. The tax on these earnings can be found by using the tax rate schedule in Table 2.1:

$$\begin{aligned}\text{Total taxes due} &= \$22{,}250 + [0.39 \times (\$250{,}000 - \$100{,}000)] \\ &= \$22{,}250 + (0.39 \times \$150{,}000) \\ &= \$22{,}250 + \$58{,}500 = \underline{\underline{\$80{,}750}}\end{aligned}$$

From a financial point of view, it is important to understand the difference between average and marginal tax rates, the treatment of interest and dividend income, and the effects of tax deductibility.

Marginal versus Average Tax Rates

marginal tax rate
The rate at which *additional income* is taxed.

The **marginal tax rate** represents the rate at which *the next dollar of income* is taxed. In the current corporate tax structure, the marginal tax rate is 15 percent

TABLE 2.1 Corporate Tax Rate Schedule

Range of taxable income	Tax calculation: Base tax	+	(Marginal rate × amount over base bracket)
\$ 0 to \$ 50,000	\$ 0	+	(15% × amount over \$ 0)
50,000 to 75,000	7,500	+	(25 × amount over 50,000)
75,000 to 100,000	13,750	+	(34 × amount over 75,000)
100,000 to 335,000	22,250	+	(39 × amount over 100,000)
335,000 to 10,000,000	113,900	+	(34 × amount over 335,000)
10,000,000 to 15,000,000	3,400,000	+	(35 × amount over 10,000,000)
15,000,000 to 18,333,333	5,150,000	+	(38 × amount over 15,000,000)
Over 18,333,333	6,416,667	+	(35 × amount over 18,333,333)

if the firm earns less than $50,000. If a firm earns more than $50,000 but less than $75,000, the marginal tax rate is 25 percent. As a firm's income rises, the marginal tax rate that it faces changes as shown in Table 2.1. In the example above, if Webster Manufacturing's earnings increase to $250,001, the last $1 in income would be taxed at the marginal rate of 39 percent.

average tax rate
A firm's taxes divided by its taxable income.

The **average tax rate** paid on the firm's ordinary income can be calculated by dividing its taxes by its taxable income. For most firms, the average tax rate does not equal the marginal tax rate because tax rates change with income levels. In the example above, Webster Manufacturing's marginal tax rate is 39 percent, but its average tax rate is 32.3 percent ($80,750 ÷ $250,000). For very large corporations with earnings in the hundreds of millions or even billions of dollars, the average tax rate is very close to the 35 percent marginal rate in the top bracket because most of the firm's income is taxed at that rate.

In most of the business decisions that managers make, *it's the marginal tax rate that really matters*. To keep matters simple, the examples in this text will use a *flat 40 percent tax rate*. That means that *both the average tax rate and the marginal tax rate equal 40 percent.*

Interest and Dividend Income

double taxation
Situation that occurs when after-tax corporate earnings are distributed as cash dividends to stockholders, who then must pay personal taxes on the dividend amount.

In the process of determining taxable income, any *interest received* by the corporation is included as ordinary income. Dividends, on the other hand, are treated differently. This different treatment moderates the effect of **double taxation,** which occurs when the already once-taxed earnings of a corporation are distributed as cash dividends to stockholders, who must pay taxes on dividends up to a maximum rate of 15 percent. Dividends that the firm receives on common and preferred stock held in other corporations are subject to a 70 percent exclusion for tax purposes.[2] The dividend exclusion in effect eliminates most of the potential tax liability from the dividends received by the second and any subsequent corporations.

Tax-Deductible Expenses

In calculating their taxes, corporations are allowed to deduct operating expenses, as well as interest expense. The tax deductibility of these expenses reduces their after-tax cost. The following example illustrates the benefit of tax deductibility.

Example 2.3 ▸

Two companies, Debt Co. and No-Debt Co., both expect in the coming year to have earnings before interest and taxes of $200,000. During the year, Debt Co. will have to pay $30,000 in interest. No-Debt Co. has no debt and therefore will

2. The 70 percent exclusion applies if the firm receiving dividends owns less than 20 percent of the shares of the firm paying the dividends. The exclusion is 80 percent if the corporation owns between 20 percent and 80 percent of the stock in the corporation paying it dividends; 100 percent of the dividends received are excluded if it owns more than 80 percent of the corporation paying it dividends. For convenience, we are assuming here that the ownership interest in the dividend-paying corporation is less than 20 percent.

have no interest expense. Calculation of the earnings after taxes for these two firms is as follows:

	Debt Co.	No-Debt Co.
Earnings before interest and taxes	$200,000	$200,000
Less: Interest expense	30,000	0
Earnings before taxes	$170,000	$200,000
Less: Taxes (40%)	68,000	80,000
Earnings after taxes	$102,000	$120,000
Difference in earnings after taxes	$18,000	

Debt Co. had $30,000 more interest expense than No-Debt Co., but Debt Co.'s earnings after taxes are only $18,000 less than those of No-Debt Co. This difference is attributable to the fact that Debt Co.'s $30,000 interest expense deduction provided a tax savings of $12,000 ($68,000 for Debt Co. versus $80,000 for No-Debt Co.). This amount can be calculated directly by multiplying the tax rate by the amount of interest expense ($0.40 \times \$30,000 = \$12,000$). Similarly, the $18,000 *after-tax cost* of the interest expense can be calculated directly by multiplying 1 minus the tax rate by the amount of interest expense [$(1 - 0.40) \times \$30,000 = \$18,000$].

The tax deductibility of expenses reduces their actual (after-tax) cost to the firm as long as the firm is profitable. If a firm experiences a net loss in a given year, its tax liability is already zero. Even in this case, losses in one year can be used to offset taxes paid on profits in prior years, and in some cases losses can be "carried forward" to offset income and lower taxes in subsequent years. Note that both for accounting and tax purposes *interest is a tax-deductible expense, whereas dividends are not.* Because dividends are not tax deductible, their after-tax cost is equal to the amount of the dividend. Thus a $30,000 cash dividend has an after-tax cost of $30,000.

CAPITAL GAINS

capital gain
The amount by which the sale price of an asset exceeds the asset's purchase price.

If a firm sells a capital asset (such as stock held as an investment) for more than it paid for the asset, the difference between the sale price and purchase price is called a **capital gain.** For corporations, capital gains are added to ordinary corporate income and taxed at the regular corporate rates.

Example 2.4 ▸

Ross Company, a manufacturer of pharmaceuticals, has pretax operating earnings of $500,000 and has just sold for $150,000 an asset that was purchased 2 years ago for $125,000. Because the asset was sold for more than its initial purchase price, there is a capital gain of $25,000 ($150,000 sale price − $125,000 initial purchase price). The corporation's taxable income will total $525,000 ($500,000 ordinary income plus $25,000 capital gain). Multiplying their taxable income by 40% produces Ross Company's tax liability of $210,000.

→ REVIEW QUESTIONS

2–15 Describe the tax treatment of *ordinary income* and that of *capital gains.* What is the difference between the *average tax rate* and the *marginal tax rate?*

2–16 How does the tax treatment of dividend income by the corporation moderate the effects of *double taxation?*

2–17 What benefit results from the tax deductibility of certain corporate expenses?

Summary

THE ROLE OF FINANCIAL INSTITUTIONS AND MARKETS

Chapter 2 described why financial institutions and markets are an integral part of managerial finance. Companies cannot get started or survive without raising capital, and financial institutions and markets give firms access to the money they need to grow. As we have seen in recent years, however, financial markets can be quite turbulent, and when large financial institutions get into trouble, access to capital is reduced and firms throughout the economy suffer as a result. Taxes are an important part of this story as well because the rules governing how business income is taxed shape the incentives of firms to make new investments.

REVIEW OF LEARNING GOALS

LG 1 **Understand the role that financial institutions play in managerial finance.** Financial institutions bring net suppliers of funds and net demanders together to help translate the savings of individuals, businesses, and governments into loans and other types of investments. The net suppliers of funds are generally individuals or households who save more money than they borrow. Businesses and governments are generally net demanders of funds, meaning that they borrow more money than they save.

LG 2 **Contrast the functions of financial institutions and financial markets.** Both financial institutions and financial markets help businesses raise the money that they need to fund new investments for growth. Financial institutions collect the savings of individuals and channel those funds to borrowers such as businesses and governments. Financial markets provide a forum in which savers and borrowers can transact business directly. Businesses and governments issue debt and equity securities directly to the public in the primary market. Subsequent trading of these securities between investors occurs in the secondary market.

LG 3 **Describe the differences between the capital markets and the money markets.** In the money market, savers who want a temporary place to deposit funds where they can earn interest interact with borrowers who have a short-term need for funds. Marketable securities including Treasury bills, commercial paper, and other instruments are the primary securities traded in the money market. The Eurocurrency market is the international equivalent of the domestic money market.

In contrast, the capital market is the forum in which savers and borrowers interact on a long-term basis. Firms issue either debt (bonds) or equity (stock) securities in the capital market. Once issued, these securities trade on secondary markets that are either broker markets or dealer markets. An important function of the capital market is to determine the underlying value of the securities issued by businesses. In an efficient market, the price of a security is an unbiased estimate of its true value.

LG 4 **Explain the root causes of the 2008 financial crisis and recession.** The financial crisis was caused by several factors related to investments in real estate. Financial institutions lowered their standards for lending to prospective homeowners, and institutions also invested heavily in mortgage-backed securities. When home prices fell and mortgage delinquencies rose, the value of the mortgage-backed securities held by banks plummeted, causing some banks to fail and many others to restrict the flow of credit to business. That in turn contributed to a severe recession in the United States and abroad.

LG 5 **Understand the major regulations and regulatory bodies that affect financial institutions and markets.** The Glass-Steagall Act created the FDIC and imposed a separation between commercial and investment banks. The act was designed to limit the risks that banks could take and to protect depositors. More recently, the Gramm-Leach-Bliley Act essentially repealed the elements of Glass-Steagall pertaining to the separation of commercial and investment banks. After the recent financial crisis, much debate has occurred regarding the proper regulation of large financial institutions.

The Securities Act of 1933 and the Securities Exchange Act of 1934 are the major pieces of legislation shaping the regulation of financial markets. The 1933 act focuses on regulating the sale of securities in the primary market, whereas the 1934 act deals with regulations governing transactions in the secondary market. The 1934 act also created the Securities and Exchange Commission, the primary body responsible for enforcing federal securities laws.

LG 6 **Discuss business taxes and their importance in financial decisions.** Corporate income is subject to corporate taxes. Corporate tax rates apply to both ordinary income (after deduction of allowable expenses) and capital gains. The average tax rate paid by a corporation ranges from 15 to 35 percent. Corporate taxpayers can reduce their taxes through certain provisions in the tax code: dividend income exclusions and tax-deductible expenses. A capital gain occurs when an asset is sold for more than its initial purchase price; gains are added to ordinary corporate income and taxed at regular corporate tax rates. (For convenience, we assume a 40 percent marginal tax rate in this book.)

Opener-in-Review

In the chapter opener you read about JPMorgan's tumultuous ride through the 2008 financial crisis, and in the chapter itself you learned about capital market efficiency. What role do you think market efficiency (or inefficiency) played in the 10 percent fall of JPMorgan's share price in a single day?

Self-Test Problem (Solution in Appendix)

LG 6 **ST2–1** **Corporate taxes** Montgomery Enterprises, Inc., had operating earnings of $280,000 for the year just ended. During the year the firm sold stock that it held in another company for $180,000, which was $30,000 above its original purchase price of $150,000, paid 1 year earlier.

a. What is the amount, if any, of capital gains realized during the year?

b. How much total taxable income did the firm earn during the year?

c. Use the corporate tax rate schedule given in Table 2.1 to calculate the firm's total taxes due.

d. Calculate both the *average tax rate* and the *marginal tax rate* on the basis of your findings.

Warm-Up Exercises All problems are available in myfinancelab.

LG 1 **E2–1** What does it mean to say that individuals as a group are net suppliers of funds for financial institutions? What do you think the consequences might be in financial markets if individuals consumed more of their incomes and thereby reduced the supply of funds available to financial institutions?

LG 2 **E2–2** You are the chief financial officer (CFO) of Gaga Enterprises, an edgy fashion design firm. Your firm needs $10 million to expand production. How do you think the process of raising this money will vary if you raise it with the help of a financial institution versus raising it directly in the financial markets?

LG 3 **E2–3** For what kinds of needs do you a think firm would issue securities in the money market versus the capital market?

LG 4 **E2–4** Your broker calls to offer you the investment opportunity of a lifetime, the chance to invest in mortgage-backed securities. The broker explains that these securities are entitled to the principal and interest payments received from a pool of residential mortgages. List some of the questions you would ask your broker to assess the risk of this investment opportunity.

LG 6 **E2–5** Reston, Inc., has asked your corporation, Pruro, Inc., for financial assistance. As a long-time customer of Reston, your firm has decided to give that assistance. The question you are debating is whether Pruro should take Reston stock with a 5% annual dividend or a promissory note paying 5% annual interest.

Assuming payment is guaranteed and the dollar amounts for annual interest and dividend income are identical, which option will result in greater after-tax income for the first year?

Problems All problems are available in myfinancelab.

LG 6 **P2–1** **Corporate taxes** Tantor Supply, Inc., is a small corporation acting as the exclusive distributor of a major line of sporting goods. During 2010 the firm earned $92,500 before taxes.

a. Calculate the firm's tax liability using the corporate tax rate schedule given in Table 2.1.

b. How much are Tantor Supply's 2010 after-tax earnings?

c. What was the firm's *average tax rate,* based on your findings in part **a?**
d. What is the firm's *marginal tax rate,* based on your findings in part **a?**

LG 6 **P2–2** **Average corporate tax rates** Using the corporate tax rate schedule given in Table 2.1, perform the following:
a. Calculate the tax liability, after-tax earnings, and average tax rates for the following levels of corporate earnings before taxes: $10,000; $80,000; $300,000; $500,000; $1.5 million; $10 million; and $20 million.
b. Plot the *average tax rates* (measured on the *y* axis) against the pretax income levels (measured on the *x* axis). What generalization can be made concerning the relationship between these variables?

LG 6 **P2–3** **Marginal corporate tax rates** Using the corporate tax rate schedule given in Table 2.1, perform the following:
a. Find the marginal tax rate for the following levels of corporate earnings before taxes: $15,000; $60,000; $90,000; $200,000; $400,000; $1 million; and $20 million.
b. Plot the *marginal tax rates* (measured on the *y* axis) against the pretax income levels (measured on the *x* axis). Explain the relationship between these variables.

LG 6 **P2–4** **Interest versus dividend income** During the year just ended, Shering Distributors, Inc., had pretax earnings from operations of $490,000. In addition, during the year it received $20,000 in income from interest on bonds it held in Zig Manufacturing and received $20,000 in income from dividends on its 5% common stock holding in Tank Industries, Inc. Shering is in the 40% tax bracket and is eligible for a 70% dividend exclusion on its Tank Industries stock.
a. Calculate the firm's tax on its operating earnings only.
b. Find the tax and the after-tax amount attributable to the interest income from Zig Manufacturing bonds.
c. Find the tax and the after-tax amount attributable to the dividend income from the Tank Industries, Inc., common stock.
d. Compare, contrast, and discuss the after-tax amounts resulting from the interest income and dividend income calculated in parts **b** and **c.**
e. What is the firm's total tax liability for the year?

LG 6 **P2–5** **Interest versus dividend expense** Michaels Corporation expects earnings before interest and taxes to be $40,000 for the current period. Assuming an ordinary tax rate of 40%, compute the firm's earnings after taxes and earnings available for common stockholders (earnings after taxes and preferred stock dividends, if any) under the following conditions:
a. The firm pays $10,000 in interest.
b. The firm pays $10,000 in preferred stock dividends.

LG 6 **P2–6** **Capital gains taxes** Perkins Manufacturing is considering the sale of two nondepreciable assets, X and Y. Asset X was purchased for $2,000 and will be sold today for $2,250. Asset Y was purchased for $30,000 and will be sold today for $35,000. The firm is subject to a 40% tax rate on capital gains.
a. Calculate the amount of capital gain, if any, realized on each of the assets.
b. Calculate the tax on the sale of each asset.

LG 6 **P2–7** **Capital gains taxes** The following table contains purchase and sale prices for the nondepreciable capital assets of a major corporation. The firm paid taxes of 40% on capital gains.

Asset	Purchase price	Sale price
A	$ 3,000	$ 3,400
B	12,000	12,000
C	62,000	80,000
D	41,000	45,000
E	16,500	18,000

a. Determine the amount of capital gain realized on each of the five assets.
b. Calculate the amount of tax paid on each of the assets.

LG 5 **P2-8** **ETHICS PROBLEM** The Securities Exchange Act of 1934 limits, but does not prohibit, corporate insiders from trading in their own firm's shares. What ethical issues might arise when a corporate insider wants to buy or sell shares in the firm where he or she works?

Spreadsheet Exercise

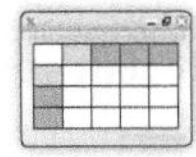

Hemingway Corporation is considering expanding its operations to boost its income, but before making a final decision they have asked you to calculate the corporate tax consequences of their decision. Currently Hemingway generates before-tax yearly income of $200,000 and has no debt outstanding. Expanding operations would allow Hemingway to increase before-tax yearly income to $350,000. Hemingway can use either cash reserves or debt to finance its expansion. If Hemingway uses debt, it will have yearly interest expense of $70,000.

TO DO

Create a spreadsheet to conduct a *tax analysis* for Hemingway Corporation and determine the following:

a. What is Hemingway's current annual corporate tax liability?
b. What is Hemingway's current average tax rate?
c. If Hemingway finances its expansion using cash reserves, what will be its new corporate tax liability and average tax rate?
d. If Hemingway finances its expansion using debt, what will be its new corporate tax liability and average tax rate?
e. What would you recommend that the firm do? Why?

Visit www.myfinancelab.com for ***Chapter Case: The Pros and Cons of Being Publicly Listed,*** Group Exercises, and numerous online resources.

Integrative Case 1

Merit Enterprise Corp.

Sara Lehn, chief financial officer of Merit Enterprise Corp., was reviewing her presentation one last time before her upcoming meeting with the board of directors. Merit's business had been brisk for the last two years, and the company's CEO was pushing for a dramatic expansion of Merit's production capacity. Executing the CEO's plans would require $4 billion in capital in addition to $2 billion in excess cash that the firm had built up. Sara's immediate task was to brief the board on options for raising the needed $4 billion.

Unlike most companies its size, Merit had maintained its status as a private company, financing its growth by reinvesting profits and, when necessary, borrowing from banks. Whether Merit could follow that same strategy to raise the $4 billion necessary to expand at the pace envisioned by the firm's CEO was uncertain, though it seemed unlikely to Sara. She had identified two options for the board to consider:

Option 1: Merit could approach JPMorgan Chase, a bank that had served Merit well for many years with seasonal credit lines as well as medium-term loans. Lehn believed that JPMorgan was unlikely to make a $4 billion loan to Merit on its own, but it could probably gather a group of banks together to make a loan of this magnitude. However, the banks would undoubtedly demand that Merit limit further borrowing and provide JPMorgan with periodic financial disclosures so that they could monitor Merit's financial condition as it expanded its operations.

Option 2: Merit could convert to public ownership, issuing stock to the public in the primary market. With Merit's excellent financial performance in recent years, Sara thought that its stock could command a high price in the market and that many investors would want to participate in any stock offering that Merit conducted.

Becoming a public company would also allow Merit, for the first time, to offer employees compensation in the form of stock or stock options, thereby creating stronger incentives for employees to help the firm succeed. On the other hand, Sara knew that public companies faced extensive disclosure requirements and other regulations that Merit had never had to confront as a private firm. Furthermore, with stock trading in the secondary market, who knew what kind of individuals or institutions might wind up holding a large chunk of Merit stock?

TO DO

a. Discuss the pros and cons of option 1, and prioritize your thoughts. What are the most positive aspects of this option, and what are the biggest drawbacks?

b. Do the same for option 2.

c. Which option do you think Sara should recommend to the board and why?

Part 2 Financial Tools

Chapters in This Part

In Part 2 you will learn about some of the basic analytical tools that financial managers use almost every day. Chapter 3 reviews the main financial statements that are the primary means by which firms communicate with investors, analysts, and the rest of the business community. Chapter 3 also illustrates some simple tools that managers use to analyze the information contained in financial statements to identify and diagnose financial problems.

Firms create financial statements using the accrual principles of accounting, but in finance it is cash flow that really matters. Chapter 4 shows how to use financial statements to determine how much cash flow a firm is generating and how it is spending that cash flow. Chapter 4 also explains how firms develop short-term and long-term financial plans.

Managers have to decide whether the up-front costs of investments are justified by the subsequent cash that those investments are likely to produce. Chapter 5 illustrates techniques that firms use to evaluate these sorts of trade-offs.

3 Financial Statements and Ratio Analysis

Learning Goals

LG 1 Review the contents of the stockholders' report and the procedures for consolidating international financial statements.

LG 2 Understand who uses financial ratios and how.

LG 3 Use ratios to analyze a firm's liquidity and activity.

LG 4 Discuss the relationship between debt and financial leverage and the ratios used to analyze a firm's debt.

LG 5 Use ratios to analyze a firm's profitability and its market value.

LG 6 Use a summary of financial ratios and the DuPont system of analysis to perform a complete ratio analysis.

Why This Chapter Matters to You

In your *professional* life

ACCOUNTING You need to understand the stockholders' report and preparation of the four key financial statements; how firms consolidate international financial statements; and how to calculate and interpret financial ratios for decision making.

INFORMATION SYSTEMS You need to understand what data are included in the firm's financial statements to design systems that will supply such data to those who prepare the statements and to those in the firm who use the data for ratio calculations.

MANAGEMENT You need to understand what parties are interested in the stockholders' report and why; how the financial statements will be analyzed by those both inside and outside the firm to assess various aspects of performance; the caution that should be exercised in using financial ratio analysis; and how the financial statements affect the value of the firm.

MARKETING You need to understand the effects your decisions will have on the financial statements, particularly the income statement and the statement of cash flows, and how analysis of ratios, especially those involving sales figures, will affect the firm's decisions about levels of inventory, credit policies, and pricing decisions.

OPERATIONS You need to understand how the costs of operations are reflected in the firm's financial statements and how analysis of ratios, particularly those involving assets, cost of goods sold, or inventory, may affect requests for new equipment or facilities.

In your *personal* life

A routine step in personal financial planning is to prepare and analyze personal financial statements, so that you can monitor progress toward your financial goals. Also, you need to understand and analyze corporate financial statements to build and monitor your investment portfolio.

Abercrombie & Fitch

The Value of Casual Luxury

A May 15, 2010, post on an investment website, Motley Fool, provided a valuation analysis for clothing retailer Abercrombie & Fitch. Abercrombie's stock price had been trending down for several weeks, and given that recent months had only just seen the end of one of the worst recessions in two generations, Motley Fool analysts did not expect the firm's financial condition to be particularly impressive. However, they noted that Abercrombie's current ratio was a healthy 2.79, and its quick ratio was also strong at 1.79. Furthermore, analysts noted that Abercrombie's receivables collection period had quickened to 43 days in the prior year, and they concluded their report with a relatively positive outlook for the stock.

Just a few days later, Abercrombie & Fitch announced that it would scale back planned overseas store openings, the markets where it had been enjoying the most rapid growth. In addition, the company reported that its gross profit margin declined in the most recent quarter. Markets responded to this information by sending Abercrombie stock down 7 percent on that day.

Valuing the shares of a company is a difficult task. Analysts try to simplify that task by drawing data from financial reports produced by the company and calculating a variety of financial ratios using those data. These ratios help analysts answer questions such as, Does the firm have enough liquidity to pay the bills that will come due in the short term? and, How effectively does the firm collect cash from its customers? In this chapter, you will learn about the main financial statements that analysts rely on for this type of analysis, and you will see how information from those statements can be used to assess the overall performance of a company.

LG 1

3.1 The Stockholders' Report

generally accepted accounting principles (GAAP) The practice and procedure guidelines used to prepare and maintain financial records and reports; authorized by the *Financial Accounting Standards Board (FASB).*

Financial Accounting Standards Board (FASB) The accounting profession's rule-setting body, which authorizes *generally accepted accounting principles (GAAP).*

Public Company Accounting Oversight Board (PCAOB) A not-for-profit corporation established by the *Sarbanes-Oxley Act of 2002* to protect the interests of investors and further the public interest in the preparation of informative, fair, and independent audit reports.

Every corporation has many and varied uses for the standardized records and reports of its financial activities. Periodically, reports must be prepared for regulators, creditors (lenders), owners, and management. The guidelines used to prepare and maintain financial records and reports are known as **generally accepted accounting principles (GAAP).** These accounting practices and procedures are authorized by the accounting profession's rule-setting body, the **Financial Accounting Standards Board (FASB).**

In addition, the *Sarbanes-Oxley Act of 2002,* enacted in an effort to eliminate the many disclosure and conflict-of-interest problems of corporations, established the **Public Company Accounting Oversight Board (PCAOB),** a not-for-profit corporation that oversees auditors of public corporations. The PCAOB is charged with protecting the interests of investors and furthering the public interest in the preparation of informative, fair, and independent audit reports. The expectation is that it will instill confidence in investors with regard to the accuracy of the audited financial statements of public companies.

Publicly owned corporations with more than $5 million in assets and 500 or more stockholders are required by the Securities and Exchange Commission (SEC)—the federal regulatory body that governs the sale and listing of securities—to provide their stockholders with an annual **stockholders' report.** The stockholders' report summarizes and documents the firm's financial activities during the past year. It begins with a letter to the stockholders from the firm's president and/or chairman of the board.

THE LETTER TO STOCKHOLDERS

The **letter to stockholders** is the primary communication from management. It describes the events that are considered to have had the greatest effect on the firm

GLOBAL focus

More Countries Adopt International Financial Reporting Standards

in practice In the United States, public companies are required to report financial results using GAAP. However, accounting standards vary around the world, and that makes comparing the financial results of firms located in different countries quite challenging. In recent years, many countries have adopted a system of accounting principles known as International Financial Reporting Standards (IFRS), which are established by an independent standards-setting body known as the International Accounting Standards Board (IASB). These standards are designed with the goal of making financial statements everywhere understandable, reliable, comparable, and accurate. More than 80 countries now require listed firms to comply with IFRS, and dozens more permit or require firms to follow IFRS to some degree.

Why hasn't the United States followed the global trend of IFRS adoption? Some argue that GAAP is still the "gold standard," and a movement to IFRS would lower the overall quality of financial reporting made by U.S. firms. It is true that IFRS generally requires less detail than GAAP. Even so, the Securities and Exchange Commission has expressed its view that U.S. investors will benefit as GAAP and IFRS converge though there is no expectation that firms in the United States will be required to switch to IFRS in the near future.

▶ ***What costs and benefits might be associated with a switch to IFRS in the United States?***

stockholders' report
Annual report that publicly owned corporations must provide to stockholders; it summarizes and documents the firm's financial activities during the past year.

letter to stockholders
Typically, the first element of the annual stockholders' report and the primary communication from management.

during the year. It also typically discusses management philosophy, corporate governance issues, strategies, and actions, as well as plans for the coming year.

THE FOUR KEY FINANCIAL STATEMENTS

The four key financial statements required by the SEC for reporting to shareholders are (1) the income statement, (2) the balance sheet, (3) the statement of stockholders' equity, and (4) the statement of cash flows. The financial statements from the 2012 stockholders' report of Bartlett Company, a manufacturer of metal fasteners, are presented and briefly discussed in this section. Most likely, you have studied these four financial statements in an accounting course, so the purpose of looking at them here is to refresh your memory of the basics, rather than provide an exhaustive review.

income statement
Provides a financial summary of the firm's operating results during a specified period.

Income Statement

The **income statement** provides a financial summary of the firm's operating results during a specified period. Most common are income statements covering a 1-year period ending at a specified date, ordinarily December 31 of the calendar year.

focus on ETHICS

Taking Earnings Reports at Face Value

in practice Near the end of each quarter, Wall Street's much anticipated "earnings season" arrives. During earnings season, many companies unveil their quarterly performance. Interest is high, as media outlets rush to report the latest announcements, analysts slice and dice the numbers, and investors buy and sell based on the news. The most anticipated performance metric for most companies is earnings per share (EPS), which is typically compared to the estimates of the analysts that cover a firm. Firms that beat analyst estimates often see their share prices jump, while those that miss estimates, by even a small amount, tend to suffer price declines.

Many investors are aware of the pitfalls of judging firms based on reported earnings. Specifically, the complexity of financial reports makes it easy for managers to mislead investors. Sometimes, the methods used to mislead investors are within the rules, albeit not the spirit, of acceptable accounting practices. Other times, firms break the rules to make their numbers. The practice of manipulating earnings to mislead investors is known as earnings management.

Some firms are notorious for consistently beating analysts' estimates. For example, for one 10-year period (1995–2004), General Electric Co. (GE) beat Wall Street earnings estimates every quarter, often by only a penny or two per share. However, in 2009, the U.S. Securities and Exchange Commission (SEC) fined GE $50 million for improper accounting practices, including recording sales that had not yet occurred. When GE went back to correct the problems identified by the SEC, they found that net earnings between 2001 and 2007 were a total of $280 million lower than originally reported.

In one of his famous letters to the shareholders of Berskshire Hathaway, Warren Buffett offers three bits of advice regarding financial reporting.[a] First, he warns that weak visible accounting practices are typically a sign of bigger problems. Second, he suggests that, when you can't understand management, the reason is probably that management doesn't want you to understand them. Third, he warns that investors should be suspicious of projections because earnings and growth do not typically progress in an orderly fashion. Finally, Buffett notes that "Managers that always promise to 'make the numbers' will at some point be tempted to *make up* the numbers."

▶ ***Why might financial managers be tempted to manage earnings?***

▶ ***Is it unethical for managers to manage earnings if they disclose their activities to investors?***

[a] www.berkshirehathaway.com/letters/2002pdf.pdf

Many large firms, however, operate on a 12-month financial cycle, or *fiscal year,* that ends at a time other than December 31. In addition, monthly income statements are typically prepared for use by management, and quarterly statements must be made available to the stockholders of publicly owned corporations.

Table 3.1 presents Bartlett Company's income statements for the years ended December 31, 2012 and 2011. The 2012 statement begins with *sales revenue*—the total dollar amount of sales during the period—from which the *cost of goods sold* is deducted. The resulting *gross profit* of $986,000 represents the amount remaining to satisfy operating, financial, and tax costs. Next, *operating expenses,* which include selling expense, general and administrative expense, lease expense, and depreciation expense, are deducted from gross profits. The resulting *operating profits* of $418,000 represent the profits earned from producing and selling products; this amount does not consider financial and tax costs. (Operating profit is often called *earnings before interest and taxes,* or *EBIT.*) Next, the financial cost—*interest expense*—is subtracted from operating profits

TABLE 3.1 Bartlett Company Income Statements ($000)

	For the years ended December 31	
	2012	2011
Sales revenue	$3,074	$2,567
Less: Cost of goods sold	2,088	1,711
Gross profits	$ 986	$ 856
Less: Operating expenses		
Selling expense	$ 100	$ 108
General and administrative expenses	194	187
Lease expense[a]	35	35
Depreciation expense	239	223
Total operating expense	$ 568	$ 553
Operating profits	$ 418	$ 303
Less: Interest expense	93	91
Net profits before taxes	$ 325	$ 212
Less: Taxes	94	64
Net profits after taxes	$ 231	$ 148
Less: Preferred stock dividends	10	10
Earnings available for common stockholders	$ 221	$ 138
Earnings per share (EPS)[b]	$2.90	$1.81
Dividend per share (DPS)[c]	$1.29	$0.75

[a]Lease expense is shown here as a separate item rather than being included as part of interest expense, as specified by the FASB for financial reporting purposes. The approach used here is consistent with tax reporting rather than financial reporting procedures.

[b]Calculated by dividing the earnings available for common stockholders by the number of shares of common stock outstanding—76,262 in 2012 and 76,244 in 2011. Earnings per share in 2012: $221,000 ÷ 76,262 = $2.90; in 2011: $138,000 ÷ 76,244 = $1.81.

[c]Calculated by dividing the dollar amount of dividends paid to common stockholders by the number of shares of common stock outstanding. Dividends per share in 2012: $98,000 ÷ 76,262 = $1.29; in 2011: $57,183 ÷ 76,244 = $0.75.

to find *net profits* (or *earnings*) *before taxes*. After subtracting $93,000 in 2012 interest, Bartlett Company had $325,000 of net profits before taxes.

Next, taxes are calculated at the appropriate tax rates and deducted to determine *net profits* (or *earnings*) *after taxes*. Bartlett Company's net profits after taxes for 2012 were $231,000. Any preferred stock dividends must be subtracted from net profits after taxes to arrive at *earnings available for common stockholders*. This is the amount earned by the firm on behalf of the common stockholders during the period.

dividend per share (DPS)
The dollar amount of cash distributed during the period on behalf of each outstanding share of common stock.

Dividing earnings available for common stockholders by the number of shares of common stock outstanding results in *earnings per share (EPS)*. EPS represent the number of dollars earned during the period on behalf of each outstanding share of common stock. In 2012, Bartlett Company earned $221,000 for its common stockholders, which represents $2.90 for each outstanding share. The actual cash **dividend per share (DPS),** which is the dollar amount of cash distributed during the period on behalf of each outstanding share of common stock, paid in 2012 was $1.29.

Personal Finance Example 3.1 ▶ Jan and Jon Smith, a mid-30s married couple with no children, prepared a personal income and expense statement, which is similar to a corporate income statement. A condensed version of their income and expense statement follows.

Jan and Jon Smith's Income and Expense Statement for the Year Ended December 31, 2012

Income	
Salaries	$72,725
Interest received	195
Dividends received	120
(1) Total income	$73,040
Expenses	
Mortgage payments	$16,864
Auto loan payments	2,520
Utilities	2,470
Home repairs and maintenance	1,050
Food	5,825
Car expense	2,265
Health care and insurance	1,505
Clothes, shoes, accessories	1,700
Insurance	1,380
Taxes	16,430
Appliance and furniture payments	1,250
Recreation and entertainment	4,630
Tuition and books for Jan	1,400
Personal care and other items	2,415
(2) Total expenses	$61,704
(3) Cash surplus (or deficit) [(1)−(2)]	$11,336

During the year, the Smiths had total income of $73,040 and total expenses of $61,704, which left them with a cash surplus of $11,336. They can use the surplus to increase their savings and investments.

Balance Sheet

balance sheet
Summary statement of the firm's financial position at a given point in time.

The **balance sheet** presents a summary statement of the firm's financial position at a given time. The statement balances the firm's *assets* (what it owns) against its financing, which can be either *debt* (what it owes) or *equity* (what was provided by owners). Bartlett Company's balance sheets as of December 31 of 2012 and 2011 are presented in Table 3.2. They show a variety of asset, liability (debt), and equity accounts.

current assets
Short-term assets, expected to be converted into cash within 1 year or less.

current liabilities
Short-term liabilities, expected to be paid within 1 year or less.

An important distinction is made between short-term and long-term assets and liabilities. The **current assets** and **current liabilities** are *short-term* assets and liabilities. This means that they are expected to be converted into cash (current assets) or paid (current liabilities) within 1 year or less. All other assets and liabilities, along with stockholders' equity, which is assumed to have an infinite life, are considered *long-term,* or *fixed,* because they are expected to remain on the firm's books for more than 1 year.

As is customary, the assets are listed from the most liquid—*cash*—down to the least liquid. *Marketable securities* are very liquid short-term investments, such as U.S. Treasury bills or certificates of deposit, held by the firm. Because they are highly liquid, marketable securities are viewed as a form of cash ("near cash"). *Accounts receivable* represent the total monies owed the firm by its customers on credit sales. *Inventories* include raw materials, work in process (partially finished goods), and finished goods held by the firm. The entry for *gross fixed assets* is the original cost of all fixed (long-term) assets owned by the firm.[1] *Net fixed assets* represent the difference between gross fixed assets and *accumulated depreciation*—the total expense recorded for the depreciation of fixed assets. The net value of fixed assets is called their *book value.*

long-term debt
Debt for which payment is not due in the current year.

Like assets, the liabilities and equity accounts are listed from short-term to long-term. Current liabilities include *accounts payable,* amounts owed for credit purchases by the firm; *notes payable,* outstanding short-term loans, typically from commercial banks; and *accruals,* amounts owed for services for which a bill may not or will not be received. Examples of accruals include taxes due the government and wages due employees. **Long-term debt** represents debt for which payment is not due in the current year. *Stockholders' equity* represents the owners' claims on the firm. The *preferred stock* entry shows the historical proceeds from the sale of preferred stock ($200,000 for Bartlett Company).

paid-in capital in excess of par
The amount of proceeds in excess of the par value received from the original sale of common stock.

Next, the amount paid by the original purchasers of common stock is shown by two entries, common stock and paid-in capital in excess of par on common stock. The *common stock* entry is the *par value* of common stock. **Paid-in capital in excess of par** represents the amount of proceeds in excess of the par value received from the original sale of common stock. The sum of the common stock and paid-in capital accounts divided by the number of shares outstanding represents the original price per share received by the firm on a single issue of common stock.

1. For convenience the term *fixed assets* is used throughout this text to refer to what, in a strict accounting sense, is captioned "property, plant, and equipment." This simplification of terminology permits certain financial concepts to be more easily developed.

TABLE 3.2 Bartlett Company Balance Sheets ($000)

	December 31	
Assets	**2012**	**2011**
Cash	$ 363	$ 288
Marketable securities	68	51
Accounts receivable	503	365
Inventories	289	300
Total current assets	$1,223	$1,004
Land and buildings	$2,072	$1,903
Machinery and equipment	1,866	1,693
Furniture and fixtures	358	316
Vehicles	275	314
Other (includes financial leases)	98	96
Total gross fixed assets (at cost)[a]	$4,669	$4,322
Less: Accumulated depreciation	2,295	2,056
Net fixed assets	$2,374	$2,266
Total assets	$3,597	$3,270
Liabilities and Stockholders' Equity		
Accounts payable	$ 382	$ 270
Notes payable	79	99
Accruals	159	114
Total current liabilities	$ 620	$ 483
Long-term debt (includes financial leases)[b]	1,023	967
Total liabilities	$1,643	$1,450
Preferred stock—cumulative 5%, $100 par, 2,000 shares authorized and issued[c]	$ 200	$ 200
Common stock—$2.50 par, 100,000 shares authorized, shares issued and outstanding in 2012: 76,262; in 2011: 76,244	191	190
Paid-in capital in excess of par on common stock	428	418
Retained earnings	1,135	1,012
Total stockholders' equity	$1,954	$1,820
Total liabilities and stockholders' equity	$3,597	$3,270

[a]In 2012, the firm has a 6-year financial lease requiring annual beginning-of-year payments of $35,000. Four years of the lease have yet to run.

[b]Annual principal repayments on a portion of the firm's total outstanding debt amount to $71,000.

[c]The annual preferred stock dividend would be $5 per share (5% × $100 par), or a total of $10,000 annually ($5 per share × 2,000 shares).

Bartlett Company therefore received about $8.12 per share [($191,000 par + $428,000 paid-in capital in excess of par) ÷ 76,262 shares] from the sale of its common stock.

retained earnings
The cumulative total of all earnings, net of dividends, that have been retained and reinvested in the firm since its inception.

Finally, **retained earnings** represent the cumulative total of all earnings, net of dividends, that have been retained and reinvested in the firm since its inception. It is important to recognize that retained earnings are not cash but rather have been utilized to finance the firm's assets.

Bartlett Company's balance sheets in Table 3.2 show that the firm's total assets increased from $3,270,000 in 2011 to $3,597,000 in 2012. The $327,000 increase was due primarily to the $219,000 increase in current assets. The asset increase, in turn, appears to have been financed primarily by an increase of $193,000 in total liabilities. Better insight into these changes can be derived from the statement of cash flows, which we will discuss shortly.

Personal Finance Example 3.2 ▶ The following personal balance sheet for Jan and Jon Smith—the couple introduced earlier, who are married, in their mid-30s, and have no children—is similar to a corporate balance sheet.

Jan and Jon Smith's Balance Sheet: December 31, 2012

Assets		Liabilities and Net Worth	
Cash on hand	$ 90	Credit card balances	$ 665
Checking accounts	575	Utility bills	120
Savings accounts	760	Medical bills	75
Money market funds	800	Other current liabilities	45
Total liquid assets	$ 2,225	Total current liabilities	$ 905
Stocks and bonds	$ 2,250	Real estate mortgage	$ 92,000
Mutual funds	1,500	Auto loans	4,250
Retirement funds, IRA	2,000	Education loan	3,800
Total investments	$ 5,750	Personal loan	4,000
Real estate	$120,000	Furniture loan	800
Cars	14,000	Total long-term liabilities	$104,850
Household furnishings	3,700	Total liabilities	$105,755
Jewelry and artwork	1,500	Net worth (N/W)	41,420
Total personal property	$139,200	Total liabilities	
Total assets	$147,175	and net worth	$147,175

statement of stockholders' equity
Shows all equity account transactions that occurred during a given year.

statement of retained earnings
Reconciles the net income earned during a given year, and any cash dividends paid, with the change in retained earnings between the start and the end of that year. An abbreviated form of the *statement of stockholders' equity.*

The Smiths have total assets of $147,175 and total liabilities of $105,755. Personal net worth (N/W) is a "plug figure"—the difference between total assets and total liabilities—which in the case of Jan and Jon Smith is $41,420.

Statement of Retained Earnings

The *statement of retained earnings* is an abbreviated form of the statement of stockholders' equity. Unlike the **statement of stockholders' equity,** which shows all equity account transactions that occurred during a given year, the **statement of retained earnings** reconciles the net income earned during a given year, and any

TABLE 3.3 Bartlett Company Statement of Retained Earnings ($000) for the Year Ended December 31, 2012

Retained earnings balance (January 1, 2012)	$1,012
Plus: Net profits after taxes (for 2012)	231
Less: Cash dividends (paid during 2012)	
Preferred stock	10
Common stock	98
Total dividends paid	$ 108
Retained earnings balance (December 31, 2012)	$1,135

cash dividends paid, with the change in retained earnings between the start and the end of that year. Table 3.3 presents this statement for Bartlett Company for the year ended December 31, 2012. The statement shows that the company began the year with $1,012,000 in retained earnings and had net profits after taxes of $231,000, from which it paid a total of $108,000 in dividends, resulting in year-end retained earnings of $1,135,000. Thus the net increase for Bartlett Company was $123,000 ($231,000 net profits after taxes minus $108,000 in dividends) during 2012.

Statement of Cash Flows

statement of cash flows
Provides a summary of the firm's operating, investment, and financing cash flows and reconciles them with changes in its cash and marketable securities during the period.

The **statement of cash flows** is a summary of the cash flows over the period of concern. The statement provides insight into the firm's operating, investment, and financing cash flows and reconciles them with changes in its cash and marketable securities during the period. Bartlett Company's statement of cash flows for the year ended December 31, 2012, is presented in Table 3.4 (see page 66). Further insight into this statement is included in the discussion of cash flow in Chapter 4.

NOTES TO THE FINANCIAL STATEMENTS

notes to the financial statements
Explanatory notes keyed to relevant accounts in the statements; they provide detailed information on the accounting policies, procedures, calculations, and transactions underlying entries in the financial statements.

Included with published financial statements are explanatory notes keyed to the relevant accounts in the statements. These **notes to the financial statements** provide detailed information on the accounting policies, procedures, calculations, and transactions underlying entries in the financial statements. Common issues addressed by these notes include revenue recognition, income taxes, breakdowns of fixed asset accounts, debt and lease terms, and contingencies. Since passage of Sarbanes-Oxley, notes to the financial statements have also included some details about compliance with that law. Professional securities analysts use the data in the statements and notes to develop estimates of the value of securities that the firm issues, and these estimates influence the actions of investors and therefore the firm's share value.

CONSOLIDATING INTERNATIONAL FINANCIAL STATEMENTS

So far, we've discussed financial statements involving only one currency, the U.S. dollar. The issue of how to consolidate a company's foreign and domestic financial statements has bedeviled the accounting profession for many years.

TABLE 3.4 Bartlett Company Statement of Cash Flows ($000) for the Year Ended December 31, 2012

Cash Flow from Operating Activities	
Net profits after taxes	$231
Depreciation	239
Increase in accounts receivable	(138)[a]
Decrease in inventories	11
Increase in accounts payable	112
Increase in accruals	45
Cash provided by operating activities	$500
Cash Flow from Investment Activities	
Increase in gross fixed assets	(347)
Change in equity investments in other firms	0
Cash provided by investment activities	($347)
Cash Flow from Financing Activities	
Decrease in notes payable	(20)
Increase in long-term debts	56
Changes in stockholders' equity[b]	11
Dividends paid	(108)
Cash provided by financing activities	($ 61)
Net increase in cash and marketable securities	$ 92

[a]As is customary, parentheses are used to denote a negative number, which in this case is a cash outflow.

[b]Retained earnings are excluded here because their change is actually reflected in the combination of the "net profits after taxes" and "dividends paid" entries.

Financial Accounting Standards Board (FASB) Standard No. 52
Mandates that U.S.–based companies translate their foreign-currency-denominated assets and liabilities into dollars, for consolidation with the parent company's financial statements. This is done by using the *current rate (translation) method.*

current rate (translation) method
Technique used by U.S.–based companies to translate their foreign-currency-denominated assets and liabilities into dollars, for consolidation with the parent company's financial statements, using the year-end (current) exchange rate.

The current policy is described in **Financial Accounting Standards Board (FASB) Standard No. 52,** which mandates that U.S.–based companies translate their foreign-currency-denominated assets and liabilities into dollars, for consolidation with the parent company's financial statements. This is done by using a technique called the **current rate (translation) method,** under which all of a U.S. parent company's foreign-currency-denominated assets and liabilities are converted into dollar values using the exchange rate prevailing at the fiscal year ending date (the current rate). Income statement items are treated similarly. Equity accounts, on the other hand, are translated into dollars by using the exchange rate that prevailed when the parent's equity investment was made (the historical rate). Retained earnings are adjusted to reflect each year's operating profits or losses.

→ REVIEW QUESTIONS

3–1 What roles do GAAP, the FASB, and the PCAOB play in the financial reporting activities of public companies?

3–2 Describe the purpose of each of the four major financial statements.

3–3 Why are the notes to the financial statements important to professional securities analysts?

3–4 How is the *current rate (translation) method* used to consolidate a firm's foreign and domestic financial statements?

LG 2

3.2 Using Financial Ratios

The information contained in the four basic financial statements is of major significance to a variety of interested parties who regularly need to have relative measures of the company's performance. *Relative* is the key word here, because the analysis of financial statements is based on the use of *ratios* or *relative values.* **Ratio analysis** involves methods of calculating and interpreting financial ratios to analyze and monitor the firm's performance. The basic inputs to ratio analysis are the firm's income statement and balance sheet.

ratio analysis
Involves methods of calculating and interpreting financial ratios to analyze and monitor the firm's performance.

INTERESTED PARTIES

Ratio analysis of a firm's financial statements is of interest to shareholders, creditors, and the firm's own management. Both current and prospective shareholders are interested in the firm's current and future level of risk and return, which directly affect share price. The firm's creditors are interested primarily in the short-term liquidity of the company and its ability to make interest and principal payments. A secondary concern of creditors is the firm's profitability; they want assurance that the business is healthy. Management, like stockholders, is concerned with all aspects of the firm's financial situation, and it attempts to produce financial ratios that will be considered favorable by both owners and creditors. In addition, management uses ratios to monitor the firm's performance from period to period.

TYPES OF RATIO COMPARISONS

Ratio analysis is not merely the calculation of a given ratio. More important is the *interpretation* of the ratio value. A meaningful basis for comparison is needed to answer such questions as "Is it too high or too low?" and "Is it good or bad?" Two types of ratio comparisons can be made, cross-sectional and time-series.

Cross-Sectional Analysis

Cross-sectional analysis involves the comparison of different firms' financial ratios at the same point in time. Analysts are often interested in how well a firm has performed in relation to other firms in its industry. Frequently, a firm will compare its ratio values to those of a key competitor or group of competitors that it wishes to emulate. This type of cross-sectional analysis, called **benchmarking,** has become very popular.

cross-sectional analysis
Comparison of different firms' financial ratios at the same point in time; involves comparing the firm's ratios to those of other firms in its industry or to industry averages.

benchmarking
A type of *cross-sectional analysis* in which the firm's ratio values are compared to those of a key competitor or group of competitors that it wishes to emulate.

Comparison to industry averages is also popular. These figures can be found in the *Almanac of Business and Industrial Financial Ratios, Dun & Bradstreet's Industry Norms and Key Business Ratios, RMA Annual Statement Studies, Value Line,* and industry sources. It is also possible to derive financial ratios for yourself using financial information reported in financial databases, such as Compustat. Table 3.5 illustrates a brief cross-sectional ratio analysis by comparing several

TABLE 3.5 Financial Ratios for Select Firms and Their Industry Median Values[a]

	Current ratio	Quick ratio	Inventory turnover	Average collection period (days)	Total asset turnover	Debt ratio	Net profit margin (%)	Return on total assets (%)	Return on Common Equity (%)
Dell	1.3	1.2	40.5	58.9	1.6	0.8	2.7	4.3	25.4
Hewlett-Packard	1.2	1.1	13.8	80.6	1.0	0.6	6.7	6.7	18.9
Computers	2.5	2.1	5.8	61.3	0.9	0.4	−3.1	−2.2	−2.6
Home Depot	1.3	0.4	4.3	5.3	1.6	0.5	4.0	6.5	13.7
Lowe's	1.3	0.2	3.7	0.0	1.4	0.4	3.7	5.4	9.3
Building Materials	2.8	0.8	3.7	5.3	1.6	0.3	4.0	6.5	13.7
Kroger	1.0	0.3	12.0	4.3	3.3	0.8	0.1	0.3	1.4
Whole Foods Market	1.3	1.0	25.6	7.0	3.6	0.4	2.3	8.0	14.5
Grocery Stores	1.3	0.7	11.1	7.5	2.4	0.6	2.1	3.1	9.8
Sears	1.3	0.3	3.7	5.4	1.8	0.6	0.5	0.9	2.6
Wal-Mart	0.9	0.3	9.0	3.7	2.4	0.6	3.5	8.4	20.3
Merchandise Stores	1.7	0.6	4.1	3.7	2.3	0.5	1.5	4.9	10.8

[a]The data used to calculate these ratios are drawn from the Compustat North American database.

ratios as of early 2010 for two select firms to each other and the median value for their particular industry.

Analysts have to be very careful when drawing conclusions from ratio comparisons. It's tempting to assume that if one ratio for a particular firm is above the industry norm, this is a sign that the firm is performing well, at least along the dimension measured by that ratio. However, ratios may be above or below the industry norm for both positive and negative reasons, and it is necessary to determine why a firm's performance differs from its industry peers. *Thus, ratio analysis on its own is probably most useful in highlighting areas for further investigation.*

Example 3.3 ▶ In early 2013, Mary Boyle, the chief financial analyst at Caldwell Manufacturing, a producer of heat exchangers, gathered data on the firm's financial performance during 2012, the year just ended. She calculated a variety of ratios and obtained industry averages. She was especially interested in inventory turnover, which reflects the speed with which the firm moves its inventory from raw materials through production into finished goods and to the customer as a completed sale. Generally, higher values of this ratio are preferred, because they indicate a quicker turnover of inventory and more efficient inventory management. Caldwell Manufacturing's calculated inventory turnover for 2012 and the industry average inventory turnover were as follows:

	Inventory Turnover, 2012
Caldwell Manufacturing	14.8
Industry average	9.7

Mary's initial reaction to these data was that the firm had managed its inventory significantly *better than* the average firm in the industry. The turnover was nearly 53% faster than the industry average. On reflection, however, she realized that a very high inventory turnover could be a sign that the firm is not holding enough inventories. The consequence of low inventory could be excessive stockouts (insufficient inventory to meet customer needs). Discussions with people in the manufacturing and marketing departments did, in fact, uncover such a problem: Inventories during the year were extremely low, the result of numerous production delays that hindered the firm's ability to meet demand and resulted in disgruntled customers and lost sales. A ratio that initially appeared to reflect extremely efficient inventory management was actually the symptom of a major problem.

Time-Series Analysis

time-series analysis
Evaluation of the firm's financial performance over time using financial ratio analysis.

Time-series analysis evaluates performance over time. Comparison of current to past performance, using ratios, enables analysts to assess the firm's progress. Developing trends can be seen by using multiyear comparisons. Any significant year-to-year changes may be symptomatic of a problem, especially if the same trend is not an industry-wide phenomenon.

Combined Analysis

The most informative approach to ratio analysis combines cross-sectional and time-series analyses. A combined view makes it possible to assess the trend in the behavior of the ratio in relation to the trend for the industry. Figure 3.1 depicts this type of approach using the average collection period ratio of Bartlett Company, over the years 2009–2012. This ratio reflects the average amount of time (in days) it takes the firm to collect bills, and lower values of this ratio generally are preferred. The figure quickly discloses that (1) Bartlett's effectiveness in collecting its receivables is poor in comparison to the industry, and (2) Bartlett's trend is toward longer collection periods. Clearly, Bartlett needs to shorten its collection period.

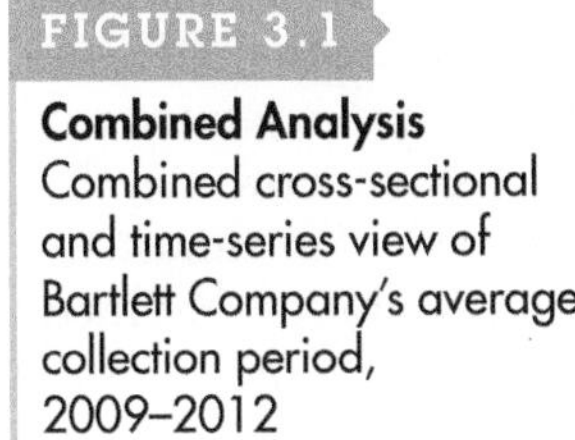
FIGURE 3.1

Combined Analysis
Combined cross-sectional and time-series view of Bartlett Company's average collection period, 2009–2012

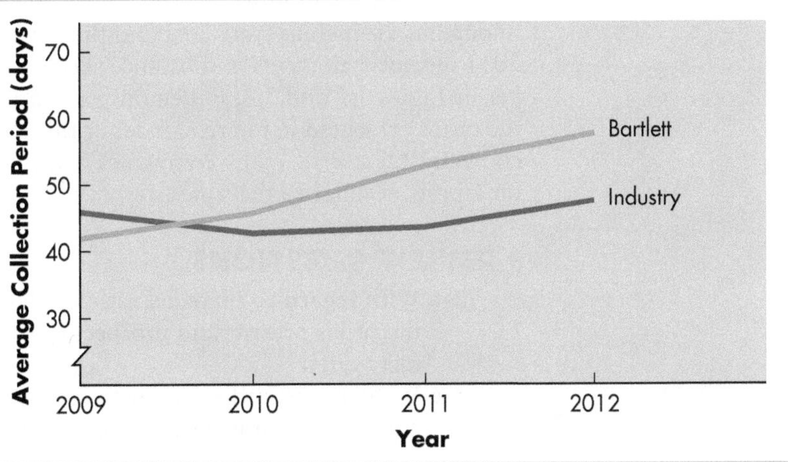

In more depth

To read about *Perils of Ratio Analysis*, go to www.myfinancelab.com

CAUTIONS ABOUT USING RATIO ANALYSIS

Before discussing specific ratios, we should consider the following cautions about their use:

1. Ratios that reveal large deviations from the norm merely indicate *the possibility* of a problem. Additional analysis is typically needed to determine whether there is a problem and to isolate the *causes* of the problem.
2. A single ratio does not generally provide sufficient information from which to judge the *overall* performance of the firm. However, if an analysis is concerned only with certain *specific* aspects of a firm's financial position, one or two ratios may suffice.
3. The ratios being compared should be calculated using financial statements dated at the same point in time during the year. If they are not, the effects of *seasonality* may produce erroneous conclusions and decisions.
4. It is preferable to use *audited financial statements* for ratio analysis. If they have not been audited, the data in them may not reflect the firm's true financial condition.
5. The financial data being compared should have been developed in the same way. The use of differing accounting treatments—especially relative to inventory and depreciation—can distort the results of ratio comparisons, regardless of whether cross-sectional or time-series analysis is used.
6. Results can be distorted by *inflation,* which can cause the book values of inventory and depreciable assets to differ greatly from their replacement values. Additionally, inventory costs and depreciation write-offs can differ from their true values, thereby distorting profits. Without adjustment, inflation tends to cause older firms (older assets) to appear more efficient and profitable than newer firms (newer assets). Clearly, in using ratios, you must be careful when comparing older to newer firms or a firm to itself over a long period of time.

CATEGORIES OF FINANCIAL RATIOS

Financial ratios can be divided for convenience into five basic categories: liquidity, activity, debt, profitability, and market ratios. Liquidity, activity, and debt ratios primarily measure risk. Profitability ratios measure return. Market ratios capture both risk and return.

As a rule, the inputs necessary for an effective financial analysis include, at a minimum, the income statement and the balance sheet. We will use the 2012 and 2011 income statements and balance sheets for Bartlett Company, presented earlier in Tables 3.1 and 3.2, to demonstrate ratio calculations. Note, however, that the ratios presented in the remainder of this chapter can be applied to almost any company. Of course, many companies in different industries use ratios that focus on aspects peculiar to their industry.

→ REVIEW QUESTIONS

3–5 With regard to financial ratio analysis, how do the viewpoints held by the firm's present and prospective shareholders, creditors, and management differ?

3–6 What is the difference between *cross-sectional* and *time-series* ratio analysis? What is *benchmarking?*

3–7 What types of deviations from the norm should the analyst pay primary attention to when performing cross-sectional ratio analysis? Why?

3–8 Why is it preferable to compare ratios calculated using financial statements that are dated at the same point in time during the year?

LG 3 3.3 Liquidity Ratios

liquidity
A firm's ability to satisfy its short-term obligations *as they come due.*

The **liquidity** of a firm is measured by its ability to satisfy its short-term obligations *as they come due.* Liquidity refers to the solvency of the firm's *overall* financial position—the ease with which it can pay its bills. Because a common precursor to financial distress and bankruptcy is low or declining liquidity, these ratios can provide early signs of cash flow problems and impending business failure. Clearly it is desirable that a firm is able to pay its bills, so having enough liquidity for day-to-day operations is important. However, liquid assets, like cash held at banks and marketable securities, do not earn a particularly high rate of return, so shareholders will not want a firm to *overinvest* in liquidity. Firms have to balance the need for safety that liquidity provides against the low returns that liquid assets generate for investors. The two basic measures of liquidity are the current ratio and the quick (acid-test) ratio.

CURRENT RATIO

current ratio
A measure of liquidity calculated by dividing the firm's current assets by its current liabilities.

The **current ratio,** one of the most commonly cited financial ratios, measures the firm's ability to meet its short-term obligations. It is expressed as follows:

$$\text{Current ratio} = \text{Current assets} \div \text{Current liabilities}$$

The current ratio for Bartlett Company in 2012 is

$$\$1{,}223{,}000 \div \$620{,}000 = 1.97$$

A higher current ratio indicates a greater degree of liquidity. How much liquidity a firm needs depends on a variety of factors, including the firm's size, its access to short-term financing sources like bank credit lines, and the volatility of its business. For example, a grocery store whose revenues are relatively predictable may not need as much liquidity as a manufacturing firm who faces sudden and unexpected shifts in demand for its products. The more predictable a firm's cash flows, the lower the acceptable current ratio. Because Bartlett Company is in a business with a relatively predictable annual cash flow, its current ratio of 1.97 should be quite acceptable.

Matter of fact

Determinants of Liquidity Needs

Glance back at the first column of data in Table 3.5 that shows the current ratio for a variety of companies and industries. Notice that the industry with the highest current ratio (that is, most liquidity) is building materials, a business that is notoriously sensitive to business cycle swings. The current ratio for that industry is 2.8, indicating that the typical firm in that business has almost three times as much in current assets as in current liabilities. Two of the largest competitors in that industry, The Home Depot and Lowe's, operate with a current ratio of 1.3, less than half the industry average. Does this mean that these firms have a liquidity problem? Not necessarily. Large enterprises generally have well-established relationships with banks that can provide lines of credit and other short-term loan products in the event that the firm has a need for liquidity. Smaller firms may not have the same access to credit, and therefore they tend to operate with more liquidity.

Personal Finance Example 3.4 ▶ Individuals, like corporations, can use financial ratios to analyze and monitor their performance. Typically, personal finance ratios are calculated using the personal income and expense statement and personal balance sheet for the period of concern. Here we use these statements, presented in the preceding personal finance examples, to demonstrate calculation of Jan and Jon Smith's liquidity ratio for calendar year 2012.

The personal *liquidity ratio* is calculated by dividing total liquid assets by total current debt. It indicates the percent of annual debt obligations that an individual can meet using current liquid assets. The Smiths' total liquid assets were \$2,225. Their total current debts are \$21,539 (total current liabilities of \$905 + mortgage payments of \$16,864 + auto loan payments of \$2,520 + appliance and furniture payments of \$1,250). Substituting these values into the ratio formula, we get:

$$\text{Liquidity ratio} = \frac{\text{Total liquid assets}}{\text{Total current debts}} = \frac{\$2{,}225}{\$21{,}539} = 0.1033, \text{ or } 10.3\%$$

That ratio indicates that the Smiths can cover only about 10% of their existing 1-year debt obligations with their current liquid assets. Clearly, the Smiths plan to meet these debt obligations from their income, but this ratio suggests that their liquid funds do not provide a large cushion. One of their goals should probably be to build up a larger fund of liquid assets to meet unexpected expenses.

QUICK (ACID-TEST) RATIO

quick (acid-test) ratio
A measure of liquidity calculated by dividing the firm's current assets minus inventory by its current liabilities.

The **quick (acid-test) ratio** is similar to the current ratio except that it excludes inventory, which is generally the least liquid current asset. The generally low liquidity of inventory results from two primary factors: (1) Many types of inventory cannot be easily sold because they are partially completed items, special-purpose items, and the like; and (2) inventory is typically sold on credit, which means that it becomes an account receivable before being converted into cash. An additional problem with inventory as a liquid asset is that the times when companies face the most dire need for liquidity, when business is bad, are precisely the times when it is most difficult to convert inventory into cash by selling it. The quick ratio is calculated as follows:

$$\text{Quick ratio} = \frac{\text{Current assets} - \text{Inventory}}{\text{Current liabilities}}$$

The quick ratio for Bartlett Company in 2012 is

$$\frac{\$1{,}223{,}000 - \$289{,}000}{\$620{,}000} = \frac{\$934{,}000}{\$620{,}000} = 1.51$$

As with the current ratio, the quick ratio level that a firm should strive to achieve depends largely on the nature of the business in which it operates. The quick ratio provides a better measure of overall liquidity only when a firm's inventory cannot be easily converted into cash. If inventory is liquid, the current ratio is a preferred measure of overall liquidity.

Matter of fact

The Importance of Inventories

Turn again to Table 3.5 and examine the columns listing current and quick ratios for different firms and industries. Notice that Dell has a current ratio of 1.3, and so do The Home Depot and Lowe's. However, although the quick ratios for The Home Depot and Lowe's are dramatically lower than their current ratios, for Dell the current and quick ratios have nearly the same value. Why? For many years, Dell operated on a "built-to-order" business model that required them to hold very little inventory. In contrast, all it takes is a trip to your local Home Depot or Lowe's store to see that the business model in this industry requires a massive investment in inventory, which implies that the quick ratio will be much less than the current ratio for building materials firms.

→ REVIEW QUESTIONS

3–9 Under what circumstances would the current ratio be the preferred measure of overall firm liquidity? Under what circumstances would the quick ratio be preferred?

3–10 In Table 3.5, most of the specific firms listed have current ratios that fall below the industry average. Why? The exception to this general pattern is Whole Foods Market, which competes at the very high end of the retail grocery market. Why might Whole Foods Market operate with greater-than-average liquidity?

LG 3

3.4 Activity Ratios

activity ratios
Measure the speed with which various accounts are converted into sales or cash—inflows or outflows.

Activity ratios measure the speed with which various accounts are converted into sales or cash—inflows or outflows. In a sense, activity ratios measure how efficiently a firm operates along a variety of dimensions such as inventory management, disbursements, and collections. A number of ratios are available for measuring the activity of the most important current accounts, which include inventory, accounts receivable, and accounts payable. The efficiency with which total assets are used can also be assessed.

INVENTORY TURNOVER

inventory turnover
Measures the activity, or liquidity, of a firm's inventory.

Inventory turnover commonly measures the activity, or liquidity, of a firm's inventory. It is calculated as follows:

$$\text{Inventory turnover} = \text{Cost of goods sold} \div \text{Inventory}$$

Applying this relationship to Bartlett Company in 2012 yields

$$\$2{,}088{,}000 \div \$289{,}000 = 7.2$$

The resulting turnover is meaningful only when it is compared with that of other firms in the same industry or to the firm's past inventory turnover. An inventory turnover of 20 would not be unusual for a grocery store, whose goods are highly perishable and must be sold quickly, whereas an aircraft manufacturer might turn its inventory just four times per year.

average age of inventory
Average number of days' sales in inventory.

Another inventory activity ratio measures how many days of inventory the firm has on hand. Inventory turnover can be easily converted into an **average age of inventory** by dividing it into 365. For Bartlett Company, the average age of inventory in 2012 is 50.7 days (365 ÷ 7.2). This value can also be viewed as the average number of days' sales in inventory.

AVERAGE COLLECTION PERIOD

average collection period
The average amount of time needed to collect accounts receivable.

The **average collection period,** or average age of accounts receivable, is useful in evaluating credit and collection policies. It is arrived at by dividing the average daily sales into the accounts receivable balance:[2]

$$\text{Average collection period} = \frac{\text{Accounts receivable}}{\text{Average sales per day}} = \frac{\text{Accounts receivable}}{\dfrac{\text{Annual sales}}{365}}$$

The average collection period for Bartlett Company in 2012 is

$$\frac{\$503{,}000}{\dfrac{\$3{,}074{,}000}{365}} = \frac{\$503{,}000}{\$8{,}422} = 59.7 \text{ days}$$

On the average, it takes the firm 59.7 days to collect an account receivable.

The average collection period is meaningful only in relation to the firm's credit terms. If Bartlett Company extends 30-day credit terms to customers, an average collection period of 59.7 days may indicate a poorly managed credit or collection department, or both. It is also possible that the lengthened collection period resulted from an intentional relaxation of credit-term enforcement in response to competitive pressures. If the firm had extended 60-day credit terms, the 59.7-day average collection period would be quite acceptable. Clearly, additional information is needed to evaluate the effectiveness of the firm's credit and collection policies.

Matter of fact

Who Gets Credit?

Notice in Table 3.5 the vast differences across industries in the average collection periods. Companies in the building materials, grocery, and merchandise store industries collect in just a few days, whereas firms in the computer industry take roughly two months to collect on their sales. The difference is primarily due to the fact that these industries serve very different customers. Grocery and retail stores serve individuals who pay cash or use credit cards (which to the store are essentially the same as cash). Computer manufacturers sell to retail chains, businesses, and other large organizations that negotiate agreements that allow them to pay for the computers they order well after the sale is made.

2. The formula as presented assumes, for simplicity, that all sales are made on a credit basis. If this is not the case, *average credit sales per day* should be substituted for average sales per day.

AVERAGE PAYMENT PERIOD

average payment period
The average amount of time needed to pay accounts payable.

The **average payment period,** or average age of accounts payable, is calculated in the same manner as the average collection period:

$$\text{Average payment period} = \frac{\text{Accounts payable}}{\text{Average purchases per day}} = \frac{\text{Accounts payable}}{\frac{\text{Annual purchases}}{365}}$$

The difficulty in calculating this ratio stems from the need to find annual purchases,[3] a value not available in published financial statements. Ordinarily, purchases are estimated as a given percentage of cost of goods sold. If we assume that Bartlett Company's purchases equaled 70 percent of its cost of goods sold in 2012, its average payment period is

$$\frac{\$382{,}000}{\frac{0.70 \times \$2{,}088{,}000}{365}} = \frac{\$382{,}000}{\$4{,}004} = 95.4 \text{ days}$$

This figure is meaningful only in relation to the average credit terms extended to the firm. If Bartlett Company's suppliers have extended, on average, 30-day credit terms, an analyst would give Bartlett a low credit rating because it was taking too long to pay its bills. Prospective lenders and suppliers of trade credit are interested in the average payment period because it provides insight into the firm's bill-paying patterns.

TOTAL ASSET TURNOVER

total asset turnover
Indicates the efficiency with which the firm uses its assets to generate sales.

The **total asset turnover** indicates the efficiency with which the firm uses its assets to generate sales. Total asset turnover is calculated as follows:

$$\text{Total asset turnover} = \text{Sales} \div \text{Total assets}$$

The value of Bartlett Company's total asset turnover in 2012 is

$$\$3{,}074{,}000 \div \$3{,}597{,}000 = 0.85$$

This means the company turns over its assets 0.85 times per year.

Generally, the higher a firm's total asset turnover, the more efficiently its assets have been used. This measure is probably of greatest interest to management because it indicates whether the firm's operations have been financially efficient.

Matter of fact

Sell It Fast

Observe in Table 3.5 that the grocery business turns over assets faster than any of the other industries listed. That makes sense because inventory is among the most valuable assets held by these firms, and grocery stores have to sell baked goods, dairy products, and produce quickly or throw them away when they spoil. It's true that some items in a grocery store have a shelf life longer than anyone really wants to know (think Twinkies), but on average a grocery store has to replace its entire inventory in just a few days or weeks, and that contributes to the rapid turnover of the firm's total assets.

3. Technically, annual *credit* purchases—rather than annual purchases—should be used in calculating this ratio. For simplicity, this refinement is ignored here.

→ **REVIEW QUESTION**

3–11 To assess the firm's average collection period and average payment period ratios, what additional information is needed, and why?

LG 4

3.5 Debt Ratios

The *debt position* of a firm indicates the amount of other people's money being used to generate profits. In general, the financial analyst is most concerned with long-term debts because these commit the firm to a stream of contractual payments over the long run. The more debt a firm has, the greater its risk of being unable to meet its contractual debt payments. Because creditors' claims must be satisfied before the earnings can be distributed to shareholders, current and prospective shareholders pay close attention to the firm's ability to repay debts. Lenders are also concerned about the firm's indebtedness.

financial leverage
The magnification of risk and return through the use of fixed-cost financing, such as debt and preferred stock.

In general, the more debt a firm uses in relation to its total assets, the greater its *financial leverage.* **Financial leverage** is the magnification of risk and return through the use of fixed-cost financing, such as debt and preferred stock. The more fixed-cost debt a firm uses, the greater will be its expected risk and return.

Example 3.5 ▸

Patty Akers is in the process of incorporating her new business. After much analysis she determined that an initial investment of $50,000—$20,000 in current assets and $30,000 in fixed assets—is necessary. These funds can be obtained in either of two ways. The first is the *no-debt plan,* under which she would invest the full $50,000 without borrowing. The other alternative, the *debt plan,* involves investing $25,000 and borrowing the balance of $25,000 at 12% annual interest.

Patty expects $30,000 in sales, $18,000 in operating expenses, and a 40% tax rate. Projected balance sheets and income statements associated with the two plans are summarized in Table 3.6. The no-debt plan results in after-tax profits of $7,200, which represent a 14.4% rate of return on Patty's $50,000 investment. The debt plan results in $5,400 of after-tax profits, which represent a 21.6% rate of return on Patty's investment of $25,000. The debt plan provides Patty with a higher rate of return, but the risk of this plan is also greater, because the annual $3,000 of interest must be paid whether Patty's business is profitable or not.

The example demonstrates that *with increased debt comes greater risk as well as higher potential return.* Therefore, the greater the financial leverage, the greater the potential risk and return. A detailed discussion of the impact of debt on the firm's risk, return, and value is included in Chapter 12. Here, we emphasize the use of financial debt ratios to assess externally a firm's debt position.

degree of indebtedness
Measures the amount of debt relative to other significant balance sheet amounts.

ability to service debts
The ability of a firm to make the payments required on a scheduled basis over the life of a debt.

There are two general types of debt measures: measures of the degree of indebtedness and measures of the ability to service debts. The **degree of indebtedness** measures the amount of debt relative to other significant balance sheet amounts. A popular measure of the degree of indebtedness is the debt ratio.

The second type of debt measure, the **ability to service debts,** reflects a firm's ability to make the payments required on a scheduled basis over the life of a debt.

TABLE 3.6 Financial Statements Associated with Patty's Alternatives

Balance Sheets	**No-debt plan**		**Debt plan**
Current assets	$20,000		$20,000
Fixed assets	30,000		30,000
Total assets	$50,000		$50,000
Debt (12% interest)	$ 0		$25,000
(1) Equity	50,000		25,000
Total liabilities and equity	$50,000		$50,000
Income Statements			
Sales	$30,000		$30,000
Less: Operating expenses	18,000		18,000
Operating profits	$12,000		$12,000
Less: Interest expense	0	0.12 × $25,000 =	3,000
Net profits before taxes	$12,000		$ 9,000
Less: Taxes (rate = 40%)	4,800		3,600
(2) Net profits after taxes	$ 7,200		$ 5,400
Return on equity [(2) ÷ (1)]	$\frac{\$7,200}{\$50,000} = 14.4\%$		$\frac{\$5,400}{\$25,000} = 21.6\%$

coverage ratios
Ratios that measure the firm's ability to pay certain fixed charges.

The term *to service debts* simply means to pay debts on time. The firm's ability to pay certain fixed charges is measured using **coverage ratios.** Typically, higher coverage ratios are preferred (especially by the firm's lenders), but a very high ratio might indicate that the firm's management is too conservative and might be able to earn higher returns by borrowing more. In general, the lower the firm's coverage ratios, the less certain it is to be able to pay fixed obligations. If a firm is unable to pay these obligations, its creditors may seek immediate repayment, which in most instances would force a firm into bankruptcy. Two popular coverage ratios are the times interest earned ratio and the fixed-payment coverage ratio.

DEBT RATIO

debt ratio
Measures the proportion of total assets financed by the firm's creditors.

The **debt ratio** measures the proportion of total assets financed by the firm's creditors. The higher this ratio, the greater the amount of other people's money being used to generate profits. The ratio is calculated as follows:

$$\text{Debt ratio} = \text{Total liabilities} \div \text{Total assets}$$

The debt ratio for Bartlett Company in 2012 is

$$\$1{,}643{,}000 \div \$3{,}597{,}000 = 0.457 = 45.7\%$$

This value indicates that the company has financed close to half of its assets with debt. The higher this ratio, the greater the firm's degree of indebtedness and the more financial leverage it has.

TIMES INTEREST EARNED RATIO

times interest earned ratio
Measures the firm's ability to make contractual interest payments; sometimes called the *interest coverage ratio.*

The **times interest earned ratio,** sometimes called the *interest coverage ratio,* measures the firm's ability to make contractual interest payments. The higher its value, the better able the firm is to fulfill its interest obligations. The times interest earned ratio is calculated as follows:

$$\text{Times interest earned ratio} = \text{Earnings before interest and taxes} \div \text{taxes}$$

The figure for *earnings before interest and taxes (EBIT)* is the same as that for *operating profits* shown in the income statement. Applying this ratio to Bartlett Company yields the following 2012 value:

$$\text{Time interest earned ratio} = \$418{,}000 \div \$93{,}000 = 4.5$$

The times interest earned ratio for Bartlett Company seems acceptable. A value of at least 3.0—and preferably closer to 5.0—is often suggested. The firm's earnings before interest and taxes could shrink by as much as 78 percent $[(4.5 - 1.0) \div 4.5]$, and the firm would still be able to pay the \$93,000 in interest it owes. Thus it has a large margin of safety.

FIXED-PAYMENT COVERAGE RATIO

fixed-payment coverage ratio
Measures the firm's ability to meet all fixed-payment obligations.

The **fixed-payment coverage ratio** measures the firm's ability to meet all fixed-payment obligations, such as loan interest and principal, lease payments, and preferred stock dividends. As is true of the times interest earned ratio, the higher this value the better. The formula for the fixed-payment coverage ratio is

$$\text{Fixed-payment coverage ratio} = \frac{\text{Earnings before interest and taxes} + \text{Lease payments}}{\text{Interest} + \text{Lease payments} + \{(\text{Principal payments} + \text{Preferred stock dividends}) \times [1/(1 - T)]\}}$$

where T is the corporate tax rate applicable to the firm's income. The term $1/(1 - T)$ is included to adjust the after-tax principal and preferred stock dividend payments back to a before-tax equivalent that is consistent with the before-tax values of all other terms. Applying the formula to Bartlett Company's 2012 data yields

$$\text{Fixed-payment coverage ratio} = \frac{\$418{,}000 + \$35{,}000}{\$93{,}000 + \$35{,}000 + \{(\$71{,}000 + \$10{,}000) \times [1/(1 - 0.29)]\}}$$

$$= \frac{\$453{,}000}{\$242{,}000} = 1.9$$

Because the earnings available are nearly twice as large as its fixed-payment obligations, the firm appears safely able to meet the latter.

Like the times interest earned ratio, the fixed-payment coverage ratio measures risk. The lower the ratio, the greater the risk to both lenders and owners, and the greater the ratio, the lower the risk. This ratio allows interested parties to assess the firm's ability to meet additional fixed-payment obligations without being driven into bankruptcy.

→ REVIEW QUESTIONS

3–12 What is *financial leverage?*

3–13 What ratio measures the firm's *degree of indebtedness?* What ratios assess the firm's *ability to service debts?*

LG 5

3.6 Profitability Ratios

There are many measures of profitability. As a group, these measures enable analysts to evaluate the firm's profits with respect to a given level of sales, a certain level of assets, or the owners' investment. Without profits, a firm could not attract outside capital. Owners, creditors, and management pay close attention to boosting profits because of the great importance the market places on earnings.

COMMON-SIZE INCOME STATEMENTS

common-size income statement
An income statement in which each item is expressed as a percentage of sales.

A useful tool for evaluating profitability in relation to sales is the **common-size income statement.** Each item on this statement is expressed as a percentage of sales. Common-size income statements are especially useful in comparing performance across years because it is easy to see if certain categories of expenses are trending up or down as a percentage of the total volume of business that the company transacts. Three frequently cited ratios of profitability that come directly from the common-size income statement are (1) the gross profit margin, (2) the operating profit margin, and (3) the net profit margin.

Common-size income statements for 2012 and 2011 for Bartlett Company are presented and evaluated in Table 3.7 on page 80. These statements reveal that the firm's cost of goods sold increased from 66.7 percent of sales in 2011 to 67.9 percent in 2012, resulting in a worsening gross profit margin. However, thanks to a decrease in total operating expenses, the firm's net profit margin rose from 5.4 percent of sales in 2011 to 7.2 percent in 2012. The decrease in expenses more than compensated for the increase in the cost of goods sold. A decrease in the firm's 2012 interest expense (3.0 percent of sales versus 3.5 percent in 2011) added to the increase in 2012 profits.

GROSS PROFIT MARGIN

gross profit margin
Measures the percentage of each sales dollar remaining after the firm has paid for its goods.

The **gross profit margin** measures the percentage of each sales dollar remaining after the firm has paid for its goods. The higher the gross profit margin, the better (that is, the lower the relative cost of merchandise sold). The gross profit margin is calculated as follows:

$$\text{Gross profit margin} = \frac{\text{Sales} - \text{Cost of goods sold}}{\text{Sales}} = \frac{\text{Gross profits}}{\text{Sales}}$$

Bartlett Company's gross profit margin for 2012 is

$$\frac{\$3{,}074{,}000 - \$2{,}088{,}000}{\$3{,}074{,}000} = \frac{\$986{,}000}{\$3{,}074{,}000} = 32.1\%$$

This value is labeled (1) on the common-size income statement in Table 3.7.

TABLE 3.7 Bartlett Company Common-Size Income Statements

	For the Years Ended December 31		Evaluation[a]
	2012	2011	2011–2012
Sales revenue	100.0%	100.0%	Same
Less: Cost of goods sold	67.9	66.7	Worse
(1) Gross profit margin	32.1%	33.3%	Worse
Less: Operating expenses			
Selling expense	3.3%	4.2%	Better
General and administrative expenses	6.8	6.7	Better
Lease expense	1.1	1.3	Better
Depreciation expense	7.3	9.3	Better
Total operating expense	18.5%	21.5%	Better
(2) Operating profit margin	13.6%	11.8%	Better
Less: Interest expense	3.0	3.5	Better
Net profits before taxes	10.6%	8.3%	Better
Less: Taxes	3.1	2.5	Worse[b]
Net profits after taxes	7.5%	5.8%	Better
Less: Preferred stock dividends	0.3	0.4	Better
(3) Net profit margin	7.2%	5.4%	Better

[a]Subjective assessments based on data provided.

[b]Taxes as a percentage of sales increased noticeably between 2011 and 2012 because of differing costs and expenses, whereas the average tax rates (taxes ÷ net profits before taxes) for 2011 and 2012 remained about the same—30% and 29%, respectively.

OPERATING PROFIT MARGIN

operating profit margin
Measures the percentage of each sales dollar remaining after all costs and expenses *other than* interest, taxes, and preferred stock dividends are deducted; the "pure profits" earned on each sales dollar.

The **operating profit margin** measures the percentage of each sales dollar remaining after all costs and expenses *other than* interest, taxes, and preferred stock dividends are deducted. It represents the "pure profits" earned on each sales dollar. Operating profits are "pure" because they measure only the profits earned on operations and ignore interest, taxes, and preferred stock dividends. A high operating profit margin is preferred. The operating profit margin is calculated as follows:

$$\text{Operating profit margin} = \text{Operating profits} \div \text{Sales}$$

Bartlett Company's operating profit margin for 2012 is

$$\$418{,}000 \div \$3{,}074{,}000 = 13.6\%$$

$$\frac{\$418{,}000}{\$3{,}074{,}000} = 13.6\%$$

This value is labeled (2) on the common-size income statement in Table 3.7.

NET PROFIT MARGIN

net profit margin
Measures the percentage of each sales dollar remaining after all costs and expenses, *including* interest, taxes, and preferred stock dividends, have been deducted.

The **net profit margin** measures the percentage of each sales dollar remaining after ali costs and expenses, *including* interest, taxes, and preferred stock dividends, have been deducted. The higher the firm's net profit margin, the bett… profit margin is calculated as follows:

$$\text{Net profit margin} = \text{Earnings available for common stockholders} \div \text{Sales}$$

Bartlett Company's net profit margin for 2012 is:

$$\$221{,}000 \div \$3{,}074{,}000 = 0.072 = 7.2\%$$

$$\frac{\$221{,}000}{\$3{,}074{,}000} = 7.2\%$$

This value is labeled (3) on the common-size income statement in Table 3.7.

The net profit margin is a commonly cited measure of the firm's success with respect to earnings on sales. "Good" net profit margins differ considerably across industries. A net profit margin of 1 percent or less would not be unusual for a grocery store, whereas a net profit margin of 10 percent would be low for a retail jewelry store.

EARNINGS PER SHARE (EPS)

The firm's *earnings per share (EPS)* is generally of interest to present or prospective stockholders and management. As we noted earlier, EPS represents the number of dollars earned during the period on behalf of each outstanding share of common stock. Earnings per share is calculated as follows:

$$\text{Earnings per share} = \frac{\text{Earnings available for common stockholders}}{\text{Number of shares of common stock outstanding}}$$

Bartlett Company's earnings per share in 2012 is

$$\$221{,}000 \div 76{,}262 = \$2.90$$

This figure represents the dollar amount earned *on behalf of* each outstanding share of common stock. The dollar amount of cash *actually distributed* to each shareholder is the *dividend per share (DPS),* which, as noted in Bartlett Company's income statement (Table 3.1), rose to $1.29 in 2012 from $0.75 in 2011. EPS is closely watched by the investing public and is considered an important indicator of corporate success.

RETURN ON TOTAL ASSETS (ROA)

return on total assets (ROA) Measures the overall effectiveness of management in generating profits with its available assets; also called the *return on investment (ROI).*

The **return on total assets (ROA),** often called the *return on investment (ROI),* measures the overall effectiveness of management in generating profits with its available assets. The higher the firm's return on total assets the better. The return on total assets is calculated as follows:

$$\text{ROA} = \text{Earnings available for common stockholders} \div \text{Total assets}$$

Bartlett Company's return on total assets in 2012 is

$$\frac{\$221{,}000}{\$3{,}597{,}000} = 6.1\%$$

$$\$221{,}000 \div \$3{,}597{,}000 = 0.061 = 6.1\%$$

This value indicates that the company earned 6.1 cents on each dollar of asset investment.

RETURN ON COMMON EQUITY (ROE)

return on common equity (ROE)
Measures the return earned on the common stockholders' investment in the firm.

The **return on common equity (ROE)** measures the return earned on the common stockholders' investment in the firm. Generally, the owners are better off the higher is this return. Return on common equity is calculated as follows:

$$\text{ROE} = \text{Earnings available for common stockholders} \div \text{Common stock equity}$$

This ratio for Bartlett Company in 2012 is

$$\$221{,}000 \div \$1{,}754{,}000 = 0.126 = 12.6\%$$

$$\frac{\$221{,}000}{\$1{,}754{,}000} = 12.6\%$$

Note that the value for common stock equity ($1,754,000) was found by subtracting the $200,000 of preferred stock equity from the total stockholders' equity of $1,954,000 (see Bartlett Company's 2012 balance sheet in Table 3.2). The calculated ROE of 12.6 percent indicates that during 2012 Bartlett earned 12.6 cents on each dollar of common stock equity.

→ REVIEW QUESTIONS

3–14 What three ratios of profitability are found on a *common-size income statement?*

3–15 What would explain a firm's having a high gross profit margin and a low net profit margin?

3–16 Which measure of profitability is probably of greatest interest to the investing public? Why?

LG 5 3.7 Market Ratios

market ratios
Relate a firm's market value, as measured by its current share price, to certain accounting values.

Market ratios relate the firm's market value, as measured by its current share price, to certain accounting values. These ratios give insight into how investors in the marketplace feel the firm is doing in terms of risk and return. They tend to reflect, on a relative basis, the common stockholders' assessment of all aspects of the firm's past and expected future performance. Here we consider two widely quoted market ratios, one that focuses on earnings and another that considers book value.

PRICE/EARNINGS (P/E) RATIO

price/earnings (P/E) ratio
Measures the amount that investors are willing to pay for each dollar of a firm's earnings; the higher the P/E ratio, the greater the investor confidence.

The **price/earnings (P/E) ratio** is commonly used to assess the owners' appraisal of share value. The P/E ratio measures the amount that investors are willing to pay for each dollar of a firm's earnings. The level of this ratio indicates the degree of confidence that investors have in the firm's future performance. The higher the P/E ratio, the greater the investor confidence. The P/E ratio is calculated as follows:

$$\text{P/E ratio} = \text{Market price per share of common stock} \div \text{Earnings per share}$$

If Bartlett Company's common stock at the end of 2012 was selling at \$32.25, using the EPS of \$2.90, the P/E ratio at year-end 2012 is

$$\$32.25 \div \$2.90 = 11.1$$

This figure indicates that investors were paying \$11.10 for each \$1.00 of earnings. The P/E ratio is most informative when applied in cross-sectional analysis using an industry average P/E ratio or the P/E ratio of a benchmark firm.

MARKET/BOOK (M/B) RATIO

market/book (M/B) ratio
Provides an assessment of how investors view the firm's performance. Firms expected to earn high returns relative to their risk typically sell at higher M/B multiples.

The **market/book (M/B) ratio** provides an assessment of how investors view the firm's performance. It relates the market value of the firm's shares to their book—strict accounting—value. To calculate the firm's M/B ratio, we first need to find the *book value per share of common stock:*

$$\text{Book value per share of common stock} = \frac{\text{Common stock equity}}{\text{Number of shares of common stock outstanding}}$$

Substituting the appropriate values for Bartlett Company from its 2012 balance sheet, we get

$$\text{Book value per share of common stock} = \frac{\$1{,}754{,}000}{76{,}262} = \$23.00$$

The formula for the market/book ratio is

$$\text{Market/book (M/B) ratio} = \frac{\text{Market price per share of common stock}}{\text{Book value per share of common stock}}$$

Substituting Bartlett Company's end of 2012 common stock price of \$32.25 and its \$23.00 book value per share of common stock (calculated above) into the M/B ratio formula, we get

$$\$32.25 \div \$23.00 = 1.40$$

This M/B ratio means that investors are currently paying \$1.40 for each \$1.00 of book value of Bartlett Company's stock.

The stocks of firms that are expected to perform well—improve profits, increase their market share, or launch successful products—typically sell at higher M/B ratios than the stocks of firms with less attractive outlooks. Simply stated, firms expected to earn high returns relative to their risk typically sell at higher M/B multiples. Clearly, Bartlett's future prospects are being viewed favorably by investors, who are willing to pay more than their book value for the firm's shares. Like P/E ratios, M/B ratios are typically assessed cross-sectionally to get a feel for the firm's return and risk compared to peer firms.

→ REVIEW QUESTION

3–17 How do the *price/earnings (P/E) ratio* and the *market/book (M/B) ratio* provide a feel for the firm's return and risk?

LG 6 3.8 A Complete Ratio Analysis

Analysts frequently wish to take an overall look at the firm's financial performance and status. Here we consider two popular approaches to a complete ratio analysis: (1) summarizing all ratios and (2) the DuPont system of analysis. The summary analysis approach tends to view *all aspects* of the firm's financial activities to isolate key areas of responsibility. The DuPont system acts as a search technique aimed at finding the *key areas* responsible for the firm's financial condition.

SUMMARIZING ALL RATIOS

We can use Bartlett Company's ratios to perform a complete ratio analysis using both cross-sectional and time-series analysis approaches. The 2012 ratio values calculated earlier and the ratio values calculated for 2010 and 2011 for Bartlett Company, along with the industry average ratios for 2012, are summarized in Table 3.8 (see pages 86 and 87), which also shows the formula used to calculate each ratio. Using these data, we can discuss the five key aspects of Bartlett's performance—liquidity, activity, debt, profitability, and market.

Liquidity

The overall liquidity of the firm seems to exhibit a reasonably stable trend, having been maintained at a level that is relatively consistent with the industry average in 2012. The firm's liquidity seems to be good.

Activity

Bartlett Company's inventory appears to be in good shape. Its inventory management seems to have improved, and in 2012 it performed at a level above that of the industry. The firm may be experiencing some problems with accounts receivable. The average collection period seems to have crept up above that of the industry. Bartlett also appears to be slow in paying its bills; it pays nearly 30 days slower than the industry average. This could adversely affect the firm's credit standing. Although overall liquidity appears to be good, the management of receivables and payables should be examined. Bartlett's total asset turnover reflects a decline in the efficiency of total asset utilization between 2010 and 2011. Although in 2012 it rose to a level considerably above the industry average, it appears that the pre-2011 level of efficiency has not yet been achieved.

Debt

Bartlett Company's indebtedness increased over the 2010–2012 period and is currently above the industry average. Although this increase in the debt ratio could be cause for alarm, the firm's ability to meet interest and fixed-payment obligations improved, from 2011 to 2012, to a level that outperforms the industry. The firm's increased indebtedness in 2011 apparently caused deterioration in its ability to pay debt adequately. However, Bartlett has evidently improved its income in 2012 so that it is able to meet its interest and fixed-payment obligations at a level consistent with the average in the industry. In summary, it appears that although 2011 was an off year, the company's improved ability to pay debts in 2012 compensates for its increased degree of indebtedness.

Profitability

Bartlett's profitability relative to sales in 2012 was better than the average company in the industry, although it did not match the firm's 2010 performance. Although the *gross* profit margin was better in 2011 and 2012 than in 2010, higher levels of operating and interest expenses in 2011 and 2012 appear to have caused the 2012 *net* profit margin to fall below that of 2010. However, Bartlett Company's 2012 net profit margin is quite favorable when compared to the industry average.

The firm's earnings per share, return on total assets, and return on common equity behaved much as its net profit margin did over the 2010–2012 period. Bartlett appears to have experienced either a sizable drop in sales between 2010 and 2011 or a rapid expansion in assets during that period. The exceptionally high 2012 level of return on common equity suggests that the firm is performing quite well. The firm's above-average returns—net profit margin, EPS, ROA, and ROE—may be attributable to the fact that it is more risky than average. A look at market ratios is helpful in assessing risk.

Market

Investors have greater confidence in the firm in 2012 than in the prior 2 years, as reflected in the price/earnings (P/E) ratio of 11.1. However, this ratio is below the industry average. The P/E ratio suggests that the firm's risk has declined but remains above that of the average firm in its industry. The firm's market/book (M/B) ratio has increased over the 2010–2012 period, and in 2012 it exceeds the industry average. This implies that investors are optimistic about the firm's future performance. The P/E and M/B ratios reflect the firm's increased profitability over the 2010–2012 period: Investors expect to earn high future returns as compensation for the firm's above-average risk.

In summary, the firm appears to be growing and has recently undergone an expansion in assets, financed primarily through the use of debt. The 2011–2012 period seems to reflect a phase of adjustment and recovery from the rapid growth in assets. Bartlett's sales, profits, and other performance factors seem to be growing with the increase in the size of the operation. In addition, the market response to these accomplishments appears to have been positive. In short, the firm seems to have done well in 2012.

DUPONT SYSTEM OF ANALYSIS

DuPont system of analysis
System used to dissect the firm's financial statements and to assess its financial condition.

The **DuPont system of analysis** is used to dissect the firm's financial statements and to assess its financial condition. It merges the income statement and balance sheet into two summary measures of profitability, return on total assets (ROA) and return on common equity (ROE). Figure 3.2 (see page 88) depicts the basic DuPont system with Bartlett Company's 2012 monetary and ratio values. The upper portion of the chart summarizes the income statement activities; the lower portion summarizes the balance sheet activities.

DuPont Formula

The DuPont system first brings together the *net profit margin,* which measures the firm's profitability on sales, with its *total asset turnover,* which indicates how

TABLE 3.8 Summary of Bartlett Company Ratios (2010–2012, Including 2012 Industry Averages)

Ratio	Formula	Year 2010[a]	Year 2011[b]	Year 2012[b]	Industry Average 2012[c]	Evaluation[d] Cross-Sectional 2012	Evaluation[d] Time-Series 2010–2012	Evaluation[d] Overall
Liquidity								
Current ratio	$\frac{\text{Current assets}}{\text{Current liabilities}}$	2.04	2.08	1.97	2.05	OK	OK	OK
Quick (acid-test) ratio	$\frac{\text{Current assets} - \text{Inventory}}{\text{Current liabilities}}$	1.32	1.46	1.51	1.43	OK	Good	Good
Activity								
Inventory turnover	$\frac{\text{Cost of goods sold}}{\text{Inventory}}$	5.1	5.7	7.2	6.6	Good	Good	Good
Average collection period	$\frac{\text{Accounts receivable}}{\text{Average sales per day}}$	43.9 days	51.2 days	59.7 days	44.3 days	Poor	Poor	Poor
Average payment period	$\frac{\text{Accounts payable}}{\text{Average purchases per day}}$	75.8 days	81.2 days	95.4 days	66.5 days	Poor	Poor	Poor
Total assets turnover	$\frac{\text{Sales}}{\text{Total assets}}$	0.94	0.79	0.85	0.75	OK	OK	OK
Debt								
Debt ratio	$\frac{\text{Total liabilities}}{\text{Total assets}}$	36.8%	44.3%	45.7%	40.0%	OK	OK	OK
Times interest earned ratio	$\frac{\text{Earnings before interest and taxes}}{\text{Interest}}$	5.6	3.3	4.5	4.3	Good	OK	OK
Fixed-payment coverage ratio	$\frac{\text{Earnings before interest and taxes} + \text{Lease payments}}{\text{Int.} + \text{Lease pay.} + \{(\text{Prin.} + \text{Pref. div.}) \times [1/(1 - T)]\}}$	2.4	1.4	1.9	1.5	Good	OK	Good
Profitability								
Gross profit margin	$\frac{\text{Gross profits}}{\text{Sales}}$	31.4%	33.3%	32.1%	30.0%	OK	OK	OK
Operating profit margin	$\frac{\text{Operating profits}}{\text{Sales}}$	14.6%	11.8%	13.6%	11.0%	Good	OK	Good
Net profit margin	$\frac{\text{Earnings available for common stockholders}}{\text{Sales}}$	8.2%	5.4%	7.2%	6.2%	Good	OK	Good

Ratio	Formula	Year			Industry Average 2012[c]	Evaluation[d]		
		2010[a]	2011[b]	2012[b]		Cross-Sectional 2012	Time-Series 2010–2012	Overall
Profitability (cont.)								
Earnings per share (EPS)	$\frac{\text{Earnings available for common stockholders}}{\text{Number of shares of common stock outstanding}}$	$3.26	$1.81	$2.90	$2.26	Good	OK	Good
Return on total assets (ROA)	$\frac{\text{Earnings available for common stockholders}}{\text{Total assets}}$	7.8%	4.2%	6.1%	4.6%	Good	OK	Good
Return on common equity (ROE)	$\frac{\text{Earnings available for common stockholders}}{\text{Common stock equity}}$	13.7%	8.5%	12.6%	8.5%	Good	OK	Good
Market								
Price/earnings (P/E) ratio	$\frac{\text{Market price per share of common stock}}{\text{Earnings per share}}$	10.5	10.0[e]	11.1	12.5	OK	OK	OK
Market/book (M/B) ratio	$\frac{\text{Market price per share of common stock}}{\text{Book value per share of common stock}}$	1.25	0.85[e]	1.40	1.30	OK	OK	OK

[a]Calculated from data not included in this chapter.

[b]Calculated by using the financial statements presented in Tables 3.1 and 3.2.

[c]Obtained from sources not included in this chapter.

[d]Subjective assessments based on data provided.

[e]The market price per share at the end of 2011 was $18.06.

FIGURE 3.2

DuPont System of Analysis
The DuPont system of analysis with application to Bartlett Company (2012)

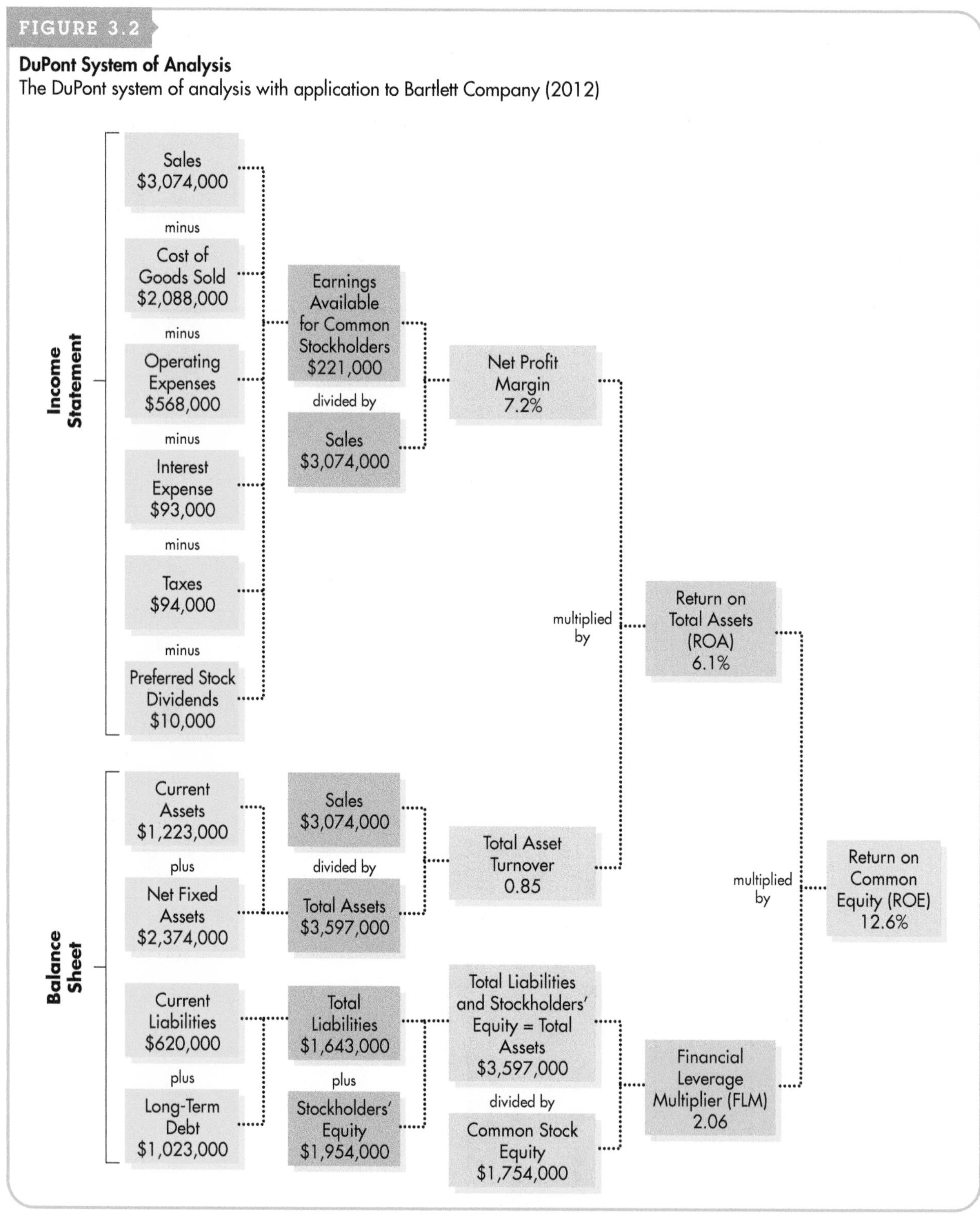

DuPont formula
Multiplies the firm's *net profit margin* by its *total asset turnover* to calculate the firm's *return on total assets (ROA).*

efficiently the firm has used its assets to generate sales. In the **DuPont formula,** the product of these two ratios results in the *return on total assets (ROA):*

$$\text{ROA} = \text{Net profit margin} \times \text{Total asset turnover}$$

Substituting the appropriate formulas into the equation and simplifying results in the formula given earlier,

$$\text{ROA} = \frac{\text{Earnings available for common stockholders}}{\text{Sales}} \times \frac{\text{Sales}}{\text{Total assets}} = \frac{\text{Earnings available for common stockholders}}{\text{Total assets}}$$

When the 2012 values of the net profit margin and total asset turnover for Bartlett Company, calculated earlier, are substituted into the DuPont formula, the result is

$$\text{ROA} = 7.2\% \times 0.85 = 6.1\%$$

This value is the same as that calculated directly in an earlier section (page 81). The DuPont formula enables the firm to break down its return into profit-on-sales and efficiency-of-asset-use components. Typically, a firm with a low net profit margin has a high total asset turnover, which results in a reasonably good return on total assets. Often, the opposite situation exists.

Matter of fact

Dissecting ROA

Return to Table 3.5, and examine the total asset turnover figures for Dell and The Home Depot. Both firms turn their assets 1.6 times per year. Now look at the return on assets column. Dell's ROA is 4.3 percent, but The Home Depot's is significantly higher at 6.5 percent. If the two firms are equal in terms of the efficiency with which they manage their assets (that is, equal asset turns), why is The Home Depot more profitable relative to assets? The answer lies in the DuPont formula. Notice that Home Depot's net profit margin is 4.0 percent compared to Dell's 2.7 percent. That drives the superior ROA figures for The Home Depot.

Modified DuPont Formula

modified DuPont formula
Relates the firm's *return on total assets (ROA)* to its *return on common equity (ROE)* using the *financial leverage multiplier (FLM).*

financial leverage multiplier (FLM)
The ratio of the firm's total assets to its common stock equity.

The second step in the DuPont system employs the **modified DuPont formula.** This formula relates the firm's *return on total assets (ROA)* to its *return on common equity (ROE)*. The latter is calculated by multiplying the return on total assets (ROA) by the **financial leverage multiplier (FLM),** which is the ratio of total assets to common stock equity:

$$\text{ROE} = \text{ROA} \times \text{FLM}$$

Substituting the appropriate formulas into the equation and simplifying results in the formula given earlier,

$$\text{ROE} = \frac{\text{Earnings available for common stockholders}}{\text{Total assets}} \times \frac{\text{Total assets}}{\text{Common stock equity}} = \frac{\text{Earnings available for common stockholders}}{\text{Common stock equity}}$$

Use of the financial leverage multiplier (FLM) to convert the ROA into the ROE reflects the impact of financial leverage on owners' return. Substituting the values for Bartlett Company's ROA of 6.1 percent, calculated earlier, and Bartlett's FLM of 2.06 (\$3,597,000 total assets ÷ \$1,754,000 common stock equity) into the modified DuPont formula yields

$$\text{ROE} = 6.1\% \times 2.06 = 12.6\%$$

The 12.6 percent ROE calculated by using the modified DuPont formula is the same as that calculated directly (page 82).

Applying the DuPont System

The advantage of the DuPont system is that it allows the firm to break its return on equity into a profit-on-sales component (net profit margin), an efficiency-of-asset-use component (total asset turnover), and a use-of-financial-leverage component (financial leverage multiplier). The total return to owners therefore can be analyzed in these important dimensions.

The use of the DuPont system of analysis as a diagnostic tool is best explained using Figure 3.2. Beginning with the rightmost value—the ROE—the financial analyst moves to the left, dissecting and analyzing the inputs to the formula to isolate the probable cause of the resulting above-average (or below-average) value.

Example 3.6 ▸

For the sake of demonstration, let's ignore all industry average data in Table 3.8 and assume that Bartlett's ROE of 12.6% is actually below the industry average. Moving to the left in Figure 3.2, we would examine the inputs to the ROE—the ROA and the FLM—relative to the industry averages. Let's assume that the FLM is in line with the industry average, but the ROA is below the industry average. Moving farther to the left, we examine the two inputs to the ROA—the net profit margin and total asset turnover. Assume that the net profit margin is in line with the industry average, but the total asset turnover is below the industry average. Moving still farther to the left, we find that whereas the firm's sales are consistent with the industry value, Bartlett's total assets have grown significantly during the past year. Looking farther to the left, we would review the firm's activity ratios for current assets. Let's say that whereas the firm's inventory turnover is in line with the industry average, its average collection period is well above the industry average.

We can readily trace the possible problem back to its cause: Bartlett's low ROE is primarily the consequence of slow collections of accounts receivable, which resulted in high levels of receivables and therefore high levels of total assets. The high total assets slowed Bartlett's total asset turnover, driving down its ROA, which then drove down its ROE. By using the DuPont system of analysis to dissect Bartlett's overall returns as measured by its ROE, we found that slow collections of receivables caused the below-industry-average ROE. Clearly, the firm needs to better manage its credit operations.

→ REVIEW QUESTIONS

3–18 Financial ratio analysis is often divided into five areas: *liquidity, activity, debt, profitability,* and *market* ratios. Differentiate each of these areas of analysis from the others. Which is of the greatest concern to creditors?

3–19 Describe how you would use a large number of ratios to perform a complete ratio analysis of the firm.

3–20 What three areas of analysis are combined in the *modified DuPont formula?* Explain how the *DuPont system of analysis* is used to dissect the firm's results and isolate their causes.

Summary

FOCUS ON VALUE

Financial managers review and analyze the firm's financial statements periodically, both to uncover developing problems and to assess the firm's progress toward achieving its goals. These actions are aimed at **preserving and creating value for the firm's owners.** Financial ratios enable financial managers to monitor the pulse of the firm and its progress toward its strategic goals. Although financial statements and financial ratios rely on accrual concepts, they can provide useful insights into important aspects of risk and return (cash flow) that affect share price.

REVIEW OF LEARNING GOALS

LG 1 **Review the contents of the stockholders' report and the procedures for consolidating international financial statements.** The annual stockholders' report, which publicly owned corporations must provide to stockholders, documents the firm's financial activities of the past year. It includes the letter to stockholders and various subjective and factual information. It also contains four key financial statements: the income statement, the balance sheet, the statement of stockholders' equity (or its abbreviated form, the statement of retained earnings), and the statement of cash flows. Notes describing the technical aspects of the financial statements follow. Financial statements of companies that have operations whose cash flows are denominated in one or more foreign currencies must be translated into dollars in accordance with *FASB Standard No. 52.*

LG 2 **Understand who uses financial ratios and how.** Ratio analysis enables stockholders, lenders, and the firm's managers to evaluate the firm's financial performance. It can be performed on a cross-sectional or a time-series basis. Benchmarking is a popular type of cross-sectional analysis. Users of ratios should understand the cautions that apply to their use.

LG 3 **Use ratios to analyze a firm's liquidity and activity.** Liquidity, or the ability of the firm to pay its bills as they come due, can be measured by the current ratio and the quick (acid-test) ratio. Activity ratios measure the speed with which accounts are converted into sales or cash—inflows or outflows. The activity of inventory can be measured by its turnover: that of accounts receivable by the average collection period and that of accounts payable by the average payment period. Total asset turnover measures the efficiency with which the firm uses its assets to generate sales.

LG 4 **Discuss the relationship between debt and financial leverage and the ratios used to analyze a firm's debt.** The more debt a firm uses, the greater its financial leverage, which magnifies both risk and return. Financial debt ratios measure both the degree of indebtedness and the ability to service debts. A common measure of indebtedness is the debt ratio. The ability to pay fixed charges can be measured by times interest earned and fixed-payment coverage ratios.

LG 5 **Use ratios to analyze a firm's profitability and its market value.** The common-size income statement, which shows each item as a percentage of sales, can be used to determine gross profit margin, operating profit margin, and net profit margin. Other measures of profitability include earnings per share, return on total assets, and return on common equity. Market ratios include the price/earnings ratio and the market/book ratio.

LG 6 **Use a summary of financial ratios and the DuPont system of analysis to perform a complete ratio analysis.** A summary of all ratios can be used to perform a complete ratio analysis using cross-sectional and time-series analysis. The

DuPont system of analysis is a diagnostic tool used to find the key areas responsible for the firm's financial performance. It enables the firm to break the return on common equity into three components: profit on sales, efficiency of asset use, and use of financial leverage.

Opener-in-Review

In the chapter opener you read about how financial analysts gave Abercrombie's stock a relatively positive outlook based on a current ratio of 2.79, a quick ratio of 1.79, and a receivables collection period of 43 days. Based on what you learned in this chapter, do you agree with the analysts' assessment? Explain why or why not.

Self-Test Problems (Solutions in Appendix)

LG 3 LG 4 LG 5 **ST3–1** **Ratio formulas and interpretations** Without referring to the text, indicate for each of the following ratios the formula for calculating it and the kinds of problems, if any, the firm may have if that ratio is too high relative to the industry average. What if the ratio is too low relative to the industry average? Create a table similar to the one that follows and fill in the empty blocks.

Ratio	Too High	Too Low
Current ratio =		
Inventory turnover =		
Times interest earned =	X	
Gross profit margin =		
Return on total assets =	X	
Price/earnings (P/E) ratio =		

LG 3 LG 4 LG 5 **ST3–2** **Balance sheet completion using ratios** Complete the 2012 balance sheet for O'Keefe Industries using the information that follows it.

O'Keefe Industries Balance Sheet December 31, 2012			
Assets		**Liabilities and Stockholders' Equity**	
Cash	$32,720	Accounts payable	$120,000
Marketable securities	25,000	Notes payable	______
Accounts receivable	______	Accruals	20,000
Inventories	______	Total current liabilities	______
Total current assets	______	Long-term debt	______
Net fixed assets	______	Stockholders' equity	$600,000
Total assets	$ ______	Total liabilities and stockholders' equity	$ ______

The following financial data for 2012 are also available:
1. Sales totaled $1,800,000.
2. The gross profit margin was 25%.
3. Inventory turnover was 6.0.
4. There are 365 days in the year.
5. The average collection period was 40 days.
6. The current ratio was 1.60.
7. The total asset turnover ratio was 1.20.
8. The debt ratio was 60%.

Warm-Up Exercises

All problems are available in myfinancelab.

LG 1 **E3–1** You are a summer intern at the office of a local tax preparer. To test your basic knowledge of financial statements, your manager, who graduated from your alma mater 2 years ago, gives you the following list of accounts and asks you to prepare a simple income statement using those accounts.

Accounts	**($000,000)**
Depreciation	25
General and administrative expenses	22
Sales	345
Sales expenses	18
Cost of goods sold	255
Lease expense	4
Interest expense	3

a. Arrange the accounts into a well-labeled income statement. Make sure you label and solve for gross profit, operating profit, and net profit before taxes.
b. Using a 35% tax rate, calculate taxes paid and net profit after taxes.
c. Assuming a dividend of $1.10 per share with 4.25 million shares outstanding, calculate EPS and additions to retained earnings.

LG 1 **E3–2** Explain why the income statement can also be called a "profit-and-loss statement." What exactly does the word *balance* mean in the title of the balance sheet? Why do we balance the two halves?

LG 1 **E3–3** Cooper Industries, Inc., began 2012 with retained earnings of $25.32 million. During the year it paid four quarterly dividends of $0.35 per share to 2.75 million common stockholders. Preferred stockholders, holding 500,000 shares, were paid two semiannual dividends of $0.75 per share. The firm had a net profit after taxes of $5.15 million. Prepare the statement of retained earnings for the year ended December 31, 2012.

LG 3 **E3–4** Bluestone Metals, Inc., is a metal fabrication firm that manufactures prefabricated metal parts for customers in a variety of industries. The firm's motto is "If you need it, we can make it." The CEO of Bluestone recently held a board meeting during which he extolled the virtues of the corporation. The company, he stated confidently, had the capability to build any product and could do so using a lean manufacturing model. The firm would soon be profitable, claimed the CEO, because the company used state-of-the-art technology to build a variety of products while keeping inventory levels low. As a business press reporter, you have calculated some ratios to analyze the financial health of the firm. Bluestone's current ratios and quick ratios for the past 6 years are shown in the table below:

	2007	2008	2009	2010	2011	2012
Current ratio	1.2	1.4	1.3	1.6	1.8	2.2
Quick ratio	1.1	1.3	1.2	0.8	0.6	0.4

What do you think of the CEO's claim that the firm is lean and soon to be profitable? (*Hint:* Is there a possible warning sign in the relationship between the two ratios?)

LG 5 **E3–5** If we know that a firm has a net profit margin of 4.5%, total asset turnover of 0.72, and a financial leverage multiplier of 1.43, what is its ROE? What is the advantage to using the DuPont system to calculate ROE over the direct calculation of earnings available for common stockholders divided by common stock equity?

Problems

All problems are available in myfinancelab.

LG 1 **P3–1** **Reviewing basic financial statements** The income statement for the year ended December 31, 2012, the balance sheets for December 31, 2012 and 2011, and the statement of retained earnings for the year ended December 31, 2012, for Technica, Inc., are given below and on the following page. Briefly discuss the form and informational content of each of these statements.

Technica, Inc. Income Statement for the Year Ended December 31, 2012

Sales revenue	$600,000
Less: Cost of goods sold	460,000
Gross profits	$140,000
Less: Operating expenses	
General and administrative expenses	$ 30,000
Depreciation expense	30,000
Total operating expense	$ 60,000
Operating profits	$ 80,000
Less: Interest expense	10,000
Net profits before taxes	$ 70,000
Less: Taxes	27,100
Earnings available for common stockholders	$ 42,900
Earnings per share (EPS)	$2.15

Technica, Inc. Balance Sheets		
	December 31	
Assets	**2012**	**2011**
Cash	$ 15,000	$ 16,000
Marketable securities	7,200	8,000
Accounts receivable	34,100	42,200
Inventories	82,000	50,000
Total current assets	$138,300	$116,200
Land and buildings	$150,000	$150,000
Machinery and equipment	200,000	190,000
Furniture and fixtures	54,000	50,000
Other	11,000	10,000
Total gross fixed assets	$415,000	$400,000
Less: Accumulated depreciation	145,000	115,000
Net fixed assets	$270,000	$285,000
Total assets	$408,000	$401,200
Liabilities and Stockholders' Equity		
Accounts payable	$ 57,000	$ 49,000
Notes payable	13,000	16,000
Accruals	5,000	6,000
Total current liabilities	$ 75,000	$ 71,000
Long-term debt	$150,000	$160,000
Common stock equity (shares outstanding: 19,500 in 2012 and 20,000 in 2011)	$110,200	$120,000
Retained earnings	73,100	50,200
Total stockholders' equity	$183,300	$170,200
Total liabilities and stockholders' equity	$408,300	$401,200

Technica, Inc. Statement of Retained Earnings for the Year Ended December 31, 2012	
Retained earnings balance (January 1, 2012)	$50,200
Plus: Net profits after taxes (for 2012)	42,900
Less: Cash dividends (paid during 2012)	20,000
Retained earnings balance (December 31, 2012)	$73,100

LG 1

P3–2 Financial statement account identification Mark each of the accounts listed in the following table as follows:

a. In column (1), indicate in which statement—income statement (IS) or balance sheet (BS)—the account belongs.

b. In column (2), indicate whether the account is a current asset (CA), current liability (CL), expense (E), fixed asset (FA), long-term debt (LTD), revenue (R), or stockholders' equity (SE).

Account name	(1) Statement	(2) Type of account
Accounts payable	____	____
Accounts receivable	____	____
Accruals	____	____
Accumulated depreciation	____	____
Administrative expense	____	____
Buildings	____	____
Cash	____	____
Common stock (at par)	____	____
Cost of goods sold	____	____
Depreciation	____	____
Equipment	____	____
General expense	____	____
Interest expense	____	____
Inventories	____	____
Land	____	____
Long-term debts	____	____
Machinery	____	____
Marketable securities	____	____
Notes payable	____	____
Operating expense	____	____
Paid-in capital in excess of par	____	____
Preferred stock	____	____
Preferred stock dividends	____	____
Retained earnings	____	____
Sales revenue	____	____
Selling expense	____	____
Taxes	____	____
Vehicles	____	____

LG 1 **P3–3 Income statement preparation** On December 31, 2012, Cathy Chen, a self-employed certified public accountant (CPA), completed her first full year in business. During the year, she billed $360,000 for her accounting services. She had two employees, a bookkeeper and a clerical assistant. In addition to her *monthly* salary of $8,000, Ms. Chen paid *annual* salaries of $48,000 and $36,000 to the bookkeeper and the clerical assistant, respectively. Employment taxes and benefit costs for Ms. Chen and her employees totaled $34,600 for the year. Expenses for office supplies, including postage, totaled $10,400 for the year. In addition, Ms. Chen spent $17,000 during the year on tax-deductible travel and entertainment associated with client visits and new business development. Lease payments for the office space rented (a tax-deductible expense) were $2,700 *per month*. Depreciation expense on the office furniture and fixtures was $15,600 for the year. During the year, Ms. Chen paid interest of $15,000 on the $120,000 borrowed to start the business. She paid an average tax rate of 30% during 2012.

a. Prepare an income statement for Cathy Chen, CPA, for the year ended December 31, 2012.

b. Evaluate her 2012 financial performance.

Personal Finance Problem

LG 1 **P3–4 Income statement preparation** Adam and Arin Adams have collected their personal income and expense information and have asked you to put together an income and expense statement for the year ended December 31, 2012. The following information is received from the Adams family.

Adam's salary	$45,000	Utilities	$ 3,200
Arin's salary	30,000	Groceries	2,200
Interest received	500	Medical	1,500
Dividends received	150	Property taxes	1,659
Auto insurance	600	Income tax, Social Security	13,000
Home insurance	750	Clothes and accessories	2,000
Auto loan payment	3,300	Gas and auto repair	2,100
Mortgage payment	14,000	Entertainment	2,000

a. Create a personal *income and expense statement* for the period ended December 31, 2012. It should be similar to a corporate income statement.
b. Did the Adams family have a cash surplus or cash deficit?
c. If the result is a surplus, how can the Adams family use that surplus?

LG 1 **P3–5 Calculation of EPS and retained earnings** Philagem, Inc., ended 2012 with a net profit *before* taxes of $218,000. The company is subject to a 40% tax rate and must pay $32,000 in preferred stock dividends before distributing any earnings on the 85,000 shares of common stock currently outstanding.
a. Calculate Philagem's 2012 earnings per share (EPS).
b. If the firm paid common stock dividends of $0.80 per share, how many dollars would go to retained earnings?

LG 1 **P3–6 Balance sheet preparation** Use the *appropriate items* from the following list to prepare in good form Owen Davis Company's balance sheet at December 31, 2012.

Item	Value ($000) at December 31, 2012	Item	Value ($000) at December 31, 2012
Accounts payable	$ 220	Inventories	$ 375
Accounts receivable	450	Land	100
Accruals	55	Long-term debts	420
Accumulated depreciation	265	Machinery	420
Buildings	225	Marketable securities	75
Cash	215	Notes payable	475
Common stock (at par)	90	Paid-in capital in excess of par	360
Cost of goods sold	2,500	Preferred stock	100
Depreciation expense	45	Retained earnings	210
Equipment	140	Sales revenue	3,600
Furniture and fixtures	170	Vehicles	25
General expense	320		

Personal Finance Problem

LG 1 **P3–7 Balance sheet preparation** Adam and Arin Adams have collected their personal asset and liability information and have asked you to put together a balance sheet as of December 31, 2012. The following information is received from the Adams family.

Cash	$ 300	Retirement funds, IRA	$ 2,000
Checking	3,000	2011 Sebring	15,000
Savings	1,200	2010 Jeep	8,000
IBM stock	2,000	Money market funds	1,200
Auto loan	8,000	Jewelry and artwork	3,000
Mortgage	100,000	Net worth	76,500
Medical bills payable	250	Household furnishings	4,200
Utility bills payable	150	Credit card balance	2,000
Real estate	150,000	Personal loan	3,000

a. Create a personal balance sheet as of December 31, 2012. It should be similar to a corporate balance sheet.
b. What must the total assets of the Adams family be equal to by December 31, 2012?
c. What was their *net working capital (NWC)* for the year? (*Hint:* NWC is the difference between total liquid assets and total current liabilities.)

LG 1 **P3–8 Impact of net income on a firm's balance sheet** Conrad Air, Inc., reported net income of $1,365,000 for the year ended December 31, 2013. Show how Conrad's balance sheet would change from 2012 to 2013 depending on how Conrad "spent" those earnings as described in the scenarios that appear below.

Conrad Air, Inc. Balance Sheet as of December 31, 2012

Assets		**Liabilities and Stockholders' Equity**	
Cash	$ 120,000	Accounts payable	$ 70,000
Marketable securities	35,000	Short-term notes	55,000
Accounts receivable	45,000	Current liabilities	$ 125,000
Inventories	130,000	Long-term debt	2,700,000
Current assets	$ 330,000	Total liabilities	$2,825,000
Equipment	$2,970,000	Common stock	$ 500,000
Buildings	1,600,000	Retained earnings	1,575,000
Fixed assets	$4,570,000	Stockholders' equity	$2,075,000
Total assets	$4,900,000	Total liabilities and equity	$4,900,000

a. Conrad paid no dividends during the year and invested the funds in marketable securities.
b. Conrad paid dividends totaling $500,000 and used the balance of the net income to retire (pay off) long-term debt.
c. Conrad paid dividends totaling $500,000 and invested the balance of the net income in building a new hangar.
d. Conrad paid out all $1,365,000 as dividends to its stockholders.

LG 1 **P3–9** **Initial sale price of common stock** Beck Corporation has one issue of preferred stock and one issue of common stock outstanding. Given Beck's stockholders' equity account that follows, determine the original price per share at which the firm sold its single issue of common stock.

Stockholders' Equity ($000)	
Preferred stock	$ 125
Common stock ($0.75 par, 300,000 shares outstanding)	225
Paid-in capital in excess of par on common stock	2,625
Retained earnings	900
Total stockholders' equity	$3,875

LG 1 **P3–10** **Statement of retained earnings** Hayes Enterprises began 2012 with a retained earnings balance of $928,000. During 2012, the firm earned $377,000 after taxes. From this amount, preferred stockholders were paid $47,000 in dividends. At year-end 2012, the firm's retained earnings totaled $1,048,000. The firm had 140,000 shares of common stock outstanding during 2012.

a. Prepare a statement of retained earnings for the year ended December 31, 2012, for Hayes Enterprises. (*Note:* Be sure to calculate and include the amount of cash dividends paid in 2012.)

b. Calculate the firm's 2012 earnings per share (EPS).

c. How large a per-share cash dividend did the firm pay on common stock during 2012?

LG 1 **P3–11** **Changes in stockholders' equity** Listed are the equity sections of balance sheets for years 2011 and 2012 as reported by Mountain Air Ski Resorts, Inc. The overall value of stockholders' equity has risen from $2,000,000 to $7,500,000. Use the statements to discover how and why this happened.

Mountain Air Ski Resorts, Inc.
Balance Sheets (partial)

Stockholders' equity	**2011**	**2012**
Common stock ($1.00 par)		
Authorized—5,000,000 shares		
Outstanding—1,500,000 shares 2012		$1,500,000
— 500,000 shares 2011	$ 500,000	
Paid-in capital in excess of par	500,000	4,500,000
Retained earnings	1,000,000	1,500,000
Total stockholders' equity	$2,000,000	$7,500,000

The company paid total dividends of $200,000 during fiscal 2012.

a. What was Mountain Air's net income for fiscal 2012?

b. How many new shares did the corporation issue and sell during the year?

c. At what average price per share did the new stock sold during 2012 sell?

d. At what price per share did Mountain Air's original 500,000 shares sell?

LG 2 LG 3 LG 4 LG 5

P3–12 Ratio comparisons Robert Arias recently inherited a stock portfolio from his uncle. Wishing to learn more about the companies in which he is now invested, Robert performs a ratio analysis on each one and decides to compare them to each other. Some of his ratios are listed below.

Ratio	Island Electric Utility	Burger Heaven	Fink Software	Roland Motors
Current ratio	1.10	1.3	6.8	4.5
Quick ratio	0.90	0.82	5.2	3.7
Debt ratio	0.68	0.46	0.0	0.35
Net profit margin	6.2%	14.3%	28.5%	8.4%

Assuming that his uncle was a wise investor who assembled the portfolio with care, Robert finds the wide differences in these ratios confusing. Help him out.

a. What problems might Robert encounter in comparing these companies to one another on the basis of their ratios?

b. Why might the current and quick ratios for the electric utility and the fast-food stock be so much lower than the same ratios for the other companies?

c. Why might it be all right for the electric utility to carry a large amount of debt, but not the software company?

d. Why wouldn't investors invest all of their money in software companies instead of in less profitable companies? (Focus on risk and return.)

LG 3

P3–13 Liquidity management Bauman Company's total current assets, total current liabilities, and inventory for each of the past 4 years follow:

Item	2009	2010	2011	2012
Total current assets	$16,950	$21,900	$22,500	$27,000
Total current liabilities	9,000	12,600	12,600	17,400
Inventory	6,000	6,900	6,900	7,200

a. Calculate the firm's current and quick ratios for each year. Compare the resulting time series for these measures of liquidity.

b. Comment on the firm's liquidity over the 2009–2010 period.

c. If you were told that Bauman Company's inventory turnover for each year in the 2009–2012 period and the industry averages were as follows, would this information support or conflict with your evaluation in part **b**? Why?

Inventory turnover	2009	2010	2011	2012
Bauman Company	6.3	6.8	7.0	6.4
Industry average	10.6	11.2	10.8	11.0

Personal Finance Problem

LG 3 **P3–14 Liquidity ratio** Josh Smith has compiled some of his personal financial data in order to determine his liquidity position. The data are as follows.

Account	Amount
Cash	$3,200
Marketable securities	1,000
Checking account	800
Credit card payables	1,200
Short-term notes payable	900

a. Calculate Josh's *liquidity ratio.*
b. Several of Josh's friends have told him that they have liquidity ratios of about 1.8. How would you analyze Josh's liquidity relative to his friends?

LG 3 **P3–15 Inventory management** Wilkins Manufacturing has annual sales of $4 million and a gross profit margin of 40%. Its *end-of-quarter inventories* are

Quarter	Inventory
1	$ 400,000
2	800,000
3	1,200,000
4	200,000

a. Find the average quarterly inventory and use it to calculate the firm's inventory turnover and the average age of inventory.
b. Assuming that the company is in an industry with an average inventory turnover of 2.0, how would you evaluate the activity of Wilkins' inventory?

LG 3 **P3–16 Accounts receivable management** An evaluation of the books of Blair Supply, which follows, gives the end-of-year accounts receivable balance, which is believed to consist of amounts originating in the months indicated. The company had annual sales of $2.4 million. The firm extends 30-day credit terms.

Month of origin	Amounts receivable
July	$ 3,875
August	2,000
September	34,025
October	15,100
November	52,000
December	193,000
Year-end accounts receivable	$300,000

a. Use the year-end total to evaluate the firm's collection system.
b. If 70% of the firm's sales occur between July and December, would this affect the validity of your conclusion in part **a**? Explain.

LG 3 **P3–17 Interpreting liquidity and activity ratios** The new owners of Bluegrass Natural Foods, Inc., have hired you to help them diagnose and cure problems that the company has had in maintaining adequate liquidity. As a first step, you perform a liquidity analysis. You then do an analysis of the company's short-term activity ratios. Your calculations and appropriate industry norms are listed.

Ratio	Bluegrass	Industry norm
Current ratio	4.5	4.0
Quick ratio	2.0	3.1
Inventory turnover	6.0	10.4
Average collection period	73 days	52 days
Average payment period	31 days	40 days

a. What recommendations relative to the amount and the handling of inventory could you make to the new owners?
b. What recommendations relative to the amount and the handling of accounts receivable could you make to the new owners?
c. What recommendations relative to the amount and the handling of accounts payable could you make to the new owners?
d. What results, overall, would you hope your recommendations would achieve? Why might your recommendations not be effective?

LG 4 **P3–18 Debt analysis** Springfield Bank is evaluating Creek Enterprises, which has requested a $4,000,000 loan, to assess the firm's financial leverage and financial risk. On the basis of the debt ratios for Creek, along with the industry averages (see top of page 103) and Creek's recent financial statements (following), evaluate and recommend appropriate action on the loan request.

Creek Enterprises Income Statement for the Year Ended December 31, 2012	
Sales revenue	$30,000,000
Less: Cost of goods sold	21,000,000
Gross profits	$ 9,000,000
Less: Operating expenses	
Selling expense	$ 3,000,000
General and administrative expenses	1,800,000
Lease expense	200,000
Depreciation expense	1,000,000
Total operating expense	$ 6,000,000
Operating profits	$ 3,000,000
Less: Interest expense	1,000,000
Net profits before taxes	$ 2,000,000
Less: Taxes (rate = 40%)	800,000
Net profits after taxes	$ 1,200,000
Less: Preferred stock dividends	100,000
Earnings available for common stockholders	$ 1,100,000

Creek Enterprises Balance Sheet December 31, 2012

Assets		Liabilities and Stockholders' Equity	
Cash	$ 1,000,000	Accounts payable	$ 8,000,000
Marketable securities	3,000,000	Notes payable	8,000,000
Accounts receivable	12,000,000	Accruals	500,000
Inventories	7,500,000	Total current liabilities	$16,500,000
Total current assets	$23,500,000	Long-term debt (includes financial leases)[b]	$20,000,000
Land and buildings	$11,000,000		
Machinery and equipment	20,500,000	Preferred stock (25,000 shares, $4 dividend)	$ 2,500,000
Furniture and fixtures	8,000,000		
Gross fixed assets (at cost)[a]	$39,500,000	Common stock (1 million shares at $5 par)	5,000,000
Less: Accumulated depreciation	13,000,000		
Net fixed assets	$26,500,000	Paid-in capital in excess of par value	4,000,000
Total assets	$50,000,000		
		Retained earnings	2,000,000
		Total stockholders' equity	$13,500,000
		Total liabilities and stockholders' equity	$50,000,000

[a]The firm has a 4-year financial lease requiring annual beginning-of-year payments of $200,000. Three years of the lease have yet to run.

[b]Required annual principal payments are $800,000.

Industry averages	
Debt ratio	0.51
Times interest earned ratio	7.30
Fixed-payment coverage ratio	1.85

LG 5

P3–19 Common-size statement analysis A common-size income statement for Creek Enterprises' 2011 operations follows. Using the firm's 2012 income statement presented in Problem 3–18, develop the 2012 common-size income statement and compare it to the 2011 statement. Which areas require further analysis and investigation?

Creek Enterprises Common-Size Income Statement for the Year Ended December 31, 2011

Sales revenue ($35,000,000)	100.0%
Less: Cost of goods sold	65.9
Gross profits	34.1%
Less: Operating expenses	
Selling expense	12.7%
General and administrative expenses	6.3
Lease expense	0.6
Depreciation expense	3.6
Total operating expense	23.2
Operating profits	10.9%
Less: Interest expense	1.5
Net profits before taxes	9.4%
Less: Taxes (rate = 40%)	3.8
Net profits after taxes	5.6%
Less: Preferred stock dividends	0.1
Earnings available for common stockholders	5.5%

LG 4 LG 5 **P3–20 The relationship between financial leverage and profitability** Pelican Paper, Inc., and Timberland Forest, Inc., are rivals in the manufacture of craft papers. Some financial statement values for each company follow. Use them in a ratio analysis that compares the firms' financial leverage and profitability.

Item	Pelican Paper, Inc.	Timberland Forest, Inc.
Total assets	$10,000,000	$10,000,000
Total equity (all common)	9,000,000	5,000,000
Total debt	1,000,000	5,000,000
Annual interest	100,000	500,000
Total sales	25,000,000	25,000,000
EBIT	6,250,000	6,250,000
Earnings available for common stockholders	3,690,000	3,450,00

a. Calculate the following debt and coverage ratios for the two companies. Discuss their financial risk and ability to cover the costs in relation to each other.
(1) Debt ratio
(2) Times interest earned ratio

b. Calculate the following profitability ratios for the two companies. Discuss their profitability relative to each other.
(1) Operating profit margin
(2) Net profit margin
(3) Return on total assets
(4) Return on common equity

c. In what way has the larger debt of Timberland Forest made it more profitable than Pelican Paper? What are the risks that Timberland's investors undertake when they choose to purchase its stock instead of Pelican's?

LG 6 **P3–21 Ratio proficiency** McDougal Printing, Inc., had sales totaling $40,000,000 in fiscal year 2012. Some ratios for the company are listed below. Use this information to determine the dollar values of various income statement and balance sheet accounts as requested.

McDougal Printing, Inc. Year Ended December 31, 2012	
Sales	$40,000,000
Gross profit margin	80%
Operating profit margin	35%
Net profit margin	8%
Return on total assets	16%
Return on common equity	20%
Total asset turnover	2
Average collection period	62.2 days

Calculate values for the following:

a. Gross profits
b. Cost of goods sold
c. Operating profits
d. Operating expenses
e. Earnings available for common stockholders
f. Total assets
g. Total common stock equity
h. Accounts receivable

LG 6 **P3–22** **Cross-sectional ratio analysis** Use the financial statements below and on page 106 for Fox Manufacturing Company for the year ended December 31, 2012, along with the industry average ratios below, to:

a. Prepare and interpret a complete ratio analysis of the firm's 2012 operations.
b. Summarize your findings and make recommendations.

Fox Manufacturing Company Income Statement for the Year Ended December 31, 2012	
Sales revenue	$600,000
Less: Cost of goods sold	460,000
Gross profits	$140,000
Less: Operating expenses	
General and administrative expenses	$30,000
Depreciation expense	30,000
Total operating expense	60,000
Operating profits	$ 80,000
Less: Interest expense	10,000
Net profits before taxes	$ 70,000
Less: Taxes	27,100
Net profits after taxes (earnings available for common stockholders)	$ 42,900
Earnings per share (EPS)	$2.15

Ratio	Industry average, 2012
Current ratio	2.35
Quick ratio	0.87
Inventory turnover[a]	4.55
Average collection period[a]	35.8 days
Total asset turnover	1.09
Debt ratio	0.300
Times interest earned ratio	12.3
Gross profit margin	0.202
Operating profit margin	0.135
Net profit margin	0.091
Return on total assets (ROA)	0.099
Return on common equity (ROE)	0.167
Earnings per share (EPS)	$3.10

[a]Based on a 365-day year and on end-of-year figures.

Fox Manufacturing Company Balance Sheet December 31, 2012	
Assets	
Cash	$ 15,000
Marketable securities	7,200
Accounts receivable	34,100
Inventories	82,000
Total current assets	$138,300
Net fixed assets	270,000
Total assets	$408,300
Liabilities and Stockholders' Equity	
Accounts payable	$ 57,000
Notes payable	13,000
Accruals	5,000
Total current liabilities	$ 75,000
Long-term debt	$150,000
Common stock equity (20,000 shares outstanding)	$110,200
Retained earnings	73,100
Total stockholders' equity	$183,300
Total liabilities and stockholders' equity	$408,300

LG 6 **P3–23 Financial statement analysis** The financial statements of Zach Industries for the year ended December 31, 2012, follow.

Zach Industries Income Statement for the Year Ended December 31, 2012	
Sales revenue	$160,000
Less: Cost of goods sold	106,000
Gross profits	$ 54,000
Less: Operating expenses	
Selling expense	$ 16,000
General and administrative expenses	10,000
Lease expense	1,000
Depreciation expense	10,000
Total operating expense	$ 37,000
Operating profits	$ 17,000
Less: Interest expense	6,100
Net profits before taxes	$ 10,900
Less: Taxes	4,360
Net profits after taxes	$ 6,540

Zach Industries Balance Sheet December 31, 2012	
Assets	
Cash	$ 500
Marketable securities	1,000
Accounts receivable	25,000
Inventories	45,500
Total current assets	$ 72,000
Land	$ 26,000
Buildings and equipment	90,000
Less: Accumulated depreciation	38,000
Net fixed assets	$ 78,000
Total assets	$150,000
Liabilities and Stockholders' Equity	
Accounts payable	$ 22,000
Notes payable	47,000
Total current liabilities	$ 69,000
Long-term debt	22,950
Common stock[a]	31,500
Retained earnings	26,550
Total liabilities and stockholders' equity	$150,000

[a]The firm's 3,000 outstanding shares of common stock closed 2012 at a price of $25 per share.

a. Use the preceding financial statements to complete the following table. Assume the industry averages given in the table are applicable for both 2011 and 2012.

Ratio	Industry average	Actual 2011	Actual 2012
Current ratio	1.80	1.84	____
Quick ratio	0.70	0.78	____
Inventory turnover[a]	2.50	2.59	____
Average collection period[a]	37.5 days	36.5 days	____
Debt ratio	65%	67%	____
Times interest earned ratio	3.8	4.0	____
Gross profit margin	38%	40%	____
Net profit margin	3.5%	3.6%	____
Return on total assets	4.0%	4.0%	____
Return on common equity	9.5%	8.0%	____
Market/book ratio	1.1	1.2	____

[a]Based on a 365-day year and on end-of-year figures.

b. Analyze Zach Industries' financial condition as it is related to (1) liquidity, (2) activity, (3) debt, (4) profitability, and (5) market. Summarize the company's overall financial condition.

LG 6 **P3–24 Integrative—Complete ratio analysis** Given the following financial statements (following and on page 109), historical ratios, and industry averages, calculate Sterling Company's financial ratios for the most recent year. (Assume a 365-day year.)

Sterling Company Income Statement for the Year Ended December 31, 2012

Sales revenue	$10,000,000
Less: Cost of goods sold	7,500,000
Gross profits	$ 2,500,000
Less: Operating expenses	
Selling expense	$300,000
General and administrative expenses	650,000
Lease expense	50,000
Depreciation expense	200,000
Total operating expense	$ 1,200,000
Operating profits	$ 1,300,000
Less: Interest expense	200,000
Net profits before taxes	$ 1,100,000
Less: Taxes (rate = 40%)	440,000
Net profits after taxes	$ 660,000
Less: Preferred stock dividends	50,000
Earnings available for common stockholders	$ 610,000
Earnings per share (EPS)	$3.05

Sterling Company Balance Sheet December 31, 2012

Assets		Liabilities and Stockholders' Equity	
Cash	$ 200,000	Accounts payable[b]	$ 900,000
Marketable securities	50,000	Notes payable	200,000
Accounts receivable	800,000	Accruals	100,000
Inventories	950,000	Total current liabilities	$ 1,200,000
Total current assets	$ 2,000,000	Long-term debt (includes financial leases)[c]	$ 3,000,000
Gross fixed assets (at cost)[a]	$12,000,000		
Less: Accumulated depreciation	3,000,000	Preferred stock (25,000 shares, $2 dividend)	$ 1,000,000
Net fixed assets	$ 9,000,000		
Other assets	1,000,000	Common stock (200,000 shares at $3 par)[d]	600,000
Total assets	$12,000,000		
		Paid-in capital in excess of par value	5,200,000
		Retained earnings	1,000,000
		Total stockholders' equity	$ 7,800,000
		Total liabilities and stockholders' equity	$12,000,000

[a]The firm has an 8-year financial lease requiring annual beginning-of-year payments of $50,000. Five years of the lease have yet to run.
[b]Annual credit purchases of $6,200,000 were made during the year.
[c]The annual principal payment on the long-term debt is $100,000.
[d]On December 31, 2012, the firm's common stock closed at $39.50 per share.

Analyze its overall financial situation from both a cross-sectional and a time-series viewpoint. Break your analysis into evaluations of the firm's liquidity, activity, debt, profitability, and market.

Historical and Industry Average Ratios for Sterling Company

Ratio	Actual 2010	Actual 2011	Industry average, 2012
Current ratio	1.40	1.55	1.85
Quick ratio	1.00	0.92	1.05
Inventory turnover	9.52	9.21	8.60
Average collection period	45.6 days	36.9 days	35.5 days
Average payment period	59.3 days	61.6 days	46.4 days
Total asset turnover	0.74	0.80	0.74
Debt ratio	0.20	0.20	0.30
Times interest earned ratio	8.2	7.3	8.0
Fixed-payment coverage ratio	4.5	4.2	4.2
Gross profit margin	0.30	0.27	0.25
Operating profit margin	0.12	0.12	0.10
Net profit margin	0.062	0.062	0.053
Return on total assets (ROA)	0.045	0.050	0.040
Return on common equity (ROE)	0.061	0.067	0.066
Earnings per share (EPS)	$1.75	$2.20	$1.50
Price/earnings (P/E) ratio	12.0	10.5	11.2
Market/book (M/B) ratio	1.20	1.05	1.10

LG 6 **P3–25 DuPont system of analysis** Use the following ratio information for Johnson International and the industry averages for Johnson's line of business to:

a. Construct the DuPont system of analysis for both Johnson and the industry.
b. Evaluate Johnson (and the industry) over the 3-year period.
c. Indicate in which areas Johnson requires further analysis. Why?

Johnson	2010	2011	2012
Financial leverage multiplier	1.75	1.75	1.85
Net profit margin	0.059	0.058	0.049
Total asset turnover	2.11	2.18	2.34
Industry Averages			
Financial leverage multiplier	1.67	1.69	1.64
Net profit margin	0.054	0.047	0.041
Total asset turnover	2.05	2.13	2.15

LG 6 **P3–26 Complete ratio analysis, recognizing significant differences** Home Health, Inc., has come to Jane Ross for a yearly financial checkup. As a first step, Jane has prepared a complete set of ratios for fiscal years 2011 and 2012. She will use them to look for significant changes in the company's situation from one year to the next.

Home Health, Inc. Financial Ratios		
Ratio	**2011**	**2012**
Current ratio	3.25	3.00
Quick ratio	2.50	2.20
Inventory turnover	12.80	10.30
Average collection period	42.6 days	31.4 days
Total asset turnover	1.40	2.00
Debt ratio	0.45	0.62
Times interest earned ratio	4.00	3.85
Gross profit margin	68%	65%
Operating profit margin	14%	16%
Net profit margin	8.3%	8.1%
Return on total assets	11.6%	16.2%
Return on common equity	21.1%	42.6%
Price/earnings ratio	10.7	9.8
Market/book ratio	1.40	1.25

a. To focus on the degree of change, calculate the year-to-year proportional change by subtracting the year 2011 ratio from the year 2012 ratio, then dividing the difference by the year 2011 ratio. Multiply the result by 100. Preserve the positive or negative sign. The result is the percentage change in the ratio from 2011 to 2012. Calculate the proportional change for the ratios shown here.

b. For any ratio that shows a year-to-year difference of 10% or more, state whether the difference is in the company's favor or not.

c. For the most significant changes (25% or more), look at the other ratios and cite at least one other change that may have contributed to the change in the ratio that you are discussing.

LG 1 **P3–27 ETHICS PROBLEM** Do some reading in periodicals and/or on the Internet to find out more about the Sarbanes-Oxley Act's provisions for companies. Select one of those provisions, and indicate why you think financial statements will be more trustworthy if company financial executives implement this provision of SOX.

Spreadsheet Exercise

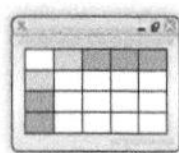

The income statement and balance sheet are the basic reports that a firm constructs for use by management and for distribution to stockholders, regulatory bodies, and the general public. They are the primary sources of historical financial information about the firm. Dayton Products, Inc., is a moderate-sized manufacturer. The company's management has asked you to perform a detailed financial statement analysis of the firm.

The income statements for the years ending December 31, 2012 and 2011, respectively, are presented in the table below. (*Note:* Purchases of inventory during 2012 amounted to $109,865.)

Annual Income Statements (Values in millions)		
	For the year ended	
	December 31, 2012	December 31, 2011
Sales	$178,909	$187,510
Cost of goods sold	?	111,631
Selling, general, and administrative expenses	12,356	12,900
Other tax expense	33,572	33,377
Depreciation and amortization	12,103	7,944
Other income (add to EBIT to arrive at EBT)	3,147	3,323
Interest expense	398	293
Income tax rate (average)	35.324%	37.945%
Dividends paid per share	$1.47	$0.91
Basic EPS from total operations	$1.71	$2.25

You also have the following balance sheet information as of December 31, 2012 and 2011, respectively.

Annual Balance Sheets (Values in millions)		
	December 31, 2012	December, 31, 2011
Cash and equivalents	$ 7,229	$ 6,547
Receivables	21,163	19,549
Inventories	8,068	7,904
Other current assets	1,831	1,681
Property, plant, and equipment, gross	204,960	187,519
Accumulated depreciation and depletion	110,020	97,917
Other noncurrent assets	19,413	17,891
Accounts payable	13,792	22,862
Short-term debt payable	4,093	3,703
Other current liabilities	15,290	3,549
Long-term debt payable	6,655	7,099
Deferred income taxes	16,484	16,359
Other noncurrent liabilities	21,733	16,441
Retained earnings	74,597	73,161
Total common shares outstanding	6.7 billion	6.8 billion

TO DO

a. Create a spreadsheet similar to Table 3.1 to model the following:
  (1) A multiple-step comparative income statement for Dayton, Inc., for the periods ending December 31, 2012 and 2011. You must calculate the cost of goods sold for the year 2012.
  (2) A common-size income statement for Dayton, Inc., covering the years 2012 and 2011.

b. Create a spreadsheet similar to Table 3.2 to model the following:
  (1) A detailed, comparative balance sheet for Dayton, Inc., for the years ended December 31, 2012 and 2011.
  (2) A common-size balance sheet for Dayton, Inc., covering the years 2012 and 2011.

c. Create a spreadsheet similar to Table 3.8 to perform the following analysis:
  (1) Create a table that reflects both 2012 and 2011 operating ratios for Dayton, Inc., segmented into (a) liquidity, (b) activity, (c) debt, (d) profitability, and (e) market. Assume that the current market price for the stock is $90.
  (2) Compare the 2012 ratios to the 2011 ratios. Indicate whether the results "outperformed the prior year" or "underperformed relative to the prior year."

Visit www.myfinancelab.com for **Chapter Case: *Assessing Martin Manufacturing's Current Financial Position,*** Group Exercises, and numerous online resources.

4 Cash Flow and Financial Planning

Learning Goals

LG 1 Understand tax depreciation procedures and the effect of depreciation on the firm's cash flows.

LG 2 Discuss the firm's statement of cash flows, operating cash flow, and free cash flow.

LG 3 Understand the financial planning process, including long-term (strategic) financial plans and short-term (operating) financial plans.

LG 4 Discuss the cash-planning process and the preparation, evaluation, and use of the cash budget.

LG 5 Explain the simplified procedures used to prepare and evaluate the pro forma income statement and the pro forma balance sheet.

LG 6 Evaluate the simplified approaches to pro forma financial statement preparation and the common uses of pro forma statements.

Why This Chapter Matters to You

In your *professional* life

ACCOUNTING You need to understand how depreciation is used for both tax and financial reporting purposes; how to develop the statement of cash flows; the primary focus on cash flows, rather than accruals, in financial decision making; and how pro forma financial statements are used within the firm.

INFORMATION SYSTEMS You need to understand the data that must be kept to record depreciation for tax and financial reporting; the information needed for strategic and operating plans; and what data are needed as inputs for preparing cash plans and profit plans.

MANAGEMENT You need to understand the difference between strategic and operating plans, and the role of each; the importance of focusing on the firm's cash flows; and how use of pro forma statements can head off trouble for the firm.

MARKETING You need to understand the central role that marketing plays in formulating the firm's long-term strategic plans, and the importance of the sales forecast as the key input for both cash planning and profit planning.

OPERATIONS You need to understand how depreciation affects the value of the firm's plant assets; how the results of operations are captured in the statement of cash flows; that operations provide key inputs into the firm's short-term financial plans; and the distinction between fixed and variable operating costs.

In your *personal* life

Individuals, like corporations, should focus on cash flow when planning and monitoring finances. You should establish short- and long-term financial goals (destinations) and develop personal financial plans (road maps) that will guide their achievement. Cash flows and financial plans are as important for individuals as for corporations.

Apple

Investors Want Apple to Take a Bite Out of Its Cash Hoard

Many people would be surprised to learn that U.S. firms emerged from the worst recession in at least two decades with more cash on their balance sheets than they had before the downturn hit. Nonfinancial firms in the S&P 500 stock index ended 2009 with $832 billion in cash and short-term marketable securities on hand, an increase of more than 25 percent from 2008 and the highest figure on record. Among the firms with the largest cash hoards were the titans of high technology—Microsoft ($39.7 billion), Cisco Systems ($39.1 billion), Google ($26.5 billion), Oracle ($17.5 billion), and Intel ($16.3 billion).

At the top of this list was Apple Inc., with $41.7 billion in cash in early 2010, equivalent to roughly one-fifth of the firm's total market value (or $40 of the $200 share price). Is holding that much cash a good thing? Investors buy Apple shares because they believe that the company will continue to produce great high-tech gadgets and generate high returns as a result, but the money that Apple held in cash earned no more than 1 percent in 2010. Thus, some investors complained that Apple should distribute a chunk of its cash via a large dividend or share repurchase program.

Steve Jobs, Apple's CEO, responded that distributing cash would not have a lasting impact on the firm's value. Instead, he argued that billions in cash could be used to do "big, bold things," and he worried, "Who knows what's around the next corner?" The latter statement may be the most revealing for Apple and the other high-tech firms. Having survived a recession in which cash was hard to come by, many executives appeared to be taking a very conservative posture and holding on to as much cash as they could—just in case.

LG 1 LG 2

4.1 Analyzing the Firm's Cash Flow

An old saying in finance is "Cash is king." Cash flow, the lifeblood of the firm, is the primary ingredient in any financial valuation model. Whether an analyst wants to put a value on an investment that a firm is considering or the objective is to value the firm itself, estimating cash flow is central to the valuation process. This chapter explains where the cash flow numbers used in valuations come from.

DEPRECIATION

For tax and financial reporting purposes, businesses generally cannot deduct as an expense the full cost of an asset that will be in use for several years. Instead, each year firms are required to charge a portion of the costs of fixed assets against revenues. This allocation of historical cost over time is called **depreciation.** Depreciation deductions, like any other business expenses, reduce the income that a firm reports on its income statement and therefore reduce the taxes that the firm must pay. However, depreciation deductions are not associated with any cash outlay. That is, when a firm deducts depreciation expense, it is allocating a portion of an asset's original cost (that the firm has already paid for) as a charge against that year's income. The net effect is that *depreciation deductions increase a firm's cash flow because they reduce a firm's tax bill.*

depreciation
A portion of the costs of fixed assets charged against annual revenues over time.

For tax purposes, the depreciation of business assets is regulated by the Internal Revenue Code. Because the objectives of financial reporting sometimes differ from those of tax legislation, firms often use different depreciation methods for financial reporting than those required for tax purposes. Keeping two different sets of records for these two purposes is legal in the United States.

Depreciation for tax purposes is determined by using the **modified accelerated cost recovery system (MACRS);** a variety of depreciation methods are available for financial reporting purposes. All depreciation methods require you to know an asset's depreciable value and its depreciable life.

modified accelerated cost recovery system (MACRS)
System used to determine the depreciation of assets for tax purposes.

Depreciable Value of an Asset

Under the basic MACRS procedures, the depreciable value of an asset (the amount to be depreciated) is its *full* cost, including outlays for installation. Even if the asset is expected to have some salvage value at the end of its useful life, the firm can still take depreciation deductions equal to the asset's full initial cost.

Example 4.1 ▶ Baker Corporation acquired a new machine at a cost of \$38,000, with installation costs of \$2,000. When the machine is retired from service, Baker expects to sell it for scrap metal and receive \$1,000. Regardless of its expected salvage value, the depreciable value of the machine is \$40,000: \$38,000 cost + \$2,000 installation cost.

Depreciable Life of an Asset

The time period over which an asset is depreciated is called its **depreciable life.** The shorter the depreciable life, the larger the annual depreciation deductions

depreciable life
Time period over which an asset is depreciated.

TABLE 4.1 First Four Property Classes under MACRS

Property class (recovery period)	Definition
3 years	Research equipment and certain special tools
5 years	Computers, printers, copiers, duplicating equipment, cars, light-duty trucks, qualified technological equipment, and similar assets
7 years	Office furniture, fixtures, most manufacturing equipment, railroad track, and single-purpose agricultural and horticultural structures
10 years	Equipment used in petroleum refining or in the manufacture of tobacco products and certain food products

recovery period
The appropriate depreciable life of a particular asset as determined by MACRS.

will be, and the larger will be the tax savings associated with those deductions, all other things being equal. Accordingly, firms generally would like to depreciate their assets as rapidly as possible. However, the firm must abide by certain Internal Revenue Service (IRS) requirements for determining depreciable life. These MACRS standards, which apply to both new and used assets, require the taxpayer to use as an asset's depreciable life the appropriate MACRS **recovery period.** There are six MACRS recovery periods—3, 5, 7, 10, 15, and 20 years—excluding real estate. It is customary to refer to the property classes as 3-, 5-, 7-, 10-, 15-, and 20-year property. The first four property classes—those routinely used by business—are defined in Table 4.1.

DEPRECIATION METHODS

For *financial reporting purposes,* companies can use a variety of depreciation methods (straight-line, double-declining balance, and sum-of-the-years'-digits). For *tax purposes,* assets in the first four MACRS property classes are depreciated by the double-declining balance method, using a half-year convention (meaning that a half-year's depreciation is taken in the year the asset is purchased) and switching to straight-line when advantageous. The *approximate percentages* (rounded to the nearest whole percent) written off each year for the first four property classes are shown in Table 4.2. Rather than using the percentages in the table, the firm can either use straight-line depreciation over the asset's recovery period with the half-year convention or use the alternative depreciation system. For purposes of this text, we will use the MACRS depreciation percentages because they generally provide for the fastest write-off and therefore the best cash flow effects for the profitable firm.

Because MACRS requires use of the half-year convention, assets are assumed to be acquired in the middle of the year; therefore, only one-half of the first year's depreciation is recovered in the first year. As a result, the final half-year of depreciation is recovered in the year immediately following the asset's stated recovery period. In Table 4.2, the depreciation percentages for an n-year class asset are given for $n + 1$ years. For example, a 5-year asset is depreciated over 6 recovery years. The application of the tax depreciation percentages given in Table 4.2 can be demonstrated by a simple example.

TABLE 4.2 Rounded Depreciation Percentages by Recovery Year Using MACRS for First Four Property Classes

	Percentage by recovery year[a]			
Recovery year	**3 years**	**5 years**	**7 years**	**10 years**
1	33%	20%	14%	10%
2	45	32	25	18
3	15	19	18	14
4	7	12	12	12
5		12	9	9
6		5	9	8
7			9	7
8			4	6
9				6
10				6
11	—	—	—	4
Totals	100%	100%	100%	100%

[a]These percentages have been rounded to the nearest whole percent to simplify calculations while retaining realism. To calculate the *actual* depreciation for tax purposes, be sure to apply the actual unrounded percentages or directly apply double-declining balance depreciation using the half-year convention.

Example 4.2 ▶

Baker Corporation acquired, for an installed cost of $40,000, a machine having a recovery period of 5 years. Using the applicable percentages from Table 4.2, Baker calculates the depreciation in each year as follows:

Year	Cost (1)	Percentages (from Table 4.2) (2)	Depreciation [(1) × (2)] (3)
1	$40,000	20%	$ 8,000
2	40,000	32	12,800
3	40,000	19	7,600
4	40,000	12	4,800
5	40,000	12	4,800
6	40,000	5	2,000
Totals		100%	$40,000

Column 3 shows that the full cost of the asset is written off over 6 recovery years.

Because financial managers focus primarily on cash flows, *only tax depreciation methods will be used throughout this textbook.*

DEVELOPING THE STATEMENT OF CASH FLOWS

The *statement of cash flows,* introduced in Chapter 3, summarizes the firm's cash flow over a given period. Keep in mind that analysts typically lump cash and

operating flows
Cash flows directly related to sale and production of the firm's products and services.

investment flows
Cash flows associated with purchase and sale of both fixed assets and equity investments in other firms.

financing flows
Cash flows that result from debt and equity financing transactions; include incurrence and repayment of debt, cash inflow from the sale of stock, and cash outflows to repurchase stock or pay cash dividends.

Matter of fact

Apple's Cash Flows

In its 2009 annual report, Apple reported over $10 billion in cash from its operating activities. In the same year, Apple used $17.4 billion in cash to invest in marketable securities and other investments. By comparison, its financing cash flows were negligible, resulting in a cash inflow of about $663 million, mostly from stock issued to employees as part of Apple's compensation plans.

marketable securities together when assessing the firm's liquidity because both cash and marketable securities represent a reservoir of liquidity. That reservoir is *increased by cash inflows* and *decreased by cash outflows*.

Also note that the firm's cash flows fall into three categories: (1) operating flows, (2) investment flows, and (3) financing flows. The **operating flows** are cash inflows and outflows directly related to the sale and production of the firm's products and services. **Investment flows** are cash flows associated with the purchase and sale of both fixed assets and equity investments in other firms. Clearly, purchase transactions would result in cash outflows, whereas sales transactions would generate cash inflows. The **financing flows** result from debt and equity financing transactions. Incurring either short-term or long-term debt would result in a corresponding cash inflow; repaying debt would result in an outflow. Similarly, the sale of the company's stock would result in a cash inflow; the repurchase of stock or payment of cash dividends would result in an outflow.

Classifying Inflows and Outflows of Cash

The statement of cash flows, in effect, summarizes the inflows and outflows of cash during a given period. Table 4.3 classifies the basic inflows (sources) and outflows (uses) of cash. For example, if a firm's accounts payable balance increased by $1,000 during the year, the change would be an *inflow of cash*. The change would be an *outflow of cash* if the firm's inventory increased by $2,500.

A few additional points can be made with respect to the classification scheme in Table 4.3:

1. A *decrease* in an asset, such as the firm's cash balance, is an *inflow of cash*. Why? Because cash that has been tied up in the asset is released and can be used for some other purpose, such as repaying a loan. On the other hand, an *increase* in the firm's cash balance is an *outflow of cash* because additional cash is being tied up in the firm's cash balance.

   The classification of decreases and increases in a firm's cash balance is difficult for many to grasp. To clarify, imagine that you store all your cash in a bucket. Your cash balance is represented by the amount of cash in the bucket. When you need cash, you withdraw it from the bucket, which *decreases your cash balance and provides an inflow* of cash to you. Conversely, when you have excess cash, you deposit it in the bucket, which *increases your cash balance and represents an outflow* of cash from you. Focus on the movement of funds *in and out of your pocket*: Clearly, a decrease in cash (from the bucket) is an inflow (to your pocket); an increase in cash (in the bucket) is an outflow (from your pocket).

TABLE 4.3 Inflows and Outflows of Cash

Inflows (sources)	Outflows (uses)
Decrease in any asset	Increase in any asset
Increase in any liability	Decrease in any liability
Net profits after taxes	Net loss
Depreciation and other noncash charges	Dividends paid
Sale of stock	Repurchase or retirement of stock

noncash charge
An expense that is deducted on the income statement but does not involve the actual outlay of cash during the period; includes depreciation, amortization, and depletion.

2. Depreciation (like amortization and depletion) is a **noncash charge**—an expense that is deducted on the income statement but does not involve an actual outlay of cash. Therefore, when measuring the amount of cash flow generated by a firm, we have to add depreciation back to net income or we will understate the cash that the firm has truly generated. For this reason, depreciation appears as a source of cash in Table 4.3.
3. Because depreciation is treated as a separate cash inflow, only *gross* rather than *net* changes in fixed assets appear on the statement of cash flows. The change in net fixed assets is equal to the change in gross fixed assets minus the depreciation charge. Therefore, if we treated depreciation as a cash inflow as well as the reduction in net (rather than gross) fixed assets, we would be double counting depreciation.
4. Direct entries of changes in retained earnings are not included on the statement of cash flows. Instead, entries for items that affect retained earnings appear as net profits or losses after taxes and dividends paid.

Preparing the Statement of Cash Flows

The statement of cash flows uses data from the income statement, along with the beginning- and end-of-period balance sheets. The income statement for the year ended December 31, 2012, and the December 31 balance sheets for 2011 and 2012 for Baker Corporation are given in Tables 4.4 and 4.5 (see page 120), respectively. The statement of cash flows for the year ended December 31, 2012, for Baker Corporation is presented in Table 4.6 (see page 121). Note that all cash inflows as well as net profits after taxes and depreciation are treated as positive values.

TABLE 4.4 Baker Corporation 2012 Income Statement ($000)

Sales revenue	$1,700
Less: Cost of goods sold	1,000
Gross profits	$ 700
Less: Operating expenses	
Selling, general, and administrative expense	$ 230
Depreciation expense	100
Total operating expense	$ 330
Earnings before interest and taxes (EBIT)	$ 370
Less: Interest expense	70
Net profits before taxes	$ 300
Less: Taxes (rate = 40%)	120
Net profits after taxes	$ 180
Less: Preferred stock dividends	10
Earnings available for common stockholders	$ 170
Earnings per share (EPS)[a]	$1.70

[a]Calculated by dividing the earnings available for common stockholders by the number of shares of common stock outstanding ($170,000 ÷ 100,000 shares = $1.70 per share).

TABLE 4.5 Baker Corporation Balance Sheets ($000)

	December 31	
Assets	**2012**	**2011**
Cash and marketable securities	$1,000	$ 500
Accounts receivable	400	500
Inventories	600	900
Total current assets	$2,000	$1,900
Land and buildings	$1,200	$1,050
Machinery and equipment, furniture and fixtures, vehicles, and other	1,300	1,150
Total gross fixed assets (at cost)	$2,500	$2,200
Less: Accumulated depreciation	1,300	1,200
Net fixed assets	$1,200	$1,000
Total assets	$3,200	$2,900
Liabilities and Stockholders' Equity		
Accounts payable	$ 700	$ 500
Notes payable	600	700
Accruals	100	200
Total current liabilities	$1,400	$1,400
Long-term debt	600	400
Total liabilities	$2,000	$1,800
Preferred stock	$ 100	$ 100
Common stock—$1.20 par, 100,000 shares outstanding in 2012 and 2011	120	120
Paid-in capital in excess of par on common stock	380	380
Retained earnings	600	500
Total stockholders' equity	$1,200	$1,100
Total liabilities and stockholders' equity	$3,200	$2,900

All cash outflows, any losses, and dividends paid are treated as negative values. The items in each category—operating, investment, and financing—are totaled, and the three totals are added to get the "Net increase (decrease) in cash and marketable securities" for the period. As a check, this value should reconcile with the actual change in cash and marketable securities for the year, which is obtained from the beginning- and end-of-period balance sheets.

Interpreting the Statement

The statement of cash flows allows the financial manager and other interested parties to analyze the firm's cash flow. The manager should pay special attention both to the major categories of cash flow and to the individual items of cash inflow and outflow, to assess whether any developments have occurred that are contrary to the company's financial policies. In addition, the statement can be used to evaluate progress toward projected goals or to isolate inefficiencies. The

TABLE 4.6 Baker Corporation Statement of Cash Flows ($000) for the Year Ended December 31, 2012

Cash Flow from Operating Activities	
Net profits after taxes	$180
Depreciation	100
Decrease in accounts receivable	100
Decrease in inventories	300
Increase in accounts payable	200
Decrease in accruals	(100)[a]
Cash provided by operating activities	$780
Cash Flow from Investment Activities	
Increase in gross fixed assets	($300)
Changes in equity investments in other firms	0
Cash provided by investment activities	($300)
Cash Flow from Financing Activities	
Decrease in notes payable	($100)
Increase in long-term debts	200
Changes in stockholders' equity[b]	0
Dividends paid	(80)
Cash provided by financing activities	$ 20
Net increase in cash and marketable securities	$500

[a]As is customary, parentheses are used to denote a negative number, which in this case is a cash outflow.

[b]Retained earnings are excluded here, because their change is actually reflected in the combination of the "Net profits after taxes" and "Dividends paid" entries.

financial manager also can prepare a statement of cash flows developed from projected financial statements to determine whether planned actions are desirable in view of the resulting cash flows.

operating cash flow (OCF)
The cash flow a firm generates from its normal operations; calculated as *net operating profits after taxes (NOPAT)* plus depreciation.

net operating profits after taxes (NOPAT)
A firm's earnings before interest and after taxes, EBIT × (1 − *T*).

Operating Cash Flow A firm's **operating cash flow (OCF)** is the cash flow it generates from its normal operations—producing and selling its output of goods or services. A variety of definitions of OCF can be found in the financial literature. The definition introduced here excludes the impact of interest on cash flow. We exclude those effects because we want a measure that captures the cash flow generated by the firm's operations, not by how those operations are financed and taxed. The first step is to calculate **net operating profits after taxes (NOPAT)**, which represent the firm's earnings before interest and after taxes. Letting T equal the applicable corporate tax rate, NOPAT is calculated as follows:

$$\text{NOPAT} = \text{EBIT} \times (1 - T) \tag{4.1}$$

To convert NOPAT to operating cash flow (OCF), we merely add back depreciation:

$$\text{OCF} = \text{NOPAT} + \text{Depreciation} \tag{4.2}$$

We can substitute the expression for NOPAT from Equation 4.1 into Equation 4.2 to get a single equation for OCF:

$$\text{OCF} = [\text{EBIT} \times (1 - T)] + \text{Depreciation} \quad (4.3)$$

Example 4.3 ▸ Substituting the values for Baker Corporation from its income statement (Table 4.4) into Equation 4.3, we get

$$\text{OCF} = [\$370 \times (1.00 - 0.40)] + \$100 = \$222 + \$100 = \$322$$

During 2012, Baker Corporation generated $322,000 of cash flow from producing and selling its output. Therefore, we can conclude that Baker's operations are generating positive cash flows.

FREE CASH FLOW

free cash flow (FCF)
The amount of cash flow available to investors (creditors and owners) after the firm has met all operating needs and paid for investments in net fixed assets and net current assets.

The firm's **free cash flow (FCF)** represents the cash available to investors—the providers of debt (creditors) and equity (owners)—after the firm has met all operating needs and paid for net investments in fixed assets and current assets. Free cash flow can be defined as follows:

$$\text{FCF} = \text{OCF} - \text{Net fixed asset investment (NFAI)} - \text{Net current asset investment (NCAI)} \quad (4.4)$$

The *net fixed asset investment (NFAI)* is the *net investment* that the firm makes in fixed assets and refers to purchases minus sales of fixed assets. You can calculate the NFAI using Equation 4.5.

$$\text{NFAI} = \text{Change in net fixed assets} + \text{Depreciation} \quad (4.5)$$

The NFAI is also equal to the change in gross fixed assets from one year to the next.

Example 4.4 ▸ Using the Baker Corporation's balance sheets in Table 4.5, we see that its change in net fixed assets between 2011 and 2012 was +$200 ($1,200 in 2012 − $1,000 in 2011). Substituting this value and the $100 of depreciation for 2012 into Equation 4.5, we get Baker's net fixed asset investment (NFAI) for 2012:

$$\text{NFAI} = \$200 + \$100 = \$300$$

Baker Corporation therefore invested a net $300,000 in fixed assets during 2012. This amount would, of course, represent a cash outflow to acquire fixed assets during 2012.

Looking at Equation 4.5, we can see that if net fixed assets decline by an amount exceeding the depreciation for the period, the NFAI would be negative. A negative NFAI represents a net cash *inflow* attributable to the fact that the firm sold more assets than it acquired during the year.

The *net current asset investment (NCAI)* represents the net investment made by the firm in its current (operating) assets. "Net" refers to the difference between current assets and the sum of accounts payable and accruals. Notes payable are not included in the NCAI calculation because they represent a negotiated creditor claim on the firm's free cash flow. Equation 4.6 shows the NCAI calculation:

$$NCAI = \text{Change in current assets} - \text{Change in (accounts payable + accruals)} \quad (4.6)$$

Example 4.5 ▶ Looking at the Baker Corporation's balance sheets for 2011 and 2012 in Table 4.5, we see that the change in current assets between 2011 and 2012 is +\$100 (\$2,000 in 2012 − \$1,900 in 2011). The difference between Baker's accounts payable plus accruals of \$800 in 2012 (\$700 in accounts payable + \$100 in accruals) and of \$700 in 2011 (\$500 in accounts payable + \$200 in accruals) is +\$100 (\$800 in 2012 − \$700 in 2011). Substituting into Equation 4.6 the change in current assets and the change in the sum of accounts payable plus accruals for Baker Corporation, we get its 2012 NCAI:

$$NCAI = \$100 - \$100 = \$0$$

This means that during 2012 Baker Corporation made no investment (\$0) in its current assets net of accounts payable and accruals.

Now we can substitute Baker Corporation's 2012 operating cash flow (OCF) of \$322, its net fixed asset investment (NFAI) of \$300, and its net current asset investment (NCAI) of \$0 into Equation 4.4 to find its free cash flow (FCF):

$$FCF = \$322 - \$300 - \$0 = \$22$$

We can see that during 2012 Baker generated \$22,000 of free cash flow, which it can use to pay its investors—creditors (payment of interest) and owners (payment of dividends). Thus, the firm generated adequate cash flow to cover all of its operating costs and investments and had free cash flow available to pay investors. However, Baker's interest expense in 2012 was \$70,000, so the firm is not generating enough FCF to provide a sufficient return to its investors.

Clearly, cash flow is the lifeblood of the firm. The *Focus on Practice* box discusses Cisco System's free cash flow.

focus on **PRACTICE**

Free Cash Flow at Cisco Systems

in practice On May 13, 2010, Cisco Systems issued what at first glance appeared to be a favorable earnings report, saying that they had achieved earnings per share of \$0.42 for the most recent quarter, ahead of the expectations of Wall Street experts who had projected EPS of \$0.39. Oddly, though, Cisco stock began to fall after the earnings announcement.

In subsequent analysis, one analyst observed that of the three cents by which Cisco beat the street's forecast, one cent could be attributed to the fact that the quarter was 14 weeks rather than the more typical 13 weeks. Another penny was attributable to unusual tax gains, and the third was classified with the somewhat vague label, "other income." Other analysts were even more skeptical. One noted that Cisco's free cash flow in the prior three quarters had been \$6.24 billion, but \$5.55 billion of that had been spent to buy shares to offset dilution from the stock options that Cisco granted its employees. The analyst complained, "Cisco is being run for the benefit of its employees and not its public shareholders."

▶ *Free cash flow is often considered a more reliable measure of a company's income than reported earnings. What are some possible ways that corporate accountants might be able to change their earnings to portray a more favorable earnings statement?*

Source: "Update Cisco Systems (CSCO)," May 13, 2010, http://jubakpicks.com; Eric Savitz, "Cisco Shares Off Despite Strong FYQ3; Focus on Q4 Guidance," May 13, 2010, http://blogs.barrons.com.

In the next section, we consider various aspects of financial planning for cash flow and profit.

→ REVIEW QUESTIONS

4–1 Briefly describe the first four *modified accelerated cost recovery system (MACRS)* property classes and recovery periods. Explain how the depreciation percentages are determined by using the MACRS recovery periods.

4–2 Describe the overall cash flow through the firm in terms of operating flows, investments flows, and financing flows.

4–3 Explain why a decrease in cash is classified as a *cash inflow (source)* and why an increase in cash is classified as a *cash outflow (use)* in preparing the statement of cash flows.

4–4 Why is depreciation (as well as amortization and depletion) considered a *noncash charge?*

4–5 Describe the general format of the statement of cash flows. How are cash inflows differentiated from cash outflows on this statement?

4–6 Why do we exclude interest expense and taxes from operating cash flow?

4–7 From a strict financial perspective, define and differentiate between a firm's *operating cash flow (OCF)* and its *free cash flow (FCF).*

LG 3

4.2 The Financial Planning Process

Financial planning is an important aspect of the firm's operations because it provides road maps for guiding, coordinating, and controlling the firm's actions to achieve its objectives. Two key aspects of the financial planning process are *cash planning* and *profit planning.* Cash planning involves preparation of the firm's cash budget. Profit planning involves preparation of pro forma statements. Both the cash budget and the pro forma statements are useful for internal financial planning. They also are routinely required by existing and prospective lenders.

financial planning process
Planning that begins with long-term, or *strategic,* financial plans that in turn guide the formulation of short-term, or *operating,* plans and budgets.

The **financial planning process** begins with long-term, or *strategic,* financial plans. These, in turn, guide the formulation of short-term, or *operating,* plans and budgets. Generally, the short-term plans and budgets implement the firm's long-term strategic objectives. Although the remainder of this chapter places primary emphasis on short-term financial plans and budgets, a few preliminary comments on long-term financial plans are in order.

LONG-TERM (STRATEGIC) FINANCIAL PLANS

long-term (strategic) financial plans
Plans that lay out a company's planned financial actions and the anticipated impact of those actions over periods ranging from 2 to 10 years.

Long-term (strategic) financial plans lay out a company's planned financial actions and the anticipated impact of those actions over periods ranging from 2 to 10 years. Five-year strategic plans, which are revised as significant new information becomes available, are common. Generally, firms that are subject to high degrees of operating uncertainty, relatively short production cycles, or both, tend to use shorter planning horizons.

Long-term financial plans are part of an integrated strategy that, along with production and marketing plans, guides the firm toward strategic goals. Those long-term plans consider proposed outlays for fixed assets, research and development activities, marketing and product development actions, capital structure, and major sources of financing. Also included would be termination of existing projects, product lines, or lines of business; repayment or retirement of outstanding debts; and any planned acquisitions. Such plans tend to be supported by a series of annual budgets. The *Focus on Ethics* box shows how one CEO dramatically reshaped his company's operating structure, although it later cost him his job.

SHORT-TERM (OPERATING) FINANCIAL PLANS

short-term (operating) financial plans
Specify short-term financial actions and the anticipated impact of those actions.

Short-term (operating) financial plans specify short-term financial actions and the anticipated impact of those actions. These plans most often cover a 1- to 2-year period. Key inputs include the sales forecast and various forms of operating and financial data. Key outputs include a number of operating budgets, the cash budget, and pro forma financial statements. The entire short-term financial planning process is outlined in Figure 4.1 on page 126. Here we focus solely on cash and profit planning from the financial manager's perspective.

focus on ETHICS

How Much Is a CEO Worth?

in practice When Jack Welch retired as chairman and CEO of General Electric in 2000, Robert L. Nardelli was part of a lengthy and well-publicized succession planning saga; he eventually lost the job to Jeff Immelt. Nardelli was quickly hired by The Home Depot, one of several companies competing for his services, who offered generous incentives for him to come on board.

Using the "Six Sigma" management strategy from GE, Nardelli dramatically overhauled The Home Depot and replaced its freewheeling entrepreneurial culture. He changed the decentralized management structure by eliminating and consolidating division executives. He also installed processes and streamlined operations, most notably implementing a computerized automated inventory system and centralizing supply orders at the Atlanta headquarters. Nardelli was credited with doubling the sales of the chain and improving its competitive position. Revenue increased from $45.7 billion in 2000 to $81.5 billion in 2005, while profit rose from $2.6 billion to $5.8 billion.

However, the company's stagnating share price; Nardelli's results-driven management style, which turned off both employees and customers; and his compensation package eventually earned the ire of investors. Despite having received the solid support of The Home Depot's board of directors, Nardelli abruptly resigned on January 3, 2007. He was not destined for poverty, as his severance package had been negotiated years earlier when he joined The Home Depot. The total severance package amounted to $210 million, including $55.3 million of life insurance coverage, reimbursement of $1.3 million of Nardelli's personal taxes related to the life insurance, $50,000 to cover his legal fees, $33.8 million in cash due July 3, 2007, an additional $18 million over 4 years for abiding by the terms of the deal, and the balance of the package from accelerated vesting of stock options. In addition, Nardelli and his family would receive health care benefits from the company for the next 3 years.

The mammoth payoff for Nardelli's departure caused uproar among many shareholder activists because The Home Depot's stock fell 8 percent during his 6-year tenure. Clearly, the mantra of shareholder activists today is, "Ask not what you can do for your company, ask what your company can do for shareholders." The spotlight will no longer be only on what a CEO does, but also on how much the CEO is paid.

► ***Do you think shareholder activists would have been as upset with Nardelli's severance package had The Home Depot's stock performed much better under his leadership?***

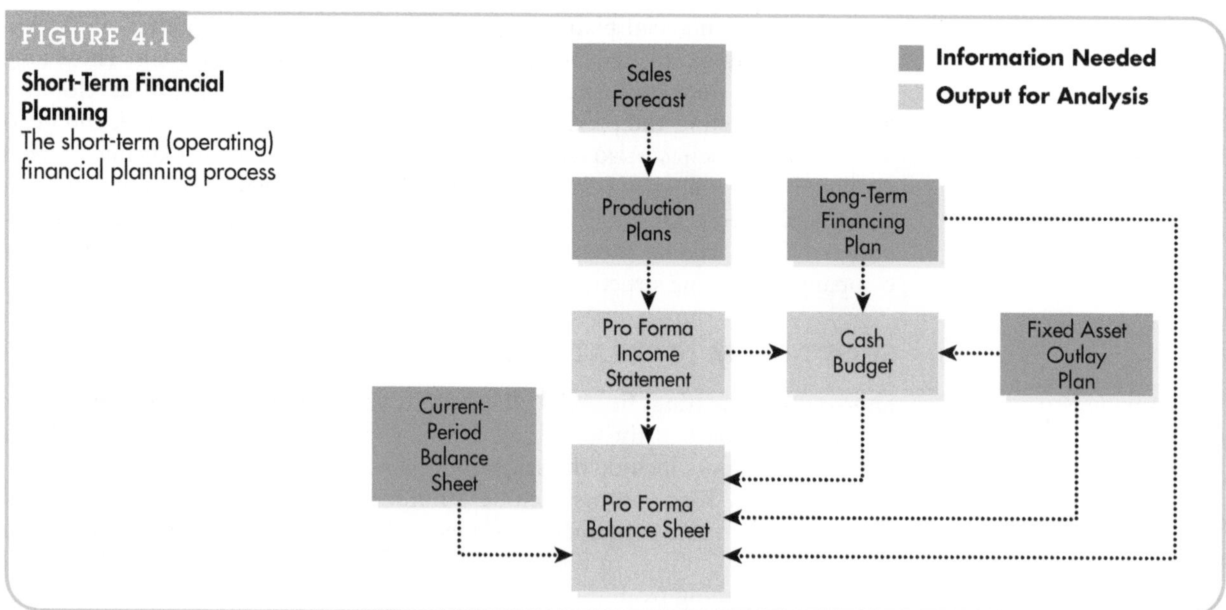

FIGURE 4.1

Short-Term Financial Planning
The short-term (operating) financial planning process

Short-term financial planning begins with the sales forecast. From it, companies develop production plans that take into account lead (preparation) times and include estimates of the required raw materials. Using the production plans, the firm can estimate direct labor requirements, factory overhead outlays, and operating expenses. Once these estimates have been made, the firm can prepare a pro forma income statement and cash budget. With these basic inputs, the firm can finally develop a pro forma balance sheet.

Personal Finance Example 4.6 ▶ The first step in personal financial planning requires you to define your goals. Whereas in a corporation, the goal is to maximize owner wealth (that is, share price), individuals typically have a number of major goals.

Generally personal goals can be short-term (1 year), intermediate-term (2 to 5 years), or long-term (6 or more years). The short- and intermediate-term goals support the long-term goals. Clearly, types of long-term personal goals depend on the individual's or family's age, and goals will continue to change with one's life situation.

You should set your personal financial goals carefully and realistically. Each goal should be clearly defined and have a priority, time frame, and cost estimate. For example, a college senior's intermediate-term goal in 2012 might include earning a master's degree at a cost of $40,000 by 2014, and his or her long-term goal might be to buy a condominium at a cost of $125,000 by 2016.

Throughout the remainder of this chapter, we will concentrate on the key outputs of the short-term financial planning process: the cash budget, the pro forma income statement, and the pro forma balance sheet.

→ **REVIEW QUESTIONS**

4–8 What is the *financial planning process?* Contrast *long-term (strategic) financial plans* and *short-term (operating) financial plans.*

4–9 Which three statements result as part of the short-term (operating) financial planning process?

LG 4 4.3 Cash Planning: Cash Budgets

cash budget (cash forecast)
A statement of the firm's planned inflows and outflows of cash that is used to estimate its short-term cash requirements.

The **cash budget,** or **cash forecast,** is a statement of the firm's planned inflows and outflows of cash. It is used by the firm to estimate its short-term cash requirements, with particular attention being paid to planning for surplus cash and for cash shortages.

Typically, the cash budget is designed to cover a 1-year period, divided into smaller time intervals. The number and type of intervals depend on the nature of the business. The more seasonal and uncertain a firm's cash flows, the greater the number of intervals. Because many firms are confronted with a seasonal cash flow pattern, the cash budget is quite often presented on a *monthly basis.* Firms with stable patterns of cash flow may use quarterly or annual time intervals.

THE SALES FORECAST

sales forecast
The prediction of the firm's sales over a given period, based on external and/or internal data; used as the key input to the short-term financial planning process.

The key input to the short-term financial planning process is the firm's **sales forecast.** This prediction of the firm's sales over a given period is ordinarily prepared by the marketing department. On the basis of the sales forecast, the financial manager estimates the monthly cash flows that will result from projected sales and from outlays related to production, inventory, and sales. The manager also determines the level of fixed assets required and the amount of financing, if any, needed to support the forecast level of sales and production. In practice, obtaining good data is the most difficult aspect of forecasting. The sales forecast may be based on an analysis of external data, internal data, or a combination of the two.

external forecast
A sales forecast based on the relationships observed between the firm's sales and certain key external economic indicators.

internal forecast
A sales forecast based on a buildup, or consensus, of sales forecasts through the firm's own sales channels.

An **external forecast** is based on the relationships observed between the firm's sales and certain key external economic indicators such as the gross domestic product (GDP), new housing starts, consumer confidence, and disposable personal income. Forecasts containing these indicators are readily available.

Internal forecasts are based on a consensus of sales forecasts through the firm's own sales channels. Typically, the firm's salespeople in the field are asked to estimate how many units of each type of product they expect to sell in the coming year. These forecasts are collected and totaled by the sales manager, who may adjust the figures using knowledge of specific markets or of the salesperson's forecasting ability. Finally, adjustments may be made for additional internal factors, such as production capabilities.

Firms generally use a combination of external and internal forecast data to make the final sales forecast. The internal data provide insight into sales expectations, and the external data provide a means of adjusting these expectations to take into account general economic factors. The nature of the firm's product also often affects the mix and types of forecasting methods used.

TABLE 4.7 The General Format of the Cash Budget

	Jan.	Feb.	...	Nov.	Dec.
Cash receipts	$XXX	$XXG		$XXM	$XXT
Less: Cash disbursements	XXA	XXH	...	XXN	XXU
Net cash flow	$XXB	$XXI		$XXO	$XXV
Add: Beginning cash	XXC	XXD	XXJ	XXP	XXQ
Ending cash	$XXD	$XXJ		$XXQ	$XXW
Less: Minimum cash balance	XXE	XXK	...	XXR	XXY
Required total financing		$XXL		$XXS	
Excess cash balance	$XXF				$XXZ

PREPARING THE CASH BUDGET

The general format of the cash budget is presented in Table 4.7. We will discuss each of its components individually.

Cash Receipts

cash receipts
All of a firm's inflows of cash during a given financial period.

Cash receipts include all of a firm's inflows of cash during a given financial period. The most common components of cash receipts are cash sales, collections of accounts receivable, and other cash receipts.

Example 4.7 ▶

Coulson Industries, a defense contractor, is developing a cash budget for October, November, and December. Coulson's sales in August and September were $100,000 and $200,000, respectively. Sales of $400,000, $300,000, and $200,000 have been forecast for October, November, and December, respectively. Historically, 20% of the firm's sales have been for cash, 50% have generated accounts receivable collected after 1 month, and the remaining 30% have generated accounts receivable collected after 2 months. Bad-debt expenses (uncollectible accounts) have been negligible. In December, the firm will receive a $30,000 dividend from stock in a subsidiary. The schedule of expected cash receipts for the company is presented in Table 4.8. It contains the following items:

Forecast sales This initial entry is *merely informational.* It is provided as an aid in calculating other sales-related items.

Cash sales The cash sales shown for each month represent 20% of the total sales forecast for that month.

Collections of A/R These entries represent the collection of accounts receivable (A/R) resulting from sales in earlier months.

Lagged 1 month These figures represent sales made in the preceding month that generated accounts receivable collected in the current month. Because 50% of the current month's sales are collected 1 month later, the collections of A/R with a 1-month lag shown for September represent 50% of the sales in August, collections for October represent 50% of September sales, and so on.

TABLE 4.8 A Schedule of Projected Cash Receipts for Coulson Industries ($000)

Sales forecast	Aug. $100	Sept. $200	Oct. $400	Nov. $300	Dec. $200
Cash sales (0.20)	$20	$40	$ 80	$ 60	$ 40
Collections of A/R:					
Lagged 1 month (0.50)		50	100	200	150
Lagged 2 months (0.30)			30	60	120
Other cash receipts					30
Total cash receipts	$20	$90	$210	$320	$340

Lagged 2 months These figures represent sales made 2 months earlier that generated accounts receivable collected in the current month. Because 30% of sales are collected 2 months later, the collections with a 2-month lag shown for October represent 30% of the sales in August, and so on.

Other cash receipts These are cash receipts expected from sources other than sales. Interest received, dividends received, proceeds from the sale of equipment, stock and bond sale proceeds, and lease receipts may show up here. For Coulson Industries, the only other cash receipt is the $30,000 dividend due in December.

Total cash receipts This figure represents the total of all the cash receipts listed for each month. For Coulson Industries, we are concerned only with October, November, and December, as shown in Table 4.8.

Cash Disbursements

cash disbursements
All outlays of cash by the firm during a given financial period.

Cash disbursements include all outlays of cash by the firm during a given financial period. The most common cash disbursements are

Cash purchases	Fixed-asset outlays
Payments of accounts payable	Interest payments
Rent (and lease) payments	Cash dividend payments
Wages and salaries	Principal payments (loans)
Tax payments	Repurchases or retirements of stock

It is important to recognize that *depreciation and other noncash charges are NOT included in the cash budget,* because they merely represent a scheduled write-off of an earlier cash outflow. The impact of depreciation, as we noted earlier, is reflected in the reduced cash outflow for tax payments.

Example 4.8 ▸

Coulson Industries has gathered the following data needed for the preparation of a cash disbursements schedule for October, November, and December.

Purchases The firm's purchases represent 70% of sales. Of this amount, 10% is paid in cash, 70% is paid in the month immediately following the month of purchase, and the remaining 20% is paid 2 months following the month of purchase.

Rent payments Rent of $5,000 will be paid each month.

Wages and salaries Fixed salaries for the year are $96,000, or $8,000 per month. In addition, wages are estimated as 10% of monthly sales.

Tax payments Taxes of $25,000 must be paid in December.

Fixed-asset outlays New machinery costing $130,000 will be purchased and paid for in November.

Interest payments An interest payment of $10,000 is due in December.

Cash dividend payments Cash dividends of $20,000 will be paid in October.

Principal payments (loans) A $20,000 principal payment is due in December.

Repurchases or retirements of stock No repurchase or retirement of stock is expected between October and December.

The firm's cash disbursements schedule, using the preceding data, is shown in Table 4.9. Some items in the table are explained in greater detail below.

Purchases This entry is *merely informational.* The figures represent 70% of the forecast sales for each month. They have been included to facilitate calculation of the cash purchases and related payments.

Cash purchases The cash purchases for each month represent 10% of the month's purchases.

Payments of A/P These entries represent the payment of accounts payable (A/P) resulting from purchases in earlier months.

Lagged 1 month These figures represent purchases made in the preceding month that are paid for in the current month. Because 70% of the firm's purchases are paid for 1 month later, the payments with a 1-month lag shown for September represent 70% of the August purchases, payments for October represent 70% of September purchases, and so on.

TABLE 4.9 A Schedule of Projected Cash Disbursements for Coulson Industries ($000)

Purchases (0.70 × sales)	Aug. $70	Sept. $140	Oct. $280	Nov. $210	Dec. $140
Cash purchases (0.10)	$7	$14	$ 28	$ 21	$ 14
Payments of A/P:					
Lagged 1 month (0.70)		49	98	196	147
Lagged 2 months (0.20)			14	28	56
Rent payments			5	5	5
Wages and salaries			48	38	28
Tax payments					25
Fixed-asset outlays				130	
Interest payments					10
Cash dividend payments			20		
Principal payments	—	—	—	—	20
Total cash disbursements	$7	$63	$213	$418	$305

net cash flow
The mathematical difference between the firm's cash receipts and its cash disbursements in each period.

ending cash
The sum of the firm's beginning cash and its net cash flow for the period.

required total financing
Amount of funds needed by the firm if the ending cash for the period is less than the desired minimum cash balance; typically represented by notes payable.

excess cash balance
The (excess) amount available for investment by the firm if the period's ending cash is greater than the desired minimum cash balance; assumed to be invested in marketable securities.

Lagged 2 months These figures represent purchases made 2 months earlier that are paid for in the current month. Because 20% of the firm's purchases are paid for 2 months later, the payments with a 2-month lag for October represent 20% of the August purchases, and so on.

Wages and salaries These amounts were obtained by adding $8,000 to 10% of the *sales* in each month. The $8,000 represents the salary component; the rest represents wages.

The remaining items on the cash disbursements schedule are self-explanatory.

Net Cash Flow, Ending Cash, Financing, and Excess Cash

Look back at the general-format cash budget in Table 4.7 on page 128. We have inputs for the first two entries, and we now continue calculating the firm's cash needs. The firm's **net cash flow** is found by subtracting the cash disbursements from cash receipts in each period. Then we add beginning cash to the firm's net cash flow to determine the **ending cash** for each period.

Finally, we subtract the desired minimum cash balance from ending cash to find the **required total financing** or the **excess cash balance.** If the ending cash is less than the minimum cash balance, *financing* is required. Such financing is typically viewed as short-term and is therefore represented by notes payable. If the ending cash is greater than the minimum cash balance, *excess cash* exists. Any excess cash is assumed to be invested in a liquid, short-term, interest-paying vehicle—that is, in marketable securities.

Example 4.9 ▶

Table 4.10 presents Coulson Industries' cash budget. The company wishes to maintain, as a reserve for unexpected needs, a minimum cash balance of $25,000. For Coulson Industries to maintain its required $25,000 ending cash balance, it will need total borrowing of $76,000 in November and $41,000 in December. In October the firm will have an excess cash balance of $22,000, which can be held

TABLE 4.10 A Cash Budget for Coulson Industries ($000)

	Oct.	Nov.	Dec.
Total cash receipts[a]	$210	$320	$340
Less: Total cash disbursements[b]	213	418	305
Net cash flow	($ 3)	($ 98)	$ 35
Add: Beginning cash	50	47	(51)
Ending cash	$ 47 ↗	($ 51) ↗	($ 16)
Less: Minimum cash balance	25	25	25
Required total financing (notes payable)[c]		$ 76	$ 41
Excess cash balance (marketable securities)[d]	$ 22		

[a]From Table 4.8.

[b]From Table 4.9.

[c]Values are placed in this line when the ending cash is less than the desired minimum cash balance. These amounts are typically financed short-term and therefore are represented by notes payable.

[d]Values are placed in this line when the ending cash is greater than the desired minimum cash balance. These amounts are typically assumed to be invested short-term and therefore are represented by marketable securities.

in an interest-earning marketable security. The required total financing figures in the cash budget refer to *how much will be owed at the end of the month;* they do *not* represent the monthly changes in borrowing.

The monthly changes in borrowing and in excess cash can be found by further analyzing the cash budget. In October the $50,000 beginning cash, which becomes $47,000 after the $3,000 net cash outflow, results in a $22,000 excess cash balance once the $25,000 minimum cash is deducted. In November the $76,000 of required total financing resulted from the $98,000 net cash outflow less the $22,000 of excess cash from October. The $41,000 of required total financing in December resulted from reducing November's $76,000 of required total financing by the $35,000 of net cash inflow during December. Summarizing, the *financial activities for each month* would be as follows:

October: **Invest the $22,000** excess cash balance in marketable securities.

November: Liquidate the $22,000 of marketable securities and **borrow $76,000** (notes payable).

December: **Repay $35,000** of notes payable to leave $41,000 of outstanding required total financing.

EVALUATING THE CASH BUDGET

The cash budget indicates whether a cash shortage or surplus is expected in each of the months covered by the forecast. Each month's figure is based on the internally imposed requirement of a minimum cash balance and *represents the total balance at the end of the month.*

At the end of each of the 3 months, Coulson expects the following balances in cash, marketable securities, and notes payable:

	End-of-month balance ($000)		
Account	**Oct.**	**Nov.**	**Dec.**
Cash	$25	$25	$25
Marketable securities	22	0	0
Notes payable	0	76	41

Note that the firm is assumed first to liquidate its marketable securities to meet deficits and then to borrow with notes payable if additional financing is needed. As a result, it will not have marketable securities and notes payable on its books at the same time. Because it may be necessary to borrow up to $76,000 for the 3-month period, the financial manager should be certain that some arrangement is made to ensure the availability of these funds.

Personal Finance Example 4.10 ▸ Because individuals receive only a finite amount of income (cash inflow) during a given period, they need to prepare budgets to make sure they can cover their expenses (cash outflows) during the period. The *personal budget* is a short-term financial planning report that helps individuals or families achieve short-term financial goals. Personal budgets typically cover a 1-year period, broken into months.

A condensed version of a personal budget for the first quarter (3 months) is shown below.

	Jan.	Feb.	Mar.
Income			
Take-home pay	$4,775	$4,775	$4,775
Investment income			90
(1) Total income	$4,775	$4,775	$4,865
Expenses			
(2) Total expenses	$4,026	$5,291	$7,396
Cash surplus or deficit [(1) − (2)]	$ 749	($ 516)	($2,531)
Cumulative cash surplus or deficit	$ 749	$ 233	($2,298)

The personal budget shows a cash surplus of $749 in January followed by monthly deficits in February and March of $516 and $2,531, resulting in a cumulative deficit of $2,298 through March. Clearly, to cover the deficit, some action—such as increasing income, reducing expenses, drawing down savings, or borrowing—will be necessary to bring the budget into balance. Borrowing by using credit can offset a deficit in the short term but can lead to financial trouble if done repeatedly.

COPING WITH UNCERTAINTY IN THE CASH BUDGET

Aside from careful estimation of cash budget inputs, there are two ways of coping with uncertainty in the cash budget. One is to prepare several cash budgets—based on pessimistic, most likely, and optimistic forecasts. From this range of cash flows, the financial manager can determine the amount of financing necessary to cover the most adverse situation. The use of several cash budgets, based on differing scenarios, also should give the financial manager a sense of the riskiness of the various alternatives. This *scenario analysis,* or "what if" approach, is often used to analyze cash flows under a variety of circumstances. Clearly, the use of electronic spreadsheets simplifies the process of performing scenario analysis.

Example 4.11 ▸

Table 4.11 presents the summary of Coulson Industries' cash budget prepared for each month using pessimistic, most likely, and optimistic estimates of total cash receipts and disbursements. The most likely estimate is based on the expected outcomes presented earlier.

During October, Coulson will, at worst, need a maximum of $15,000 of financing and, at best, will have a $62,000 excess cash balance. During November, its financing requirement will be between $0 and $185,000, or it could experience an excess cash balance of $5,000. The December projections show maximum borrowing of $190,000 with a possible excess cash balance of $107,000. By considering the extreme values in the pessimistic and optimistic

TABLE 4.11 A Scenario Analysis of Coulson Industries' Cash Budget ($000)

	October			November			December		
	Pessimistic	Most likely	Optimistic	Pessimistic	Most likely	Optimistic	Pessimistic	Most likely	Optimistic
Total cash receipts	$160	$210	$285	$210	$320	$410	$275	$340	$422
Less: Total cash disbursements	200	213	248	380	418	467	280	305	320
Net cash flow	($ 40)	($ 3)	$ 37	($170)	($ 98)	($ 57)	($ 5)	$ 35	$102
Add: Beginning cash	50	50	50	10	47	87	(160)	(51)	30
Ending cash	$ 10	$ 47	$ 87	($160)	($ 51)	$ 30	($165)	($ 16)	$132
Less: Minimum cash balance	25	25	25	25	25	25	25	25	25
Required total financing	$ 15			$185	$ 76		$190	$ 41	
Excess cash balance		$ 22	$ 62			$ 5			$107

outcomes, Coulson Industries should be better able to plan its cash requirements. For the 3-month period, the peak borrowing requirement under the worst circumstances would be $190,000, which happens to be considerably greater than the most likely estimate of $76,000 for this period.

A second and much more sophisticated way of coping with uncertainty in the cash budget is *simulation* (discussed in Chapter 12). By simulating the occurrence of sales and other uncertain events, the firm can develop a probability distribution of its ending cash flows for each month. The financial decision maker can then use the probability distribution to determine the amount of financing needed to protect the firm adequately against a cash shortage.

CASH FLOW WITHIN THE MONTH

Because the cash budget shows cash flows only on a total monthly basis, the information provided by the cash budget is not necessarily adequate for ensuring solvency. A firm must look more closely at its pattern of daily cash receipts and cash disbursements to ensure that adequate cash is available for paying bills as they come due.

The synchronization of cash flows in the cash budget at month-end does not ensure that the firm will be able to meet its daily cash requirements. Because a firm's cash flows are generally quite variable when viewed on a daily basis, effective cash planning requires a look *beyond* the cash budget. The financial manager must therefore plan and monitor cash flow more frequently than on a monthly basis. The greater the variability of cash flows from day to day, the greater the amount of attention required.

→ **REVIEW QUESTIONS**

4–10 What is the purpose of the *cash budget*? What role does the sales forecast play in its preparation?

4–11 Briefly describe the basic format of the cash budget.

4–12 How can the two "bottom lines" of the cash budget be used to determine the firm's short-term borrowing and investment requirements?

4–13 What is the cause of uncertainty in the cash budget, and what two techniques can be used to cope with this uncertainty?

LG 5

4.4 Profit Planning: Pro Forma Statements

pro forma statements
Projected, or forecast, income statements and balance sheets.

Whereas cash planning focuses on forecasting cash flows, *profit planning* relies on accrual concepts to project the firm's profit and overall financial position. Shareholders, creditors, and the firm's management pay close attention to the **pro forma statements** which are projected income statements and balance sheets. The basic steps in the short-term financial planning process were shown in the flow diagram of Figure 4.1. The approaches for estimating the pro forma statements are all based on the belief that the financial relationships reflected in the firm's past financial statements will not change in the coming period. The commonly used simplified approaches are presented in subsequent discussions.

Two inputs are required for preparing pro forma statements: (1) financial statements for the preceding year and (2) the sales forecast for the coming year. A variety of assumptions must also be made. The company that we will use to illustrate the simplified approaches to pro forma preparation is Vectra Manufacturing, which manufactures and sells one product. It has two basic product models, X and Y, which are produced by the same process but require different amounts of raw material and labor.

PRECEDING YEAR'S FINANCIAL STATEMENTS

The income statement for the firm's 2012 operations is given in Table 4.12 on page 136. It indicates that Vectra had sales of $100,000, total cost of goods sold of $80,000, net profits before taxes of $9,000, and net profits after taxes of $7,650. The firm paid $4,000 in cash dividends, leaving $3,650 to be transferred to retained earnings. The firm's balance sheet for 2012 is given in Table 4.13 on page 136.

SALES FORECAST

Just as for the cash budget, the key input for pro forma statements is the sales forecast. Vectra Manufacturing's sales forecast for the coming year (2013), based on both external and internal data, is presented in Table 4.14 on page 136. The unit sale prices of the products reflect an increase from $20 to $25 for model X and from $40 to $50 for model Y. These increases are necessary to cover anticipated increases in costs.

→ **REVIEW QUESTION**

4–14 What is the purpose of *pro forma statements*? What inputs are required for preparing them using the simplified approaches?

TABLE 4.12 Vectra Manufacturing's Income Statement for the Year Ended December 31, 2012

Sales revenue	
Model X (1,000 units at $20/unit)	$ 20,000
Model Y (2,000 units at $40/unit)	80,000
Total sales	$100,000
Less: Cost of goods sold	
Labor	$ 28,500
Material A	8,000
Material B	5,500
Overhead	38,000
Total cost of goods sold	$ 80,000
Gross profits	$ 20,000
Less: Operating expenses	10,000
Operating profits	$ 10,000
Less: Interest expense	1,000
Net profits before taxes	$ 9,000
Less: Taxes (0.15 × $9,000)	1,350
Net profits after taxes	$ 7,650
Less: Common stock dividends	4,000
To retained earnings	$ 3,650

TABLE 4.13 Vectra Manufacturing's Balance Sheet, December 31, 2012

Assets		Liabilities and Stockholders' Equity	
Cash	$ 6,000	Accounts payable	$ 7,000
Marketable securities	4,000	Taxes payable	300
Accounts receivable	13,000	Notes payable	8,300
Inventories	16,000	Other current liabilities	3,400
Total current assets	$39,000	Total current liabilities	$19,000
Net fixed assets	51,000	Long-term debt	18,000
Total assets	$90,000	Total liabilities	$37,000
		Common stock	30,000
		Retained earnings	23,000
		Total liabilities and stockholders' equity	$90,000

TABLE 4.14 2013 Sales Forecast for Vectra Manufacturing

Unit sales		Dollar sales	
Model X	1,500	Model X ($25/unit)	$ 37,500
Model Y	1,950	Model Y ($50/unit)	97,500
		Total	$135,000

LG 5

4.5 Preparing the Pro Forma Income Statement

percent-of-sales method
A simple method for developing the pro forma income statement; it forecasts sales and then expresses the various income statement items as percentages of projected sales.

A simple method for developing a pro forma income statement is the **percent-of-sales method.** It forecasts sales and then expresses the various income statement items as percentages of projected sales. The percentages used are likely to be the percentages of sales for those items in the previous year. By using dollar values taken from Vectra's 2012 income statement (Table 4.12), we find that these percentages are

$$\frac{\text{Cost of goods sold}}{\text{Sales}} = \frac{\$80{,}000}{\$100{,}000} = 80.0\%$$

$$\frac{\text{Operating expenses}}{\text{Sales}} = \frac{\$10{,}000}{\$100{,}000} = 10.0\%$$

$$\frac{\text{Interest expense}}{\text{Sales}} = \frac{\$1{,}000}{\$100{,}000} = 1.0\%$$

Applying these percentages to the firm's forecast sales of $135,000 (developed in Table 4.14), we get the 2013 pro forma income statement shown in Table 4.15. We have assumed that Vectra will pay $4,000 in common stock dividends, so the expected contribution to retained earnings is $6,327. This represents a considerable increase over $3,650 in the preceding year (see Table 4.12).

CONSIDERING TYPES OF COSTS AND EXPENSES

The technique that is used to prepare the pro forma income statement in Table 4.15 assumes that all the firm's costs and expenses are *variable*. That is, for a given percentage increase in sales, the same percentage increase in cost of goods sold, operating expenses, and interest expense would result. For example, as Vectra's sales increased by 35 percent, we assumed that its costs of goods sold also increased by 35 percent. On the basis of this assumption, the firm's net profits before taxes also increased by 35 percent.

TABLE 4.15 A Pro Forma Income Statement, Using the Percent-of-Sales Method, for Vectra Manufacturing for the Year Ended December 31, 2013

Sales revenue	$135,000
Less: Cost of goods sold (0.80)	108,000
Gross profits	$ 27,000
Less: Operating expenses (0.10)	13,500
Operating profits	$ 13,500
Less: Interest expense (0.01)	1,350
Net profits before taxes	$ 12,150
Less: Taxes (0.15 × $12,150)	1,823
Net profits after taxes	$ 10,327
Less: Common stock dividends	4,000
To retained earnings	$ 6,327

In more depth

To read about *What Costs Are Fixed?* go to www.myfinancelab.com

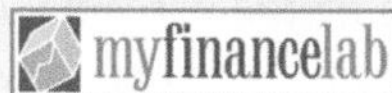

Because this approach assumes that all costs are variable, it may understate the increase in profits that will occur when sales increase if some of the firm's costs are fixed. Similarly, if sales decline, the percentage-of-sales method may overstate profits if some costs are fixed and do not fall when revenues decline. Therefore, a pro forma income statement constructed using the percentage-of-sales method generally *tends to understate profits when sales are increasing and overstate profits when sales are decreasing.* The best way to adjust for the presence of fixed costs when preparing a pro forma income statement is to break the firm's historical costs and expenses into *fixed* and *variable* components. The potential returns as well as risks resulting from use of fixed (operating and financial) costs to create "leverage" are discussed in Chapter 13. The key point to recognize here is that fixed costs make a firm's profits more variable than its revenues. That is, when both profits and sales are rising, profits tend to increase at a faster rate, but when profits and sales are in decline, the percentage drop in profits is often greater than the rate of decline in sales.

Example 4.12 ▸

Vectra Manufacturing's 2012 actual and 2013 pro forma income statements, broken into fixed and variable cost and expense components, follow:

Vectra Manufacturing Income Statements

	2012 Actual	2013 Pro forma
Sales revenue	$100,000	$135,000
Less: Cost of goods sold		
Fixed cost	40,000	40,000
Variable cost (0.40 × sales)	40,000	54,000
Gross profits	$ 20,000	$ 41,000
Less: Operating expenses		
Fixed expense	$ 5,000	$ 5,000
Variable expense (0.05 × sales)	5,000	6,750
Operating profits	$ 10,000	$ 29,250
Less: Interest expense (all fixed)	1,000	1,000
Net profits before taxes	$ 9,000	$ 28,250
Less: Taxes (0.15 × net profits before taxes)	1,350	4,238
Net profits after taxes	$ 7,650	$ 24,012

Breaking Vectra's costs and expenses into fixed and variable components provides a more accurate projection of its pro forma profit. By assuming that *all* costs are variable (as shown in Table 4.15), we find that projected net profits before taxes would continue to equal 9% of sales (in 2012, $9,000 net profits before taxes ÷ $100,000 sales). Therefore, the 2013 net profits before taxes would have been $12,150 (0.09 × $135,000 projected sales) instead of the $28,250 obtained by using the firm's fixed-cost–variable-cost breakdown.

Clearly, when using a simplified approach to prepare a pro forma income statement, we should break down costs and expenses into fixed and variable components.

→ **REVIEW QUESTIONS**

4–15 How is the *percent-of-sales method* used to prepare pro forma income statements?

4–16 Why does the presence of fixed costs cause the percent-of-sales method of pro forma income statement preparation to fail? What is a better method?

LG 5

4.6 Preparing the Pro Forma Balance Sheet

judgmental approach
A simplified approach for preparing the pro forma balance sheet under which the firm estimates the values of certain balance sheet accounts and uses its external financing as a balancing, or "plug," figure.

A number of simplified approaches are available for preparing the pro forma balance sheet. One involves estimating all balance sheet accounts as a strict percentage of sales. A better and more popular approach is the **judgmental approach,** under which the firm estimates the values of certain balance sheet accounts and uses its external financing as a balancing, or "plug," figure. The judgmental approach represents an improved version of the percent-of-sales approach to pro forma balance sheet preparation. Because the judgmental approach requires only slightly more information and should yield better estimates than the somewhat naive percent-of-sales approach, it is presented here.

To apply the judgmental approach to prepare Vectra Manufacturing's 2013 pro forma balance sheet, a number of assumptions must be made about levels of various balance sheet accounts:

1. A minimum cash balance of $6,000 is desired.
2. Marketable securities will remain unchanged from their current level of $4,000.
3. Accounts receivable on average represent about 45 days of sales (about 1/8 of a year). Because Vectra's annual sales are projected to be $135,000, accounts receivable should average $16,875 (1/8 × $135,000).
4. The ending inventory should remain at a level of about $16,000, of which 25 percent (approximately $4,000) should be raw materials and the remaining 75 percent (approximately $12,000) should consist of finished goods.
5. A new machine costing $20,000 will be purchased. Total depreciation for the year is $8,000. Adding the $20,000 acquisition to the existing net fixed assets of $51,000 and subtracting the depreciation of $8,000 yields net fixed assets of $63,000.
6. Purchases will represent approximately 30 percent of annual sales, which in this case is approximately $40,500 (0.30 × $135,000). The firm estimates that it can take 73 days on average to satisfy its accounts payable. Thus accounts payable should equal one-fifth (73 days ÷ 365 days) of the firm's purchases, or $8,100 (1/5 × $40,500).
7. Taxes payable will equal one-fourth of the current year's tax liability, which equals $455 (one-fourth of the tax liability of $1,823 shown in the pro forma income statement in Table 4.15).
8. Notes payable will remain unchanged from their current level of $8,300.
9. No change in other current liabilities is expected. They remain at the level of the previous year: $3,400.

10. The firm's long-term debt and its common stock will remain unchanged at $18,000 and $30,000, respectively; no issues, retirements, or repurchases of bonds or stocks are planned.
11. Retained earnings will increase from the beginning level of $23,000 (from the balance sheet dated December 31, 2012, in Table 4.13) to $29,327. The increase of $6,327 represents the amount of retained earnings calculated in the year-end 2013 pro forma income statement in Table 4.15.

external financing required ("plug" figure)
Under the judgmental approach for developing a pro forma balance sheet, the amount of external financing needed to bring the statement into balance. It can be either a positive or a negative value.

A 2013 pro forma balance sheet for Vectra Manufacturing based on these assumptions is presented in Table 4.16. A **"plug" figure**—called the **external financing required**—of $8,293 is needed to bring the statement into balance. This means that the firm will have to obtain about $8,300 of additional external financing to support the increased sales level of $135,000 for 2013.

A *positive* value for "external financing required," like that shown in Table 4.16, means that, based on its plans, the firm will not generate enough internal financing to support its forecast growth in assets. To support the forecast level of operation, the firm must raise funds externally by using debt and/or equity financing or by reducing dividends. Once the form of financing is determined, the pro forma balance sheet is modified to replace "external financing required" with the planned increases in the debt and/or equity accounts.

A *negative* value for "external financing required" indicates that, based on its plans, the firm will generate more financing internally than it needs to support its forecast growth in assets. In this case, funds are available for use in repaying debt, repurchasing stock, or increasing dividends. Once the specific actions are determined, "external financing required" is replaced in the pro forma balance sheet with the planned reductions in the debt and/or equity accounts. Obviously, besides

TABLE 4.16 A Pro Forma Balance Sheet, Using the Judgmental Approach, for Vectra Manufacturing (December 31, 2013)

Assets			**Liabilities and Stockholders' Equity**	
Cash		$ 6,000	Accounts payable	$ 8,100
Marketable securities		4,000	Taxes payable	455
Accounts receivable		16,875	Notes payable	8,300
Inventories			Other current liabilities	3,400
Raw materials	$ 4,000		Total current liabilities	$ 20,255
Finished goods	12,000		Long-term debt	18,000
Total inventory		16,000	Total liabilities	$ 38,255
Total current assets		$ 42,875	Common stock	30,000
Net fixed assets		63,000	Retained earnings	29,327
Total assets		$105,875	Total	$ 97,582
			External financing required[a]	8,293
			Total liabilities and stockholders' equity	$105,875

[a]The amount of external financing needed to force the firm's balance sheet to balance. Because of the nature of the judgmental approach, the balance sheet is not expected to balance without some type of adjustment.

being used to prepare the pro forma balance sheet, the judgmental approach is frequently used specifically to estimate the firm's financing requirements.

→ REVIEW QUESTIONS

4–17 Describe the *judgmental approach* for simplified preparation of the pro forma balance sheet.

4–18 What is the significance of the "plug" figure, *external financing required?* Differentiate between strategies associated with positive values and with negative values for external financing required.

LG 6

4.7 Evaluation of Pro Forma Statements

It is difficult to forecast the many variables involved in preparing pro forma statements. As a result, investors, lenders, and managers frequently use the techniques presented in this chapter to make rough estimates of pro forma financial statements. Yet, it is important to recognize the basic weaknesses of these simplified approaches. The weaknesses lie in two assumptions: (1) that the firm's past financial condition is an accurate indicator of its future; and (2) that certain variables (such as cash, accounts receivable, and inventories) can be forced to take on certain "desired" values. These assumptions cannot be justified solely on the basis of their ability to simplify the calculations involved. However, despite their weaknesses, the simplified approaches to pro forma statement preparation are likely to remain popular because of their relative simplicity. The widespread use of spreadsheets certainly helps to streamline the financial planning process.

However pro forma statements are prepared, analysts must understand how to use them to make financial decisions. Both financial managers and lenders can use pro forma statements to analyze the firm's inflows and outflows of cash, as well as its liquidity, activity, debt, profitability, and market value. Various ratios can be calculated from the pro forma income statement and balance sheet to evaluate performance. Cash inflows and outflows can be evaluated by preparing a pro forma statement of cash flows. After analyzing the pro forma statements, the financial manager can take steps to adjust planned operations to achieve short-term financial goals. For example, if projected profits on the pro forma income statement are too low, a variety of pricing and/or cost-cutting actions might be initiated. If the projected level of accounts receivable on the pro forma balance sheet is too high, changes in credit or collection policy may be called for. Pro forma statements are therefore of great importance in solidifying the firm's financial plans for the coming year.

→ REVIEW QUESTIONS

4–19 What are the two basic weaknesses of the simplified approaches to preparing pro forma statements?

4–20 What is the financial manager's objective in evaluating pro forma statements?

Summary

FOCUS ON VALUE

Cash flow, the lifeblood of the firm, is a key determinant of the value of the firm. The financial manager must plan and manage the firm's cash flow. The goal is to ensure the firm's solvency and to generate positive cash flow for the firm's owners. Both the magnitude and the risk of the cash flows generated on behalf of the owners determine the firm's value.

To carry out the responsibility **to create value for owners,** the financial manager uses tools such as cash budgets and pro forma financial statements as part of the process of generating positive cash flow. Good financial plans should result in large free cash flows. Clearly, the financial manager must deliberately and carefully plan and manage the firm's cash flows to achieve the firm's goal of maximizing share price.

REVIEW OF LEARNING GOALS

LG 1 **Understand tax depreciation procedures and the effect of depreciation on the firm's cash flows.** Depreciation is an important factor affecting a firm's cash flow. An asset's depreciable value and depreciable life are determined by using the MACRS standards in the federal tax code. MACRS groups assets (excluding real estate) into six property classes based on length of recovery period.

LG 2 **Discuss the firm's statement of cash flows, operating cash flow, and free cash flow.** The statement of cash flows is divided into operating, investment, and financing flows. It reconciles changes in the firm's cash flows with changes in cash and marketable securities for the period. Interpreting the statement of cash flows involves both the major categories of cash flow and the individual items of cash inflow and outflow. From a strict financial point of view, a firm's operating cash flow is defined to exclude interest. Of greater importance is a firm's free cash flow, which is the amount of cash flow available to creditors and owners.

LG 3 **Understand the financial planning process, including long-term (strategic) financial plans and short-term (operating) financial plans.** The two key aspects of the financial planning process are cash planning and profit planning. Cash planning involves the cash budget or cash forecast. Profit planning relies on the pro forma income statement and balance sheet. Long-term (strategic) financial plans act as a guide for preparing short-term (operating) financial plans. Long-term plans tend to cover periods ranging from 2 to 10 years; short-term plans most often cover a 1- to 2-year period.

LG 4 **Discuss the cash-planning process and the preparation, evaluation, and use of the cash budget.** The cash-planning process uses the cash budget, based on a sales forecast, to estimate short-term cash surpluses and shortages. The cash budget is typically prepared for a 1-year period divided into months. It nets cash receipts and disbursements for each period to calculate net cash flow.

Ending cash is estimated by adding beginning cash to the net cash flow. By subtracting the desired minimum cash balance from the ending cash, the firm can determine required total financing or the excess cash balance. To cope with uncertainty in the cash budget, scenario analysis or simulation can be used. A firm must also consider its pattern of daily cash receipts and cash disbursements.

LG 5 **Explain the simplified procedures used to prepare and evaluate the pro forma income statement and the pro forma balance sheet.** A pro forma income statement can be developed by calculating past percentage relationships between certain cost and expense items and the firm's sales and then applying these percentages to forecasts. Because this approach implies that all costs and expenses are variable, it tends to understate profits when sales are increasing and to overstate profits when sales are decreasing. This problem can be avoided by breaking down costs and expenses into fixed and variable components. In this case, the fixed components remain unchanged from the most recent year, and the variable costs and expenses are forecast on a percent-of-sales basis.

Under the judgmental approach, the values of certain balance sheet accounts are estimated and the firm's external financing is used as a balancing, or "plug," figure. A positive value for "external financing required" means that the firm will not generate enough internal financing to support its forecast growth in assets and will have to raise funds externally or reduce dividends. A negative value for "external financing required" indicates that the firm will generate more financing internally than it needs to support its forecast growth in assets and funds will be available for use in repaying debt, repurchasing stock, or increasing dividends.

LG 6 **Evaluate the simplified approaches to pro forma financial statement preparation and the common uses of pro forma statements.** Simplified approaches for preparing pro forma statements assume that the firm's past financial condition is an accurate indicator of the future. Pro forma statements are commonly used to forecast and analyze the firm's level of profitability and overall financial performance so that adjustments can be made to planned operations to achieve short-term financial goals.

Opener-in-Review

The chapter opener mentions that in 2010, Apple's stock sold for approximately $200. Apple had just over $40 billion in cash on its balance sheet and just fewer than 1 billion shares outstanding, so each Apple share represented a claim on $40 of Apple's cash. Suppose that when Apple invests in the resources necessary to create new technology products, it expects to earn a 20% rate of return. Suppose also that when it invests its cash, Apple earns just 1%. Given this, what rate of return should investors expect if they pay $200 to acquire one share of Apple?

Self-Test Problems (Solutions in Appendix)

LG 1 LG 2 **ST4–1 Depreciation and cash flow** A firm expects to have earnings before interest and taxes (EBIT) of $160,000 in each of the next 6 years. It pays annual interest of $15,000. The firm is considering the purchase of an asset that costs $140,000, requires $10,000 in installation cost, and has a recovery period of 5 years. It will be the firm's only asset, and the asset's depreciation is already reflected in its EBIT estimates.

a. Calculate the annual depreciation for the asset purchase using the MACRS depreciation percentages in Table 4.2 on page 117.

b. Calculate the firm's operating cash flows for each of the 6 years, using Equation 4.3. Assume that the firm is subject to a 40% tax rate on all the profit that it earns.

c. Suppose the firm's net fixed assets, current assets, accounts payable, and accruals had the following values at the start and end of the final year (year 6). Calculate the firm's free cash flow (FCF) for that year.

Account	Year 6 start	Year 6 end
Net fixed assets	$ 7,500	$ 0
Current assets	90,000	110,000
Accounts payable	40,000	45,000
Accruals	8,000	7,000

d. Compare and discuss the significance of each value calculated in parts **b** and **c.**

LG 4 LG 5 **ST4–2 Cash budget and pro forma balance sheet inputs** Jane McDonald, a financial analyst for Carroll Company, has prepared the following sales and cash disbursement estimates for the period February–June of the current year.

Month	Sales	Cash disbursements
February	$500	$400
March	600	300
April	400	600
May	200	500
June	200	200

McDonald notes that historically, 30% of sales have been for cash. Of *credit sales,* 70% are collected 1 month after the sale, and the remaining 30% are collected 2 months after the sale. The firm wishes to maintain a minimum ending balance in its cash account of $25. Balances above this amount would be invested in short-term government securities (marketable securities), whereas any deficits would be financed through short-term bank borrowing (notes payable). The beginning cash balance at April 1 is $115.

a. Prepare cash budgets for April, May, and June.

b. How much financing, if any, at a maximum would Carroll Company require to meet its obligations during this 3-month period?

c. A pro forma balance sheet dated at the end of June is to be prepared from the information presented. Give the size of each of the following: cash, notes payable, marketable securities, and accounts receivable.

LG 5 **ST4–3** **Pro forma income statement** Euro Designs, Inc., expects sales during 2013 to rise from the 2012 level of $3.5 million to $3.9 million. Because of a scheduled large loan payment, the interest expense in 2013 is expected to drop to $325,000. The firm plans to increase its cash dividend payments during 2013 to $320,000. The company's year-end 2012 income statement follows.

Euro Designs, Inc. Income Statement for the Year Ended December 31, 2012	
Sales revenue	$3,500,000
Less: Cost of goods sold	1,925,000
Gross profits	$1,575,000
Less: Operating expenses	420,000
Operating profits	$1,155,000
Less: Interest expense	400,000
Net profits before taxes	$ 755,000
Less: Taxes (rate = 40%)	302,000
Net profits after taxes	$ 453,000
Less: Cash dividends	250,000
To retained earnings	$ 203,000

a. Use the *percent-of-sales method* to prepare a 2013 pro forma income statement for Euro Designs, Inc.

b. Explain why the statement may underestimate the company's actual 2013 pro forma income.

Warm-Up Exercises

All problems are available in myfinancelab.

LG 1 **E4–1** The installed cost of a new computerized controller was $65,000. Calculate the depreciation schedule by year assuming a recovery period of 5 years and using the appropriate MACRS depreciation percentages given in Table 4.2 on page 117.

LG 2 **E4–2** Classify the following changes in each of the accounts as either an *inflow* or an *outflow* of cash. During the year (a) marketable securities increased, (b) land and buildings decreased, (c) accounts payable increased, (d) vehicles decreased, (e) accounts receivable increased, and (f) dividends were paid.

LG 2 **E4–3** Determine the *operating cash flow (OCF)* for Kleczka, Inc., based on the following data. (All values are in thousands of dollars.) During the year the firm had sales of $2,500, cost of goods sold totaled $1,800, operating expenses totaled $300, and depreciation expenses were $200. The firm is in the 35% tax bracket.

LG 2 **E4–4** During the year, Xero, Inc., experienced an increase in net fixed assets of $300,000 and had depreciation of $200,000. It also experienced an increase in current assets of $150,000 and an increase in accounts payable and accruals of $75,000. If operating cash flow (OCF) for the year was $700,000, calculate the firm's *free cash flow (FCF)* for the year.

LG 5 **E4–5** Rimier Corp. forecasts sales of $650,000 for 2013. Assume the firm has fixed costs of $250,000 and variable costs amounting to 35% of sales. Operating expenses are estimated to include fixed costs of $28,000 and a variable portion equal to 7.5% of sales. Interest expenses for the coming year are estimated to be $20,000. Estimate Rimier's net profits before taxes for 2013.

Problems

All problems are available in myfinancelab.

LG 1 **P4–1** **Depreciation** On March 20, 2012, Norton Systems acquired two new assets. Asset A was research equipment costing $17,000 and having a 3-year recovery period. Asset B was duplicating equipment having an installed cost of $45,000 and a 5-year recovery period. Using the MACRS depreciation percentages in Table 4.2 on page 117, prepare a depreciation schedule for each of these assets.

LG 1 **P4–2** **Depreciation** In early 2012, Sosa Enterprises purchased a new machine for $10,000 to make cork stoppers for wine bottles. The machine has a 3-year recovery period and is expected to have a salvage value of $2,000. Develop a depreciation schedule for this asset using the MACRS depreciation percentages in Table 4.2.

LG 1 LG 2 **P4–3** **MACRS depreciation expense and accounting cash flow** Pavlovich Instruments, Inc., a maker of precision telescopes, expects to report pretax income of $430,000 this year. The company's financial manager is considering the timing of a purchase of new computerized lens grinders. The grinders will have an installed cost of $80,000 and a cost recovery period of 5 years. They will be depreciated using the MACRS schedule.

a. If the firm purchases the grinders before year-end, what depreciation expense will it be able to claim this year? (Use Table 4.2 on page 117.)

b. If the firm reduces its reported income by the amount of the depreciation expense calculated in part **a,** what tax savings will result?

LG 1 LG 2 **P4–4** **Depreciation and accounting cash flow** A firm in the third year of depreciating its only asset, which originally cost $180,000 and has a 5-year MACRS recovery period, has gathered the following data relative to the current year's operations:

Accruals	$ 15,000
Current assets	120,000
Interest expense	15,000
Sales revenue	400,000
Inventory	70,000
Total costs before depreciation, interest, and taxes	290,000
Tax rate on ordinary income	40%

a. Use the *relevant data* to determine the operating cash flow (see Equation 4.2) for the current year.

b. Explain the impact that depreciation, as well as any other noncash charges, has on a firm's cash flows.

LG 2 **P4–5 Classifying inflows and outflows of cash** Classify each of the following items as an inflow (I) or an outflow (O) of cash, or as neither (N).

Item	Change ($)	Item	Change ($)
Cash	+100	Accounts receivable	−700
Accounts payable	−1,000	Net profits	+600
Notes payable	+500	Depreciation	+100
Long-term debt	−2,000	Repurchase of stock	+600
Inventory	+200	Cash dividends	+800
Fixed assets	+400	Sale of stock	+1,000

LG 2 **P4–6 Finding operating and free cash flows** Consider the balance sheets and selected data from the income statement of Keith Corporation that appear below and on the next page.

Keith Corporation Balance Sheets

	December 31	
Assets	**2012**	**2011**
Cash	$ 1,500	$ 1,000
Marketable securities	1,800	1,200
Accounts receivable	2,000	1,800
Inventories	2,900	2,800
Total current assets	$ 8,200	$ 6,800
Gross fixed assets	$29,500	$28,100
Less: Accumulated depreciation	14,700	13,100
Net fixed assets	$14,800	$15,000
Total assets	$23,000	$21,800
Liabilities and Stockholders' Equity		
Accounts payable	$ 1,600	$ 1,500
Notes payable	2,800	2,200
Accruals	200	300
Total current liabilities	$ 4,600	$ 4,000
Long-term debt	5,000	5,000
Total liabilities	$ 9,600	$ 9,000
Common stock	$10,000	$10,000
Retained earnings	3,400	2,800
Total stockholders' equity	$13,400	$12,800
Total liabilities and stockholders' equity	$23,000	$21,800

Keith Corporation Income Statement Data (2012)	
Depreciation expense	$1,600
Earnings before interest and taxes (EBIT)	2,700
Interest expense	367
Net profits after taxes	1,400
Tax rate	40%

a. Calculate the firm's *net operating profit after taxes (NOPAT)* for the year ended December 31, 2012, using Equation 4.1.
b. Calculate the firm's *operating cash flow* (*OCF*) for the year ended December 31, 2012, using Equation 4.3.
c. Calculate the firm's *free cash flow* (*FCF*) for the year ended December 31, 2012, using Equation 4.5.
d. Interpret, compare, and contrast your cash flow estimates in parts **b** and **c.**

LG 4 **P4–7 Cash receipts** A firm has actual sales of $65,000 in April and $60,000 in May. It expects sales of $70,000 in June and $100,000 in July and in August. Assuming that sales are the only source of cash inflows and that half of them are for cash and the remainder are collected evenly over the following 2 months, what are the firm's expected cash receipts for June, July, and August?

LG 4 **P4–8 Cash disbursements schedule** Maris Brothers, Inc., needs a cash disbursement schedule for the months of April, May, and June. Use the format of Table 4.9 (on page 130) and the following information in its preparation.

Sales: February = $500,000; March = $500,000; April = $560,000; May = $610,000; June = $650,000; July = $650,000

Purchases: Purchases are calculated as 60% of the next month's sales, 10% of purchases are made in cash, 50% of purchases are paid for 1 month after purchase, and the remaining 40% of purchases are paid for 2 months after purchase.

Rent: The firm pays rent of $8,000 per month.

Wages and salaries: Base wage and salary costs are fixed at $6,000 per month plus a variable cost of 7% of the current month's sales.

Taxes: A tax payment of $54,500 is due in June.

Fixed asset outlays: New equipment costing $75,000 will be bought and paid for in April.

Interest payments: An interest payment of $30,000 is due in June.

Cash dividends: Dividends of $12,500 will be paid in April.

Principal repayments and retirements: No principal repayments or retirements are due during these months.

LG 4 **P4–9 Cash budget—Basic** Grenoble Enterprises had sales of $50,000 in March and $60,000 in April. Forecast sales for May, June, and July are $70,000, $80,000, and $100,000, respectively. The firm has a cash balance of $5,000 on May 1 and wishes to maintain a minimum cash balance of $5,000. Given the following data, prepare and interpret a cash budget for the months of May, June, and July.

(1) The firm makes 20% of sales for cash, 60% are collected in the next month, and the remaining 20% are collected in the second month following sale.

(2) The firm receives other income of $2,000 per month.
(3) The firm's actual or expected purchases, all made for cash, are $50,000, $70,000, and $80,000 for the months of May through July, respectively.
(4) Rent is $3,000 per month.
(5) Wages and salaries are 10% of the previous month's sales.
(6) Cash dividends of $3,000 will be paid in June.
(7) Payment of principal and interest of $4,000 is due in June.
(8) A cash purchase of equipment costing $6,000 is scheduled in July.
(9) Taxes of $6,000 are due in June.

Personal Finance Problem

LG 4 **P4–10 Preparation of cash budget** Sam and Suzy Sizeman need to prepare a cash budget for the last quarter of 2013 to make sure they can cover their expenditures during the period. Sam and Suzy have been preparing budgets for the past several years and have been able to establish specific percentages for most of their cash outflows. These percentages are based on their take-home pay (that is, monthly utilities normally run 5% of monthly take-home pay). The information in the following table can be used to create their fourth-quarter budget for 2013.

Income	
Monthly take-home pay	$4,900
Expenses	
Housing	30%
Utilities	5%
Food	10%
Transportation	7%
Medical/dental	.5%
Clothing for October and November	3%
Clothing for December	$440
Property taxes (November only)	11.5%
Appliances	1%
Personal care	2%
Entertainment for October and November	6%
Entertainment for December	$1,500
Savings	7.5%
Other	5%
Excess cash	4.5%

a. Prepare a quarterly cash budget for Sam and Suzy covering the months October through December 2013.
b. Are there individual months that incur a deficit?
c. What is the cumulative cash surplus or deficit by the end of December 2013?

LG 4 **P4–11 Cash budget—Advanced** The actual sales and purchases for Xenocore, Inc., for September and October 2012, along with its forecast sales and purchases for the period November 2012 through April 2013, follow.

The firm makes 20% of all sales for cash and collects on 40% of its sales in each of the 2 months following the sale. Other cash inflows are expected to be $12,000 in September and April, $15,000 in January and March, and $27,000 in February. The firm pays cash for 10% of its purchases. It pays for 50% of its purchases in the following month and for 40% of its purchases 2 months later.

Year	Month	Sales	Purchases
2012	September	$210,000	$120,000
2012	October	250,000	150,000
2012	November	170,000	140,000
2012	December	160,000	100,000
2013	January	140,000	80,000
2013	February	180,000	110,000
2013	March	200,000	100,000
2013	April	250,000	90,000

Wages and salaries amount to 20% of the preceding month's sales. Rent of $20,000 per month must be paid. Interest payments of $10,000 are due in January and April. A principal payment of $30,000 is also due in April. The firm expects to pay cash dividends of $20,000 in January and April. Taxes of $80,000 are due in April. The firm also intends to make a $25,000 cash purchase of fixed assets in December.

a. Assuming that the firm has a cash balance of $22,000 at the beginning of November, determine the end-of-month cash balances for each month, November through April.

b. Assuming that the firm wishes to maintain a $15,000 minimum cash balance, determine the required total financing or excess cash balance for each month, November through April.

c. If the firm were requesting a line of credit to cover needed financing for the period November to April, how large would this line have to be? Explain your answer.

LG 4 **P4–12 Cash flow concepts** The following represent financial transactions that Johnsfield & Co. will be undertaking in the next planning period. For each transaction, check the statement or statements that will be affected immediately.

Transaction	Statement		
	Cash budget	Pro forma income statement	Pro forma balance sheet
Cash sale			
Credit sale			
Accounts receivable are collected			
Asset with 5-year life is purchased			
Depreciation is taken			
Amortization of goodwill is taken			
Sale of common stock			
Retirement of outstanding bonds			
Fire insurance premium is paid for the next 3 years			

LG 4 **P4–13 Cash budget—Scenario analysis** Trotter Enterprises, Inc., has gathered the following data to plan for its cash requirements and short-term investment opportunities for October, November, and December. All amounts are shown in thousands of dollars.

	October			November			December		
	Pessimistic	Most likely	Optimistic	Pessimistic	Most likely	Optimistic	Pessimistic	Most likely	Optimistic
Total cash receipts	$260	$342	$462	$200	$287	$366	$191	$294	$353
Total cash disbursements	285	326	421	203	261	313	287	332	315

a. Prepare a *scenario analysis* of Trotter's cash budget using –$20,000 as the beginning cash balance for October and a minimum required cash balance of $18,000.

b. Use the analysis prepared in part **a** to predict Trotter's financing needs and investment opportunities over the months of October, November, and December. Discuss how knowledge of the timing and amounts involved can aid the planning process.

LG 4 **P4–14 Multiple cash budgets—Scenario analysis** Brownstein, Inc., expects sales of $100,000 during each of the next 3 months. It will make monthly purchases of $60,000 during this time. Wages and salaries are $10,000 per month plus 5% of sales. Brownstein expects to make a tax payment of $20,000 in the next month and a $15,000 purchase of fixed assets in the second month and to receive $8,000 in cash from the sale of an asset in the third month. All sales and purchases are for cash. Beginning cash and the minimum cash balance are assumed to be zero.

a. Construct a cash budget for the next 3 months.

b. Brownstein is unsure of the sales levels, but all other figures are certain. If the most pessimistic sales figure is $80,000 per month and the most optimistic is $120,000 per month, what are the monthly minimum and maximum ending cash balances that the firm can expect for each of the 1-month periods?

c. Briefly discuss how the financial manager can use the data in parts **a** and **b** to plan for financing needs.

LG 5 **P4–15 Pro forma income statement** The marketing department of Metroline Manufacturing estimates that its sales in 2013 will be $1.5 million. Interest expense is expected to remain unchanged at $35,000, and the firm plans to pay $70,000 in cash dividends during 2013. Metroline Manufacturing's income statement for the year ended December 31, 2012, is given on page 152, along with a breakdown of the firm's cost of goods sold and operating expenses into their fixed and variable components.

a. Use the *percent-of-sales method* to prepare a pro forma income statement for the year ended December 31, 2013.

b. Use *fixed and variable cost data* to develop a pro forma income statement for the year ended December 31, 2013.

c. Compare and contrast the statements developed in parts **a** and **b.** Which statement probably provides the better estimate of 2013 income? Explain why.

Metroline Manufacturing Income Statement for the Year Ended December 31, 2012	
Sales revenue	$1,400,000
Less: Cost of goods sold	910,000
Gross profits	$ 490,000
Less: Operating expenses	120,000
Operating profits	$ 370,000
Less: Interest expense	35,000
Net profits before taxes	$ 335,000
Less: Taxes (rate = 40%)	134,000
Net profits after taxes	$ 201,000
Less: Cash dividends	66,000
To retained earnings	$ 135,000

Metroline Manufacturing Breakdown of Costs and Expenses into Fixed and Variable Components for the Year Ended December 31, 2012	
Cost of goods sold	
Fixed cost	$210,000
Variable cost	700,000
Total costs	$910,000
Operating expenses	
Fixed expenses	$ 36,000
Variable expenses	84,000
Total expenses	$120,000

LG 5 **P4–16 Pro forma income statement—Scenario analysis** Allen Products, Inc., wants to do a *scenario analysis* for the coming year. The pessimistic prediction for sales is $900,000; the most likely amount of sales is $1,125,000; and the optimistic prediction is $1,280,000. Allen's income statement for the most recent year follows.

Allen Products, Inc. Income Statement for the Year Ended December 31, 2012	
Sales revenue	$937,500
Less: Cost of goods sold	421,875
Gross profits	$515,625
Less: Operating expenses	234,375
Operating profits	$281,250
Less: Interest expense	30,000
Net profits before taxes	$251,250
Less: Taxes (rate = 25%)	62,813
Net profits after taxes	$188,437

a. Use the *percent-of-sales method,* the income statement for December 31, 2012, and the sales revenue estimates to develop pessimistic, most likely, and optimistic pro forma income statements for the coming year.

b. Explain how the percent-of-sales method could result in an overstatement of profits for the pessimistic case and an understatement of profits for the most likely and optimistic cases.

c. Restate the pro forma income statements prepared in part **a** to incorporate the following assumptions about the 2012 costs:

$250,000 of the cost of goods sold is fixed; the rest is variable.
$180,000 of the operating expenses is fixed; the rest is variable.
All of the interest expense is fixed.

d. Compare your findings in part **c** to your findings in part **a.** Do your observations confirm your explanation in part **b?**

LG 5 **P4–17 Pro forma balance sheet—Basic** Leonard Industries wishes to prepare a pro forma balance sheet for December 31, 2013. The firm expects 2013 sales to total $3,000,000. The following information has been gathered.

(1) A minimum cash balance of $50,000 is desired.
(2) Marketable securities are expected to remain unchanged.
(3) Accounts receivable represent 10% of sales.
(4) Inventories represent 12% of sales.
(5) A new machine costing $90,000 will be acquired during 2013. Total depreciation for the year will be $32,000.
(6) Accounts payable represent 14% of sales.
(7) Accruals, other current liabilities, long-term debt, and common stock are expected to remain unchanged.
(8) The firm's net profit margin is 4%, and it expects to pay out $70,000 in cash dividends during 2013.
(9) The December 31, 2012, balance sheet follows.

Leonard Industries Balance Sheet December 31, 2012

Assets		Liabilities and Stockholders' Equity	
Cash	$ 45,000	Accounts payable	$ 395,000
Marketable securities	15,000	Accruals	60,000
Accounts receivable	255,000	Other current liabilities	30,000
Inventories	340,000	Total current liabilities	$ 485,000
Total current assets	$ 655,000	Long-term debt	350,000
Net fixed assets	600,000	Total liabilities	$ 835,000
Total assets	$1,255,000	Common stock	200,000
		Retained earnings	220,000
		Total liabilities and stockholders' equity	$1,255,000

a. Use the *judgmental approach* to prepare a pro forma balance sheet dated December 31, 2013, for Leonard Industries.

b. How much, if any, additional financing will Leonard Industries require in 2013? Discuss.

c. Could Leonard Industries adjust its planned 2013 dividend to avoid the situation described in part **b?** Explain how.

LG 5 **P4–18 Pro forma balance sheet** Peabody & Peabody has 2012 sales of $10 million. It wishes to analyze expected performance and financing needs for 2014—2 years ahead. Given the following information, respond to parts **a** and **b.**

(1) The percents of sales for items that vary directly with sales are as follows:

Accounts receivable, 12%
Inventory, 18%
Accounts payable, 14%
Net profit margin, 3%

(2) Marketable securities and other current liabilities are expected to remain unchanged.

(3) A minimum cash balance of $480,000 is desired.
(4) A new machine costing $650,000 will be acquired in 2013, and equipment costing $850,000 will be purchased in 2014. Total depreciation in 2013 is forecast as $290,000, and in 2014 $390,000 of depreciation will be taken.
(5) Accruals are expected to rise to $500,000 by the end of 2014.
(6) No sale or retirement of long-term debt is expected.
(7) No sale or repurchase of common stock is expected.
(8) The dividend payout of 50% of net profits is expected to continue.
(9) Sales are expected to be $11 million in 2013 and $12 million in 2014.
(10) The December 31, 2012, balance sheet follows.

Peabody & Peabody Balance Sheet December 31, 2012 ($000)

Assets		Liabilities and Stockholders' Equity	
Cash	$ 400	Accounts payable	$1,400
Marketable securities	200	Accruals	400
Accounts receivable	1,200	Other current liabilities	80
Inventories	1,800	Total current liabilities	$1,880
Total current assets	$3,600	Long-term debt	2,000
Net fixed assets	4,000	Total liabilities	$3,880
Total assets	$7,600	Common equity	3,720
		Total liabilities and stockholders' equity	$7,600

a. Prepare a pro forma balance sheet dated December 31, 2014.
b. Discuss the financing changes suggested by the statement prepared in part **a.**

LG 5 P4–19 **Integrative—Pro forma statements** Red Queen Restaurants wishes to prepare financial plans. Use the financial statements on page 155 and the other information provided below to prepare the financial plans.

The following financial data are also available:
(1) The firm has estimated that its sales for 2013 will be $900,000.
(2) The firm expects to pay $35,000 in cash dividends in 2013.
(3) The firm wishes to maintain a minimum cash balance of $30,000.
(4) Accounts receivable represent approximately 18% of annual sales.
(5) The firm's ending inventory will change directly with changes in sales in 2013.
(6) A new machine costing $42,000 will be purchased in 2013. Total depreciation for 2013 will be $17,000.
(7) Accounts payable will change directly in response to changes in sales in 2013.
(8) Taxes payable will equal one-fourth of the tax liability on the pro forma income statement.
(9) Marketable securities, other current liabilities, long-term debt, and common stock will remain unchanged.

a. Prepare a pro forma income statement for the year ended December 31, 2013, using the *percent-of-sales method.*
b. Prepare a pro forma balance sheet dated December 31, 2013, using the *judgmental approach.*
c. Analyze these statements, and discuss the resulting *external financing required.*

Red Queen Restaurants Income Statement for the Year Ended December 31, 2012	
Sales revenue	$800,000
Less: Cost of goods sold	600,000
Gross profits	$200,000
Less: Operating expenses	100,000
Net profits before taxes	$100,000
Less: Taxes (rate = 40%)	40,000
Net profits after taxes	$ 60,000
Less: Cash dividends	20,000
To retained earnings	$ 40,000

Red Queen Restaurants Balance Sheet December 31, 2012			
Assets		**Liabilities and Stockholders' Equity**	
Cash	$ 32,000	Accounts payable	$100,000
Marketable securities	18,000	Taxes payable	20,000
Accounts receivable	150,000	Other current liabilities	5,000
Inventories	100,000	Total current liabilities	$125,000
Total current assets	$300,000	Long-term debt	200,000
Net fixed assets	350,000	Total liabilities	$325,000
Total assets	$650,000	Common stock	150,000
		Retained earnings	175,000
		Total liabilities and stockholders' equity	$650,000

LG 5

P4–20 Integrative—Pro forma statements Provincial Imports, Inc., has assembled past (2012) financial statements (income statement below and balance sheet on page 156) and financial projections for use in preparing financial plans for the coming year (2013).

Provincial Imports, Inc. Income Statement for the Year Ended December 31, 2012	
Sales revenue	$5,000,000
Less: Cost of goods sold	2,750,000
Gross profits	$2,250,000
Less: Operating expenses	850,000
Operating profits	$1,400,000
Less: Interest expense	200,000
Net profits before taxes	$1,200,000
Less: Taxes (rate = 40%)	480,000
Net profits after taxes	$ 720,000
Less: Cash dividends	288,000
To retained earnings	$ 432,000

Information related to financial projections for the year 2013:

Provincial Imports, Inc. Balance Sheet December 31, 2012			
Assets		**Liabilities and Stockholders' Equity**	
Cash	$ 200,000	Accounts payable	$ 700,000
Marketable securities	225,000	Taxes payable	95,000
Accounts receivable	625,000	Notes payable	200,000
Inventories	500,000	Other current liabilities	5,000
Total current assets	$1,550,000	Total current liabilities	$1,000,000
Net fixed assets	1,400,000	Long-term debt	500,000
Total assets	$2,950,000	Total liabilities	$1,500,000
		Common stock	75,000
		Retained earnings	1,375,000
		Total liabilities and equity	$2,950,000

(1) Projected sales are $6,000,000.
(2) Cost of goods sold in 2012 includes $1,000,000 in fixed costs.
(3) Operating expense in 2012 includes $250,000 in fixed costs.
(4) Interest expense will remain unchanged.
(5) The firm will pay cash dividends amounting to 40% of net profits after taxes.
(6) Cash and inventories will double.
(7) Marketable securities, notes payable, long-term debt, and common stock will remain unchanged.
(8) Accounts receivable, accounts payable, and other current liabilities will change in direct response to the change in sales.
(9) A new computer system costing $356,000 will be purchased during the year. Total depreciation expense for the year will be $110,000.
(10) The tax rate will remain at 40%.

a. Prepare a pro forma income statement for the year ended December 31, 2013, using the *fixed cost data* given to improve the accuracy of the *percent-of-sales method.*

b. Prepare a pro forma balance sheet as of December 31, 2013, using the information given and the *judgmental approach*. Include a reconciliation of the retained earnings account.

c. Analyze these statements, and discuss the resulting *external financing required.*

LG 3 **P4–21 ETHICS PROBLEM** The SEC is trying to get companies to notify the investment community more quickly when a "material change" will affect their forthcoming financial results. In what sense might a financial manager be seen as "more ethical" if he or she follows this directive and issues a press release indicating that sales will not be as high as previously anticipated?

Spreadsheet Exercise

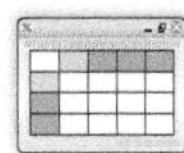

You have been assigned the task of putting together a statement for the ACME Company that shows its expected inflows and outflows of cash over the months of July 2013 through December 2013.

You have been given the following data for ACME Company:

(1) Expected gross sales for May through December, respectively, are $300,000, $290,000, $425,000, $500,000, $600,000, $625,000, $650,000, and $700,000.

(2) 12% of the sales in any given month are collected during that month. However, the firm has a credit policy of 3/10 net 30, so factor a 3% discount into the current month's sales collection.

(3) 75% of the sales in any given month are collected during the following month after the sale.

(4) 13% of the sales in any given month are collected during the second month following the sale.

(5) The expected purchases of raw materials in any given month are based on 60% of the expected sales during the following month.

(6) The firm pays 100% of its current month's raw materials purchases in the following month.

(7) Wages and salaries are paid on a monthly basis and are based on 6% of the current month's expected sales.

(8) Monthly lease payments are 2% of the current month's expected sales.

(9) The monthly advertising expense amounts to 3% of sales.

(10) R&D expenditures are expected to be allocated to August, September, and October at the rate of 12% of sales in those months.

(11) During December a prepayment of insurance for the following year will be made in the amount of $24,000.

(12) During the months of July through December, the firm expects to have miscellaneous expenditures of $15,000, $20,000, $25,000, $30,000, $35,000, and $40,000, respectively.

(13) Taxes will be paid in September in the amount of $40,000 and in December in the amount of $45,000.

(14) The beginning cash balance in July is $15,000.

(15) The target cash balance is $15,000.

TO DO

a. Prepare a cash budget for July 2013 through December 2013 by creating a combined spreadsheet that incorporates spreadsheets similar to those in Tables 4.8, 4.9, and 4.10. Divide your spreadsheet into three sections:

(1) Total cash receipts

(2) Total cash disbursements

(3) Cash budget covering the period of July through December

The cash budget should reflect the following:

(1) Beginning and ending monthly cash balances

(2) The required total financing in each month required

(3) The excess cash balance in each month with excess

b. Based on your analysis, briefly describe the outlook for this company over the next 6 months. Discuss its specific obligations and the funds available to meet them. What could the firm do in the case of a cash deficit? (Where could it get the money?) What should the firm do if it has a cash surplus?

Visit www.myfinancelab.com for **Chapter Case: *Preparing Martin Manufacturing's 2013 Pro Forma Financial Statements,*** Group Exercises, and numerous online resources.

5 Time Value of Money

Learning Goals

LG 1 Discuss the role of time value in finance, the use of computational tools, and the basic patterns of cash flow.

LG 2 Understand the concepts of future value and present value, their calculation for single amounts, and the relationship between them.

LG 3 Find the future value and the present value of both an ordinary annuity and an annuity due, and find the present value of a perpetuity.

LG 4 Calculate both the future value and the present value of a mixed stream of cash flows.

LG 5 Understand the effect that compounding interest more frequently than annually has on future value and on the effective annual rate of interest.

LG 6 Describe the procedures involved in (1) determining deposits needed to accumulate a future sum, (2) loan amortization, (3) finding interest or growth rates, and (4) finding an unknown number of periods.

Why This Chapter Matters to You

In your *professional* life

ACCOUNTING You need to understand time-value-of-money calculations to account for certain transactions such as loan amortization, lease payments, and bond interest rates.

INFORMATION SYSTEMS You need to understand time-value-of-money calculations to design systems that accurately measure and value the firm's cash flows.

MANAGEMENT You need to understand time-value-of-money calculations so that you can manage cash receipts and disbursements in a way that will enable the firm to receive the greatest value from its cash flows.

MARKETING You need to understand time value of money because funding for new programs and products must be justified financially using time-value-of-money techniques.

OPERATIONS You need to understand time value of money because the value of investments in new equipment, in new processes, and in inventory will be affected by the time value of money.

In your *personal* life

Time-value-of-money techniques are widely used in personal financial planning. You can use them to calculate the value of savings at given future dates and to estimate the amount you need now to accumulate a given amount at a future date. You also can apply them to value lump-sum amounts or streams of periodic cash flows and to the interest rate or amount of time needed to achieve a given financial goal.

Eli Lilly and Company

Riding the Pipeline

Companies spend money on new investments if they believe that those investments will later generate enough cash flow to justify the up-front cost. For pharmaceutical companies like Eli Lilly, the average length of time from the discovery of a new drug until delivery to a patient is 10 to 15 years. After R&D produces a promising lead, a drug is still a long way from being ready for human testing. Researchers must probe further to determine what dosage will be required and at what level it might be toxic to the patient. They also must explore practical issues such as whether Lilly will be able to manufacture the compound on a large scale. The clinical trials themselves can take years.

To help recoup its investment, a drug manufacturer can get a 20-year patent that grants the company exclusive rights to the new drug. However, with the lengthy research and approval process, companies may have fewer than 10 years to sell the drug while the patent is in force. Once patent protection expires, generic drug manufacturers enter the market with low-priced alternatives to the name-brand drug.

For Eli Lilly, the cost of bringing a new drug to market runs from $800 million to $1.2 billion. To keep its drug pipeline full, Eli Lilly plows some 20 percent of sales back into the R&D programs on which its future depends. With large cash expenditures occurring years before any cash return, the time value of money is an important factor in calculating the economic viability of a new drug. In this chapter, you will learn how to determine the present value of future cash flows and other time-value-of-money calculations.

LG 1

5.1 The Role of Time Value in Finance

The *time value of money* refers to the observation that it is better to receive money sooner than later. Money that you have in hand today can be invested to earn a positive rate of return, producing more money tomorrow. For that reason, a dollar today is worth more than a dollar in the future. In business, managers constantly face trade-offs in situations where actions that require outflows of cash today may produce inflows of cash later. Because the cash that comes in the future is worth less than the cash that firms spend up front, managers need a set of tools to help them compare cash inflows and outflows that occur at different times. This chapter introduces you to those tools.

In more depth

To read about *The Royalty Treatment*, go to www.myfinancelab.com

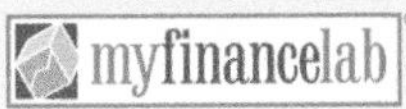

FUTURE VALUE VERSUS PRESENT VALUE

Suppose a firm has an opportunity to spend $15,000 today on some investment that will produce $17,000 spread out over the next five years as follows:

Year 1	$3,000
Year 2	$5,000
Year 3	$4,000
Year 4	$3,000
Year 5	$2,000

Is this a wise investment? It might seem that the obvious answer is yes because the firm spends $15,000 and receives $17,000. Remember, though, that the value of the dollars the firm receives in the future is less than the value of the dollars that they spend today. Therefore, it is not clear whether the $17,000 inflows are enough to justify the initial investment.

Time-value-of-money analysis helps managers answer questions like these. The basic idea is that managers need a way to compare cash today versus cash in the future. There are two ways of doing this. One way is to ask the question, What amount of money in the future is equivalent to $15,000 today? In other words, what is the *future value* of $15,000? The other approach asks, What amount today is equivalent to $17,000 paid out over the next 5 years as outlined above? In other words, what is the *present value* of the stream of cash flows coming in the next 5 years?

time line
A horizontal line on which time zero appears at the leftmost end and future periods are marked from left to right; can be used to depict investment cash flows.

A **time line** depicts the cash flows associated with a given investment. It is a horizontal line on which time zero appears at the leftmost end and future periods are marked from left to right. A time line illustrating our hypothetical investment problem appears in Figure 5.1. The cash flows occurring at time zero (today) and

FIGURE 5.1

Time Line
Time line depicting an investment's cash flows

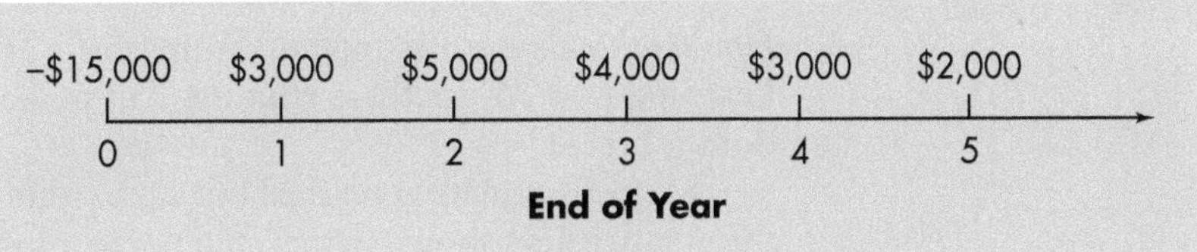

FIGURE 5.2

Compounding and Discounting
Time line showing compounding to find future value and discounting to find present value

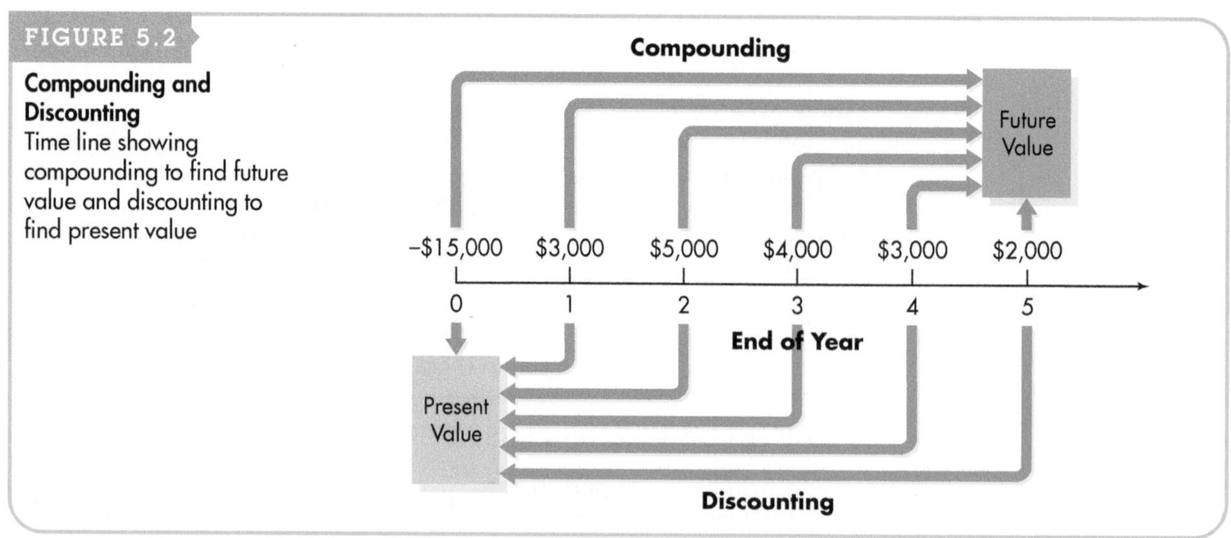

at the end of each subsequent year are above the line; the negative values represent *cash outflows* ($15,000 invested today at time zero), and the positive values represent *cash inflows* ($3,000 inflow in 1 year, $5,000 inflow in 2 years, and so on).

To make the right investment decision, managers need to compare the cash flows depicted in Figure 5.1 at a single point in time. Typically, that point is either the end or the beginning of the investment's life. The future value technique uses *compounding* to find the *future value* of each cash flow at the end of the investment's life and then sums these values to find the investment's future value. This approach is depicted above the time line in Figure 5.2. The figure shows that the future value of each cash flow is measured at the end of the investment's 5-year life. Alternatively, the present value technique uses *discounting* to find the *present value* of each cash flow at time zero and then sums these values to find the investment's value today. Application of this approach is depicted below the time line in Figure 5.2. In practice, when making investment decisions, *managers usually adopt the present value approach.*

COMPUTATIONAL TOOLS

Finding present and future values can involve time-consuming calculations. Although you should understand the concepts and mathematics underlying these calculations, financial calculators and spreadsheets streamline the application of time value techniques.

Financial Calculators

Financial calculators include numerous preprogrammed financial routines. Learning how to use these routines can make present and future values calculations a breeze.

We focus primarily on the keys pictured in Figure 5.3. We typically use four of the first five keys shown in the left column, along with the compute (**CPT**) key. One of the four keys represents the unknown value being calculated. The keystrokes on

FIGURE 5.3

Calculator Keys
Important financial keys on the typical calculator

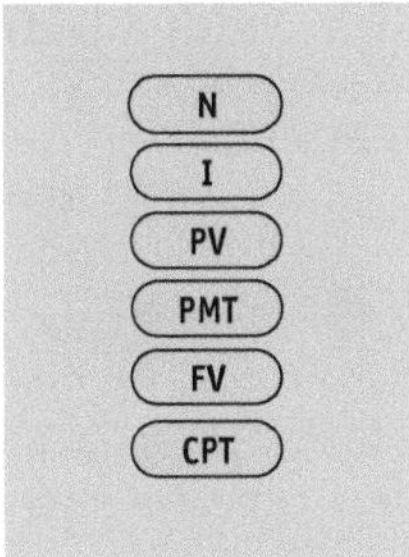

N — Number of periods
I — Interest rate per period
PV — Present value
PMT — Amount of payment (used only for annuities)
FV — Future value
CPT — Compute key used to initiate financial calculation once all values are input

some of the more sophisticated calculators are menu-driven: After you select the appropriate routine, the calculator prompts you to input each value. Regardless, any calculator with the basic future and present value functions can simplify time-value-of-money calculations. The keystrokes for financial calculators are explained in the reference guides that accompany them.

Once you understand the basic underlying concepts, you probably will want to use a calculator to streamline calculations. With a little practice, you can increase both the speed and the accuracy of your financial computations. Remember that *conceptual understanding of the material is the objective.* An ability to solve problems with the aid of a calculator does not necessarily reflect such an understanding, so don't just settle for answers. Work with the material until you are sure you also understand the concepts.

Electronic Spreadsheets

Like financial calculators, electronic spreadsheets have built-in routines that simplify time value calculations. We provide in the text a number of spreadsheet solutions that identify the cell entries for calculating time values. The value for each variable is entered in a cell in the spreadsheet, and the calculation is programmed using an equation that links the individual cells. Changing any of the input variables automatically changes the solution as a result of the equation linking the cells.

BASIC PATTERNS OF CASH FLOW

The cash flow—both inflows and outflows—of a firm can be described by its general pattern. It can be defined as a single amount, an annuity, or a mixed stream.

Single amount: A lump-sum amount either currently held or expected at some future date. Examples include \$1,000 today and \$650 to be received at the end of 10 years.

Annuity: A level periodic stream of cash flow. For our purposes, we'll work primarily with *annual* cash flows. Examples include either paying out or receiving \$800 at the end of each of the next 7 years.

Mixed stream: A stream of cash flow that is *not* an annuity; a stream of unequal periodic cash flows that reflect no particular pattern. Examples include the following two cash flow streams A and B.

End of year	Mixed cash flow stream A	B
1	$ 100	−$ 50
2	800	100
3	1,200	80
4	1,200	− 60
5	1,400	
6	300	

Note that neither cash flow stream has equal, periodic cash flows and that A is a 6-year mixed stream and B is a 4-year mixed stream.

In the next three sections of this chapter, we develop the concepts and techniques for finding future and present values of single amounts, annuities, and mixed streams, respectively. Detailed demonstrations of these cash flow patterns are included.

→ REVIEW QUESTIONS

5–1 What is the difference between *future value* and *present value?* Which approach is generally preferred by financial managers? Why?

5–2 Define and differentiate among the three basic patterns of cash flow: (1) a single amount, (2) an annuity, and (3) a mixed stream.

LG 2

5.2 Single Amounts

Imagine that at age 25 you began investing $2,000 per year in an investment that earns 5 percent interest. At the end of 40 years, at age 65, you would have invested a total of $80,000 (40 years × $2,000 per year). How much would you have accumulated at the end of the fortieth year? $100,000? $150,000? $200,000? No, your $80,000 would have grown to $242,000! Why? Because the time value of money allowed your investments to generate returns that built on each other over the 40 years.

FUTURE VALUE OF A SINGLE AMOUNT

The most basic future value and present value concepts and computations concern single amounts, either present or future amounts. We begin by considering problems that involve finding the future value of cash that is on hand immediately. Then we will use the underlying concepts to solve problems that determine the value today of cash that will be received or paid in the future.

future value
The value at a given future date of an amount placed on deposit today and earning interest at a specified rate. Found by applying *compound interest* over a specified period of time.

We often need to find the value at some future date of a given amount of money placed on deposit today. For example, if you deposit $500 today into an account that pays 5 percent annual interest, how much would you have in the account in 10 years? **Future value** is the value at a given future date of an amount placed on deposit today and earning interest at a specified rate. The future value depends on the rate of interest earned and the length of time the money is left on deposit. Here we explore the future value of a single amount.

The Concept of Future Value

compound interest
Interest that is earned on a given deposit and has become part of the *principal* at the end of a specified period.

principal
The amount of money on which interest is paid.

We speak of **compound interest** to indicate that the amount of interest earned on a given deposit has become part of the *principal* at the end of a specified period. The term **principal** refers to the amount of money on which the interest is paid. Annual compounding is the most common type.

The *future value* of a present amount is found by applying *compound interest* over a specified period of time. Savings institutions advertise compound interest returns at a rate of x percent, or x percent interest, compounded annually, semi-annually, quarterly, monthly, weekly, daily, or even continuously. The concept of future value with annual compounding can be illustrated by a simple example.

Personal Finance Example 5.1 ▶ If Fred Moreno places \$100 in a savings account paying 8% interest compounded annually, at the end of 1 year he will have \$108 in the account—the initial principal of \$100 plus 8% (\$8) in interest. The future value at the end of the first year is calculated by using Equation 5.1:

$$\text{Future value at end of year 1} = \$100 \times (1 + 0.08) = \$108 \tag{5.1}$$

If Fred were to leave this money in the account for another year, he would be paid interest at the rate of 8% on the new principal of \$108. At the end of this second year there would be \$116.64 in the account. This amount would represent the principal at the beginning of year 2 (\$108) plus 8% of the \$108 (\$8.64) in interest. The future value at the end of the second year is calculated by using Equation 5.2:

$$\begin{aligned}\text{Future value at end of year 2} &= \$108 \times (1 + 0.08) \\ &= \$116.64\end{aligned} \tag{5.2}$$

Substituting the expression between the equals signs in Equation 5.1 for the \$108 figure in Equation 5.2 gives us Equation 5.3:

$$\begin{aligned}\text{Future value at end of year 2} &= \$100 \times (1 + 0.08) \times (1 + 0.08) \\ &= \$100 \times (1 + 0.08)^2 \\ &= \$116.64\end{aligned} \tag{5.3}$$

The equations in the preceding example lead to a more general formula for calculating future value.

The Equation for Future Value

The basic relationship in Equation 5.3 can be generalized to find the future value after any number of periods. We use the following notation for the various inputs:

FV_n = future value at the end of period n

PV = initial principal, or present value

r = annual rate of interest paid. (Note: On financial calculators, **I** is typically used to represent this rate.)

n = number of periods (typically years) that the money is left on deposit

The general equation for the future value at the end of period n is

$$FV_n = PV \times (1 + r)^n \tag{5.4}$$

A simple example will illustrate how to apply Equation 5.4.

Personal Finance Example 5.2 ▸ Jane Farber places \$800 in a savings account paying 6% interest compounded annually. She wants to know how much money will be in the account at the end of 5 years. Substituting $PV = \$800$, $r = 0.06$, and $n = 5$ into Equation 5.4 gives the amount at the end of year 5:

$$FV_5 = \$800 \times (1 + 0.06)^5 = \$800 \times (1.33823) = \$1{,}070.58$$

This analysis can be depicted on a time line as follows:

Time line for future value of a single amount (\$800 initial principal, earning 6%, at the end of 5 years)

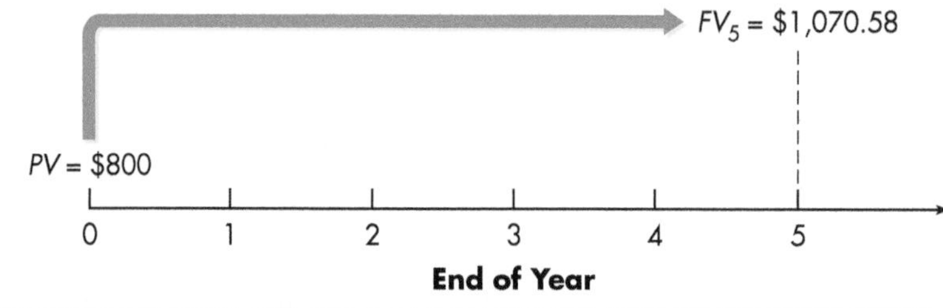

In more depth

To read about *The Rule of 72*, go to www.myfinancelab.com

myfinancelab

Solving the equation in the preceding example involves raising 1.06 to the fifth power. Using a financial calculator or electronic spreadsheet greatly simplifies the calculation.

Personal Finance Example 5.3 ▸ In Personal Finance Example 5.2, Jane Farber placed \$800 in her savings account at 6% interest compounded annually and wishes to find out how much will be in the account at the end of 5 years.

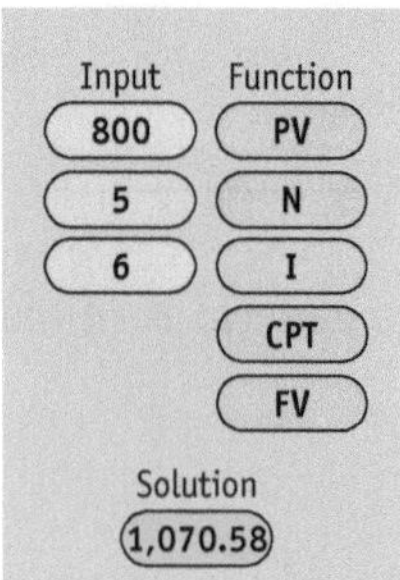

Calculator Use[1] The financial calculator can be used to calculate the future value directly. First punch in \$800 and depress **PV;** next punch in 5 and depress **N;** then punch in 6 and depress **I** (which is equivalent to "r" in our notation); finally, to calculate the future value, depress **CPT** and then **FV.** The future value of \$1,070.58 should appear on the calculator display as shown at the left. On many calculators, this value will be preceded by a minus sign (–1,070.58). *If a minus sign appears on your calculator, ignore it here as well as in all other*

1. Many calculators allow the user to set the number of payments per year. Most of these calculators are preset for monthly payments—12 payments per year. Because we work primarily with annual payments—one payment per year—it is important to *be sure that your calculator is set for one payment per year.* And although most calculators are preset to recognize that all payments occur at the end of the period, it is important to *make sure that your calculator is correctly set on the END mode.* To avoid including previous data in current calculations, *always clear all registers of your calculator before inputting values and making each computation.* The known values *can be punched into the calculator in any order;* the order specified in this as well as other demonstrations of calculator use included in this text merely reflects convenience and personal preference.

"Calculator Use" illustrations in this text.[2] (*Note:* In future examples of calculator use, we will use only a display similar to that shown on page 166. If you need a reminder of the procedures involved, go back and review this paragraph.)

Spreadsheet Use Excel offers a mathematical function that makes the calculation of future values easy. The format of that function is FV(rate,nper,pmt,pv, type). The terms inside the parentheses are inputs that Excel requires to calculate the future value. The terms *rate* and *nper* refer to the interest rate and the number of time periods respectively. The term *pv* represents the lump sum (or present value) that you are investing today. For now, we will ignore the other two inputs, *pmt* and *type,* and enter a value of zero. The future value of the single amount also can be calculated as shown on the following Excel spreadsheet.

	A	B
1	FUTURE VALUE OF A SINGLE AMOUNT	
2	Present value	$800
3	Interest rate, pct per year compounded annually	6%
4	Number of years	5
5	Future value	$1,070.58

Entry in Cell B5 is =FV(B3,B4,0,–B2,0)
The minus sign appears before B2 because the present value is an outflow (i.e., a deposit made by Jane Farber).

Changing any of the values in cells B2, B3, or B4 automatically changes the result shown in cell B5 because the formula in that cell links back to the others. As with the calculator, Excel reports cash inflows as positive numbers and cash outflows as negative numbers. In the example here, we have entered the $800 present value as a negative number, which causes Excel to report the future value as a positive number. Logically, Excel treats the $800 present value as a cash outflow, as if you are paying for the investment you are making, and it treats the future value as a cash inflow when you reap the benefits of your investment 5 years later.

A Graphical View of Future Value

Remember that we measure future value at the *end* of the given period. Figure 5.4 (see page 168) illustrates how the future value depends on the interest rate and the number of periods that money is invested. The figure shows that (1) the higher the interest rate, the higher the future value, and (2) the longer the period of time, the higher the future value. Note that for an interest rate of 0 percent, the future value always equals the present value ($1.00). But for any interest rate greater than zero, the future value is greater than the present value of $1.00.

2. The calculator differentiates inflows from outflows by preceding the outflows with a negative sign. For example, in the problem just demonstrated, the $800 present value (PV), because it was keyed as a positive number, is considered an inflow. Therefore, the calculated future value (FV) of –1,070.58 is preceded by a minus sign to show that it is the resulting outflow. Had the $800 present value been keyed in as a negative number (–800), the future value of $1,070.58 would have been displayed as a positive number (1,070.58). Simply stated, *the cash flows—present value* (PV) *and future value* (FV)*—will have opposite signs.*

Future Value Relationship
Interest rates, time periods, and future value of one dollar

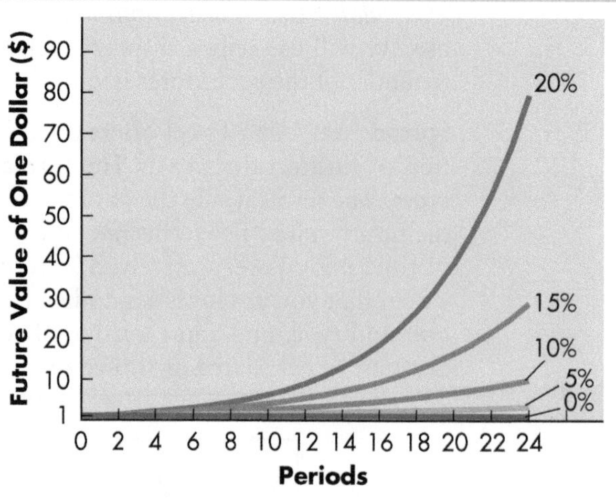

PRESENT VALUE OF A SINGLE AMOUNT

present value
The current dollar value of a future amount—the amount of money that would have to be invested today at a given interest rate over a specified period to equal the future amount.

It is often useful to determine the value today of a future amount of money. For example, how much would I have to deposit today into an account paying 7 percent annual interest to accumulate $3,000 at the end of 5 years? **Present value** is the current dollar value of a future amount—the amount of money that would have to be invested today at a given interest rate over a specified period to equal the future amount. Like future value, the present value depends largely on the interest rate and the point in time at which the amount is to be received. This section explores the present value of a single amount.

The Concept of Present Value

discounting cash flows
The process of finding present values; the inverse of compounding interest.

The process of finding present values is often referred to as **discounting cash flows.** It is concerned with answering the following question: If I can earn r percent on my money, what is the most I would be willing to pay now for an opportunity to receive FV_n dollars n periods from today?

This process is actually the inverse of compounding interest. Instead of finding the future value of present dollars invested at a given rate, discounting determines the present value of a future amount, assuming an opportunity to earn a certain return on the money. This annual rate of return is variously referred to as the *discount rate, required return, cost of capital,* and *opportunity cost.* These terms will be used interchangeably in this text.

Personal Finance Example 5.4 ▸ Paul Shorter has an opportunity to receive $300 one year from now. If he can earn 6% on his investments in the normal course of events, what is the most he should pay now for this opportunity? To answer this question, Paul must determine how many dollars he would have to invest at 6% today to have $300 one year from now. Letting PV equal this unknown amount and using the same notation as in the future value discussion, we have

$$PV \times (1 + 0.06) = \$300 \tag{5.5}$$

Solving Equation 5.5 for PV gives us Equation 5.6:

$$PV = \frac{\$300}{(1 + 0.06)} \tag{5.6}$$
$$= \$283.02$$

The value today ("present value") of \$300 received one year from today, given an interest rate of 6%, is \$283.02. That is, investing \$283.02 today at 6% would result in \$300 at the end of one year.

The Equation for Present Value

The present value of a future amount can be found mathematically by solving Equation 5.4 for PV. In other words, the present value, PV, of some future amount, FV_n, to be received n periods from now, assuming an interest rate (or opportunity cost) of r, is calculated as follows:

$$PV = \frac{FV_n}{(1 + r)^n} \tag{5.7}$$

Note the similarity between this general equation for present value and the equation in the preceding example (Equation 5.6). Let's use this equation in an example.

Personal Finance Example 5.5 ▸ Pam Valenti wishes to find the present value of \$1,700 that she will receive 8 years from now. Pam's opportunity cost is 8%. Substituting FV_8 = \$1,700, $n = 8$, and $r = 0.08$ into Equation 5.7 yields Equation 5.8:

$$PV = \frac{\$1{,}700}{(1 \times 0.08)^8} = \frac{\$1{,}700}{1.85093} = \$918.46 \tag{5.8}$$

The following time line shows this analysis.

Time line for present value of a single amount (\$1,700 future amount, discounted at 8%, from the end of 8 years)

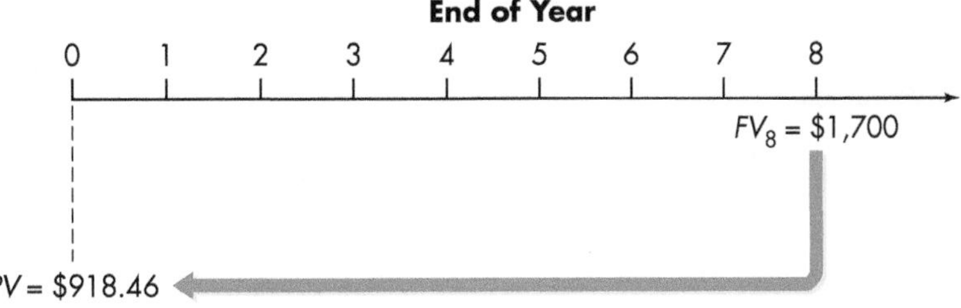

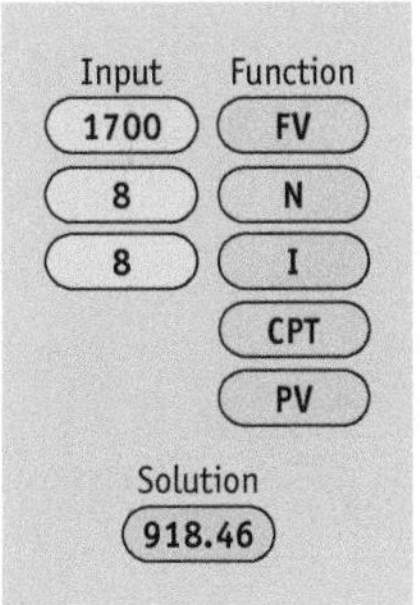

Calculator Use Using the calculator's financial functions and the inputs shown at the left, you should find the present value to be \$918.46.

Spreadsheet Use The format of Excel's present value function is very similar to the future value function covered earlier. The appropriate syntax is PV(rate,nper, pmt,fv,type). The input list inside the parentheses is the same as in Excel's future value function with one exception. The present value function contains the term *fv*, which represents the future lump sum payment (or receipt) whose present value you are trying to calculate. The present value of the single future amount also can be calculated as shown on the following Excel spreadsheet.

	A	B
1	PRESENT VALUE OF A SINGLE AMOUNT	
2	Future value	$1,700
3	Interest rate, pct per year compounded annually	8%
4	Number of years	8
5	Present value	$918.46

Entry in Cell B5 is =–PV(B3,B4,0,B2)
The minus sign appears before PV to change the present value to a positive amount.

A Graphical View of Present Value

Remember that present value calculations assume that the future values are measured at the *end* of the given period. The relationships among the factors in a present value calculation are illustrated in Figure 5.5. The figure clearly shows that, everything else being equal, (1) the higher the discount rate, the lower the present value, and (2) the longer the period of time, the lower the present value. Also note that given a discount rate of 0 percent, the present value always equals the future value ($1.00). But for any discount rate greater than zero, the present value is less than the future value of $1.00.

→ REVIEW QUESTIONS

5–3 How is the *compounding process* related to the payment of interest on savings? What is the general equation for future value?

5–4 What effect would a *decrease* in the interest rate have on the future value of a deposit? What effect would an *increase* in the holding period have on future value?

5–5 What is meant by "the present value of a future amount"? What is the general equation for present value?

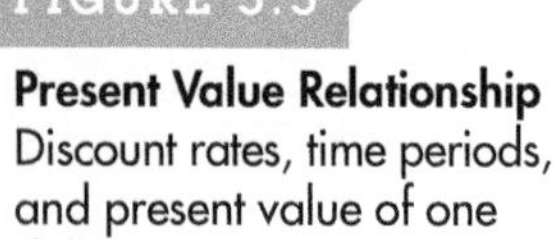

Present Value Relationship
Discount rates, time periods, and present value of one dollar

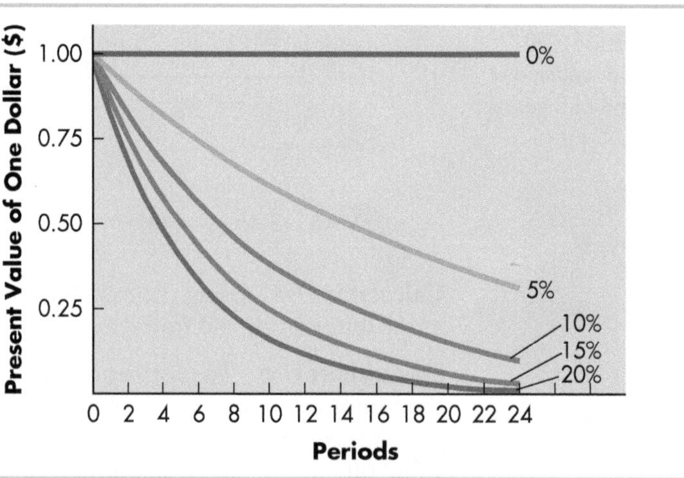

5–6 What effect does *increasing* the required return have on the present value of a future amount? Why?

5–7 How are present value and future value calculations related?

LG 3

5.3 Annuities

annuity
A stream of equal periodic cash flows over a specified time period. These cash flows can be *inflows* of returns earned on investments or *outflows* of funds invested to earn future returns.

ordinary annuity
An annuity for which the cash flow occurs at the *end* of each period.

annuity due
An annuity for which the cash flow occurs at the *beginning* of each period.

How much would you pay today, given that you can earn 7 percent on low-risk investments, to receive a guaranteed $3,000 at the end of *each* of the next 20 years? How much will you have at the end of 5 years if your employer withholds and invests $1,000 of your bonus at the end of *each* of the next 5 years, guaranteeing you a 9 percent annual rate of return? To answer these questions, you need to understand the application of the time value of money to *annuities.*

An **annuity** is a stream of equal periodic cash flows, over a specified time period. These cash flows are usually annual but can occur at other intervals, such as monthly rent or car payments. The cash flows in an annuity can be *inflows* (the $3,000 received at the end of each of the next 20 years) or *outflows* (the $1,000 invested at the end of each of the next 5 years).

TYPES OF ANNUITIES

There are two basic types of annuities. For an **ordinary annuity,** the cash flow occurs at the *end* of each period. For an **annuity due,** the cash flow occurs at the *beginning* of each period.

Personal Finance Example 5.6 ▸ Fran Abrams is evaluating two annuities. Both are 5-year, $1,000 annuities; annuity A is an ordinary annuity and annuity B is an annuity due. To better understand the difference between these annuities, she has listed their cash flows in Table 5.1. Note that the amount of each annuity totals $5,000. The two annuities differ only in the timing of their cash flows: The cash flows are received sooner with the annuity due than with the ordinary annuity.

TABLE 5.1 Comparison of Ordinary Annuity and Annuity Due Cash Flows ($1,000, 5 Years)

	Annual cash flows	
Year	**Annuity A (*ordinary*)**	**Annuity B (*annuity due*)**
0	$ 0	$1,000
1	1,000	1,000
2	1,000	1,000
3	1,000	1,000
4	1,000	1,000
5	1,000	0
Totals	$5,000	$5,000

Although the cash flows of both annuities in Table 5.1 total \$5,000, the annuity due would have a higher future value than the ordinary annuity because each of its five annual cash flows can earn interest for 1 year more than each of the ordinary annuity's cash flows. In general, as will be demonstrated later in this chapter, *the value (present or future) of an annuity due is always greater than the value of an otherwise identical ordinary annuity.*

Because ordinary annuities are more frequently used in finance, *unless otherwise specified, the term* annuity *is intended throughout this book to refer to ordinary annuities.*

FINDING THE FUTURE VALUE OF AN ORDINARY ANNUITY

One way to find the future value of an ordinary annuity is to calculate the future value of each of the individual cash flows and then add up those figures. Fortunately, there are several shortcuts to get to the answer. You can calculate the future value of an ordinary annuity that pays an annual cash flow equal to *CF* by using Equation 5.9:

$$FV_n = CF \times \left\{ \frac{[(1+r)^n - 1]}{r} \right\} \tag{5.9}$$

As before, in this equation r represents the interest rate, and n represents the number of payments in the annuity (or equivalently, the number of years over which the annuity is spread). The calculations required to find the future value of an ordinary annuity are illustrated in the following example.

Personal Finance Example 5.7 ▶ Fran Abrams wishes to determine how much money she will have at the end of 5 years if she chooses annuity A, the ordinary annuity. She will deposit \$1,000 annually, at the *end of each* of the next 5 years, into a savings account paying 7% annual interest. This situation is depicted on the following time line:

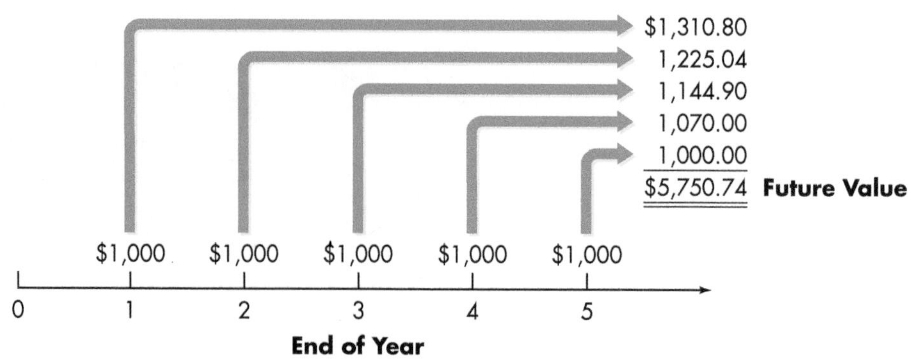

Time line for future value of an ordinary annuity (\$1,000 end-of-year deposit, earning 7%, at the end of 5 years)

As the figure shows, at the end of year 5, Fran will have \$5,750.74 in her account. Note that because the deposits are made at the end of the year the first deposit will earn interest for 4 years, the second for 3 years, and so on. Plugging the relevant values into Equation 5.9 we have

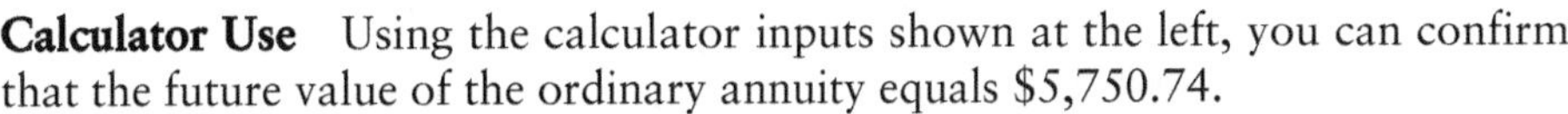

$$FV_5 = \$1{,}000 \times \left\{\frac{[(1 + 0.07)^5 - 1]}{0.07}\right\} = \$5{,}750.74 \tag{5.10}$$

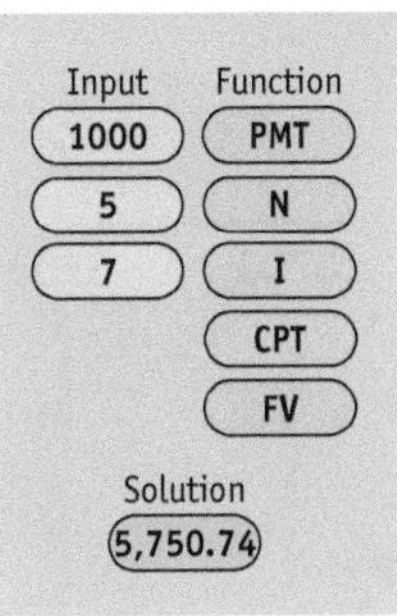

Calculator Use Using the calculator inputs shown at the left, you can confirm that the future value of the ordinary annuity equals $5,750.74.

Spreadsheet Use To calculate the future value of an annuity in Excel, we will use the same future value function that we used to calculate the future value of a lump sum, but we will add two new input values. Recall that the future value function's syntax is FV(rate,nper,pmt,pv,type). We have already explained the terms *rate, nper,* and *pv* in this function. The term *pmt* refers to the annual payment that the annuity offers. The term *type* is an input that lets Excel know whether the annuity being valued is an ordinary annuity (in which case the input value for *type* is 0 or omitted) or an annuity due (in which case the correct input value for *type* is 1). In this particular problem, the input value for *pv* is 0 or omitted because there is no up-front money received. The only cash flows are those that are part of the annuity stream. The future value of the ordinary annuity can be calculated as shown on the following Excel spreadsheet.

	A	B
1	FUTURE VALUE OF AN ORDINARY ANNUITY	
2	Annual payment	$1,000
3	Annual rate of interest, compounded annually	7%
4	Number of years	5
5	Future value of an ordinary annuity	$5,750.74
	Entry in Cell B5 is =FV(B3,B4,–B2) The minus sign appears before B2 because the annual payment is a cash outflow.	

FINDING THE PRESENT VALUE OF AN ORDINARY ANNUITY

Quite often in finance, there is a need to find the present value of a *stream* of cash flows to be received in future periods. An annuity is, of course, a stream of equal periodic cash flows. The method for finding the present value of an ordinary annuity is similar to the method just discussed. One approach would be to calculate the present value of each cash flow in the annuity and then add up those present values. Alternatively, the algebraic shortcut for finding the present value of an ordinary annuity that makes an annual payment of CF for n years looks like this:

$$PV_n = \left(\frac{CF}{r}\right) \times \left[1 - \frac{1}{(1 + r)^n}\right] \tag{5.11}$$

Of course the simplest approach is to solve problems like these with a financial calculator or spreadsheet program.

Example 5.8 ▶ Braden Company, a small producer of plastic toys, wants to determine the most it should pay to purchase a particular ordinary annuity. The annuity consists of cash flows of \$700 at the end of each year for 5 years. The firm requires the annuity to provide a minimum return of 8%. This situation is depicted on the following time line:

Time line for present value of an ordinary annuity (\$700 end-of-year cash flows, discounted at 8%, over 5 years)

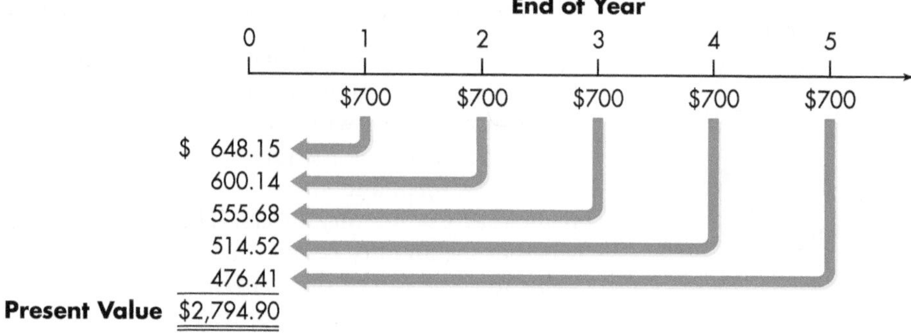

Table 5.2 shows one way to find the present value of the annuity—simply calculate the present values of all the cash payments using the present value equation (Equation 5.7 on page 169) and sum them. This procedure yields a present value of \$2,794.90. Calculators and spreadsheets offer streamlined methods for arriving at this figure.

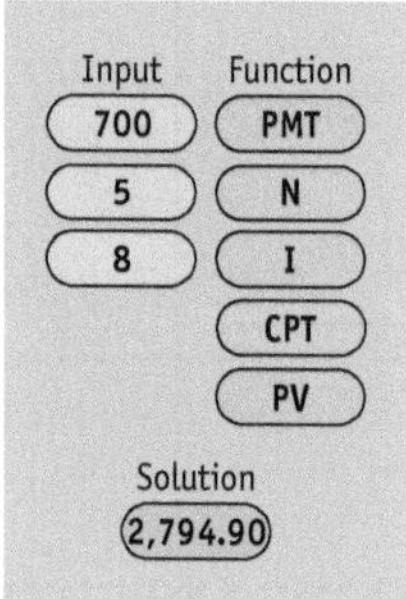

Calculator Use Using the calculator's inputs shown at the left, you will find the present value of the ordinary annuity to be \$2,794.90.

Spreadsheet Use The present value of the ordinary annuity also can be calculated as shown on the Excel spreadsheet on the next page.

TABLE 5.2 Long Method for Finding the Present Value of an Ordinary Annuity

Year (n)	Cash flow	Present value calculation	Present value
1	\$700	$\frac{700}{(1 + 0.08)^1} =$	\$ 648.15
2	700	$\frac{700}{(1 + 0.08)^2} =$	600.14
3	700	$\frac{700}{(1 + 0.08)^3} =$	555.68
4	700	$\frac{700}{(1 + 0.08)^4} =$	514.52
5	700	$\frac{700}{(1 + 0.08)^5} =$	476.41
		Present value of annuity	\$2,794.90

	A	B
1	PRESENT VALUE OF AN ORDINARY ANNUITY	
2	Annual payment	$700
3	Annual rate of interest, compounded annually	8%
4	Number of years	5
5	Present value of an ordinary annuity	$2,794.90
	Entry in Cell B5 is =PV(B3,B4,–B2) The minus sign appears before B2 because the annual payment is a cash outflow.	

FINDING THE FUTURE VALUE OF AN ANNUITY DUE

We now turn our attention to annuities due. Remember that the cash flows of an annuity due occur at the *start of the period.* In other words, if we are dealing with annual payments, each payment in an annuity due comes one year earlier than it would in an ordinary annuity. This in turn means that each payment can earn an extra year's worth of interest, which is why the future value of an annuity due exceeds the future value of an otherwise identical ordinary annuity.

The algebraic shortcut for the future value of an annuity due that makes annual payments of CF for n years is

$$FV_n = CF \times \left\{\frac{[(1 + r)^n - 1]}{r}\right\} \times (1 + r) \quad (5.12)$$

Compare this to Equation 5.9 on page 172, which shows how to calculate the future value of an ordinary annuity. The two equations are nearly identical, but Equation 5.12 has an added term, $(1 + r)$, at the end. In other words, the value obtained from Equation 5.12 will be $(1 + r)$ times greater than the value in Equation 5.9 if the other inputs (CF and n) are the same, and that makes sense because all the payments in the annuity due earn one more year's worth of interest compared to the ordinary annuity.

Personal Finance Example 5.9 ▶ Recall from an earlier example, illustrated in Table 5.1 on page 171, that Fran Abrams wanted to choose between an ordinary annuity and an annuity due, both offering similar terms except for the timing of cash flows. We calculated the future value of the ordinary annuity in Example 5.7. We now will calculate the future value of the annuity due.

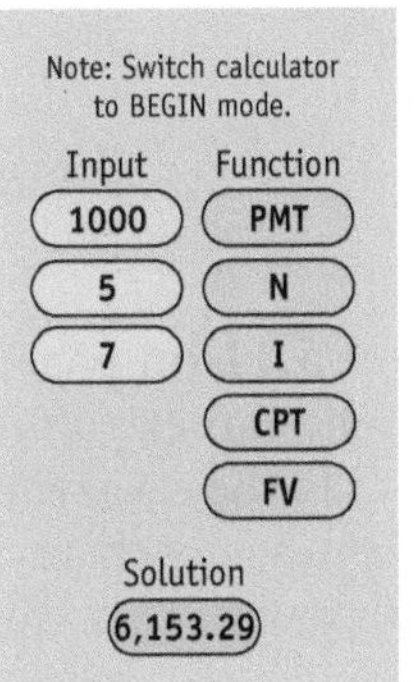

Calculator Use Before using your calculator to find the future value of an annuity due, depending on the specific calculator, you must either switch it to BEGIN mode or use the DUE key. Then, using the inputs shown at the left, you will find the future value of the annuity due to be $6,153.29. (*Note:* Because we nearly always assume end-of-period cash flows, *be sure to switch your calculator back to END mode when you have completed your annuity-due calculations.*)

Spreadsheet Use The future value of the annuity due also can be calculated as shown on the following Excel spreadsheet. Remember that for an annuity due the *type* input value must be set to 1, and we must also specify the *pv* input value as 0 since the inputs are in an ordered series.

	A	B
1	FUTURE VALUE OF AN ANNUITY DUE	
2	Annual payment	$1,000
3	Annual rate of interest, compounded annually	7%
4	Number of years	5
5	Future value of an annuity due	$6,153.29
	Entry in Cell B5 is =FV(B3,B4,–B2,0,1) The minus sign appears before B2 because the annual payment is a cash outflow.	

Comparison of an Annuity Due with an Ordinary Annuity Future Value

The future value of an annuity due is *always greater* than the future value of an otherwise identical ordinary annuity. We can see this by comparing the future values at the end of year 5 of Fran Abrams's two annuities:

$$\text{Ordinary annuity} = \$5{,}750.74 \qquad \text{versus} \qquad \text{Annuity due} = \$6{,}153.29$$

Because the cash flow of the annuity due occurs at the beginning of the period rather than at the end (that is, each payment comes one year sooner in the annuity due), its future value is greater. How much greater? It is interesting to calculate the percentage difference between the value of the annuity and the value of the annuity due:

$$(\$6{,}153.29 - \$5{,}750.74) \div \$5{,}750.74 = 0.07 = 7\%$$

Recall that the interest rate in this example is 7 percent. It is no coincidence that the annuity due is 7 percent more valuable than the annuity. An extra year's interest on each of the annuity due's payments make the annuity due 7 percent more valuable than the annuity.

FINDING THE PRESENT VALUE OF AN ANNUITY DUE

We can also find the present value of an annuity due. This calculation can be easily performed by adjusting the ordinary annuity calculation. Because the cash flows of an annuity due occur at the beginning rather than the end of the period, to find their present value, each annuity due cash flow is discounted back one less year than for an ordinary annuity. The algebraic formula for the present value of an annuity due looks like this:

$$PV_n = \left(\frac{CF}{r}\right) \times \left[1 - \frac{1}{(1+r)^n}\right] \times (1 + r) \tag{5.13}$$

Notice the similarity between this equation and Equation 5.11 on page 173. The two equations are identical except that Equation 5.13 has an extra term at the end, $(1 + r)$. The reason for this extra term is the same as in the case when we calculated the future value of the annuity due. In the annuity due, each payment arrives one year earlier (compared to the annuity), so each payment is worth a little more—one year's interest more.

Example 5.10 ▸ In Example 5.8 of Braden Company, we found the present value of Braden's \$700, 5-year ordinary annuity discounted at 8% to be \$2,794.90. If we now assume that Braden's \$700 annual cash flow occurs at the *start* of each year and is thereby an annuity due, we can calculate its present value using a calculator or a spreadsheet.

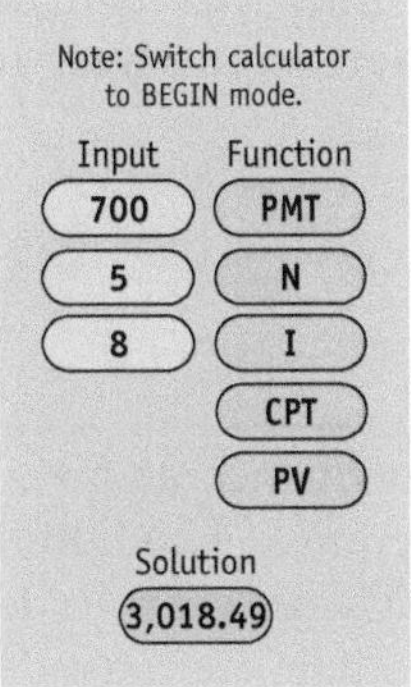

Calculator Use Before using your calculator to find the present value of an annuity due, depending on the specifics of your calculator, you must either switch it to BEGIN mode or use the DUE key. Then, using the inputs shown at the left, you will find the present value of the annuity due to be \$3,018.49 (*Note:* Because we nearly always assume end-of-period cash flows, *be sure to switch your calculator back to END mode when you have completed your annuity-due calculations.*)

Spreadsheet Use The present value of the annuity due also can be calculated as shown on the following Excel spreadsheet.

	A	B
1	PRESENT VALUE OF AN ANNUITY DUE	
2	Annual payment	\$700
3	Annual rate of interest, compounded annually	8%
4	Number of years	5
5	Present value of an annuity due	\$3,018.49

Entry in Cell B5 is =PV(B3,B4,–B2,0,1)
The minus sign appears before B2 because the annual payment is a cash outflow.

Comparison of an Annuity Due with an Ordinary Annuity Present Value

The present value of an annuity due is always greater than the present value of an otherwise identical ordinary annuity. We can see this by comparing the present values of the Braden Company's two annuities:

$$\text{Ordinary annuity} = \$2{,}794.90 \qquad \text{versus} \qquad \text{Annuity due} = \$3{,}018.49$$

Because the cash flow of the annuity due occurs at the beginning of the period rather than at the end, its present value is greater. If we calculate the percentage difference in the values of these two annuities, we will find that the annuity due is 8 percent more valuable than the annuity:

$$(\$3{,}018.49 - \$2{,}794.90) \div \$2{,}794.90 = 0.08 = 8\%$$

Matter of fact

Getting Your (Annuity) Due

Kansas truck driver Donald Damon got the surprise of his life when he learned he held the winning ticket for the Powerball lottery drawing held November 11, 2009. The advertised lottery jackpot was \$96.6 million. Damon could have chosen to collect his prize in 30 annual payments of \$3,220,000 (30 × \$3.22 million = \$96.6 million), but instead he elected to accept a lump sum payment of \$48,367,329.08, roughly half the stated jackpot total.

FINDING THE PRESENT VALUE OF A PERPETUITY

perpetuity
An annuity with an infinite life, providing continual annual cash flow.

A **perpetuity** is an annuity with an infinite life—in other words, an annuity that never stops providing its holder with a cash flow at the end of each year (for example, the right to receive $500 at the end of each year forever).

It is sometimes necessary to find the present value of a perpetuity. Fortunately, the calculation for the present value of a perpetuity is one of the easiest in all of finance. If a perpetuity pays an annual cash flow of *CF*, starting one year from now, the present value of the cash flow stream is

$$PV = CF \div r \tag{5.14}$$

Personal Finance Example 5.11 ▸ Ross Clark wishes to endow a chair in finance at his alma mater. The university indicated that it requires $200,000 per year to support the chair, and the endowment would earn 10% per year. To determine the amount Ross must give the university to fund the chair, we must determine the present value of a $200,000 perpetuity discounted at 10%. Using equation 5.14, we can determine that the present value of a perpetuity paying $200,000 per year is $2 million when the interest rate is 10%:

$$PV = \$200{,}000 \div 0.10 = \$2{,}000{,}000$$

In other words, to generate $200,000 every year for an indefinite period requires $2,000,000 today if Ross Clark's alma mater can earn 10% on its investments. If the university earns 10% interest annually on the $2,000,000, it can withdraw $200,000 per year indefinitely.

→ REVIEW QUESTIONS

5–8 What is the difference between an *ordinary annuity* and an *annuity due?* Which is more valuable? Why?

5–9 What are the most efficient ways to calculate the present value of an ordinary annuity?

5–10 How can the formula for the future value of an annuity be modified to find the future value of an annuity due?

5–11 How can the formula for the present value of an ordinary annuity be modified to find the present value of an annuity due?

5–12 What is a *perpetuity?* Why is the present value of a perpetuity equal to the annual cash payment divided by the interest rate?

LG 4

5.4 Mixed Streams

mixed stream
A stream of unequal periodic cash flows that reflect no particular pattern.

Two basic types of cash flow streams are possible, the annuity and the mixed stream. Whereas an *annuity* is a pattern of equal periodic cash flows, a **mixed stream** is a stream of unequal periodic cash flows that reflect no particular pattern. Financial managers frequently need to evaluate opportunities that are expected to provide mixed streams of cash flows. Here we consider both the future value and the present value of mixed streams.

FUTURE VALUE OF A MIXED STREAM

Determining the future value of a mixed stream of cash flows is straightforward. We determine the future value of each cash flow at the specified future date and then add all the individual future values to find the total future value.

Example 5.12 ▸ Shrell Industries, a cabinet manufacturer, expects to receive the following mixed stream of cash flows over the next 5 years from one of its small customers.

End of year	Cash flow
1	$11,500
2	14,000
3	12,900
4	16,000
5	18,000

If Shrell expects to earn 8% on its investments, how much will it accumulate by the end of year 5 if it immediately invests these cash flows when they are received? This situation is depicted on the following time line:

Time line for future value of a mixed stream (end-of-year cash flows, compounded at 8% to the end of year 5)

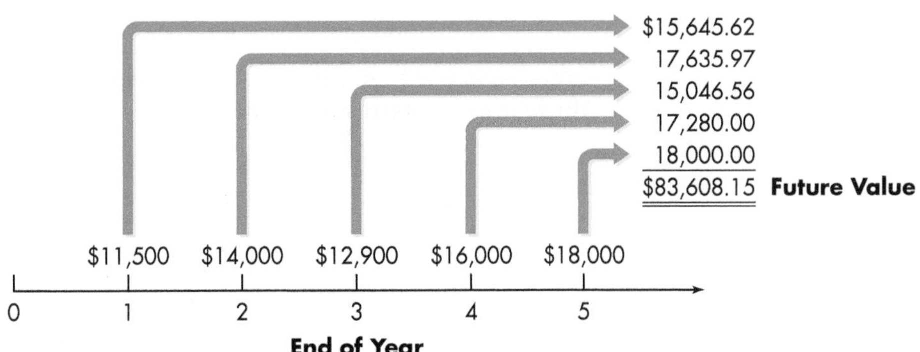

Calculator Use You can use your calculator to find the future value of each individual cash flow, as demonstrated earlier (on page 167), and then sum the future values to get the future value of the stream. Unfortunately, unless you can program your calculator, most calculators lack a function that would allow you to input *all of the cash flows,* specify the interest rate, and directly calculate the future value of the entire cash flow stream. Had you used your calculator to find the individual cash flow future values and then summed them, the future value of Shrell Industries' cash flow stream at the end of year 5 would have been $83,608.15.

Spreadsheet Use A relatively simple way to use Excel to calculate the future value of a mixed stream is to use the Excel future value (FV) function discussed on page 167 combined with the net present value (NPV) function (which will be discussed on page 181). The trick is to use the NPV function to first find the present value of the mixed stream and then find the future of this present value amount. The following Excel spreadsheet illustrates this approach:

	A	B
1	FUTURE VALUE OF A MIXED STREAM	
2	Interest rate, pct/year	8%
3	Year	Year-End Cash Flow
4	1	$11,500
5	2	$14,000
6	3	$12,900
7	4	$16,000
8	5	$18,000
9	Future value	$83,608.15

Entry in Cell B9 is =–FV(B2,A8,0,NPV(B2,B4:B8)).
The minus sign appears before FV to convert the future value to a positive amount.

PRESENT VALUE OF A MIXED STREAM

Finding the present value of a mixed stream of cash flows is similar to finding the future value of a mixed stream. We determine the present value of each future amount and then add all the individual present values together to find the total present value.

Example 5.13 ▸ Frey Company, a shoe manufacturer, has been offered an opportunity to receive the following mixed stream of cash flows over the next 5 years:

End of year	Cash flow
1	$400
2	800
3	500
4	400
5	300

If the firm must earn at least 9% on its investments, what is the most it should pay for this opportunity? This situation is depicted on the following time line:

Time line for present value of a mixed stream (end-of-year cash flows, discounted at 9% over the corresponding number of years)

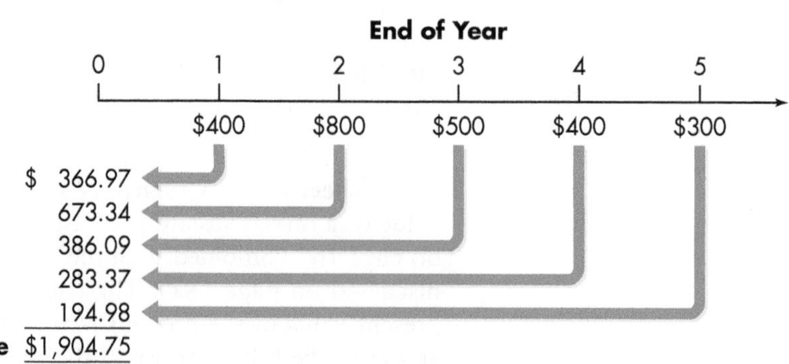

Calculator Use You can use a calculator to find the present value of each individual cash flow, as demonstrated earlier (on page 169), and then sum the present values, to get the present value of the stream. However, most financial calculators have a function that allows you to punch in *all cash flows,* specify the discount rate, and then directly calculate the present value of the entire cash flow stream. The present value of Frey Company's cash flow stream found using a calculator is $1,904.75.

Spreadsheet Use To calculate the present value of a mixed stream in Excel, we will make use of a new function. The syntax of that function is NPV(rate,value1, value2,value3, . . .). The *rate* argument is the interest rate, and *value1, value2,value3, . . .* represent the stream of cash flows. The NPV function assumes that the first payment in the stream arrives one year in the future, and all subsequent payments arrive at one-year intervals. The present value of the mixed stream of future cash flows can be calculated as shown on the following Excel spreadsheet:

	A	B
1	PRESENT VALUE OF A MIXED STREAM OF CASH FLOWS	
2	Interest rate, pct/year	9%
3	Year	Year-End Cash Flow
4	1	$400
5	2	$800
6	3	$500
7	4	$400
8	5	$300
9	Present value	$1,904.75
	Entry in Cell B9 is =NPV(B2,B4:B8).	

→ **REVIEW QUESTION**

5–13 How is the future value of a mixed stream of cash flows calculated? How is the present value of a mixed stream of cash flows calculated?

LG 5

5.5 Compounding Interest More Frequently Than Annually

Interest is often compounded more frequently than once a year. Savings institutions compound interest semiannually, quarterly, monthly, weekly, daily, or even continuously. This section discusses various issues and techniques related to these more frequent compounding intervals.

SEMIANNUAL COMPOUNDING

semiannual compounding
Compounding of interest over two periods within the year.

Semiannual compounding of interest involves two compounding periods within the year. Instead of the stated interest rate being paid once a year, one-half of the stated interest rate is paid twice a year.

TABLE 5.3 Future Value from Investing $100 at 8% Interest Compounded Semiannually over 24 Months (2 Years)

Period	Beginning principal	Future value calculation	Future value at end of period
6 months	$100.00	$100.00 \times (1 + 0.04) =$	$104.00
12 months	104.00	$104.00 \times (1 + 0.04) =$	108.16
18 months	108.16	$108.16 \times (1 + 0.04) =$	112.49
24 months	112.49	$112.49 \times (1 + 0.04) =$	116.99

Personal Finance Example 5.14 ▶ Fred Moreno has decided to invest $100 in a savings account paying 8% interest *compounded semiannually.* If he leaves his money in the account for 24 months (2 years), he will be paid 4% interest compounded over four periods, each of which is 6 months long. Table 5.3 shows that at the end of 12 months (1 year) with 8% semiannual compounding, Fred will have $108.16; at the end of 24 months (2 years), he will have $116.99.

QUARTERLY COMPOUNDING

quarterly compounding
Compounding of interest over four periods within the year.

Quarterly compounding of interest involves four compounding periods within the year. One-fourth of the stated interest rate is paid four times a year.

Personal Finance Example 5.15 ▶ Fred Moreno has found an institution that will pay him 8% interest *compounded quarterly.* If he leaves his money in this account for 24 months (2 years), he will be paid 2% interest compounded over eight periods, each of which is 3 months long. Table 5.4 shows the amount Fred will have at the end of each period. At the end of 12 months (1 year), with 8% quarterly compounding, Fred will have $108.24; at the end of 24 months (2 years), he will have $117.17.

TABLE 5.4 Future Value from Investing $100 at 8% Interest Compounded Quarterly over 24 Months (2 Years)

Period	Beginning principal	Future value calculation	Future value at end of period
3 months	$100.00	$100.00 \times (1 + 0.02) =$	$102.00
6 months	102.00	$102.00 \times (1 + 0.02) =$	104.04
9 months	104.04	$104.04 \times (1 + 0.02) =$	106.12
12 months	106.12	$106.12 \times (1 + 0.02) =$	108.24
15 months	108.24	$108.24 \times (1 + 0.02) =$	110.41
18 months	110.41	$110.41 \times (1 + 0.02) =$	112.62
21 months	112.62	$112.62 \times (1 + 0.02) =$	114.87
24 months	114.87	$114.87 \times (1 + 0.02) =$	117.17

TABLE 5.5 **Future Value at the End of Years 1 and 2 from Investing \$100 at 8% Interest, Given Various Compounding Periods**

	Compounding period		
End of year	**Annual**	**Semiannual**	**Quarterly**
1	\$108.00	\$108.16	\$108.24
2	116.64	116.99	117.17

Table 5.5 compares values for Fred Moreno's \$100 at the end of years 1 and 2 given annual, semiannual, and quarterly compounding periods at the 8 percent rate. The table shows that *the more frequently interest is compounded, the greater the amount of money accumulated.* This is true for *any interest rate* for *any period of time.*

A GENERAL EQUATION FOR COMPOUNDING MORE FREQUENTLY THAN ANNUALLY

The future value formula (Equation 5.4) can be rewritten for use when compounding takes place more frequently. If m equals the number of times per year interest is compounded, the formula for the future value of a lump sum becomes

$$FV_n = PV \times \left(1 + \frac{r}{m}\right)^{m \times n} \tag{5.15}$$

If $m = 1$, Equation 5.15 reduces to Equation 5.4. Thus, if interest compounds annually, Equation 5.15 will provide the same result as Equation 5.4. The general use of Equation 5.15 can be illustrated with a simple example.

Personal Finance Example 5.16 ▸ The preceding examples calculated the amount that Fred Moreno would have at the end of 2 years if he deposited \$100 at 8% interest compounded semiannually and compounded quarterly. For semiannual compounding, m would equal 2 in Equation 5.15; for quarterly compounding, m would equal 4. Substituting the appropriate values for semiannual and quarterly compounding into Equation 5.14, we find that

1. *For semiannual compounding:*

$$FV_2 = \$100 \times \left(1 + \frac{0.08}{2}\right)^{2 \times 2} = \$100 \times (1 + 0.04)^4 = \$116.99$$

2. *For quarterly compounding:*

$$FV_2 = \$100 \times \left(1 + \frac{0.08}{4}\right)^{4 \times 2} = \$100 \times (1 + 0.02)^8 = \$117.17$$

These results agree with the values for FV_2 in Tables 5.5 and 5.6.

If the interest were compounded monthly, weekly, or daily, m would equal 12, 52, or 365, respectively.

USING COMPUTATIONAL TOOLS FOR COMPOUNDING MORE FREQUENTLY THAN ANNUALLY

As before, we can simplify the process of doing the calculations by using a calculator or spreadsheet program.

Personal Finance Example 5.17 ▸ Fred Moreno wished to find the future value of $100 invested at 8% interest compounded both semiannually and quarterly for 2 years.

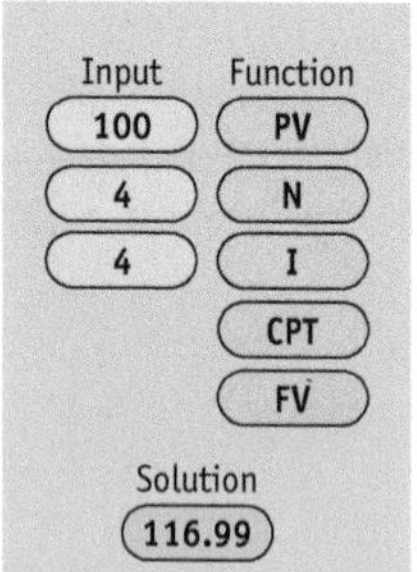

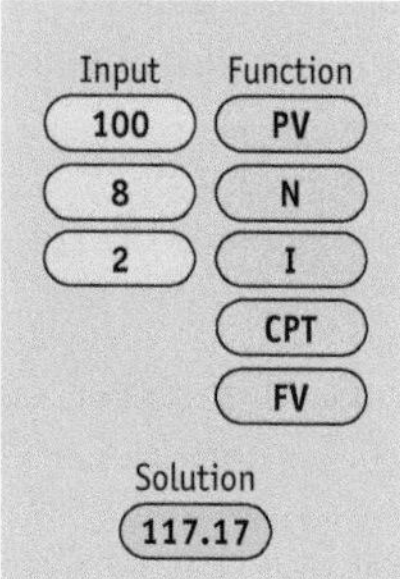

Calculator Use If the calculator were used for the semiannual compounding calculation, the number of periods would be 4 and the interest rate would be 4%. The future value of $116.99 will appear on the calculator display as shown at the top left.

For the quarterly compounding case, the number of periods would be 8 and the interest rate would be 2%. The future value of $117.17 will appear on the calculator display as shown in the second display at the left.

Spreadsheet Use The future value of the single amount with semiannual and quarterly compounding also can be calculated as shown on the following Excel spreadsheet:

	A	B
1	FUTURE VALUE OF A SINGLE AMOUNT WITH SEMIANNUAL AND QUARTERLY COMPOUNDING	
2	Present value	$100
3	Interest rate, pct per year compounded semiannually	8%
4	Number of years	2
5	Future value with semiannual compounding	$116.99
6	Present value	$100
7	Interest rate, pct per year compounded quarterly	8%
8	Number of years	2
9	Future value with quarterly compounding	$117.17

Entry in Cell B5 is =FV(B3/2,B4*2,0,–B2,0).
Entry in Cell B9 is =FV(B7/4,B8*4,0,–B2,0).
The minus sign appears before B2 because the present value is a cash outflow (i.e., a deposit made by Fred Moreno).

CONTINUOUS COMPOUNDING

continuous compounding Compounding of interest an infinite number of times per year at intervals of microseconds.

In the extreme case, interest can be compounded continuously. **Continuous compounding** involves compounding over every nanosecond—the smallest time period imaginable. In this case, m in Equation 5.15 would approach infinity. Through the use of calculus, we know that as m approaches infinity, Equation 5.15 converges to

$$FV_n = (PV) \times (e^{r \times n}) \tag{5.16}$$

where e is the exponential function,[3] which has a value of approximately 2.7183.

3. Most calculators have the exponential function, typically noted by $\mathbf{e^x}$, built into them. The use of this key is especially helpful in calculating future value when interest is compounded continuously.

Personal Finance Example 5.18 ▶ To find the value at the end of 2 years ($n = 2$) of Fred Moreno's \$100 deposit ($PV = \$100$) in an account paying 8% annual interest ($r = 0.08$) compounded continuously, we can substitute into Equation 5.16:

$$\begin{aligned} FV_2 \text{ (continuous compounding)} &= \$100 \times e^{0.08 \times 2} \\ &= \$100 \times 2.7183^{0.16} \\ &= \$100 \times 1.1735 = \$117.35 \end{aligned}$$

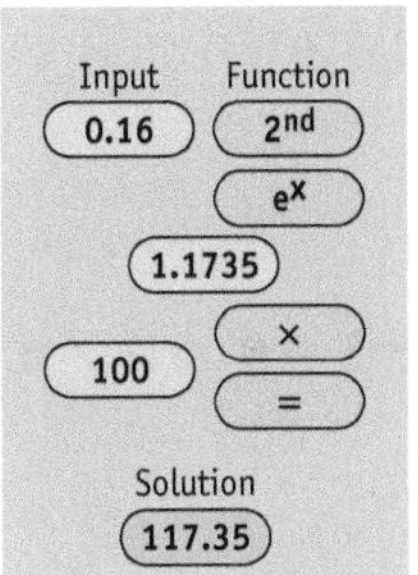

Calculator Use To find this value using the calculator, you need first to find the value of $e^{0.16}$ by punching in 0.16 and then pressing **2nd** and then $\mathbf{e^x}$ to get 1.1735. Next multiply this value by \$100 to get the future value of \$117.35 as shown at the left. (*Note:* On some calculators, you may not have to press **2nd** before pressing $\mathbf{e^x}$.)

Spreadsheet Use The future value of the single amount with continuous compounding of Fred's deposit also can be calculated as shown on the following Excel spreadsheet:

	A	B
1	FUTURE VALUE OF A SINGLE AMOUNT WITH CONTINUOUS COMPOUNDING	
2	Present value	\$100
3	Annual rate of interest, compounded continuously	8%
4	Number of years	2
5	Future value with continuous compounding	\$117.35
	Entry in Cell B5 is =B2*EXP(B3*B4).	

The future value with continuous compounding therefore equals \$117.35. As expected, the continuously compounded value is larger than the future value of interest compounded semiannually (\$116.99) or quarterly (\$117.17). In fact, continuous compounding produces a greater future value than any other compounding frequency.

NOMINAL AND EFFECTIVE ANNUAL RATES OF INTEREST

nominal (stated) annual rate
Contractual annual rate of interest charged by a lender or promised by a borrower.

effective (true) annual rate (EAR)
The annual rate of interest actually paid or earned.

Both businesses and investors need to make objective comparisons of loan costs or investment returns over different compounding periods. To put interest rates on a common basis, so as to allow comparison, we distinguish between nominal and effective annual rates. The **nominal,** or **stated, annual rate** is the contractual annual rate of interest charged by a lender or promised by a borrower. The **effective,** or **true, annual rate (EAR)** is the annual rate of interest actually paid or earned. The effective annual rate reflects the effects of compounding frequency, whereas the nominal annual rate does not.

Using the notation introduced earlier, we can calculate the effective annual rate, EAR, by substituting values for the nominal annual rate, r, and the compounding frequency, m, into Equation 5.17:

$$EAR = \left(1 + \frac{r}{m}\right)^m - 1 \tag{5.17}$$

We can apply this equation using data from preceding examples.

Personal Finance Example 5.19 ▸ Fred Moreno wishes to find the effective annual rate associated with an 8% nominal annual rate ($r = 0.08$) when interest is compounded (1) annually ($m = 1$); (2) semiannually ($m = 2$); and (3) quarterly ($m = 4$). Substituting these values into Equation 5.17, we get

1. *For annual compounding:*

$$EAR = \left(1 + \frac{0.08}{1}\right)^1 - 1 = (1 + 0.08)^1 - 1 = 1 + 0.08 - 1 = 0.08 = 8\%$$

2. *For semiannual compounding:*

$$EAR = \left(1 + \frac{0.08}{2}\right)^2 - 1 = (1 + 0.04)^2 - 1 = 1.0816 - 1 = 0.0816 = 8.16\%$$

3. *For quarterly compounding:*

$$EAR = \left(1 + \frac{0.08}{4}\right)^4 - 1 = (1 + 0.02)^4 - 1 = 1.0824 - 1 = 0.0824 = 8.24\%$$

These values demonstrate two important points: The first is that nominal and effective annual rates are equivalent for annual compounding. The second is that the effective annual rate increases with increasing compounding frequency, up to a limit that occurs with *continuous compounding.*[4]

---

annual percentage rate (APR)
The *nominal annual rate* of interest, found by multiplying the periodic rate by the number of periods in one year, that must be disclosed to consumers on credit cards and loans as a result of "truth-in-lending laws."

annual percentage yield (APY)
The *effective annual rate* of interest that must be disclosed to consumers by banks on their savings products as a result of "truth-in-savings laws."

For an EAR example related to the "payday loan" business, with discussion of the ethical issues involved, see the *Focus on Ethics* box.

At the consumer level, "truth-in-lending laws" require disclosure on credit card and loan agreements of the **annual percentage rate (APR).** The APR is the *nominal annual rate* found by multiplying the periodic rate by the number of periods in one year. For example, a bank credit card that charges 1.5 percent per month (the periodic rate) would have an APR of 18 percent (1.5% per month × 12 months per year).

"Truth-in-savings laws," on the other hand, require banks to quote the **annual percentage yield (APY)** on their savings products. The APY is the *effective annual rate* a savings product pays. For example, a savings account that pays 0.5 percent per month would have an APY of 6.17 percent $[(1.005)^{12} - 1]$.

---

4. The effective annual rate for this extreme case can be found by using the following equation:

$$EAR \text{ (continuous compounding)} = e^r - 1 \qquad (5.17a)$$

For the 8% nominal annual rate ($r = 0.08$), substitution into Equation 5.24a results in an effective annual rate of

$$e^{0.08} - 1 = 1.0833 - 1 = 0.0833 = 8.33\%$$

in the case of continuous compounding. This is the highest effective annual rate attainable with an 8% nominal rate.

focus on ETHICS

How Fair Is "Check Into Cash"?

in practice In 1993, the first Check Into Cash location opened in Cleveland, Tennessee. Today there are more than 1,100 Check Into Cash centers among an estimated 22,000 payday-advance lenders in the United States. There is no doubt about the demand for such organizations, but the debate continues on the "fairness" of payday-advance loans.

A payday loan is a small, unsecured, short-term loan ranging from $100 to $1,000 (depending on the state) offered by a payday lender such as Check Into Cash. A payday loan can solve temporary cash-flow problems without bouncing a check or incurring late-payment penalties. To receive a payday advance, borrowers simply write a personal post-dated check for the amount they wish to borrow, plus the payday loan fee. Check Into Cash holds their checks until payday when the loans are either paid off in person or the check is presented to the borrowers' bank for payment.

Although payday-advance borrowers usually pay a flat fee in lieu of interest, it is the size of the fee in relation to the amount borrowed that is particularly aggravating to opponents of the payday-advance industry. A typical fee is $15 for every $100 borrowed. Payday advance companies that belong to the Community Financial Services Association of America (CFSA), an organization dedicated to promoting responsible regulation of the industry, limit their member companies to a maximum of four rollovers of the original amount borrowed. Thus, a borrower who rolled over an initial $100 loan for the maximum of four times would accumulate a total of $75 in fees all within a 10-week period. On an annualized basis, the fees would amount to a whopping 391 percent.

An annual rate of 391 percent is a huge cost in relation to interest charged on home equity loans, personal loans, and even credit cards. However, advocates of the payday-advance industry make the following arguments: Most payday loan recipients do so either because funds are unavailable through conventional loans or because the payday loan averts a penalty or bank fee which is, in itself, onerous. According to Check Into Cash, the cost for $100 of overdraft protection is $26.90, a credit card late fee on $100 is $37, and the late/disconnect fee on a $100 utility bill is $46.16. Bankrate.com reports that nonsufficient funds (NSF) fees average $26.90 per occurrence.

A payday advance could be useful, for example, if you have six outstanding checks at the time you are notified that the first check has been returned for insufficient funds and you have been charged an NSF fee of $26. A payday advance could potentially avert subsequent charges of $26 per check for each of the remaining five checks and allow you time to rearrange your finances. When used judiciously, a payday advance can be a viable option to meet a short-term cash flow problem despite its high cost. Used unwisely, or by someone who continuously relies on a payday loan to try to make ends meet, payday advances can seriously harm one's personal finances.

▶ ***The 391 percent mentioned above is an annual nominal rate [15% × (365 ÷ 14)]. Should the 2-week rate (15 percent) be compounded to calculate the effective annual interest rate?***

Quoting loan interest rates at their lower nominal annual rate (the APR) and savings interest rates at the higher effective annual rate (the APY) offers two advantages: It tends to standardize disclosure to consumers, and it enables financial institutions to quote the most attractive interest rates: low loan rates and high savings rates.

→ REVIEW QUESTIONS

5–14 What effect does compounding interest more frequently than annually have on (**a**) future value and (**b**) the *effective annual rate (EAR)*? Why?

5–15 How does the future value of a deposit subject to continuous compounding compare to the value obtained by annual compounding?

5–16 Differentiate between a *nominal annual rate* and an *effective annual rate (EAR)*. Define *annual percentage rate (APR)* and *annual percentage yield (APY)*.

LG 6 5.6 Special Applications of Time Value

Future value and present value techniques have a number of important applications in finance. We'll study four of them in this section: (1) determining deposits needed to accumulate a future sum, (2) loan amortization, (3) finding interest or growth rates, and (4) finding an unknown number of periods.

DETERMINING DEPOSITS NEEDED TO ACCUMULATE A FUTURE SUM

Suppose you want to buy a house 5 years from now, and you estimate that an initial down payment of $30,000 will be required at that time. To accumulate the $30,000, you will wish to make equal annual end-of-year deposits into an account paying annual interest of 6 percent. The solution to this problem is closely related to the process of finding the future value of an annuity. You must determine what size annuity will result in a single amount equal to $30,000 at the end of year 5.

Earlier in the chapter, Equation 5.9 was provided for the future value of an ordinary annuity that made a payment, *CF*, each year. In the current problem, we know the future value we want to achieve, $30,000, but we want to solve for the annual cash payment that we'd have to save to achieve that goal. Solving Equation 5.9 for *CF* gives the following:

$$CF = FV_n \div \left\{ \frac{[(1 + r)^n - 1]}{r} \right\} \tag{5.18}$$

As a practical matter, to solve problems like this one, analysts nearly always use a calculator or Excel as demonstrated in the following example.

Personal Finance Example 5.20 ▶ As just stated, you want to determine the equal annual end-of-year deposits required to accumulate $30,000 at the end of 5 years, given an interest rate of 6%.

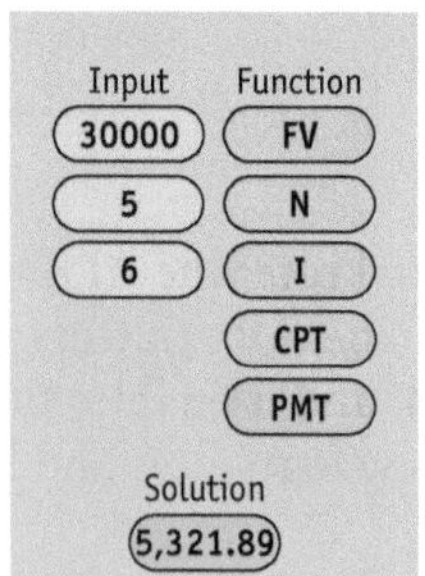

Calculator Use Using the calculator inputs shown at the left, you will find the annual deposit amount to be $5,321.89. Thus, if $5,321.89 is deposited at the end of each year for 5 years at 6% interest, there will be $30,000 in the account at the end of 5 years.

Spreadsheet Use In Excel, solving for the annual cash flow that helps you reach the $30,000 means using the payment function. Its syntax is PMT(rate,nper,pv, fv,type). All of the inputs in this function have been discussed previously. The following Excel spreadsheet illustrates how to use this function to find the annual payment required to save $30,000.

	A	B
1	ANNUAL DEPOSITS NEEDED TO ACCUMULATE A FUTURE SUM	
2	Future value	$30,000
3	Number of years	5
4	Annual rate of interest	6%
5	Annual deposit	$5,321.89
	Entry in Cell B5 is =–PMT(B4,B3,0,B2). The minus sign appears before PMT because the annual deposits are cash outflows.	

LOAN AMORTIZATION

loan amortization
The determination of the equal periodic loan payments necessary to provide a lender with a specified interest return and to repay the loan principal over a specified period.

loan amortization schedule
A schedule of equal payments to repay a loan. It shows the allocation of each loan payment to interest and principal.

The term **loan amortization** refers to the determination of equal periodic loan payments. These payments provide a lender with a specified interest return and repay the loan principal over a specified period. The loan amortization process involves finding the future payments, over the term of the loan, whose present value at the loan interest rate equals the amount of initial principal borrowed. Lenders use a **loan amortization schedule** to determine these payment amounts and the allocation of each payment to interest and principal. In the case of home mortgages, these tables are used to find the equal *monthly* payments necessary to *amortize,* or pay off, the mortgage at a specified interest rate over a 15- to 30-year period.

Amortizing a loan actually involves creating an annuity out of a present amount. For example, say you borrow \$6,000 at 10 percent and agree to make equal annual end-of-year payments over 4 years. To find the size of the payments, the lender determines the amount of a 4-year annuity discounted at 10 percent that has a present value of \$6,000. This process is actually the inverse of finding the present value of an annuity.

Earlier in the chapter, Equation 5.11 demonstrated how to find the present value of an ordinary annuity given information about the number of time periods, the interest rate, and the annuity's periodic payment. We can rearrange that equation to solve for the payment, our objective in this problem:

$$CF = (PV \times r) \div \left[1 - \frac{1}{(1 + r)^n}\right] \tag{5.19}$$

Personal Finance Example 5.21 ▶ As just stated, you want to determine the equal annual end-of-year payments necessary to amortize fully a \$6,000, 10% loan over 4 years.

Input	Function
6000	PV
4	N
10	I
	CPT
	PMT

Solution
1,892.82

Calculator Use Using the calculator inputs shown at the left, you will find the annual payment amount to be \$1,892.82. Thus, to repay the interest and principal on a \$6,000, 10%, 4-year loan, equal annual end-of-year payments of \$1,892.82 are necessary.

The allocation of each loan payment to interest and principal can be seen in columns 3 and 4 of the *loan amortization schedule* in Table 5.6 on page 190. The portion of each payment that represents interest (column 3) declines over the repayment period, and the portion going to principal repayment (column 4) increases. This pattern is typical of amortized loans; as the principal is reduced, the interest component declines, leaving a larger portion of each subsequent loan payment to repay principal.

Spreadsheet Use The annual payment to repay the loan also can be calculated as shown on the first Excel spreadsheet shown on page 190. The amortization schedule, shown in Table 5.6, allocating each loan payment to interest and principal can be calculated precisely as shown on the second spreadsheet on page 190.

TABLE 5.6 Loan Amortization Schedule ($6,000 Principal, 10% Interest, 4-Year Repayment Period)

			Payments		
End of-year	Beginning-of-year principal (1)	Loan payment (2)	Interest [0.10 × (1)] (3)	Principal [(2) − (3)] (4)	End-of-year principal [(1) − (4)] (5)
1	$6,000.00	$1,892.82	$600.00	$1,292.82	$4,707.18
2	4,707.18	1,892.82	470.72	1,422.10	3,285.08
3	3,285.08	1,892.82	328.51	1,564.31	1,721.77
4	1,720.77	1,892.82	172.08	1,720.74	—[a]

[a]Because of rounding, a slight difference ($0.03) exists between the beginning-of-year-4 principal (in column 1) and the year-4 principal payment (in column 4).

	A	B
1	ANNUAL PAYMENT TO REPAY A LOAN	
2	Loan principal (present value)	$6,000
3	Annual rate of interest	10%
4	Number of years	4
5	Annual payment	$1,892.82

Entry in Cell B5 is =–PMT(B3,B4,B2).
The minus sign appears before PMT because the annual payments are cash outflows.

	A	B	C	D	E
1	LOAN AMORTIZATION SCHEDULE				
2		Data: Loan principal		$6,000	
3		Annual rate of interest		10%	
4		Number of years		4	
5		Annual Payments			
6	Year	Total	To Interest	To Principal	Year-End Principal
7	0				$6,000.00
8	1	$1,892.82	$600.00	$1,292.82	4,707.18
9	2	$1,892.82	$470.72	$1,422.11	3,285.07
10	3	$1,892.82	$328.51	$1,564.32	1,720.75
11	4	$1,892.82	$172.07	$1,720.75	0.00

Key Cell Entries
Cell B8: =–PMT(D3,D4,D2), copy to B9:B11
Cell C8: =–CUMIPMT(D3,D4,D2,A8,A8,0), copy to C9:C11
Cell D8: =–CUMPRINC(D3,D4,D2,A8,A8,0), copy to D9:D11
Cell E8: =E7–D8, copy to E9:E11
The minus signs appear before the entries in Cells B8, C8, and D8 because these are cash outflows.

To attract buyers who could not immediately afford 15- to 30-year mortgages of equal annual payments, lenders offered mortgages whose interest rates adjusted at certain points. The *Focus on Practice* box discusses how such mortgages have worked out for some "subprime" borrowers.

focus on **PRACTICE**

New Century Brings Trouble for Subprime Mortgages

in practice As the housing market began to boom at the end of the twentieth century and into the early twenty-first, the market share of subprime mortgages climbed from near 0 percent in 1997 to about 20 percent of mortgage originations in 2006. Several factors combined to fuel the rapid growth of lending to borrowers with tarnished credit, including a low interest rate environment, loose underwriting standards, and innovations in mortgage financing such as "affordability programs" to increase rates of homeownership among lower-income borrowers.

Particularly attractive to new home buyers was the hybrid adjustable rate mortgage (ARM), which featured a low introductory interest rate that reset upward after a preset period of time. Interest rates began a steady upward trend beginning in late 2004. In 2006, some $300 billion worth of adjustable ARMs were reset to higher rates. In a market with rising home values, a borrower has the option to refinance the mortgage, using some of the equity created by the home's increasing value to reduce the mortgage payment. But after 2006, home prices started a 3-year slide, so refinancing was not an option for many subprime borrowers. Instead, borrowers in trouble could try to convince their lenders to allow a "short sale," in which the borrower sells the home for whatever the market will bear, and the lender agrees to accept the proceeds from that sale as settlement for the mortgage debt. For lenders and borrowers alike, foreclosure is the last, worst option.

► ***As a reaction to problems in the subprime area, lenders tightened lending standards. What effect do you think this had on the housing market?***

FINDING INTEREST OR GROWTH RATES

It is often necessary to calculate the compound annual interest or *growth rate* (that is, the annual rate of change in values) of a series of cash flows. Examples include finding the interest rate on a loan, the rate of growth in sales, and the rate of growth in earnings. In doing this, we again make use of Equation 5.4. In this case, we want to solve for the interest rate (or growth rate) representing the increase in value of some investment between two time periods. Solving Equation 5.4 for r we have

$$r = \left(\frac{FV_n}{PV}\right)^{1/n} - 1 \qquad (5.20)$$

The simplest situation is one in which an investment's value has increased over time, and you want to know the annual rate of growth (that is, interest) that is represented by the increase in the investment.

Personal Finance Example 5.22 ► Ray Noble purchased an investment four years ago for $1,250. Now it is worth $1,520. What compound annual rate of return has Ray earned on this investment? Plugging the appropriate values into Equation 5.20, we have

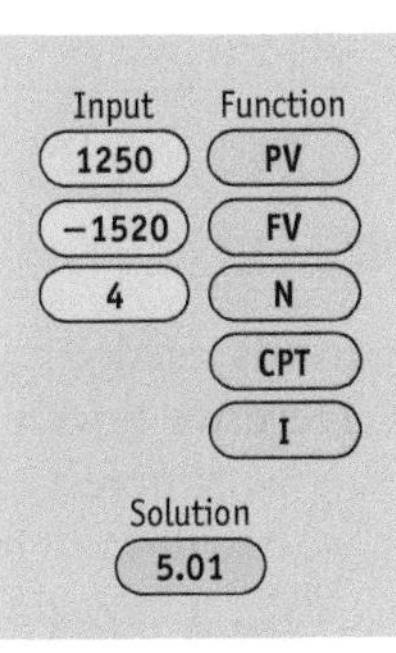

$$r = (\$1{,}520 \div \$1{,}250)^{(1/4)} - 1 = 0.0501 = 5.01\% \text{ per year}$$

Calculator Use Using the calculator to find the interest or growth rate, we treat the earliest value as a present value, PV, and the latest value as a future value, FV_n. (*Note:* Most calculators require *either* the PV or the FV value to be input as a negative number to calculate an unknown interest or growth rate. That approach is used here.) Using the inputs shown at the left, you will find the interest or growth rate to be 5.01%.

Spreadsheet Use The interest or growth rate for the series of cash flows also can be calculated as shown on the following Excel spreadsheet:

	A	B
1	INTEREST OR GROWTH RATE– SERIES OF CASH FLOWS	
2	Year	Cash Flow
3	2008	$1,250
4	2012	$1,520
5	Annual growth rate	5.01%

Entry in Cell B5 is =RATE(A4–A3,0,–B3,B4,0). The expression A4–A3 in the entry calculates the number of years of growth. The minus sign appears before B3 because the investment in 2008 is treated as a cash outflow.

Another type of interest-rate problem involves finding the interest rate associated with an *annuity,* or equal-payment loan.

Personal Finance Example 5.23 ▸ Jan Jacobs can borrow \$2,000 to be repaid in equal annual end-of-year amounts of \$514.14 for the next 5 years. She wants to find the interest rate on this loan.

Input	Function
514.14	PMT
–2000	PV
5	N
	CPT
	I

Solution
9.00

Calculator Use (*Note:* Most calculators require *either* the *PMT* or the *PV* value to be input as a negative number to calculate an unknown interest rate on an equal-payment loan. That approach is used here.) Using the inputs shown at the left, you will find the interest rate to be 9.00%.

Spreadsheet Use The interest or growth rate for the annuity also can be calculated as shown on the following Excel spreadsheet:

	A	B
1	INTEREST OR GROWTH RATE– ANNUITY	
2	Present value (loan principal)	$2,000
3	Number of years	5
4	Annual payments	$514.14
5	Annual interest rate	9.00%

Entry in Cell B5 is =RATE(B3,B4,–B2). The minus sign appears before B2 because the loan principal is treated as a cash outflow.

FINDING AN UNKNOWN NUMBER OF PERIODS

Sometimes it is necessary to calculate the number of time periods needed to generate a given amount of cash flow from an initial amount. Here we briefly consider this calculation for both single amounts and annuities. This simplest case is when a person wishes to determine the number of periods, n, it will take for an initial deposit, PV, to grow to a specified future amount, FV_n, given a stated interest rate, r.

Personal Finance Example 5.24 ▸ Ann Bates wishes to determine the number of years it will take for her initial \$1,000 deposit, earning 8% annual interest, to grow to equal \$2,500. Simply stated, at an 8% annual rate of interest, how many years, *n*, will it take for Ann's \$1,000, *PV*, to grow to \$2,500, FV_n?

Input Function
1000 PV
−2500 FV
8 I
CPT
N
Solution
11.91

Calculator Use Using the calculator, we treat the initial value as the present value, *PV*, and the latest value as the future value, FV_n. (*Note:* Most calculators require *either* the *PV* or the *FV* value to be input as a negative number to calculate an unknown number of periods. That approach is used here.) Using the inputs shown at the left, we find the number of periods to be 11.91 years.

Spreadsheet Use The number of years for the present value to grow to a specified future value can be calculated as shown on the following Excel spreadsheet:

	A	B
1	YEARS FOR A PRESENT VALUE TO GROW TO A SPECIFIED FUTURE VALUE	
2	Present value (deposit)	\$1,000
3	Annual rate of interest, compounded annually	8%
4	Future value	\$2,500
5	Number of years	11.91

Entry in Cell B5 is =NPER(B3,0,B2,–B4).
The minus sign appears before B4 because
the future value is treated as a cash outflow.

Another type of number-of-periods problem involves finding the number of periods associated with an *annuity.* Occasionally we wish to find the unknown life, *n*, of an annuity that is intended to achieve a specific objective, such as repaying a loan of a given amount.

Personal Finance Example 5.25 ▸ Bill Smart can borrow \$25,000 at an 11% annual interest rate; equal, annual, end-of-year payments of \$4,800 are required. He wishes to determine how long it will take to fully repay the loan. In other words, he wishes to determine how many years, *n*, it will take to repay the \$25,000, 11% loan, PV_n, if the payments of \$4,800 are made at the end of each year.

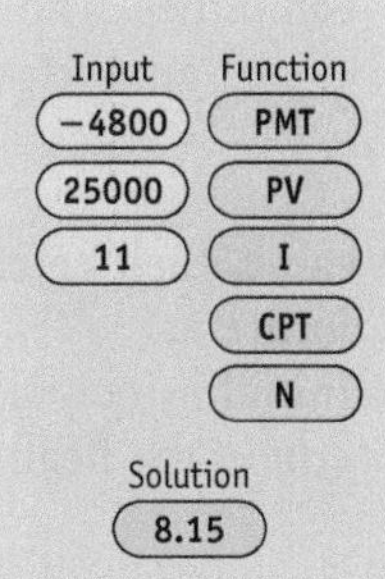

Calculator Use (*Note:* Most calculators require *either* the *PV* or the *PMT* value to be input as a negative number to calculate an unknown number of periods. That approach is used here.) Using the inputs shown at the left, you will find the number of periods to be 8.15 years. This means that after making 8 payments of \$4,800, Bill will still have a small outstanding balance.

Spreadsheet Use The number of years to pay off the loan also can be calculated as shown on the following Excel spreadsheet:

	A	B
1	YEARS TO PAY OFF A LOAN	
2	Annual payment	\$4,800
3	Annual rate of interest, compounded annually	11%
4	Present value (loan principal)	\$25,000
5	Number of years to pay off the loan	8.15

Entry in Cell B5 is =NPER(B3,–B2,B4).
The minus sign appears before B2 because
the payments are treated as cash outflows.

→ **REVIEW QUESTIONS**

5–17 How can you determine the size of the equal, annual, end-of-period deposits necessary to accumulate a certain future sum at the end of a specified future period at a given annual interest rate?

5–18 Describe the procedure used to amortize a loan into a series of equal periodic payments.

5–19 How can you determine the unknown number of periods when you know the present and future values—single amount or annuity—and the applicable rate of interest?

Summary

FOCUS ON VALUE

Time value of money is an important tool that financial managers and other market participants use to assess the effects of proposed actions. Because firms have long lives and some decisions affect their long-term cash flows, the effective application of time-value-of-money techniques is extremely important. These techniques enable financial managers to evaluate cash flows occurring at different times so as to combine, compare, and evaluate them and link them to the firm's **overall goal of share price maximization.** It will become clear in Chapters 6 and 7 that the application of time value techniques is a key part of the value determination process needed to make intelligent value-creating decisions.

REVIEW OF LEARNING GOALS

LG 1 **Discuss the role of time value in finance, the use of computational tools, and the basic patterns of cash flow.** Financial managers and investors use time-value-of-money techniques when assessing the value of expected cash flow streams. Alternatives can be assessed by either compounding to find future value or discounting to find present value. Financial managers rely primarily on present value techniques. Financial calculators, electronic spreadsheets, and financial tables can streamline the application of time value techniques. The cash flow of a firm can be described by its pattern—single amount, annuity, or mixed stream.

LG 2 **Understand the concepts of future value and present value, their calculation for single amounts, and the relationship between them.** Future value (FV) relies on compound interest to measure future amounts. The initial principal or deposit in one period, along with the interest earned on it, becomes the beginning principal of the following period.

The present value (PV) of a future amount is the amount of money today that is equivalent to the given future amount, considering the return that can be earned. Present value is the inverse of future value.

LG 3 **Find the future value and the present value of both an ordinary annuity and an annuity due, and find the present value of a perpetuity.** An annuity is a pattern of equal periodic cash flows. For an ordinary annuity, the cash flows occur at the end of the period. For an annuity due, cash flows occur at the beginning of the period.

The future or present value of an ordinary annuity can be found by using algebraic equations, a financial calculator, or a spreadsheet program. The value of an annuity due is always $r\%$ greater than the value of an identical annuity. The present value of a perpetuity—an infinite-lived annuity—equals the annual cash payment divided by the discount rate.

LG 4 **Calculate both the future value and the present value of a mixed stream of cash flows.** A mixed stream of cash flows is a stream of unequal periodic cash flows that reflect no particular pattern. The future value of a mixed stream of cash flows is the sum of the future values of each individual cash flow. Similarly, the present value of a mixed stream of cash flows is the sum of the present values of the individual cash flows.

LG 5 **Understand the effect that compounding interest more frequently than annually has on future value and on the effective annual rate of interest.** Interest can be compounded at intervals ranging from annually to daily and even continuously. The more often interest is compounded, the larger the future amount that will be accumulated, and the higher the effective, or true, annual rate (EAR).

The annual percentage rate (APR)—a nominal annual rate—is quoted on credit cards and loans. The annual percentage yield (APY)—an effective annual rate—is quoted on savings products.

LG 6 **Describe the procedures involved in (1) determining deposits needed to accumulate a future sum, (2) loan amortization, (3) finding interest or growth rates, and (4) finding an unknown number of periods.** (1) The periodic deposit to accumulate a given future sum can be found by solving the equation for the future value of an annuity for the annual payment. (2) A loan can be amortized into equal periodic payments by solving the equation for the present value of an annuity for the periodic payment. (3) Interest or growth rates can be estimated by finding the unknown interest rate in the equation for the present value of a single amount or an annuity. (4) The number of periods can be estimated by finding the unknown number of periods in the equation for the present value of a single amount or an annuity.

Opener-in-Review

In the chapter opener you learned that it costs Eli Lilly close to $1 billion to bring a new drug to market, and by the time all of the R&D and clinical trials are completed, Lilly may have fewer than 10 years left to sell the drug under patent protection.

Assume that the $1 billion cost of bringing a new drug to market is spread out evenly over 10 years, and then 10 years remain for Lilly to recover their investment. How much cash would a new drug have to generate in the last 10 years to justify the $1 billion spent in the first 10 years? Assume that Lilly uses a required rate of return of 10%.

Self-Test Problems (Solutions in Appendix)

LG 2 LG 5 **ST5–1** **Future values for various compounding frequencies** Delia Martin has $10,000 that she can deposit in any of three savings accounts for a 3-year period. Bank A compounds interest on an annual basis, bank B compounds interest twice each year, and bank C compounds interest each quarter. All three banks have a stated annual interest rate of 4%.

a. What amount would Ms. Martin have at the end of the third year, leaving all interest paid on deposit, in each bank?

b. What *effective annual rate* (*EAR*) would she earn in each of the banks?

c. On the basis of your findings in parts **a** and **b,** which bank should Ms. Martin deal with? Why?

d. If a fourth bank (bank D), also with a 4% stated interest rate, compounds interest continuously, how much would Ms. Martin have at the end of the third year? Does this alternative change your recommendation in part **c**? Explain why or why not.

LG 3 **ST5–2** **Future values of annuities** Ramesh Abdul wishes to choose the better of two equally costly cash flow streams: annuity X and annuity Y. X is an *annuity due* with a cash inflow of $9,000 for each of 6 years. Y is an *ordinary annuity* with a cash inflow of $10,000 for each of 6 years. Assume that Ramesh can earn 15% on his investments.

a. On a purely subjective basis, which annuity do you think is more attractive? Why?

b. Find the future value at the end of year 6 for both annuities.

c. Use your finding in part **b** to indicate which annuity is more attractive. Why? Compare your finding to your subjective response in part **a.**

LG 2 LG 3 LG 4 **ST5–3** **Present values of single amounts and streams** You have a choice of accepting either of two 5-year cash flow streams or single amounts. One cash flow stream is an ordinary annuity, and the other is a mixed stream. You may accept alternative A or B—either as a cash flow stream or as a single amount. Given the cash flow stream and single amounts associated with each (see the following table), and assuming a 9% opportunity cost, which alternative (A or B) and in which form (cash flow stream or single amount) would you prefer?

	Cash flow stream	
End of year	**Alternative A**	**Alternative B**
1	$700	$1,100
2	700	900
3	700	700
4	700	500
5	700	300
	Single amount	
At time zero	$2,825	$2,800

LG 6 **ST5–4** **Deposits needed to accumulate a future sum** Judi Janson wishes to accumulate $8,000 by the end of 5 years by making equal, annual, end-of-year deposits over the next 5 years. If Judi can earn 7% on her investments, how much must she deposit at the *end of each year* to meet this goal?

Warm-Up Exercises

All problems are available in myfinancelab.

LG 2 **E5–1** Assume a firm makes a $2,500 deposit into its money market account. If this account is currently paying 0.7% (yes, that's right, less than 1%!), what will the account balance be after 1 year?

LG 2 LG 5 **E5–2** If Bob and Judy combine their savings of $1,260 and $975, respectively, and deposit this amount into an account that pays 2% annual interest, compounded monthly, what will the account balance be after 4 years?

LG 3 **E5–3** Gabrielle just won $2.5 million in the state lottery. She is given the option of receiving a total of $1.3 million now, or she can elect to be paid $100,000 at the end of each of the next 25 years. If Gabrielle can earn 5% annually on her investments, from a strict economic point of view which option should she take?

LG 4 **E5–4** Your firm has the option of making an investment in new software that will cost $130,000 today and is estimated to provide the savings shown in the following table over its 5-year life:

Year	Savings estimate
1	$35,000
2	50,000
3	45,000
4	25,000
5	15,000

Should the firm make this investment if it requires a minimum annual return of 9% on all investments?

LG 5 **E5–5** Joseph is a friend of yours. He has plenty of money but little financial sense. He received a gift of $12,000 for his recent graduation and is looking for a bank in which to deposit the funds. Partners' Savings Bank offers an account with an annual interest rate of 3% compounded semiannually, while Selwyn's offers an account with a 2.75% annual interest rate compounded continuously. Calculate the value of the two accounts at the end of one year, and recommend to Joseph which account he should choose.

LG 6 **E5–6** Jack and Jill have just had their first child. If college is expected to cost $150,000 per year in 18 years, how much should the couple begin depositing annually at the end of each year to accumulate enough funds to pay the first year's tuition at the beginning of the 19th year? Assume that they can earn a 6% annual rate of return on their investment.

Problems

All problems are available in myfinancelab.

LG 1 **P5–1 Using a time line** The financial manager at Starbuck Industries is considering an investment that requires an initial outlay of \$25,000 and is expected to result in cash inflows of \$3,000 at the end of year 1, \$6,000 at the end of years 2 and 3, \$10,000 at the end of year 4, \$8,000 at the end of year 5, and \$7,000 at the end of year 6.

a. Draw and label a time line depicting the cash flows associated with Starbuck Industries' proposed investment.

b. Use arrows to demonstrate, on the time line in part **a,** how compounding to find future value can be used to measure all cash flows at the end of year 6.

c. Use arrows to demonstrate, on the time line in part **b,** how discounting to find present value can be used to measure all cash flows at time zero.

d. Which of the approaches—*future value* or *present value*—do financial managers rely on most often for decision making? Why?

LG 2 **P5–2 Future value calculation** *Without referring to the preprogrammed function on your financial calculator,* use the basic formula for future value along with the given interest rate, r, and the number of periods, n, to calculate the future value of \$1 in each of the cases shown in the following table.

Case	Interest rate, r	Number of periods, n
A	12%	2
B	6	3
C	9	2
D	3	4

LG 1 **P5–3 Future value** You have \$100 to invest. If you can earn 12% interest, about how long does it take for your \$100 investment to grow to \$200? Suppose the interest rate is just half that, at 6%. At half the interest rate, does it take twice as long to double your money? Why or why not? How long does it take?

LG 2 **P5–4 Future values** For each of the cases shown in the following table, calculate the future value of the single cash flow deposited today at the end of the deposit period if the interest is compounded annually at the rate specified.

Case	Single cash flow	Interest rate	Deposit period (years)
A	\$ 200	5%	20
B	4,500	8	7
C	10,000	9	10
D	25,000	10	12
E	37,000	11	5
F	40,000	12	9

Personal Finance Problem

LG 2 **P5–5** **Time value** You have $1,500 to invest today at 7% interest compounded annually.

a. Find how much you will have accumulated in the account at the end of (1) 3 years, (2) 6 years, and (3) 9 years.

b. Use your findings in part **a** to calculate the amount of interest earned in (1) the first 3 years (years 1 to 3), (2) the second 3 years (years 4 to 6), and (3) the third 3 years (years 7 to 9).

c. Compare and contrast your findings in part **b.** Explain why the amount of interest earned increases in each succeeding 3-year period.

Personal Finance Problem

LG 2 **P5–6** **Time value** As part of your financial planning, you wish to purchase a new car exactly 5 years from today. The car you wish to purchase costs $14,000 today, and your research indicates that its price will increase by 2% to 4% per year over the next 5 years.

a. Estimate the price of the car at the end of 5 years if inflation is (1) 2% per year and (2) 4% per year.

b. How much more expensive will the car be if the rate of inflation is 4% rather than 2%?

c. Estimate the price of the car if inflation is 2% for the next 2 years and 4% for 3 years after that.

Personal Finance Problem

LG 2 **P5–7** **Time value** You can deposit $10,000 into an account paying 9% annual interest either today or exactly 10 years from today. How much better off will you be at the end of 40 years if you decide to make the initial deposit today rather than 10 years from today?

Personal Finance Problem

LG 2 **P5–8** **Time value** Misty needs to have $15,000 at the end of 5 years to fulfill her goal of purchasing a small sailboat. She is willing to invest a lump sum today and leave the money untouched for 5 years until it grows to $15,000, but she wonders what sort of investment return she will need to earn to reach her goal. Use your calculator or spreadsheet to figure out the approximate annually compounded rate of return needed in each of these cases:

a. Misty can invest $10,200 today.

b. Misty can invest $8,150 today.

c. Misty can invest $7,150 today.

Personal Finance Problem

LG 2 **P5–9** **Single-payment loan repayment** A person borrows $200 to be repaid in 8 years with 14% annually compounded interest. The loan may be repaid at the end of any earlier year with no prepayment penalty.

a. What amount will be due if the loan is repaid at the end of year 1?

b. What is the repayment at the end of year 4?

c. What amount is due at the end of the eighth year?

LG 2 **P5–10** **Present value calculation** *Without referring to the preprogrammed function on your financial calculator*, use the basic formula for present value, along with the given opportunity cost, r, and the number of periods, n, to calculate the present value of $1 in each of the cases shown in the following table.

Case	Opportunity cost, r	Number of periods, n
A	2%	4
B	10	2
C	5	3
D	13	2

LG 2 **P5–11 Present values** For each of the cases shown in the following table, calculate the present value of the cash flow, discounting at the rate given and assuming that the cash flow is received at the end of the period noted.

Case	Single cash flow	Discount rate	End of period (years)
A	$ 7,000	12%	4
B	28,000	8	20
C	10,000	14	12
D	150,000	11	6
E	45,000	20	8

LG 2 **P5–12 Present value concept** Answer each of the following questions.

a. What single investment made today, earning 12% annual interest, will be worth $6,000 at the end of 6 years?

b. What is the present value of $6,000 to be received at the end of 6 years if the discount rate is 12%?

c. What is the most you would pay today for a promise to repay you $6,000 at the end of 6 years if your opportunity cost is 12%?

d. Compare, contrast, and discuss your findings in parts **a** through **c.**

Personal Finance Problem

LG 2 **P5–13 Time value** Jim Nance has been offered an investment that will pay him $500 three years from today.

a. If his opportunity cost is 7% compounded annually, what value should he place on this opportunity today?

b. What is the most he should pay to purchase this payment today?

c. If Jim can purchase this investment for less than the amount calculated in part **a,** what does that imply about the rate of return that he will earn on the investment?

LG 2 **P5–14 Time value** An Iowa state savings bond can be converted to $100 at maturity 6 years from purchase. If the state bonds are to be competitive with U.S. savings bonds, which pay 8% annual interest (compounded annually), at what price must the state sell its bonds? Assume no cash payments on savings bonds prior to redemption.

Personal Finance Problem

LG 2 **P5–15 Time value and discount rates** You just won a lottery that promises to pay you $1,000,000 exactly 10 years from today. Because the $1,000,000 payment is guaranteed by the state in which you live, opportunities exist to sell the claim today for an immediate single cash payment.

a. What is the least you will sell your claim for if you can earn the following rates of return on similar-risk investments during the 10-year period?
(1) 6%
(2) 9%
(3) 12%
b. Rework part **a** under the assumption that the $1,000,000 payment will be received in 15 rather than 10 years.
c. On the basis of your findings in parts **a** and **b,** discuss the effect of both the size of the rate of return and the time until receipt of payment on the present value of a future sum.

Personal Finance Problem

LG 2 **P5–16 Time value comparisons of single amounts** In exchange for a $20,000 payment today, a well-known company will allow you to choose *one* of the alternatives shown in the following table. Your opportunity cost is 11%.

Alternative	Single amount
A	$28,500 at end of 3 years
B	$54,000 at end of 9 years
C	$160,000 at end of 20 years

a. Find the value today of each alternative.
b. Are all the alternatives acceptable—that is, worth $20,000 today?
c. Which alternative, if any, will you take?

Personal Finance Problem

LG 2 **P5–17 Cash flow investment decision** Tom Alexander has an opportunity to purchase any of the investments shown in the following table. The purchase price, the amount of the single cash inflow, and its year of receipt are given for each investment. Which purchase recommendations would you make, assuming that Tom can earn 10% on his investments?

Investment	Price	Single cash inflow	Year of receipt
A	$18,000	$30,000	5
B	600	3,000	20
C	3,500	10,000	10
D	1,000	15,000	40

LG 2 **P5–18 Calculating deposit needed** You put $10,000 in an account earning 5%. After 3 years, you make another deposit into the same account. Four years later (that is, 7 years after your original $10,000 deposit), the account balance is $20,000. What was the amount of the deposit at the end of year 3?

LG 3 **P5–19 Future value of an annuity** For each case in the accompanying table, answer the questions that follow.

Case	Amount of annuity	Interest rate	Deposit period (years)
A	$ 2,500	8%	10
B	500	12	6
C	30,000	20	5
D	11,500	9	8
E	6,000	14	30

a. Calculate the future value of the annuity assuming that it is
(1) An ordinary annuity.
(2) An annuity due.

b. Compare your findings in parts **a**(1) and **a**(2). All else being identical, which type of annuity—ordinary or annuity due—is preferable? Explain why.

LG 3 **P5-20 Present value of an annuity** Consider the following cases.

Case	Amount of annuity	Interest rate	Period (years)
A	$ 12,000	7%	3
B	55,000	12	15
C	700	20	9
D	140,000	5	7
E	22,500	10	5

a. Calculate the present value of the annuity assuming that it is
(1) An ordinary annuity.
(2) An annuity due.

b. Compare your findings in parts **a**(1) and **a**(2). All else being identical, which type of annuity—ordinary or annuity due—is preferable? Explain why.

Personal Finance Problem

LG 3 **P5–21 Time value—Annuities** Marian Kirk wishes to select the better of two 10-year annuities, C and D. Annuity C is an *ordinary annuity* of $2,500 per year for 10 years. Annuity D is an *annuity due* of $2,200 per year for 10 years.

a. Find the *future value* of both annuities at the end of year 10, assuming that Marian can earn (1) 10% annual interest and (2) 20% annual interest.

b. Use your findings in part **a** to indicate which annuity has the greater future value at the end of year 10 for both the (1) 10% and (2) 20% interest rates.

c. Find the *present value* of both annuities, assuming that Marian can earn (1) 10% annual interest and (2) 20% annual interest.

d. Use your findings in part **c** to indicate which annuity has the greater present value for both (1) 10% and (2) 20% interest rates.

e. Briefly compare, contrast, and explain any differences between your findings using the 10% and 20% interest rates in parts **b** and **d.**

Personal Finance Problem

LG 3 **P5–22** **Retirement planning** Hal Thomas, a 25-year-old college graduate, wishes to retire at age 65. To supplement other sources of retirement income, he can deposit $2,000 each year into a tax-deferred individual retirement arrangement (IRA). The IRA will earn a 10% return over the next 40 years.

a. If Hal makes annual end-of-year $2,000 deposits into the IRA, how much will he have accumulated by the end of his sixty-fifth year?

b. If Hal decides to wait until age 35 to begin making annual end-of-year $2,000 deposits into the IRA, how much will he have accumulated by the end of his sixty-fifth year?

c. Using your findings in parts **a** and **b,** discuss the impact of delaying making deposits into the IRA for 10 years (age 25 to age 35) on the amount accumulated by the end of Hal's sixty-fifth year.

d. Rework parts **a, b,** and **c,** assuming that Hal makes all deposits at the beginning, rather than the end, of each year. Discuss the effect of beginning-of-year deposits on the future value accumulated by the end of Hal's sixty-fifth year.

Personal Finance Problem

LG 3 **P5–23** **Value of a retirement annuity** An insurance agent is trying to sell you an immediate-retirement annuity, which for a single amount paid today will provide you with $12,000 at the end of each year for the next 25 years. You currently earn 9% on low-risk investments comparable to the retirement annuity. Ignoring taxes, what is the most you would pay for this annuity?

Personal Finance Problem

LG 2 LG 3 **P5–24** **Funding your retirement** You plan to retire in exactly 20 years. Your goal is to create a fund that will allow you to receive $20,000 at the end of each year for the 30 years between retirement and death (a psychic told you would die exactly 30 years after you retire). You know that you will be able to earn 11% per year during the 30-year retirement period.

a. How large a fund will you need *when you retire* in 20 years to provide the 30-year, $20,000 retirement annuity?

b. How much will you need *today* as a single amount to provide the fund calculated in part **a** if you earn only 9% per year during the 20 years preceding retirement?

c. What effect would an increase in the rate you can earn both during and prior to retirement have on the values found in parts **a** and **b**? Explain.

d. Now assume that you will earn 10% from now through the end of your retirement. You want to make 20 end-of-year deposits into your retirement account that will fund the 30-year stream of $20,000 annual annuity payments. How large do your annual deposits have to be?

Personal Finance Problem

LG 2 LG 3 **P5–25** **Value of an annuity versus a single amount** Assume that you just won the state lottery. Your prize can be taken either in the form of $40,000 at the end of each of the next 25 years (that is, $1,000,000 over 25 years) or as a single amount of $500,000 paid immediately.

a. If you expect to be able to earn 5% annually on your investments over the next 25 years, ignoring taxes and other considerations, which alternative should you take? Why?

b. Would your decision in part **a** change if you could earn 7% rather than 5% on your investments over the next 25 years? Why?

c. On a strictly economic basis, at approximately what earnings rate would you be indifferent between the two plans?

LG 3 **P5–26 Perpetuities** Consider the data in the following table.

Perpetuity	Annual amount	Discount rate
A	$ 20,000	8%
B	100,000	10
C	3,000	6
D	60,000	5

Determine the present value of each perpetuity.

Personal Finance Problem

LG 3 **P5–27 Creating an endowment** On completion of her introductory finance course, Marla Lee was so pleased with the amount of useful and interesting knowledge she gained that she convinced her parents, who were wealthy alumni of the university she was attending, to create an endowment. The endowment is to allow three needy students to take the introductory finance course each year in perpetuity. The guaranteed annual cost of tuition and books for the course is $600 per student. The endowment will be created by making a single payment to the university. The university expects to earn exactly 6% per year on these funds.

a. How large an initial single payment must Marla's parents make to the university to fund the endowment?

b. What amount would be needed to fund the endowment if the university could earn 9% rather than 6% per year on the funds?

LG 4 **P5–28 Value of a mixed stream** For each of the mixed streams of cash flows shown in the following table, determine the future value at the end of the final year if deposits are made into an account paying annual interest of 12%, assuming that no withdrawals are made during the period and that the deposits are made:

a. At the *end* of each year.

b. At the *beginning* of each year.

	Cash flow stream		
Year	A	B	C
1	$ 900	$30,000	$1,200
2	1,000	25,000	1,200
3	1,200	20,000	1,000
4		10,000	1,900
5		5,000	

Personal Finance Problem

LG 4 **P5–29** **Value of a single amount versus a mixed stream** Gina Vitale has just contracted to sell a small parcel of land that she inherited a few years ago. The buyer is willing to pay $24,000 at the closing of the transaction or will pay the amounts shown in the following table at the *beginning* of each of the next 5 years. Because Gina doesn't really need the money today, she plans to let it accumulate in an account that earns 7% annual interest. Given her desire to buy a house at the end of 5 years after closing on the sale of the lot, she decides to choose the payment alternative—$24,000 single amount or the mixed stream of payments in the following table—that provides the higher future value at the end of 5 years. Which alternative will she choose?

Mixed stream	
Beginning of year	**Cash flow**
1	$ 2,000
2	4,000
3	6,000
4	8,000
5	10,000

LG 4 **P5-30** **Value of mixed streams** Find the present value of the streams of cash flows shown in the following table. Assume that the firm's opportunity cost is 12%.

A		B		C	
Year	**Cash flow**	**Year**	**Cash flow**	**Year**	**Cash flow**
1	–$2,000	1	$10,000	1–5	$10,000/yr
2	3,000	2–5	5,000/yr	6–10	8,000/yr
3	4,000	6	7,000		
4	6,000				
5	8,000				

LG 4 **P5–31** **Present value—Mixed streams** Consider the mixed streams of cash flows shown in the following table.

	Cash flow stream	
Year	**A**	**B**
1	$ 50,000	$ 10,000
2	40,000	20,000
3	30,000	30,000
4	20,000	40,000
5	10,000	50,000
Totals	$150,000	$150,000

a. Find the present value of each stream using a 15% discount rate.
b. Compare the calculated present values and discuss them in light of the fact that the undiscounted cash flows total $150,000 in each case.

LG 1 LG 4 **P5–32 Value of a mixed stream** Harte Systems, Inc., a maker of electronic surveillance equipment, is considering selling to a well-known hardware chain the rights to market its home security system. The proposed deal calls for the hardware chain to pay Harte $30,000 and $25,000 at the end of years 1 and 2 and to make annual year-end payments of $15,000 in years 3 through 9. A final payment to Harte of $10,000 would be due at the end of year 10.
a. Lay out the cash flows involved in the offer on a time line.
b. If Harte applies a required rate of return of 12% to them, what is the present value of this series of payments?
c. A second company has offered Harte an immediate one-time payment of $100,000 for the rights to market the home security system. Which offer should Harte accept?

Personal Finance Problem

LG 4 **P5–33 Funding budget shortfalls** As part of your personal budgeting process, you have determined that in each of the next 5 years you will have budget shortfalls. In other words, you will need the amounts shown in the following table at the end of the given year to balance your budget—that is, to make inflows equal outflows. You expect to be able to earn 8% on your investments during the next 5 years and wish to fund the budget shortfalls over the next 5 years with a single amount.

End of year	Budget shortfall
1	$ 5,000
2	4,000
3	6,000
4	10,000
5	3,000

a. How large must the single deposit today into an account paying 8% annual interest be to provide for full coverage of the anticipated budget shortfalls?
b. What effect would an increase in your earnings rate have on the amount calculated in part **a?** Explain.

LG 4 **P5–34 Relationship between future value and present value—Mixed stream** Using the information in the accompanying table, answer the questions that follow.

Year (*t*)	Cash flow
1	$ 800
2	900
3	1,000
4	1,500
5	2,000

a. Determine the *present value* of the mixed stream of cash flows using a 5% discount rate.
b. How much would you be willing to pay for an opportunity to buy this stream, assuming that you can at best earn 5% on your investments?
c. What effect, if any, would a 7% rather than a 5% opportunity cost have on your analysis? (Explain verbally.)

LG 4 **P5–35 Relationship between future value and present value—Mixed stream** The table below shows a mixed cash flow stream, except that the cash flow for year 3 is missing.

Year 1	$10,000
Year 2	5,000
Year 3	
Year 4	20,000
Year 5	3,000

Suppose that somehow you know that the present value of the entire stream is $32,911.03, and the discount rate is 4%. What is the amount of the missing cash flow in year 3?

LG 5 **P5–36 Changing compounding frequency** Using annual, semiannual, and quarterly compounding periods for each of the following, (1) calculate the future value if $5,000 is deposited initially, and (2) determine the *effective annual rate* (*EAR*).
a. At 12% annual interest for 5 years.
b. At 16% annual interest for 6 years.
c. At 20% annual interest for 10 years.

LG 5 **P5–37 Compounding frequency, time value, and effective annual rates** For each of the cases in the following table:
a. Calculate the future value at the end of the specified deposit period.
b. Determine the *effective annual rate, EAR*.
c. Compare the nominal annual rate, r, to the effective annual rate, EAR. What relationship exists between compounding frequency and the nominal and effective annual rates?

Case	Amount of initial deposit	Nominal annual rate, r	Compounding frequency, m (times/year)	Deposit period (years)
A	$ 2,500	6%	2	5
B	50,000	12	6	3
C	1,000	5	1	10
D	20,000	16	4	6

LG 5 **P5–38 Continuous compounding** For each of the cases in the following table, find the future value at the end of the deposit period, assuming that interest is compounded continuously at the given nominal annual rate.

Case	Amount of initial deposit	Nominal annual rate, r	Deposit period (years), n
A	$1,000	9%	2
B	600	10	10
C	4,000	8	7
D	2,500	12	4

Personal Finance Problem

LG 5 **P5–39 Compounding frequency and time value** You plan to invest $2,000 in an individual retirement arrangement (IRA) today at a *nominal annual rate* of 8%, which is expected to apply to all future years.

a. How much will you have in the account at the end of 10 years if interest is compounded (1) annually, (2) semiannually, (3) daily (assume a 365-day year), and (4) continuously?

b. What is the *effective annual rate, EAR,* for each compounding period in part **a?**

c. How much greater will your IRA balance be at the end of 10 years if interest is compounded continuously rather than annually?

d. How does the compounding frequency affect the future value and effective annual rate for a given deposit? Explain in terms of your findings in parts **a** through **c.**

Personal Finance Problem

LG 5 **P5–40 Comparing compounding periods** René Levin wishes to determine the future value at the end of 2 years of a $15,000 deposit made today into an account paying a nominal annual rate of 12%.

a. Find the future value of René's deposit, assuming that interest is compounded (1) annually, (2) quarterly, (3) monthly, and (4) continuously.

b. Compare your findings in part **a**, and use them to demonstrate the relationship between compounding frequency and future value.

c. What is the maximum future value obtainable given the $15,000 deposit, the 2-year time period, and the 12% nominal annual rate? Use your findings in part **a** to explain.

Personal Finance Problem

LG 3 LG 5 **P5-41 Annuities and compounding** Janet Boyle intends to deposit $300 per year in a credit union for the next 10 years, and the credit union pays an annual interest rate of 8%.

a. Determine the future value that Janet will have at the end of 10 years, given that end-of-period deposits are made and no interest is withdrawn, if

(1) $300 is deposited annually and the credit union pays interest annually.

(2) $150 is deposited semiannually and the credit union pays interest semiannually.

(3) $75 is deposited quarterly and the credit union pays interest quarterly.

b. Use your finding in part **a** to discuss the effect of more frequent deposits and compounding of interest on the future value of an annuity.

LG 6 **P5–42** **Deposits to accumulate future sums** For each of the cases shown in the following table, determine the amount of the equal, annual, end-of-year deposits necessary to accumulate the given sum at the end of the specified period, assuming the stated annual interest rate.

Case	Sum to be accumulated	Accumulation period (years)	Interest rate
A	$ 5,000	3	12%
B	100,000	20	7
C	30,000	8	10
D	15,000	12	8

Personal Finance Problem

LG 6 **P5–43** **Creating a retirement fund** To supplement your planned retirement in exactly 42 years, you estimate that you need to accumulate $220,000 by the end of 42 years from today. You plan to make equal, annual, end-of-year deposits into an account paying 8% annual interest.

a. How large must the annual deposits be to create the $220,000 fund by the end of 42 years?

b. If you can afford to deposit only $600 per year into the account, how much will you have accumulated by the end of the forty-second year?

Personal Finance Problem

LG 6 **P5–44** **Accumulating a growing future sum** A retirement home at Deer Trail Estates now costs $185,000. Inflation is expected to cause this price to increase at 6% per year over the 20 years before C. L. Donovan retires. How large an equal, annual, end-of-year deposit must be made each year into an account paying an annual interest rate of 10% for Donovan to have the cash needed to purchase a home at retirement?

Personal Finance Problem

LG 3 LG 6 **P5–45** **Deposits to create a perpetuity** You have decided to endow your favorite university with a scholarship. It is expected to cost $6,000 per year to attend the university into perpetuity. You expect to give the university the endowment in 10 years and will accumulate it by making equal annual (end-of-year) deposits into an account. The rate of interest is expected to be 10% for all future time periods.

a. How large must the endowment be?

b. How much must you deposit at the end of each of the next 10 years to accumulate the required amount?

Personal Finance Problem

LG 2 LG 3 LG 6 **P5–46** **Inflation, time value, and annual deposits** While vacationing in Florida, John Kelley saw the vacation home of his dreams. It was listed with a sale price of $200,000. The only catch is that John is 40 years old and plans to continue working until he is 65. Still, he believes that prices generally increase at the overall rate of inflation. John believes that he can earn 9% annually after taxes on his investments. He is willing to invest a fixed amount at the end of each of the next 25 years to fund the cash purchase of such a house (one that can be purchased today for $200,000) when he retires.

a. Inflation is expected to average 5% per year for the next 25 years. What will John's dream house cost when he retires?
b. How much must John invest at the *end* of each of the next 25 years to have the cash purchase price of the house when he retires?
c. If John invests at the *beginning* instead of at the end of each of the next 25 years, how much must he invest each year?

LG 6 **P5–47** **Loan payment** Determine the equal, annual, end-of-year payment required each year over the life of the loans shown in the following table to repay them fully during the stated term of the loan.

Loan	Principal	Interest rate	Term of loan (years)
A	$12,000	8%	3
B	60,000	12	10
C	75,000	10	30
D	4,000	15	5

Personal Finance Problem

LG 6 **P5–48** **Loan amortization schedule** Joan Messineo borrowed $15,000 at a 14% annual rate of interest to be repaid over 3 years. The loan is amortized into three equal, annual, end-of-year payments.
a. Calculate the annual, end-of-year loan payment.
b. Prepare a loan amortization schedule showing the interest and principal breakdown of each of the three loan payments.
c. Explain why the interest portion of each payment declines with the passage of time.

LG 6 **P5–49** **Loan interest deductions** Liz Rogers just closed a $10,000 business loan that is to be repaid in three equal, annual, end-of-year payments. The interest rate on the loan is 13%. As part of her firm's detailed financial planning, Liz wishes to determine the annual interest deduction attributable to the loan. (Because it is a business loan, the interest portion of each loan payment is tax-deductible to the business.)
a. Determine the firm's annual loan payment.
b. Prepare an amortization schedule for the loan.
c. How much interest expense will Liz's firm have in *each* of the next 3 years as a result of this loan?

Personal Finance Problem

LG 6 **P5–50** **Monthly loan payments** Tim Smith is shopping for a used car. He has found one priced at $4,500. The dealer has told Tim that if he can come up with a down payment of $500, the dealer will finance the balance of the price at a 12% annual rate over 2 years (24 months).
a. Assuming that Tim accepts the dealer's offer, what will his *monthly* (end-of-month) payment amount be?
b. Use a financial calculator or spreadsheet to help you figure out what Tim's *monthly* payment would be if the dealer were willing to finance the balance of the car price at a 9% annual rate.

LG 6 **P5–51 Growth rates** You are given the series of cash flows shown in the following table.

Year	Cash flows A	B	C
1	$500	$1,500	$2,500
2	560	1,550	2,600
3	640	1,610	2,650
4	720	1,680	2,650
5	800	1,760	2,800
6		1,850	2,850
7		1,950	2,900
8		2,060	
9		2,170	
10		2,280	

a. Calculate the compound annual growth rate between the first and last payment in each stream.

b. If year-1 values represent initial deposits in a savings account paying annual interest, what is the annual rate of interest earned on each account?

c. Compare and discuss the growth rate and interest rate found in parts **a** and **b,** respectively.

Personal Finance Problem

LG 6 **P5–52 Rate of return** Rishi Singh has $1,500 to invest. His investment counselor suggests an investment that pays no stated interest but will return $2,000 at the end of 3 years.

a. What annual rate of return will Rishi earn with this investment?

b. Rishi is considering another investment, of equal risk, that earns an annual return of 8%. Which investment should he make, and why?

Personal Finance Problem

LG 6 **P5–53 Rate of return and investment choice** Clare Jaccard has $5,000 to invest. Because she is only 25 years old, she is not concerned about the length of the investment's life. What she is sensitive to is the rate of return she will earn on the investment. With the help of her financial advisor, Clare has isolated four equally risky investments, each providing a single amount at the end of its life, as shown in the following table. All of the investments require an initial $5,000 payment.

Investment	Single amount	Investment life (years)
A	$ 8,400	6
B	15,900	15
C	7,600	4
D	13,000	10

a. Calculate, to the nearest 1%, the rate of return on each of the four investments available to Clare.

b. Which investment would you recommend to Clare, given her goal of maximizing the rate of return?

LG 6 **P5–54 Rate of return—Annuity** What is the rate of return on an investment of $10,606 if the company will receive $2,000 each year for the next 10 years?

Personal Finance Problem

LG 6 **P5–55 Choosing the best annuity** Raina Herzig wishes to choose the best of four immediate-retirement annuities available to her. In each case, in exchange for paying a single premium today, she will receive equal, annual, end-of-year cash benefits for a specified number of years. She considers the annuities to be equally risky and is not concerned about their differing lives. Her decision will be based solely on the rate of return she will earn on each annuity. The key terms of the four annuities are shown in the following table.

Annuity	Premium paid today	Annual benefit	Life (years)
A	$30,000	$3,100	20
B	25,000	3,900	10
C	40,000	4,200	15
D	35,000	4,000	12

a. Calculate to the nearest 1% the rate of return on each of the four annuities Raina is considering.
b. Given Raina's stated decision criterion, which annuity would you recommend?

Personal Finance Problem

LG 6 **P5–56 Interest rate for an annuity** Anna Waldheim was seriously injured in an industrial accident. She sued the responsible parties and was awarded a judgment of $2,000,000. Today, she and her attorney are attending a settlement conference with the defendants. The defendants have made an initial offer of $156,000 per year for 25 years. Anna plans to counteroffer at $255,000 per year for 25 years. Both the offer and the counteroffer have a present value of $2,000,000, the amount of the judgment. Both assume payments at the end of each year.
a. What interest rate assumption have the defendants used in their offer (rounded to the nearest whole percent)?
b. What interest rate assumption have Anna and her lawyer used in their counteroffer (rounded to the nearest whole percent)?
c. Anna is willing to settle for an annuity that carries an interest rate assumption of 9%. What annual payment would be acceptable to her?

Personal Finance Problem

LG 6 **P5–57 Loan rates of interest** John Flemming has been shopping for a loan to finance the purchase of a used car. He has found three possibilities that seem attractive and wishes to select the one with the lowest interest rate. The information available with respect to each of the three $5,000 loans is shown in the following table.

Loan	Principal	Annual payment	Term (years)
A	$5,000	$1,352.81	5
B	5,000	1,543.21	4
C	5,000	2,010.45	3

a. Determine the interest rate associated with each of the loans.
b. Which loan should John take?

LG 6 **P5–58** **Number of years to equal future amount** For each of the following cases, determine the number of years it will take for the initial deposit to grow to equal the future amount at the given interest rate.

Case	Initial deposit	Future amount	Interest rate
A	$ 300	$ 1,000	7%
B	12,000	15,000	5
C	9,000	20,000	10
D	100	500	9
E	7,500	30,000	15

Personal Finance Problem

LG 6 **P5–59** **Time to accumulate a given sum** Manuel Rios wishes to determine how long it will take an initial deposit of $10,000 to double.

a. If Manuel earns 10% annual interest on the deposit, how long will it take for him to double his money?
b. How long will it take if he earns only 7% annual interest?
c. How long will it take if he can earn 12% annual interest?
d. Reviewing your findings in parts **a, b,** and **c,** indicate what relationship exists between the interest rate and the amount of time it will take Manuel to double his money.

LG 6 **P5–60** **Number of years to provide a given return** In each of the following cases, determine the number of years that the given annual *end-of-year* cash flow must continue to provide the given rate of return on the given initial amount.

Case	Initial amount	Annual cash flow	Rate of return
A	$ 1,000	$ 250	11%
B	150,000	30,000	15
C	80,000	10,000	10
D	600	275	9
E	17,000	3,500	6

Personal Finance Problem

LG 6 **P5–61** **Time to repay installment loan** Mia Salto wishes to determine how long it will take to repay a loan with initial proceeds of $14,000 where annual *end-of-year* installment payments of $2,450 are required.

a. If Mia can borrow at a 12% annual rate of interest, how long will it take for her to repay the loan fully?
b. How long will it take if she can borrow at a 9% annual rate?
c. How long will it take if she has to pay 15% annual interest?
d. Reviewing your answers in parts **a, b,** and **c,** describe the general relationship between the interest rate and the amount of time it will take Mia to repay the loan fully.

LG 6 **P5–62 ETHICS PROBLEM** A manager at a "Check Into Cash" business (see *Focus on Ethics* box on page 187) defends his business practice as simply "charging what the market will bear." "After all," says the manager, "we don't force people to come in the door." How would you respond to this ethical defense of the payday-advance business?

Spreadsheet Exercise

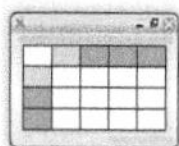

At the end of 2012, Uma Corporation was considering undertaking a major long-term project in an effort to remain competitive in its industry. The production and sales departments determined the potential annual cash flow savings that could accrue to the firm if it acts soon. Specifically, they estimate that a mixed stream of future cash flow savings will occur at the end of the years 2013 through 2018. The years 2019 through 2023 will see consecutive and equal cash flow savings at the end of each year. The firm estimates that its discount rate over the first 6 years will be 7%. The expected discount rate over the years 2019 through 2023 will be 11%.

The project managers will find the project acceptable if it results in present cash flow savings of at least $860,000. The following cash flow savings data are supplied to the finance department for analysis.

End of year	Cash flow savings
2013	$110,000
2014	120,000
2015	130,000
2016	150,000
2017	160,000
2018	150,000
2019	90,000
2020	90,000
2021	90,000
2022	90,000
2023	90,000

TO DO

Create spreadsheets similar to Table 5.2, and then answer the following questions:

a. Determine the value (at the beginning of 2013) of the future cash flow savings expected to be generated by this project.

b. Based solely on the one criterion set by management, should the firm undertake this specific project? Explain.

c. What is the "interest rate risk," and how might it influence the recommendation made in part **b?** Explain.

Visit www.myfinancelab.com for **Chapter Case: *Funding Jill Moran's Retirement Annuity,*** Group Exercises, and numerous online resources.

Integrative Case 2

Track Software, Inc.

Seven years ago, after 15 years in public accounting, Stanley Booker, CPA, resigned his position as manager of cost systems for Davis, Cohen, and O'Brien Public Accountants and started Track Software, Inc. In the 2 years preceding his departure from Davis, Cohen, and O'Brien, Stanley had spent nights and weekends developing a sophisticated cost-accounting software program that became Track's initial product offering. As the firm grew, Stanley planned to develop and expand the software product offerings—all of which would be related to streamlining the accounting processes of medium- to large-sized manufacturers.

Although Track experienced losses during its first 2 years of operation—2006 and 2007—its profit has increased steadily from 2008 to the present (2012). The firm's profit history, including dividend payments and contributions to retained earnings, is summarized in Table 1.

Stanley started the firm with a $100,000 investment—his savings of $50,000 as equity and a $50,000 long-term loan from the bank. He had hoped to maintain his initial 100 percent ownership in the corporation, but after experiencing a $50,000 loss during the first year of operation (2006), he sold 60 percent of the stock to a group of investors to obtain needed funds. Since then, no other stock transactions have taken place. Although he owns only 40 percent of the firm, Stanley actively manages all aspects of its activities; the other stockholders are not active in management of the firm. The firm's stock was valued at $4.50 per share in 2011 and at $5.28 per share in 2012.

TABLE 1

Track Software, Inc.
Profit, Dividends, and Retained Earnings, 2006–2012

Year	Net profits after taxes (1)	Dividends paid (2)	Contribution to retained earnings [(1) − (2)] (3)
2006	($50,000)	$ 0	($50,000)
2007	(20,000)	0	(20,000)
2008	15,000	0	15,000
2009	35,000	0	35,000
2010	40,000	1,000	39,000
2011	43,000	3,000	40,000
2012	48,000	5,000	43,000

Stanley has just prepared the firm's 2012 income statement, balance sheet, and statement of retained earnings, shown in Tables 2, 3, and 4, along with the 2011 balance sheet. In addition, he has compiled the 2011 ratio values and industry average ratio values for 2012, which are applicable to both 2011 and 2012 and are summarized in Table 5 (on page 218). He is quite pleased to have achieved record earnings of $48,000 in 2012, but he is concerned about the firm's cash flows. Specifically, he is finding it more and more difficult to pay the firm's bills in a timely manner and generate cash flows to investors—both creditors and owners. To gain insight into these cash flow problems, Stanley is planning to determine the firm's 2012 operating cash flow (OCF) and free cash flow (FCF).

Stanley is further frustrated by the firm's inability to afford to hire a software developer to complete development of a cost estimation package that is believed to have "blockbuster" sales potential. Stanley began development of this package 2 years ago, but the firm's growing complexity has forced him to devote more of his time to administrative duties, thereby halting the development of this product. Stanley's reluctance to fill this position stems from his concern that the added $80,000 per year in salary and benefits for the position would certainly lower the firm's earnings per share (EPS) over the next couple of years. Although the project's success is in no way guaranteed, Stanley believes that if the money were spent to hire the software developer, the firm's sales and earnings would significantly rise once the 2- to 3-year development, production, and marketing process was completed.

With all of these concerns in mind, Stanley set out to review the various data to develop strategies that would help to ensure a bright future for Track Software. Stanley believed that as part of this process, a thorough ratio analysis of the firm's 2012 results would provide important additional insights.

TABLE 2

Track Software, Inc. Income Statement ($000) for the Year Ended December 31, 2012

Sales revenue	$ 1,550
Less: Cost of goods sold	$1,030
Gross profits	$ 520
Less: Operating expenses	
Selling expense	$ 150
General and administrative expenses	270
Depreciation expense	11
Total operating expense	431
Operating profits (EBIT)	$ 89
Less: Interest expense	29
Net profits before taxes	$ 60
Less: Taxes (20%)	12
Net profits after taxes	$ 48

TABLE 3

Track Software, Inc. Balance Sheet ($000)

	December 31	
Assets	**2012**	**2011**
Cash	$ 12	$ 31
Marketable securities	66	82
Accounts receivable	152	104
Inventories	191	145
Total current assets	$421	$362
Gross fixed assets	$195	$180
Less: Accumulated depreciation	63	52
Net fixed assets	$132	$128
Total assets	$553	$490
Liabilities and Stockholders' Equity		
Accounts payable	$136	$126
Notes payable	200	190
Accruals	27	25
Total current liabilities	$363	$341
Long-term debt	$ 38	$ 40
Total liabilities	$401	$381
Common stock (50,000 shares outstanding at $0.40 par value)	$ 20	$ 20
Paid-in capital in excess of par	30	30
Retained earnings	102	59
Total stockholders' equity	$152	$109
Total liabilities and stockholders' equity	$553	$490

TABLE 4

Track Software, Inc.
Statement of Retained Earnings ($000)
for the Year Ended December 31, 2012

Retained earnings balance (January 1, 2012)	$ 59
Plus: Net profits after taxes (for 2012)	48
Less: Cash dividends on common stock (paid during 2012)	5
Retained earnings balance (December 31, 2012)	$102

TABLE 5

Ratio	Actual 2011	Industry average 2012
Current ratio	1.06	1.82
Quick ratio	0.63	1.10
Inventory turnover	10.40	12.45
Average collection period	29.6 days	20.2 days
Total asset turnover	2.66	3.92
Debt ratio	0.78	0.55
Times interest earned ratio	3.0	5.6
Gross profit margin	32.1%	42.3%
Operating profit margin	5.5%	12.4%
Net profit margin	3.0%	4.0%
Return on total assets (ROA)	8.0%	15.6%
Return on common equity (ROE)	36.4%	34.7%
Price/earnings (P/E) ratio	5.2	7.1
Market/book (M/B) ratio	2.1	2.2

TO DO

a. (1) On what financial goal does Stanley seem to be focusing? Is it the correct goal? Why or why not?
(2) Could a potential *agency problem* exist in this firm? Explain.

b. Calculate the firm's earnings per share (EPS) for each year, recognizing that the number of shares of common stock outstanding has remained *unchanged* since the firm's inception. Comment on the EPS performance in view of your response in part **a.**

c. Use the financial data presented to determine Track's *operating cash flow (OCF)* and *free cash flow (FCF)* in 2012. Evaluate your findings in light of Track's current cash flow difficulties.

d. Analyze the firm's financial condition in 2012 as it relates to (1) liquidity, (2) activity, (3) debt, (4) profitability, and (5) market, using the financial statements provided in Tables 2 and 3 and the ratio data included in Table 5. Be sure to *evaluate* the firm on both a cross-sectional and a time-series basis.

e. What recommendation would you make to Stanley regarding hiring a new software developer? Relate your recommendation here to your responses in part **a.**

f. Track Software paid $5,000 in dividends in 2012. Suppose an investor approached Stanley about buying 100% of his firm. If this investor believed that by owning the company he could extract $5,000 per year in cash from the company in perpetuity, what do you think the investor would be willing to pay for the firm if the required return on this investment is 10%?

g. Suppose that you believed that the FCF generated by Track Software in 2012 could continue forever. You are willing to buy the company in order to receive this perpetual stream of free cash flow. What are you willing to pay if you require a 10% return on your investment?

Part 3 Valuation of Securities

Chapters in This Part

In Part 2, you learned how to use time-value-of-money tools to compare cash flows at different times. In the next two chapters you'll put those tools to practice valuing the two most common types of securities—bonds and stocks.

Chapter 6 introduces you to the world of interest rates and bonds. Though bonds are considered to be among the safest investments available, they are not without risk. The primary risk that bond investors face is the risk that market interest rates will fluctuate. Those fluctuations cause bond prices to move, and those movements affect the returns that bond investors earn. Chapter 6 explains why interest rates vary from one bond to another and the factors that cause interest rates to move.

Chapter 7 focuses on stock valuation. Chapter 7 explains the characteristics of stock that distinguish it from debt and the chapter describes how companies issue stock to investors. You'll have another chance to practice time-value-of-money techniques as the chapter illustrates how to value stocks by discounting either (1) the dividends that stockholders receive or (2) the free cash flows that the firm generates over time.

6 Interest Rates and Bond Valuation

Learning Goals

LG 1 Describe interest rate fundamentals, the term structure of interest rates, and risk premiums.

LG 2 Review the legal aspects of bond financing and bond cost.

LG 3 Discuss the general features, yields, prices, ratings, popular types, and international issues of corporate bonds.

LG 4 Understand the key inputs and basic model used in the bond valuation process.

LG 5 Apply the basic valuation model to bonds, and describe the impact of required return and time to maturity on bond values.

LG 6 Explain yield to maturity (YTM), its calculation, and the procedure used to value bonds that pay interest semiannually.

Why This Chapter Matters to You

In your *professional* life

ACCOUNTING You need to understand interest rates and the various types of bonds to be able to account properly for amortization of bond premiums and discounts and for bond issues and retirements.

INFORMATION SYSTEMS You need to understand the data that is necessary to track bond valuations and bond amortization schedules.

MANAGEMENT You need to understand the behavior of interest rates and how they affect the types of funds the firm can raise and the timing and cost of bond issues and retirements.

MARKETING You need to understand how the interest rate level and the firm's ability to issue bonds may affect the availability of financing for marketing research projects and new-product development.

OPERATIONS You need to understand how the interest rate level may affect the firm's ability to raise funds to maintain and grow the firm's production capacity.

In your *personal* life

Interest rates have a direct impact on personal financial planning. Movements in interest rates occur frequently and affect the returns from and values of savings and investments. The rate of interest you are charged on credit cards and loans can have a profound effect on your personal finances. Understanding the basics of interest rates is important to your personal financial success.

The Federal Debt

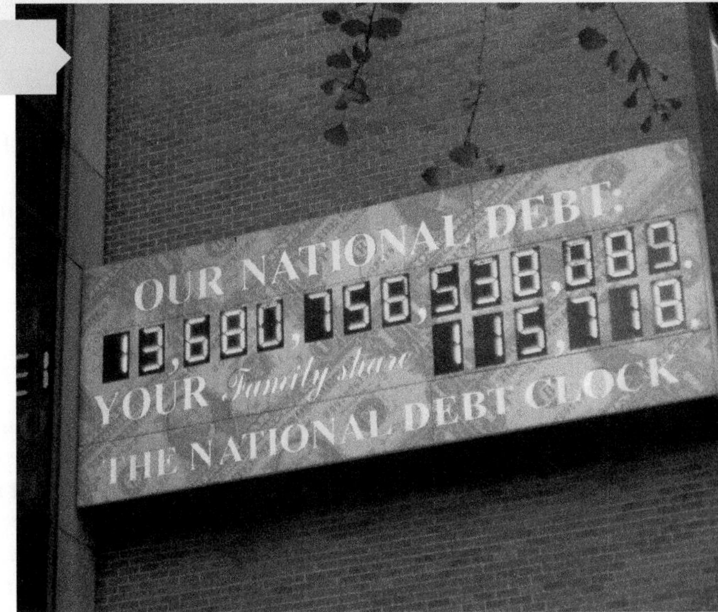

A Huge Appetite for Money

Who is the largest debtor in the world? The U.S. federal government, of course. As of October 6, 2010, the national debt was more than \$13 trillion, more than \$1 trillion of which accrued in 2009 alone. About half of the outstanding U.S. government debt is held by the U.S. Federal Reserve and other U.S. intragovernmental bodies, and another quarter is held by foreign investors. Interest on the national debt is one of the largest items in the federal budget, totaling \$383 billion in 2009. With Congressional Budget Office estimates projecting that from 2010 to 2019 the cumulative deficits will exceed \$7 trillion, the federal government has a huge need for outside financing, which dwarfs the capital needs of any corporation.

To feed this huge demand, the U.S. Treasury Department can issue T-bills, debt securities that mature in less than 1 year, Treasury notes that mature in 1 to 10 years, Treasury bonds that mature in more than 10 years, and savings bonds. Treasury securities can be purchased at banks (EE- and I-series savings bonds), at public auctions, and through TreasuryDirect, a Web-based system that allows investors to establish accounts to conduct transactions in Treasury securities online. Despite the government's massive past and projected future deficits, U.S. Treasury securities are still regarded as the safest investments in the world. In this chapter, you'll learn about the pricing of these and other debt instruments.

LG 1 6.1 Interest Rates and Required Returns

As noted in Chapter 2, financial institutions and markets create the mechanism through which funds flow between savers (funds suppliers) and borrowers (funds demanders). All else being equal, savers would like to earn as much interest as possible, and borrowers would like to pay as little as possible. The interest rate prevailing in the market at any given time reflects the equilibrium between savers and borrowers.

INTEREST RATE FUNDAMENTALS

The *interest rate* or *required return* represents the cost of money. It is the compensation that a supplier of funds expects and a demander of funds must pay. Usually the term **interest rate** is applied to debt instruments such as bank loans or bonds, and the term **required return** is applied to equity investments, such as common stock, that give the investor an ownership stake in the issuer. In fact, the meaning of these two terms is quite similar because, in both cases, the supplier is compensated for providing funds to the demander.

interest rate
Usually applied to debt instruments such as bank loans or bonds; the compensation paid by the borrower of funds to the lender; from the borrower's point of view, the cost of borrowing funds.

required return
Usually applied to equity instruments such as common stock; the cost of funds obtained by selling an ownership interest.

inflation
A rising trend in the prices of most goods and services.

liquidity preference
A general tendency for investors to prefer short-term (that is, more liquid) securities.

A variety of factors can influence the equilibrium interest rate. One factor is **inflation**, a rising trend in the prices of most goods and services. Typically, savers demand higher returns (that is, higher interest rates) when inflation is high because they want their investments to more than keep pace with rising prices. A second factor influencing interest rates is risk. When people perceive that a particular investment is riskier, they will expect a higher return on that investment as compensation for bearing the risk. A third factor that can affect the interest rate is a **liquidity preference** among investors. The term *liquidity preference* refers to the general tendency of investors to prefer short-term securities (that is, securities that are more liquid). If, all other things being equal, investors would prefer to buy short-term rather than long-term securities, interest rates on short-term instruments such as Treasury bills will be lower than rates on longer-term securities. Investors will hold these securities, despite the relatively low return that they offer, because they meet investors' preferences for liquidity.

Matter of fact

Fear Turns T-Bill Rates Negative

Near the height of the financial crisis in December 2008, interest rates on Treasury bills briefly turned negative, meaning that investors paid more to the Treasury than the Treasury promised to pay back. Why would anyone put their money into an investment that they *know* will lose money? Remember that 2008 saw the demise of Lehman Brothers, and fears that other commercial banks and investments banks might fail were rampant. Evidently, some investors were willing to pay the U.S. Treasury to keep their money safe for a short time.

real rate of interest
The rate that creates equilibrium between the supply of savings and the demand for investment funds in a perfect world, without inflation, where suppliers and demanders of funds have no liquidity preferences and there is no risk.

The Real Rate of Interest

Imagine a *perfect world* in which there is no inflation, in which investors have no liquidity preferences, and in which there is no risk. In this world, there would be one cost of money—the **real rate of interest**. The real rate of interest creates equilibrium

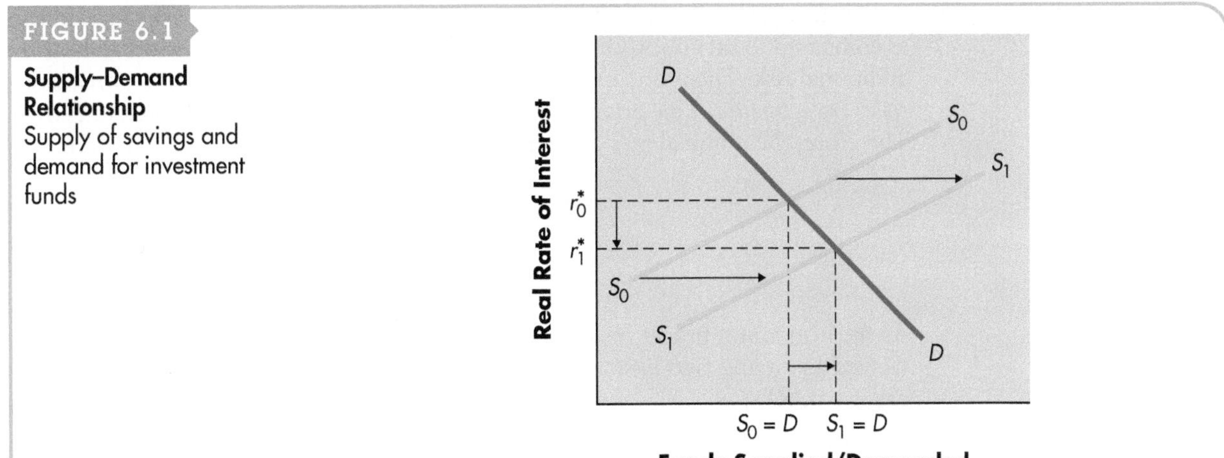

FIGURE 6.1
Supply–Demand Relationship
Supply of savings and demand for investment funds

between the supply of savings and the demand for funds. It represents the most basic cost of money. Historically, the real rate of interest in the United States has averaged about 1 percent per year, but that figure does fluctuate over time. This supply–demand relationship is shown in Figure 6.1 by the supply function (labeled S_0) and the demand function (labeled D). An equilibrium between the supply of funds and the demand for funds ($S_0 = D$) occurs at a rate of interest $r_0{}^*$, the real rate of interest.

Clearly, the real rate of interest changes with changing economic conditions, tastes, and preferences. To combat a recession, the Board of Governors of the Federal Reserve System might initiate actions to increase the supply of credit in the economy, causing the supply function in Figure 6.1 to shift to, say, S_1. This could result in a lower real rate of interest, $r_1{}^*$, at equilibrium ($S_1 = D$). With a lower cost of money, firms might find that investments that were previously unattractive are now worth undertaking, and as firms hire more workers and spend more on plant and equipment, the economy begins to expand again.

Nominal or Actual Rate of Interest (Return)

nominal rate of interest
The actual rate of interest charged by the supplier of funds and paid by the demander.

The **nominal rate of interest** is the actual rate of interest charged by the supplier of funds and paid by the demander. *Throughout this book, interest rates and required rates of return are nominal rates unless otherwise noted.* The nominal rate of interest differs from the real rate of interest, r^*, as a result of two factors, inflation and risk. When people save money and invest it, they are sacrificing consumption today (that is, they are spending less than they could) in return for higher future consumption. When investors expect inflation to occur, they believe that the price of consuming goods and services will be higher in the future than in the present. Therefore, they will be reluctant to sacrifice today's consumption unless the return they can earn on the money they save (or invest) will be high enough to allow them to purchase the goods and services they desire at a higher future price. That is, *investors will demand a higher nominal rate of return if they expect inflation.* This higher rate of return is called the expected inflation premium (IP).

Similarly, investors generally demand higher rates of return on risky investments as compared to safe ones. Otherwise, there is little incentive for investors to bear the additional risk. Therefore, *investors will demand a higher nominal rate of return on risky investments*. This additional rate of return is called the risk premium (RP). Therefore, the nominal rate of interest for security 1, r_1, is given in Equation 6.1:

$$r_1 = \underbrace{r^* + IP}_{\substack{\text{risk-free} \\ \text{rate, } R_F}} + \underbrace{RP_1}_{\substack{\text{risk} \\ \text{premium}}} \tag{6.1}$$

As the horizontal braces below the equation indicate, the nominal rate, r_1, can be viewed as having two basic components: a risk-free rate of return, R_F, and a risk premium, RP_1:

$$r_1 = R_F + RP_1 \tag{6.2}$$

For the moment, ignore the risk premium, RP_1, and focus exclusively on the risk-free rate. Equation 6.1 says that the risk-free rate can be represented as

$$R_F = r^* + IP \tag{6.3}$$

The risk-free rate (as shown in Equation 6.3) embodies the real rate of interest plus the expected inflation premium. The inflation premium is driven by investors' expectations about inflation—the more inflation they expect, the higher will be the inflation premium and the higher will be the nominal interest rate.

Three-month *U.S. Treasury bills (T-bills)* are short-term IOUs issued by the U.S. Treasury, and they are widely regarded as the safest investments in the world. They are as close as we can get in the real world to a risk-free investment. To estimate the real rate of interest, analysts typically try to determine what rate of inflation investors expect over the coming 3 months. Next, *they subtract the expected inflation rate from the nominal rate on the 3-month T-bill to arrive at the underlying real rate of interest*. For the risk-free asset in Equation 6.3, the real rate of interest, r^*, would equal $R_F - IP$. A simple personal finance example can demonstrate the practical distinction between nominal and real rates of interest.

Personal Finance Example 6.1 ▶ Marilyn Carbo has \$10 that she can spend on candy costing \$0.25 per piece. She could buy 40 pieces of candy (\$10.00 ÷ \$0.25) today. The nominal rate of interest on a 1-year deposit is currently 7%, and the expected rate of inflation over the coming year is 4%. Instead of buying the 40 pieces of candy today, Marilyn could invest the \$10. After one year she would have \$10.70 because she would have earned 7% interest—an additional \$0.70 (0.07 × \$10.00)—on her \$10 deposit. During that year, inflation would have increased the cost of the candy by 4%—an additional \$0.01 (0.04 × \$0.25)—to \$0.26 per piece. As a result, at the end of the 1-year period Marilyn would be able to buy about 41.2 pieces of candy (\$10.70 ÷ \$0.26), or roughly 3% more (41.2 ÷ 40.0 = 1.03). The 3% increase in Marilyn's buying power represents her real rate of return. The nominal rate of return on her investment (7%), is partly eroded by inflation (4%), so her real return during the year is the difference between the nominal rate and the inflation rate (7% − 4% = 3%).

focus on **PRACTICE**

I-Bonds Adjust for Inflation

in practice One of the disadvantages of bonds is that they usually offer a fixed interest rate. Once a bond is issued, its interest rate typically cannot adjust as expected inflation changes. This presents a serious risk to bond investors because if inflation rises while the nominal rate on the bond remains fixed, the real rate of return falls.

The U.S. Treasury Department now offers the I-bond, which is an inflation-adjusted savings bond. A Series-I bond earns interest through the application of a *composite rate*. The composite rate consists of a *fixed rate* that remains the same for the life of the bond and an *adjustable rate* equal to the actual rate of inflation. The adjustable rate changes twice per year and is based on movements in the Consumer Price Index for All Urban Consumers (CPI-U). This index tracks the prices of thousands of goods and services, so an increase in this index indicates that inflation has occurred. As the rate of inflation moves up and down, I-bond interest rates adjust (with a short lag). Interest earnings are exempt from state and local income taxes, and are payable only when an investor redeems an I-bond. I-bonds are issued at face value in denominations of $50, $75, $100, $200, $500, $1,000, $5,000, and $10,000.

The I-bond is not without its drawbacks. Any redemption within the first 5 years results in a 3-month interest penalty. Also, you should redeem an I-bond only at the first of the month because none of the interest earned during a month is included in the redemption value until the first day of the following month. The adjustable-rate feature of I-bonds can work against investors (that is, it can lower their returns) if deflation occurs. **Deflation** refers to a general trend of falling prices, so when deflation occurs, the change in the CPI-U is negative, and the adjustable portion of an I-bond's interest also turns negative. For example, if the fixed-rate component on an I-bond is 2 percent and prices fall 0.5 percent (stated equivalently, the inflation rate is –0.5 percent), then the nominal rate on an I-bond will be just 1.5 percent (2 percent minus 0.5 percent). Nevertheless, in the past 80 years, periods of deflation have been very rare, whereas inflation has been an almost ever-present feature of the economy, so investors are likely to enjoy the inflation protection that I-bonds offer in the future.

► ***What effect do you think the inflation-adjusted interest rate has on the price of an I-bond in comparison with similar bonds with no allowance for inflation?***

deflation
A general trend of falling prices.

The premium for *expected inflation* in Equation 6.3 represents the average rate of *inflation* expected over the life of an investment. It is *not* the rate of inflation experienced over the immediate past, although investors' inflation expectations are undoubtedly influenced by the rate of inflation that has occurred in the recent past. Even so, the inflation premium reflects the expected rate of inflation. The expected inflation premium changes over time in response to many factors, such as changes in monetary and fiscal policies, currency movements, and international political events. For a discussion of a U.S. debt security whose interest rate is adjusted for inflation, see the *Focus on Practice* box.

Figure 6.2 (see page 226) illustrates the annual movement of the rate of inflation and the risk-free rate of return from 1961 through 2009. During this period the two rates tended to move in a similar fashion. Note that T-bill rates were slightly above the inflation rate most of the time, meaning that T-bills generally offered a small positive real return. Between 1978 and the early 1980s, inflation and interest rates were quite high, peaking at over 13 percent in 1980–1981. Since then, rates have gradually declined. To combat a severe recession, the Federal Reserve pushed interest rates down to almost 0% in 2009, and for the first time in decades, the rate of inflation turned slightly negative (that is, there was slight deflation that year).

Impact of Inflation
Relationship between annual rate of inflation and 3-month U.S. Treasury bill average annual returns, 1961–2009

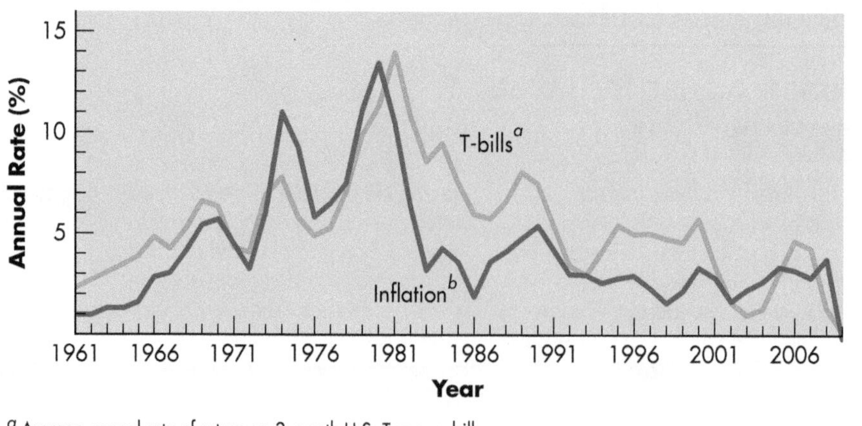

[a] Average annual rate of return on 3-month U.S. Treasury bills.
[b] Annual pecentage change in the consumer price index.

Sources: Data from selected *Federal Reserve Bulletins* and *U.S. Department of Labor Bureau of Labor Statistics.*

TERM STRUCTURE OF INTEREST RATES

term structure of interest rates
The relationship between the maturity and rate of return for bonds with similar levels of risk.

yield curve
A graphic depiction of the term structure of interest rates.

The **term structure of interest rates** is the relationship between the maturity and rate of return for bonds with similar levels of risk. A graph of this relationship is called the **yield curve.** A quick glance at the yield curve tells analysts how rates vary between short-, medium-, and long-term bonds, but it may also provide information on where interest rates and the economy in general are headed in the future. Usually, when analysts examine the term structure of interest rates, they focus on Treasury securities because these are generally considered to be free of default risk.

Yield Curves

yield to maturity (YTM)
Compound annual rate of return earned on a debt security purchased on a given day and held to maturity.

A bond's **yield to maturity (YTM)** (discussed later in this chapter) represents the compound annual rate of return that an investor earns on the bond assuming that the bond makes all promised payments and the investor holds the bond to maturity. In a yield curve, the yield to maturity is plotted on the vertical axis and time to maturity is plotted on the horizontal axis. Figure 6.3 shows three yield curves for U.S. Treasury securities: one at May 22, 1981, a second at September 29, 1989, and a third at May 28, 2010.

inverted yield curve
A *downward-sloping* yield curve indicates that short-term interest rates are generally higher than long-term interest rates.

normal yield curve
An *upward-sloping* yield curve indicates that long-term interest rates are generally higher than short-term interest rates.

Observe that both the position and the shape of the yield curves change over time. The yield curve of May 22, 1981, indicates that short-term interest rates at that time were above longer-term rates. For reasons that a glance at the figure makes obvious, this curve is described as *downward-sloping*. Interest rates in May 1981 were also quite high by historical standards, so the overall level of the yield curve is high. Historically, a downward-sloping yield curve, which is often called an **inverted yield curve,** occurs infrequently and is often a sign that the economy is weakening. Most recessions in the United States have been preceded by an inverted yield curve.

Usually, short-term interest rates are lower than long-term interest rates, as they were on May 28, 2010. That is, the **normal yield curve** is *upward-sloping*. Notice that the May 2010 yield curve lies entirely beneath the other two curves

FIGURE 6.3

Treasury Yield Curves
Yield curves for U.S. Treasury securities: May 22, 1981; September 29, 1989; and May 28, 2010

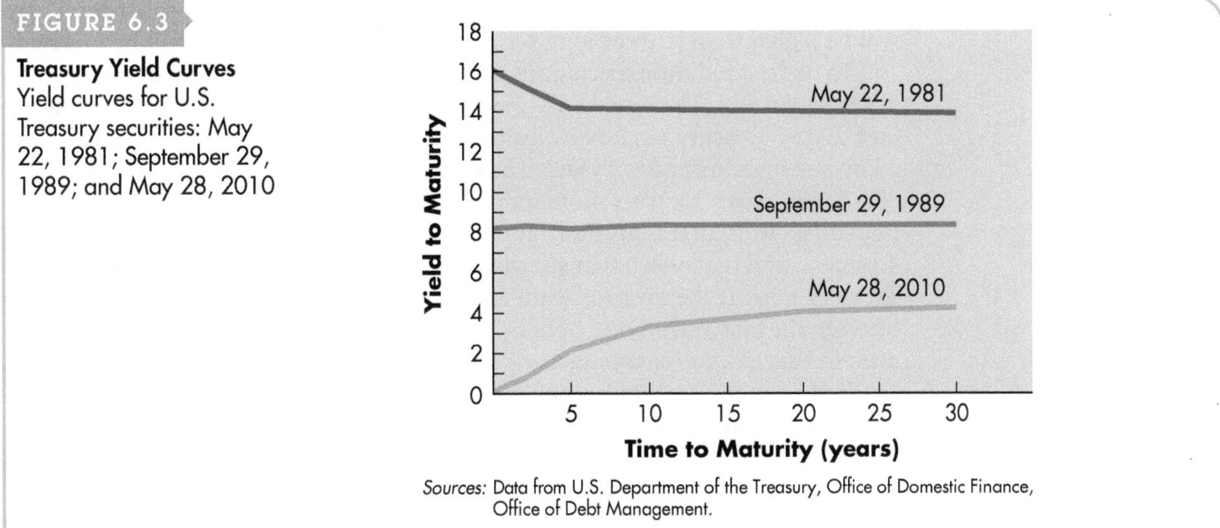

Sources: Data from U.S. Department of the Treasury, Office of Domestic Finance, Office of Debt Management.

flat yield curve
A yield curve that indicates that interest rates do not vary much at different maturities.

In more depth

To read about *Yield Curve Animation,* go to www.myfinancelab.com

shown in Figure 6.3. In other words, interest rates in May 2010 were unusually low, largely because at that time the economy was just beginning to recover from a deep recession and inflation was very low. Sometimes, a **flat yield curve,** similar to that of September 29, 1989, exists. A flat yield curve simply means that rates do not vary much at different maturities.

The shape of the yield curve may affect the firm's financing decisions. A financial manager who faces a downward-sloping yield curve may be tempted to rely more heavily on cheaper, long-term financing. However, a risk in following this strategy is that interest rates may fall in the future, so long-term rates that seem cheap today may be relatively expensive tomorrow. Likewise, when the yield curve is upward-sloping, the manager may feel that it is wise to use cheaper, short-term financing. Relying on short-term financing has its own risks. Firms that borrow on a short-term basis may see their costs rise if interest rates go up. Even more serious is the risk that a firm may not be able to refinance a short-term loan when it comes due. A variety of factors influence the choice of loan maturity, but the shape of the yield curve is something that managers must consider when making decisions about borrowing short-term versus long-term.

Theories of Term Structure

Three theories are frequently cited to explain the general shape of the yield curve: the expectations theory, the liquidity preference theory, and the market segmentation theory.

expectations theory
The theory that the yield curve reflects investor expectations about future interest rates; an expectation of rising interest rates results in an upward-sloping yield curve, and an expectation of declining rates results in a downward-sloping yield curve.

Expectations Theory One theory of the term structure of interest rates, the **expectations theory,** suggests that the yield curve reflects investor expectations about future interest rates. According to this theory, when investors expect short-term interest rates to rise in the future (perhaps because investors believe that inflation will rise in the future), today's long-term rates will be higher than current short-term rates, and the yield curve will be upward sloping. The opposite is true when investors expect declining short-term rates—today's short-term rates will be higher than current long-term rates, and the yield curve will be inverted.

To understand the expectations theory, consider this example. Suppose that the yield curve is flat. The rate on a 1-year Treasury note is 4 percent, and so is the rate on a 2-year Treasury note. Now, consider an investor who has money to place into a low-risk investment for 2 years. The investor has two options. First, he could purchase the 2-year Treasury note and receive a total of 8 percent (ignoring compounding) in 2 years. Second, he could invest in the 1-year Treasury earning 4 percent, and then when that security matures, he could reinvest in another 1-year Treasury note. If the investor wants to maximize his expected return, the decision between the first and second options above depends on whether he expects interest rates to rise, fall, or remain unchanged during the next year.

If the investor believes that interest rates will rise, that means next year's return on a 1-year Treasury note will be greater than 4 percent (that is, greater than the 1-year Treasury rate right now). Let's say the investor believes that the interest rate on a 1-year note next year will be 5 percent. If the investor expects rising rates, then his expected return is higher if he follows the second option, buying a 1-year Treasury note now (paying 4 percent) and reinvesting in a new security that pays 5 percent next year. Over 2 years, the investor would expect to earn about 9 percent (ignoring compounding) in interest, compared to just 8 percent earned by holding the 2-year bond.

If the current 1-year rate is 4 percent and investors generally expect that rate to go up to 5 percent next year, what would the 2-year Treasury note rate have to be right now to remain competitive? The answer is 4.5 percent. An investor who buys this security and holds it for 2 years would earn about 9 percent interest (again, ignoring compounding), the same as the expected return from investing in two consecutive 1-year bonds. In other words, *if investors expect interest rates to rise, the 2-year rate today must be higher than the 1-year rate today, and that in turn means that the yield curve must have an upward slope.*

Example 6.2 ▸

Suppose that a 5-year Treasury note currently offers a 3% annual return. Investors believe that interest rates are going to decline, and 5 years from now, they expect the rate on a 5-year Treasury note to be 2.5%. According to the expectations theory, what is the return that a 10-year Treasury note has to offer today? What does this imply about the slope of the yield curve?

Consider an investor who purchases a 5-year note today and plans to reinvest in another 5-year note in the future. Over the 10-year investment horizon, this investor expects to earn about 27.5%, ignoring compounding (that's 3% per year for the first 5 years and 2.5% per year for the next 5 years). To compete with that return, a 10-year bond today could offer 2.75% per year. That is, a bond that pays 2.75% for each of the next 10 years produces the same 27.5% total return that the series of two 5-year notes is expected to produce. Therefore, the 5-year rate today is 3% and the 10-year rate today is 2.75%, and the yield curve is downward sloping.

---

liquidity preference theory
Theory suggesting that long-term rates are generally higher than short-term rates (hence, the yield curve is upward sloping) because investors perceive short-term investments to be more liquid and less risky than long-term investments. Borrowers must offer higher rates on long-term bonds to entice investors away from their preferred short-term securities.

Liquidity Preference Theory Most of the time, yield curves are upward sloping. According to the expectations theory, this means that investors expect interest rates to rise. An alternative explanation for the typical upward slope of the yield curve is the **liquidity preference theory.** This theory holds that, all else being equal, investors generally prefer to buy short-term securities, while issuers prefer to sell long-term securities. For investors, short-term securities are attractive because they are highly liquid and their prices are not particularly volatile.[1] Hence, investors will accept somewhat lower rates on short-term bonds because they are less risky than long-term bonds. Conversely, when firms or governments want to lock in their borrowing costs for a long period of time by selling long-term bonds, those bonds have to offer higher rates to entice investors away from the short-term securities that they prefer. Borrowers are willing to pay somewhat higher rates because long-term debt allows them to eliminate or reduce the risk of not being able to refinance short-term debts when they come due. Borrowing on a long-term basis also reduces uncertainty about future borrowing costs.

market segmentation theory
Theory suggesting that the market for loans is segmented on the basis of maturity and that the supply of and demand for loans within each segment determine its prevailing interest rate; the slope of the yield curve is determined by the general relationship between the prevailing rates in each market segment.

Market Segmentation Theory The **market segmentation theory** suggests that the market for loans is totally segmented on the basis of maturity and that the supply of and demand for loans within each segment determine its prevailing interest rate. In other words, the equilibrium between suppliers and demanders of short-term funds, such as seasonal business loans, would determine prevailing short-term interest rates, and the equilibrium between suppliers and demanders of long-term funds, such as real estate loans, would determine prevailing long-term interest rates. The slope of the yield curve would be determined by the general relationship between the prevailing rates in each market segment. Simply stated, an upward-sloping yield curve indicates greater borrowing demand relative to the supply of funds in the long-term segment of the debt market relative to the short-term segment.

All three term structure theories have merit. From them we can conclude that at any time the slope of the yield curve is affected by (1) interest rate expectations, (2) liquidity preferences, and (3) the comparative equilibrium of supply and demand in the short- and long-term market segments. Upward-sloping yield curves result from expectations of rising interest rates, lender preferences for shorter-maturity loans, and greater supply of short-term loans than of long-term loans relative to demand. The opposite conditions would result in a downward-sloping yield curve. At any time, the interaction of these three forces determines the prevailing slope of the yield curve.

RISK PREMIUMS: ISSUER AND ISSUE CHARACTERISTICS

So far we have considered only risk-free U.S. Treasury securities. We now reintroduce the risk premium and assess it in view of risky non-Treasury issues. Recall Equation 6.1:

$$r_1 = \underbrace{r^* + IP}_{\substack{\text{risk-free} \\ \text{rate, } R_F}} + \underbrace{RP_1}_{\substack{\text{risk} \\ \text{premium}}}$$

In words, the nominal rate of interest for security 1 (r_1) is equal to the risk-free rate, consisting of the real rate of interest (r^*) plus the inflation expectation

1. Later in this chapter we demonstrate that debt instruments with longer maturities are more sensitive to changing market interest rates. For a given change in market rates, the price or value of longer-term debts will be more significantly changed (up or down) than the price or value of debts with shorter maturities.

premium (IP), plus the risk premium (RP_1). The *risk premium* varies with specific issuer and issue characteristics.

Example 6.3 ▶ The nominal interest rates on a number of classes of long-term securities in May 2010 were as follows:

Security	Nominal interest rate
U.S. Treasury bonds (average)	3.30%
Corporate bonds (by risk ratings):	
High quality (Aaa–Aa)	3.95
Medium quality (A–Baa)	4.98
Speculative (Ba–C)	8.97

Because the U.S. Treasury bond would represent the risk-free, long-term security, we can calculate the risk premium of the other securities by subtracting the risk-free rate, 3.30%, from each nominal rate (yield):

Security	Risk premium
Corporate bonds (by ratings):	
High quality (Aaa–Aa)	3.95% − 3.30% = 0.65%
Medium quality (A–Baa)	4.98 − 3.30 = 1.68
Speculative (Ba–C)	8.97 − 3.30 = 5.67

These risk premiums reflect differing issuer and issue risks. The lower-rated (speculative) corporate issues have a far higher risk premium than that of the higher-rated corporate issues (high quality and medium quality), and that risk premium is the compensation that investors demand for bearing the higher default risk of lower quality bonds.

The risk premium consists of a number of issuer- and issue-related components, including business risk, financial risk, interest rate risk, liquidity risk, and tax risk, as well as the purely debt-specific risks—default risk, maturity risk, and contractual provision risk, briefly defined in Table 6.1. In general, the highest risk premiums and therefore the highest returns result from securities issued by firms with a high risk of default and from long-term maturities that have unfavorable contractual provisions.

→ REVIEW QUESTIONS

6–1 What is the *real rate of interest?* Differentiate it from the *nominal rate of interest* for the risk-free asset, a 3-month U.S. Treasury bill.

6–2 What is the *term structure of interest rates,* and how is it related to the *yield curve?*

TABLE 6.1 Debt-Specific Issuer- and Issue-Related Risk Premium Components

Component	Description
Default risk	The possibility that the issuer of debt will not pay the contractual interest or principal as scheduled. The greater the uncertainty as to the borrower's ability to meet these payments, the greater the risk premium. High bond ratings reflect low default risk, and low bond ratings reflect high default risk.
Maturity risk	The fact that the longer the maturity, the more the value of a security will change in response to a given change in interest rates. If interest rates on otherwise similar-risk securities suddenly rise as a result of a change in the money supply, the prices of long-term bonds will decline by more than the prices of short-term bonds, and vice versa.[a]
Contractual provision risk	Conditions that are often included in a debt agreement or a stock issue. Some of these reduce risk, whereas others may increase risk. For example, a provision allowing a bond issuer to retire its bonds prior to their maturity under favorable terms increases the bond's risk.

[a]A detailed discussion of the effects of interest rates on the price or value of bonds and other fixed-income securities is presented later in this chapter.

6–3 For a given class of similar-risk securities, what does each of the following yield curves reflect about interest rates: (**a**) downward-sloping; (**b**) upward-sloping; and (**c**) flat? What is the "normal" shape of the yield curve?

6–4 Briefly describe the following theories of the general shape of the yield curve: (**a**) expectations theory; (**b**) liquidity preference theory; and (**c**) market segmentation theory.

6–5 List and briefly describe the potential issuer- and issue-related risk components that are embodied in the risk premium. Which are the purely debt-specific risks?

LG 2 LG 3 6.2 Corporate Bonds

corporate bond
A long-term debt instrument indicating that a corporation has borrowed a certain amount of money and promises to repay it in the future under clearly defined terms.

A **corporate bond** is a long-term debt instrument indicating that a corporation has borrowed a certain amount of money and promises to repay it in the future under clearly defined terms. Most bonds are issued with maturities of 10 to 30 years and with a par value, or face value, of $1,000. The **coupon interest rate** on a bond represents the percentage of the bond's par value that will be paid annually, typically in two equal semiannual payments, as interest. The bondholders, who are the lenders, are promised the semiannual interest payments and, at maturity, repayment of the principal amount.

coupon interest rate
The percentage of a bond's par value that will be paid annually, typically in two equal semiannual payments, as interest.

bond indenture
A legal document that specifies both the rights of the bondholders and the duties of the issuing corporation.

standard debt provisions
Provisions in a *bond indenture* specifying certain record-keeping and general business practices that the bond issuer must follow; normally, they do not place a burden on a financially sound business.

restrictive covenants
Provisions in a *bond indenture* that place operating and financial constraints on the borrower.

subordination
In a bond indenture, the stipulation that subsequent creditors agree to wait until all claims of the *senior debt* are satisfied.

sinking-fund requirement
A restrictive provision often included in a bond indenture, providing for the systematic retirement of bonds prior to their maturity.

LEGAL ASPECTS OF CORPORATE BONDS

Certain legal arrangements are required to protect purchasers of bonds. Bondholders are protected primarily through the indenture and the trustee.

Bond Indenture

A **bond indenture** is a legal document that specifies both the rights of the bondholders and the duties of the issuing corporation. Included in the indenture are descriptions of the amount and timing of all interest and principal payments, various standard and restrictive provisions, and, frequently, sinking-fund requirements and security interest provisions. The borrower commonly must (1) *maintain satisfactory accounting records* in accordance with generally accepted accounting principles (GAAP); (2) periodically *supply audited financial statements;* (3) *pay taxes and other liabilities when due;* and (4) *maintain all facilities in good working order.*

Standard Provisions The **standard debt provisions** in the bond indenture specify certain record-keeping and general business practices that the bond issuer must follow.

Restrictive Provisions Bond indentures also normally include certain **restrictive covenants,** which place operating and financial constraints on the borrower. These provisions help protect the bondholder against increases in borrower risk. Without them, the borrower could increase the firm's risk but not have to pay increased interest to compensate for the increased risk.

The most common restrictive covenants do the following:

1. Require a *minimum level of liquidity,* to ensure against loan default.
2. *Prohibit the sale of accounts receivable* to generate cash. Selling receivables could cause a long-run cash shortage if proceeds were used to meet current obligations.
3. Impose *fixed-asset restrictions.* The borrower must maintain a specified level of fixed assets to guarantee its ability to repay the bonds.
4. *Constrain subsequent borrowing.* Additional long-term debt may be prohibited, or additional borrowing may be *subordinated* to the original loan. **Subordination** means that subsequent creditors agree to wait until all claims of the *senior debt* are satisfied.
5. *Limit the firm's annual cash dividend payments* to a specified percentage or amount.

Other restrictive covenants are sometimes included in bond indentures.

The violation of any standard or restrictive provision by the borrower gives the bondholders the right to demand immediate repayment of the debt. Generally, bondholders evaluate any violation to determine whether it jeopardizes the loan. They may then decide to demand immediate repayment, continue the loan, or alter the terms of the bond indenture.

Sinking-Fund Requirements Another common restrictive provision is a **sinking-fund requirement.** Its objective is to provide for the systematic retirement of bonds prior to their maturity. To carry out this requirement, the corporation makes semiannual or annual payments that are used to retire bonds by purchasing them in the marketplace.

Security Interest The bond indenture identifies any collateral pledged against the bond and specifies how it is to be maintained. The protection of bond collateral is crucial to guarantee the safety of a bond issue.

Trustee

trustee
A paid individual, corporation, or commercial bank trust department that acts as the third party to a *bond indenture* and can take specified actions on behalf of the bondholders if the terms of the indenture are violated.

A **trustee** is a third party to a *bond indenture*. The trustee can be an individual, a corporation, or (most often) a commercial bank trust department. The trustee is paid to act as a "watchdog" on behalf of the bondholders and can take specified actions on behalf of the bondholders if the terms of the indenture are violated.

COST OF BONDS TO THE ISSUER

The cost of bond financing is generally greater than the issuer would have to pay for short-term borrowing. The major factors that affect the cost, which is the rate of interest paid by the bond issuer, are the bond's maturity, the size of the offering, the issuer's risk, and the basic cost of money.

Impact of Bond Maturity

Generally, as we noted earlier, long-term debt pays higher interest rates than short-term debt. In a practical sense, the longer the maturity of a bond, the less accuracy there is in predicting future interest rates, and therefore the greater the bondholders' risk of giving up an opportunity to lend money at a higher rate. In addition, the longer the term, the greater the chance that the issuer might default.

Impact of Offering Size

The size of the bond offering also affects the interest cost of borrowing but in an inverse manner: Bond flotation and administration costs per dollar borrowed are likely to decrease with increasing offering size. On the other hand, the risk to the bondholders may increase, because larger offerings result in greater risk of default.

Impact of Issuer's Risk

The greater the issuer's *default risk,* the higher the interest rate. Some of this risk can be reduced through inclusion of appropriate restrictive provisions in the bond indenture. Clearly, bondholders must be compensated with higher returns for taking greater risk. Frequently, bond buyers rely on bond ratings (discussed later) to determine the issuer's overall risk.

Impact of the Cost of Money

The cost of money in the capital market is the basis for determining a bond's coupon interest rate. Generally, the rate on U.S. Treasury securities of equal maturity is used as the lowest-risk cost of money. To that basic rate is added a *risk premium* (as described earlier in this chapter) that reflects the factors mentioned above (maturity, offering size, and issuer's risk).

GENERAL FEATURES OF A BOND ISSUE

Three features sometimes included in a corporate bond issue are a conversion feature, a call feature, and stock purchase warrants. These features provide the issuer or the purchaser with certain opportunities for replacing or retiring the bond or supplementing it with some type of equity issue.

conversion feature
A feature of *convertible bonds* that allows bondholders to change each bond into a stated number of shares of common stock.

Convertible bonds offer a **conversion feature** that allows bondholders to change each bond into a stated number of shares of common stock. Bondholders convert their bonds into stock only when the market price of the stock is such that conversion will provide a profit for the bondholder. Inclusion of the conversion feature by the issuer lowers the interest cost and provides for automatic conversion of the bonds to stock if future stock prices appreciate noticeably.

call feature
A feature included in nearly all corporate bond issues that gives the issuer the opportunity to repurchase bonds at a stated *call price* prior to maturity.

call price
The stated price at which a bond may be repurchased, by use of a *call feature*, prior to maturity.

call premium
The amount by which a bond's *call price* exceeds its par value.

The **call feature** is included in nearly all corporate bond issues. It gives the issuer the opportunity to repurchase bonds prior to maturity. The **call price** is the stated price at which bonds may be repurchased prior to maturity. Sometimes the call feature can be exercised only during a certain period. As a rule, the call price exceeds the par value of a bond by an amount equal to 1 year's interest. For example, a $1,000 bond with a 10 percent coupon interest rate would be callable for around $1,100 [$1,000 + (10% × $1,000)]. The amount by which the call price exceeds the bond's par value is commonly referred to as the **call premium.** This premium compensates bondholders for having the bond called away from them; to the issuer, it is the cost of calling the bonds.

The call feature enables an issuer to call an outstanding bond when interest rates fall and issue a new bond at a lower interest rate. When interest rates rise, the call privilege will not be exercised, except possibly to meet *sinking-fund requirements.* Of course, to sell a callable bond in the first place, the issuer must pay a higher interest rate than on noncallable bonds of equal risk, to compensate bondholders for the risk of having the bonds called away from them.

stock purchase warrants
Instruments that give their holders the right to purchase a certain number of shares of the issuer's common stock at a specified price over a certain period of time.

Bonds occasionally have stock purchase warrants attached as "sweeteners" to make them more attractive to prospective buyers. **Stock purchase warrants** are instruments that give their holders the right to purchase a certain number of shares of the issuer's common stock at a specified price over a certain period of time. Their inclusion typically enables the issuer to pay a slightly lower coupon interest rate than would otherwise be required.

BOND YIELDS

The *yield,* or rate of return, on a bond is frequently used to assess a bond's performance over a given period of time, typically 1 year. Because there are a number of ways to measure a bond's yield, it is important to understand popular yield measures. The three most widely cited bond yields are (1) *current yield,* (2) *yield to maturity (YTM),* and (3) *yield to call (YTC).* Each of these yields provides a unique measure of the return on a bond.

current yield
A measure of a bond's cash return for the year; calculated by dividing the bond's annual interest payment by its current price.

The simplest yield measure is the **current yield,** the annual interest payment divided by the current price. For example, a $1,000 par value bond with an 8 percent coupon interest rate that currently sells for $970 would have a current yield of 8.25% [(0.08 × $1,000) ÷ $970]. This measure indicates the cash return for the year from the bond. However, because current yield ignores any change in bond value, it does not measure the total return. As we'll see later in this chapter, both the yield to maturity and the yield to call measure the total return.

BOND PRICES

Because most corporate bonds are purchased and held by institutional investors, such as banks, insurance companies, and mutual funds, rather than individual investors, bond trading and price data are not readily available to individuals. Table 6.2 includes some assumed current data on the bonds of five companies, noted A through E. Looking at the data for Company C's bond, which is highlighted

TABLE 6.2 Data on Selected Bonds

Company	Coupon	Maturity	Price	Yield (YTM)
Company A	6.125%	Nov. 15, 2011	105.336	4.788%
Company B	6.000	Oct. 31, 2036	94.007	6.454
Company C	7.200	Jan. 15, 2014	103.143	6.606
Company D	5.150	Jan. 15, 2017	95.140	5.814
Company E	5.850	Jan. 14, 2012	100.876	5.631

in the table, we see that the bond has a coupon interest rate of 7.200 percent and a maturity date of January 15, 2017. These data identify a specific bond issued by Company C. (The company could have more than a single bond issue outstanding.) The price represents the final price at which the bond traded on the current day.

Although most corporate bonds are issued with a *par,* or *face, value* of $1,000, *all bonds are quoted as a percentage of par.* A $1,000-par-value bond quoted at 94.007 is priced at $940.07 (94.007% × $1,000). Corporate bonds are quoted in dollars and cents. Thus, Company C's price of 103.143 for the day was $1,031.43—that is, 103.143% × $1,000.

The final column of Table 6.2 represents the bond's *yield to maturity (YTM),* which is the compound annual rate of return that would be earned on the bond if it were purchased and held to maturity. (YTM is discussed in detail later in this chapter.)

BOND RATINGS

Independent agencies such as Moody's, Fitch, and Standard & Poor's assess the riskiness of publicly traded bond issues. These agencies derive their ratings by using financial ratio and cash flow analyses to assess the likely payment of bond interest and principal. Table 6.3 summarizes these ratings. For

TABLE 6.3 Moody's and Standard & Poor's Bond Ratings[a]

Moody's	Interpretation	Standard & Poor's	Interpretation
Aaa	Prime quality	AAA	Investment grade
Aa	High grade	AA	
A	Upper medium grade	A	
Baa	Medium grade	BBB	
Ba	Lower medium grade or speculative	BB	Speculative
		B	
B	Speculative		
Caa	From very speculative to near or in default	CCC	
Ca		CC	
C	Lowest grade	C	Income bond
		D	In default

[a]Some ratings may be modified to show relative standing within a major rating category; for example, Moody's uses numerical modifiers (1, 2, 3), whereas Standard & Poor's uses plus (+) and minus (−) signs.

Sources: Moody's Investors Service, Inc., and Standard & Poor's Corporation.

focus on ETHICS

Can We Trust the Bond Raters?

in practice Moody's Investors Service, Standard & Poor's, and Fitch Ratings play a crucial role in the financial markets. These credit-rating agencies evaluate and attach ratings to credit instruments (for example, bonds). Historically, bonds that received higher ratings were almost always repaid, while lower-rated, more speculative "junk" bonds experienced much higher default rates. The agencies' ratings have a direct impact on firms' cost of raising external capital and investors' appraisals of fixed-income investments.

Recently, the credit-rating agencies have been criticized for their role in the subprime crisis. The agencies attached ratings to complex securities that did not reflect the true risk of the underlying investments. For example, securities backed by mortgages issued to borrowers with bad credit and no documented income often received investment-grade ratings that implied almost zero probability of default. However, when home prices began to decline in 2006, securities backed by risky mortgages did default, including many that had been rated investment grade.

It is not entirely clear why the rating agencies assigned such high ratings to these securities. Did the agencies believe that complex financial engineering could create investment-grade securities out of risky mortgage loans? Did the agencies understand the securities they were rating? Were they unduly influenced by the security issuers, who also happened to pay for the ratings? Apparently, some within the rating agencies were suspicious. In a December, 2006 e-mail exchange between colleagues at Standard & Poor's, one individual proclaimed, "Let's hope we are all wealthy and retired by the time this house of cards falters."[a]

▶ ***What ethical issues may arise because the companies that issue bonds pay the rating agencies to rate their bonds?***

[a]http://oversight.house.gov/images/stories/Hearings/Committee_on_Oversight/E-mail_from_Belinda_Ghetti_to_Nicole_Billick_et_al._December_16_2006.pdf

discussion of ethical issues related to the bond-rating agencies, see the *Focus on Ethics* box.

Normally an inverse relationship exists between the quality of a bond and the rate of return that it must provide bondholders: High-quality (high-rated) bonds provide lower returns than lower-quality (low-rated) bonds. This reflects the lender's risk–return trade-off. When considering bond financing, the financial manager must be concerned with the expected ratings of the bond issue, because these ratings affect salability and cost.

COMMON TYPES OF BONDS

debentures
subordinated debentures
income bonds
mortgage bonds
collateral trust bonds
equipment trust certificates
See Table 6.4.

Bonds can be classified in a variety of ways. Here we break them into traditional bonds (the basic types that have been around for years) and contemporary bonds (newer, more innovative types). The traditional types of bonds are summarized in terms of their key characteristics and priority of lender's claim in Table 6.4. Note that the first three types—**debentures, subordinated debentures,** and **income bonds**—are unsecured, whereas the last three—**mortgage bonds, collateral trust bonds,** and **equipment trust certificates**—are secured.

zero- (or low-) coupon bonds
junk bonds
floating-rate bonds
extendible notes
putable bonds
See Table 6.5 on page 238.

Table 6.5 (see page 238) describes the key characteristics of five contemporary types of bonds: **zero- (or low-) coupon bonds, junk bonds, floating-rate bonds, extendible notes,** and **putable bonds.** These bonds can be either unsecured or secured. Changing capital market conditions and investor preferences have spurred further innovations in bond financing in recent years and will probably continue to do so.

TABLE 6.4 Characteristics and Priority of Lender's Claim of Traditional Types of Bonds

Bond type	Characteristics	Priority of lender's claim
Unsecured bonds		
Debentures	Unsecured bonds that only creditworthy firms can issue. Convertible bonds are normally debentures.	Claims are the same as those of any general creditor. May have other unsecured bonds subordinated to them.
Subordinated debentures	Claims are not satisfied until those of the creditors holding certain (senior) debts have been fully satisfied.	Claim is that of a general creditor but not as good as a senior debt claim.
Income bonds	Payment of interest is required only when earnings are available. Commonly issued in reorganization of a failing firm.	Claim is that of a general creditor. Are not in default when interest payments are missed, because they are contingent only on earnings being available.
Secured Bonds		
Mortgage bonds	Secured by real estate or buildings.	Claim is on proceeds from sale of mortgaged assets; if not fully satisfied, the lender becomes a general creditor. The *first-mortgage* claim must be fully satisfied before distribution of proceeds to *second-mortgage* holders, and so on. A number of mortgages can be issued against the same collateral.
Collateral trust bonds	Secured by stock and (or) bonds that are owned by the issuer. Collateral value is generally 25% to 35% greater than bond value.	Claim is on proceeds from stock and (or) bond collateral; if not fully satisfied, the lender becomes a general creditor.
Equipment trust certificates	Used to finance "rolling stock"—airplanes, trucks, boats, railroad cars. A trustee buys the asset with funds raised through the sale of trust certificates and then leases it to the firm; after making the final scheduled lease payment, the firm receives title to the asset. A type of leasing.	Claim is on proceeds from the sale of the asset; if proceeds do not satisfy outstanding debt, trust certificate lenders become general creditors.

INTERNATIONAL BOND ISSUES

Companies and governments borrow internationally by issuing bonds in two principal financial markets: the Eurobond market and the foreign bond market. Both give borrowers the opportunity to obtain large amounts of long-term debt financing quickly, in the currency of their choice and with flexible repayment terms.

Eurobond
A bond issued by an international borrower and sold to investors in countries with currencies other than the currency in which the bond is denominated.

A **Eurobond** is issued by an international borrower and sold to investors in countries with currencies other than the currency in which the bond is denominated. An example is a dollar-denominated bond issued by a U.S. corporation and sold to Belgian investors. From the founding of the Eurobond market in the 1960s until the mid-1980s, "blue chip" U.S. corporations were the largest single class of Eurobond issuers. Some of these companies were able to borrow in this market at interest rates below those the U.S. government paid on Treasury bonds. As the market matured, issuers became able to choose the currency in which they borrowed, and European and Japanese borrowers rose to prominence. In more recent years, the Eurobond market has become much more balanced in terms of the mix of borrowers, total issue volume, and currency of denomination.

TABLE 6.5 Characteristics of Contemporary Types of Bonds

Bond type	Characteristics[a]
Zero- (or low-) coupon bonds	Issued with no (zero) or a very low coupon (stated interest) rate and sold at a large discount from par. A significant portion (or all) of the investor's return comes from gain in value (that is, par value minus purchase price). Generally callable at par value. Because the issuer can annually deduct the current year's interest accrual without having to pay the interest until the bond matures (or is called), its cash flow each year is increased by the amount of the tax shield provided by the interest deduction.
Junk bonds	Debt rated Ba or lower by Moody's or BB or lower by Standard & Poor's. Commonly used by rapidly growing firms to obtain growth capital, most often as a way to finance mergers and takeovers. High-risk bonds with high yields—often yielding 2% to 3% more than the best-quality corporate debt.
Floating-rate bonds	Stated interest rate is adjusted periodically within stated limits in response to changes in specified money market or capital market rates. Popular when future inflation and interest rates are uncertain. Tend to sell at close to par because of the automatic adjustment to changing market conditions. Some issues provide for annual redemption at par at the option of the bondholder.
Extendible notes	Short maturities, typically 1 to 5 years, that can be renewed for a similar period at the option of holders. Similar to a floating-rate bond. An issue might be a series of 3-year renewable notes over a period of 15 years; every 3 years, the notes could be extended for another 3 years, at a new rate competitive with market interest rates at the time of renewal.
Putable bonds	Bonds that can be redeemed at par (typically, $1,000) at the option of their holder either at specific dates after the date of issue and every 1 to 5 years thereafter or when and if the firm takes specified actions, such as being acquired, acquiring another company, or issuing a large amount of additional debt. In return for its conferring the right to "put the bond" at specified times or when the firm takes certain actions, the bond's yield is lower than that of a nonputable bond.

[a] The claims of lenders (that is, bondholders) against issuers of each of these types of bonds vary, depending on the bonds' other features. Each of these bonds can be unsecured or secured.

foreign bond
A bond that is issued by a foreign corporation or government and is denominated in the investor's home currency and sold in the investor's home market.

In contrast, a **foreign bond** is issued by a foreign corporation or government and is denominated in the investor's home currency and sold in the investor's home market. A Swiss-franc–denominated bond issued in Switzerland by a U.S. company is an example of a foreign bond. The three largest foreign-bond markets are Japan, Switzerland, and the United States.

→ REVIEW QUESTIONS

6–6 What are typical maturities, denominations, and interest payments of a corporate bond? What mechanisms protect bondholders?

6–7 Differentiate between *standard debt provisions* and *restrictive covenants* included in a bond indenture. What are the consequences if a bond issuer violates any of these covenants?

6–8 How is the cost of bond financing typically related to the cost of short-term borrowing? In addition to a bond's maturity, what other major factors affect its cost to the issuer?

6–9 What is a *conversion feature?* A *call feature?* What are *stock purchase warrants?*

6–10 What is the *current yield* for a bond? How are bond prices quoted? How are bonds rated, and why?

6–11 Compare the basic characteristics of *Eurobonds* and *foreign bonds.*

LG 4 6.3 Valuation Fundamentals

valuation
The process that links risk and return to determine the worth of an asset.

Valuation is the process that links risk and return to determine the worth of an asset. It is a relatively simple process that can be applied to *expected* streams of benefits from bonds, stocks, income properties, oil wells, and so on. To determine an asset's worth at a given point in time, a financial manager uses the time-value-of-money techniques presented in Chapter 5 and the concepts of risk and return that we will develop in Chapter 8.

KEY INPUTS

There are three key inputs to the valuation process: (1) cash flows (returns), (2) timing, and (3) a measure of risk, which determines the required return. Each is described below.

Cash Flows (Returns)

The value of any asset depends on the cash flow(s) it is *expected* to provide over the ownership period. To have value, an asset does not have to provide an annual cash flow; it can provide an intermittent cash flow or even a single cash flow over the period.

Personal Finance Example 6.4 ▸ Celia Sargent wishes to estimate the value of three assets she is considering investing in: common stock in Michaels Enterprises, an interest in an oil well, and an original painting by a well-known artist. Her cash flow estimates for each are as follows:

Stock in Michaels Enterprises *Expect* to receive cash dividends of $300 per year indefinitely.

Oil well *Expect* to receive cash flow of $2,000 at the end of year 1, $4,000 at the end of year 2, and $10,000 at the end of year 4, when the well is to be sold.

Original painting *Expect* to be able to sell the painting in 5 years for $85,000.

With these cash flow estimates, Celia has taken the first step toward placing a value on each of the assets.

Timing

In addition to making cash flow estimates, we must know the timing of the cash flows.[2] For example, Celia expects the cash flows of $2,000, $4,000, and $10,000 for the oil well to occur at the ends of years 1, 2, and 4, respectively. The combination of the cash flow and its timing fully defines the return expected from the asset.

2. Although cash flows can occur at any time during a year, for computational convenience as well as custom, we will assume they occur at the *end of the year* unless otherwise noted.

Risk and Required Return

The level of risk associated with a given cash flow can significantly affect its value. In general, the greater the risk of (or the less certain) a cash flow, the lower its value. Greater risk can be incorporated into a valuation analysis by using a higher required return or discount rate. The higher the risk, the greater the required return, and the lower the risk, the less the required return.

Personal Finance Example 6.5 ▸ Let's return to Celia Sargent's task of placing a value on the original painting and consider two scenarios.

Scenario 1—Certainty A major art gallery has contracted to buy the painting for \$85,000 at the end of 5 years. Because this is considered a certain situation, Celia views this asset as "money in the bank." She thus would use the prevailing risk-free rate of 3% as the required return when calculating the value of the painting.

Scenario 2—High risk The values of original paintings by this artist have fluctuated widely over the past 10 years. Although Celia expects to be able to sell the painting for \$85,000, she realizes that its sale price in 5 years could range between \$30,000 and \$140,000. Because of the high uncertainty surrounding the painting's value, Celia believes that a 15% required return is appropriate.

These two estimates of the appropriate required return illustrate how this rate captures risk. The often subjective nature of such estimates is also evident.

BASIC VALUATION MODEL

Simply stated, the value of any asset is *the present value of all future cash flows it is expected to provide over the relevant time period.* The time period can be any length, even infinity. The value of an asset is therefore determined by discounting the expected cash flows back to their present value, using the required return commensurate with the asset's risk as the appropriate discount rate. Using the present value techniques explained in Chapter 5, we can express the value of any asset at time zero, V_0, as

$$V_0 = \frac{CF_1}{(1+r)^1} + \frac{CF_2}{(1+r)^2} + \cdots + \frac{CF_n}{(1+r)^n} \tag{6.4}$$

where

V_0 = value of the asset at time zero
CF_t = cash flow *expected* at the end of year t
r = appropriate required return (discount rate)
n = relevant time period

We can use Equation 6.4 to determine the value of any asset.

Personal Finance Example 6.6 ▸ Celia Sargent uses Equation 6.4 to calculate the value of each asset. She values Michaels Enterprises stock using Equation 5.14 on page 178, which says that the present value of a perpetuity equals the annual payment divided by the required return. In the case of Michaels stock, the annual cash flow is \$300, and Celia decides that a 12% discount rate is appropriate for this investment. Therefore, her estimate of the value of Michaels Enterprises stock is

$$\$300 \div 0.12 = \$2{,}500$$

Next, Celia values the oil well investment, which she believes is the most risky of the three investments. Using a 20% required return, Celia estimates the oil well's value to be

$$\frac{\$2{,}000}{(1 + 0.20)^1} + \frac{\$4{,}000}{(1 + 0.20)^2} + \frac{\$10{,}000}{(1 + 0.20)^4} = \$9{,}266.98$$

Finally, Celia estimates the value of the painting by discounting the expected \$85,000 lump sum payment in 5 years at 15%:

$$\$85{,}000 \div (1 + 0.15)^5 = \$42{,}260.02$$

Note that, regardless of the pattern of the expected cash flow from an asset, the basic valuation equation can be used to determine its value.

→ REVIEW QUESTIONS

6–12 Why is it important for financial managers to understand the valuation process?

6–13 What are the three key inputs to the valuation process?

6–14 Does the valuation process apply only to assets that provide an annual cash flow? Explain.

6–15 Define and specify the general equation for the value of any asset, V_0.

LG 5 LG 6

6.4 Bond Valuation

The basic valuation equation can be customized for use in valuing specific securities: bonds, common stock, and preferred stock. We describe bond valuation in this chapter, and valuation of common stock and preferred stock in Chapter 7.

BOND FUNDAMENTALS

As noted earlier in this chapter, *bonds* are long-term debt instruments used by business and government to raise large sums of money, typically from a diverse group of lenders. Most corporate bonds pay interest *semiannually* (every 6 months) at a stated *coupon interest rate,* have an initial *maturity* of 10 to 30 years, and have a *par value,* or *face value,* of \$1,000 that must be repaid at maturity.

Example 6.7 ▶ Mills Company, a large defense contractor, on January 1, 2013, issued a 10% coupon interest rate, 10-year bond with a \$1,000 par value that pays interest annually. Investors who buy this bond receive the contractual right to two cash flows: (1) \$100 annual interest (10% coupon interest rate × \$1,000 par value) distributed at the end of each year and (2) the \$1,000 par value at the end of the tenth year.

We will use data for Mills's bond issue to look at basic bond valuation.

BASIC BOND VALUATION

The value of a bond is the present value of the payments its issuer is contractually obligated to make, from the current time until it matures. The basic model for the value, B_0, of a bond is given by Equation 6.5:

$$B_0 = I \times \left[\sum_{t=1}^{n} \frac{1}{(1 + r_d)^t}\right] + M \times \left[\frac{1}{(1 + r_d)^n}\right] \quad (6.5)$$

where

B_0 = value of the bond at time zero
I = *annual* interest paid in dollars
n = number of years to maturity
M = par value in dollars
r_d = required return on the bond

We can calculate bond value by using Equation 6.5 and a financial calculator or by using a spreadsheet.

Personal Finance Example 6.8 ▶ Tim Sanchez wishes to determine the current value of the Mills Company bond. *Assuming that interest on the Mills Company bond issue is paid annually* and that the required return is equal to the bond's coupon interest rate, $I = \$100$, $r_d = 10\%$, $M = \$1{,}000$, and $n = 10$ years.

The computations involved in finding the bond value are depicted graphically on the following time line.

Time line for bond valuation (Mills Company's 10% coupon interest rate, 10-year maturity, $1,000 par, January 1, 2013, issue date, paying annual interest, and required return of 10%)

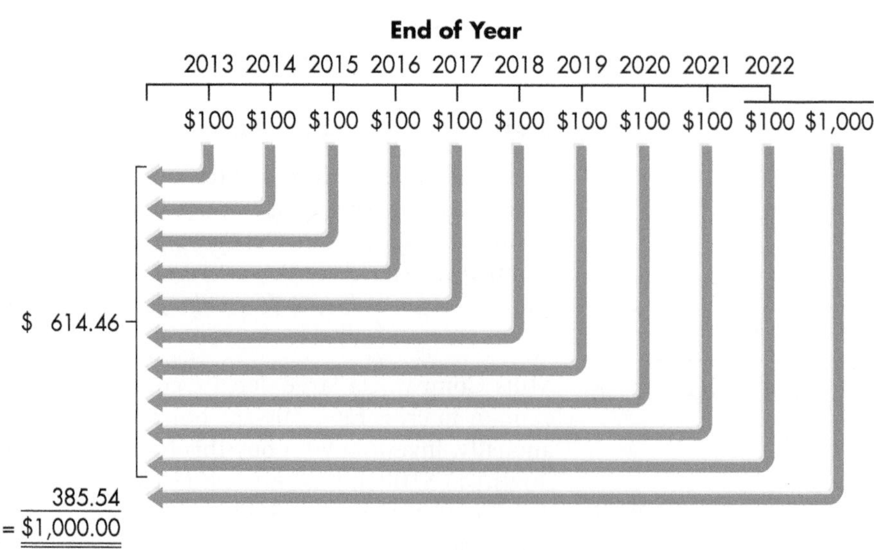

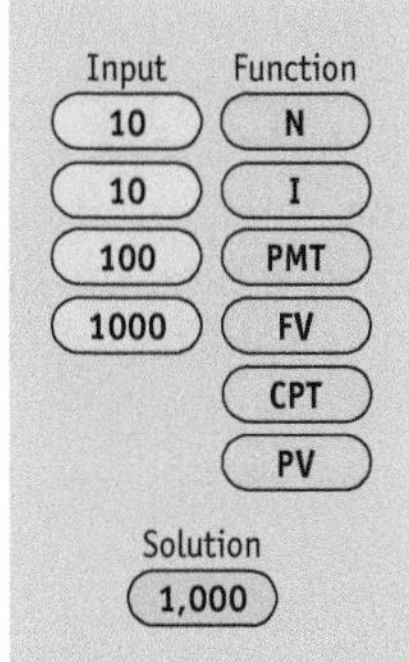

Calculator Use Using the Mills Company's inputs shown at the left, you should find the bond value to be exactly $1,000. Note that *the calculated bond value is equal to its par value; this will always be the case when the required return is equal to the coupon interest rate.*[3]

Spreadsheet Use The value of the Mills Company bond also can be calculated as shown in the following Excel spreadsheet.

	A	B
1	BOND VALUE, ANNUAL INTEREST, REQUIRED RETURN = COUPON INTEREST RATE	
2	Annual interest payment	$100
3	Coupon interest rate	10%
4	Number of years to maturity	10
5	Par value	$1,000
6	Bond value	$1,000.00
	Entry in Cell B6 is =PV(B3,B4,B2,B5,0) Note that Excel will return a negative $1000 as the price that must be paid to acquire this bond.	

BOND VALUE BEHAVIOR

In practice, the value of a bond in the marketplace is rarely equal to its par value. In the bond data (see Table 6.2 on page 235), you can see that the prices of bonds often differ from their par values of 100 (100 percent of par, or $1,000). Some bonds are valued below par (current price below 100), and others are valued above par (current price above 100). A variety of forces in the economy, as well as the passage of time, tend to affect value. Although these external forces are in no way controlled by bond issuers or investors, it is useful to understand the impact that required return and time to maturity have on bond value.

Required Returns and Bond Values

Whenever the required return on a bond differs from the bond's coupon interest rate, the bond's value will differ from its par value. The required return is likely to differ from the coupon interest rate because either (1) economic conditions have changed, causing a shift in the basic cost of long-term funds; or (2) the firm's risk has changed. Increases in the basic cost of long-term funds or in risk will raise the required return; decreases in the cost of funds or in risk will lower the required return.

3. Note that because bonds pay interest in arrears, the prices at which they are quoted and traded reflect their value *plus* any accrued interest. For example, a $1,000 par value, 10% coupon bond paying interest semiannually and having a calculated value of $900 would pay interest of $50 at the end of each 6-month period. If it is now 3 months since the beginning of the interest period, three-sixths of the $50 interest, or $25 (that is, 3/6 × $50), would be accrued. The bond would therefore be quoted at $925—its $900 value plus the $25 in accrued interest. For convenience, *throughout this book, bond values will always be assumed to be calculated at the beginning of the interest period,* thereby avoiding the need to consider accrued interest.

discount
The amount by which a bond sells at a value that is less than its par value.

premium
The amount by which a bond sells at a value that is greater than its par value.

Regardless of the exact cause, what is important is the relationship between the required return and the coupon interest rate: When the required return is greater than the coupon interest rate, the bond value, B_0, will be less than its par value, M. In this case, the bond is said to sell at a **discount,** which will equal $M - B_0$. When the required return falls below the coupon interest rate, the bond value will be greater than par. In this situation, the bond is said to sell at a **premium,** which will equal $B_0 - M$.

Example 6.9 ▶

The preceding example showed that when the required return equaled the coupon interest rate, the bond's value equaled its $1,000 par value. If for the same bond the required return were to rise to 12% or fall to 8%, its value in each case could be found using Equation 6.5 or as follows.

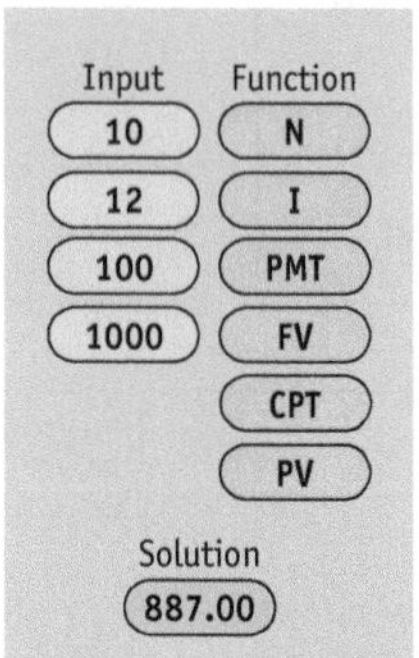

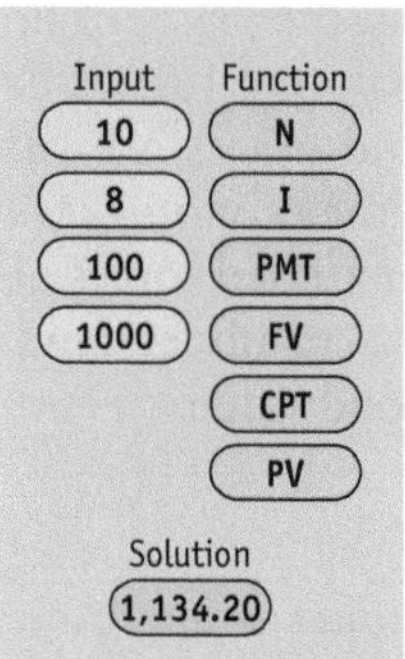

Calculator Use Using the inputs shown at the left for the two different required returns, you will find the value of the bond to be below or above par. At a 12% required return, the bond would sell at a *discount* of $113.00 ($1,000 par value − $887.00 value). At the 8% required return, the bond would sell for a *premium* of $134.20 ($1,134.20 value − $1,000 par value). The results of these calculations for Mills Company's bond values are summarized in Table 6.6 and graphically depicted in Figure 6.4. The inverse relationship between bond value and required return is clearly shown in the figure.

Spreadsheet Use The values for the Mills Company bond at required returns of 12% and 8% also can be calculated as shown in the following Excel spreadsheet. Once this spreadsheet has been configured you can compare bond values for any two required returns by simply changing the input values.

	A	B	C
1	BOND VALUE, ANNUAL INTEREST, REQUIRED RETURN NOT EQUAL TO COUPON INTEREST RATE		
2	Annual interest payment	$100	$100
3	Coupon interest rate	10%	10%
4	Annual required return	12%	8%
5	Number of years to maturity	10	10
6	Par value	$1,000	$1,000
7	Bond value	$887.00	$1,134.20

Entry in Cell B7 is =PV(B4,B5,B2,B6,0)
Note that the bond trades at a discount (i.e., below par) because the bond's coupon rate is below investors' required return.

Entry in Cell C7 is =PV(C4,C5,C2,C6,0)
Note that the bond trades at a premium because the bond's coupon rate is above investors' required return.

TABLE 6.6 Bond Values for Various Required Returns (Mills Company's 10% Coupon Interest Rate, 10-Year Maturity, $1,000 Par, January 1, 2013, Issue Date, Paying Annual Interest)

Required return, r_d	Bond value, B_0	Status
12%	$ 887.00	Discount
10	1,000.00	Par value
8	1,134.20	Premium

FIGURE 6.4

Bond Values and Required Returns
Bond values and required returns (Mills Company's 10% coupon interest rate, 10-year maturity, $1,000 par, January 1, 2013, issue date, paying annual interest)

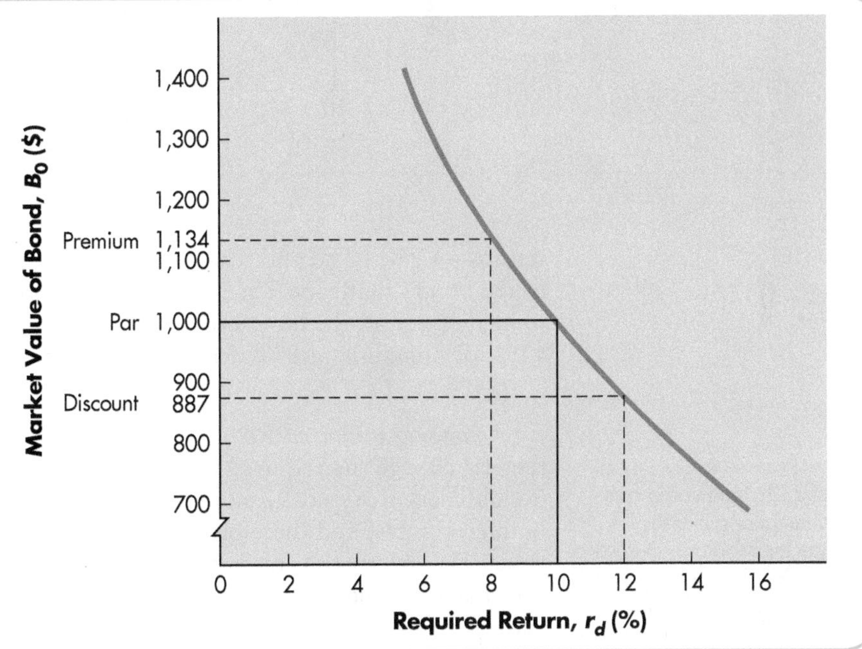

Time to Maturity and Bond Values

Whenever the required return is different from the coupon interest rate, the amount of time to maturity affects bond value. An additional factor is whether required returns are constant or change over the life of the bond.

Constant Required Returns When the required return is different from the coupon interest rate and is *constant until maturity,* the value of the bond will approach its par value as the passage of time moves the bond's value closer to maturity. (Of course, when the required return *equals* the coupon interest rate, the bond's value will remain at par until it matures.)

Example 6.10 ▸ Figure 6.5 depicts the behavior of the bond values calculated earlier and presented in Table 6.6 for Mills Company's 10% coupon interest rate bond paying annual interest and having 10 years to maturity. Each of the three required

FIGURE 6.5

Time to Maturity and Bond Values
Relationship among time to maturity, required returns, and bond values (Mills Company's 10% coupon interest rate, 10-year maturity, $1,000 par, January 1, 2013, issue date, paying annual interest)

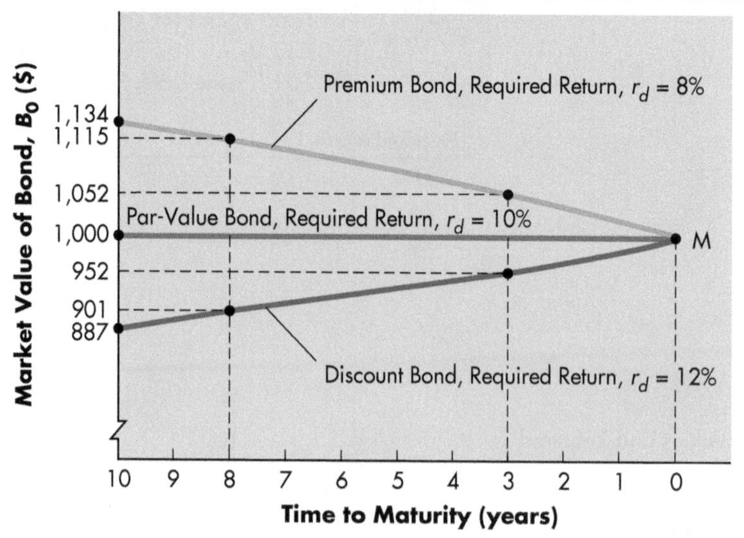

returns—12%, 10%, and 8%—is assumed to remain constant over the 10 years to the bond's maturity. The bond's value at both 12% and 8% approaches and ultimately equals the bond's $1,000 par value at its maturity, as the discount (at 12%) or premium (at 8%) declines with the passage of time.

interest rate risk
The chance that interest rates will change and thereby change the required return and bond value. Rising rates, which result in decreasing bond values, are of greatest concern.

Changing Required Returns The chance that interest rates will change and thereby change the required return and bond value is called **interest rate risk.**[4] Bondholders are typically more concerned with rising interest rates because a rise in interest rates, and therefore in the required return, causes a decrease in bond value. The shorter the amount of time until a bond's maturity, the less responsive is its market value to a given change in the required return. In other words, *short maturities have less interest rate risk than long maturities when all other features (coupon interest rate, par value, and interest payment frequency) are the same.* This is because of the mathematics of time value; the present values of short-term cash flows change far less than the present values of longer-term cash flows in response to a given change in the discount rate (required return).

Example 6.11 ▶

The effect of changing required returns on bonds with differing maturities can be illustrated by using Mills Company's bond and Figure 6.5. If the required return rises from 10% to 12% when the bond has 8 years to maturity (see the dashed line at 8 years), the bond's value decreases from $1,000 to $901—a 9.9% decrease. If the same change in required return had occurred with only 3 years to

4. A more robust measure of a bond's response to interest rate changes is *duration.* Duration measures the sensitivity of a bond's prices to changing interest rates. It incorporates both the interest rate (coupon rate) and the time to maturity into a single statistic. Duration is simply a weighted average of the maturity of the present values of all the contractual cash flows yet to be paid by the bond. Duration is stated in years, so a bond with a 5-year duration will decrease in value by 5 percent if interest rates rise by 1 percent or will increase in value by 5 percent if interest rates fall by 1 percent.

maturity (see the dashed line at 3 years), the bond's value would have dropped to just $952—only a 4.8% decrease. Similar types of responses can be seen for the change in bond value associated with decreases in required returns. The shorter the time to maturity, the less the impact on bond value caused by a given change in the required return.

YIELD TO MATURITY (YTM)

When investors evaluate bonds, they commonly consider yield to maturity (YTM). This is the compound annual rate of return earned on a debt security purchased on a given day and held to maturity. (The measure assumes, of course, that the issuer makes all scheduled interest and principal payments as promised.)[5] The yield to maturity on a bond with a current price equal to its par value (that is, $B_0 = M$) will always equal the coupon interest rate. When the bond value differs from par, the yield to maturity will differ from the coupon interest rate.

Assuming that interest is paid annually, the yield to maturity on a bond can be found by solving Equation 6.5 for r_d. In other words, the current value, the annual interest, the par value, and the number of years to maturity are known, and the required return must be found. The required return is the bond's yield to maturity. The YTM can be found by using a financial calculator, by using an Excel spreadsheet, or by trial and error. The calculator provides accurate YTM values with minimum effort.

Personal Finance Example 6.12 ▸ Earl Washington wishes to find the YTM on Mills Company's bond. The bond currently sells for $1,080, has a 10% coupon interest rate and $1,000 par value, pays interest annually, and has 10 years to maturity.

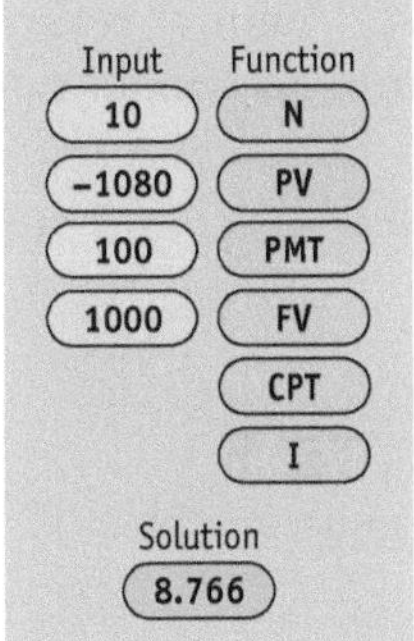

Calculator Use Most calculators require *either* the present value (B_0 in this case) or the future values (I and M in this case) to be input as negative numbers to calculate yield to maturity. That approach is employed here. Using the inputs shown at the left, you should find the YTM to be 8.766%.

Spreadsheet Use The yield to maturity of Mills Company's bond also can be calculated as shown in the following Excel spreadsheet. First, enter all the bond's cash flows. Notice that you begin with the bond's price as an outflow (a negative number). In other words, an investor has to pay the price up front to receive the cash flows over the next 10 years. Next, use Excel's *internal rate of return* function. This function calculates the discount rate that makes the present value of a series of cash flows equal to zero. In this case, when the present value of all cash flows is zero, the present value of the inflows (interest and principal) equals the present value of the outflows (the bond's initial price). In other words, the internal rate of return function is giving us the bond's YTM, the discount rate that equates the bond's price to the present value of its cash flows.

5. Many bonds have a *call feature,* which means they may not reach maturity if the issuer, after a specified time period, calls them back. Because the call feature typically cannot be exercised until a specific future date, investors often calculate the *yield to call (YTC)*. The yield to call represents the rate of return that investors earn if they buy a callable bond at a specific price and hold it until it is called back and they receive the *call price,* which would be set above the bond's par value. Here our focus is solely on the more general measure of yield to maturity.

	A	B
1	YIELD TO MATURITY, ANNUAL INTEREST	
2	Year	Cash Flow
3	0	($1,080)
4	1	$100
5	2	$100
6	3	$100
7	4	$100
8	5	$100
9	6	$100
10	7	$100
11	8	$100
12	9	$100
13	10	$1,100
14	YTM	8.766%
	Entry in Cell B14 is =IRR(B3:B13)	

SEMIANNUAL INTEREST AND BOND VALUES

The procedure used to value bonds paying interest semiannually is similar to that shown in Chapter 5 for compounding interest more frequently than annually, except that here we need to find present value instead of future value. It involves

1. Converting annual interest, I, to semiannual interest by dividing I by 2.
2. Converting the number of years to maturity, n, to the number of 6-month periods to maturity by multiplying n by 2.
3. Converting the required stated (rather than effective)[6] annual return for similar-risk bonds that also pay semiannual interest from an annual rate, r_d, to a semiannual rate by dividing r_d by 2.

Substituting these three changes into Equation 6.5 yields

$$B_0 = \frac{I}{2} \times \left[\sum_{t=1}^{2n} \frac{1}{\left(1 + \frac{r_d}{2}\right)^t} \right] + M \times \left[\frac{1}{\left(1 + \frac{r_d}{2}\right)^{2n}} \right] \qquad (6.6)$$

6. As we noted in Chapter 5, the effective annual rate of interest, EAR, for stated interest rate r, when interest is paid semiannually ($m = 2$), can be found by using Equation 5.17:

$$EAR = \left(1 + \frac{r}{2}\right)^2 - 1$$

For example, a bond with a 12% required stated annual return, r_d, that pays semiannual interest would have an effective annual rate of

$$EAR = \left(1 + \frac{0.12}{2}\right)^2 - 1 = (1.06)^2 - 1 = 1.1236 - 1 = 0.1236 = 12.36\%$$

Because most bonds pay semiannual interest at semiannual rates equal to 50 percent of the stated annual rate, their effective annual rates are generally higher than their stated annual rates.

Example 6.13 ▸ Assuming that the Mills Company bond pays interest semiannually and that the required stated annual return, r_d, is 12% for similar-risk bonds that also pay semiannual interest, substituting these values into Equation 6.6 yields

$$B_0 = \frac{\$100}{2} \times \left[\sum_{t=1}^{20} \frac{1}{\left(1 + \frac{0.12}{2}\right)^t} \right] + \$1{,}000 \times \left[\frac{1}{\left(1 + \frac{0.12}{2}\right)^{20}} \right] = \$885.30$$

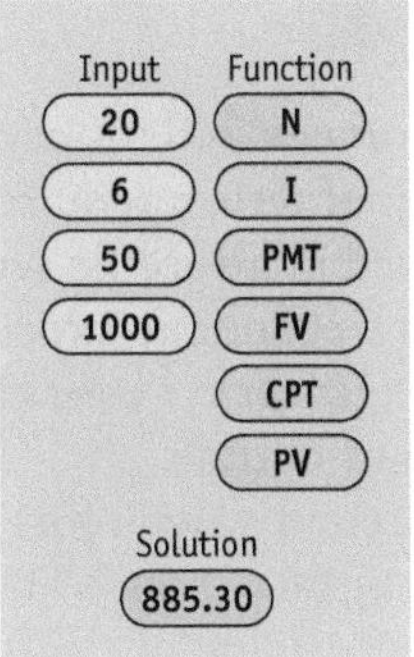

Calculator Use In using a calculator to find bond value when interest is paid semiannually, we must double the number of periods and divide both the required stated annual return and the annual interest by 2. For the Mills Company bond, we would use 20 periods (2 × 10 years), a required return of 6% (12% ÷ 2), and an interest payment of \$50 (\$100 ÷ 2). Using these inputs, you should find the bond value with semiannual interest to be \$885.30, as shown at the left.

Spreadsheet Use The value of the Mills Company bond paying semiannual interest at a required return of 12% also can be calculated as shown in the following Excel spreadsheet.

	A	B
1	BOND VALUE, SEMIANNUAL INTEREST	
2	Semiannual interest payment	\$50
3	Semiannual required return	6%
4	Number of periods to maturity	20
5	Par value	\$1,000
6	Bond value	\$885.30

Entry in Cell B6 is =PV(B3,B4,B2,B5,0)
Note that Excel will produce a negative value for the bond's price

Comparing this result with the \$887.00 value found earlier for annual compounding, we can see that the bond's value is lower when semiannual interest is paid. *This will always occur when the bond sells at a discount.* For bonds selling at a premium, the opposite will occur: The value with semiannual interest will be greater than with annual interest.

→ REVIEW QUESTIONS

6–16 What basic procedure is used to value a bond that pays annual interest? Semiannual interest?

6–17 What relationship between the required return and the coupon interest rate will cause a bond to sell at a *discount?* At a *premium?* At its *par value?*

6–18 If the required return on a bond differs from its coupon interest rate, describe the behavior of the bond value over time as the bond moves toward maturity.

6–19 As a risk-averse investor, would you prefer bonds with short or long periods until maturity? Why?

6–20 What is a bond's *yield to maturity* (*YTM*)? Briefly describe the use of a financial calculator and the use of an Excel spreadsheet for finding YTM.

Summary

FOCUS ON VALUE

Interest rates and required returns embody the real cost of money, inflationary expectations, and issuer and issue risk. They reflect the level of return required by market participants as compensation for the risk perceived in a specific security or asset investment. Because these returns are affected by economic expectations, they vary as a function of time, typically rising for longer-term maturities. The yield curve reflects such market expectations at any point in time.

The value of an asset can be found by calculating the present value of its expected cash flows, using the required return as the discount rate. Bonds are the easiest financial assets to value; both the amounts and the timing of their cash flows are contractual and, therefore, known with certainty (at least for high-grade bonds). The financial manager needs to understand how to apply valuation techniques to bonds, stocks, and tangible assets (as we will demonstrate in the following chapters) to make decisions that are consistent with the firm's **share price maximization goal.**

REVIEW OF LEARNING GOALS

LG 1 **Describe interest rate fundamentals, the term structure of interest rates, and risk premiums.** The flow of funds between savers and borrowers is regulated by the interest rate or required return. In a perfect, inflation-free, certain world there would be one cost of money—the real rate of interest. The nominal or actual interest rate is the sum of the risk-free rate and a risk premium reflecting issuer and issue characteristics. The risk-free rate is the real rate of interest plus an inflation premium.

For any class of similar-risk bonds, the term structure of interest rates reflects the relationship between the interest rate or rate of return and the time to maturity. Yield curves can be downward sloping (inverted), upward sloping (normal), or flat. The expectations theory, liquidity preference theory, and market segmentation theory are cited to explain the shape of the yield curve. Risk premiums for non-Treasury debt issues result from business risk, financial risk, interest rate risk, liquidity risk, tax risk, default risk, maturity risk, and contractual provision risk.

LG 2 **Review the legal aspects of bond financing and bond cost.** Corporate bonds are long-term debt instruments indicating that a corporation has borrowed an amount that it promises to repay in the future under clearly defined terms. Most bonds are issued with maturities of 10 to 30 years and a par value of $1,000. The bond indenture, enforced by a trustee, states all conditions of the bond issue. It contains both standard debt provisions and restrictive covenants, which may include a sinking-fund requirement and/or a security interest. The cost of a bond to an issuer depends on its maturity, offering size, and issuer risk and on the basic cost of money.

LG 3 **Discuss the general features, yields, prices, ratings, popular types, and international issues of corporate bonds.** A bond issue may include a conversion feature, a call feature, or stock purchase warrants. The yield, or rate of return, on a bond can be measured by its current yield, yield to maturity (YTM), or yield to call (YTC). Bond prices are typically reported along with their coupon, maturity date, and yield to maturity (YTM). Bond ratings by independent agencies indicate the risk of a bond issue. Various types of traditional and contemporary bonds are available. Eurobonds and foreign bonds enable established creditworthy companies and governments to borrow large amounts internationally.

LG 4 **Understand the key inputs and basic model used in the valuation process.** Key inputs to the valuation process include cash flows (returns), timing, and risk and the required return. The value of any asset is equal to the present value of all future cash flows it is *expected* to provide over the relevant time period.

LG 5 **Apply the basic valuation model to bonds, and describe the impact of required return and time to maturity on bond values.** The value of a bond is the present value of its interest payments plus the present value of its par value. The discount rate used to determine bond value is the required return, which may differ from the bond's coupon interest rate. A bond can sell at a discount, at par, or at a premium, depending on whether the required return is greater than, equal to, or less than its coupon interest rate. The amount of time to maturity affects bond values. The value of a bond will approach its par value as the bond moves closer to maturity. The chance that interest rates will change and thereby change the required return and bond value is called interest rate risk. The shorter the amount of time until a bond's maturity, the less responsive is its market value to a given change in the required return.

LG 6 **Explain yield to maturity (YTM), its calculation, and the procedure used to value bonds that pay interest semiannually.** Yield to maturity is the rate of return investors earn if they buy a bond at a specific price and hold it until maturity. YTM can be calculated by using a financial calculator or by using an Excel spreadsheet. Bonds that pay interest semiannually are valued by using the same procedure used to value bonds paying annual interest, except that the interest payments are one-half of the annual interest payments, the number of periods is twice the number of years to maturity, and the required return is one-half of the stated annual required return on similar-risk bonds.

Opener-in-Review

In the chapter opener you learned that the United States government had more than $13 trillion in debt outstanding in the form of Treasury bills, notes, and bonds in 2010. From time to time, the Treasury changes the mix of securities that it issues to finance government debt, issuing more bills than bonds or vice versa.

a. With short-term interest rates near 0 percent in 2010, suppose the Treasury decided to replace maturing notes and bonds by issuing new Treasury bills, thus shortening the average maturity of U.S. debt outstanding. Discuss the pros and cons of this strategy.

b. The average maturity of outstanding U.S. Treasury debt is about 5 years. Suppose a newly issued 5-year Treasury note has a coupon rate of 2 percent and sells at par. What happens to the value of this bond if the inflation rate rises 1 percentage point, causing the yield-to-maturity on the 5-year note to jump to 3 percent shortly after it is issued?

c. Assume that the "average" Treasury security outstanding has the features described in part **b**. If total U.S. debt is $13 trillion and an increase in inflation causes yields on Treasury securities to increase by 1 percentage point, by how much would the market value of the outstanding debt fall? What does this suggest about the incentives of government policy makers to pursue policies that could lead to higher inflation?

Self-Test Problems (Solutions in Appendix)

LG 5 LG 6 **ST6–1 Bond valuation** Lahey Industries has outstanding a $1,000 par-value bond with an 8% coupon interest rate. The bond has 12 years remaining to its maturity date.

a. If interest is paid *annually,* find the value of the bond when the required return is (1) 7%, (2) 8%, and (3) 10%.

b. Indicate for each case in part **a** whether the bond is selling at a discount, at a premium, or at its par value.

c. Using the 10% required return, find the bond's value when interest is paid *semiannually.*

LG 3 LG 6 **ST6–2 Bond yields** Elliot Enterprises' bonds currently sell for $1,150, have an 11% coupon interest rate and a $1,000 par value, pay interest *annually,* and have 18 years to maturity.

a. Calculate the bonds' *current yield.*

b. Calculate the bonds' *yield to maturity (YTM).*

c. Compare the YTM calculated in part **b** to the bonds' coupon interest rate and current yield (calculated in part **a**). Use a comparison of the bonds' current price and par value to explain these differences.

Warm-Up Exercises All problems are available in myfinancelab.

LG 1 **E6–1** The risk-free rate on T-bills recently was 1.23%. If the real rate of interest is estimated to be 0.80%, what was the expected level of inflation?

LG 1 **E6–2** The yields for Treasuries with differing maturities on a recent day were as shown in the table on page 253.

a. Use the information to plot a *yield curve* for this date.

b. If the expectations hypothesis is true, approximately what rate of return do investors expect a 5-year Treasury note to pay 5 years from now?

Maturity	Yield
3 months	1.41%
6 months	1.71
2 years	2.68
3 years	3.01
5 years	3.70
10 years	4.51
30 years	5.25

c. If the expectations hypothesis is true, approximately (ignoring compounding) what rate of return do investors expect a 1-year Treasury security to pay starting 2 years from now?

d. Is it possible that even though the yield curve slopes up in this problem, investors do not expect rising interest rates? Explain.

LG 1 **E6–3** The yields for Treasuries with differing maturities, including an estimate of the real rate of interest, on a recent day were as shown in the following table:

Maturity	Yield	Real rate of interest
3 months	1.41%	0.80%
6 months	1.71	0.80
2 years	2.68	0.80
3 years	3.01	0.80
5 years	3.70	0.80
10 years	4.51	0.80
30 years	5.25	0.80

Use the information in the preceding table to calculate the *inflation expectation* for each maturity.

LG 1 **E6–4** Recently, the annual inflation rate measured by the Consumer Price Index (CPI) was forecast to be 3.3%. How could a T-bill have had a negative real rate of return over the same period? How could it have had a zero real rate of return? What minimum rate of return must the T-bill have earned to meet your requirement of a 2% real rate of return?

LG 1 **E6–5** Calculate the *risk premium* for each of the following rating classes of long-term securities, assuming that the yield to maturity (YTM) for comparable Treasuries is 4.51%.

Rating class	Nominal interest rate
AAA	5.12%
BBB	5.78
B	7.82

LG 4 **E6–6** You have two assets and must calculate their values today based on their different payment streams and appropriate required returns. Asset 1 has a required return of 15% and will produce a stream of $500 at the end of each year indefinitely. Asset 2 has a required return of 10% and will produce an end-of-year cash flow of $1,200 in the first year, $1,500 in the second year, and $850 in its third and final year.

LG 5 **E6–7** A bond with 5 years to maturity and a coupon rate of 6% has a par, or face, value of $20,000. Interest is paid annually. If you required a return of 8% on this bond, what is the value of this bond to you?

LG 5 **E6–8** Assume a 5-year Treasury bond has a coupon rate of 4.5%.

a. Give examples of required rates of return that would make the bond sell at a discount, at a premium, and at par.

b. If this bond's par value is $10,000, calculate the differing values for this bond given the required rates you chose in part **a.**

Problems

All problems are available in myfinancelab.

LG 1 **P6–1** **Interest rate fundamentals: The real rate of return** Carl Foster, a trainee at an investment banking firm, is trying to get an idea of what real rate of return investors are expecting in today's marketplace. He has looked up the rate paid on 3-month U.S. Treasury bills and found it to be 5.5%. He has decided to use the rate of change in the Consumer Price Index as a proxy for the inflationary expectations of investors. That annualized rate now stands at 3%. On the basis of the information that Carl has collected, what estimate can he make of the *real rate of return?*

LG 1 **P6–2** **Real rate of interest** To estimate the real rate of interest, the economics division of Mountain Banks—a major bank holding company—has gathered the data summarized in the following table. Because there is a high likelihood that new tax legislation will be passed in the near future, current data as well as data reflecting the probable impact of passage of the legislation on the demand for funds are also

	Currently		With passage of tax legislation
Amount of funds supplied/demanded ($ billion)	**Interest rate required by funds suppliers**	**Interest rate required by funds demanders**	**Interest rate required by funds demanders**
$ 1	2%	7%	9%
5	3	6	8
10	4	4	7
20	6	3	6
50	7	2	4
100	9	1	3

included in the table. (*Note:* The proposed legislation will not affect the supply schedule of funds. Assume a perfect world in which inflation is expected to be zero, funds suppliers and demanders have no liquidity preference, and all outcomes are certain.)

a. Draw the supply curve and the demand curve for funds using the current data. (*Note:* Unlike the functions in Figure 6.1 on page 223, the functions here will not appear as straight lines.)
b. Using your graph, label and note the *real rate of interest* using the current data.
c. Add to the graph drawn in part **a** the new demand curve expected in the event that the proposed tax legislation is passed.
d. What is the new real rate of interest? Compare and analyze this finding in light of your analysis in part **b.**

Personal Finance Problem

LG 1 **P6–3 Real and nominal rates of interest** Zane Perelli currently has $100 that he can spend today on polo shirts costing $25 each. Alternatively, he could invest the $100 in a risk-free U.S. Treasury security that is expected to earn a 9% nominal rate of interest. The consensus forecast of leading economists is a 5% rate of inflation over the coming year.

a. How many polo shirts can Zane purchase today?
b. How much money will Zane have at the end of 1 year if he forgoes purchasing the polo shirts today?
c. How much would you expect the polo shirts to cost at the end of 1 year in light of the expected inflation?
d. Use your findings in parts **b** and **c** to determine how many polo shirts (fractions are OK) Zane can purchase at the end of 1 year. In percentage terms, how many more or fewer polo shirts can Zane buy at the end of 1 year?
e. What is Zane's *real rate of return* over the year? How is it related to the percentage change in Zane's buying power found in part **d**? Explain.

LG 1 **P6–4 Yield curve** A firm wishing to evaluate interest rate behavior has gathered yield data on five U.S. Treasury securities, each having a different maturity and all measured at the same point in time. The summarized data follow.

U.S. Treasury security	Time to maturity	Yield
A	1 year	12.6%
B	10 years	11.2
C	6 months	13.0
D	20 years	11.0
E	5 years	11.4

a. Draw the yield curve associated with these data.
b. Describe the resulting yield curve in part **a,** and explain the general expectations embodied in it.

LG 1 **P6–5 Nominal interest rates and yield curves** A recent study of inflationary expectations has revealed that the consensus among economic forecasters yields the following average annual rates of inflation expected over the periods noted. (*Note:* Assume that the risk that future interest rate movements will affect longer maturities more than shorter maturities is zero; that is, there is no *maturity risk.*)

Period	Average annual rate of inflation
3 months	5%
2 years	6
5 years	8
10 years	8.5
20 years	9

a. If the real rate of interest is currently 2.5%, find the *nominal rate of interest* on each of the following U.S. Treasury issues: 20-year bond, 3-month bill, 2-year note, and 5-year bond.
b. If the real rate of interest suddenly dropped to 2% without any change in inflationary expectations, what effect, if any, would this have on your answers in part **a?** Explain.
c. Using your findings in part **a,** draw a yield curve for U.S. Treasury securities. Describe the general shape and expectations reflected by the curve.
d. What would a follower of the *liquidity preference theory* say about how the preferences of lenders and borrowers tend to affect the shape of the yield curve drawn in part **c?** Illustrate that effect by placing on your graph a dotted line that approximates the yield curve without the effect of liquidity preference.
e. What would a follower of the *market segmentation theory* say about the supply and demand for long-term loans versus the supply and demand for short-term loans given the yield curve constructed for part **c** of this problem?

LG 1 **P6–6 Nominal and real rates and yield curves** A firm wishing to evaluate interest rate behavior has gathered data on the nominal rate of interest and on inflationary expectations for five U.S. Treasury securities, each having a different maturity and each measured at a different point in time during the year just ended. (*Note:* Assume that the risk that future interest rate movements will affect longer maturities more than shorter maturities is zero; that is, there is no *maturity risk.*) These data are summarized in the following table.

U.S. Treasury security	Point in time	Maturity	Nominal rate of interest	Inflationary expectation
A	Jan. 7	2 years	12.6%	9.5%
B	Mar. 12	10 years	11.2	8.2
C	May 30	6 months	13.0	10.0
D	Aug. 15	20 years	11.0	8.1
E	Dec. 30	5 years	11.4	8.3

a. Using the preceding data, find the *real rate of interest* at each point in time.
b. Describe the behavior of the real rate of interest over the year. What forces might be responsible for such behavior?
c. Draw the yield curve associated with these data, assuming that the nominal rates were measured at the same point in time.
d. Describe the resulting yield curve in part **c,** and explain the general expectations embodied in it.

LG 1 **P6–7 Term structure of interest rates** The following yield data for a number of highest-quality corporate bonds existed at each of the three points in time noted.

	Yield		
Time to maturity (years)	**5 years ago**	**2 years ago**	**Today**
1	9.1%	14.6%	9.3%
3	9.2	12.8	9.8
5	9.3	12.2	10.9
10	9.5	10.9	12.6
15	9.4	10.7	12.7
20	9.3	10.5	12.9
30	9.4	10.5	13.5

a. On the same set of axes, draw the yield curve at each of the three given times.
b. Label each curve in part **a** with its general shape (downward-sloping, upward-sloping, flat).
c. Describe the general interest rate expectation existing at each of the three times.
d. Examine the data from 5 years ago. According to the expectations theory, what approximate return did investors expect a 5-year bond to pay as of today?

LG 1 **P6–8 Risk-free rate and risk premiums** The real rate of interest is currently 3%; the inflation expectation and risk premiums for a number of securities follow.

	Inflation expectation	
Security	**Premium**	**Risk premium**
A	6%	3%
B	9	2
C	8	2
D	5	4
E	11	1

a. Find the *risk-free rate of interest*, R_F, that is applicable to each security.
b. Although not noted, what factor must be the cause of the differing risk-free rates found in part **a?**
c. Find the *nominal rate of interest* for each security.

LG 1 **P6–9 Risk premiums** Eleanor Burns is attempting to find the nominal rate of interest for each of two securities—A and B—issued by different firms at the same point in time. She has gathered the following data:

Characteristic	Security A	Security B
Time to maturity	3 years	15 years
Inflation expectation premium	9.0%	7.0%
Risk premium for:		
Liquidity risk	1.0%	1.0%
Default risk	1.0%	2.0%
Maturity risk	0.5%	1.5%
Other risk	0.5%	1.5%

a. If the real rate of interest is currently 2%, find the *risk-free rate of interest* applicable to each security.
b. Find the total risk premium attributable to each security's issuer and issue characteristics.
c. Calculate the *nominal rate of interest* for each security. Compare and discuss your findings.

LG 2 **P6–10 Bond interest payments before and after taxes** Charter Corp. has issued 2,500 debentures with a total principal value of $2,500,000. The bonds have a coupon interest rate of 7%.
a. What dollar amount of interest per bond can an investor expect to receive each year from Charter?
b. What is Charter's total interest expense per year associated with this bond issue?
c. Assuming that Charter is in a 35% corporate tax bracket, what is the company's net after-tax interest cost associated with this bond issue?

LG 4 **P6–11 Bond prices and yields** Assume that the Financial Management Corporation's $1,000-par-value bond had a 5.700% coupon, matured on May 15, 2020, had a current price quote of 97.708, and had a yield to maturity (YTM) of 6.034%. Given this information, answer the following questions:
a. What was the dollar price of the bond?
b. What is the bond's *current yield?*
c. Is the bond selling at par, at a discount, or at a premium? Why?
d. Compare the bond's current yield calculated in part **b** to its YTM and explain why they differ.

Personal Finance Problem

LG 4 **P6–12 Valuation fundamentals** Imagine that you are trying to evaluate the economics of purchasing an automobile. You expect the car to provide annual after-tax cash benefits of $1,200 at the end of each year and assume that you can sell the car for after-tax proceeds of $5,000 at the end of the planned 5-year ownership period. All funds for purchasing the car will be drawn from your savings, which are currently earning 6% after taxes.
a. Identify the cash flows, their timing, and the required return applicable to valuing the car.
b. What is the maximum price you would be willing to pay to acquire the car? Explain.

LG 4 **P6–13 Valuation of assets** Using the information provided in the following table, find the value of each asset.

	Cash flow		
Asset	**End of year**	**Amount**	**Appropriate required return**
A	1	$ 5,000	18%
	2	5,000	
	3	5,000	
B	1 through ∞	$ 300	15%
C	1	$ 0	16%
	2	0	
	3	0	
	4	0	
	5	35,000	
D	1 through 5	$ 1,500	12%
	6	8,500	
E	1	$ 2,000	14%
	2	3,000	
	3	5,000	
	4	7,000	
	5	4,000	
	6	1,000	

Personal Finance Problem

LG 4 **P6–14 Asset valuation and risk** Laura Drake wishes to estimate the value of an asset expected to provide cash inflows of $3,000 per year at the end of years 1 through 4 and $15,000 at the end of year 5. Her research indicates that she must earn 10% on low-risk assets, 15% on average-risk assets, and 22% on high-risk assets.

a. Determine what is the most Laura should pay for the asset if it is classified as (1) low-risk, (2) average-risk, and (3) high-risk.

b. Suppose Laura is unable to assess the risk of the asset and wants to be certain she's making a good deal. On the basis of your findings in part **a,** what is the most she should pay? Why?

c. All else being the same, what effect does increasing risk have on the value of an asset? Explain in light of your findings in part **a.**

LG 5 **P6–15 Basic bond valuation** Complex Systems has an outstanding issue of $1,000-par-value bonds with a 12% coupon interest rate. The issue pays interest *annually* and has 16 years remaining to its maturity date.

a. If bonds of similar risk are currently earning a 10% rate of return, how much should the Complex Systems bond sell for today?

b. Describe the *two* possible reasons why the rate on similar-risk bonds is below the coupon interest rate on the Complex Systems bond.

c. If the required return were at 12% instead of 10%, what would the current value of Complex Systems' bond be? Contrast this finding with your findings in part **a** and discuss.

LG 5 **P6–16** **Bond valuation—Annual interest** Calculate the value of each of the bonds shown in the following table, all of which pay interest *annually.*

Bond	Par value	Coupon interest rate	Years to maturity	Required return
A	$1,000	14%	20	12%
B	1,000	8	16	8
C	100	10	8	13
D	500	16	13	18
E	1,000	12	10	10

LG 5 **P6–17** **Bond value and changing required returns** Midland Utilities has outstanding a bond issue that will mature to its $1,000 par value in 12 years. The bond has a coupon interest rate of 11% and pays interest *annually.*

a. Find the value of the bond if the required return is (1) 11%, (2) 15%, and (3) 8%.

b. Plot your findings in part **a** on a set of "required return (*x* axis)–market value of bond (*y* axis)" axes.

c. Use your findings in parts **a** and **b** to discuss the relationship between the coupon interest rate on a bond and the required return and the market value of the bond relative to its par value.

d. What *two* possible reasons could cause the required return to differ from the coupon interest rate?

LG 5 **P6–18** **Bond value and time—Constant required returns** Pecos Manufacturing has just issued a 15-year, 12% coupon interest rate, $1,000-par bond that pays interest *annually.* The required return is currently 14%, and the company is certain it will remain at 14% until the bond matures in 15 years.

a. Assuming that the required return does remain at 14% until maturity, find the value of the bond with (1) 15 years, (2) 12 years, (3) 9 years, (4) 6 years, (5) 3 years, and (6) 1 year to maturity.

b. Plot your findings on a set of "time to maturity (*x* axis)–market value of bond (*y* axis)" axes constructed similarly to Figure 6.5 on page 246.

c. All else remaining the same, when the required return differs from the coupon interest rate and is assumed to be constant to maturity, what happens to the bond value as time moves toward maturity? Explain in light of the graph in part **b.**

Personal Finance Problem

LG 5 **P6–19** **Bond value and time—Changing required returns** Lynn Parsons is considering investing in either of two outstanding bonds. The bonds both have $1,000 par values and 11% coupon interest rates and pay *annual* interest. Bond A has exactly 5 years to maturity, and bond B has 15 years to maturity.

a. Calculate the value of bond A if the required return is (1) 8%, (2) 11%, and (3) 14%.

b. Calculate the value of bond B if the required return is (1) 8%, (2) 11%, and (3) 14%.

c. From your findings in parts **a** and **b**, complete the following table, and discuss the relationship between time to maturity and changing required returns.

Required return	Value of bond A	Value of bond B
8%	?	?
11	?	?
14	?	?

d. If Lynn wanted to minimize *interest rate risk*, which bond should she purchase? Why?

LG 6 **P6–20 Yield to maturity** The relationship between a bond's yield to maturity and coupon interest rate can be used to predict its pricing level. For each of the bonds listed, state whether the price of the bond will be at a premium to par, at par, or at a discount to par.

Bond	Coupon interest rate	Yield to maturity	Price
A	6%	10%	______
B	8	8	______
C	9	7	______
D	7	9	______
E	12	10	______

LG 6 **P6–21 Yield to maturity** The Salem Company bond currently sells for $955, has a 12% coupon interest rate and a $1,000 par value, pays interest *annually*, and has 15 years to maturity.

a. Calculate the *yield to maturity* (*YTM*) on this bond.

b. Explain the relationship that exists between the coupon interest rate and yield to maturity and the par value and market value of a bond.

LG 6 **P6–22 Yield to maturity** Each of the bonds shown in the following table pays interest *annually*.

Bond	Par value	Coupon interest rate	Years to maturity	Current value
A	$1,000	9%	8	$ 820
B	1,000	12	16	1,000
C	500	12	12	560
D	1,000	15	10	1,120
E	1,000	5	3	900

a. Calculate the *yield to maturity* (*YTM*) for each bond.

b. What relationship exists between the coupon interest rate and yield to maturity and the par value and market value of a bond? Explain.

Personal Finance Problem

LG 2 LG 5 LG 6 **P6–23 Bond valuation and yield to maturity** Mark Goldsmith's broker has shown him two bonds. Each has a maturity of 5 years, a par value of $1,000, and a yield to maturity of 12%. Bond A has a coupon interest rate of 6% paid annually. Bond B has a coupon interest rate of 14% paid annually.

a. Calculate the selling price for each of the bonds.

b. Mark has $20,000 to invest. Judging on the basis of the price of the bonds, how many of either one could Mark purchase if he were to choose it over the other? (Mark cannot really purchase a fraction of a bond, but for purposes of this question, pretend that he can.)

c. Calculate the yearly interest income of each bond on the basis of its coupon rate and the number of bonds that Mark could buy with his $20,000.

d. Assume that Mark will reinvest the interest payments as they are paid (at the end of each year) and that his rate of return on the reinvestment is only 10%. For each bond, calculate the value of the principal payment plus the value of Mark's reinvestment account at the end of the 5 years.

e. Why are the two values calculated in part **d** different? If Mark were worried that he would earn less than the 12% yield to maturity on the reinvested interest payments, which of these two bonds would be a better choice?

LG 6 **P6–24 Bond valuation—Semiannual interest** Find the value of a bond maturing in 6 years, with a $1,000 par value and a coupon interest rate of 10% (5% paid semiannually) if the required return on similar-risk bonds is 14% annual interest (7% paid semiannually).

LG 6 **P6–25 Bond valuation—Semiannual interest** Calculate the value of each of the bonds shown in the following table, all of which pay interest *semiannually.*

Bond	Par value	Coupon interest rate	Years to maturity	Required stated annual return
A	$1,000	10%	12	8%
B	1,000	12	20	12
C	500	12	5	14
D	1,000	14	10	10
E	100	6	4	14

LG 6 **P6–26 Bond valuation—Quarterly interest** Calculate the value of a $5,000-par-value bond paying quarterly interest at an annual coupon interest rate of 10% and having 10 years until maturity if the required return on similar-risk bonds is currently a 12% annual rate paid *quarterly.*

LG 1 **P6–27 ETHICS PROBLEM** Bond rating agencies have invested significant sums of money in an effort to determine which quantitative and nonquantitative factors best predict bond defaults. Furthermore, some of the raters invest time and money to meet privately with corporate personnel to get nonpublic information that is used in assigning the issue's bond rating. To recoup those costs, some bond rating agencies have tied their ratings to the purchase of additional services. Do you believe that this is an acceptable practice? Defend your position.

Spreadsheet Exercise

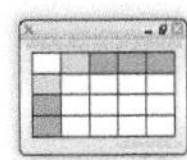

CSM Corporation has a bond issue outstanding at the end of 2012. The bond has 15 years remaining to maturity and carries a coupon interest rate of 6%. Interest on the bond is compounded on a semiannual basis. The par value of the CSM bond is $1,000 and it is currently selling for $874.42.

TO DO

Create a spreadsheet similar to the Excel spreadsheet examples located in the chapter for yield to maturity and semiannual interest to model the following:

a. Create a spreadsheet similar to the Excel spreadsheet examples located in the chapter to solve for the yield to maturity.

b. Create a spreadsheet similar to the Excel spreadsheet examples located in the chapter to solve for the price of the bond if the yield to maturity is 2% higher.

c. Create a spreadsheet similar to the Excel spreadsheet examples located in the chapter to solve for the price of the bond if the yield to maturity is 2% lower.

d. What can you summarize about the relationship between the price of the bond, the par value, the yield to maturity, and the coupon rate?

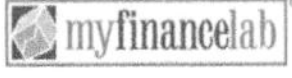

Visit www.myfinancelab.com for **Chapter Case: *Evaluating Annie Hegg's Proposed Investment in Atilier Industries Bonds,*** Group Exercises, and other numerous resources.

7 Stock Valuation

Learning Goals

LG 1 Differentiate between debt and equity.

LG 2 Discuss the features of both common and preferred stock.

LG 3 Describe the process of issuing common stock, including venture capital, going public, and the investment banker.

LG 4 Understand the concept of market efficiency and basic stock valuation using zero-growth, constant-growth, and variable-growth models.

LG 5 Discuss the free cash flow valuation model and the book value, liquidation value, and price/earnings (P/E) multiple approaches.

LG 6 Explain the relationships among financial decisions, return, risk, and the firm's value.

Why This Chapter Matters to You

In your *professional* life

ACCOUNTING You need to understand the difference between debt and equity in terms of tax treatment; the ownership claims of capital providers, including venture capitalists and stockholders; and the differences between book value per share and other market-based valuations.

INFORMATION SYSTEMS You need to understand the procedures used to issue common stock, the information needed to value stock, how to collect and process the necessary information from each functional area, and how to disseminate information to investors.

MANAGEMENT You need to understand the difference between debt and equity capital, the rights and claims of stockholders, the process of issuing common stock, and the effects each functional area has on the value of the firm's stock.

MARKETING You need to understand that the firm's ideas for products and services will greatly affect investors' beliefs regarding the likely success of the firm's projects; projects that are viewed as more likely to succeed are also viewed as more valuable and therefore lead to a higher stock value.

OPERATIONS You need to understand that the evaluations of venture capitalists and other would-be investors will in part depend on the efficiency of the firm's operations; more cost-efficient operations lead to better growth prospects and, therefore, higher stock valuations.

In your *personal* life

At some point, you are likely to hold stocks as an asset in your retirement program. You may want to estimate a stock's value. If the stock is selling below its estimated value, you may buy the stock; if its market price is above its value, you may sell it. Some individuals rely on financial advisors to make such buy or sell recommendations. Regardless of how you approach investment decisions, it will be helpful for you to understand how stocks are valued.

A123 Systems Inc.

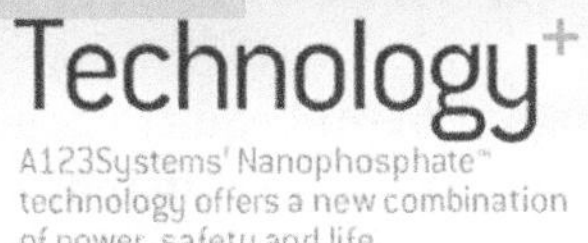

Going Green to Find Value

One of the most "hotly" debated topics of our day has been the issue of global warming and the benefits and costs of lower emissions. Many companies are investing in radical new technologies with the hope of capitalizing on the going green movement. On September 24, 2009, A123 Systems Inc. raised $378 million in its initial public offering (IPO) of common stock. A123, whose shares trade on the Nasdaq stock exchange, uses a patented nanotechnology developed at the Massachusetts Institute of Technology to produce more powerful and longer-lasting lithium ion batteries that go in products ranging from cordless hand tools to electric vehicles. Even though A123 reported a loss of $40.7 million on revenue of just $42.9 million in the first half of 2009, investors welcomed the IPO, boosting the share price 50 percent on the first day of trading.

Excitement about A123's prospects was fueled in part by major investments in the company from a few high-profile companies including General Electric, Qualcomm, and Motorola. Furthermore, the company secured almost $250 million in grants from the federal government as part of the American Recovery and Reinvestment Act of 2009, a bill passed by Congress designed to help the U.S. economy emerge from a deep recession. Some likely customers of A123 also received stimulus funds, including electric car makers Tesla Motors and Fisker Automotive. In the weeks following the IPO, A123's stock price was as high as $28 per share, but by the middle of 2010 it was trading below $10 a share. A123 is not a stock for the faint of heart. In the long run, A123's stock price will depend on its ability to generate positive cash flows and convince the market of its ability to do so into the future.

LG 1 7.1 Differences between Debt and Equity

debt
Includes all borrowing incurred by a firm, including bonds, and is repaid according to a fixed schedule of payments.

equity
Funds provided by the firm's owners (investors or stockholders) that are repaid subject to the firm's performance.

Although debt and equity capital are both sources of external financing used by firms, they are very different in several important respects. Most importantly, debt financing is obtained from creditors, and equity financing is obtained from investors who then become part owners of the firm. Creditors (lenders or debtholders) have a legal right to be repaid, whereas investors have only an expectation of being repaid. **Debt** includes all borrowing incurred by a firm, including bonds, and is repaid according to a fixed schedule of payments. **Equity** consists of funds provided by the firm's owners (investors or stockholders) and is repaid subject to the firm's performance. A firm can obtain equity either *internally,* by retaining earnings rather than paying them out as dividends to its stockholders, or *externally,* by selling common or preferred stock. The key differences between debt and equity capital are summarized in Table 7.1 and discussed in the following pages.

VOICE IN MANAGEMENT

Unlike creditors, holders of equity (stockholders) are owners of the firm. Stockholders generally have voting rights that permit them to select the firm's directors and vote on special issues. In contrast, debtholders do not receive voting privileges but instead rely on the firm's contractual obligations to them to be their voice.

CLAIMS ON INCOME AND ASSETS

Equityholders' claims on income and assets are secondary to the claims of creditors. Their *claims on income* cannot be paid until the claims of all creditors, including both interest and scheduled principal payments, have been satisfied. After satisfying creditor's claims, the firm's board of directors decides whether to distribute dividends to the owners.

Matter of fact

How Are Assets Divided in Bankruptcy?

According to the U.S. Securities and Exchange Commission, in bankruptcy assets are divided up as follows:

1. **Secured creditors:** Secured bank loans or secured bonds are paid first.
2. **Unsecured creditors:** Unsecured bank loans or unsecured bonds, suppliers, or customers have the next claim.
3. **Equityholders:** Equityholders or the owners of the company have the last claim on assets, and they may not receive anything if the secured and unsecured creditors' claims are not fully repaid.

In more depth

To read about *The Bankruptcy Process,* go to www.myfinancelab.com

Equityholders' *claims on assets* also are secondary to the claims of creditors. If the firm fails, its assets are sold, and the proceeds are distributed in this order: secured creditors, unsecured creditors, and equityholders. Because equityholders are the last to receive any distribution of assets, they expect greater returns from their investment in the firm's stock than the returns creditors require on the firm's

TABLE 7.1 Key Differences between Debt and Equity

Characteristic	Type of capital: Debt	Type of capital: Equity
Voice in management[a]	No	Yes
Claims on income and assets	Senior to equity	Subordinate to debt
Maturity	Stated	None
Tax treatment	Interest deduction	No deduction

[a]Debtholders do not have voting rights, but instead they rely on the firm's contractual obligations to them to be their voice.

borrowings. The higher rate of return expected by equityholders leads to a higher cost of equity financing relative to the cost of debt financing for the firm.

MATURITY

Unlike debt, equity is a *permanent form* of financing for the firm. It does not "mature," so repayment is not required. Because equity is liquidated only during bankruptcy proceedings, stockholders must recognize that, although a ready market may exist for their shares, the price that can be realized may fluctuate. This fluctuation of the market price of equity makes the overall returns to a firm's stockholders even more risky.

TAX TREATMENT

Interest payments to debtholders are treated as tax-deductible expenses by the issuing firm, whereas dividend payments to a firm's stockholders are not tax deductible. The tax deductibility of interest lowers the corporation's cost of debt financing, further causing it to be lower than the cost of equity financing.

→ REVIEW QUESTION

7–1 What are the key differences between *debt* and *equity?*

LG 2 LG 3

7.2 Common and Preferred Stock

A firm can obtain equity capital by selling either common or preferred stock. All corporations initially issue common stock to raise equity capital. Some of these firms later issue either additional common stock or preferred stock to raise more equity capital. Although both common and preferred stock are forms of equity capital, preferred stock has some similarities to debt that significantly differentiate it from common stock. Here we first consider the features of both common and preferred stock and then describe the process of issuing common stock, including the use of venture capital.

privately owned (stock)
The common stock of a firm is owned by private investors; this stock is not publicly traded.

publicly owned (stock)
The common stock of a firm is owned by public investors; this stock is publicly traded.

closely owned (stock)
The common stock of a firm is owned by an individual or a small group of investors (such as a family); these are usually privately owned companies.

widely owned (stock)
The common stock of a firm is owned by many unrelated individual or institutional investors.

par-value common stock
An arbitrary value established for legal purposes in the firm's corporate charter and which can be used to find the total number of shares outstanding by dividing it into the book value of common stock.

preemptive right
Allows common stockholders to maintain their proportionate ownership in the corporation when new shares are issued, thus protecting them from dilution of their ownership.

dilution of ownership
A reduction in each previous shareholder's fractional ownership resulting from the issuance of additional shares of common stock.

dilution of earnings
A reduction in each previous shareholder's fractional claim on the firm's earnings resulting from the issuance of additional shares of common stock.

rights
Financial instruments that allow stockholders to purchase additional shares at a price below the market price, in direct proportion to their number of owned shares.

COMMON STOCK

The true owners of a corporate business are the common stockholders. Common stockholders are sometimes referred to as *residual owners* because they receive what is left—the residual—after all other claims on the firm's income and assets have been satisfied. They are assured of only one thing: that they cannot lose any more than they have invested in the firm. As a result of this generally uncertain position, common stockholders expect to be compensated with adequate dividends and, ultimately, capital gains.

Ownership

The common stock of a firm can be **privately owned** by private investors or **publicly owned** by public investors. Private companies are often **closely owned** by an individual investor or a small group of private investors (such as a family). Public companies are **widely owned** by many unrelated individual or institutional investors. The shares of privately owned firms, which are typically small corporations, are generally not traded; if the shares are traded, the transactions are among private investors and often require the firm's consent. Large corporations, which are emphasized in the following discussions, are publicly owned, and their shares are generally actively traded in the broker or dealer markets described in Chapter 2.

Par Value

The market value of common stock is completely unrelated to its par value. The **par value** of common stock is an arbitrary value established for legal purposes in the firm's corporate charter and is generally set quite low, often an amount of $1 or less. Recall that when a firm sells new shares of common stock, the par value of the shares sold is recorded in the capital section of the balance sheet as part of common stock. One benefit of this recording is that at any time the total number of shares of common stock outstanding can be found by dividing the book value of common stock by the par value.

Setting a low par value is advantageous in states where certain corporate taxes are based on the par value of stock. A low par value is also beneficial in states that have laws against selling stock at a discount to par. For example, a company whose common stock has a par value of $20 per share would be unable to issue stock if investors are unwilling to pay more than $16 per share.

Preemptive Rights

The **preemptive right** allows common stockholders to maintain their *proportionate* ownership in the corporation when new shares are issued, thus protecting them from dilution of their ownership. A **dilution of ownership** is a reduction in each previous shareholder's fractional ownership resulting from the issuance of additional shares of common stock. Preemptive rights allow preexisting shareholders to maintain their preissuance voting control and protects them against the dilution of earnings. Preexisting shareholders experience a **dilution of earnings** when their claim on the firm's earnings is *diminished* as a result of new shares being issued.

In a *rights offering,* the firm grants **rights** to its shareholders. These financial instruments allow stockholders to purchase additional shares at a price below the market price, in direct proportion to their number of owned shares. In these

authorized shares
Shares of common stock that a firm's corporate charter allows it to issue.

outstanding shares
Issued shares of common stock held by investors, including both private and public investors.

treasury stock
Issued shares of common stock held by the firm; often these shares have been repurchased by the firm.

issued shares
Shares of common stock that have been put into circulation; the sum of *outstanding shares* and *treasury stock*.

situations, *rights* are an important financing tool without which shareholders would run the risk of losing their proportionate control of the corporation. From the firm's viewpoint, the use of rights offerings to raise new equity capital may be less costly than a public offering of stock.

Authorized, Outstanding, and Issued Shares

A firm's corporate charter indicates how many **authorized shares** it can issue. The firm cannot sell more shares than the charter authorizes without obtaining approval through a shareholder vote. To avoid later having to amend the charter, firms generally attempt to authorize more shares than they initially plan to issue.

Authorized shares become **outstanding shares** when they are issued or sold to investors. If the *firm* repurchases any of its outstanding shares, these shares are recorded as **treasury stock** and are no longer considered to be outstanding shares. **Issued shares** are the shares of common stock that have been put into circulation; they represent the sum of *outstanding shares* and *treasury stock*.

Example 7.1 ▸

Golden Enterprises, a producer of medical pumps, has the following stockholders' equity account on December 31:

Stockholders' Equity

Common stock—$0.80 par value:	
Authorized 35,000,000 shares; issued 15,000,000 shares	$ 12,000,000
Paid-in capital in excess of par	63,000,000
Retained earnings	31,000,000
	$106,000,000
Less: Cost of treasury stock (1,000,000 shares)	4,000,000
Total stockholders' equity	$102,000,000

How many shares of additional common stock can Golden sell without gaining approval from its shareholders? The firm has 35 million authorized shares, 15 million issued shares, and 1 million shares of treasury stock. Thus 14 million shares are outstanding (15 million issued shares minus 1 million shares of treasury stock), and Golden can issue 21 million additional shares (35 million authorized shares minus 14 million outstanding shares) without seeking shareholder approval. This total includes the treasury shares currently held, which the firm can reissue to the public without obtaining shareholder approval.

Voting Rights

Generally, each share of common stock entitles its holder to one vote in the election of directors and on special issues. Votes are generally assignable and may be cast at the annual stockholders' meeting.

proxy statement
A statement transferring the votes of a stockholder to another party.

Because most small stockholders do not attend the annual meeting to vote, they may sign a **proxy statement** transferring their votes to another party. The solicitation of proxies from shareholders is closely controlled by the Securities and Exchange Commission to ensure that proxies are not being solicited on the

proxy battle
The attempt by a nonmanagement group to gain control of the management of a firm by soliciting a sufficient number of proxy votes.

supervoting shares
Stock that carries with it multiple votes per share rather than the single vote per share typically given on regular shares of common stock.

nonvoting common stock
Common stock that carries no voting rights; issued when the firm wishes to raise capital through the sale of common stock but does not want to give up its voting control.

basis of false or misleading information. Existing management generally receives the stockholders' proxies because it is able to solicit them at company expense.

Occasionally, when the firm is widely owned, outsiders may wage a **proxy battle** to unseat the existing management and gain control of the firm. To win a corporate election, votes from a majority of the shares voted are required. However, the odds of an outside group winning a proxy battle are generally slim.

In recent years, many firms have issued two or more classes of common stock with unequal voting rights. A firm can use different classes of stock as a defense against a *hostile takeover* in which an outside group, without management support, tries to gain voting control of the firm by buying its shares in the marketplace. **Supervoting shares**, which have multiple votes per share, allow "insiders" to maintain control against an outside group whose shares have only one vote each. At other times, a class of **nonvoting common stock** is issued when the firm wishes to raise capital through the sale of common stock but does not want to give up its voting control.

When different classes of common stock are issued on the basis of unequal voting rights, class A common typically—but not universally—has one vote per share, and class B common has supervoting rights. In most cases, the multiple share classes are equal with respect to all other aspects of ownership, although there are some exceptions to this general rule. In particular, there is usually no difference in the distribution of earnings (dividends) and assets. Treasury stock, which is held within the corporation, generally *does not* have voting rights, *does not* earn dividends, and *does not* have a claim on assets in liquidation.

Dividends

The payment of dividends to the firm's shareholders is at the discretion of the company's board of directors. Most corporations that pay dividends pay them quarterly. Dividends may be paid in cash, stock, or merchandise. Cash dividends are the most common, merchandise dividends the least.

Common stockholders are not promised a dividend, but they come to expect certain payments on the basis of the historical dividend pattern of the firm. Before firms pay dividends to common stockholders, they must pay any past due dividends owed to preferred stockholders. The firm's ability to pay dividends can be affected by restrictive debt covenants designed to ensure that the firm can repay its creditors.

Since passage of the *Jobs and Growth Tax Relief Reconciliation Act of 2003*, many firms now pay larger dividends to shareholders, who are subject to a maximum tax rate of 15 percent on dividends rather than the maximum tax rate of 39 percent in effect prior to passage of the act. Because of the importance of the dividend decision to the growth and valuation of the firm, dividends are discussed in greater detail in Chapter 14.

International Stock Issues

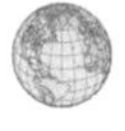

Although the international market for common stock is not as large as the international market for bonds, cross-border issuance and trading of common stock have increased dramatically in the past 30 years.

Some corporations *issue stock in foreign markets.* For example, the stock of General Electric trades in Frankfurt, London, Paris, and Tokyo; the stocks of Time Warner and Microsoft trade in Frankfurt and London; and the stock of McDonalds trades in Frankfurt, London, and Paris. The Frankfurt, London, and Tokyo markets are the most popular. Issuing stock internationally broadens the ownership base and helps a company to integrate into the local business environment. Having locally traded stock can facilitate corporate acquisitions because shares can be used as an acceptable method of payment.

American depositary shares (ADSs)
Dollar-denominated receipts for the stocks of foreign companies that are held by a U.S. financial institution overseas.

American depositary receipts (ADRs)
Securities, backed by *American depositary shares (ADSs),* that permit U.S. investors to hold shares of non-U.S. companies and trade them in U.S. markets.

Foreign corporations have also discovered the benefits of trading their stock in the United States. The disclosure and reporting requirements mandated by the U.S. Securities and Exchange Commission have historically discouraged all but the largest foreign firms from directly listing their shares on the New York Stock Exchange or the American Stock Exchange.

As an alternative, most foreign companies choose to tap the U.S. market through **American depositary shares (ADSs).** These are dollar-denominated receipts for the stocks of foreign companies that are held by a U.S. financial institution overseas. They serve as backing for **American depositary receipts (ADRs),** which are securities that permit U.S. investors to hold shares of non-U.S. companies and trade them in U.S. markets. Because ADRs are issued, in dollars, to U.S. investors, they are subject to U.S. securities laws. At the same time, they give investors the opportunity to diversify their portfolios internationally.

PREFERRED STOCK

par-value preferred stock
Preferred stock with a stated face value that is used with the specified dividend percentage to determine the annual dollar dividend.

no-par preferred stock
Preferred stock with no stated face value but with a stated annual dollar dividend.

Preferred stock gives its holders certain privileges that make them senior to common stockholders. Preferred stockholders are promised a fixed periodic dividend, which is stated either as a percentage or as a dollar amount. How the dividend is specified depends on whether the preferred stock has a *par value.* **Par-value preferred stock** has a stated face value, and its annual dividend is specified as a percentage of this value. **No-par preferred stock** has no stated face value, but its annual dividend is stated in dollars. Preferred stock is most often issued by public utilities, by acquiring firms in merger transactions, and by firms that are experiencing losses and need additional financing.

Basic Rights of Preferred Stockholders

The basic rights of preferred stockholders are somewhat stronger than the rights of common stockholders. Preferred stock is often considered *quasi-debt* because, much like interest on debt, it specifies a fixed periodic payment (dividend). Preferred stock is unlike debt in that it has no maturity date. Because they have a fixed claim on the firm's income that takes precedence over the claim of common stockholders, preferred stockholders are exposed to less risk.

Preferred stockholders are also given *preference over common stockholders in the liquidation of assets* in a legally bankrupt firm, although they must "stand in line" behind creditors. The amount of the claim of preferred stockholders in liquidation is normally equal to the par or stated value of the preferred stock. Preferred stockholders are *not normally given a voting right,* although preferred stockholders are sometimes allowed to elect one member of the board of directors.

Features of Preferred Stock

A preferred stock issue generally includes a number of features, which, along with the stock's par value, the amount of dividend payments, the dividend payment dates, and any restrictive covenants, are specified in an agreement similar to a *bond indenture.*

Restrictive Covenants The restrictive covenants in a preferred stock issue focus on ensuring the firm's continued existence and regular payment of the dividend. These covenants include provisions about passing dividends, the sale of senior securities, mergers, sales of assets, minimum liquidity requirements, and repurchases of common stock. The violation of preferred stock covenants usually permits preferred stockholders either to obtain representation on the firm's board of directors or to force the retirement of their stock at or above its par or stated value.

cumulative (preferred stock)
Preferred stock for which all passed (unpaid) dividends in arrears, along with the current dividend, must be paid before dividends can be paid to common stockholders.

noncumulative (preferred stock)
Preferred stock for which passed (unpaid) dividends do not accumulate.

Cumulation Most preferred stock is **cumulative** with respect to any dividends passed. That is, all dividends in arrears, along with the current dividend, must be paid before dividends can be paid to common stockholders. If preferred stock is **noncumulative,** passed (unpaid) dividends do not accumulate. In this case, only the current dividend must be paid before dividends can be paid to common stockholders. Because the common stockholders can receive dividends only after the dividend claims of preferred stockholders have been satisfied, it is in the firm's best interest to pay preferred dividends when they are due.

callable feature (preferred stock)
A feature of *callable preferred stock* that allows the issuer to retire the shares within a certain period of time and at a specified price.

conversion feature (preferred stock)
A feature of *convertible preferred stock* that allows holders to change each share into a stated number of shares of common stock.

Other Features Preferred stock can be *callable* or *convertible.* Preferred stock with a **callable feature** allows the issuer to retire outstanding shares within a certain period of time at a specified price. The call price is normally set above the initial issuance price, but it may decrease as time passes. Making preferred stock callable provides the issuer with a way to bring the fixed-payment commitment of the preferred issue to an end if conditions make it desirable to do so.

Preferred stock with a **conversion feature** allows *holders* to change each share into a stated number of shares of common stock, usually anytime after a predetermined date. The conversion ratio can be fixed, or the number of shares of common stock that the preferred stock can be exchanged for changes through time according to a predetermined formula.

ISSUING COMMON STOCK

Because of the high risk associated with a business startup, a firm's initial financing typically comes from its founders in the form of a common stock investment. Until the founders have made an equity investment, it is highly unlikely that others will contribute either equity or debt capital. Early-stage investors in the firm's equity, as well as lenders who provide debt capital, want to be assured that they are taking no more risk than the founders. In addition, they want confirmation that the founders are confident enough in their vision for the firm that they are willing to risk their own money.

Typically, the initial nonfounder financing for business startups with attractive growth prospects comes from private equity investors. Then, as the firm establishes the viability of its product or service offering and begins to generate revenues, cash flow, and profits, it will often "go public" by issuing shares of common stock to a much broader group of investors.

Before we consider the initial *public* sale of equity, let's discuss some of the key aspects of early-stage equity financing in firms that have attractive growth prospects.

venture capital
Privately raised external equity capital used to fund early-stage firms with attractive growth prospects.

Venture Capital

The initial external equity financing privately raised by firms, typically early-stage firms with attractive growth prospects, is called **venture capital.** Those who

venture capitalists (VCs) Providers of venture capital; typically, formal businesses that maintain strong oversight over the firms they invest in and that have clearly defined exit strategies.

angel capitalists (angels) Wealthy individual investors who do not operate as a business but invest in promising early-stage companies in exchange for a portion of the firm's equity.

provide venture capital are known as **venture capitalists (VCs).** They typically are formal business entities that maintain strong oversight over the firms they invest in and that have clearly defined exit strategies. Less visible early-stage investors called **angel capitalists** (or **angels**) tend to be investors who do not actually operate as a business; they are often wealthy individual investors who are willing to invest in promising early-stage companies in exchange for a portion of the firm's equity. Although angels play a major role in early-stage equity financing, we will focus on VCs because of their more formal structure and greater public visibility.

Organization and Investment Stages Venture capital investors tend to be organized in one of four basic ways, as described in Table 7.2. The *VC limited partnership* is by far the dominant structure. These funds have as their sole objective to earn high returns, rather than to obtain access to the companies in order to sell or buy other products or services.

VCs can invest in early-stage companies, later-stage companies, or buyouts and acquisitions. Generally, about 40 to 50 percent of VC investments are devoted to early-stage companies (for startup funding and expansion) and a similar percentage to later-stage companies (for marketing, production expansion, and preparation for public offering); the remaining 5 to 10 percent are devoted to the buyout or acquisition of other companies. Generally, VCs look for compound annual rates of return ranging from 20 to 50 percent or more, depending on both the development stage and the attributes of each company. Earlier-stage investments tend to demand higher returns than later-stage investments because of the higher risk associated with the earlier stages of a firm's growth.

Deal Structure and Pricing Regardless of the development stage, venture capital investments are made under a legal contract that clearly allocates responsibilities and ownership interests between existing owners (founders) and the VC fund or limited partnership. The terms of the agreement will depend on numerous

TABLE 7.2 Organization of Venture Capital Investors

Organization	Description
Small business investment companies (SBICs)	Corporations chartered by the federal government that can borrow at attractive rates from the U.S. Treasury and use the funds to make venture capital investments in private companies.
Financial VC funds	Subsidiaries of financial institutions, particularly banks, set up to help young firms grow and, it is hoped, become major customers of the institution.
Corporate VC funds	Firms, sometimes subsidiaries, established by nonfinancial firms, typically to gain access to new technologies that the corporation can access to further its own growth.
VC limited partnerships	Limited partnerships organized by professional VC firms, which serve as the general partner and organize, invest, and manage the partnership using the limited partners' funds; the professional VCs ultimately liquidate the partnership and distribute the proceeds to all partners.

factors related to the founders; the business structure, stage of development, and outlook; and other market and timing issues. The specific financial terms will, of course, depend on the value of the enterprise, the amount of funding, and the perceived risk. To control the VC's risk, various covenants are included in the agreement, and the actual funding may be pegged to the achievement of *measurable milestones.* The VC will negotiate numerous other provisions into the contract, both to ensure the firm's success and to control its risk exposure. The contract will have an explicit exit strategy for the VC that may be tied both to measurable milestones and to time.

The amount of equity to which the VC is entitled will, of course, depend on the value of the firm, the terms of the contract, the exit terms, and the minimum compound annual rate of return required by the VC on its investment. Although each VC investment is unique and no standard contract exists, the transaction will be structured to provide the VC with a high rate of return that is consistent with the typically high risk of such transactions. The exit strategy of most VC investments is to take the firm public through an initial public offering.

Going Public

When a firm wishes to sell its stock in the primary market, it has three alternatives. It can make (1) a *public offering,* in which it offers its shares for sale to the general public; (2) a *rights offering,* in which new shares are sold to existing stockholders; or (3) a *private placement,* in which the firm sells new securities directly to an investor or group of investors. Here we focus on public offerings, particularly the **initial public offering (IPO),** which is the first public sale of a firm's stock. IPOs are typically made by small, rapidly growing companies that either require additional capital to continue expanding or have met a milestone for going public that was established in a contract signed earlier in order to obtain VC funding.

initial public offering (IPO)
The first public sale of a firm's stock.

To go public, the firm must first obtain the approval of its current shareholders, the investors who own its privately issued stock. Next, the company's auditors and lawyers must certify that all documents for the company are legitimate. The company then finds an investment bank willing to *underwrite* the offering. This underwriter is responsible for promoting the stock and facilitating the sale of the company's IPO shares. The underwriter often brings in other investment banking firms as participants. We'll discuss the role of the investment banker in more detail in the next section.

The company files a registration statement with the SEC. One portion of the registration statement is called the **prospectus.** It describes the key aspects of the issue, the issuer, and its management and financial position. During the waiting period between the statement's filing and its approval, prospective investors can receive a preliminary prospectus. This preliminary version is called a **red herring,** because a notice printed in red on the front cover indicates the tentative nature of the offer. The cover of the preliminary prospectus describing the 2010 stock issue of Convio, Inc., is shown in Figure 7.1. Note the red herring printed across the top of the page.

prospectus
A portion of a security registration statement that describes the key aspects of the issue, the issuer, and its management and financial position.

red herring
A preliminary prospectus made available to prospective investors during the waiting period between the registration statement's filing with the SEC and its approval.

After the SEC approves the registration statement, the investment community can begin analyzing the company's prospects. However, from the time it files until at least one month after the IPO is complete, the company must observe a *quiet period,* during which there are restrictions on what company officials may say

FIGURE 7.1

Cover of a Preliminary Prospectus for a Stock Issue
Some of the key factors related to the 2010 common stock issue by Convio, Inc., are summarized on the cover of the preliminary prospectus. The disclaimer printed in red across the top of the page is what gives the preliminary prospectus its "red herring" name.

The information in this preliminary prospectus is not complete and may be changed. These securities may not be sold until the registration statement filed with the Securities and Exchange Commission is effective. This preliminary prospectus is not an offer to sell nor does it seek an offer to buy these securities in any jurisdiction where the offer or sale is not permitted.

SUBJECT TO COMPLETION. DATED APRIL 23, 2010.

IPO PRELIMINARY PROSPECTUS

5,132,728 Shares
Common Stock
$ per share

Convio, Inc. is selling 3,636,364 shares of our common stock and the selling stockholders identified in this prospectus are selling additional 1,496,364 shares. We will not receive any of the proceeds from the sale of the shares being sold by the selling stockholders. We have granted the underwriters a 30-day option to purchase up to an additional 769,909 shares from us to cover over-allotments, if any.

This is an initial public offering of our common stock. We currently expect the initial public offering price to be between $10.00 and $12.00 per share. We have applied for the listing of our common stock on the NASDAQ Global Market under the symbol "CNVO."

INVESTING IN OUR COMMON STOCK INVOLVES RISKS. SEE "RISK FACTORS" BEGINNING ON PAGE 10

	Per Share	Total
Initial public offering price	$	$
Underwriting discount	$	$
Proceeds, before expenses, to Convio	$	$
Proceeds, before expenses, to the selling stockholders	$	$

Neither the Securities and Exchange Commission nor any state securities commission has approved or disapproved of these securities or passed upon the accuracy or adequacy of this prospectus. Any representation to the contrary is a criminal offense.

Thomas Weisel Partners LLC **Piper Jaffray**

William Blair & Company

JMP Securities

Pacific Crest Securities

The date of this prospectus is , 2010.

Source: SEC filing Form S-1/A, Convio, Inc., filed April 26, 2010, p. 4.

about the company. The purpose of the quiet period is to make sure that all potential investors have access to the same information about the company—the information presented in the preliminary prospectus—and not to any unpublished data that might give them an unfair advantage.

The investment bankers and company executives promote the company's stock offering through a *road show,* a series of presentations to potential investors around the country and sometimes overseas. In addition to providing investors with information about the new issue, road show sessions help the investment bankers gauge the demand for the offering and set an expected pricing range. After the underwriter sets terms and prices the issue, the SEC must approve the offering.

investment banker
Financial intermediary that specializes in selling new security issues and advising firms with regard to major financial transactions.

underwriting
The role of the *investment banker* in bearing the risk of reselling, at a profit, the securities purchased from an issuing corporation at an agreed-on price.

The Investment Banker's Role

Most public offerings are made with the assistance of an **investment banker.** The investment banker is a financial intermediary (such as Morgan Stanley or Goldman Sachs) that specializes in selling new security issues and advising firms with regard to major financial transactions. The main activity of the investment banker is **underwriting.** This process involves purchasing the security issue from the issuing corporation at an agreed-on price and bearing the risk of reselling it to the public at a profit. The investment banker also provides the issuer with advice about pricing and other important aspects of the issue.

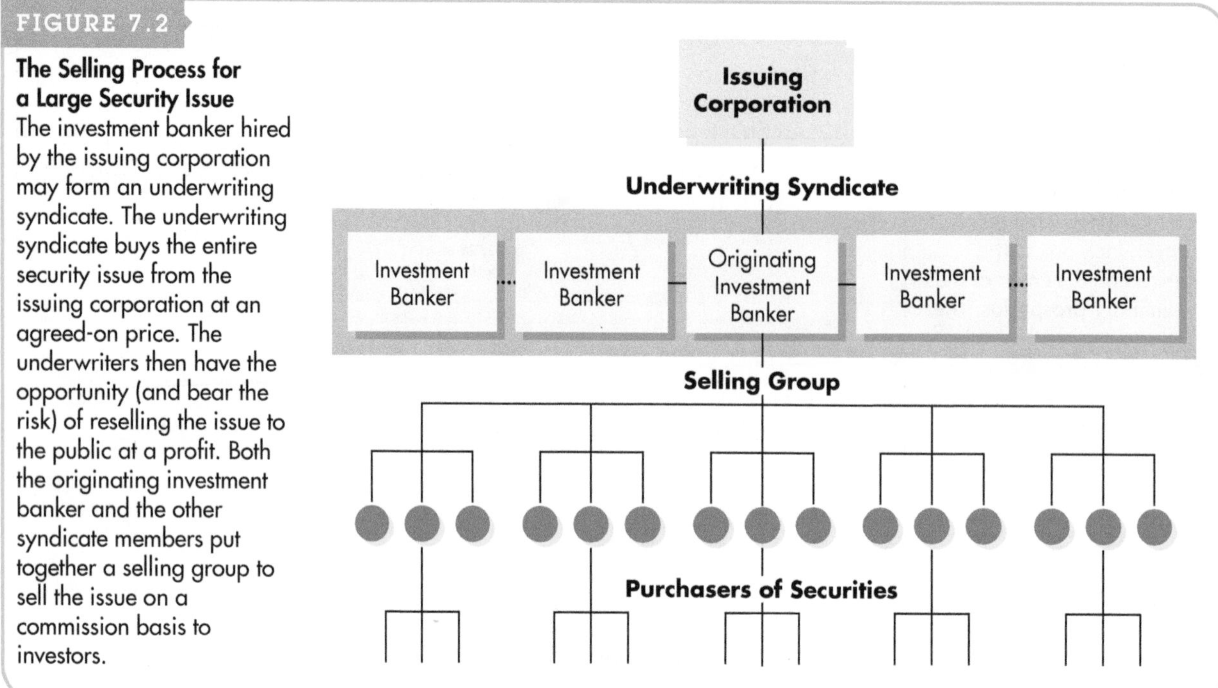

FIGURE 7.2

The Selling Process for a Large Security Issue
The investment banker hired by the issuing corporation may form an underwriting syndicate. The underwriting syndicate buys the entire security issue from the issuing corporation at an agreed-on price. The underwriters then have the opportunity (and bear the risk) of reselling the issue to the public at a profit. Both the originating investment banker and the other syndicate members put together a selling group to sell the issue on a commission basis to investors.

underwriting syndicate
A group of other bankers formed by an investment banker to share the financial risk associated with *underwriting* new securities.

selling group
A large number of brokerage firms that join the originating investment banker(s); each accepts responsibility for selling a certain portion of a new security issue on a commission basis.

In the case of very large security issues, the investment banker brings in other bankers as partners to form an **underwriting syndicate.** The syndicate shares the financial risk associated with buying the entire issue from the issuer and reselling the new securities to the public. The originating investment banker and the syndicate members put together a **selling group,** normally made up of themselves and a large number of brokerage firms. Each member of the selling group accepts the responsibility for selling a certain portion of the issue and is paid a commission on the securities it sells. The selling process for a large security issue is depicted in Figure 7.2.

Compensation for underwriting and selling services typically comes in the form of a discount on the sale price of the securities. For example, an investment banker may pay the issuing firm $24 per share for stock that will be sold for $26 per share. The investment banker may then sell the shares to members of the selling group for $25.25 per share. In this case, the original investment banker earns $1.25 per share ($25.25 sale price minus $24 purchase price). The members of the selling group earn 75 cents for each share they sell ($26 sale price minus $25.25 purchase price). Although some primary security offerings are directly placed by the issuer, the majority of new issues are sold through public offering via the mechanism just described.

→ REVIEW QUESTIONS

7–2 What risks do common stockholders take that other suppliers of capital do not?

7–3 How does a *rights offering* protect a firm's stockholders against the *dilution of ownership?*

7–4 Explain the relationships among authorized shares, outstanding shares, treasury stock, and issued shares.
7–5 What are the advantages to both U.S.-based and foreign corporations of issuing stock outside their home markets? What are *American depositary receipts (ADRs)?* What are *American depositary shares (ADSs)?*
7–6 What claims do preferred stockholders have with respect to distribution of earnings (dividends) and assets?
7–7 Explain the *cumulative feature* of preferred stock. What is the purpose of a *call feature* in a preferred stock issue?
7–8 What is the difference between a *venture capitalist (VC)* and an *angel capitalist (angel)?*
7–9 What are the four ways that VCs are most commonly organized? How are their deals structured and priced?
7–10 What general procedures must a private firm follow to go public via an *initial public offering (IPO)?*
7–11 What role does an *investment banker* play in a public offering? Describe an underwriting syndicate.

LG 4 LG 5

7.3 Common Stock Valuation

Common stockholders expect to be rewarded through periodic cash dividends and an increasing share value. Some of these investors decide which stocks to buy and sell based on a plan to maintain a broadly diversified portfolio. Other investors have a more speculative motive for trading. They try to spot companies whose shares are *undervalued*—meaning that the true value of the shares is greater than the current market price. These investors buy shares that they believe to be undervalued and sell shares that they think are *overvalued* (that is, the market price is greater than the true value). Regardless of one's motive for trading, understanding how to value common stocks is an important part of the investment process. Stock valuation is also an important tool for financial managers—how can they work to maximize the stock price without understanding the factors that determine the value of the stock? In this section, we will describe specific stock valuation techniques. First, we will consider the relationship between market efficiency and stock valuation.

MARKET EFFICIENCY

Economically rational buyers and sellers use their assessment of an asset's risk and return to determine its value. To a buyer, the asset's value represents the maximum purchase price, and to a seller it represents the minimum sale price. In competitive markets with many active participants, such as the New York Stock Exchange, the interactions of many buyers and sellers result in an equilibrium price—the *market value*—for each security. This price reflects the collective actions that buyers and sellers take on the basis of all available information. Buyers and sellers digest new information quickly as it becomes available and, through their purchase and sale activities, create a new market equilibrium price. Because the flow of new information is almost constant, stock prices fluctuate, continuously moving toward a new equilibrium that reflects the most recent information available. This general concept is known as *market efficiency*.

efficient-market hypothesis (EMH)
Theory describing the behavior of an assumed "perfect" market in which (1) securities are in equilibrium, (2) security prices fully reflect all available information and react swiftly to new information, and (3), because stocks are fully and fairly priced, investors need not waste time looking for mispriced securities.

In more depth

To read about *The Hierarchy of the Efficient-Market Hypothesis*, go to www.myfinancelab.com

THE EFFICIENT-MARKET HYPOTHESIS

As noted in Chapter 2, active broker and dealer markets, such as the New York Stock Exchange and the Nasdaq market, are *efficient*—they are made up of many rational investors who react quickly and objectively to new information. The **efficient-market hypothesis (EMH),** which is the basic theory describing the behavior of such a "perfect" market, specifically states that

1. Securities are typically in equilibrium, which means that they are fairly priced and that their expected returns equal their required returns.
2. At any point in time, security prices fully reflect all information available about the firm and its securities, and these prices react swiftly to new information.
3. Because stocks are fully and fairly priced, investors need not waste their time trying to find mispriced (undervalued or overvalued) securities.

Not all market participants are believers in the efficient-market hypothesis. Some feel that it is worthwhile to search for undervalued or overvalued securities and to trade them to profit from market inefficiencies. Others argue that it is mere luck that would allow market participants to anticipate new information correctly and as a result earn *abnormal returns*—that is, actual returns greater than average market returns. They believe it is unlikely that market participants can *over the long run* earn abnormal returns. Contrary to this belief, some well-known investors such as Warren Buffett and Bill Gross *have* over the long run consistently earned abnormal returns on their portfolios. It is unclear whether their success is the result of their superior ability to anticipate new information or of some form of market inefficiency.

The Behavioral Finance Challenge

Although considerable evidence supports the concept of market efficiency, a growing body of academic evidence has begun to cast doubt on the validity of this notion. The research documents various *anomalies*—outcomes that are inconsistent with efficient markets—in stock returns. A number of academics and practitioners have also recognized that emotions and other subjective factors play a role in investment decisions.

behavioral finance
A growing body of research that focuses on investor behavior and its impact on investment decisions and stock prices. Advocates are commonly referred to as "behaviorists."

This focus on investor behavior has resulted in a significant body of research, collectively referred to as **behavioral finance.** Advocates of behavioral finance are commonly referred to as "behaviorists." Daniel Kahneman was awarded the 2002 Nobel Prize in economics for his work in behavioral finance, specifically for integrating insights from psychology and economics. Ongoing research into the psychological factors that can affect investor behavior and the resulting effects on stock prices will likely result in growing acceptance of behavioral finance. The *Focus on Practice* box further explains some of the findings of behavioral finance.

While challenges to the efficient market hypothesis, such as those presented by advocates of behavioral finance, are interesting and worthy of study, in this text we generally take the position that markets are efficient. This means that the terms *expected return* and *required return* will be used interchangeably because they should be equal in an efficient market. In other words, we will operate under the assumption that a stock's market price at any point in time is the best estimate of its value. We're now ready to look closely at the mechanics of common stock valuation.

focus on PRACTICE

Understanding Human Behavior Helps Us Understand Investor Behavior

in practice Market anomalies are patterns inconsistent with the efficient market hypothesis. Behavioral finance has a number of theories to help explain how human emotions influence people in their investment decision-making processes.

Regret theory deals with the emotional reaction people experience after realizing they have made an error in judgment. When deciding whether to sell a stock, investors become emotionally affected by the price at which they purchased the stock. A sale at a loss would confirm that the investor miscalculated the value of the stock when it was purchased. The correct approach when considering whether to sell a stock is, "Would I buy this stock today if it were already liquidated?" If the answer is "no," it is time to sell. Regret theory also holds true for investors who passed up buying a stock that now is selling at a much higher price. Again, the correct approach is to value the stock today without regard to its prior value.

Herding is another market behavior affecting investor decisions. Some investors rationalize their decision to buy certain stocks with "everyone else is doing it." Investors may feel less embarrassment about losing money on a popular stock than about losing money on an unknown or unpopular stock.

People have a tendency to place particular events into *mental accounts*, and the difference between these compartments sometimes influences behavior more than the events themselves. Researchers have asked people the following question: "Would you purchase a $20 ticket at the local theater if you realize after you get there that you have lost a $20 bill?" Roughly 88 percent of people would do so. Under another scenario, people were asked whether they would buy a second $20 ticket if they arrived at the theater and realized that they had left at home a ticket purchased in advance for $20. Only 40 percent of respondents would buy another. In both scenarios the person is out $40, but mental accounting leads to a different outcome. In investing, compartmentalization is best illustrated by the hesitation to sell an investment that once had monstrous gains and now has a modest gain. During bull markets, people get accustomed to paper gains. When a market correction deflates investors' net worth, they are hesitant to sell, causing them to wait for the return of that gain.

Other investor behaviors are prospect theory and anchoring. According to *prospect theory*, people express a different degree of emotion toward gains than losses. Individuals are stressed more by prospective losses than they are buoyed by the prospect of equal gains. *Anchoring* is the tendency of investors to place more value on recent information. People tend to give too much credence to recent market opinions and events and mistakenly extrapolate recent trends that differ from historical, long-term averages and probabilities. Anchoring is a partial explanation for the longevity of some bull markets.

Most stock-valuation techniques require that all relevant information be available to properly determine a stock's value and potential for future gain. Behavioral finance may explain the connection between valuation and an investor's actions based on that valuation.

► ***Theories of behavioral finance can apply to other areas of human behavior in addition to investing. Think of a situation in which you may have demonstrated one of these behaviors. Share your situation with a classmate.***

BASIC COMMON STOCK VALUATION EQUATION

Like the value of a bond, which we discussed in Chapter 6, *the value of a share of common stock is equal to the present value of all future cash flows (dividends) that it is expected to provide.* Although a stockholder can earn capital gains by selling stock at a price above that originally paid, what the buyer really pays for is the right to all future dividends. What about stocks that do not currently pay dividends? Such stocks have a value attributable to a future dividend stream or to the proceeds from the sale of the company. Therefore, *from a valuation viewpoint, future dividends are relevant.*

The basic valuation model for common stock is given in Equation 7.1:

$$P_0 = \frac{D_1}{(1 + r_s)^1} + \frac{D_2}{(1 + r_s)^2} + \cdots + \frac{D_\infty}{(1 + r_s)^\infty} \tag{7.1}$$

where

P_0 = value today of common stock
D_t = per-share dividend *expected* at the end of year t
r_s = required return on common stock

The equation can be simplified somewhat by redefining each year's dividend, D_t, in terms of anticipated growth. We will consider three models here: zero growth, constant growth, and variable growth.

Zero-Growth Model

zero-growth model
An approach to dividend valuation that assumes a constant, nongrowing dividend stream.

The simplest approach to dividend valuation, the **zero-growth model,** assumes a constant, nongrowing dividend stream. In terms of the notation already introduced,

$$D_1 = D_2 = \cdots = D_\infty$$

When we let D_1 represent the amount of the annual dividend, Equation 7.1 under zero growth reduces to

$$P_0 = D_1 \times \sum_{t=1}^{\infty} \frac{1}{(1 + r_s)^t} = D_1 \times \frac{1}{r_s} = \frac{D_1}{r_s} \tag{7.2}$$

The equation shows that with zero growth, the value of a share of stock would equal the present value of a perpetuity of D_1 dollars discounted at a rate r_s. (Perpetuities were introduced in Chapter 5; see Equation 5.14 and the related discussion.)

Personal Finance Example 7.2 ▸ Chuck Swimmer estimates that the dividend of Denham Company, an established textile producer, is expected to remain constant at $3 per share indefinitely. If his required return on its stock is 15%, the stock's value is $20 ($3 ÷ 0.15) per share.

Preferred Stock Valuation Because preferred stock typically provides its holders with a fixed annual dividend over its assumed infinite life, *Equation 7.2 can be used to find the value of preferred stock*. The value of preferred stock can be estimated by substituting the stated dividend on the preferred stock for D_1 and the required return for r_s in Equation 7.2. For example, a preferred stock paying a $5 stated annual dividend and having a required return of 13 percent would have a value of $38.46 ($5 ÷ 0.13) per share.

constant-growth model
A widely cited dividend valuation approach that assumes that dividends will grow at a constant rate, but a rate that is less than the required return.

Constant-Growth Model

The most widely cited dividend valuation approach, the **constant-growth model,** assumes that dividends will grow at a constant rate, but a rate that is less than the required return. (The assumption that the constant rate of growth, g, is less than the required return, r_s, is a necessary mathematical condition for deriving this model.[1]) By letting D_0 represent the most recent dividend, we can rewrite Equation 7.1 as follows:

In more depth

To read about *Deriving the Constant-Growth Model*, go to www.myfinancelab.com

$$P_0 = \frac{D_0 \times (1+g)^1}{(1+r_s)^1} + \frac{D_0 \times (1+g)^2}{(1+r_s)^2} + \cdots + \frac{D_0 \times (1+g)^\infty}{(1+r_s)^\infty} \tag{7.3}$$

If we simplify Equation 7.3, it can be rewritten as:

$$P_0 = \frac{D_1}{r_s - g} \tag{7.4}$$

Gordon growth model
A common name for the *constant-growth model* that is widely cited in dividend valuation.

The constant-growth model in Equation 7.4 is commonly called the **Gordon growth model.** An example will show how it works.

Example 7.3 ▶

Lamar Company, a small cosmetics company, from 2007 through 2012 paid the following per-share dividends:

Year	Dividend per share
2012	$1.40
2011	1.29
2010	1.20
2009	1.12
2008	1.05
2007	1.00

We assume that the historical annual growth rate of dividends is an accurate estimate of the future constant annual rate of dividend growth, g. To find the historical annual growth rate of dividends, we must solve the following for g:

$$D_{2012} = D_{2007} \times (1+g)^5$$

$$\frac{D_{2007}}{D_{2012}} = \frac{1}{(1+g)^5}$$

$$\frac{\$1.00}{\$1.40} = \frac{1}{(1+g)^5}$$

1. Another assumption of the constant-growth model as presented is that earnings and dividends grow at the same rate. This assumption is true only in cases in which a firm pays out a fixed percentage of its earnings each year (has a fixed payout ratio). In the case of a declining industry, a negative growth rate ($g < 0\%$) might exist. In such a case, the constant-growth model, as well as the variable-growth model presented in the next section, remains fully applicable to the valuation process.

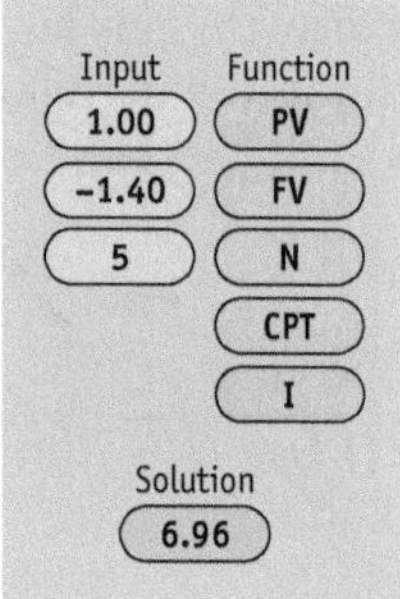

Using a financial calculator or a spreadsheet, we find that the historical annual growth rate of Lamar Company dividends equals 7%.[2] The company estimates that its dividend in 2013, D_1, will equal \$1.50 (about 7% more than the last dividend). The required return, r_s, is 15%. By substituting these values into Equation 7.4, we find the value of the stock to be

$$P_0 = \frac{\$1.50}{0.15 - 0.07} = \frac{\$1.50}{0.08} = \underline{\underline{\$18.75}} \text{ per share}$$

Assuming that the values of D_1, r_s, and g are accurately estimated, Lamar Company's stock value is \$18.75 per share.

Variable-Growth Model

variable-growth model
A dividend valuation approach that allows for a change in the dividend growth rate.

The zero- and constant-growth common stock models do not allow for any shift in expected growth rates. Because future growth rates might shift up or down because of changing business conditions, it is useful to consider a **variable-growth model** that allows for a change in the dividend growth rate.[3] We will assume that a single shift in growth rates occurs at the end of year N, and we will use g_1 to represent the initial growth rate and g_2 for the growth rate after the shift. To determine the value of a share of stock in the case of variable growth, we use a four-step procedure:

Step 1 Find the value of the cash dividends at the end of *each year*, D_t, during the initial growth period, years 1 through N. This step may require adjusting the most recent dividend, D_0, using the initial growth rate, g_1, to calculate the dividend amount for each year. Therefore, for the first N years,

$$D_t = D_0 \times (1 + g_1)^t$$

Step 2 Find the present value of the dividends expected during the initial growth period. Using the notation presented earlier, we can give this value as

$$\sum_{t=1}^{N} \frac{D_0 \times (1 + g_1)^t}{(1 + r_s)^t} = \sum_{t=1}^{N} \frac{D_t}{(1 + r_s)^t}$$

Step 3 Find the value of the stock *at the end of the initial growth period,* $P_N = (D_{N+1})/(r_s - g_2)$, which is the present value of all dividends expected from year $N + 1$ to infinity, assuming a constant dividend growth rate, g_2. This value is found by applying the constant-growth model (Equation 7.4) to the dividends expected from year $N + 1$ to infinity.

---

2. A financial calculator can be used. (*Note:* Most calculators require *either* the *PV* or *FV* value to be input as a negative number to calculate an unknown interest or growth rate. That approach is used here.) Using the inputs shown at the left, you should find the growth rate to be 6.96%, which we round to 7%.

An electronic spreadsheet could also be used to make this computation. Given space considerations, we have forgone that computational aid here.

3. More than one change in the growth rate can be incorporated into the model, but to simplify the discussion we will consider only a single growth-rate change. The number of variable-growth valuation models is technically unlimited, but concern over all possible shifts in growth is unlikely to yield much more accuracy than a simpler model.

The present value of P_N would represent the value *today* of all dividends that are expected to be received from year $N + 1$ to infinity. This value can be represented by

$$\frac{1}{(1 + r_s)^N} \times \frac{D_{N+1}}{r_s - g_2}$$

Step 4 Add the present value components found in Steps 2 and 3 to find the value of the stock, P_0, given in Equation 7.5:

$$P_0 = \underbrace{\sum_{t=1}^{N} \frac{D_0 \times (1 + g_1)^t}{(1 + r_s)^t}}_{\substack{\text{Present value of} \\ \text{dividends} \\ \text{during initial} \\ \text{growth period}}} + \underbrace{\left[\frac{1}{(1 + r_s)^N} \times \frac{D_{N+1}}{r_s - g_2}\right]}_{\substack{\text{Present value of} \\ \text{price of stock} \\ \text{at end of initial} \\ \text{growth period}}} \qquad (7.5)$$

The following example illustrates the application of these steps to a variable-growth situation with only one change in growth rate.

Personal Finance Example 7.4 ▸ Victoria Robb is considering purchasing the common stock of Warren Industries, a rapidly growing boat manufacturer. She finds that the firm's most recent (2012) annual dividend payment was $1.50 per share. Victoria estimates that these dividends will increase at a 10% annual rate, g_1, over the next 3 years (2013, 2014, and 2015) because of the introduction of a hot new boat. At the end of the 3 years (the end of 2015), she expects the firm's mature product line to result in a slowing of the dividend growth rate to 5% per year, g_2, for the foreseeable future. Victoria's required return, r_s, is 15%. To estimate the current (end-of-2012) value of Warren's common stock, $P_0 = P_{2012}$, she applies the four-step procedure to these data.

Step 1 The value of the cash dividends in each of the next 3 years is calculated in columns 1, 2, and 3 of Table 7.3. The 2013, 2014, and 2015 dividends are $1.65, $1.82, and $2.00, respectively.

TABLE 7.3 Calculation of Present Value of Warren Industries Dividends (2013–2015)

t	End of year	$D_0 = D_{2012}$ (1)	$(1 + g_1)^t$ (2)	D_t [(1) × (2)] (3)	$(1 + r_s)^t$ (4)	Present value of dividends [(3) ÷ (4)] (5)
1	2013	$1.50	1.100	$1.65	1.150	$1.43
2	2014	1.50	1.210	1.82	1.323	1.37
3	2015	1.50	1.331	2.00	1.521	1.32

$$\text{Sum of present value of dividends} = \sum_{t=1}^{3} \frac{D_0 \times (1 + g_1)^t}{(1 + r_s)^t} = \underline{\underline{\$4.12}}$$

Step 2 The present value of the three dividends expected during the 2013–2015 initial growth period is calculated in columns 3, 4, and 5 of Table 7.3. The sum of the present values of the three dividends is \$4.12.

Step 3 The value of the stock at the end of the initial growth period ($N = 2015$) can be found by first calculating $D_{N+1} = D_{2016}$:

$$D_{2016} = D_{2015} \times (1 + 0.05) = \$2.00 \times (1.05) = \$2.10$$

By using $D_{2016} = \$2.10$, a 15% required return, and a 5% dividend growth rate, the value of the stock at the end of 2015 is calculated as follows:

$$P_{2015} = \frac{D_{2016}}{r_s - g_2} = \frac{\$2.10}{0.15 - 0.05} = \frac{\$2.10}{0.10} = \$21.00$$

Finally, in Step 3, the share value of \$21 at the end of 2015 must be converted into a present (end-of-2012) value. Using the 15% required return, we get

$$\frac{P_{2015}}{(1 + r_s)^3} = \frac{\$21}{(1 + 0.15)^3} = \$13.81$$

Step 4 Adding the present value of the initial dividend stream (found in Step 2) to the present value of the stock at the end of the initial growth period (found in Step 3) as specified in Equation 7.5, the current (end-of-2012) value of Warren Industries stock is:

$$P_{2012} = \$4.12 + \$13.81 = \underline{\underline{\$17.93}} \text{ per share}$$

Victoria's calculations indicate that the stock is currently worth \$17.93 per share.

FREE CASH FLOW VALUATION MODEL

As an alternative to the dividend valuation models presented earlier in this chapter, a firm's value can be estimated by using its projected *free cash flows (FCFs)*. This approach is appealing when one is valuing firms that have no dividend history or are startups or when one is valuing an operating unit or division of a larger public company. Although dividend valuation models are widely used and accepted, in these situations it is preferable to use a more general free cash flow valuation model.

free cash flow valuation model
A model that determines the value of an entire company as the present value of its expected *free cash flows* discounted at the firm's *weighted average cost of capital,* which is its expected average future cost of funds over the long run.

The **free cash flow valuation model** is based on the same basic premise as dividend valuation models: The value of a share of common stock is the present value of all future cash flows it is expected to provide over an infinite time horizon. However, in the free cash flow valuation model, instead of valuing the firm's expected dividends, we value the firm's expected *free cash flows,* defined in Equation 4.4 (on page 122). They represent the amount of cash flow available to investors—the providers of debt (creditors) and equity (owners)—after all other obligations have been met.

The free cash flow valuation model estimates the value of the entire company by finding the present value of its expected free cash flows discounted at its *weighted average cost of capital,* which is its expected average future cost of funds (we'll say more about this in Chapter 9), as specified in Equation 7.6:

$$V_C = \frac{FCF_1}{(1 + r_a)^1} + \frac{FCF_2}{(1 + r_a)^2} + \cdots + \frac{FCF_\infty}{(1 + r_a)^\infty} \tag{7.6}$$

where

V_C = value of the entire company
FCF_t = free cash flow *expected* at the end of year t
r_a = the firm's weighted average cost of capital

Note the similarity between Equations 7.6 and 7.1, the general stock valuation equation.

Because the value of the entire company, V_C, is the market value of the entire enterprise (that is, of all assets), to find common stock value, V_S, we must subtract the market value of all of the firm's debt, V_D, and the market value of preferred stock, V_P, from V_C:

$$V_S = V_C - V_D - V_P \tag{7.7}$$

Because it is difficult to forecast a firm's free cash flow, specific annual cash flows are typically forecast for only about 5 years, beyond which a constant growth rate is assumed. Here we assume that the first 5 years of free cash flows are explicitly forecast and that a constant rate of free cash flow growth occurs beyond the end of year 5 to infinity. This model is methodologically similar to the variable-growth model presented earlier. Its application is best demonstrated with an example.

Example 7.5 ▶ Dewhurst, Inc., wishes to determine the value of its stock by using the free cash flow valuation model. To apply the model, the firm's CFO developed the data given in Table 7.4. Application of the model can be performed in four steps.

Step 1 Calculate the present value of the free cash flow occurring from the end of 2018 to infinity, measured at the beginning of 2018 (that is, at the end of 2017). Because a constant rate of growth in FCF is forecast beyond 2017, we can use the constant-growth dividend valuation model

TABLE 7.4 Dewhurst, Inc.'s, Data for the Free Cash Flow Valuation Model

Free cash flow		
Year (t)	**(FCF_t)**	**Other data**
2013	\$400,000	Growth rate of FCF, beyond 2017 to infinity, g_{FCF} = 3%
2014	450,000	Weighted average cost of capital, r_a = 9%
2015	520,000	Market value of all debt, V_D = \$3,100,000
2016	560,000	Market value of preferred stock, V_P = \$800,000
2017	600,000	Number of shares of common stock outstanding = 300,000

(Equation 7.4) to calculate the value of the free cash flows from the end of 2018 to infinity:

$$\text{Value of } FCF_{2018\rightarrow\infty} = \frac{FCF_{2018}}{r_a - g_{FCF}}$$

$$= \frac{\$600{,}000 \times (1 + 0.03)}{0.09 - 0.03}$$

$$= \frac{\$618{,}000}{0.06} = \$10{,}300{,}000$$

Note that to calculate the FCF in 2018, we had to increase the 2017 FCF value of \$600,000 by the 3% FCF growth rate, g_{FCF}.

Step 2 Add the present value of the FCF from 2018 to infinity, which is measured at the end of 2017, to the 2017 FCF value to get the total FCF in 2017.

$$\text{Total } FCF_{2017} = \$600{,}000 + \$10{,}300{,}000 = \$10{,}900{,}000$$

Step 3 Find the sum of the present values of the FCFs for 2013 through 2017 to determine the value of the entire company, V_C. This calculation is shown in Table 7.5.

TABLE 7.5 Calculation of the Value of the Entire Company for Dewhurst, Inc.

Year (t)	FCF_t (1)	$(1 + r_a)^t$ (2)	Present value of FCF_t [(1) ÷ (2)] (3)
2013	\$ 400,000	1.090	\$ 366,972
2014	450,000	1.188	378,788
2015	520,000	1.295	401,544
2016	560,000	1.412	396,601
2017	10,900,000[a]	1.539	7,082,521
		Value of entire company, V_C =	\$8,626,426[b]

[a]This amount is the sum of the FCF_{2017} of \$600,000 from Table 7.4 and the \$10,300,000 value of the $FCF_{2018\rightarrow\infty}$ calculated in Step 1.

[b]This value of the entire company is based on the rounded values that appear in the table. The precise value found without rounding is \$8,628,234.

Step 4 Calculate the value of the common stock using Equation 7.7. Substituting into Equation 7.7 the value of the entire company, V_C, calculated in Step 3, and the market values of debt, V_D, and preferred stock, V_P, given in Table 7.4, yields the value of the common stock, V_S:

$$V_S = \$8{,}626{,}426 - \$3{,}100{,}000 - \$800{,}000 = \underline{\underline{\$4{,}726{,}426}}$$

The value of Dewhurst's common stock is therefore estimated to be \$4,726,426. By dividing this total by the 300,000 shares of common stock that the firm has outstanding, we get a common stock value of *\$15.76 per share* (\$4,726,426 ÷ 300,000).

It should now be clear that the free cash flow valuation model is consistent with the dividend valuation models presented earlier. The appeal of this approach is its focus on the free cash flow estimates rather than on forecasted dividends, which are far more difficult to estimate given that they are paid at the discretion of the firm's board. The more general nature of the free cash flow model is responsible for its growing popularity, particularly with CFOs and other financial managers.

OTHER APPROACHES TO COMMON STOCK VALUATION

Many other approaches to common stock valuation exist. The more popular approaches include book value, liquidation value, and some type of price/earnings multiple.

book value per share
The amount per share of common stock that would be received if all of the firm's assets were *sold for their exact book (accounting) value* and the proceeds remaining after paying all liabilities (including preferred stock) were divided among the common stockholders.

Book Value

Book value per share is simply the amount per share of common stock that would be received if all of the firm's assets were *sold for their exact book (accounting) value* and the proceeds remaining after paying all liabilities (including preferred stock) were divided among the common stockholders. This method lacks sophistication and can be criticized on the basis of its reliance on historical balance sheet data. It ignores the firm's expected earnings potential and generally lacks any true relationship to the firm's value in the marketplace. Let us look at an example.

Example 7.6 ▸

At year-end 2012, Lamar Company's balance sheet shows total assets of $6 million, total liabilities (including preferred stock) of $4.5 million, and 100,000 shares of common stock outstanding. Its book value per share therefore would be

$$\frac{\$6{,}000{,}000 - \$4{,}500{,}000}{100{,}000 \text{ shares}} = \underline{\underline{\$15}} \text{ per share}$$

Because this value assumes that assets could be sold for their book value, it may not represent the minimum price at which shares are valued in the marketplace. As a matter of fact, although most stocks sell above book value, it is not unusual to find stocks selling below book value when investors believe either that assets are overvalued or that the firm's liabilities are understated.

liquidation value per share
The *actual amount* per share of common stock that would be received if all of the firm's assets were *sold for their market value*, liabilities (including preferred stock) were paid, and any remaining money were divided among the common stockholders.

Liquidation Value

Liquidation value per share is the *actual amount* per share of common stock that would be received if all of the firm's assets were *sold for their market value*, liabilities (including preferred stock) were paid, and any remaining money were divided among the common stockholders. This measure is more realistic than book value—because it is based on the current market value of the firm's assets—but it still fails to consider the earning power of those assets. An example will illustrate.

Example 7.7 ▸

Lamar Company found on investigation that it could obtain only $5.25 million if it sold its assets today. The firm's liquidation value per share therefore would be

$$\frac{\$5{,}250{,}000 - \$4{,}500{,}000}{100{,}000 \text{ shares}} = \underline{\underline{\$7.50}} \text{ per share}$$

Ignoring liquidation expenses, this amount would be the firm's minimum value.

Price/Earnings (P/E) Multiples

price/earnings multiple approach
A popular technique used to estimate the firm's share value; calculated by multiplying the firm's expected earnings per share (EPS) by the average price/earnings (P/E) ratio for the industry.

The *price/earnings (P/E) ratio,* introduced in Chapter 3, reflects the amount investors are willing to pay for each dollar of earnings. The average P/E ratio in a particular industry can be used as a guide to a firm's value—if it is assumed that investors value the earnings of that firm in the same way they do the "average" firm in the industry. The **price/earnings multiple approach** is a popular technique used to estimate the firm's share value; it is calculated by multiplying the firm's expected earnings per share (EPS) by the average price/earnings (P/E) ratio for the industry. The average P/E ratio for the industry can be obtained from a source such as *Standard & Poor's Industrial Ratios.*

The P/E ratio valuation technique is a simple method of determining a stock's value and can be quickly calculated after firms make earnings announcements, which accounts for its popularity. Naturally, this has increased the demand for more frequent announcements or "guidance" regarding future earnings. Some firms feel that pre-earnings guidance creates additional costs and can lead to ethical issues, as discussed in the *Focus on Ethics* box below.

focus on ETHICS

Psst—Have You Heard Any Good Quarterly Earnings Forecasts Lately?

in practice Corporate managers have long complained about the pressure to focus on the short term, and now business groups are coming to their defense. "The focus on the short term is a huge problem," says William Donaldson, former chairman of the Securities and Exchange Commission. "With all of the attention paid to quarterly performance, managers are taking their eyes off long-term strategic goals."

Donaldson, the U.S. Chamber of Commerce, and others believe that the best way to focus companies toward long-term goals is to do away with the practice of giving quarterly earnings guidance. In March 2007 the CFA Centre for Financial Market Integrity and the Business Roundtable Institute for Corporate Ethics proposed a template for quarterly earnings reports that would, in their view, obviate the need for earnings guidance.

Meanwhile, many companies are hesitant to give up issuing quarterly guidance. The practice of issuing earnings forecasts began in the early 1980s, a few years after the SEC's decision to allow companies to include forward-looking projections, provided they were accompanied by appropriate cautionary language. The result was what former SEC chairman Arthur Levitt once called a "game of winks and nods." Companies used earnings guidance to lower analysts' estimates; when the actual numbers came in higher, their stock prices jumped. The practice reached a fever pitch during the late 1990s when companies that missed the consensus earnings estimate, even by just a penny, saw their stock prices tumble.

One of the first companies to stop issuing earnings guidance was Gillette, in 2001. Others that abandoned quarterly guidance were Coca-Cola, Intel, and McDonald's. It became a trend. By 2005, just 61 percent of companies were offering quarterly projections to the public; according to the National Investor Relations Institute, the number declined to 52 percent in 2006.

Not everyone agrees with eliminating quarterly guidance. A survey conducted by New York University's Stern School of Business finance professor Baruch Lev, along with University of Florida professors Joel Houston and Jennifer Tucker, showed that companies that ended quarterly guidance reaped almost no benefit from doing so. Their study found no evidence that guidance stoppers increased capital investments or research and development. So when should companies give up earnings guidance? According to Lev, they should do so only when they are not very good at predicting their earnings. "If you are not better than others at forecasting, then don't bother," he says.

► *What temptations might managers face if they have provided earnings guidance to investors and later find it difficult to meet the expectations that they helped create?*

The use of P/E multiples is especially helpful in valuing firms that are not publicly traded, but analysts use this approach for public companies too. In any case, the price/earnings multiple approach is considered superior to the use of book or liquidation values because it considers *expected* earnings. An example will demonstrate the use of price/earnings multiples.

Personal Finance Example 7.8 ▸ Ann Perrier plans to use the price/earnings multiple approach to estimate the value of Lamar Company's stock, which she currently holds in her retirement account. She estimates that Lamar Company will earn $2.60 per share next year (2013). This expectation is based on an analysis of the firm's historical earnings trend and of expected economic and industry conditions. She finds the price/earnings (P/E) ratio for firms in the same industry to average 7. Multiplying Lamar's expected earnings per share (EPS) of $2.60 by this ratio gives her a value for the firm's shares of $18.20, assuming that investors will continue to value the average firm at 7 times its earnings.

So how much is Lamar Company's stock really worth? That's a trick question because there's no one right answer. It is important to recognize that the answer depends on the assumptions made and the techniques used. Professional securities analysts typically use a variety of models and techniques to value stocks. For example, an analyst might use the constant-growth model, liquidation value, and a price/earnings (P/E) multiple to estimate the worth of a given stock. If the analyst feels comfortable with his or her estimates, the stock would be valued at no more than the largest estimate. Of course, should the firm's estimated liquidation value per share exceed its "going concern" value per share, estimated by using one of the valuation models (zero-, constant-, or variable-growth or free cash flow) or the P/E multiple approach, the firm would be viewed as being "worth more dead than alive." In such an event, the firm would lack sufficient earning power to justify its existence and should probably be liquidated.

Matter of fact

Problems with P/E Valuation

The P/E multiple approach is a fast and easy way to estimate a stock's value. However, P/E ratios vary widely over time. In 1980, the average stock had a P/E ratio below 9, but by the year 2000, the ratio had risen above 40. Therefore, analysts using the P/E approach in the 1980s would have come up with much lower estimates of value than analysts using the model 20 years later. In other words, when using this approach to estimate stock values, the estimate will depend more on whether stock market valuations generally are high or low rather than on whether the particular company is doing well or not.

→ REVIEW QUESTIONS

7–12 Describe the events that occur in an *efficient market* in response to new information that causes the expected return to exceed the required return. What happens to the market value?

7–13 What does the *efficient-market hypothesis (EMH)* say about **(a)** securities prices, **(b)** their reaction to new information, and **(c)** investor opportunities to profit? What is the *behavioral finance* challenge to this hypothesis?

7–14 Describe, compare, and contrast the following common stock dividend valuation models: **(a)** zero-growth, **(b)** constant-growth, and **(c)** variable-growth.

7–15 Describe the *free cash flow valuation model* and explain how it differs from the dividend valuation models. What is the appeal of this model?

7–16 Explain each of the three other approaches to common stock valuation: **(a)** book value, **(b)** liquidation value, and **(c)** price/earnings (P/E) multiples. Which of these is considered the best?

LG 6

7.4 Decision Making and Common Stock Value

Valuation equations measure the stock value at a point in time based on expected return and risk. Any decisions of the financial manager that affect these variables can cause the value of the firm to change. Figure 7.3 depicts the relationship among financial decisions, return, risk, and stock value.

CHANGES IN EXPECTED DIVIDENDS

Assuming that economic conditions remain stable, any management action that would cause current and prospective stockholders to raise their dividend expectations should increase the firm's value. In Equation 7.4, we can see that P_0 will increase for any increase in D_1 or g. Any action of the financial manager that will increase the level of expected dividends without changing risk (the required return) should be undertaken, because it will positively affect owners' wealth.

Example 7.9 ▸ Using the constant-growth model in an earlier example (on pages 281 and 282), we found Lamar Company to have a share value of \$18.75. On the following day, the firm announced a major technological breakthrough that would revolutionize its industry. Current and prospective stockholders would not be expected to adjust their required return of 15%, but they would expect that future dividends will increase. Specifically, they expect that although the dividend next year, D_1, will remain at \$1.50, the expected rate of growth thereafter will increase from 7% to 9%. If we substitute $D_1 = \$1.50$, $r_s = 0.15$, and $g = 0.09$ into Equation 7.4, the resulting share value is \$25 [\$1.50 ÷ (0.15 − 0.09)]. The increased value therefore resulted from the higher expected future dividends reflected in the increase in the growth rate.

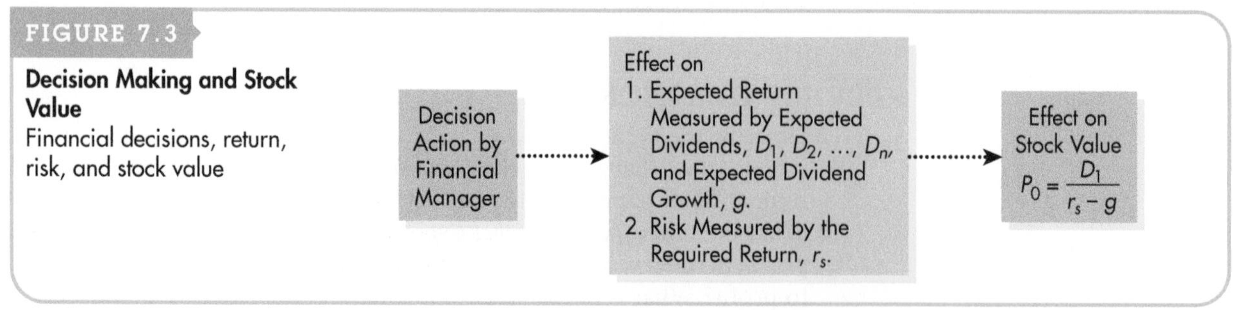

FIGURE 7.3

Decision Making and Stock Value

Financial decisions, return, risk, and stock value

CHANGES IN RISK

Although the required return, r_s, is the focus of Chapters 8 and 9, at this point we can consider its fundamental components. Any measure of required return consists of two components, a risk-free rate and a risk premium. We expressed this relationship as Equation 6.1 in the previous chapter, which we repeat here in terms of r_s:

$$r_s = \underbrace{r^* + IP}_{\text{risk-free rate, } R_F} + \underbrace{RP_s}_{\text{risk premium}}$$

In the next chapter you will learn that the real challenge in finding the required return is determining the appropriate risk premium. In Chapters 8 and 9 we will discuss how investors and managers can estimate the risk premium for any particular asset. For now, recognize that r_s represents the minimum return that the firm's stock must provide to shareholders to compensate them for bearing the risk of holding the firm's equity.

Any action taken by the financial manager that increases the risk shareholders must bear will also increase the risk premium required by shareholders, and hence the required return. Additionally, the required return can be affected by changes in the risk free rate—even if the risk premium remains constant. For example, if the risk-free rate increases due to a shift in government policy, then the required return goes up too. In Equation 7.1, we can see that an increase in the required return, r_s, will reduce share value, P_0, and a decrease in the required return will increase share value. Thus, any action of the financial manager that increases risk contributes to a reduction in value, and any action that decreases risk contributes to an increase in value.

Example 7.10 ▸ Assume that Lamar Company's 15% required return resulted from a risk-free rate of 9% and a risk premium of 6%. With this return, the firm's share value was calculated in an earlier example (on pages 280 and 281) to be $18.75.

Now imagine that the financial manager makes a decision that, without changing expected dividends, causes the firm's risk premium to increase to 7%. Assuming that *the risk-free rate remains at 9%, the new required return on Lamar stock will be 16% (9% + 7%)*, substituting $D_1 = \$1.50$, $r_s = 0.16$, and $g = 0.07$ into the valuation equation (Equation 7.3), results in a new share value of $16.67 [$1.50 ÷ (0.16 − 0.07)]. As expected, raising the required return, without any corresponding increase in expected dividends, causes the firm's stock value to decline. Clearly, the financial manager's action was not in the owners' best interest.

COMBINED EFFECT

A financial decision rarely affects dividends and risk independently; most decisions affect both factors often in the same direction. As firms take on more risk, their shareholders expect to see higher dividends. The net effect on value depends on the relative size of the changes in these two variables.

Example 7.11 ▶ If we assume that the two changes illustrated for Lamar Company in the preceding examples occur simultaneously, the key variable values would be $D_1 = \$1.50$, $r_s = 0.16$, and $g = 0.09$. Substituting into the valuation model, we obtain a share price of \$21.43 [\$1.50 ÷ (0.16 − 0.09)]. The net result of the decision, which increased dividend growth (g, from 7% to 9%) as well as required return (r_s, from 15% to 16%), is positive. The share price increased from \$18.75 to \$21.43. Even with the combined effects, the decision appears to be in the best interest of the firm's owners because it increases their wealth.

→ REVIEW QUESTIONS

7–17 Explain the linkages among financial decisions, return, risk, and stock value.

7–18 Assuming that all other variables remain unchanged, what impact would *each* of the following have on stock price? **(a)** The firm's risk premium increases. **(b)** The firm's required return decreases. **(c)** The dividend expected next year decreases. **(d)** The rate of growth in dividends is expected to increase.

Summary

FOCUS ON VALUE

The price of each share of a firm's common stock is the value of each ownership interest. Although common stockholders typically have voting rights, which indirectly give them a say in management, their most significant right is their claim on the residual cash flows of the firm. This claim is subordinate to those of vendors, employees, customers, lenders, the government (for taxes), and preferred stockholders. The value of the common stockholders' claim is embodied in the future cash flows they are entitled to receive. The present value of those expected cash flows is the firm's share value.

To determine this present value, forecast cash flows are discounted at a rate that reflects their risk. Riskier cash flows are discounted at higher rates, resulting in lower present values than less risky expected cash flows, which are discounted at lower rates. The value of the firm's common stock is therefore driven by its expected cash flows (returns) and risk (certainty of the expected cash flows).

In pursuing the firm's goal of **maximizing the stock price,** the financial manager must carefully consider the balance of return and risk associated with each proposal and must undertake only those actions that create value for owners. By focusing on value creation and by managing and monitoring the firm's cash flows and risk, the financial manager should be able to achieve the firm's goal of share price maximization.

REVIEW OF LEARNING GOALS

LG 1 **Differentiate between debt and equity.** Holders of equity capital (common and preferred stock) are owners of the firm. Typically, only common stockholders have a voice in management. Equityholders' claims on income and assets are secondary to creditors' claims, there is no maturity date, and dividends paid to stockholders are not tax deductible.

LG 2 **Discuss the features of both common and preferred stock.** The common stock of a firm can be privately owned, closely owned, or publicly owned. It can be sold with or without a par value. Preemptive rights allow common stockholders to avoid dilution of ownership when new shares are issued. Not all shares authorized in the corporate charter are outstanding. If a firm has treasury stock, it will have issued more shares than are outstanding. Some firms have two or more classes of common stock that differ mainly in having unequal voting rights. Proxies transfer voting rights from one party to another. The decision to pay dividends to common stockholders is made by the firm's board of directors. Firms can issue stock in foreign markets. The stock of many foreign corporations is traded in U.S. markets in the form of American depositary receipts (ADRs), which are backed by American depositary shares (ADSs).

Preferred stockholders have preference over common stockholders with respect to the distribution of earnings and assets. They do not normally have voting privileges. Preferred stock issues may have certain restrictive covenants, cumulative dividends, a call feature, and a conversion feature.

LG 3 **Describe the process of issuing common stock, including venture capital, going public, and the investment banker.** The initial nonfounder financing for business startups with attractive growth prospects typically comes from private equity investors. These investors can be either angel capitalists or venture capitalists (VCs). VCs usually invest in both early-stage and later-stage companies that they hope to take public so as to cash out their investments.

The first public issue of a firm's stock is called an initial public offering (IPO). The company selects an investment banker to advise it and to sell the securities. The lead investment banker may form a selling syndicate with other investment bankers. The IPO process includes getting SEC approval, promoting the offering to investors, and pricing the issue.

LG 4 **Understand the concept of market efficiency and basic stock valuation using zero-growth, constant-growth, and variable-growth models.** Market efficiency assumes that the quick reactions of rational investors to new information cause the market value of common stock to adjust upward or downward quickly. The efficient-market hypothesis (EMH) suggests that securities are fairly priced, that they reflect fully all publicly available information, and that investors should therefore not waste time trying to find and capitalize on mispriced securities. Behavioral finance advocates challenge this hypothesis by arguing that emotion and other factors play a role in investment decisions.

The value of a share of stock is the present value of all future dividends it is expected to provide over an infinite time horizon. Three dividend growth models—zero-growth, constant-growth, and variable-growth—can be considered in common stock valuation. The most widely cited model is the constant-growth model.

LG 5 **Discuss the free cash flow valuation model and the book value, liquidation value, and price/earnings (P/E) multiple approaches.** The free cash flow valuation model values firms that have no dividend history, startups, or an operating unit or division of a larger public company. The model finds the value of the entire company by discounting the firm's expected free cash flow at its weighted average cost of capital. The common stock value is found by subtracting the market values of the firm's debt and preferred stock from the value of the entire company.

Book value per share is the amount per share of common stock that would be received if all of the firm's assets were *sold for their exact book (accounting) value* and the proceeds remaining after paying all liabilities (including preferred stock) were divided among the common stockholders. Liquidation value per share is the *actual amount* per share of common stock that would be received if all of the firm's assets were *sold for their market value,* liabilities (including preferred stock) were paid, and the remaining money were divided among the common stockholders. The price/earnings (P/E) multiple approach estimates stock value by multiplying the firm's expected earnings per share (EPS) by the average price/earnings (P/E) ratio for the industry.

LG 6 **Explain the relationships among financial decisions, return, risk, and the firm's value.** In a stable economy, any action of the financial manager that increases the level of expected dividends without changing risk should increase share value; any action that reduces the level of expected dividends without changing risk should reduce share value. Similarly, any action that increases risk (required return) will reduce share value; any action that reduces risk will increase share value. An assessment of the combined effect of return and risk on stock value must be part of the financial decision-making process.

Opener-in-Review

A123 shares were originally offered for sale at a price of \$13.50. Three months later, the stock traded for about \$18. What return did investors earn over this period? On November 10, 2009, A123 reported its 3rd quarter financial results. From November 9 to November 11, the firm's stock price fell from \$17.85 to \$16.88. Given that A123 has 102 million shares outstanding, what were the dollar and percentage losses that shareholders endured in the days surrounding the earnings release? Over the same three days (November 9–11), the Nasdaq stock index moved up 0.6%. How does this influence your thinking about A123's stock performance around this time?

Self-Test Problems (Solutions in Appendix)

LG 4 **ST7–1 Common stock valuation** Perry Motors' common stock just paid its annual dividend of \$1.80 per share. The required return on the common stock is 12%. Estimate the value of the common stock under each of the following assumptions about the dividend:

a. Dividends are expected to grow at an annual rate of 0% to infinity.
b. Dividends are expected to grow at a constant annual rate of 5% to infinity.
c. Dividends are expected to grow at an annual rate of 5% for each of the next 3 years, followed by a constant annual growth rate of 4% in years 4 to infinity.

LG 5 **ST7–2** **Free cash flow valuation** Erwin Footwear wishes to assess the value of its Active Shoe Division. This division has debt with a market value of $12,500,000 and no preferred stock. Its weighted average cost of capital is 10%. The Active Shoe Division's estimated free cash flow each year from 2013 through 2016 is given in the following table. Beyond 2016 to infinity, the firm expects its free cash flow to grow at 4% annually.

Year (t)	Free cash flow (FCF_t)
2013	$ 800,000
2014	1,200,000
2015	1,400,000
2016	1,500,000

a. Use the *free cash flow valuation model* to estimate the value of Erwin's entire Active Shoe Division.
b. Use your finding in part **a** along with the data provided above to find this division's common stock value.
c. If the Active Shoe Division as a public company will have 500,000 shares outstanding, use your finding in part **b** to calculate its value per share.

Warm-Up Exercises

All problems are available in myfinancelab.

LG 1 **E7–1** A balance sheet balances assets with their sources of debt and equity financing. If a corporation has assets equal to $5.2 million and a debt ratio of 75.0%, how much debt does the corporation have on its books?

LG 2 **E7–2** Angina, Inc., has 5 million shares outstanding. The firm is considering issuing an additional 1 million shares. After selling these shares at their $20 per share offering price and netting 95% of the sale proceeds, the firm is obligated by an earlier agreement to sell an additional 250,000 shares at 90% of the offering price. In total, how much cash will the firm net from these stock sales?

LG 2 **E7–3** Figurate Industries has 750,000 shares of cumulative preferred stock outstanding. It has passed the last three quarterly dividends of $2.50 per share and now (at the end of the current quarter) wishes to distribute a total of $12 million to its shareholders. If Figurate has 3 million shares of common stock outstanding, how large a per-share common stock dividend will it be able to pay?

LG 3 **E7–4** Today the common stock of Gresham Technology closed at $24.60 per share, down $0.35 from yesterday. If the company has 4.6 million shares outstanding and annual earnings of $11.2 million, what is its P/E ratio today? What was its P/E ratio yesterday?

LG 4 **E7–5** Stacker Weight Loss currently pays an annual year-end dividend of $1.20 per share. It plans to increase this dividend by 5% next year and maintain it at the new level for the foreseeable future. If the required return on this firm's stock is 8%, what is the value of Stacker's stock?

LG 6 **E7–6** Brash Corporation initiated a new corporate strategy that fixes its annual dividend at $2.25 per share forever. If the risk-free rate is 4.5% and the risk premium on Brash's stock is 10.8%, what is the value of Brash's stock?

Problems

All problems are available in myfinancelab.

LG 2 **P7–1** **Authorized and available shares** Aspin Corporation's charter authorizes issuance of 2,000,000 shares of common stock. Currently, 1,400,000 shares are outstanding, and 100,000 shares are being held as treasury stock. The firm wishes to raise $48,000,000 for a plant expansion. Discussions with its investment bankers indicate that the sale of new common stock will net the firm $60 per share.

a. What is the maximum number of new shares of common stock that the firm can sell without receiving further authorization from shareholders?

b. Judging on the basis of the data given and your finding in part **a,** will the firm be able to raise the needed funds without receiving further authorization?

c. What must the firm do to obtain authorization to issue more than the number of shares found in part **a?**

LG 2 **P7–2** **Preferred dividends** Slater Lamp Manufacturing has an outstanding issue of preferred stock with an $80 par value and an 11% annual dividend.

a. What is the annual dollar dividend? If it is paid quarterly, how much will be paid each quarter?

b. If the preferred stock is *noncumulative* and the board of directors has passed the preferred dividend for the last 3 quarters, how much must be paid to preferred stockholders in the current quarter before dividends are paid to common stockholders?

c. If the preferred stock is *cumulative* and the board of directors has passed the preferred dividend for the last 3 quarters, how much must be paid to preferred stockholders in the current quarter before dividends are paid to common stockholders?

LG 2 **P7–3** **Preferred dividends** In each case in the following table, how many dollars of preferred dividends per share must be paid to preferred stockholders in the current period before common stock dividends are paid?

Case	Type	Par value	Dividend per share per period	Periods of dividends passed
A	Cumulative	$ 80	$ 5	2
B	Noncumulative	110	8%	3
C	Noncumulative	100	$11	1
D	Cumulative	60	8.5%	4
E	Cumulative	90	9%	0

LG 2 **P7–4** **Convertible preferred stock** Valerian Corp. convertible preferred stock has a fixed conversion ratio of 5 common shares per 1 share of preferred stock. The preferred

stock pays a dividend of $10.00 per share per year. The common stock currently sells for $20.00 per share and pays a dividend of $1.00 per share per year.

a. Judging on the basis of the conversion ratio and the price of the common shares, what is the current conversion value of each preferred share?

b. If the preferred shares are selling at $96.00 each, should an investor convert the preferred shares to common shares?

c. What factors might cause an investor not to convert from preferred to common stock?

Personal Finance Problem

LG 4 **P7–5 Common stock valuation—Zero growth** Scotto Manufacturing is a mature firm in the machine tool component industry. The firm's most recent common stock dividend was $2.40 per share. Because of its maturity as well as its stable sales and earnings, the firm's management feels that dividends will remain at the current level for the foreseeable future.

a. If the required return is 12%, what will be the value of Scotto's common stock?

b. If the firm's risk as perceived by market participants suddenly increases, causing the required return to rise to 20%, what will be the common stock value?

c. Judging on the basis of your findings in parts **a** and **b,** what impact does risk have on value? Explain.

Personal Finance Problem

LG 4 **P7–6 Common stock value—Zero growth** Kelsey Drums, Inc., is a well-established supplier of fine percussion instruments to orchestras all over the United States. The company's class A common stock has paid a dividend of $5.00 per share per year for the last 15 years. Management expects to continue to pay at that amount for the foreseeable future. Sally Talbot purchased 100 shares of Kelsey class A common 10 years ago at a time when the required rate of return for the stock was 16%. She wants to sell her shares today. The current required rate of return for the stock is 12%. How much capital gain or loss will Sally have on her shares?

LG 4 **P7–7 Preferred stock valuation** Jones Design wishes to estimate the value of its outstanding preferred stock. The preferred issue has an $80 par value and pays an annual dividend of $6.40 per share. Similar-risk preferred stocks are currently earning a 9.3% annual rate of return.

a. What is the market value of the outstanding preferred stock?

b. If an investor purchases the preferred stock at the value calculated in part **a,** how much does she gain or lose per share if she sells the stock when the required return on similar-risk preferred stocks has risen to 10.5%? Explain.

LG 4 **P7–8 Common stock value—Constant growth** Use the constant-growth model (Gordon growth model) to find the value of each firm shown in the following table.

Firm	Dividend expected next year	Dividend growth rate	Required return
A	$1.20	8%	13%
B	4.00	5	15
C	0.65	10	14
D	6.00	8	9
E	2.25	8	20

LG 4 **P7–9** **Common stock value—Constant growth** McCracken Roofing, Inc., common stock paid a dividend of \$1.20 per share last year. The company expects earnings and dividends to grow at a rate of 5% per year for the foreseeable future.

a. What required rate of return for this stock would result in a price per share of \$28?

b. If McCracken expects both earnings and dividends to grow at an annual rate of 10%, what required rate of return would result in a price per share of \$28?

Personal Finance Problem

LG 4 **P7–10** **Common stock value—Constant growth** Elk County Telephone has paid the dividends shown in the following table over the past 6 years.

Year	Dividend per share
2012	\$2.87
2011	2.76
2010	2.60
2009	2.46
2008	2.37
2007	2.25

The firm's dividend per share next year is expected to be \$3.02.

a. If you can earn 13% on similar-risk investments, what is the most you would be willing to pay per share?

b. If you can earn only 10% on similar-risk investments, what is the most you would be willing to pay per share?

c. Compare and contrast your findings in parts **a** and **b,** and discuss the impact of changing risk on share value.

LG 4 **P7–11** **Common stock value—Variable growth** Newman Manufacturing is considering a cash purchase of the stock of Grips Tool. During the year just completed, Grips earned \$4.25 per share and paid cash dividends of \$2.55 per share (D_0 = \$2.55). Grips' earnings and dividends are expected to grow at 25% per year for the next 3 years, after which they are expected to grow at 10% per year to infinity. What is the maximum price per share that Newman should pay for Grips if it has a required return of 15% on investments with risk characteristics similar to those of Grips?

Personal Finance Problem

LG 4 **P7–12** **Common stock value—Variable growth** Home Place Hotels, Inc., is entering into a 3-year remodeling and expansion project. The construction will have a limiting effect on earnings during that time, but when it is complete, it should allow the company to enjoy much improved growth in earnings and dividends. Last year, the company paid a dividend of \$3.40. It expects zero growth in the next year. In years 2 and 3, 5% growth is expected, and in year 4, 15% growth. In year 5 and thereafter, growth should be a constant 10% per year. What is the maximum price per share that an investor who requires a return of 14% should pay for Home Place Hotels common stock?

LG 4 **P7–13 Common stock value—Variable growth** Lawrence Industries' most recent annual dividend was \$1.80 per share (D_0 = \$1.80), and the firm's required return is 11%. Find the market value of Lawrence's shares when:

a. Dividends are expected to grow at 8% annually for 3 years, followed by a 5% constant annual growth rate in years 4 to infinity.

b. Dividends are expected to grow at 8% annually for 3 years, followed by a 0% constant annual growth rate in years 4 to infinity.

c. Dividends are expected to grow at 8% annually for 3 years, followed by a 10% constant annual growth rate in years 4 to infinity.

Personal Finance Problem

LG 4 **P7–14 Common stock value—All growth models** You are evaluating the potential purchase of a small business currently generating \$42,500 of after-tax cash flow (D_0 = \$42,500). On the basis of a review of similar-risk investment opportunities, you must earn an 18% rate of return on the proposed purchase. Because you are relatively uncertain about future cash flows, you decide to estimate the firm's value using several possible assumptions about the growth rate of cash flows.

a. What is the firm's value if cash flows are expected to grow at an annual rate of 0% from now to infinity?

b. What is the firm's value if cash flows are expected to grow at a constant annual rate of 7% from now to infinity?

c. What is the firm's value if cash flows are expected to grow at an annual rate of 12% for the first 2 years, followed by a constant annual rate of 7% from year 3 to infinity?

LG 5 **P7–15 Free cash flow valuation** Nabor Industries is considering going public but is unsure of a fair offering price for the company. Before hiring an investment banker to assist in making the public offering, managers at Nabor have decided to make their own estimate of the firm's common stock value. The firm's CFO has gathered data for performing the valuation using the free cash flow valuation model.

The firm's weighted average cost of capital is 11%, and it has \$1,500,000 of debt at market value and \$400,000 of preferred stock at its assumed market value. The estimated free cash flows over the next 5 years, 2013 through 2017, are given below. Beyond 2017 to infinity, the firm expects its free cash flow to grow by 3% annually.

Year (t)	Free cash flow (FCF_t)
2013	\$200,000
2014	250,000
2015	310,000
2016	350,000
2017	390,000

a. Estimate the value of Nabor Industries' entire company by using the *free cash flow valuation model.*

b. Use your finding in part **a,** along with the data provided above, to find Nabor Industries' common stock value.

c. If the firm plans to issue 200,000 shares of common stock, what is its estimated value per share?

Personal Finance Problem

LG 5 **P7–16 Using the free cash flow valuation model to price an IPO** Assume that you have an opportunity to buy the stock of CoolTech, Inc., an IPO being offered for $12.50 per share. Although you are very much interested in owning the company, you are concerned about whether it is fairly priced. To determine the value of the shares, you have decided to apply the free cash flow valuation model to the firm's financial data that you've developed from a variety of data sources. The key values you have compiled are summarized in the following table.

Free cash flow		
Year (t)	FCF_t	**Other data**
2013	$ 700,000	Growth rate of FCF, beyond 2013 to infinity = 2%
2014	800,000	Weighted average cost of capital = 8%
2015	950,000	Market value of all debt = $2,700,000
2016	1,100,000	Market value of preferred stock = $1,000,000
		Number of shares of common stock outstanding = 1,100,000

a. Use the *free cash flow valuation model* to estimate CoolTech's common stock value per share.

b. Judging on the basis of your finding in part **a** and the stock's offering price, should you buy the stock?

c. On further analysis, you find that the growth rate in FCF beyond 2016 will be 3% rather than 2%. What effect would this finding have on your responses in parts **a** and **b?**

LG 5 **P7–17 Book and liquidation value** The balance sheet for Gallinas Industries is as follows.

Gallinas Industries Balance Sheet December 31

Assets		**Liabilities and Stockholders' Equity**	
Cash	$ 40,000	Accounts payable	$100,000
Marketable securities	60,000	Notes payable	30,000
Accounts receivable	120,000	Accrued wages	30,000
Inventories	160,000	Total current liabilities	$160,000
Total current assets	$380,000	Long-term debt	$180,000
Land and buildings (net)	$150,000	Preferred stock	$ 80,000
Machinery and equipment	250,000	Common stock (10,000 shares)	260,000
Total fixed assets (net)	$400,000	Retained earnings	100,000
Total assets	$780,000	Total liabilities and stockholders' equity	$780,000

Additional information with respect to the firm is available:
(1) Preferred stock can be liquidated at book value.
(2) Accounts receivable and inventories can be liquidated at 90% of book value.
(3) The firm has 10,000 shares of common stock outstanding.
(4) All interest and dividends are currently paid up.

(5) Land and buildings can be liquidated at 130% of book value.
(6) Machinery and equipment can be liquidated at 70% of book value.
(7) Cash and marketable securities can be liquidated at book value.

Given this information, answer the following:

a. What is Gallinas Industries' *book value per share?*

b. What is its *liquidation value per share?*

c. Compare, contrast, and discuss the values found in parts **a** and **b.**

LG 5 **P7–18** **Valuation with price/earnings multiples** For each of the firms shown in the following table, use the data given to estimate its common stock value employing price/earnings (P/E) multiples.

Firm	Expected EPS	Price/earnings multiple
A	$3.00	6.2
B	4.50	10.0
C	1.80	12.6
D	2.40	8.9
E	5.10	15.0

LG 6 **P7–19** **Management action and stock value** REH Corporation's most recent dividend was $3 per share, its expected annual rate of dividend growth is 5%, and the required return is now 15%. A variety of proposals are being considered by management to redirect the firm's activities. Determine the impact on share price for each of the following proposed actions, and indicate the best alternative.

a. Do nothing, which will leave the key financial variables unchanged.

b. Invest in a new machine that will increase the dividend growth rate to 6% and lower the required return to 14%.

c. Eliminate an unprofitable product line, which will increase the dividend growth rate to 7% and raise the required return to 17%.

d. Merge with another firm, which will reduce the growth rate to 4% and raise the required return to 16%.

e. Acquire a subsidiary operation from another manufacturer. The acquisition should increase the dividend growth rate to 8% and increase the required return to 17%.

LG 4 LG 6 **P7–20** **Integrative—Risk and Valuation** Given the following information for the stock of Foster Company, calculate the risk premium on its common stock.

Current price per share of common	$50.00
Expected dividend per share next year	$ 3.00
Constant annual dividend growth rate	9%
Risk-free rate of return	7%

LG 4 LG 6 **P7–21** **Integrative—Risk and valuation** Giant Enterprises' stock has a required return of 14.8%. The company, which plans to pay a dividend of $2.60 per share in the coming year, anticipates that its future dividends will increase at an annual rate

consistent with that experienced over the 2006–2012 period, when the following dividends were paid:

Year	Dividend per share
2012	$2.45
2011	2.28
2010	2.10
2009	1.95
2008	1.82
2007	1.80
2006	1.73

a. If the risk-free rate is 10%, what is the risk premium on Giant's stock?
b. Using the constant-growth model, estimate the value of Giant's stock.
c. Explain what effect, if any, a decrease in the risk premium would have on the value of Giant's stock.

LG 4 LG 6 **P7–22 Integrative—Risk and Valuation** Hamlin Steel Company wishes to determine the value of Craft Foundry, a firm that it is considering acquiring for cash. Hamlin wishes to determine the applicable discount rate to use as an input to the constant-growth valuation model. Craft's stock is not publicly traded. After studying the required returns of firms similar to Craft that are publicly traded, Hamlin believes that an appropriate risk premium on Craft stock is about 5%. The risk-free rate is currently 9%. Craft's dividend per share for each of the past 6 years is shown in the following table.

Year	Dividend per share
2012	$3.44
2011	3.28
2010	3.15
2009	2.90
2008	2.75
2007	2.45

a. Given that Craft is expected to pay a dividend of $3.68 next year, determine the maximum cash price that Hamlin should pay for each share of Craft.
b. Describe the effect on the resulting value of Craft of:
(1) A decrease in its dividend growth rate of 2% from that exhibited over the 2007–2012 period.
(2) A decrease in its risk premium to 4%.

LG 4 **P7–23 ETHICS PROBLEM** Melissa is trying to value Generic Utility, Inc.'s, stock, which is clearly not growing at all. Generic declared and paid a $5 dividend last year. The required rate of return for utility stocks is 11%, but Melissa is unsure about the financial reporting integrity of Generic's finance team. She decides to add an extra

1% "credibility" risk premium to the required return as part of her valuation analysis.

a. What is the value of Generic's stock, assuming that the financials are trustworthy?

b. What is the value of Generic's stock, assuming that Melissa includes the extra 1% "credibility" risk premium?

c. What is the difference between the values found in parts **a** and **b,** and how might one interpret that difference?

Spreadsheet Exercise

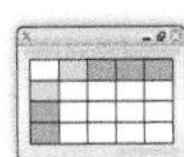

You are interested in purchasing the common stock of Azure Corporation. The firm recently paid a dividend of $3 per share. It expects its earnings—and hence its dividends—to grow at a rate of 7% for the foreseeable future. Currently, similar-risk stocks have required returns of 10%.

TO DO

a. Given the data above, calculate the present value of this security. Use the constant-growth model (Equation 7.4) to find the stock value.

b. One year later, your broker offers to sell you additional shares of Azure at $73. The most recent dividend paid was $3.21, and the expected growth rate for earnings remains at 7%. If you determine that the appropriate risk premium is 6.74% and you observe that the risk-free rate, R_F, is currently 5.25%, what is the firm's current required return, r_{Azure}?

c. Applying Equation 7.4, determine the value of the stock using the new dividend and required return from part **b.**

d. Given your calculation in part **c,** would you buy the additional shares from your broker at $73 per share? Explain.

e. Given your calculation in part **c,** would you sell your old shares for $73? Explain.

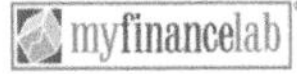

Visit www.myfinancelab.com for **Chapter Case: *Assessing the Impact of Suarez Manufacturing's Proposed Risky Investment on Its Stock Value,*** Group Exercises, and numerous online resources.

Integrative Case 3

Encore International

In the world of trendsetting fashion, instinct and marketing savvy are prerequisites to success. Jordan Ellis had both. During 2012, his international casual-wear company, Encore, rocketed to $300 million in sales after 10 years in business. His fashion line covered the young woman from head to toe with hats, sweaters, dresses, blouses, skirts, pants, sweatshirts, socks, and shoes. In Manhattan, there was an Encore shop every five or six blocks, each featuring a different color. Some shops showed the entire line in mauve, and others featured it in canary yellow.

Encore had made it. The company's historical growth was so spectacular that no one could have predicted it. However, securities analysts speculated that Encore could not keep up the pace. They warned that competition is fierce in the fashion industry and that the firm might encounter little or no growth in the future. They estimated that stockholders also should expect no growth in future dividends.

Contrary to the conservative securities analysts, Jordan Ellis felt that the company could maintain a constant annual growth rate in dividends per share of 6% in the future, or possibly 8% for the next 2 years and 6% thereafter. Ellis based his estimates on an established long-term expansion plan into European and Latin American markets. Venturing into these markets was expected to cause the risk of the firm, as measured by the risk premium on its stock, to increase immediately from 8.8% to 10%. Currently, the risk-free rate is 6%.

In preparing the long-term financial plan, Encore's chief financial officer has assigned a junior financial analyst, Marc Scott, to evaluate the firm's current stock price. He has asked Marc to consider the conservative predictions of the securities analysts and the aggressive predictions of the company founder, Jordan Ellis.

Marc has compiled these 2012 financial data to aid his analysis:

Data item	2012 value
Earnings per share (EPS)	$6.25
Price per share of common stock	$40.00
Book value of common stock equity	$60,000,000
Total common shares outstanding	2,500,000
Common stock dividend per share	$4.00

TO DO

a. What is the firm's current book value per share?

b. What is the firm's current P/E ratio?

c. (1) What is the current required return for Encore stock?

(2) What will be the new required return for Encore stock assuming that they expand into European and Latin American markets as planned?

d. If the securities analysts are correct and there is no growth in future dividends, what will be the value per share of the Encore stock? (*Note:* Use the new required return on the company's stock here.)

e. (1) If Jordan Ellis's predictions are correct, what will be the value per share of Encore stock if the firm maintains a constant annual 6% growth rate in future dividends? (*Note:* Continue to use the new required return here.)

(2) If Jordan Ellis's predictions are correct, what will be the value per share of Encore stock if the firm maintains a constant annual 8% growth rate in dividends per share over the next 2 years and 6% thereafter?

f. Compare the current (2012) price of the stock and the stock values found in parts **a, d,** and **e.** Discuss why these values may differ. Which valuation method do you believe most clearly represents the true value of the Encore stock?

Part 4 Risk and the Required Rate of Return

Chapters in This Part

Most people intuitively understand the principle that risk and return are linked. After all, as the old saying goes, "Nothing ventured, nothing gained." In the next two chapters, we'll explore how investors and financial managers quantify the notion of risk and how they determine how much additional return is appropriate compensation for taking extra risk.

Chapter 8 lays the groundwork, defining the terms *risk* and *return* and explaining why investors think about risk in different ways depending on whether they want to understand the risk of a specific investment or the risk of a broad portfolio of investments. Perhaps the most famous and widely applied theory in all of finance, the Capital Asset Pricing Model (or CAPM), is introduced here. The CAPM tells investors and managers alike what return they should expect given the risk of the asset they want to invest in.

Chapter 9 applies these lessons in a managerial finance setting. Firms raise money from two broad sources, owners and lenders. Owners provide equity financing, and lenders provide debt. To maximize the value of the firm, managers have to satisfy both groups, and doing so means earning returns high enough to meet investors' expectations. Chapter 9's focus is on the cost of capital or, more precisely, the weighted average cost of capital (WACC). The WACC tells managers exactly what kind of return their investments in plant and equipment, advertising, and human resources have to earn if the firm is to satisfy its investors. Essentially, the WACC is a hurdle rate, the minimum acceptable return that a firm should earn on any investment that it makes.

8 Risk and Return

Learning Goals

LG 1 Understand the meaning and fundamentals of risk, return, and risk preferences.

LG 2 Describe procedures for assessing and measuring the risk of a single asset.

LG 3 Discuss the measurement of return and standard deviation for a portfolio and the concept of correlation.

LG 4 Understand the risk and return characteristics of a portfolio in terms of correlation and diversification and the impact of international assets on a portfolio.

LG 5 Review the two types of risk and the derivation and role of beta in measuring the relevant risk of both a security and a portfolio.

LG 6 Explain the capital asset pricing model (CAPM), its relationship to the security market line (SML), and the major forces causing shifts in the SML.

Why This Chapter Matters to You

In your *professional* life

ACCOUNTING You need to understand the relationship between risk and return because of the effect that riskier projects will have on the firm's financial statements.

INFORMATION SYSTEMS You need to understand how to do scenario and correlation analyses to build decision packages that help management analyze the risk and return of various business opportunities.

MANAGEMENT You need to understand the relationship between risk and return and how to measure that relationship to evaluate data that come from finance personnel and translate those data into decisions that increase the value of the firm.

MARKETING You need to understand that although higher-risk projects may produce higher returns, they may not be the best choice for the firm if they produce erratic financial results and fail to maximize firm value.

OPERATIONS You need to understand why investments in plant, equipment, and systems need to be evaluated in light of their impact on the firm's risk and return, which together will affect the firm's value.

In your *personal* life

The tradeoff between risk and return enters into numerous personal financial decisions. You will use risk and return concepts when you invest your savings, buy real estate, finance major purchases, purchase insurance, invest in securities, and implement retirement plans. Although risk and return are difficult to measure precisely, you can get a feel for them and make decisions based on the trade-offs between risk and return in light of your personal disposition toward risk.

Mutual Funds

Fund's Returns Not Even Close to Average

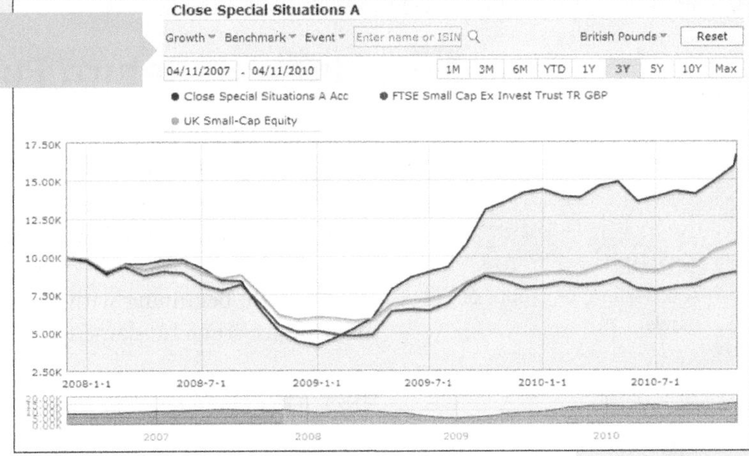

For most investors, 2008 was a miserable year. In the United States the Standard & Poor's 500 stock index, a barometer of the overall market, fell 37.2 percent. Returns were even worse in many other countries. The Morgan Stanley Europe, Australasia, and Far East (EAFE) Index dropped 45 percent, wiping out the previous five years worth of gains. For Deryck Noble-Nesbitt, manager of the Close Special Situations Fund in the United Kingdom, 2008 was close to a career-ending catastrophe. The Close Fund, which invests in small companies, lost nearly 60 percent of its value that year and ranked in the bottom 2 percent of all funds in its category. That performance followed a loss of nearly 5 percent in 2007, so the Close Fund was on a two-year losing streak going into 2009.

What a difference a year makes. In 2009, the Close Fund earned a return of 247 percent and ranked first among all funds specializing in small stocks. An investor who put £1,000 in the fund at the beginning of 2007 would have had roughly £1,411 by December 31, 2009, far ahead of what investors in most other funds would have earned over the same period. However, the first five months of 2010 were unkind to the Close Fund as it experienced another 5 percent loss, once again falling in the bottom 3 percent of all funds in the small stock category.

The experience of the Close Special Situations Fund illustrates two key points. First, investments with high returns tend to be associated with high risk. Small stocks as a category, and the recent performance of the Close Fund, clearly demonstrate that principle. In fact, investors ought to be suspicious of investment opportunities that appear to offer high returns without also having high risk. (See the *Focus on Ethics* box on page 310.) Second, predicting how any particular fund or investment will perform in any given period is difficult. In three consecutive years, the Close Fund ranked near the bottom, at the very top, and then near the bottom again of its peer group. Together, these two points suggest that investors must be very mindful of risk and should diversify their investments. This chapter explains how to put that advice into action.

LG 1

8.1 Risk and Return Fundamentals

portfolio
A collection, or group, of assets.

In most important business decisions there are two key financial considerations: risk and return. Each financial decision presents certain risk and return characteristics, and the combination of these characteristics can increase or decrease a firm's share price. Analysts use different methods to quantify risk, depending on whether they are looking at a single asset or a **portfolio**—a collection, or group, of assets. We will look at both, beginning with the risk of a single asset. First, though, it is important to introduce some fundamental ideas about risk, return, and risk preferences.

RISK DEFINED

risk
A measure of the uncertainty surrounding the return that an investment will earn or, more formally, the *variability of returns associated with a given asset.*

In the most basic sense, **risk** is a measure of the uncertainty surrounding the return that an investment will earn. Investments whose returns are more uncertain are generally viewed as being riskier. More formally, the term *risk* is used interchangeably with *uncertainty* to refer to the *variability of returns associated with a given asset.* A $1,000 government bond that guarantees its holder $5 interest after 30 days has no risk, because there is no variability associated with the return. A $1,000 investment in a firm's common stock, the value of which over the same 30 days may move up or down a great deal, is very risky because of the high variability of its return.

focus on ETHICS

If It Seems Too Good to Be True Then It Probably Is

in practice For many years, investors around the world clamored to invest with Bernard Madoff. Those fortunate enough to invest with "Bernie" might not have understood his secret trading system, but they were happy with the double-digit returns that they earned. Madoff was well connected, having been the chairman of the board of directors of the NASDAQ Stock Market and a founding member of the International Securities Clearing Corporation. His credentials seemed to be impeccable.

However, as the old saying goes, if something sounds too good to be true, it probably is. Madoff's investors learned this lesson the hard way when, on December 11, 2008, the U.S. Securities and Exchange Commission (SEC) charged Madoff with securities fraud. Madoff's hedge fund, Ascot Partners, turned out to be a giant Ponzi scheme.

Over the years, suspicions were raised about Madoff. Madoff generated high returns year after year, seemingly with very little risk. Madoff credited his complex trading strategy for his investment performance, but other investors employed similar strategies with much different results than Madoff reported. Harry Markopolos went as far as to submit a report to the SEC three years prior to Madoff's arrest titled "The World's Largest Hedge Fund Is a Fraud" that detailed his concerns.[a]

On June 29, 2009, Madoff was sentenced to 150 years in prison. Madoff's investors are still working to recover what they can. Fraudulent account statements sent just prior to Madoff's arrest indicated that investors' accounts contained over $64 billion, in aggregate. Many investors pursued claims based on the balance reported in these statements. However, a recent court ruling permits claims up to the difference between the amount an investor deposited with Madoff and the amount they withdrew. The judge also ruled that investors who managed to withdraw at least their initial investment before the fraud was uncovered are not eligible to recover additional funds. Total out-of-pocket cash losses as a result of Madoff's fraud were recently estimated at slightly over $20 billion.

► ***What are some hazards of allowing investors to pursue claims based on their most recent account statements?***

[a]www.sec.gov/news/studies/2009/oig-509/exhibit-0293.pdf

RETURN DEFINED

total rate of return
The total gain or loss experienced on an investment over a given period of time; calculated by dividing the asset's cash distributions during the period, plus change in value, by its beginning-of-period investment value.

Obviously, if we are going to assess risk on the basis of variability of return, we need to be certain we know what *return* is and how to measure it. The **total rate of return** is the total gain or loss experienced on an investment over a given period. Mathematically, an investment's total return is the sum of any cash distributions (for example, dividends or interest payments) plus the change in the investment's value, divided by the beginning-of-period value. The expression for calculating the total rate of return earned on any asset over period t, r_t, is commonly defined as

$$r_t = \frac{C_t + P_t - P_{t-1}}{P_{t-1}} \tag{8.1}$$

where

r_t = actual, expected, or required rate of return during period t
C_t = cash (flow) received from the asset investment in the time period $t - 1$ to t
P_t = price (value) of asset at time t
P_{t-1} = price (value) of asset at time $t - 1$

The return, r_t, reflects the combined effect of cash flow, C_t, and changes in value, $P_t - P_{t-1}$, over the period.[1]

Equation 8.1 is used to determine the rate of return over a time period as short as 1 day or as long as 10 years or more. However, in most cases, t is 1 year, and r therefore represents an annual rate of return.

Example 8.1 ▶

Robin wishes to determine the return on two stocks that she owned during 2009, Apple Inc. and Wal-Mart. At the beginning of the year, Apple stock traded for $90.75 per share, and Wal-Mart was valued at $55.33. During the year, Apple paid no dividends, but Wal-Mart shareholders received dividends of $1.09 per share. At the end of the year, Apple stock was worth $210.73 and Wal-Mart sold for $52.84. Substituting into Equation 8.1, we can calculate the annual rate of return, r, for each stock.

Apple: ($0 + $210.73 − $90.75) ÷ $90.75 = 132.2%
Wal-Mart: ($1.09 + $52.84 − $55.33) ÷ $55.33 = −2.5%

Robin made money on Apple and lost money on Wal-Mart in 2009, but notice that her losses on Wal-Mart would have been greater had it not been for the dividends that she received on her Wal-Mart shares. When calculating the total rate of return, it is important to take into account the effects of both cash disbursements and changes in the price of the investment during the year.

1. This expression does not imply that an investor necessarily buys the asset at time $t - 1$ and sells it at time t. Rather, it represents the increase (or decrease) in wealth that the investor has experienced during the period by holding a particular investment. If the investor sells the asset at time t, we say that the investor has *realized* the return on the investment. If the investor continues to hold the investment, we say that the return is *unrealized*.

TABLE 8.1 Historical Returns on Selected Investments (1900–2009)

Investment	Average nominal return	Average real return
Treasury bills	3.9%	0.9%
Treasury bonds	5.0	1.9
Common stocks	9.3	6.2

Source: Elroy Dimson, Paul Marsh, and Mike Staunton, *Triumph of the Optimists: 101 Years of Global Investment Returns* (Princeton, NJ: Princeton University Press, 2002).

Investment returns vary both over time and between different types of investments. By averaging historical returns over a long period of time, we can focus on the differences in returns that different kinds of investments tend to generate. Table 8.1 shows both the nominal and real average annual rates of return from 1900 to 2009 for three different types of investments: Treasury bills, Treasury bonds, and common stocks. Although bills and bonds are both issued by the U.S. government and are therefore viewed as relatively safe investments, bills have maturities of 1 year or less, while bonds have maturities ranging up to 30 years. Consequently, the interest rate risk associated with Treasury bonds is much higher than with bills. Over the last 109 years, bills earned the lowest returns, just 3.9 percent per year on average in nominal returns and only 0.9 percent annually in real terms. The latter number means that average Treasury bill returns barely exceeded the average rate of inflation. Bond returns were higher, 5.0 percent in nominal terms and 1.9 percent in real terms. Clearly, though, stocks outshined the other types of investments, earning average annual nominal returns of 9.3 percent and average real returns of 6.2 percent.

In more depth

To read about *Inflation and Returns*, go to www.myfinancelab.com

myfinancelab

In light of these statistics, you might wonder, "Why would anyone invest in bonds or bills if the returns on stocks are so much higher?" The answer, as you will soon see, is that stocks are much riskier than either bonds or bills and that risk leads some investors to prefer the safer, albeit lower, returns on Treasury securities.

RISK PREFERENCES

Different people react to risk in different ways. Economists use three categories to describe how investors respond to risk. The first category, *and the one that describes the behavior of most people most of the time*, is called risk aversion. A person who is a **risk-averse** investor prefers less risky over more risky investments, holding the rate of return fixed. A risk-averse investor who believes that two different investments have the same expected return will choose the investment whose returns are more certain. Stated another way, when choosing between two investments, *a risk-averse investor will not make the riskier investment unless it offers a higher expected return to compensate the investor for bearing the additional risk.*

risk averse
The attitude toward risk in which investors would require an increased return as compensation for an increase in risk.

A second attitude toward risk is called risk neutrality. An investor who is **risk neutral** chooses investments based solely on their expected returns, disregarding the risks. When choosing between two investments, *a risk-neutral investor will always choose the investment with the higher expected return regardless of its risk.*

risk neutral
The attitude toward risk in which investors choose the investment with the higher return regardless of its risk.

risk seeking
The attitude toward risk in which investors prefer investments with greater risk even if they have lower expected returns.

Finally, a **risk-seeking** investor is one who prefers investments with higher risk and may even sacrifice some expected return when choosing a riskier investment. By design, the average person who buys a lottery ticket or gambles in a casino loses money. After all, state governments and casinos make money off of these endeavors, so individuals lose on average. This implies that the expected return on these activities is negative. Yet people do buy lottery tickets and visit casinos, and in doing so they exhibit risk-seeking behavior.

→ REVIEW QUESTIONS

8–1 What is *risk* in the context of financial decision making?

8–2 Define *return,* and describe how to find the rate of return on an investment.

8–3 Compare the following risk preferences: **(a)** risk averse, **(b)** risk neutral, and **(c)** risk seeking. Which is most common among financial managers?

LG 2

8.2 Risk of a Single Asset

In this section we refine our understanding of risk. Surprisingly, the concept of risk changes when the focus shifts from the risk of a single asset held in isolation to the risk of a portfolio of assets. Here, we examine different statistical methods to quantify risk, and next we apply those methods to portfolios.

RISK ASSESSMENT

The notion that risk is somehow connected to uncertainty is intuitive. The more uncertain you are about how an investment will perform, the riskier that investment seems. Scenario analysis provides a simple way to quantify that intuition, and probability distributions offer an even more sophisticated way to analyze the risk of an investment.

scenario analysis
An approach for assessing risk that uses several possible alternative outcomes (scenarios) to obtain a sense of the variability among returns.

range
A measure of an asset's risk, which is found by subtracting the return associated with the pessimistic (worst) outcome from the return associated with the optimistic (best) outcome.

Scenario Analysis

Scenario analysis uses several possible alternative outcomes (scenarios) to obtain a sense of the variability of returns.[2] One common method involves considering pessimistic (worst), most likely (expected), and optimistic (best) outcomes and the returns associated with them for a given asset. In this one measure of an investment's risk is the range of possible outcomes. The **range** is found by subtracting the return associated with the pessimistic outcome from the return associated with the optimistic outcome. The greater the range, the more variability, or risk, the asset is said to have.

Example 8.2 ▶

Norman Company, a manufacturer of custom golf equipment, wants to choose the better of two investments, A and B. Each requires an initial outlay of $10,000, and each has a *most likely* annual rate of return of 15%. Management has estimated

2. The term *scenario analysis* is intentionally used in a general rather than a technically correct fashion here to simplify this discussion. A more technical and precise definition and discussion of this technique and of *sensitivity analysis* are presented in Chapter 12.

TABLE 8.2 Assets A and B

	Asset A	Asset B
Initial investment	$10,000	$10,000
Annual rate of return		
Pessimistic	13%	7%
Most likely	15%	15%
Optimistic	17%	23%
Range	4%	16%

returns associated with each investment's *pessimistic* and *optimistic* outcomes. The three estimates for each asset, along with its range, are given in Table 8.2. Asset A appears to be less risky than asset B; its range of 4% (17% minus 13%) is less than the range of 16% (23% minus 7%) for asset B. The risk-averse decision maker would prefer asset A over asset B, because A offers the same most likely return as B (15%) with lower risk (smaller range).

It's not unusual for financial managers to think about the best and worst possible outcomes when they are in the early stages of analyzing a new investment project. No matter how great the intuitive appeal of this approach, looking at the range of outcomes that an investment might produce is a very unsophisticated way of measuring its risk. More sophisticated methods require some basic statistical tools.

Probability Distributions

probability
The *chance* that a given outcome will occur.

Probability distributions provide a more quantitative insight into an asset's risk. The **probability** of a given outcome is its *chance* of occurring. An outcome with an 80 percent probability of occurrence would be expected to occur 8 out of 10 times. An outcome with a probability of 100 percent is certain to occur. Outcomes with a probability of zero will never occur.

Matter of fact

Beware of the Black Swan

Is it ever possible to know for sure that a particular outcome can never happen, that the chance of it occurring is 0 percent? In the 2007 best seller, *The Black Swan: The Impact of the Highly Improbable*, Nassim Nicholas Taleb argues that seemingly improbable or even impossible events are more likely to occur than most people believe, especially in the area of finance. The book's title refers to the fact that for many years, people believed that all swans were white until a black variety was discovered in Australia. Taleb reportedly earned a large fortune during the 2007–2008 financial crisis by betting that financial markets would plummet.

Example 8.3 ▶

Norman Company's past estimates indicate that the probabilities of the pessimistic, most likely, and optimistic outcomes are 25%, 50%, and 25%, respectively. Note that the sum of these probabilities must equal 100%; that is, they must be based on all the alternatives considered.

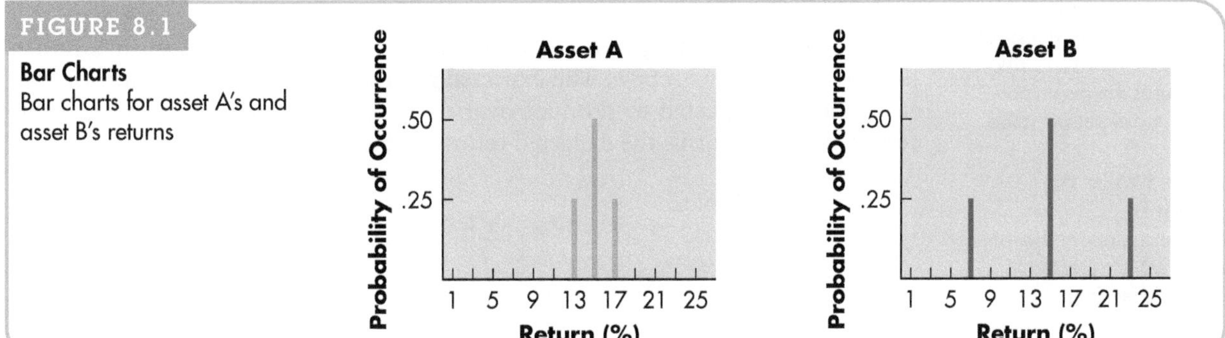

FIGURE 8.1

Bar Charts

Bar charts for asset A's and asset B's returns

probability distribution
A model that relates probabilities to the associated outcomes.

bar chart
The simplest type of probability distribution; shows only a limited number of outcomes and associated probabilities for a given event.

continuous probability distribution
A probability distribution showing all the possible outcomes and associated probabilities for a given event.

A **probability distribution** is a model that relates probabilities to the associated outcomes. The simplest type of probability distribution is the **bar chart**. The bar charts for Norman Company's assets A and B are shown in Figure 8.1. Although both assets have the same average return, the range of return is much greater, or more dispersed, for asset B than for asset A—16 percent versus 4 percent.

Most investments have more than two or three possible outcomes. In fact, the number of possible outcomes in most cases is practically infinite. If we knew all the possible outcomes and associated probabilities, we could develop a **continuous probability distribution.** This type of distribution can be thought of as a bar chart for a very large number of outcomes. Figure 8.2 presents continuous probability distributions for assets C and D. Note that although the two assets have the same average return (15 percent), the distribution of returns for asset D has much greater *dispersion* than the distribution for asset C. Apparently, asset D is more risky than asset C.

RISK MEASUREMENT

In addition to considering the *range* of returns that an investment might produce, the risk of an asset can be measured quantitatively by using statistics. The most common statistical measure used to describe an investment's risk is its standard deviation.

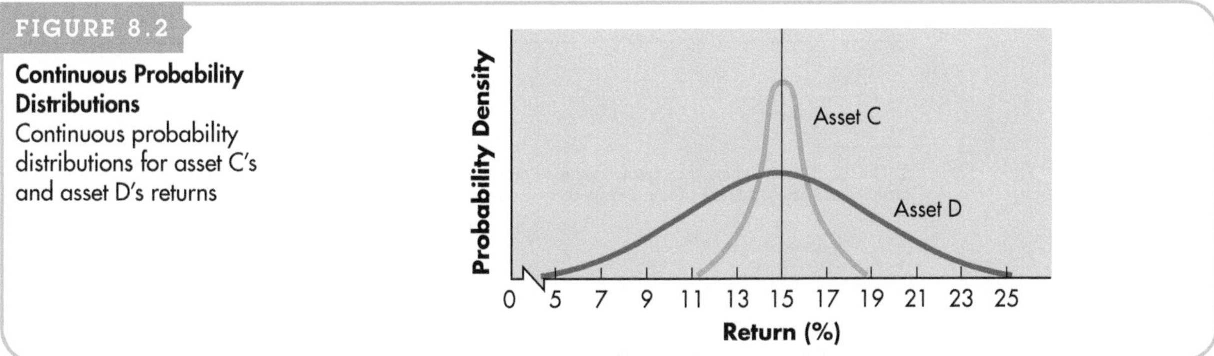

FIGURE 8.2

Continuous Probability Distributions

Continuous probability distributions for asset C's and asset D's returns

standard deviation (σ_r) The most common statistical indicator of an asset's risk; it measures the dispersion around the *expected value.*

expected value of a return ($\bar{r}$) The average return that an investment is expected to produce over time.

Standard Deviation

The **standard deviation, σ_r,** measures the dispersion of an investment's return around the *expected return.* The **expected return, $\bar{r}$,** is the average return that an investment is expected to produce over time. For an investment that has *j* different possible returns, the expected return is calculated as follows:[3]

$$\bar{r} = \sum_{j=1}^{n} r_j \times Pr_j \tag{8.2}$$

where

r_j = return for the *j*th outcome
Pr_j = probability of occurrence of the *j*th outcome
n = number of outcomes considered

Example 8.4 ▸ The expected values of returns for Norman Company's assets A and B are presented in Table 8.3. Column 1 gives the Pr_j's and column 2 gives the r_j's. In each case *n* equals 3. The expected value for each asset's return is 15%.

TABLE 8.3 Expected Values of Returns for Assets A and B

Possible outcomes	Probability (1)	Returns (2)	Weighted value [(1) × (2)] (3)
Asset A			
Pessimistic	0.25	13%	3.25%
Most likely	0.50	15	7.50
Optimistic	0.25	17	4.25
Total	1.00		Expected return 15.00%
Asset B			
Pessimistic	0.25	7%	1.75%
Most likely	0.50	15	7.50
Optimistic	0.25	23	5.75
Total	1.00		Expected return 15.00%

3. The formula for finding the expected value of return, $\bar{r}$, when all of the outcomes, r_j, are known *and* their related probabilities are equal, is a simple arithmetic average:

$$\bar{r} = \frac{\sum_{j=1}^{n} r_j}{n} \tag{8.2a}$$

where *n* is the number of observations.

The expression for the *standard deviation of returns,* σ_r, is[4]

$$\sigma_r = \sqrt{\sum_{j=1}^{n} (r_j - \bar{r})^2 \times Pr_j} \tag{8.3}$$

In general, the higher the standard deviation, the greater the risk.

Example 8.5 ▶ Table 8.4 presents the standard deviations for Norman Company's assets A and B, based on the earlier data. The standard deviation for asset A is 1.41%, and the standard deviation for asset B is 5.66%. The higher risk of asset B is clearly reflected in its higher standard deviation.

TABLE 8.4 The Calculation of the Standard Deviation of the Returns for Assets A and B[a]

j	r_j	$\bar{r}$	$r_j - \bar{r}$	$(r_j - \bar{r})^2$	Pr_j	$(r_j - \bar{r})^2 \times Pr_j$
Asset A						
1	13%	15%	−2%	4%	.25	1%
2	15	15	0	0	.50	0
3	17	15	2	4	.25	1

$$\sum_{j=1}^{3} (r_j - \bar{r})^2 \times Pr_j = 2\%$$

$$\sigma_{r_A} = \sqrt{\sum_{j=1}^{3} (r_j - \bar{r})^2 \times Pr_j} = \sqrt{2\%} = \underline{\underline{1.41\%}}$$

j	r_j	$\bar{r}$	$r_j - \bar{r}$	$(r_j - \bar{r})^2$	Pr_j	$(r_j - \bar{r})^2 \times Pr_j$
Asset B						
1	7%	15%	−8%	64%	.25	16%
2	15	15	0	0	.50	0
3	23	15	8	64	.25	16

$$\sum_{j=1}^{3} (r_j - \bar{r})^2 \times Pr_j = 32\%$$

$$\sigma_{r_B} = \sqrt{\sum_{j=1}^{3} (r_j - \bar{r})^2 \times Pr_j} = \sqrt{32\%} = \underline{\underline{5.66\%}}$$

[a]Calculations in this table are made in percentage form rather than decimal form—for example, 13% rather than 0.13. As a result, some of the intermediate computations may appear to be inconsistent with those that would result from using decimal form. Regardless, the resulting standard deviations are correct and identical to those that would result from using decimal rather than percentage form.

4. In practice, analysts rarely know the full range of possible investment outcomes and their probabilities. In these cases, analysts use historical data to estimate the standard deviation. The formula that applies in this situation is

$$\sigma_r = \sqrt{\frac{\sum_{j=1}^{n} (r_j - \bar{r})^2}{n-1}} \tag{8.3a}$$

TABLE 8.5 **Historical Returns and Standard Deviations on Selected Investments (1900–2009)**

Investment	Average nominal return	Standard deviation	Coefficient of variation
Treasury bills	3.9%	4.7%	1.21
Treasury bonds	5.0	10.2	2.04
Common stocks	9.3	20.4	2.19

Source: Elroy Dimson, Paul Marsh, and Mike Staunton, *Triumph of the Optimists: 101 Years of Global Investment Returns* (Princeton, NJ: Princeton University Press, 2002).

Historical Returns and Risk We can now use the standard deviation as a measure of risk to assess the historical (1900–2009) investment return data in Table 8.1. Table 8.5 repeats the historical nominal average returns in column 1 and shows the standard deviations associated with each of them in column 2. A close relationship can be seen between the investment returns and the standard deviations: Investments with higher returns have higher standard deviations. For example, stocks have the highest average return at 9.3 percent, which is more than double the average return on Treasury bills. At the same time, stocks are much more volatile, with a standard deviation of 20.4 percent, more than four times greater than the standard deviation of Treasury bills. Because higher standard deviations are associated with greater risk, the historical data confirm the existence of a positive relationship between risk and return. That relationship reflects *risk aversion* by market participants, who require higher returns as compensation for greater risk. The historical data in columns 1 and 2 of Table 8.5 clearly show that during the 1900–2009 period, investors were, on average, rewarded with higher returns on higher-risk investments.

Matter of fact

All Stocks Are Not Created Equal

Table 8.5 shows that stocks are riskier than bonds, but are some stocks riskier than others? The answer is emphatically *yes*. A recent study examined the historical returns of large stocks and small stocks and found that the average annual return on large stocks from 1926 through 2009 was 11.8 percent, while small stocks earned 16.7 percent per year on average. The higher returns on small stocks came with a cost, however. The standard deviation of small stock returns was a whopping 32.8 percent, whereas the standard deviation on large stocks was just 20.5 percent.

normal probability distribution
A symmetrical probability distribution whose shape resembles a "bell-shaped" curve.

Normal Distribution A **normal probability distribution,** depicted in Figure 8.3, resembles a symmetrical "bell-shaped" curve. The symmetry of the curve means that half the probability is associated with the values to the left of the peak and half with the values to the right. As noted on the figure, for normal probability distributions, 68 percent of the possible outcomes will lie between ± 1 standard deviation from the expected value, 95 percent of all outcomes will lie between ± 2 standard deviations from the expected value, and 99 percent of all outcomes will lie between ± 3 standard deviations from the expected value.

FIGURE 8.3

Bell-Shaped Curve
Normal probability distribution, with ranges

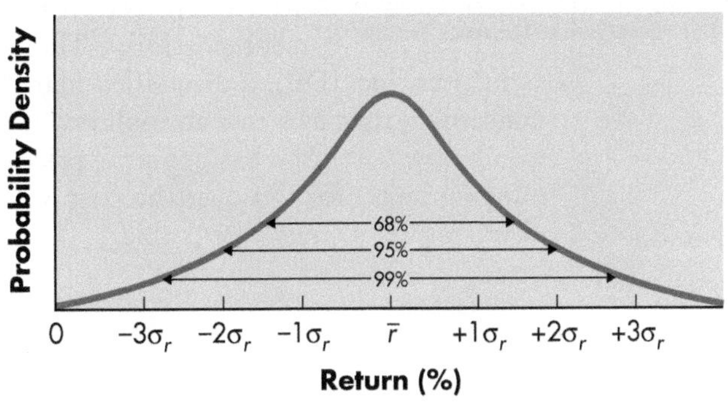

Example 8.6 ▶

Using the data in Table 8.5 and assuming that the probability distributions of returns for common stocks and bonds are normal, we can surmise that 68% of the possible outcomes would have a return ranging between −11.1% and 29.7% for stocks and between −5.2% and 15.2% for bonds; 95% of the possible return outcomes would range between −31.5% and 50.1% for stocks and between −15.4% and 25.4% for bonds. The greater risk of stocks is clearly reflected in their much wider range of possible returns for each level of confidence (68% or 95%).

Coefficient of Variation—Trading Off Risk and Return

coefficient of variation (*CV*) A measure of relative dispersion that is useful in comparing the risks of assets with differing expected returns.

The **coefficient of variation,** *CV,* is a measure of relative dispersion that is useful in comparing the risks of assets with differing expected returns. Equation 8.4 gives the expression for the coefficient of variation:

$$CV = \frac{\sigma_r}{\bar{r}} \tag{8.4}$$

A higher coefficient of variation means that an investment has more volatility relative to its expected return. Because investors prefer higher returns and less risk, intuitively one might expect investors to gravitate towards investments with a low coefficient of variation. However, this logic doesn't always apply for reasons that will emerge in the next section. For now, consider the coefficients of variation in column 3 of Table 8.5. That table reveals that Treasury bills have the lowest coefficient of variation and therefore the lowest risk relative to their return. Does this mean that investors should load up on Treasury bills and divest themselves of stocks? Not necessarily.

Example 8.7 ▶

When the standard deviations (from Table 8.4) and the expected returns (from Table 8.3) for assets A and B are substituted into Equation 8.4, the coefficients of variation for A and B are 0.094 (1.41% ÷ 15%) and 0.377 (5.66% ÷ 15%), respectively. Asset B has the higher coefficient of variation and is therefore more risky than asset A—which we already know from the standard deviation. (Because both assets have the same expected return, the coefficient of variation has not provided any new information.)

Personal Finance Example 8.8 ▸ Marilyn Ansbro is reviewing stocks for inclusion in her investment portfolio. The stock she wishes to analyze is Danhaus Industries, Inc. (DII), a diversified manufacturer of pet products. One of her key concerns is risk; as a rule she will invest only in stocks with a coefficient of variation below 0.75. She has gathered price and dividend data (shown in the accompanying table) for DII over the past 3 years, 2010–2012, and assumes that each year's return is equally probable.

	Stock Price		
Year	**Beginning**	**End**	**Dividend paid**
2010	$35.00	$36.50	$3.50
2011	36.50	34.50	3.50
2012	34.50	35.00	4.00

Substituting the price and dividend data for each year into Equation 8.1, we get:

Year	Returns
2010	[$3.50 + ($36.50 − $35.00)] ÷ $35.00 = $5.00 ÷ $35.00 = 14.3%
2011	[$3.50 + ($34.50 − $36.50)] ÷ $36.50 = $1.50 ÷ $36.50 = 4.1%
2012	[$4.00 + ($35.00 − $34.50)] ÷ $34.50 = $4.50 ÷ $34.50 = 13.0%

Substituting into Equation 8.2a, given that the returns are equally probable, we get the average return, $\bar{r}_{2010-2012}$:

$$\bar{r}_{2010-2012} = (14.3\% + 4.1\% + 13.0\%) \div 3 = 10.5\%$$

Substituting the average return and annual returns into Equation 8.3a, we get the standard deviation, $\sigma_{r2010-2012}$:

$$\sigma_{r2010-2012} = \sqrt{[(14.3\%-10.5\%)^2+(4.1\%-10.5\%)^2+(13.0\%-10.5\%)^2] \div (3-1)}$$
$$= \sqrt{(14.44\% + 40.96\% + 6.25\%) \div 2} = \sqrt{30.825\%} = 5.6\%$$

Finally, substituting the standard deviation of returns and the average return into Equation 8.4, we get the coefficient of variation, *CV*:

$$CV = 5.6\% \div 10.5\% = 0.53$$

Because the coefficient of variation of returns on the DII stock over the 2010–2012 period of 0.53 is well below Marilyn's maximum coefficient of variation of 0.75, she concludes that the DII stock would be an acceptable investment.

→ REVIEW QUESTIONS

8–4 Explain how the *range* is used in scenario analysis.

8–5 What does a plot of the *probability distribution* of outcomes show a decision maker about an asset's risk?

8–6 What relationship exists between the size of the *standard deviation* and the degree of asset risk?

8–7 What does the *coefficient of variation* reveal about an investment's risk that the standard deviation does not?

LG 3 LG 4

8.3 Risk of a Portfolio

efficient portfolio
A portfolio that maximizes return for a given level of risk.

In real-world situations, the risk of any single investment would not be viewed independently of other assets. New investments must be considered in light of their impact on the risk and return of an investor's *portfolio* of assets. The financial manager's goal is to create an **efficient portfolio,** one that provides the maximum return for a given level of risk. We therefore need a way to measure the return and the standard deviation of a portfolio of assets. As part of that analysis, we will look at the statistical concept of *correlation,* which underlies the process of diversification that is used to develop an efficient portfolio.

PORTFOLIO RETURN AND STANDARD DEVIATION

The *return on a portfolio* is a weighted average of the returns on the individual assets from which it is formed. We can use Equation 8.5 to find the portfolio return, r_p:

$$r_p = (w_1 \times r_1) + (w_2 \times r_2) + \cdots + (w_n \times r_n) = \sum_{j=1}^{n} w_j \times r_j \tag{8.5}$$

where

w_j = proportion of the portfolio's total dollar value represented by asset j

r_j = return on asset j

Of course, $\sum_{j=1}^{n} w_j = 1$, which means that 100 percent of the portfolio's assets must be included in this computation.

Example 8.9 ▸

James purchases 100 shares of Wal-Mart at a price of \$55 per share, so his total investment in Wal-Mart is \$5,500. He also buys 100 shares of Cisco Systems at \$25 per share, so the total investment in Cisco stock is \$2,500. Combining these two holdings, James's total portfolio is worth \$8,000. Of the total, 68.75% is invested in Wal-Mart (\$5,500 ÷ \$8,000) and 31.25% is invested in Cisco Systems (\$2,500 ÷ \$8,000). Thus, $w_1 = 0.6875$, $w_2 = 0.3125$, and $w_1 + w_2 = 1.0$.

The *standard deviation of a portfolio's returns* is found by applying the formula for the standard deviation of a single asset. Specifically, Equation 8.3 is used when the probabilities of the returns are known, and Equation 8.3a (from footnote 4) is applied when analysts use historical data to estimate the standard deviation.

Example 8.10 ▶ Assume that we wish to determine the expected value and standard deviation of returns for portfolio XY, created by combining equal portions (50% each) of assets X and Y. The forecasted returns of assets X and Y for each of the next 5 years (2013–2017) are given in columns 1 and 2, respectively, in part A of Table 8.6. In column 3, the weights of 50% for both assets X and Y along with their respective returns from columns 1 and 2 are substituted into Equation 8.5. Column 4 shows the results of the calculation—an expected portfolio return of 12% for each year, 2013 to 2017.

Furthermore, as shown in part B of Table 8.6, the expected value of these portfolio returns over the 5-year period is also 12% (calculated by using Equation 8.2a, in footnote 3). In part C of Table 8.6, portfolio XY's standard deviation is calculated to be 0% (using Equation 8.3a, in footnote 4). This value should not be surprising because the portfolio return each year is the same—12%. Portfolio returns do not vary through time.

TABLE 8.6 Expected Return, Expected Value, and Standard Deviation of Returns for Portfolio XY

A. Expected Portfolio Returns

	Forecasted return			
Year	**Asset X (1)**	**Asset Y (2)**	**Portfolio return calculation[a] (3)**	**Expected portfolio return, r_p (4)**
2013	8%	16%	(0.50 × 8%) + (0.50 × 16%) =	12%
2014	10	14	(0.50 × 10%) + (0.50 × 14%) =	12
2015	12	12	(0.50 × 12%) + (0.50 × 12%) =	12
2016	14	10	(0.50 × 14%) + (0.50 × 10%) =	12
2017	16	8	(0.50 × 16%) + (0.50 × 8%) =	12

B. Expected Value of Portfolio Returns, 2013–2017[b]

$$\bar{r}_p = \frac{12\% + 12\% + 12\% + 12\% + 12\%}{5} = \frac{60\%}{5} = \underline{\underline{12\%}}$$

C. Standard Deviation of Expected Portfolio Returns[c]

$$\sigma_{r_p} = \sqrt{\frac{(12\% - 12\%)^2 + (12\% - 12\%)^2 + (12\% - 12\%)^2 + (12\% - 12\%)^2 + (12\% - 12\%)^2}{5-1}}$$

$$= \sqrt{\frac{0\% + 0\% + 0\% + 0\% + 0\%}{4}}$$

$$= \sqrt{\frac{0\%}{4}} = \underline{\underline{0\%}}$$

[a]Using Equation 8.5.
[b]Using Equation 8.2a found in footnote 3.
[c]Using Equation 8.3a found in footnote 4.

correlation
A statistical measure of the relationship between any two series of numbers.

positively correlated
Describes two series that move in the same direction.

negatively correlated
Describes two series that move in opposite directions.

correlation coefficient
A measure of the degree of correlation between two series.

perfectly positively correlated
Describes two *positively correlated* series that have a *correlation coefficient* of +1.

perfectly negatively correlated
Describes two *negatively correlated* series that have a *correlation coefficient* of −1.

CORRELATION

Correlation is a statistical measure of the relationship between any two series of numbers. The numbers may represent data of any kind, from returns to test scores. If two series tend to vary in the same direction, they are **positively correlated.** If the series vary in opposite directions, they are **negatively correlated.** For example, suppose we gathered data on the retail price and weight of new cars. It is likely that we would find that larger cars cost more than smaller ones, so we would say that among new cars weight and price are positively correlated. If we also measured the fuel efficiency of these vehicles (as measured by the number of miles they can travel per gallon of gasoline), we would find that lighter cars are more fuel efficient than heavier cars. In that case, we would say that fuel economy and vehicle weight are negatively correlated.[5]

The degree of correlation is measured by the **correlation coefficient,** which ranges from +1 for **perfectly positively correlated** series to −1 for **perfectly negatively correlated** series. These two extremes are depicted for series M and N in Figure 8.4. The perfectly positively correlated series move exactly together without exception; the perfectly negatively correlated series move in exactly opposite directions.

DIVERSIFICATION

The concept of correlation is essential to developing an efficient portfolio. To reduce overall risk, it is best to *diversify* by combining, or adding to the portfolio, assets that have the lowest possible correlation. Combining assets that have a low correlation with each other can reduce the overall variability of a portfolio's returns. Figure 8.5 (see page 324) shows the returns that two assets, F and G, earn over time. Both assets earn the same average or expected return, $\bar{r}$, but note that when F's return is above average, the return on G is below average and vice versa. In other words, returns on F and G are negatively correlated, and when these two assets are combined in a portfolio, the risk of that portfolio falls without reducing the average return (that is, the portfolio's average return is also $\bar{r}$).

FIGURE 8.4

Correlations
The correlation between series M and series N

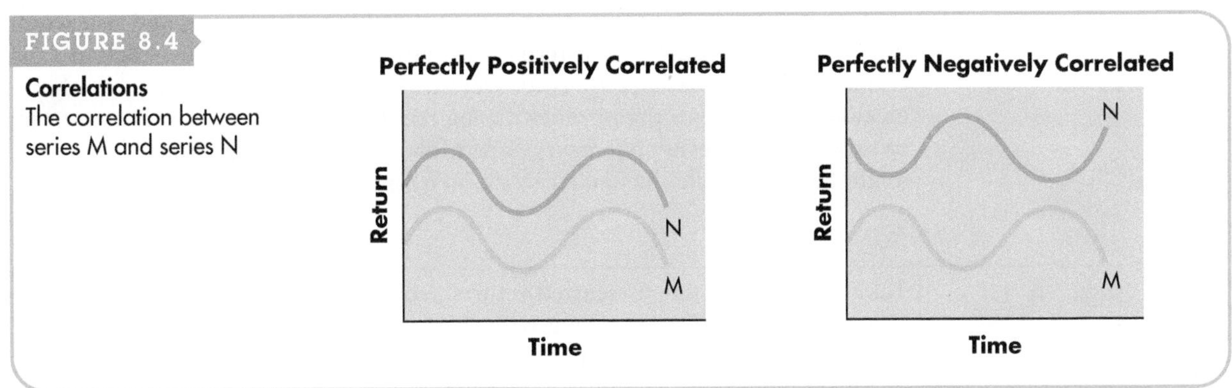

5. Note here that we are talking about general tendencies. For instance, a large hybrid SUV might have better fuel economy than a smaller sedan powered by a conventional gas engine. This does not change the fact that the general tendency is for lighter cars to achieve better fuel economy.

FIGURE 8.5

Diversification
Combining negatively correlated assets to reduce, or diversify, risk

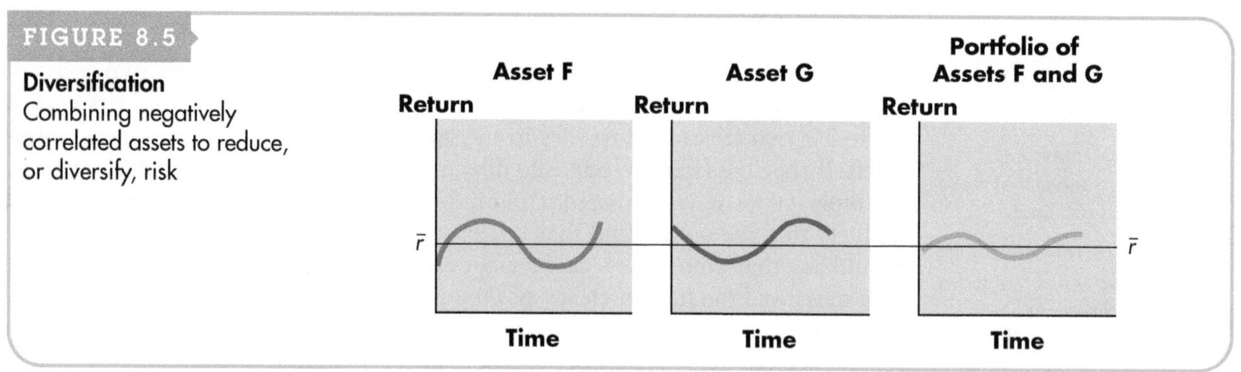

For risk-averse investors, this is very good news. They get rid of something that they don't like (risk) without having to sacrifice what they do like (return). Even if assets are positively correlated, the lower the correlation between them, the greater the risk reduction that can be achieved through diversification.

uncorrelated
Describes two series that lack any interaction and therefore have a *correlation coefficient* close to zero.

Some assets are **uncorrelated**—that is, there is no interaction between their returns. Combining uncorrelated assets can reduce risk, not as effectively as combining negatively correlated assets but more effectively than combining positively correlated assets. The *correlation coefficient for uncorrelated assets is close to zero* and acts as the midpoint between perfectly positive and perfectly negative correlation.

The creation of a portfolio that combines two assets with perfectly positively correlated returns results in overall portfolio risk that at minimum equals that of the least risky asset and at maximum equals that of the most risky asset. However, a portfolio combining two assets with less than perfectly positive correlation *can* reduce total risk to a level below that of either of the components. For example, assume that you buy stock in a company that manufactures machine tools. The business is very *cyclical*, so the stock will do well when the economy is expanding, and it will do poorly during a recession. If you bought shares in another machine-tool company, with sales positively correlated with those of your firm, the combined portfolio would still be cyclical and risk would not be reduced a great deal. Alternatively, however, you could buy stock in a discount retailer, whose sales are *countercyclical*. It typically performs worse during economic expansions than it does during recessions (when consumers are trying to save money on every purchase). A portfolio that contained both of these stocks might be less volatile than either stock on its own.

Example 8.11 ▸

Table 8.7 presents the forecasted returns from three different assets—X, Y, and Z—over the next 5 years, along with their expected values and standard deviations. Each of the assets has an expected return of 12% and a standard deviation of 3.16%. The assets therefore have equal return and equal risk. The return patterns of assets X and Y are perfectly negatively correlated. When X enjoys its highest return, Y experiences its lowest return, and vice versa. The returns of assets X and Z are perfectly positively correlated. They move in precisely the same direction, so when the return on X is high, so is the return on Z. (*Note:* The

TABLE 8.7 **Forecasted Returns, Expected Values, and Standard Deviations for Assets X, Y, and Z and Portfolios XY and XZ**

	Assets			Portfolios	
Year	**X**	**Y**	**Z**	**XY**[a] **(50% X + 50% Y)**	**XZ**[b] **(50% X + 50% Z)**
2013	8%	16%	8%	12%	8%
2014	10	14	10	12	10
2015	12	12	12	12	12
2016	14	10	14	12	14
2017	16	8	16	12	16
Statistics:[c]					
Expected value	12%	12%	12%	12%	12%
Standard deviation[d]	3.16%	3.16%	3.16%	0%	3.16%

[a]Portfolio XY, which consists of 50 percent of asset X and 50 percent of asset Y, illustrates *perfect negative correlation* because these two return streams behave in completely opposite fashion over the 5-year period. Its return values shown here were calculated in part A of Table 8.6.

[b]Portfolio XZ, which consists of 50 percent of asset X and 50 percent of asset Z, illustrates *perfect positive correlation* because these two return streams behave identically over the 5-year period. Its return values were calculated by using the same method demonstrated for portfolio XY in part A of Table 8.6.

[c]Because the probabilities associated with the returns are not given, the general equations, Equation 8.2a in footnote 3 and Equation 8.3a in footnote 4, were used to calculate expected values and standard deviations, respectively. Calculation of the expected value and standard deviation for portfolio XY is demonstrated in parts B and C, respectively, of Table 8.6.

[d]The portfolio standard deviations can be directly calculated from the standard deviations of the component assets with the following formula:

$$\sigma_{r_p} = \sqrt{w_1^2\sigma_1^2 + w_2^2\sigma_2^2 + 2w_1w_2c_{1,2}\sigma_1\sigma_2}$$

where w_1 and w_2 are the proportions of component assets 1 and 2, σ_1 and σ_2 are the standard deviations of component assets 1 and 2, and $c_{1,2}$ is the correlation coefficient between the returns of component assets 1 and 2.

returns for X and Z are identical.)[6] Now let's consider what happens when we combine these assets in different ways to form portfolios.

Portfolio XY Portfolio XY (shown in Table 8.7) is created by combining equal portions of assets X and Y, the perfectly negatively correlated assets. (Calculation of portfolio XY's annual returns, the expected portfolio return, and the standard deviation of returns was demonstrated in Table 8.6 on page 322.) The risk in this portfolio, as reflected by its standard deviation, is reduced to 0%, whereas the expected return remains at 12%. Thus, the combination results in the complete elimination of risk because in each and every year the portfolio earns a 12% return.[7] *Whenever assets are perfectly negatively correlated, some combination of the two assets exists such that the resulting portfolio's returns are risk free.*

Portfolio XZ Portfolio XZ (shown in Table 8.7) is created by combining equal portions of assets X and Z, the perfectly positively correlated assets. Individually, assets X and Z have the same standard deviation, 3.16%, and because they

6. Identical return streams are used in this example to permit clear illustration of the concepts, but it is *not* necessary for return streams to be identical for them to be perfectly positively correlated. Any return streams that move exactly together—regardless of the relative magnitude of the returns—are perfectly positively correlated.

7. Perfect negative correlation means that the ups and downs experienced by one asset are exactly offset by movements in the other asset. Therefore, the portfolio return does not vary over time.

always move together, combining them in a portfolio does nothing to reduce risk—the portfolio standard deviation is also 3.16%. As was the case with portfolio XY, the expected return of portfolio XZ is 12%. Because both of these portfolios provide the same expected return, but portfolio XY achieves that expected return with no risk, portfolio XY is clearly preferred by risk-averse investors over portfolio XZ.

CORRELATION, DIVERSIFICATION, RISK, AND RETURN

In general, the lower the correlation between asset returns, the greater the risk reduction that investors can achieve by diversifying. The following example illustrates how correlation influences the risk of a portfolio but not the portfolio's expected return.

Example 8.12 ▸ Consider two assets—Lo and Hi—with the characteristics described in the table below:

Asset	Expected return, $\bar{r}$	Risk (standard deviation), σ
Lo	6%	3%
Hi	8	8

Clearly, asset Lo offers a lower return than Hi does, but Lo is also less risky than Hi. It is natural to think that a portfolio combining Lo and Hi would offer a return that is between 6% and 8% and that the portfolio's risk would also fall between the risk of Lo and Hi (between 3% and 8%). That intuition is only partly correct.

The performance of a portfolio consisting of assets Lo and Hi depends not only on the expected return and standard deviation of each asset (given above), but also on how the returns on the two assets are correlated. We will illustrate the results of three specific scenarios: (1) returns on Lo and Hi are perfectly positively correlated, (2) returns on Lo and Hi are uncorrelated, and (3) returns on Lo and Hi are perfectly negatively correlated.

The results of the analysis appear in Figure 8.6. Whether the correlation between Lo and Hi is +1, 0, or −1, a portfolio of those two assets must have an expected return between 6% and 8%. That is why the line segments at left in Figure 8.6 all range between 6% and 8%. However, the standard deviation of a portfolio depends critically on the correlation between Lo and Hi. Only when Lo and Hi are perfectly positively correlated can it be said that the portfolio standard deviation must fall between 3% (Lo's standard deviation) and 8% (Hi's standard deviation). As the correlation between Lo and Hi becomes weaker (that is, as the correlation coefficient falls), investors may find that they can form portfolios of Lo and Hi with standard deviations that are even less than 3% (that is, portfolios that are less risky than holding asset Lo by itself). That is why the line segments at right in Figure 8.6 vary. In the special case when Lo and Hi are perfectly negatively correlated, it is possible to diversify away all of the risk and form a portfolio that is risk free.

FIGURE 8.6

Possible Correlations
Range of portfolio return ($\bar{r}_p$) and risk (σ_{r_p}) for combinations of assets Lo and Hi for various correlation coefficients

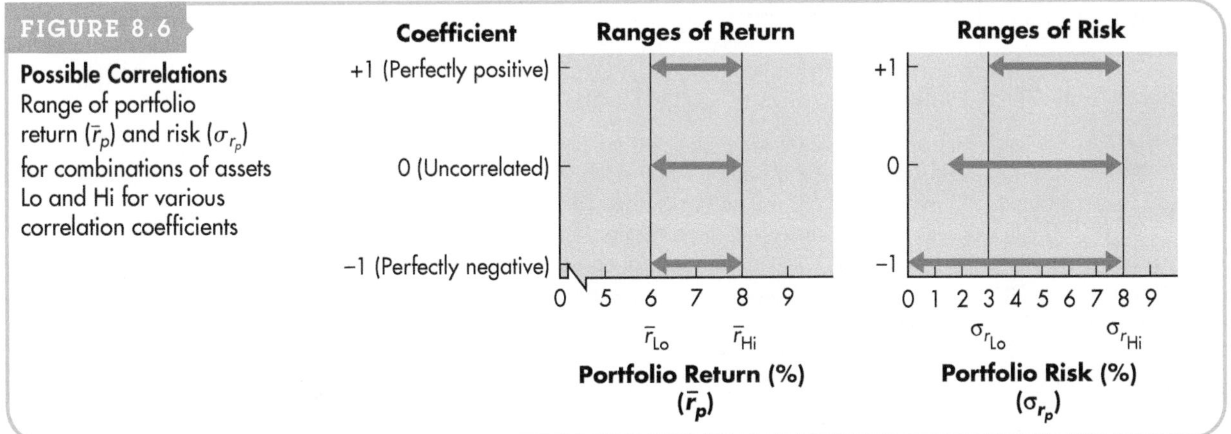

INTERNATIONAL DIVERSIFICATION

One excellent practical example of portfolio diversification involves including foreign assets in a portfolio. The inclusion of assets from countries with business cycles that are not highly correlated with the U.S. business cycle reduces the portfolio's responsiveness to market movements. The ups and the downs of different markets around the world offset each other, at least to some extent, and the result is a portfolio that is less risky than one invested entirely in the U.S. market.

Returns from International Diversification

Over long periods, internationally diversified portfolios tend to perform better (meaning that they earn higher returns relative to the risks taken) than purely domestic portfolios. However, over shorter periods such as a year or two, internationally diversified portfolios may perform better or worse than domestic portfolios. For example, consider what happens when the U.S. economy is performing relatively poorly and the dollar is depreciating in value against most foreign currencies. At such times, the dollar returns to U.S. investors on a portfolio of foreign assets can be very attractive. However, international diversification can yield subpar returns, particularly when the dollar is appreciating in value relative to other currencies. When the U.S. currency appreciates, the dollar value of a foreign-currency-denominated portfolio of assets declines. Even if this portfolio yields a satisfactory return in foreign currency, the return to U.S. investors will be reduced when foreign profits are translated into dollars. Subpar local currency portfolio returns, coupled with an appreciating dollar, can yield truly dismal dollar returns to U.S. investors.

Overall, though, the logic of international portfolio diversification assumes that these fluctuations in currency values and relative performance will average out over long periods. Compared to similar, purely domestic portfolios, an internationally diversified portfolio will tend to yield a comparable return at a lower level of risk.

political risk
Risk that arises from the possibility that a host government will take actions harmful to foreign investors or that political turmoil will endanger investments.

Risks of International Diversification

In addition to the risk induced by currency fluctuations, several other financial risks are unique to international investing. Most important is **political risk,** which

GLOBAL focus

An International Flavor to Risk Reduction

in practice Earlier in this chapter (see Table 8.5 on page 318), we learned that from 1900 through 2009 the U.S. stock market produced an average annual nominal return of 9.3 percent, but that return was associated with a relatively high standard deviation: 20.4 percent per year. Could U.S. investors have done better by diversifying globally? The answer is a qualified yes. Elroy Dimson, Paul Marsh, and Mike Staunton calculated the historical returns on a portfolio that included U.S. stocks as well as stocks from 18 other countries. This diversified portfolio produced returns that were not quite as high as the U.S. average, just 8.6 percent per year. However, the globally diversified portfolio was also less volatile, with an annual standard deviation of 17.8 percent. Dividing the standard deviation by the annual return produces a coefficient of variation for the globally diversified portfolio of 2.07, slightly lower than the 2.10 coefficient of variation reported for U.S. stocks in Table 8.5.

► ***International mutual funds do not include any domestic assets whereas global mutual funds include both foreign and domestic assets. How might this difference affect their correlation with U.S. equity mutual funds?***

Source: Elroy Dimson, Paul Marsh, and Mike Staunton, *Triumph of the Optimists: 101 Years of Global Investment Returns* (Princeton University Press, 2002).

arises from the possibility that a host government will take actions harmful to foreign investors or that political turmoil will endanger investments. Political risks are particularly acute in developing countries, where unstable or ideologically motivated governments may attempt to block return of profits by foreign investors or even seize (nationalize) their assets in the host country. For example, reflecting President Chavez's desire to broaden the country's socialist revolution, Venezuela issued a list of priority goods for import that excluded a large percentage of the necessary inputs to the automobile production process. As a result, Toyota halted auto production in Venezuela, and three other auto manufacturers temporarily closed or deeply cut their production there. Chavez also has forced most foreign energy firms to reduce their stakes and give up control of oil projects in Venezuela.

For more discussion of reducing risk through international diversification, see the *Global Focus* box above.

→ REVIEW QUESTIONS

8–8 What is an *efficient portfolio?* How can the return and standard deviation of a portfolio be determined?

8–9 Why is the *correlation* between asset returns important? How does diversification allow risky assets to be combined so that the risk of the portfolio is less than the risk of the individual assets in it?

8–10 How does international diversification enhance risk reduction? When might international diversification result in subpar returns? What are *political risks,* and how do they affect international diversification?

LG 5 LG 6

8.4 Risk and Return: The Capital Asset Pricing Model (CAPM)

Thus far we have observed a tendency for riskier investments to earn higher returns, and we have learned that investors can reduce risk through diversification. Now we want to quantify the relationship between risk and return. In other words, we want to measure how much additional return an investor should expect from taking a little extra risk. The classic theory that links risk and return for all assets is the **capital asset pricing model (CAPM).** We will use the CAPM to understand the basic risk–return tradeoffs involved in all types of financial decisions.

capital asset pricing model (CAPM)
The basic theory that links risk and return for all assets.

TYPES OF RISK

In the last section we saw that the standard deviation of a portfolio is often less than the standard deviation of the individual assets in the portfolio. That's the power of diversification. To see this more clearly, consider what happens to the risk of a portfolio consisting of a single security (asset), to which we add securities randomly selected from, say, the population of all actively traded securities. Using the standard deviation of return, $\sigma_r p$, to measure the total portfolio risk, Figure 8.7 depicts the behavior of the total portfolio risk (y axis) as more securities are added (x axis). With the addition of securities, the total portfolio risk declines, as a result of diversification, and tends to approach a lower limit.

The **total risk** of a security can be viewed as consisting of two parts:

total risk
The combination of a security's *nondiversifiable risk* and *diversifiable risk.*

diversifiable risk
The portion of an asset's risk that is attributable to firm-specific, random causes; can be eliminated through diversification. Also called *unsystematic risk.*

nondiversifiable risk
The relevant portion of an asset's risk attributable to market factors that affect all firms; cannot be eliminated through diversification. Also called *systematic risk.*

$$\text{Total security risk} = \text{Nondiversifiable risk} + \text{Diversifiable risk} \tag{8.6}$$

Diversifiable risk (sometimes called *unsystematic risk*) represents the portion of an asset's risk that is associated with random causes that can be eliminated through diversification. It is attributable to firm-specific events, such as strikes, lawsuits, regulatory actions, or the loss of a key account. Figure 8.7 shows that diversifiable risk gradually disappears as the number of stocks in the portfolio increases. **Nondiversifiable risk** (also called *systematic risk*) is attributable to

FIGURE 8.7

Risk Reduction
Portfolio risk and diversification

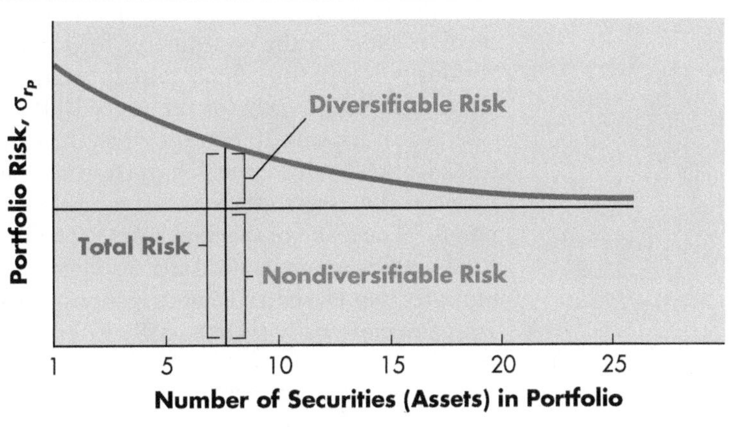

market factors that affect all firms; it cannot be eliminated through diversification. Factors such as war, inflation, the overall state of the economy, international incidents, and political events account for nondiversifiable risk. In Figure 8.7, nondiversifiable risk is represented by the horizontal black line below which the blue curve can never go, no matter how diversified the portfolio becomes.

Because any investor can easily create a portfolio of assets that will eliminate virtually all diversifiable risk, *the only relevant risk is nondiversifiable risk.* Any investor or firm therefore must be concerned solely with nondiversifiable risk. The measurement of nondiversifiable risk is thus of primary importance in selecting assets with the most desired risk–return characteristics.

THE MODEL: CAPM

The capital asset pricing model (CAPM) links nondiversifiable risk to expected returns. We will discuss the model in five sections. The first section deals with the beta coefficient, which is a measure of nondiversifiable risk. The second section presents an equation of the model itself, and the third section graphically describes the relationship between risk and return. The fourth section discusses the effects of changes in inflationary expectations and risk aversion on the relationship between risk and return. The fifth section offers some comments on the CAPM.

Beta Coefficient

beta coefficient (*b*)
A relative measure of nondiversifiable risk. An *index* of the degree of movement of an asset's return in response to a change in the *market return.*

market return
The return on the market portfolio of all traded securities.

The **beta coefficient, *b*,** is a relative measure of nondiversifiable risk. It is an *index* of the degree of movement of an asset's return in response to a change in the *market return.* An asset's historical returns are used in finding the asset's beta coefficient. The **market return** is the return on the market portfolio of all traded securities. The *Standard & Poor's 500 Stock Composite Index* or some similar stock index is commonly used as the market return. Betas for actively traded stocks can be obtained from a variety of sources, but you should understand how they are derived and interpreted and how they are applied to portfolios.

Deriving Beta from Return Data An asset's historical returns are used in finding the asset's beta coefficient. Figure 8.8 plots the relationship between the returns of two assets—R and S—and the market return. Note that the horizontal (x) axis measures the historical market returns and that the vertical (y) axis measures the individual asset's historical returns. The first step in deriving beta involves plotting the coordinates for the market return and asset returns from various points in time. Such annual "market return–asset return" coordinates are shown *for asset S only* for the years 2005 through 2012. For example, in 2012, asset S's return was 20 percent when the market return was 10 percent. By use of statistical techniques, the "characteristic line" that best explains the relationship between the asset return and the market return coordinates is fit to the data points.[8] The slope of this line is *beta.* The beta for asset R is about 0.80, and that for asset S is about 1.30. Asset S's higher beta (steeper characteristic line slope) indicates that its return is more responsive to changing market returns. *Therefore asset S is more risky than asset R.*

---

8. The empirical measurement of beta is approached by using *least-squares regression analysis.*

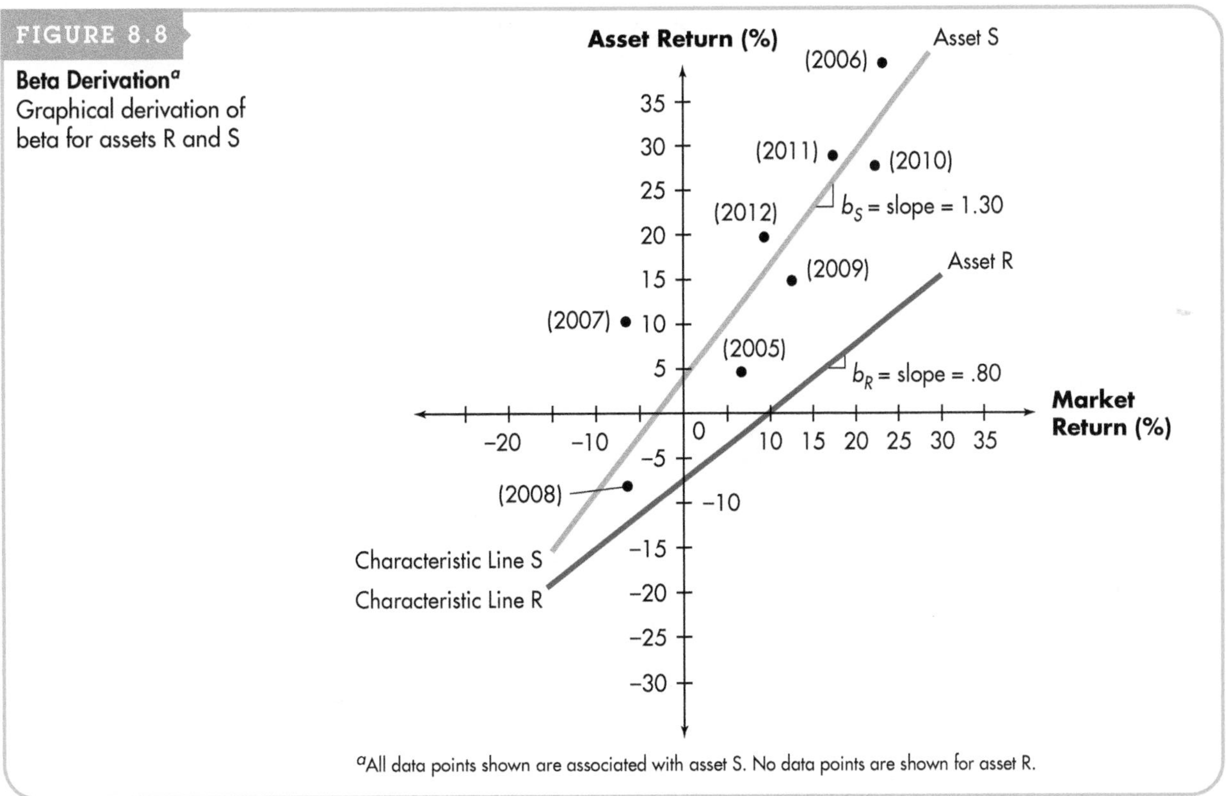

FIGURE 8.8

Beta Derivation[a]

Graphical derivation of beta for assets R and S

[a]All data points shown are associated with asset S. No data points are shown for asset R.

Interpreting Betas The beta coefficient for the entire market equals 1.0. All other betas are viewed in relation to this value. Asset betas may be positive or negative, but positive betas are the norm. The majority of beta coefficients fall between 0.5 and 2.0. The return of a stock that is half as responsive as the market ($b = 0.5$) should change by 0.5 percent for each 1 percent change in the return of the market portfolio. A stock that is twice as responsive as the market ($b = 2.0$) should experience a 2 percent change in its return for each 1 percent change in the return of the market portfolio. Table 8.8 provides various beta values and their interpretations. Beta coefficients for actively traded stocks can be obtained from published sources such as *Value Line Investment Survey,* via the Internet, or through brokerage firms. Betas for some selected stocks are given in Table 8.9.

TABLE 8.8 **Selected Beta Coefficients and Their Interpretations**

Beta	Comment	Interpretation
2.0 1.0 0.5	Move in same direction as market	Twice as responsive as the market Same response as the market Only half as responsive as the market
0		Unaffected by market movement
−0.5 −1.0 −2.0	Move in opposite direction to market	Only half as responsive as the market Same response as the market Twice as responsive as the market

TABLE 8.9 Beta Coefficients for Selected Stocks (June 7, 2010)

Stock	Beta	Stock	Beta
Amazon.com	0.99	JP Morgan Chase & Co.	1.16
Anheuser-Busch	1.00	Bank of America	2.58
Ford Motor	2.72	Microsoft	0.99
Disney	1.25	Nike, Inc.	0.92
eBay	1.75	PepsiCo, Inc.	0.57
ExxonMobil Corp.	0.37	Qualcomm	0.89
Gap (The), Inc.	1.31	Sempra Energy	0.60
General Electric	1.68	Wal-Mart Stores	0.29
Intel	1.12	Xerox	1.50
Int'l Business Machines	0.68	Yahoo! Inc.	0.92

Source: www.finance.yahoo.com

Portfolio Betas The beta of a portfolio can be easily estimated by using the betas of the individual assets it includes. Letting w_j represent the proportion of the portfolio's total dollar value represented by asset j, and letting b_j equal the beta of asset j, we can use Equation 8.7 to find the portfolio beta, b_p:

$$b_p = (w_1 \times b_1) + (w_2 \times b_2) + \cdots + (w_n \times b_n) = \sum_{j=1}^{n} w_j \times b_j \tag{8.7}$$

Of course, $\sum_{j=1}^{n} w_j = 1$, which means that 100 percent of the portfolio's assets must be included in this computation.

Portfolio betas are interpreted in the same way as the betas of individual assets. They indicate the degree of responsiveness of the *portfolio's* return to changes in the market return. For example, when the market return increases by 10 percent, a portfolio with a beta of 0.75 will experience a 7.5 percent increase in its return (0.75 × 10%); a portfolio with a beta of 1.25 will experience a 12.5 percent increase in its return (1.25 × 10%). Clearly, a portfolio containing mostly low-beta assets will have a low beta, and one containing mostly high-beta assets will have a high beta.

Personal Finance Example 8.13 ▸ Mario Austino, an individual investor, wishes to assess the risk of two small portfolios he is considering—V and W. Both portfolios contain five assets, with the proportions and betas shown in Table 8.10. The betas for the two portfolios, b_V and b_W, can be calculated by substituting data from the table into Equation 8.7:

$$\begin{aligned} b_V &= (0.10 \times 1.65) + (0.30 \times 1.00) + (0.20 \times 1.30) + (0.20 \times 1.10) + (0.20 \times 1.25) \\ &= 0.165 + 0.300 + 0.260 + 0.220 + 0.250 = 1.195 \approx \underline{\underline{1.20}} \end{aligned}$$

$$\begin{aligned} b_W &= (0.10 \times .80) + (0.10 \times 1.00) + (0.20 \times .65) + (0.10 \times .75) + (0.50 \times 1.05) \\ &= 0.080 + 0.100 + 0.130 + 0.075 + 0.525 = \underline{\underline{0.91}} \end{aligned}$$

TABLE 8.10 Mario Austino's Portfolios V and W

	Portfolio V		Portfolio W	
Asset	Proportion	Beta	Proportion	Beta
1	0.10	1.65	0.10	0.80
2	0.30	1.00	0.10	1.00
3	0.20	1.30	0.20	0.65
4	0.20	1.10	0.10	0.75
5	0.20	1.25	0.50	1.05
Totals	1.00		1.00	

Portfolio V's beta is about 1.20, and portfolio W's is 0.91. These values make sense because portfolio V contains relatively high-beta assets, and portfolio W contains relatively low-beta assets. Mario's calculations show that portfolio V's returns are more responsive to changes in market returns and are therefore more risky than portfolio W's. He must now decide which, if either, portfolio he feels comfortable adding to his existing investments.

The Equation

Using the beta coefficient to measure nondiversifiable risk, the *capital asset pricing model (CAPM)* is given in Equation 8.8:

$$r_j = R_F + [b_j \times (r_m - R_F)] \qquad (8.8)$$

where

r_j = required return on asset j

R_F = risk-free rate of return, commonly measured by the return on a U.S. Treasury bill

b_j = beta coefficient or index of nondiversifiable risk for asset j

r_m = market return; return on the market portfolio of assets

risk-free rate of return, (R_F) The required return on a *risk-free asset,* typically a 3-month *U.S. Treasury bill.*

U.S. Treasury bills (T-bills) Short-term IOUs issued by the U.S. Treasury; considered the *risk-free asset.*

The CAPM can be divided into two parts: (1) the **risk-free rate of return, R_F,** which is the required return on a *risk-free asset,* typically a 3-month **U.S. Treasury bill (T-bill),** a short-term IOU issued by the U.S. Treasury, and (2) the *risk premium.* These are, respectively, the two elements on either side of the plus sign in Equation 8.8. The $(r_m - R_F)$ portion of the risk premium is called the *market risk premium* because it represents the premium the investor must receive for taking the average amount of risk associated with holding the market portfolio of assets.

Historical Risk Premiums Using the historical return data for stocks, bonds, and Treasury bills for the 1900–2009 period shown in Table 8.1, we can calculate the risk premiums for each investment category. The calculation (consistent with Equation 8.8) involves merely subtracting the historical

U.S. Treasury bill's average return from the historical average return for a given investment:

Investment	Risk premium[a]
Stocks	9.3% − 3.9% = 5.4%
Treasury bonds	5.0 − 3.9 = 1.1

[a]Return values obtained from Table 8.1.

Reviewing the risk premiums calculated above, we can see that the risk premium is higher for stocks than for bonds. This outcome makes sense intuitively because stocks are riskier than bonds (equity is riskier than debt).

Example 8.14 ▸ Benjamin Corporation, a growing computer software developer, wishes to determine the required return on an asset Z, which has a beta of 1.5. The risk-free rate of return is 7%; the return on the market portfolio of assets is 11%. Substituting $b_Z = 1.5$, $R_F = 7\%$, and $r_m = 11\%$ into the capital asset pricing model given in Equation 8.8 yields a required return of

$$r_Z = 7\% + [1.5 \times (11\% - 7\%)] = 7\% + 6\% = \underline{\underline{13\%}}$$

The market risk premium of 4% (11% − 7%), when adjusted for the asset's index of risk (beta) of 1.5, results in a risk premium of 6% (1.5 × 4%). That risk premium, when added to the 7% risk-free rate, results in a 13% required return.

Other things being equal, *the higher the beta, the higher the required return, and the lower the beta, the lower the required return.*

The Graph: The Security Market Line (SML)

security market line (SML) The depiction of the *capital asset pricing model* (*CAPM*) as a graph that reflects the required return in the marketplace for each level of nondiversifiable risk (beta).

When the capital asset pricing model (Equation 8.8) is depicted graphically, it is called the **security market line (SML).** The SML will, in fact, be a straight line. It reflects the required return in the marketplace for each level of nondiversifiable risk (beta). In the graph, risk as measured by beta, b, is plotted on the x axis, and required returns, r, are plotted on the y axis. The risk–return trade-off is clearly represented by the SML.

Example 8.15 ▸ In the preceding example for Benjamin Corporation, the risk-free rate, R_F, was 7%, and the market return, r_m, was 11%. The SML can be plotted by using the two sets of coordinates for the betas associated with R_F and r_m, b_{R_F} and b_m (that is, $b_{R_F} = 0$,[9] $R_F = 7\%$; and $b_m = 1.0$, $r_m = 11\%$). Figure 8.9 presents the resulting security market line. As traditionally shown, the security market line in

9. Because R_F is the rate of return on a risk-free asset, the beta associated with the risk-free asset, b_{R_F}, would equal 0. The zero beta on the risk-free asset reflects not only its absence of risk but also that the asset's return is unaffected by movements in the market return.

FIGURE 8.9

Security Market Line
Security market line (SML) with Benjamin Corporation's asset Z data shown

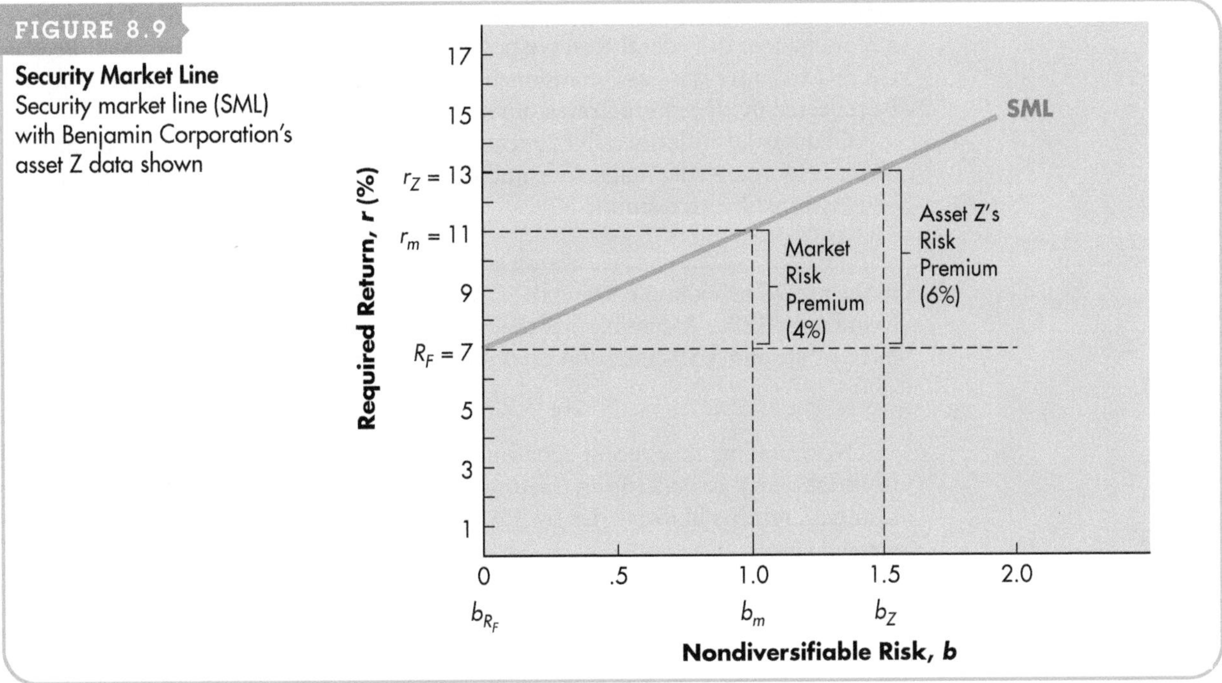

Figure 8.9 presents the required return associated with all positive betas. The market risk premium of 4% (r_m of 11% − R_F of 7%) has been highlighted. For a beta for asset Z, b_Z, of 1.5, its corresponding required return, r_Z, is 13%. Also shown in the figure is asset Z's risk premium of 6% (r_Z of 13% − R_F of 7%). It should be clear that for assets with betas greater than 1, the risk premium is greater than that for the market; for assets with betas less than 1, the risk premium is less than that for the market.

Shifts in the Security Market Line

The security market line is not stable over time, and shifts in the security market line can result in a change in required return. The position and slope of the SML are affected by two major forces—inflationary expectations and risk aversion—which are analyzed next.[10]

Changes in Inflationary Expectations Changes in inflationary expectations affect the risk-free rate of return, R_F. The equation for the risk-free rate of return is

$$R_F = r^* + IP \tag{8.9}$$

This equation shows that, assuming a constant real rate of interest, r^*, changes in inflationary expectations, reflected in an inflation premium, IP, will result in corresponding changes in the risk-free rate. Therefore, a change in inflationary

10. A firm's beta can change over time as a result of changes in the firm's asset mix, in its financing mix, or in external factors not within management's control, such as earthquakes, toxic spills, and so on.

expectations that results from events such as international trade embargoes or major changes in Federal Reserve policy will result in a shift in the SML. Because the risk-free rate is a basic component of all rates of return, any change in R_F will be reflected in *all* required rates of return.

Changes in inflationary expectations result in parallel shifts in the SML in direct response to the magnitude and direction of the change. This effect can best be illustrated by an example.

Example 8.16 ▶ In the preceding example, using the CAPM, the required return for asset Z, r_Z, was found to be 13%. Assuming that the risk-free rate of 7% includes a 2% real rate of interest, r^*, and a 5% inflation premium, IP, then Equation 8.9 confirms that

$$R_F = 2\% + 5\% = 7\%$$

Now assume that recent economic events have resulted in an *increase of 3% in inflationary expectations, raising the inflation premium* to 8% (IP_1). As a result, all returns likewise rise by 3%. In this case, the new returns (noted by subscript 1) are

$$R_{F_1} = 10\% \text{ (rises from 7\% to 10\%)}$$
$$r_{m_1} = 14\% \text{ (rises from 11\% to 14\%)}$$

Substituting these values, along with asset Z's beta (b_Z) of 1.5, into the CAPM (Equation 8.8), we find that asset Z's new required return (r_{Z_1}) can be calculated:

$$r_{Z_1} = 10\% + [1.5 \times (14\% - 10\%)] = 10\% + 6\% = \underline{\underline{16\%}}$$

Comparing r_{Z_1} of 16% to r_Z of 13%, we see that the change of 3% in asset Z's required return exactly equals the change in the inflation premium. The same 3% increase results for all assets.

Figure 8.10 depicts the situation just described. It shows that the 3% increase in inflationary expectations results in a parallel shift upward of 3% in the SML. Clearly, the required returns on all assets rise by 3%. Note that the rise in the inflation premium from 5% to 8% (IP to IP_1) causes the risk-free rate to rise from 7% to 10% (R_F to R_{F_1}) and the market return to increase from 11% to 14% (r_m to r_{m_1}). The security market line therefore shifts upward by 3% (SML to SML_1), causing the required return on all risky assets, such as asset Z, to rise by 3%. The important lesson here is that *a given change in inflationary expectations will be fully reflected in a corresponding change in the returns of all assets, as reflected graphically in a parallel shift of the SML.*

Changes in Risk Aversion The slope of the security market line reflects the general risk preferences of investors in the marketplace. As discussed earlier, most investors are *risk averse*—they require increased returns for increased risk. This positive relationship between risk and return is graphically represented by the SML, which depicts the relationship between nondiversifiable risk as measured by beta (x axis) and the required return (y axis). The slope of the SML reflects the degree of risk aversion: *the steeper its slope, the greater the degree of risk aversion* because a higher level of return will be required for each level of risk as measured by beta. In other words, *risk premiums increase with increasing risk avoidance.*

FIGURE 8.10

Inflation Shifts SML
Impact of increased inflationary expectations on the SML

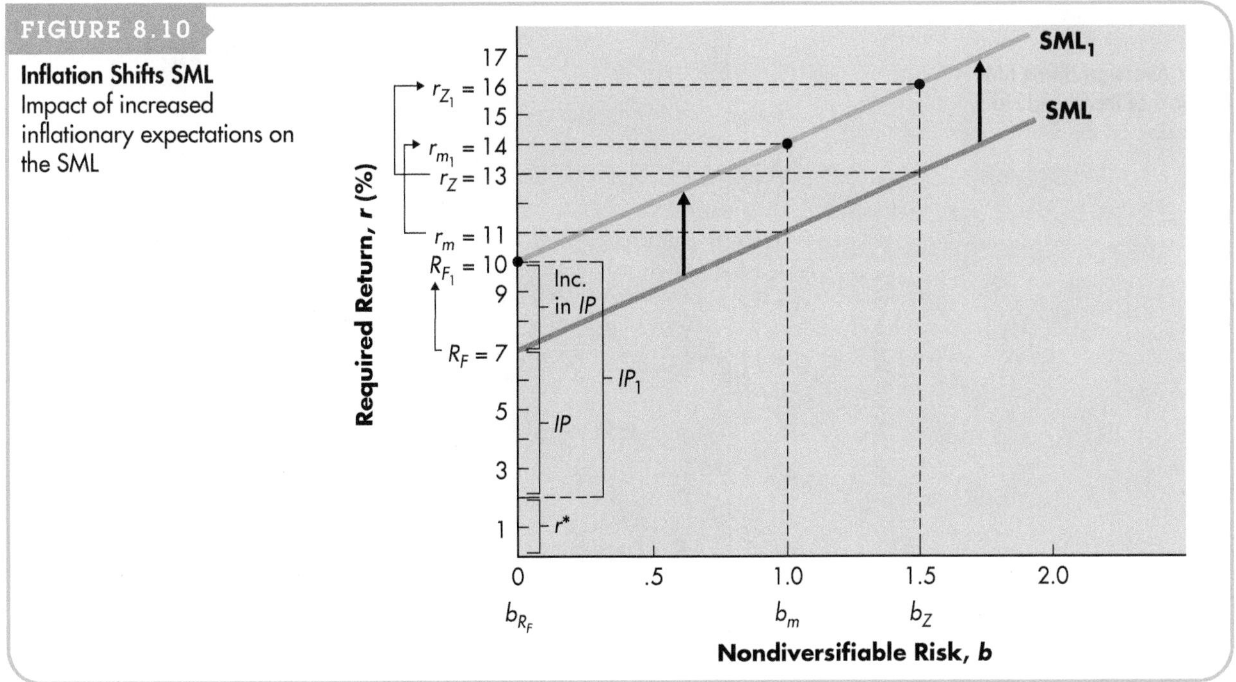

Changes in risk aversion, and therefore shifts in the SML, result from changing preferences of investors, which generally result from economic, political, and social events. Examples of events that *increase* risk aversion include a stock market crash, assassination of a key political leader, and the outbreak of war. In general, widely shared expectations of hard times ahead tend to cause investors to become more risk averse, requiring higher returns as compensation for accepting a given level of risk. The impact of increased risk aversion on the SML can best be demonstrated by an example.

Example 8.17 ▶

In the preceding examples, the SML in Figure 8.9 reflected a risk-free rate (R_F) of 7%, a market return (r_m) of 11%, a market risk premium ($r_m - R_F$) of 4%, and a required return on asset Z (r_Z) of 13% with a beta (b_Z) of 1.5. Assume that recent economic events have made investors more risk averse, causing a new higher market return (r_{m_1}) of 14%. Graphically, this change would cause the SML to pivot upward as shown in Figure 8.11, causing a new market risk premium ($r_{m_1} - R_F$) of 7%. As a result, the required return on all risky assets will increase. For asset Z, with a beta of 1.5, the new required return (r_{Z_1}) can be calculated by using the CAPM (Equation 8.8):

$$r_{Z_1} = 7\% + [1.5 \times (14\% - 7\%)] = 7\% + 10.5\% = \underline{\underline{17.5\%}}$$

This value can be seen on the new security market line (SML_1) in Figure 8.11. Note that although asset Z's risk, as measured by beta, did not change, its required return has increased because of the increased risk aversion reflected in the market risk premium. To summarize, *greater risk aversion results in higher required returns for each level of risk. Similarly, a reduction in risk aversion causes the required return for each level of risk to decline.*

FIGURE 8.11

Risk Aversion Shifts SML
Impact of increased risk aversion on the SML

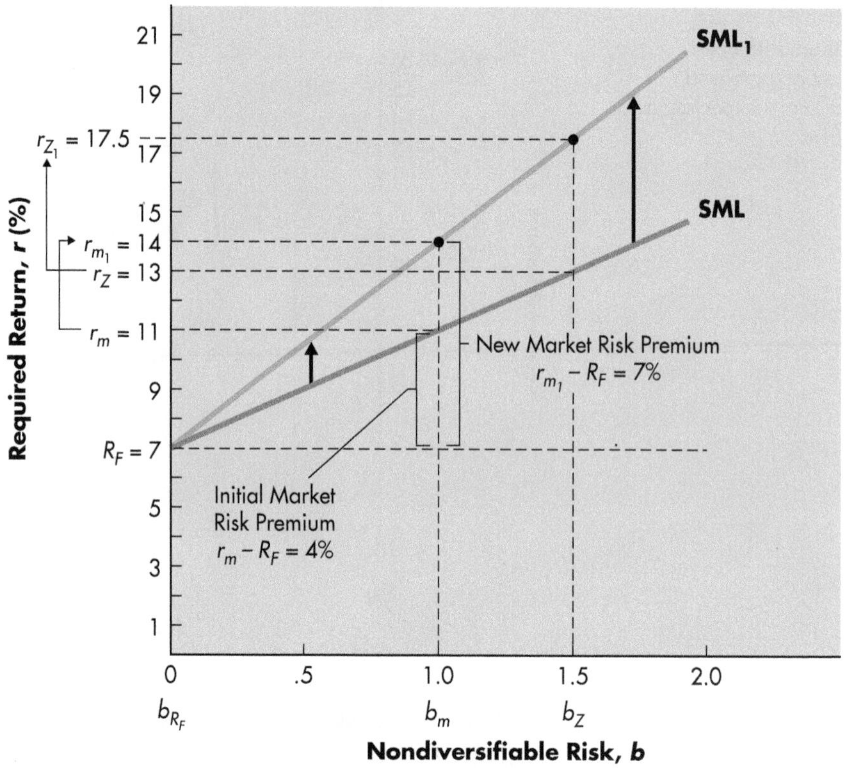

Some Comments on the CAPM

The capital asset pricing model generally relies on historical data. The betas may or may not actually reflect the *future* variability of returns. Therefore, the required returns specified by the model can be viewed only as rough approximations. Users of betas commonly make subjective adjustments to the historically determined betas to reflect their expectations of the future.

The CAPM was developed to explain the behavior of security prices and provide a mechanism whereby investors could assess the impact of a proposed security investment on their portfolio's overall risk and return. It is based on an assumed efficient market with the following characteristics: many small investors, all having the same information and expectations with respect to securities; no restrictions on investment, no taxes, and no transaction costs; and rational investors, who view securities similarly and are risk averse, preferring higher returns and lower risk.

In more depth

To read about *CAPM Survives Criticism*, go to www.myfinancelab.com

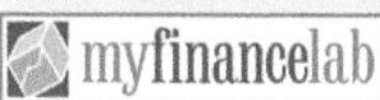

Although the perfect world described in the preceding paragraph appears to be unrealistic, studies have provided support for the existence of the expectational relationship described by the CAPM in active markets such as the New York Stock Exchange. The CAPM also sees widespread use in corporations that use the model to assess the required returns that their shareholders demand (and therefore, the returns that the firm's managers need to achieve when they invest shareholders' money).

→ **REVIEW QUESTIONS**

8–11 How are total risk, nondiversifiable risk, and diversifiable risk related? Why is nondiversifiable risk the *only relevant risk?*

8–12 What risk does *beta* measure? How can you find the beta of a portfolio?

8–13 Explain the meaning of each variable in the *capital asset pricing model (CAPM)* equation. What is the *security market line (SML)?*

8–14 What impact would the following changes have on the security market line and therefore on the required return for a given level of risk? **(a)** An *increase* in inflationary expectations. **(b)** Investors become *less* risk-averse.

Summary

FOCUS ON VALUE

A firm's risk and expected return directly affect its share price. Risk and return are the two key determinants of the firm's value. It is therefore the financial manager's responsibility to assess carefully the risk and return of all major decisions to ensure that the expected returns justify the level of risk being introduced.

The financial manager can expect to achieve **the firm's goal of increasing its share price** (and thereby benefiting its owners) by taking only those actions that earn returns at least commensurate with their risk. Clearly, financial managers need to recognize, measure, and evaluate risk–return trade-offs to ensure that their decisions contribute to the creation of value for owners.

REVIEW OF LEARNING GOALS

LG 1 **Understand the meaning and fundamentals of risk, return, and risk preferences.** Risk is a measure of the uncertainty surrounding the return that an investment will produce. The total rate of return is the sum of cash distributions, such as interest or dividends, plus the change in the asset's value over a given period, divided by the investment's beginning-of-period value. Investment returns vary both over time and between different types of investments. Investors may be risk averse, risk neutral, or risk seeking. Most financial decision makers are risk averse. A risk averse decision maker requires a higher expected return on a more risky investment alternative.

LG 2 **Describe procedures for assessing and measuring the risk of a single asset.** The risk of a single asset is measured in much the same way as the risk of a portfolio of assets. Scenario analysis and probability distributions can be used to assess risk. The range, the standard deviation, and the coefficient of variation can be used to measure risk quantitatively.

LG 3 **Discuss the measurement of return and standard deviation for a portfolio and the concept of correlation.** The return of a portfolio is calculated as the weighted average of returns on the individual assets from which it is formed. The portfolio standard deviation is found by using the formula for the standard deviation of a single asset.

Correlation—the statistical relationship between any two series of numbers—can be positively correlated, negatively correlated, or uncorrelated. At the extremes, the series can be perfectly positively correlated or perfectly negatively correlated.

LG 4 **Understand the risk and return characteristics of a portfolio in terms of correlation and diversification and the impact of international assets on a portfolio.** Diversification involves combining assets with low correlation to reduce the risk of the portfolio. The range of risk in a two-asset portfolio depends on the correlation between the two assets. If they are perfectly positively correlated, the portfolio's risk will be between the individual assets' risks. If they are perfectly negatively correlated, the portfolio's risk will be between the risk of the more risky asset and zero.

International diversification can further reduce a portfolio's risk. Foreign assets have the risk of currency fluctuation and political risks.

LG 5 **Review the two types of risk and the derivation and role of beta in measuring the relevant risk of both a security and a portfolio.** The total risk of a security consists of nondiversifiable and diversifiable risk. Diversifiable risk can be eliminated through diversification. Nondiversifiable risk is the only relevant risk. Nondiversifiable risk is measured by the beta coefficient, which is a relative measure of the relationship between an asset's return and the market return. Beta is derived by finding the slope of the "characteristic line" that best explains the historical relationship between the asset's return and the market return. The beta of a portfolio is a weighted average of the betas of the individual assets that it includes.

LG 6 **Explain the capital asset pricing model (CAPM), its relationship to the security market line (SML), and the major forces causing shifts in the SML.** The CAPM uses beta to relate an asset's risk relative to the market to the asset's required return. The graphical depiction of the CAPM is SML, which shifts over time in response to changing inflationary expectations and/or changes in investor risk aversion. Changes in inflationary expectations result in parallel shifts in the SML. Increasing risk aversion results in a steepening in the slope of the SML. Decreasing risk aversion reduces the slope of the SML. Although it has some shortcomings, the CAPM provides a useful conceptual framework for evaluating and linking risk and return.

Opener-in-Review

The table below shows the annual returns in each year from 2007 through 2009 of the Close Special Situations Fund (a British fund specializing in small stocks), and the Financial Times Stock Index (FTSE), an index that tracks the performance of the 100 largest companies on the U.K. stock market:

Year	Close Fund	FTSE
2007	−4.8%	2.1%
2008	−57.3%	−30.9%
2009	246.9%	22.1%

For both the Close Fund and the FTSE, calculate the average annual return and its standard deviation. What are the general patterns that you see? Provide one reason that the performance of the FTSE differs from that of the Close Fund.

Self-Test Problems (Solutions in Appendix)

LG 3 LG 4 **ST8–1 Portfolio analysis** You have been asked for your advice in selecting a portfolio of assets and have been given the following data:

	Expected return		
Year	**Asset A**	**Asset B**	**Asset C**
2013	12%	16%	12%
2014	14	14	14
2015	16	12	16

You have been told that you can create two portfolios—one consisting of assets A and B and the other consisting of assets A and C—by investing equal proportions (50%) in each of the two component assets.

a. What is the expected return for each asset over the 3-year period?
b. What is the standard deviation for each asset's return?
c. What is the expected return for each of the two portfolios?
d. How would you characterize the correlations of returns of the two assets making up each of the two portfolios identified in part **c?**
e. What is the standard deviation for each portfolio?
f. Which portfolio do you recommend? Why?

LG 5 LG 6 **ST8–2 Beta and CAPM** Currently under consideration is an investment with a beta, b, of 1.50. At this time, the risk-free rate of return, R_F, is 7%, and the return on the market portfolio of assets, r_m, is 10%. You believe that this investment will earn an annual rate of return of 11%.

a. If the return on the market portfolio were to increase by 10%, what would you expect to happen to the investment's return? What if the market return were to decline by 10%?
b. Use the capital asset pricing model (CAPM) to find the *required return* on this investment.
c. On the basis of your calculation in part **b,** would you recommend this investment? Why or why not?
d. Assume that as a result of investors becoming less risk-averse, the market return drops by 1% to 9%. What impact would this change have on your responses in parts **b** and **c?**

Warm-Up Exercises

All problems are available in myfinancelab.

LG 1 **E8–1** An analyst predicted last year that the stock of Logistics, Inc., would offer a total return of at least 10% in the coming year. At the beginning of the year, the firm had a stock market value of $10 million. At the end of the year, it had a market value of $12 million even though it experienced a loss, or negative net income, of $2.5 million. Did the analyst's prediction prove correct? Explain using the values for total annual return.

LG 2 **E8–2** Four analysts cover the stock of Fluorine Chemical. One forecasts a 5% return for the coming year. A second expects the return to be negative 5%. A third predicts a 10% return. A fourth expects a 3% return in the coming year. You are relatively confident that the return will be positive but not large, so you arbitrarily assign probabilities of being correct of 35%, 5%, 20%, and 40%, respectively, to the analysts' forecasts. Given these probabilities, what is Fluorine Chemical's *expected return* for the coming year?

LG 2 **E8–3** The expected annual returns are 15% for investment 1 and 12% for investment 2. The standard deviation of the first investment's return is 10%; the second investment's return has a standard deviation of 5%. Which investment is less risky based solely on *standard deviation*? Which investment is less risky based on *coefficient of variation*? Which is a better measure given that the expected returns of the two investments are not the same?

LG 3 **E8–4** Your portfolio has three asset classes. U.S. government T-bills account for 45% of the portfolio, large-company stocks constitute another 40%, and small-company stocks make up the remaining 15%. If the expected returns are 3.8% for the T-bills, 12.3% for the large-company stocks, and 17.4% for the small-company stocks, what is the expected return of the portfolio?

LG 5 **E8–5** You wish to calculate the risk level of your portfolio based on its beta. The five stocks in the portfolio with their respective weights and betas are shown in the accompanying table. Calculate the beta of your portfolio.

Stock	Portfolio weight	Beta
Alpha	20%	1.15
Centauri	10	0.85
Zen	15	1.60
Wren	20	1.35
Yukos	35	1.85

LG 6 **E8–6** **a.** Calculate the required rate of return for an asset that has a beta of 1.8, given a risk-free rate of 5% and a market return of 10%.

b. If investors have become more risk-averse due to recent geopolitical events, and the market return rises to 13%, what is the required rate of return for the same asset?

c. Use your findings in part **a** to graph the initial *security market line (SML)*, and then use your findings in part **b** to graph (on the same set of axes) the shift in the SML.

Problems

All problems are available in myfinancelab.

LG 1 **P8–1 Rate of return** Douglas Keel, a financial analyst for Orange Industries, wishes to estimate the rate of return for two similar-risk investments, X and Y. Douglas's research indicates that the immediate past returns will serve as reasonable estimates of future returns. A year earlier, investment X had a market value of $20,000; investment Y had a market value of $55,000. During the year, investment X generated cash flow of $1,500 and investment Y generated cash flow of $6,800. The current market values of investments X and Y are $21,000 and $55,000, respectively.

a. Calculate the expected rate of return on investments X and Y using the most recent year's data.

b. Assuming that the two investments are equally risky, which one should Douglas recommend? Why?

LG 1 **P8–2 Return calculations** For each of the investments shown in the following table, calculate the rate of return earned over the unspecified time period.

Investment	Cash flow during period	Beginning-of-period value	End-of-period value
A	−$ 800	$ 1,100	$ 100
B	15,000	120,000	118,000
C	7,000	45,000	48,000
D	80	600	500
E	1,500	12,500	12,400

LG 1 **P8–3 Risk preferences** Sharon Smith, the financial manager for Barnett Corporation, wishes to evaluate three prospective investments: X, Y, and Z. Sharon will evaluate each of these investments to decide whether they are superior to investments that her company already has in place, which have an expected return of 12% and a standard deviation of 6%. The expected returns and standard deviations of the investments are as follows:

Investment	Expected return	Standard deviation
X	14%	7%
Y	12	8
Z	10	9

a. If Sharon were *risk neutral,* which investments would she select? Explain why.

b. If she were *risk averse,* which investments would she select? Why?

c. If she were *risk seeking,* which investments would she select? Why?

d. Given the traditional risk preference behavior exhibited by financial managers, which investment would be preferred? Why?

LG 2 **P8–4 Risk analysis** Solar Designs is considering an investment in an expanded product line. Two possible types of expansion are being considered. After investigating the possible outcomes, the company made the estimates shown in the following table.

	Expansion A	Expansion B
Initial investment	$12,000	$12,000
Annual rate of return		
Pessimistic	16%	10%
Most likely	20%	20%
Optimistic	24%	30%

a. Determine the *range* of the rates of return for each of the two projects.
b. Which project is less risky? Why?
c. If you were making the investment decision, which one would you choose? Why? What does this imply about your feelings toward risk?
d. Assume that expansion B's most likely outcome is 21% per year and that all other facts remain the same. Does this change your answer to part **c?** Why?

LG 2 **P8–5 Risk and probability** Micro-Pub, Inc., is considering the purchase of one of two microfilm cameras, R and S. Both should provide benefits over a 10-year period, and each requires an initial investment of $4,000. Management has constructed the accompanying table of estimates of rates of return and probabilities for pessimistic, most likely, and optimistic results.

a. Determine the *range* for the rate of return for each of the two cameras.
b. Determine the *expected value* of return for each camera.
c. Purchase of which camera is riskier? Why?

	Camera R		Camera S	
	Amount	Probability	Amount	Probability
Initial investment	$4,000	1.00	$4,000	1.00
Annual rate of return				
Pessimistic	20%	0.25	15%	0.20
Most likely	25%	0.50	25%	0.55
Optimistic	30%	0.25	35%	0.25

LG 2 **P8–6 Bar charts and risk** Swan's Sportswear is considering bringing out a line of designer jeans. Currently, it is negotiating with two different well-known designers. Because of the highly competitive nature of the industry, the two lines of jeans have been given code names. After market research, the firm has established the expectations shown in the following table about the annual rates of return:

		Annual rate of return	
Market acceptance	Probability	Line J	Line K
Very poor	0.05	0.0075	0.010
Poor	0.15	0.0125	0.025
Average	0.60	0.0850	0.080
Good	0.15	0.1475	0.135
Excellent	0.05	0.1625	0.150

Use the table to:

a. Construct a bar chart for each line's annual rate of return.
b. Calculate the *expected value* of return for each line.
c. Evaluate the relative riskiness for each jean line's rate of return using the bar charts.

LG 2 **P8–7** **Coefficient of variation** Metal Manufacturing has isolated four alternatives for meeting its need for increased production capacity. The following table summarizes data gathered relative to each of these alternatives.

Alternative	Expected return	Standard deviation of return
A	20%	7.0%
B	22	9.5
C	19	6.0
D	16	5.5

a. Calculate the *coefficient of variation* for each alternative.
b. If the firm wishes to minimize risk, which alternative do you recommend? Why?

LG 2 **P8–8** **Standard deviation versus coefficient of variation as measures of risk** Greengage, Inc., a successful nursery, is considering several expansion projects. All of the alternatives promise to produce an acceptable return. Data on four possible projects follow.

Project	Expected return	Range	Standard deviation
A	12.0%	4.0%	2.9%
B	12.5	5.0	3.2
C	13.0	6.0	3.5
D	12.8	4.5	3.0

a. Which project is least risky, judging on the basis of *range?*
b. Which project has the lowest *standard deviation?* Explain why standard deviation may not be an entirely appropriate measure of risk for purposes of this comparison.
c. Calculate the *coefficient of variation* for each project. Which project do you think Greengage's owners should choose? Explain why.

Personal Finance Problem

LG 1 LG 2 **P8–9** **Rate of return, standard deviation, coefficient of variation** Mike is searching for a stock to include in his current stock portfolio. He is interested in Hi-Tech Inc.; he has been impressed with the company's computer products and believes Hi-Tech is an innovative market player. However, Mike realizes that any time you consider a technology stock, risk is a major concern. The rule he follows is to include only securities with a coefficient of variation of returns below 0.90.

Mike has obtained the following price information for the period 2009 through 2012. Hi-Tech stock, being growth-oriented, did not pay any dividends during these 4 years.

	Stock price	
Year	**Beginning**	**End**
2009	$14.36	$21.55
2010	21.55	64.78
2011	64.78	72.38
2012	72.38	91.80

a. Calculate the *rate of return* for each year, 2009 through 2012, for Hi-Tech stock.
b. Assume that each year's return is equally probable, and calculate the *average return* over this time period.
c. Calculate the *standard deviation* of returns over the past 4 years. (*Hint:* Treat these data as a sample.)
d. Based on **b** and **c** determine the *coefficient of variation* of returns for the security.
e. Given the calculation in **d** what should be Mike's decision regarding the inclusion of Hi-Tech stock in his portfolio?

LG 2 P8–10 **Assessing return and risk** Swift Manufacturing must choose between two asset purchases. The annual rate of return and the related probabilities given in the following table summarize the firm's analysis to this point.

Project 257		Project 432	
Rate of return	**Probability**	**Rate of return**	**Probability**
−10%	0.01	10%	0.05
10	0.04	15	0.10
20	0.05	20	0.10
30	0.10	25	0.15
40	0.15	30	0.20
45	0.30	35	0.15
50	0.15	40	0.10
60	0.10	45	0.10
70	0.05	50	0.05
80	0.04		
100	0.01		

a. For each project, compute:
(1) The range of possible rates of return.
(2) The expected return.
(3) The standard deviation of the returns.
(4) The coefficient of variation of the returns.
b. Construct a bar chart of each distribution of rates of return.
c. Which project would you consider less risky? Why?

LG 2 **P8–11 Integrative—Expected return, standard deviation, and coefficient of variation** Three assets—F, G, and H—are currently being considered by Perth Industries. The probability distributions of expected returns for these assets are shown in the following table.

	Asset F		Asset G		Asset H	
j	Pr_j	Return, r_j	Pr_j	Return, r_j	Pr_j	Return, r_j
1	0.10	40%	0.40	35%	0.10	40%
2	0.20	10	0.30	10	0.20	20
3	0.40	0	0.30	−20	0.40	10
4	0.20	−5			0.20	0
5	0.10	−10			0.10	−20

a. Calculate the expected value of return, $\bar{r}$, for each of the three assets. Which provides the largest expected return?

b. Calculate the standard deviation, σ_r, for each of the three assets' returns. Which appears to have the greatest risk?

c. Calculate the coefficient of variation, CV, for each of the three assets' returns. Which appears to have the greatest *relative* risk?

LG 2 **P8–12 Normal probability distribution** Assuming that the rates of return associated with a given asset investment are normally distributed; that the expected return, $\bar{r}$, is 18.9%; and that the coefficient of variation, CV, is 0.75; answer the following questions:

a. Find the standard deviation of returns, σ_r.

b. Calculate the range of expected return outcomes associated with the following probabilities of occurrence: (1) 68%, (2) 95%, (3) 99%.

c. Draw the probability distribution associated with your findings in parts **a** and **b.**

Personal Finance Problem

LG 3 **P8–13 Portfolio return and standard deviation** Jamie Wong is considering building an investment portfolio containing two stocks, L and M. Stock L will represent 40% of the dollar value of the portfolio, and stock M will account for the other 60%. The expected returns over the next 6 years, 2013–2018, for each of these stocks are shown in the following table.

	Expected return	
Year	Stock L	Stock M
2013	14%	20%
2014	14	18
2015	16	16
2016	17	14
2017	17	12
2018	19	10

a. Calculate the expected portfolio return, r_p, for *each* of the 6 years.
b. Calculate the expected value of portfolio returns, $\bar{r}_p$, over the 6-year period.
c. Calculate the standard deviation of expected portfolio returns, σ_{r_p}, over the 6-year period.
d. How would you characterize the correlation of returns of the two stocks L and M?
e. Discuss any benefits of diversification achieved by Jamie through creation of the portfolio.

LG 3 **P8–14 Portfolio analysis** You have been given the expected return data shown in the first table on three assets—F, G, and H—over the period 2013–2016.

	Expected return		
Year	**Asset F**	**Asset G**	**Asset H**
2013	16%	17%	14%
2014	17	16	15
2015	18	15	16
2016	19	14	17

Using these assets, you have isolated the three investment alternatives shown in the following table.

Alternative	Investment
1	100% of asset F
2	50% of asset F and 50% of asset G
3	50% of asset F and 50% of asset H

a. Calculate the expected return over the 4-year period for each of the three alternatives.
b. Calculate the standard deviation of returns over the 4-year period for each of the three alternatives.
c. Use your findings in parts **a** and **b** to calculate the coefficient of variation for each of the three alternatives.
d. On the basis of your findings, which of the three investment alternatives do you recommend? Why?

LG 4 **P8–15 Correlation, risk, and return** Matt Peters wishes to evaluate the risk and return behaviors associated with various combinations of assets V and W under three assumed degrees of correlation: perfectly positive, uncorrelated, and perfectly negative. The expected returns and standard deviations calculated for each of the assets are shown in the following table.

Asset	Expected return, $\bar{r}$	Risk (standard deviation), σ_r
V	8%	5%
W	13	10

a. If the returns of assets V and W are *perfectly positively correlated* (correlation coefficient = +1), describe the *range* of (1) expected return and (2) risk associated with all possible portfolio combinations.

b. If the returns of assets V and W are *uncorrelated* (correlation coefficient = 0), describe the *approximate range* of (1) expected return and (2) risk associated with all possible portfolio combinations.

c. If the returns of assets V and W are *perfectly negatively correlated* (correlation coefficient = −1), describe the *range* of (1) expected return and (2) risk associated with all possible portfolio combinations.

Personal Finance Problem

LG 1 LG 4 **P8–16 International investment returns** Joe Martinez, a U.S. citizen living in Brownsville, Texas, invested in the common stock of Telmex, a Mexican corporation. He purchased 1,000 shares at 20.50 pesos per share. Twelve months later, he sold them at 24.75 pesos per share. He received no dividends during that time.

a. What was Joe's investment return (in percentage terms) for the year, on the basis of the peso value of the shares?

b. The exchange rate for pesos was 9.21 pesos per US$1.00 at the time of the purchase. At the time of the sale, the exchange rate was 9.85 pesos per US$1.00. Translate the purchase and sale prices into US$.

c. Calculate Joe's investment return on the basis of the US$ value of the shares.

d. Explain why the two returns are different. Which one is more important to Joe? Why?

LG 5 **P8–17 Total, nondiversifiable, and diversifiable risk** David Talbot randomly selected securities from all those listed on the New York Stock Exchange for his portfolio. He began with a single security and added securities one by one until a total of 20 securities were held in the portfolio. After each security was added, David calculated the portfolio standard deviation, σ_{r_p}. The calculated values are shown in the following table.

Number of securities	Portfolio risk, σ_{r_p}	Number of securities	Portfolio risk, σ_{r_p}
1	14.50%	11	7.00%
2	13.30	12	6.80
3	12.20	13	6.70
4	11.20	14	6.65
5	10.30	15	6.60
6	9.50	16	6.56
7	8.80	17	6.52
8	8.20	18	6.50
9	7.70	19	6.48
10	7.30	20	6.47

a. Plot the data from the table above on a graph that has the number of securities on the *x*-axis and the portfolio standard deviation on the *y*-axis.

b. Divide the total portfolio risk in the graph into its *nondiversifiable* and *diversifiable* risk components, and label each of these on the graph.

c. Describe which of the two risk components is the *relevant risk,* and explain why it is relevant. How much of this risk exists in David Talbot's portfolio?

LG 5 **P8–18 Graphical derivation of beta** A firm wishes to estimate graphically the betas for two assets, A and B. It has gathered the return data shown in the following table for the market portfolio and for both assets over the last 10 years, 2003–2012.

	Actual return		
Year	Market portfolio	Asset A	Asset B
2003	6%	11%	16%
2004	2	8	11
2005	−13	−4	−10
2006	−4	3	3
2007	−8	0	−3
2008	16	19	30
2009	10	14	22
2010	15	18	29
2011	8	12	19
2012	13	17	26

a. On a set of "market return (x axis)–asset return (y axis)" axes, use the data given to draw the characteristic line for asset A and for asset B.

b. Use the characteristic lines from part **a** to estimate the betas for assets A and B.

c. Use the betas found in part **b** to comment on the relative risks of assets A and B.

LG 5 **P8–19 Graphical derivation and interpreting beta** You are analyzing the performance of two stocks. The first, shown in Panel A, is Cyclical Industries Incorporated. Cyclical

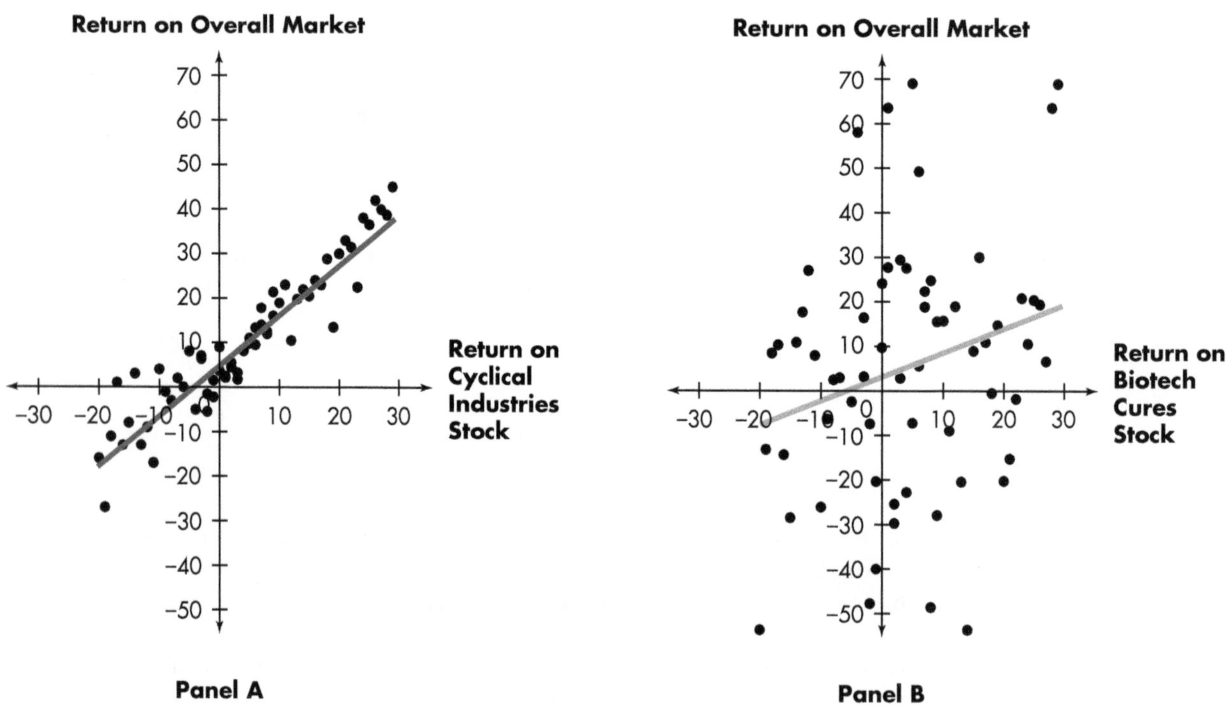

Industries makes machine tools and other heavy equipment, the demand for which rises and falls closely with the overall state of the economy. The second stock, shown in Panel B, is Biotech Cures Corporation. Biotech Cures uses biotechnology to develop new pharmaceutical compounds to treat incurable diseases. Biotech's fortunes are driven largely by the success or failure of its scientists to discover new and effective drugs. Each data point on the graph shows the monthly return on the stock of interest and the monthly return on the overall stock market. The lines drawn through the data points represent the characteristic lines for each security.

a. Which stock do you think has a higher standard deviation? Why?
b. Which stock do you think has a higher beta? Why?
c. Which stock do you think is riskier? What does the answer to this question depend on?

LG 5 **P8–20** **Interpreting beta** A firm wishes to assess the impact of changes in the market return on an asset that has a beta of 1.20.

a. If the market return increased by 15%, what impact would this change be expected to have on the asset's return?
b. If the market return decreased by 8%, what impact would this change be expected to have on the asset's return?
c. If the market return did not change, what impact, if any, would be expected on the asset's return?
d. Would this asset be considered more or less risky than the market? Explain.

LG 5 **P8–21** **Betas** Answer the questions below for assets A to D shown in the table.

Asset	Beta
A	0.50
B	1.60
C	−0.20
D	0.90

a. What impact would a *10% increase* in the market return be expected to have on each asset's return?
b. What impact would a *10% decrease* in the market return be expected to have on each asset's return?
c. If you believed that the market return would *increase* in the near future, which asset would you prefer? Why?
d. If you believed that the market return would *decrease* in the near future, which asset would you prefer? Why?

Personal Finance Problem

LG 5 **P8–22** **Betas and risk rankings** You are considering three stocks—A, B, and C—for possible inclusion in your investment portfolio. Stock A has a beta of 0.80, stock B has a beta of 1.40, and stock C has a beta of −0.30.

a. Rank these stocks from the most risky to the least risky.
b. If the return on the market portfolio increased by 12%, what change would you expect in the return for each of the stocks?
c. If the return on the market portfolio decreased by 5%, what change would you expect in the return for each of the stocks?

d. If you felt that the stock market was getting ready to experience a significant decline, which stock would you probably add to your portfolio? Why?

e. If you anticipated a major stock market rally, which stock would you add to your portfolio? Why?

Personal Finance Problem

LG 5 **P8–23 Portfolio betas** Rose Berry is attempting to evaluate two possible portfolios, which consist of the same five assets held in different proportions. She is particularly interested in using beta to compare the risks of the portfolios, so she has gathered the data shown in the following table.

		Portfolio weights	
Asset	**Asset beta**	**Portfolio A**	**Portfolio B**
1	1.30	10%	30%
2	0.70	30	10
3	1.25	10	20
4	1.10	10	20
5	0.90	40	20
Totals		100%	100%

a. Calculate the betas for portfolios A and B.

b. Compare the risks of these portfolios to the market as well as to each other. Which portfolio is more risky?

LG 6 **P8–24 Capital asset pricing model (CAPM)** For each of the cases shown in the following table, use the capital asset pricing model to find the required return.

Case	**Risk-free rate, R_F**	**Market return, r_m**	**Beta, b**
A	5%	8%	1.30
B	8	13	0.90
C	9	12	−0.20
D	10	15	1.00
E	6	10	0.60

Personal Finance Problem

LG 5 LG 6 **P8–25 Beta coefficients and the capital asset pricing model** Katherine Wilson is wondering how much risk she must undertake to generate an acceptable return on her portfolio. The risk-free return currently is 5%. The return on the overall stock market is 16%. Use the CAPM to calculate how high the beta coefficient of Katherine's portfolio would have to be to achieve each of the following expected portfolio returns.

a. 10%

b. 15%

c. 18%

d. 20%

e. Katherine is risk averse. What is the highest return she can expect if she is unwilling to take more than an average risk?

LG 6 **P8-26 Manipulating CAPM** Use the basic equation for the capital asset pricing model (CAPM) to work each of the following problems.

a. Find the *required return* for an asset with a beta of 0.90 when the risk-free rate and market return are 8% and 12%, respectively.

b. Find the *risk-free rate* for a firm with a required return of 15% and a beta of 1.25 when the market return is 14%.

c. Find the *market return* for an asset with a required return of 16% and a beta of 1.10 when the risk-free rate is 9%.

d. Find the *beta* for an asset with a required return of 15% when the risk-free rate and market return are 10% and 12.5%, respectively.

Personal Finance Problem

LG 1 LG 3 LG 5 LG 6 **P8-27 Portfolio return and beta** Jamie Peters invested $100,000 to set up the following portfolio one year ago:

Asset	Cost	Beta at purchase	Yearly income	Value today
A	$20,000	0.80	$1,600	$20,000
B	35,000	0.95	1,400	36,000
C	30,000	1.50	—	34,500
D	15,000	1.25	375	16,500

a. Calculate the portfolio beta on the basis of the original cost figures.

b. Calculate the percentage return of each asset in the portfolio for the year.

c. Calculate the percentage return of the portfolio on the basis of original cost, using income and gains during the year.

d. At the time Jamie made his investments, investors were estimating that the market return for the coming year would be 10%. The estimate of the risk-free rate of return averaged 4% for the coming year. Calculate an expected rate of return for each stock on the basis of its beta and the expectations of market and risk-free returns.

e. On the basis of the actual results, explain how each stock in the portfolio performed relative to those CAPM-generated expectations of performance. What factors could explain these differences?

LG 6 **P8-28 Security market line (SML)** Assume that the risk-free rate, R_F, is currently 9% and that the market return, r_m, is currently 13%.

a. Draw the security market line (SML) on a set of "nondiversifiable risk (x axis)–required return (y axis)" axes.

b. Calculate and label the *market risk premium* on the axes in part **a.**

c. Given the previous data, calculate the required return on asset A having a beta of 0.80 and asset B having a beta of 1.30.

d. Draw in the betas and required returns from part **c** for assets A and B on the axes in part **a.** Label the *risk premium* associated with each of these assets, and discuss them.

LG 6 **P8-29 Shifts in the security market line** Assume that the risk-free rate, R_F, is currently 8%, the market return, r_m, is 12%, and asset A has a beta, b_A, of 1.10.

a. Draw the security market line (SML) on a set of "nondiversifiable risk (x axis)–required return (y axis)" axes.

b. Use the CAPM to calculate the required return, r_A, on asset A, and depict asset A's beta and required return on the SML drawn in part **a.**

c. Assume that as a result of recent economic events, inflationary expectations have declined by 2%, lowering R_F and r_m to 6% and 10%, respectively. Draw the new SML on the axes in part **a,** and calculate and show the new required return for asset A.

d. Assume that as a result of recent events, investors have become more risk averse, causing the market return to rise by 1%, to 13%. Ignoring the shift in part **c,** draw the new SML on the same set of axes that you used before, and calculate and show the new required return for asset A.

e. From the previous changes, what conclusions can be drawn about the impact of (1) decreased inflationary expectations and (2) increased risk aversion on the required returns of risky assets?

LG 6 **P8–30 Integrative—Risk, return, and CAPM** Wolff Enterprises must consider several investment projects, A through E, using the capital asset pricing model (CAPM) and its graphical representation, the security market line (SML). Relevant information is presented in the following table.

Item	Rate of return	Beta, b
Risk-free asset	9%	0.00
Market portfolio	14	1.00
Project A	—	1.50
Project B	—	0.75
Project C	—	2.00
Project D	—	0.00
Project E	—	−0.50

a. Calculate (1) the required rate of return and (2) the risk premium for each project, given its level of nondiversifiable risk.

b. Use your findings in part **a** to draw the security market line (required return relative to nondiversifiable risk).

c. Discuss the relative nondiversifiable risk of projects A through E.

d. Assume that recent economic events have caused investors to become less risk-averse, causing the market return to decline by 2%, to 12%. Calculate the new required returns for assets A through E, and draw the new security market line on the same set of axes that you used in part **b.**

e. Compare your findings in parts **a** and **b** with those in part **d.** What conclusion can you draw about the impact of a decline in investor risk aversion on the required returns of risky assets?

LG 1 **P8–31 ETHICS PROBLEM** Risk is a major concern of almost all investors. When shareholders invest their money in a firm, they expect managers to take risks with those funds. What do you think are the ethical limits that managers should observe when taking risks with other people's money?

Spreadsheet Exercise

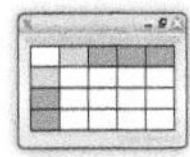

Jane is considering investing in three different stocks or creating three distinct two-stock portfolios. Jane considers herself to be a rather conservative investor. She is able to obtain forecasted returns for the three securities for the years 2013 through 2019. The data are as follows:

Year	Stock A	Stock B	Stock C
2013	10%	10%	12%
2014	13	11	14
2015	15	8	10
2016	14	12	11
2017	16	10	9
2018	14	15	9
2019	12	15	10

In any of the possible two-stock portfolios, the weight of each stock in the portfolio will be 50%. The three possible portfolio combinations are AB, AC, and BC.

TO DO

Create a spreadsheet similar to Tables 8.6 and 8.7 to answer the following:

a. Calculate the expected return for each individual stock.
b. Calculate the standard deviation for each individual stock.
c. Calculate the expected returns for portfolio AB, AC, and BC.
d. Calculate the standard deviations for portfolios AB, AC, and BC.
e. Would you recommend that Jane invest in the single stock A or the portfolio consisting of stocks A and B? Explain your answer from a risk–return viewpoint.
f. Would you recommend that Jane invest in the single stock B or the portfolio consisting of stocks B and C? Explain your answer from a risk–return viewpoint.

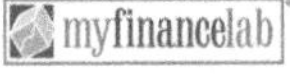

Visit www.myfinancelab.com for **Chapter Case: *Analyzing Risk and Return on Chargers Products' Investments,*** Group Exercises, and numerous online resources.

9 The Cost of Capital

Learning Goals

LG 1 Understand the basic concept and sources of capital associated with the cost of capital.

LG 2 Explain what is meant by the marginal cost of capital.

LG 3 Determine the cost of long-term debt, and explain why the after-tax cost of debt is the relevant cost of debt.

LG 4 Determine the cost of preferred stock.

LG 5 Calculate the cost of common stock equity, and convert it into the cost of retained earnings and the cost of new issues of common stock.

LG 6 Calculate the weighted average cost of capital (WACC), and discuss alternative weighting schemes.

Why This Chapter Matters to You

In your *professional* life

ACCOUNTING You need to understand the various sources of capital and how their costs are calculated to provide the data necessary to determine the firm's overall cost of capital.

INFORMATION SYSTEMS You need to understand the various sources of capital and how their costs are calculated to develop systems that will estimate the costs of those sources of capital, as well as the overall cost of capital.

MANAGEMENT You need to understand the cost of capital to select long-term investments after assessing their acceptability and relative rankings.

MARKETING You need to understand the firm's cost of capital because proposed projects must earn returns in excess of it to be acceptable.

OPERATIONS You need to understand the firm's cost of capital to assess the economic viability of investments in plant and equipment needed to improve or grow the firm's capacity.

In your *personal* life

Knowing your *personal cost of capital* will allow you to make informed decisions about your personal consuming, borrowing, and investing. Managing your personal wealth is a lot like managing the wealth of a business—you need to understand the trade-offs between consuming wealth and growing wealth and how growing wealth can be accomplished by investing your own monies or borrowed monies. Understanding the cost of capital concepts will allow you to make better long-term decisions and maximize the value of your personal wealth.

General Electric

Falling Short of Expectations

For years, General Electric was perhaps the most admired company in the world. From 1990 through 2000, its stock rose more than 800 percent, making it one of the world's most valuable companies and earning its long-time CEO, Jack Welch, the title of "Manager of the Century" from *Fortune* magazine. GE's stock price peaked in August 2000 at $60.50. Since then, however, GE stock has lost its luster, falling by roughly 50 percent and trailing far behind benchmarks such as the Standard & Poor's 500 Stock Index. In 2009, GE cut its dividend for the first time since the Great Depression and lost its coveted AAA credit rating.

Why did GE perform so poorly? A simple answer is that GE's business investments failed to earn a return sufficient to meet the expectations of investors. When a firm's operating results disappoint investors, its stock price will fall as investors sell their shares and move to a more attractive investment. As one expert explained, "GE has been destroying shareholder capital for years. Their cost of capital is about 5 percent, and their return on assets is about 1 percent. That mathematic equation can't remain too much longer."[1]

For companies to succeed, their investments have to earn a rate of return that exceeds investors' expectations. But how do companies know what investors expect? The answer is that companies have to measure their cost of capital. Read on to learn how firms do that.

1. *Pros Say,* December 15, 2009, cnbc.com, www.cnbc.com/id/34440926.

LG 1 LG 2 9.1 Overview of the Cost of Capital

Chapter 1 established that the goal of the firm is to maximize shareholder wealth, and it told us that financial managers achieve this goal by investing in risky projects that add value to the firm. In this chapter, you will learn about the cost of capital, which is the rate of return that financial managers use to evaluate all possible investment opportunities to determine which ones to invest in on behalf of the firm's shareholders. The **cost of capital** represents the firm's cost of financing and is the minimum rate of return that a project must earn to increase firm value. In particular, the cost of capital refers to the cost of the next dollar of financing necessary to finance a new investment opportunity. Investments with a rate of return above the cost of capital will increase the value of the firm, and projects with a rate of return below the cost of capital will decrease firm value.

cost of capital
Represents the firm's cost of financing and is the minimum rate of return that a project must earn to increase firm value.

The cost of capital is an extremely important financial concept. It acts as a major link between the firm's long-term investment decisions and the wealth of the firm's owners as determined by the market value of their shares. Financial managers are ethically bound to invest only in projects that they expect to exceed the cost of capital; see the *Focus on Ethics* box for more discussion of this responsibility.

THE BASIC CONCEPT

A firm's cost of capital is estimated at a given point in time and reflects the *expected average future cost of funds over the long run.* Although firms typically raise

focus on ETHICS

The Ethics of Profit

in practice *Business Week* once referred to Peter Drucker as "The Man Who Invented Management." In his role as writer and management consultant, Drucker stressed the importance of ethics to business leaders. He believed that it was the ethical responsibility of a business to earn a profit. In his mind, profitable businesses create opportunities, while unprofitable ones waste society's resources. Drucker once said, "Profit is not the explanation, cause, or rationale of business behavior and business decisions, but rather the test of their validity. If archangels instead of businessmen sat in directors' chairs, they would still have to be concerned with profitability, despite their total lack of personal interest in making profits."[a]

But what happens when businesses abandon ethics for profits? Consider Merck's experience with the drug, Vioxx. Introduced in 1999, Vioxx was an immediate success, quickly reaching $2.5 billion in annual sales. However, a Merck study launched in 1999 eventually found that patients who took Vioxx suffered from an increased risk of heart attacks and strokes. Despite the risks, Merck continued to market and sell Vioxx. By the time Vioxx was withdrawn from the market, an estimated 20 million Americans had taken the drug, 88,000 had suffered Vioxx-related heart attacks, and 38,000 had died.

News of the 2004 Vioxx withdrawal hit Merck's stock hard. The company's shares fell 27 percent on the day of the announcement, slashing $27 billion off the firm's market capitalization. Moody's, Standard & Poor's, and Fitch cut Merck's credit ratings, costing the firm its coveted AAA rating. The company's bottom line also suffered, as net income fell 21 percent in the final three months of 2004.

The recall dealt a major blow to Merck's reputation. The company was criticized for aggressively marketing Vioxx despite its serious side effects. Questions were also raised about the research reports Merck had submitted in support of the drug. Lawsuits followed. In 2008, Merck agreed to fund a $4.85 billion settlement to resolve approximately 50,000 Vioxx-related lawsuits. The company had also incurred $1.53 billion in legal costs by the time of the settlement.

► ***The Vioxx recall increased Merck's cost of capital. What effect would an increased cost of capital have on a firm's future investments?***

[a]Peter F. Drucker, *The Essential Drucker* (New York: Collins Business Essentials, 2001).

money in lumps, the cost of capital reflects the entirety of the firm's financing activities. For example, if a firm raises funds with debt (borrowing) today and at some future point sells common stock to raise additional financing, then the respective costs of both forms of capital should be reflected in the firm's cost of capital. Most firms attempt to maintain an optimal mix of debt and equity financing. In practice, this mix is commonly a range, such as 40 percent to 50 percent debt, rather than a point, such as 55 percent debt. This range is called a *target capital structure*—a topic that will be addressed in Chapter 13. Here, it is sufficient to say that although firms raise money in lumps, they tend toward some desired *mix of financing*.

To capture all of the relevant financing costs, assuming some desired mix of financing, we need to look at the *overall cost of capital* rather than just the cost of any single source of financing.

Example 9.1 ▸ A firm is *currently* faced with an investment opportunity. Assume the following:

Best project available today

Cost = \$100,000
Life = 20 years
Expected Return = 7%

Least costly financing source available

Debt = 6%

Because it can earn 7% on the investment of funds costing only 6%, the firm undertakes the opportunity. Imagine that *1 week later* a new investment opportunity is available:

Best project available 1 week later

Cost = \$100,000
Life = 20 years
Expected Return = 12%

Least costly financing source available

Equity = 14%

In this instance, the firm rejects the opportunity because the 14% financing cost is greater than the 12% expected return.

What if instead the firm used a *combined* cost of financing? By weighting the cost of each source of financing by its relative *proportion* in the firm's target capital structure, the firm can obtain a *weighted average cost of capital*. Assuming that a 50–50 mix of debt and equity is targeted, the weighted average cost here would be 10% [(0.50 × 6% debt) + (0.50 × 14% equity)]. With this average cost of financing, the first opportunity would have been rejected (7% expected return < 10% weighted average cost), and the second would have been accepted (12% expected return > 10% weighted average cost).

SOURCES OF LONG-TERM CAPITAL

In this chapter, our concern is only with the *long-term* sources of capital available to a firm because these are the sources that supply the financing necessary to support the firm's *capital budgeting* activities. Capital budgeting is the process of evaluating and selecting long-term investments. This process is intended to achieve the firm's goal of maximizing shareholders' wealth. Although the entire capital budgeting process is discussed throughout Part 5, at this point it is sufficient to say that capital budgeting activities are chief among the responsibilities of financial managers and that they cannot be carried out without knowing the appropriate cost of capital with which to judge the firm's investment opportunities.

There are four basic sources of long-term capital for firms: long-term debt, preferred stock, common stock, and retained earnings. All entries on the right-hand side of the balance sheet, other than current liabilities, represent these sources:

Balance Sheet		
Assets	Current liabilities	
	Long-term debt	Sources of long-term capital
	Stockholders' equity Preferred stock Common stock equity Common stock Retained earnings	

Not every firm will use all of these sources of financing, but most firms will have some mix of funds from these sources in their capital structures. Although a firm's existing mix of financing sources may reflect its target capital structure, it is ultimately the marginal cost of capital necessary to raise the next marginal dollar of financing that is relevant for evaluating the firm's future investment opportunities.

→ REVIEW QUESTIONS

9–1 What is the *cost of capital?*

9–2 What role does the cost of capital play in the firm's long-term investment decisions? How does it relate to the firm's ability to maximize shareholder wealth?

9–3 What does the firm's capital structure represent?

9–4 What are the typical sources of long-term capital available to the firm?

LG 3

9.2 Cost of Long-Term Debt

cost of long-term debt
The financing cost associated with new funds raised through long-term borrowing.

The **cost of long-term debt** is the financing cost associated with new funds raised through long-term borrowing. Typically, the funds are raised through the sale of corporate bonds.

NET PROCEEDS

net proceeds
Funds actually received by the firm from the sale of a security.

The **net proceeds** from the sale of a bond, or any security, are the funds that the firm receives from the sale. The total proceeds are reduced by the **flotation costs,**

flotation costs
The total costs of issuing and selling a security.

which represent the total costs of issuing and selling securities. These costs apply to all public offerings of securities—debt, preferred stock, and common stock. They include two components: (1) *underwriting costs*—compensation earned by investment bankers for selling the security—and (2) *administrative costs*—issuer expenses such as legal, accounting, and printing.

Example 9.2 ▸

Duchess Corporation, a major hardware manufacturer, is contemplating selling \$10 million worth of 20-year, 9% coupon (stated *annual* interest rate) bonds, each with a par value of \$1,000. Because bonds with similar risk earn returns greater than 9%, the firm must sell the bonds for \$980 to compensate for the lower coupon interest rate. The flotation costs are 2% of the par value of the bond ($0.02 \times \$1{,}000$), or \$20. The *net proceeds* to the firm from the sale of each bond are therefore \$960 (\$980 minus \$20).

BEFORE-TAX COST OF DEBT

The before-tax cost of debt, r_d, is simply the rate of return the firm must pay on new borrowing. A firm's before-tax cost of debt for bonds can be found in any of three ways: quotation, calculation, or approximation.

Using Market Quotations

A relatively quick method for finding the before-tax cost of debt is to observe the *yield to maturity (YTM)* on the firm's existing bonds or bonds of similar risk issued by other companies. The market price of existing bonds reflects the rate of return required by the market. For example, if the market requires a YTM of 9.7 percent for a similar-risk bond, then this value can be used as the before-tax cost of debt, r_d, for new bonds. Bond yields are widely reported by sources such as *The Wall Street Journal.*

Calculating the Cost

This approach finds the before-tax cost of debt by calculating the YTM generated by the bond cash flows. From the issuer's point of view, this value is the *cost to maturity* of the cash flows associated with the debt. The yield to maturity can be calculated by using a financial calculator or an electronic spreadsheet. It represents the annual before-tax percentage cost of the debt.

Example 9.3 ▸

In the preceding example, \$960 were the net proceeds of a 20-year bond with a \$1,000 par value and 9% coupon interest rate. The calculation of the annual cost is quite simple. The cash flow pattern associated with this bond's sales consists of an initial inflow (the net proceeds) followed by a series of annual outlays (the interest payments). In the final year, when the debt is retired, an outlay representing the repayment of the principal also occurs. The cash flows associated with Duchess Corporation's bond issue are as follows:

End of year(s)	Cash flow
0	\$ 960
1–20	−\$ 90
20	−\$1,000

The initial \$960 inflow is followed by annual interest outflows of \$90 (9% coupon interest rate × \$1,000 par value) over the 20-year life of the bond. In year 20, an outflow of \$1,000 (the repayment of the principal) occurs. We can determine the cost of debt by finding the YTM, which is the discount rate that equates the present value of the bond outflows to the initial inflow.

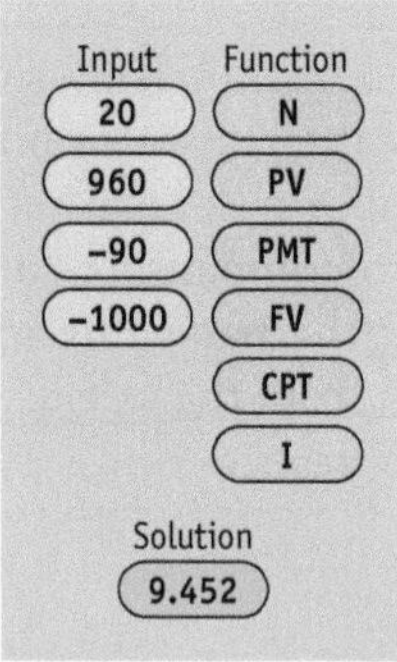

Calculator Use (*Note:* Most calculators require either the present value [net proceeds] or the future value [annual interest payments and repayment of principal] to be input as negative numbers when we calculate yield to maturity. That approach is used here.) Using the calculator and the inputs shown at the left, you should find the before-tax cost of debt (yield to maturity) to be 9.452%.

Spreadsheet Use The before-tax cost of debt on the Duchess Corporation bond can be calculated using an Excel spreadsheet. The following Excel spreadsheet shows that by referencing the cells containing the bond's net proceeds, coupon payment, years to maturity, and par value as part of Excel's RATE function you can quickly determine that the appropriate before-tax cost of debt for Duchess Corporation's bond is 9.452%.

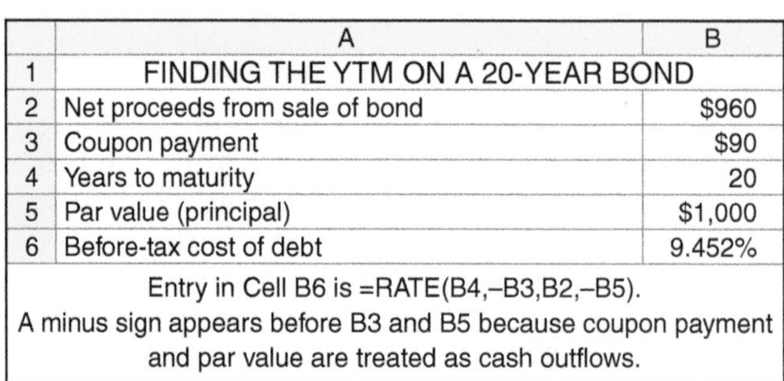

	A	B
1	FINDING THE YTM ON A 20-YEAR BOND	
2	Net proceeds from sale of bond	\$960
3	Coupon payment	\$90
4	Years to maturity	20
5	Par value (principal)	\$1,000
6	Before-tax cost of debt	9.452%

Entry in Cell B6 is =RATE(B4,–B3,B2,–B5).
A minus sign appears before B3 and B5 because coupon payment and par value are treated as cash outflows.

Although you may not recognize it, both the calculator and the Excel function are using trial-and-error to find the bond's YTM—they just do it faster than you can.

Approximating the Cost

Although not as precise as using a calculator, there is a method for quickly approximating the before-tax cost of debt. The before-tax cost of debt, r_d, for a bond with a \$1,000 par value can be approximated by using the following equation:

$$r_d = \frac{I + \dfrac{\$1{,}000 - N_d}{n}}{\dfrac{N_d + \$1{,}000}{2}} \quad (9.1)$$

where

I = annual interest in dollars

N_d = net proceeds from the sale of debt (bond)

n = number of years to the bond's maturity

Example 9.4 ▶ Substituting the appropriate values from the Duchess Corporation example into the approximation formula given in Equation 9.1, we get:

$$r_d = \frac{\$90 + \frac{\$1{,}000 - \$960}{20}}{\frac{\$960 + \$1{,}000}{2}} = \frac{\$90 + \$2}{\$980}$$

$$= \frac{\$92}{\$980} = 0.09388 \text{ or } \underline{\underline{9.388\%}}$$

This approximate value of before-tax cost of debt is close to the 9.452%, but it lacks the precision of the value derived using the calculator or spreadsheet.

AFTER-TAX COST OF DEBT

Unlike the dividends paid to equityholders, the interest payments paid to bondholders are tax deductable for the firm, so the interest expense on debt reduces the firm's taxable income and, therefore, the firm's tax liability. To find the firm's *net* cost of debt, we must account for the tax savings created by debt and solve for the cost of long-term debt on an after-tax basis. The after-tax cost of debt, r_i, can be found by multiplying the before-tax cost, r_d, by 1 minus the tax rate, T, as stated in the following equation:

$$r_i = r_d \times (1 - T) \tag{9.2}$$

Example 9.5 ▶ Duchess Corporation has a 40% tax rate. Using the 9.452% before-tax debt cost calculated above, and applying Equation 9.2, we find an after-tax cost of debt of 5.67% [9.452% × (1 − 0.40)]. Typically, the cost of long-term debt for a given firm is less than the cost of preferred or common stock, partly because of the tax deductibility of interest.

Personal Finance Example 9.6 ▶ Kait and Kasim Sullivan, a married couple in the 28% federal income-tax bracket, wish to borrow $60,000 to pay for a new luxury car. To finance the purchase, they can either borrow the $60,000 through the auto dealer at an annual interest rate of 6.0%, or they can take a $60,000 second mortgage on their home. The best annual rate they can get on the second mortgage is 7.2%. They already have qualified for both of the loans being considered.

If they borrow from the auto dealer, the interest on this "consumer loan" will not be deductible for federal tax purposes. However, the interest on the second mortgage would be tax deductible because the tax law allows individuals to deduct interest paid on a home mortgage. To choose the least-cost financing, the Sullivans calculated the after-tax cost of both sources of long-term debt. Because interest on the auto loan is *not* tax deductible, its after-tax cost equals its stated cost of 6.0%. Because the interest on the second mortgage *is* tax deductible, its after-tax cost can be found using Equation 9.2:

$$\text{After-tax cost of debt} = \text{Before-tax cost of debt} \times (1 - \text{Tax rate})$$
$$7.2\% \times (1 - 0.28) = 7.2\% \times 0.72 = \underline{\underline{5.2\%}}$$

Because the 5.2% after-tax cost of the second mortgage is less than the 6.0% cost of the auto loan, the Sullivans should use the second mortgage to finance the auto purchase.

→ **REVIEW QUESTIONS**

9–5 What are the *net proceeds* from the sale of a bond? What are *flotation costs,* and how do they affect a bond's net proceeds?

9–6 What methods can be used to find the before-tax cost of debt?

9–7 How is the before-tax cost of debt converted into the after-tax cost?

LG 4

9.3 Cost of Preferred Stock

Preferred stock represents a special type of ownership interest in the firm. It gives preferred stockholders the right to receive their *stated* dividends before the firm can distribute any earnings to common stockholders. The key characteristics of preferred stock were described in Chapter 7. However, the one aspect of preferred stock that requires review is dividends.

PREFERRED STOCK DIVIDENDS

Most preferred stock dividends are stated as a *dollar amount:* "*x* dollars per year." When dividends are stated this way, the stock is often referred to as "*x*-dollar preferred stock." Thus a "$4 preferred stock" is expected to pay preferred stockholders $4 in dividends each year on each share of preferred stock owned.

Sometimes preferred stock dividends are stated as an *annual percentage rate.* This rate represents the percentage of the stock's par, or face, value that equals the annual dividend. For instance, an 8 percent preferred stock with a $50 par value would be expected to pay an annual dividend of $4 per share (0.08 × $50 par = $4). Before the cost of preferred stock is calculated, any dividends stated as percentages should be converted to annual dollar dividends.

CALCULATING THE COST OF PREFERRED STOCK

cost of preferred stock, r_p
The ratio of the preferred stock dividend to the firm's net proceeds from the sale of preferred stock.

The **cost of preferred stock, r_p,** is the ratio of the preferred stock dividend to the firm's net proceeds from the sale of the preferred stock. The net proceeds represent the amount of money to be received minus any flotation costs. Equation 9.3 gives the cost of preferred stock, r_p, in terms of the annual dollar dividend, D_p, and the net proceeds from the sale of the stock, N_p:

$$r_p = \frac{D_p}{N_p} \tag{9.3}$$

Example 9.7 ▶ Duchess Corporation is contemplating issuance of a 10% preferred stock that they expect to sell for \$87 per share. The cost of issuing and selling the stock will be \$5 per share. The first step in finding the cost of the stock is to calculate the dollar amount of the annual preferred dividend, which is \$8.70 (0.10 × \$87). The net proceeds per share from the proposed sale of stock equals the sale price minus the flotation costs (\$87 − \$5 = \$82). Substituting the annual dividend, D_p, of \$8.70 and the net proceeds, N_p, of \$82 into Equation 9.3 gives the cost of preferred stock, 10.6% (\$8.70 ÷ \$82).

The cost of Duchess's preferred stock (10.6%) is much greater than the cost of its long-term debt (5.67%). This difference exists both because the cost of long-term debt (the interest) is tax deductible and because preferred stock is riskier than long-term debt.

→ REVIEW QUESTION

9–8 How would you calculate the cost of preferred stock?

LG 5

9.4 Cost of Common Stock

In more depth

To read about *Subjective Techniques,* go to www.myfinancelab.com

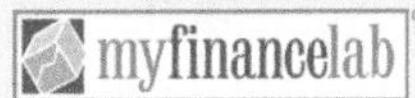

The *cost of common stock* is the return required on the stock by investors in the marketplace. There are two forms of common stock financing: (1) retained earnings and (2) new issues of common stock. As a first step in finding each of these costs, we must estimate the cost of common stock equity.

FINDING THE COST OF COMMON STOCK EQUITY

cost of common stock equity, r_s
The rate at which investors discount the expected dividends of the firm to determine its share value.

The **cost of common stock equity, r_s,** is the rate at which investors discount the expected common stock dividends of the firm to determine its share value. Two techniques are used to measure the cost of common stock equity. One relies on the constant-growth valuation model, the other on the capital asset pricing model (CAPM).

Using the Constant-Growth Valuation (Gordon Growth) Model

constant-growth valuation (Gordon growth) model
Assumes that the value of a share of stock equals the present value of all future dividends (assumed to grow at a constant rate) that it is expected to provide over an infinite time horizon.

In Chapter 7 we found the value of a share of stock to be equal to the present value of all future dividends, which in one model were assumed to grow at a constant annual rate over an infinite time horizon. This is the **constant-growth valuation model,** also known as the **Gordon growth model.** The key expression derived for this model was presented as Equation 7.4 and is restated here:

$$P_0 = \frac{D_1}{r_s - g} \qquad (9.4)$$

where

P_0 = value of common stock
D_1 = per-share dividend *expected* at the end of year 1
r_s = required return on common stock
g = constant rate of growth in dividends

Solving Equation 9.4 for r_s results in the following expression for the *cost of common stock equity:*

$$r_s = \frac{D_1}{P_0} + g \tag{9.5}$$

Equation 9.5 indicates that the cost of common stock equity can be found by dividing the dividend expected at the end of year 1 by the current market price of the stock (the "dividend yield") and adding the expected growth rate (the "capital gains yield").

Example 9.8 ▸

Duchess Corporation wishes to determine its cost of common stock equity, r_s. The market price, P_0, of its common stock is $50 per share. The firm expects to pay a dividend, D_1, of $4 at the end of the coming year, 2013. The dividends paid on the outstanding stock over the past 6 years (2007 through 2012) were as follows:

Year	Dividend
2012	$3.80
2011	3.62
2010	3.47
2009	3.33
2008	3.12
2007	2.97

Using a financial calculator or electronic spreadsheet, in conjunction with the technique described for finding growth rates in Chapter 5, we can calculate the annual rate at which dividends have grown, g, from 2007 to 2012. It turns out to be approximately 5% (more precisely, it is 5.05%). Substituting $D_1 = \$4$, $P_0 = \$50$, and $g = 5\%$ into Equation 9.5 yields the cost of common stock equity:

$$r_s = \frac{\$4}{\$50} + 0.05 = 0.08 + 0.05 = 0.130 \text{ or } \underline{\underline{13.0\%}}$$

The 13.0% cost of common stock equity represents the return required by *existing* shareholders on their investment. If the actual return is less than that, shareholders are likely to begin selling their stock.

Using the Capital Asset Pricing Model (CAPM)

capital asset pricing model (CAPM)
Describes the relationship between the required return, r_s, and the nondiversifiable risk of the firm as measured by the beta coefficient, b.

Recall from Chapter 8 that the **capital asset pricing model (CAPM)** describes the relationship between the required return, r_s, and the nondiversifiable risk of the firm as measured by the beta coefficient, b. The basic CAPM is:

$$r_s = R_F + [b \times (r_m - R_F)] \tag{9.6}$$

where

R_F = risk-free rate of return

r_m = market return; return on the market portfolio of assets

Using the CAPM indicates that the cost of common stock equity is the return required by investors as compensation for the firm's nondiversifiable risk, measured by beta.

Example 9.9 ▸

Duchess Corporation now wishes to calculate its cost of common stock equity, r_s, by using the CAPM. The firm's investment advisors and its own analysts indicate that the risk-free rate, R_F, equals 7%; the firm's beta, b, equals 1.5; and the market return, r_m, equals 11%. Substituting these values into Equation 9.6, the company estimates the cost of common stock equity, r_s, to be:

$$r_s = 7.0\% + [1.5 \times (11.0\% - 7.0\%)] = 7.0\% + 6.0\% = \underline{\underline{13.0}}\%$$

The 13.0% cost of common stock equity represents the required return of investors in Duchess Corporation common stock. It is the same as that found by using the constant-growth valuation model.

Comparing Constant-Growth and CAPM Techniques

The CAPM technique differs from the constant-growth valuation model in that it directly considers the firm's risk, as reflected by beta, in determining the *required* return or cost of common stock equity. The constant-growth model does not look at risk; it uses the market price, P_0, as a reflection of the *expected* risk–return preference of investors in the marketplace. The constant-growth valuation and CAPM techniques for finding r_s are theoretically equivalent, though in practice estimates from the two methods do not always agree. The two methods can produce different estimates because they require (as inputs) estimates of other quantities, such as the expected dividend growth rate or the firm's beta.

Another difference is that when the constant-growth valuation model is used to find the cost of common stock equity, it can easily be adjusted for flotation costs to find the cost of new common stock; the CAPM does not provide a simple adjustment mechanism. The difficulty in adjusting the cost of common stock equity calculated by using the CAPM occurs because in its common form the model does not include the market price, P_0, a variable needed to make such an adjustment. Although the CAPM has a stronger theoretical foundation, the computational appeal of the traditional constant-growth valuation model justifies its use throughout this text to measure financing costs of common stock. As a practical matter, analysts might want to estimate the cost of equity using both approaches and then take an average of the results to arrive at a final estimate of the cost of equity.

COST OF RETAINED EARNINGS

As you know, dividends are paid out of a firm's earnings. Their payment, made in cash to common stockholders, reduces the firm's retained earnings. Suppose a firm needs common stock equity financing of a certain amount. It has two choices relative to retained earnings: It can issue additional common stock in that amount and still pay dividends to stockholders out of retained earnings, or it can increase common stock equity by retaining the earnings (not paying the cash dividends) in the needed amount. In a strict accounting sense, the retention of earnings increases common stock equity in the same way that the sale of additional shares of common stock does. Thus the **cost of retained earnings, r_r,** to the firm is the same as the cost of an *equivalent fully subscribed issue of additional common stock.*

cost of retained earnings, r_r
The same as the cost of an *equivalent fully subscribed issue of additional common stock,* which is equal to the cost of common stock equity, r_s.

Stockholders find the firm's retention of earnings acceptable only if they expect that it will earn at least their required return on the reinvested funds.

Viewing retained earnings as a fully subscribed issue of additional common stock, we can set the firm's cost of retained earnings, r_r, equal to the cost of common stock equity as given by Equations 9.5 and 9.6.

$$r_r = r_s \tag{9.7}$$

It is not necessary to adjust the cost of retained earnings for flotation costs because by retaining earnings the firm "raises" equity capital without incurring these costs.

Example 9.10 ▶ The cost of retained earnings for Duchess Corporation was actually calculated in the preceding examples: It is equal to the cost of common stock equity. Thus r_r equals 13.0%. As we will show in the next section, the cost of retained earnings is always lower than the cost of a new issue of common stock because it entails no flotation costs.

Matter of fact

Retained Earnings, the Preferred Source of Financing

In the United States and most other countries, firms rely more heavily on retained earnings than any other financing source. For example, a 2010 survey of CEOs by the Australian Industry Group and Deloitte reported that the vast majority of Australian firms see retained earnings as their most important source of finance. Almost 65% of CEOs surveyed said that retained earnings was their most preferred source of financing, with bank debt coming in as a distant second choice.[2]

COST OF NEW ISSUES OF COMMON STOCK

cost of a new issue of common stock, r_n
The cost of common stock, net of underpricing and associated flotation costs.

underpriced
Stock sold at a price below its current market price, P_0.

Our purpose in finding the firm's overall cost of capital is to determine the after-tax cost of *new* funds required for financing projects. The **cost of a new issue of common stock, r_n,** is determined by calculating the cost of common stock, net of underpricing and associated flotation costs. Normally, when new shares are issued they are **underpriced**—sold at a discount relative to the current market price, P_0. Underpricing is the difference between the market price and the issue price, which is the price paid by the primary market investors discussed in Chapter 2.

We can use the constant-growth valuation model expression for the cost of existing common stock, r_s, as a starting point. If we let N_n represent the net proceeds from the sale of new common stock after subtracting underpricing and flotation costs, the cost of the new issue, r_n, can be expressed as follows:[3]

$$r_n = \frac{D_1}{N_n} + g \tag{9.8}$$

2. Australian Industry Group and Deloitte, *National CEO Survey: Growth Strategies for Business,* Report, October 2010.

3. An alternative, but computationally less straightforward, form of this equation is

$$r_n = \frac{D_1}{P_0 \times (1 - f)} + g \tag{9.8a}$$

where f represents the *percentage* reduction in current market price expected as a result of underpricing and flotation costs. Simply stated, N_n in Equation 9.8 is equivalent to $P_0 \times (1 - f)$ in Equation 9.8a. For convenience, Equation 9.8 is used to define the cost of a new issue of common stock, r_n.

The net proceeds from sale of new common stock, N_n, will be less than the current market price, P_0. Therefore, the cost of new issues, r_n, will always be greater than the cost of existing issues, r_s, which is equal to the cost of retained earnings, r_r. *The cost of new common stock is normally greater than any other long-term financing cost.*

Example 9.11 ▶ In the constant-growth valuation example, we found Duchess Corporation's cost of common stock equity, r_s, to be 13%, using the following values: an expected dividend, D_1, of \$4; a current market price, P_0, of \$50; and an expected growth rate of dividends, g, of 5%.

To determine its cost of *new* common stock, r_n, Duchess Corporation has estimated that on average, new shares can be sold for \$47. The \$3-per-share underpricing is due to the competitive nature of the market. A second cost associated with a new issue is flotation costs of \$2.50 per share that would be paid to issue and sell the new shares. The total underpricing and flotation costs per share are therefore \$5.50.

Subtracting the \$5.50-per-share underpricing and flotation cost from the current \$50 share price results in expected net proceeds of \$44.50 per share (\$50.00 minus \$5.50). Substituting $D_1 = \$4$, $N_n = \$44.50$, and $g = 5\%$ into Equation 9.8 results in a cost of new common stock, r_n, as follows:

$$r_n = \frac{\$4.00}{\$44.50} + 0.05 = 0.09 + 0.05 = 0.140 \text{ or } \underline{\underline{14.0\%}}$$

Duchess Corporation's cost of new common stock is therefore 14.0%. This is the value to be used in subsequent calculations of the firm's overall cost of capital.

→ REVIEW QUESTIONS

9–9 What premise about share value underlies the constant-growth valuation (Gordon growth) model that is used to measure the cost of common stock equity, r_s?

9–10 How do the constant-growth valuation model and capital asset pricing model methods for finding the cost of common stock differ?

9–11 Why is the cost of financing a project with retained earnings less than the cost of financing it with a new issue of common stock?

LG 6

9.5 Weighted Average Cost of Capital

weighted average cost of capital (WACC), r_a
Reflects the expected average future cost of capital over the long run; found by weighting the cost of each specific type of capital by its proportion in the firm's capital structure.

Now that we have calculated the cost of specific sources of financing, we can determine the overall cost of capital. As noted earlier, the **weighted average cost of capital (WACC), r_a,** reflects the expected average future cost of capital over the long run. It is found by weighting the cost of each specific type of capital by its proportion in the firm's capital structure.

CALCULATING WEIGHTED AVERAGE COST OF CAPITAL (WACC)

Calculating the weighted average cost of capital (WACC) is straightforward: Multiply the individual cost of each form of financing by its proportion in the firm's capital structure and sum the weighted values. As an equation, the weighted average cost of capital, r_a, can be specified as follows:

$$r_a = (w_i \times r_i) + (w_p \times r_p) + (w_s \times r_{r \text{ or } n}) \tag{9.9}$$

where

w_i = proportion of long-term debt in capital structure
w_p = proportion of preferred stock in capital structure
w_s = proportion of common stock equity in capital structure
$w_i + w_p + w_s = 1.0$

Three important points should be noted in Equation 9.9:

1. For computational convenience, it is best to convert the weights into decimal form and leave the individual costs in percentage terms.
2. *The weights must be nonnegative and sum to 1.0.* Simply stated, WACC must account for all financing costs within the firm's capital structure.
3. The firm's common stock equity weight, w_s, is multiplied by either the cost of retained earnings, r_r, or the cost of new common stock, r_n. Which cost is used depends on whether the firm's common stock equity will be financed using retained earnings, r_r, or new common stock, r_n.

Example 9.12 ▸ In earlier examples, we found the costs of the various types of capital for Duchess Corporation to be as follows:

Cost of debt, r_i = 5.6%
Cost of preferred stock, r_p = 10.6%
Cost of retained earnings, r_r = 13.0%
Cost of new common stock, r_n = 14.0%

The company uses the following weights in calculating its weighted average cost of capital:

Source of capital	Weight
Long-term debt	40%
Preferred stock	10
Common stock equity	50
Total	100%

Because the firm expects to have a sizable amount of retained earnings available ($300,000), it plans to use its cost of retained earnings, r_r, as the cost of common stock equity. Duchess Corporation's weighted average cost of capital is calculated in Table 9.1. The resulting weighted average cost of capital for Duchess is 9.8%. Assuming an unchanged risk level, the firm should accept all projects that will earn a return greater than 9.8%.

TABLE 9.1 **Calculation of the Weighted Average Cost of Capital for Duchess Corporation**

Source of capital	Weight (1)	Cost (2)	Weighted cost [(1) × (2)] (3)
Long-term debt	0.40	5.6%	2.2%
Preferred stock	0.10	10.6	1.1
Common stock equity	0.50	13.0	6.5
Totals	1.00		WACC = 9.8%

focus on **PRACTICE**

Uncertain Times Make for an Uncertain Weighted Average Cost of Capital

in practice As U.S. financial markets experienced and recovered from the 2008 financial crisis and 2009 "great recession," firms struggled to keep track of their weighted average cost of capital. The individual component costs were moving rapidly in response to the financial market turmoil. Volatile financial markets can make otherwise manageable cost-of-capital calculations exceedingly complex and inherently error prone—possibly wreaking havoc with investment decisions. If a firm underestimates its cost of capital it risks making investments that are not economically justified, and if a firm overestimates its financing costs it risks foregoing value-maximizing investments.

Although the WACC computation does not change when markets become unstable, the uncertainty surrounding the components that comprise the WACC increases dramatically. The financial crisis pushed credit costs to a point where long-term debt was largely inaccessible, and the great recession saw Treasury bond yields fall to historic lows, making cost of equity projections appear unreasonably low. With these key components in flux, it is exceedingly difficult, if not impossible, for firms to get a handle on a cost of long-term capital.

According to *CFO Magazine*, at least one firm resorted to a two-pronged approach for determining its cost of capital during the uncertain times. Ron Domanico is the chief financial officer (CFO) at Caraustar Industries, Inc., and he reported that his company dealt with the cost-of-capital uncertainty by abandoning the conventional one-size-fits-all approach. "In the past, we had one cost of capital that we applied to all our investment decisions . . . today that's not the case. We have a short-term cost of capital we apply to short-term opportunities, and a longer-term cost of capital we apply to longer-term opportunities . . . and the reality is that the longer-term cost is so high that it has forced us to focus only on those projects that have immediate returns," Mr. Domanico is quoted saying.[a]

Part of Caraustar's motivation for implementing this two-pronged approach was to account for the excessively large spread between short- and long-term debt rates that emerged during the financial market crisis. Mr. Domanico reported that during the crisis Caraustar could borrow short-term funds at the lower of Prime plus 4 percent or LIBOR plus 5 percent—where either rate was reasonable for making short-term investment decisions. Alternatively, long-term investment decisions were being required to clear Caraustar's long-term cost-of-capital calculation accounting for borrowing rates in excess of 12 percent.

▶ ***Why don't firms generally use both short- and long-run weighted average costs of capital?***

[a]Randy Myers, "A Losing Formula" (May 2009), **www.cfo.com/article.cfm/13522582/c_13526469.**

WEIGHTING SCHEMES

Firms can calculate weights on the basis of either *book value* or *market value* using either *historical* or *target* proportions.

book value weights
Weights that use accounting values to measure the proportion of each type of capital in the firm's financial structure.

market value weights
Weights that use market values to measure the proportion of each type of capital in the firm's financial structure.

historical weights
Either book or market value weights based on *actual* capital structure proportions.

target weights
Either book or market value weights based on *desired* capital structure proportions.

Book Value versus Market Value

Book value weights use accounting values to measure the proportion of each type of capital in the firm's financial structure. **Market value weights** measure the proportion of each type of capital at its market value. Market value weights are appealing because the market values of securities closely approximate the actual dollars to be received from their sale. Moreover, because firms calculate the costs of the various types of capital by using prevailing market prices, it seems reasonable to use market value weights. In addition, the long-term investment cash flows to which the cost of capital is applied are estimated in terms of current as well as future market values. *Market value weights are clearly preferred over book value weights.*

Historical versus Target

Historical weights can be either book or market value weights based on *actual* capital structure proportions. For example, past or current book value proportions would constitute a form of historical weighting, as would past or current market value proportions. Such a weighting scheme would therefore be based on real—rather than desired—proportions.

Target weights, which can also be based on either book or market values, reflect the firm's *desired* capital structure proportions. Firms using target weights establish such proportions on the basis of the "optimal" capital structure they wish to achieve. (The development of these proportions and the optimal structure are discussed in detail in Chapter 13.)

When one considers the somewhat approximate nature of the calculation of weighted average cost of capital, the choice of weights may not be critical. However, from a strictly theoretical point of view, the *preferred weighting scheme is target market value proportions,* and we assume these throughout this chapter.

In more depth

To read about *Changes in the Weighted Average Cost of Capital,* go to www.myfinancelab.com

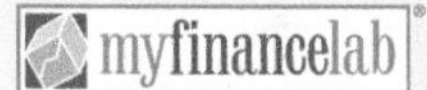

Personal Finance Example 9.13 ▸ Chuck Solis currently has three loans outstanding, all of which mature in exactly 6 years and can be repaid without penalty any time prior to maturity. The outstanding balances and annual interest rates on these loans are noted in the following table.

Loan	Outstanding balance	Annual interest rate
1	$26,000	9.6%
2	9,000	10.6
3	45,000	7.4

After a thorough search, Chuck found a lender who would loan him $80,000 for 6 years at an annual interest rate of 9.2% on the condition that the loan proceeds be used to fully repay the three outstanding loans, which combined have an outstanding balance of $80,000 ($26,000 + $9,000 + $45,000).

Chuck wishes to choose the least costly alternative: (1) to do nothing or (2) to borrow the $80,000 and pay off all three loans. He calculates the weighted average cost of his current debt by weighting each debt's annual interest cost by the proportion of the \$80,000 total it represents and then summing the three weighted values as follows:

$$\begin{aligned}\text{Weighted average cost of current debt} &= [(\$26{,}000 \div \$80{,}000) \times 9.6\%] + [(\$9{,}000 \div \$80{,}000) \\ &\quad \times 10.6\%] + [(\$45{,}000 \div \$80{,}000) \times 7.4\%] \\ &= (.3250 \times 9.6\%) + (.1125 \times 10.6\%) + (.5625 \times 7.4\%) \\ &= 3.12\% + 1.19\% + 4.16\% = 8.47\% \approx \underline{\underline{8.5}}\%\end{aligned}$$

Given that the weighted average cost of the \$80,000 of current debt of 8.5% is below the 9.2% cost of the new \$80,000 loan, Chuck should do nothing, and just continue to pay off the three loans as originally scheduled.

→ REVIEW QUESTIONS

9–12 What is the *weighted average cost of capital (WACC)*, and how is it calculated?

9–13 What is the relationship between the firm's target capital structure and the *weighted average cost of capital (WACC)?*

9–14 Describe the logic underlying the use of *target weights* to calculate the WACC, and compare and contrast this approach with the use of *historical weights*. What is the preferred weighting scheme?

Summary

FOCUS ON VALUE

The cost of capital is an extremely important rate of return, particularly in capital budgeting decisions. It is the expected average future cost to the firm of funds over the long run. Because the cost of capital is the pivotal rate of return used in the investment decision process, its accuracy can significantly affect the quality of these decisions.

Underestimation of the cost of capital can make poor projects look attractive; overestimation can make good projects look unattractive. By applying the techniques presented in this chapter to estimate the firm's cost of capital, the financial manager will improve the likelihood that the firm's long-term decisions will be consistent with the firm's overall goal of **maximizing stock price (owner wealth).**

REVIEW OF LEARNING GOALS

LG 1 **Understand the basic concept and sources of capital associated with the cost of capital.** The cost of capital is the minimum rate of return that a firm must earn on its investments to grow firm value. A weighted average cost of capital should be used to find the expected average future cost of funds over the long run. The individual costs of the basic sources of capital (long-term debt, preferred stock, retained earnings, and common stock) can be calculated separately.

LG 2 **Explain what is meant by the marginal cost of capital.** The relevant cost of capital for a firm is the marginal cost of capital necessary to raise the next marginal dollar of financing to fund the firm's future investment opportunities. A firm's future investment opportunities in expectation will be required to exceed the firm's cost of capital.

LG 3 **Determine the cost of long-term debt, and explain why the after-tax cost of debt is the relevant cost of debt.** The before-tax cost of long-term debt can be found by using cost quotations, calculations (either by calculator or spreadsheet), or an approximation. The after-tax cost of debt is calculated by multiplying the before-tax cost of debt by 1 minus the tax rate. The after-tax cost of debt is the relevant cost of debt because it is the lowest possible cost of debt for the firm due to the deductibility of interest expenses.

LG 4 **Determine the cost of preferred stock.** The cost of preferred stock is the ratio of the preferred stock dividend to the firm's net proceeds from the sale of preferred stock.

LG 5 **Calculate the cost of common stock equity, and convert it into the cost of retained earnings and the cost of new issues of common stock.** The cost of common stock equity can be calculated by using the constant-growth valuation (Gordon growth) model or the CAPM. The cost of retained earnings is equal to the cost of common stock equity. An adjustment in the cost of common stock equity to reflect underpricing and flotation costs is necessary to find the cost of new issues of common stock.

LG 6 **Calculate the weighted average cost of capital (WACC), and discuss alternative weighting schemes.** The firm's WACC reflects the expected average future cost of funds over the long run. It combines the costs of specific types of capital after weighting each of them by its proportion. The theoretically preferred approach uses target weights based on market values.

Opener-in-Review

The chapter opener claimed that GE's cost of capital in late 2009 was about 5%. Suppose that GE could use $1 billion to make an investment that would generate positive cash flow of $60 million every year in perpetuity. At a 5 percent discount rate, what would be the value of this cash flow to investors? How much would such an investment add to GE's market value? Now suppose that the investment actually produces just $10 million per year in perpetuity (or about 1 percent per year relative to the cost of the investment). What is the value of this investment to shareholders, and by how much would GE's market value fall because of this investment?

Self-Test Problem (Solutions in Appendix)

LG 3 LG 4 LG 5 LG 6

ST9–1 Individual costs and WACC Humble Manufacturing is interested in measuring its overall cost of capital. The firm is in the 40% tax bracket. Current investigation has gathered the following data:

Debt The firm can raise debt by selling $1,000-par-value, 10% coupon interest rate, 10-year bonds on which *annual interest* payments will be made. To sell the issue, an average discount of $30 per bond must be given. The firm must also pay flotation costs of $20 per bond.

Preferred stock The firm can sell 11% (annual dividend) preferred stock at its $100-per-share par value. The cost of issuing and selling the preferred stock is expected to be $4 per share.

Common stock The firm's common stock is currently selling for $80 per share. The firm expects to pay cash dividends of $6 per share next year. The firm's dividends have been growing at an annual rate of 6%, and this rate is expected to continue in the future. The stock will have to be underpriced by $4 per share, and flotation costs are expected to amount to $4 per share.

Retained earnings The firm expects to have $225,000 of retained earnings available in the coming year. Once these retained earnings are exhausted, the firm will use new common stock as the form of common stock equity financing.

a. Calculate the individual cost of each source of financing. (Round to the nearest 0.1%.)

b. Calculate the firm's weighted average cost of capital using the weights shown in the following table, which are based on the firm's target capital structure proportions. (Round to the nearest 0.1%.)

Source of capital	Weight
Long-term debt	40%
Preferred stock	15
Common stock equity	45
Total	100%

c. In which, if any, of the investments shown in the following table do you recommend that the firm invest? Explain your answer. How much new financing is required?

Investment opportunity	Expected rate of return	Initial investment
A	11.2%	$100,000
B	9.7	500,000
C	12.9	150,000
D	16.5	200,000
E	11.8	450,000
F	10.1	600,000
G	10.5	300,000

Warm-Up Exercises

All problems are available in myfinancelab.

LG 3 **E9–1** A firm raises capital by selling $20,000 worth of debt with flotation costs equal to 2% of its par value. If the debt matures in 10 years and has a coupon interest rate of 8%, what is the bond's YTM?

LG 4 **E9–2** Your firm, People's Consulting Group, has been asked to consult on a potential preferred stock offering by Brave New World. This 15% preferred stock issue would be sold at its par value of $35 per share. Flotation costs would total $3 per share. Calculate the cost of this preferred stock.

LG 5 **E9–3** Duke Energy has been paying dividends steadily for 20 years. During that time, dividends have grown at a compound annual rate of 7%. If Duke Energy's current stock price is $78 and the firm plans to pay a dividend of $6.50 next year, what is Duke's *cost of common stock equity*?

LG 6 **E9–4** Weekend Warriors, Inc., has 35% debt and 65% equity in its capital structure. The firm's estimated after-tax cost of debt is 8% and its estimated cost of equity is 13%. Determine the firm's *weighted average cost of capital (WACC)*.

LG 6 **E9–5** Oxy Corporation uses debt, preferred stock, and common stock to raise capital. The firm's capital structure targets the following proportions: debt, 55%; preferred stock, 10%; and common stock, 35%. If the cost of debt is 6.7%, preferred stock costs 9.2%, and common stock costs 10.6%, what is Oxy's *weighted average cost of capital (WACC)*?

Problems

All problems are available in myfinancelab.

LG 1 **P9–1 Concept of cost of capital** Wren Manufacturing is in the process of analyzing its investment decision-making procedures. The two projects evaluated by the firm during the past month were projects 263 and 264. The basic variables surrounding each project analysis and the resulting decision actions are summarized in the following table.

Basic variables	Project 263	Project 264
Cost	$64,000	$58,000
Life	15 years	15 years
Expected return	8%	15%
Least-cost financing		
Source	Debt	Equity
Cost (after-tax)	7%	16%
Decision		
Action	Invest	Don't invest
Reason	8% > 7% cost	15% < 16% cost

a. Evaluate the firm's decision-making procedures, and explain why the acceptance of project 263 and rejection of project 264 may not be in the owners' best interest.

b. If the firm maintains a capital structure containing 40% debt and 60% equity, find its *weighted average cost* using the data in the table.

c. If the firm had used the weighted average cost calculated in part **b,** what actions would have been indicated relative to projects 263 and 264?

d. Compare and contrast the firm's actions with your findings in part **c.** Which decision method seems more appropriate? Explain why.

LG 3 **P9–2 Cost of debt using both methods** Currently, Warren Industries can sell 15-year, $1,000-par-value bonds paying *annual interest* at a 12% coupon rate. As a result of current interest rates, the bonds can be sold for $1,010 each; flotation costs of $30 per bond will be incurred in this process. The firm is in the 40% tax bracket.

a. Find the net proceeds from sale of the bond, N_d.
b. Show the cash flows from the firm's point of view over the maturity of the bond.
c. Calculate the before-tax and after-tax costs of debt.
d. Use the *approximation formula* to estimate the before-tax and after-tax costs of debt.
e. Compare and contrast the costs of debt calculated in parts **c** and **d.** Which approach do you prefer? Why?

Personal Finance Problem

LG 3 **P9–3 Before-tax cost of debt and after-tax cost of debt** David Abbot is interested in purchasing a bond issued by Sony. He has obtained the following information on the security:

Sony bond			
Par value	$1,000	Coupon interest rate 6%	Tax bracket 20%
Cost	$ 930	Years to maturity 10	

Answer the following questions.

a. Calculate the *before-tax cost* of the Sony bond.
b. Calculate the *after-tax cost* of the Sony bond given David's tax bracket.

LG 3 **P9–4 Cost of debt using the approximation formula** For each of the following $1,000-par-value bonds, assuming *annual interest* payment and a 40% tax rate, calculate the *after-tax* cost to maturity using the *approximation formula.*

Bond	Life (years)	Underwriting fee	Discount (−) or premium (+)	Coupon interest rate
A	20	$25	−$20	9%
B	16	40	+10	10
C	15	30	−15	12
D	25	15	Par	9
E	22	20	−60	11

LG 3 **P9–5 The cost of debt** Gronseth Drywall Systems, Inc., is in discussions with its investment bankers regarding the issuance of new bonds. The investment banker has informed the firm that different maturities will carry different coupon rates and sell at different prices. The firm must choose among several alternatives. In each case, the bonds will have a $1,000 par value and flotation costs will be $30 per bond. The company is taxed at a rate of 40%. Calculate the *after-tax cost of financing* with each of the following alternatives.

Alternative	Coupon rate	Time to maturity (years)	Premium or discount
A	9%	16	$250
B	7	5	50
C	6	7	par
D	5	10	− 75

Personal Finance Problem

LG 3 **P9–6 After-tax cost of debt** Rick and Stacy Stark, a married couple, are interested in purchasing their first boat. They have decided to borrow the boat's purchase price of $100,000. The family is in the 28% federal income tax bracket. There are two choices for the Stark family: They can borrow the money from the boat dealer at an annual interest rate of 8%, or they could take out a $100,000 second mortgage on their home. Currently, home equity loans are at rates of 9.2%. There is no problem securing either of these two alternative financing choices.

Rick and Stacy learn that if they borrow from the boat dealership, the interest will not be tax deductible. However, the interest on the second mortgage will qualify as being tax deductible on their federal income tax return.

a. Calculate the *after-tax cost* of borrowing from the boat dealership.

b. Calculate the *after-tax cost* of borrowing through a second mortgage on their home.

c. Which source of borrowing is less costly for the Stark family?

LG 4 **P9–7 Cost of preferred stock** Taylor Systems has just issued preferred stock. The stock has a 12% annual dividend and a $100 par value and was sold at $97.50 per share. In addition, flotation costs of $2.50 per share must be paid.

a. Calculate the *cost of the preferred stock*.

b. If the firm sells the preferred stock with a 10% annual dividend and nets $90.00 after flotation costs, what is its cost?

LG 4 **P9–8 Cost of preferred stock** Determine the cost for each of the following preferred stocks.

Preferred stock	Par value	Sale price	Flotation cost	Annual dividend
A	$100	$101	$9.00	11%
B	40	38	$3.50	8%
C	35	37	$4.00	$5.00
D	30	26	5% of par	$3.00
E	20	20	$2.50	9%

LG 5 **P9–9 Cost of common stock equity—CAPM** J&M Corporation common stock has a beta, b, of 1.2. The risk-free rate is 6%, and the market return is 11%.

a. Determine the risk premium on J&M common stock.

b. Determine the required return that J&M common stock should provide.

c. Determine J&M's *cost of common stock equity* using the CAPM.

LG 5 **P9–10 Cost of common stock equity** Ross Textiles wishes to measure its cost of common stock equity. The firm's stock is currently selling for $57.50. The firm expects to pay a $3.40 dividend at the end of the year (2013). The dividends for the past 5 years are shown in the following table.

Year	Dividend
2012	$3.10
2011	2.92
2010	2.60
2009	2.30
2008	2.12

After underpricing and flotation costs, the firm expects to net $52 per share on a new issue.

a. Determine the growth rate of dividends from 2008 to 2012.

b. Determine the net proceeds, N_n, that the firm will actually receive.

c. Using the constant-growth valuation model, determine the *cost of retained earnings*, r_r.

d. Using the constant-growth valuation model, determine the *cost of new common stock*, r_n.

LG 5 **P9–11 Retained earnings versus new common stock** Using the data for each firm shown in the following table, calculate the *cost of retained earnings* and the *cost of new common stock* using the constant-growth valuation model.

Firm	Current market price per share	Dividend growth rate	Projected dividend per share next year	Underpricing per share	Flotation cost per share
A	$50.00	8%	$2.25	$2.00	$1.00
B	20.00	4	1.00	0.50	1.50
C	42.50	6	2.00	1.00	2.00
D	19.00	2	2.10	1.30	1.70

LG 3 LG 4 LG 5 LG 6 **P9–12 The effect of tax rate on WACC** Equity Lighting Corp. wishes to explore the effect on its cost of capital of the rate at which the company pays taxes. The firm wishes to maintain a capital structure of 30% debt, 10% preferred stock, and 60% common stock. The cost of financing with retained earnings is 14%, the cost of preferred stock financing is 9%, and the before-tax cost of debt financing is 11%. Calculate the weighted average cost of capital (WACC) given the tax rate assumptions in parts **a** to **c.**

a. Tax rate = 40%

b. Tax rate = 35%

c. Tax rate = 25%

d. Describe the relationship between changes in the rate of taxation and the weighted average cost of capital.

LG 6 **P9–13 WACC—Book weights** Ridge Tool has on its books the amounts and specific (after-tax) costs shown in the following table for each source of capital.

Source of capital	Book value	Individual cost
Long-term debt	$700,000	5.3%
Preferred stock	50,000	12.0
Common stock equity	650,000	16.0

a. Calculate the firm's *weighted average cost of capital using book value weights.*
b. Explain how the firm can use this cost in the investment decision-making process.

LG 6 **P9–14 WACC—Book weights and market weights** Webster Company has compiled the information shown in the following table.

Source of capital	Book value	Market value	After-tax cost
Long-term debt	$4,000,000	$3,840,000	6.0%
Preferred stock	40,000	60,000	13.0
Common stock equity	1,060,000	3,000,000	17.0
Totals	$5,100,000	$6,900,000	

a. Calculate the weighted average cost of capital using *book value weights.*
b. Calculate the weighted average cost of capital using *market value weights.*
c. Compare the answers obtained in parts **a** and **b.** Explain the differences.

LG 6 **P9–15 WACC and target weights** After careful analysis, Dexter Brothers has determined that its optimal capital structure is composed of the sources and target market value weights shown in the following table.

Source of capital	Target market value weight
Long-term debt	30%
Preferred stock	15
Common stock equity	55
Total	100%

The cost of debt is estimated to be 7.2%; the cost of preferred stock is estimated to be 13.5%; the cost of retained earnings is estimated to be 16.0%; and the cost of new common stock is estimated to be 18.0%. All of these are after-tax rates. The company's debt represents 25%, the preferred stock represents 10%, and the common stock equity represents 65% of total capital on the basis of the market values of the three components. The company expects to have a significant amount of retained earnings available and does not expect to sell any new common stock.

a. Calculate the weighted average cost of capital on the basis of *historical market value weights.*
b. Calculate the weighted average cost of capital on the basis of *target market value weights.*
c. Compare the answers obtained in parts **a** and **b.** Explain the differences.

LG 3 LG 4 LG 5 LG 6

P9–16 Cost of capital Edna Recording Studios, Inc., reported earnings available to common stock of $4,200,000 last year. From those earnings, the company paid a dividend of $1.26 on each of its 1,000,000 common shares outstanding. The capital structure of the company includes 40% debt, 10% preferred stock, and 50% common stock. It is taxed at a rate of 40%.

a. If the market price of the common stock is $40 and dividends are expected to grow at a rate of 6% per year for the foreseeable future, what is the company's *cost of retained earnings* financing?
b. If underpricing and flotation costs on new shares of common stock amount to $7.00 per share, what is the company's *cost of new common stock* financing?
c. The company can issue $2.00 dividend preferred stock for a market price of $25.00 per share. Flotation costs would amount to $3.00 per share. What is the *cost of preferred stock* financing?
d. The company can issue $1,000-par-value, 10% coupon, 5-year bonds that can be sold for $1,200 each. Flotation costs would amount to $25.00 per bond. Use the estimation formula to figure the approximate *cost of debt* financing.
e. What is the *WACC?*

LG 3 LG 4 LG 5 LG 6

P9–17 Calculation of individual costs and WACC Dillon Labs has asked its financial manager to measure the cost of each specific type of capital as well as the weighted average cost of capital. The weighted average cost is to be measured by using the following weights: 40% long-term debt, 10% preferred stock, and 50% common stock equity (retained earnings, new common stock, or both). The firm's tax rate is 40%.

Debt The firm can sell for $980 a 10-year, $1,000-par-value bond paying *annual interest* at a 10% coupon rate. A flotation cost of 3% of the par value is required in addition to the discount of $20 per bond.

Preferred stock Eight percent (annual dividend) preferred stock having a par value of $100 can be sold for $65. An additional fee of $2 per share must be paid to the underwriters.

Common stock The firm's common stock is currently selling for $50 per share. The dividend expected to be paid at the end of the coming year (2013) is $4. Its dividend payments, which have been approximately 60% of earnings per share in each of the past 5 years, were as shown in the following table.

Year	Dividend
2012	$3.75
2011	3.50
2010	3.30
2009	3.15
2008	2.85

It is expected that to attract buyers, new common stock must be underpriced $5 per share, and the firm must also pay $3 per share in flotation costs. Dividend payments are expected to continue at 60% of earnings. (Assume that $r_r = r_s$.)

a. Calculate the after-tax cost of debt.

b. Calculate the cost of preferred stock.

c. Calculate the cost of common stock.

d. Calculate the WACC for Dillon Labs.

Personal Finance Problem

LG 6 **P9–18** **Weighted average cost of capital** John Dough has just been awarded his degree in business. He has three education loans outstanding. They all mature in 5 years and can be repaid without penalty any time before maturity. The amounts owed on each loan and the annual interest rate associated with each loan are given in the following table.

Loan	Balance due	Annual interest rate
1	$20,000	6%
2	12,000	9
3	32,000	5

John can also combine the total of his three debts (that is, $64,000) and create a consolidated loan from his bank. His bank will charge a 7.2% annual interest rate for a period of 5 years.

Should John do nothing (leave the three individual loans as is) or create a consolidated loan (the $64,000 question)?

LG 3 LG 4 LG 5 LG 6 **P9–19** **Calculation of individual costs and WACC** Lang Enterprises is interested in measuring its overall cost of capital. Current investigation has gathered the following data. The firm is in the 40% tax bracket.

Debt The firm can raise debt by selling $1,000-par-value, 8% coupon interest rate, 20-year bonds on which *annual interest* payments will be made. To sell the issue, an average discount of $30 per bond would have to be given. The firm also must pay flotation costs of $30 per bond.

Preferred stock The firm can sell 8% preferred stock at its $95-per-share par value. The cost of issuing and selling the preferred stock is expected to be $5 per share. Preferred stock can be sold under these terms.

Common stock The firm's common stock is currently selling for $90 per share. The firm expects to pay cash dividends of $7 per share next year. The firm's dividends have been growing at an annual rate of 6%, and this growth is expected to continue into the future. The stock must be underpriced by $7 per share, and flotation costs are expected to amount to $5 per share. The firm can sell new common stock under these terms.

Retained earnings When measuring this cost, the firm does not concern itself with the tax bracket or brokerage fees of owners. It expects to have available $100,000 of retained earnings in the coming year; once these retained earnings are exhausted, the firm will use new common stock as the form of common stock equity financing.

a. Calculate the after-tax cost of debt.
b. Calculate the cost of preferred stock.
c. Calculate the cost of common stock.
d. Calculate the firm's weighted average cost of capital using the capital structure weights shown in the following table. (Round answer to the nearest 0.1%.)

Source of capital	Weight
Long-term debt	30%
Preferred stock	20
Common stock equity	50
Total	100%

LG 6 **P9–20** **Weighted average cost of capital** American Exploration, Inc., a natural gas producer, is trying to decide whether to revise its target capital structure. Currently it targets a 50–50 mix of debt and equity, but it is considering a target capital structure with 70% debt. American Exploration currently has 6% after-tax cost of debt and a 12% cost of common stock. The company does not have any preferred stock outstanding.

a. What is American Exploration's current WACC?
b. Assuming that its cost of debt and equity remain unchanged, what will be American Exploration's WACC under the revised target capital structure?
c. Do you think shareholders are affected by the increase in debt to 70%? If so, how are they affected? Are their common stock claims riskier now?
d. Suppose that in response to the increase in debt, American Exploration's shareholders increase their required return so that cost of common equity is 16%. What will its new WACC be in this case?
e. What does your answer in part **b** suggest about the tradeoff between financing with debt versus equity?

LG 1 **P9–21** **ETHICS PROBLEM** During the 1990s, General Electric put together a long string of consecutive quarters in which the firm managed to meet or beat the earnings forecasts of Wall Street stock analysts. Some skeptics wondered if GE "managed" earnings to meet Wall Street's expectations, meaning that GE used accounting gimmicks to conceal the true volatility in its business. How do you think GE's long run of meeting or beating earnings forecasts affected its cost of capital? If investors learn that GE's performance was achieved largely through accounting gimmicks, how do you think they would respond?

Spreadsheet Exercise

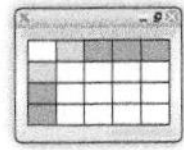

Nova Corporation is interested in measuring the cost of each specific type of capital as well as the weighted average cost of capital. Historically, the firm has raised capital in the following manner:

Source of capital	Weight
Long-term debt	35%
Preferred stock	12
Common stock equity	53

The tax rate of the firm is currently 40%. The needed financial information and data are as follows:

Debt Nova can raise debt by selling $1,000-par-value, 6.5% coupon interest rate, 10-year bonds on which *annual interest payments* will be made. To sell the issue, an average discount of $20 per bond needs to be given. There is an associated flotation cost of 2% of par value.

Preferred stock Preferred stock can be sold under the following terms: The security has a par value of $100 per share, the annual dividend rate is 6% of the par value, and the flotation cost is expected to be $4 per share. The preferred stock is expected to sell for $102 before cost considerations.

Common stock The current price of Nova's common stock is $35 per share. The cash dividend is expected to be $3.25 per share next year. The firm's dividends have grown at an annual rate of 5%, and it is expected that the dividend will continue at this rate for the foreseeable future. The flotation costs are expected to be approximately $2 per share. Nova can sell new common stock under these terms.

Retained earnings The firm expects to have available $100,000 of retained earnings in the coming year. Once these retained earnings are exhausted, the firm will use new common stock as the form of common stock equity financing. (*Note:* When measuring this cost, the firm does not concern itself with the tax bracket or brokerage fees of owners.)

TO DO

Create a spreadsheet to answer the following questions:

a. Calculate the after-tax cost of debt.
b. Calculate the cost of preferred stock.
c. Calculate the cost of retained earnings.
d. Calculate the cost of new common stock.
e. Calculate the firm's weighted average cost of capital using retained earnings and the capital structure weights shown in the table above.
f. Calculate the firm's weighted average cost of capital using new common stock and the capital structure weights shown in the table above.

Visit www.myfinancelab.com for **Chapter Case: *Making Star Products' Financing/Investment Decision,*** Group Exercises, and numerous online resources.

Integrative Case 4

Eco Plastics Company

Since its inception, Eco Plastics Company has been revolutionizing plastic and trying to do its part to save the environment. Eco's founder, Marion Cosby, developed a biodegradable plastic that her company is marketing to manufacturing companies throughout the southeastern United States. After operating as a private company for six years, Eco went public in 2009 and is listed on the Nasdaq stock exchange.

As the chief financial officer of a young company with lots of investment opportunities, Eco's CFO closely monitors the firm's cost of capital. The CFO keeps tabs on each of the individual costs of Eco's three main financing sources: long-term debt, preferred stock, and common stock. The target capital structure for ECO is given by the weights in the following table:

Source of capital	Weight
Long-term debt	30%
Preferred stock	20
Common stock equity	50
Total	100%

At the present time, Eco can raise debt by selling 20-year bonds with a $1,000 par value and a 10.5% annual coupon interest rate. Eco's corporate tax rate is 40%, and its bonds generally require an average discount of $45 per bond and flotation costs of $32 per bond when being sold. Eco's outstanding preferred stock pays a 9% dividend and has a $95-per-share par value. The cost of issuing and selling additional preferred stock is expected to be $7 per share. Because Eco is a young firm that requires lots of cash to grow it does not currently pay a dividend to common stock holders. To track the cost of common stock the CFO uses the capital asset pricing model (CAPM). The CFO and the firm's investment advisors believe that the appropriate risk-free rate is 4% and that the market's expected return equals 13%. Using data from 2009 through 2012, Eco's CFO estimates the firm's beta to be 1.3.

Although Eco's current target capital structure includes 20% preferred stock, the company is considering using debt financing to retire the outstanding preferred stock, thus shifting their target capital structure to 50% long-term debt and 50% common stock. If Eco shifts its capital mix from preferred stock to debt, its financial advisors expect its beta to increase to 1.5.

TO DO

a. Calculate Eco's current after-tax cost of long-term debt.
b. Calculate Eco's current cost of preferred stock.
c. Calculate Eco's current cost of common stock.
d. Calculate Eco's current weighted average cost capital.
e. (1) Assuming that the debt financing costs do not change, what effect would a shift to a more highly leveraged *capital structure* consisting of 50% long-term debt, 0% preferred stock, and 50% common stock have on the risk premium for Eco's common stock? What would be Eco's new cost of common equity?
(2) What would be Eco's new weighted average cost of capital?
(3) Which capital structure—the original one or this one—seems better? Why?

Part 5 Long-Term Investment Decisions

Chapters in This Part

Probably nothing that financial managers do is more important to the long-term success of a company than making good investment decisions. The term *capital budgeting* describes the process for evaluating and selecting investment projects. Often, capital expenditures can be very large, such as building a new plant or launching a new product line. These endeavors can create enormous value for shareholders, but they can also bankrupt the company. In this section, you'll learn how financial managers decide which investment opportunities to pursue.

Chapter 10 covers the capital budgeting tools that financial managers and analysts use to evaluate the merits of an investment. Some of these techniques are quite intuitive and simple to use, such as payback analysis. Other techniques are a little more complex, such as the NPV and IRR approaches. In general, the more complex techniques provide more comprehensive evaluations, however, the simpler approaches often lead to the same value-maximizing decisions.

Chapter 11 illustrates how to develop the capital budgeting cash flows that the techniques covered in Chapter 10 require. After studying this chapter, you will understand the inputs that are necessary to build the relevant cash flows that are required to determine whether a particular investment is likely to create or destroy value for shareholders.

Chapter 12 introduces additional techniques for evaluating the risks inherent with capital investment projects. Because of the often huge scale of capital investments and their importance to the firm's financial well-being, managers invest a tremendous amount of time and energy trying to understand the risks associated with these projects.

10 Capital Budgeting Techniques

Learning Goals

LG 1 Understand the key elements of the capital budgeting process.

LG 2 Calculate, interpret, and evaluate the payback period.

LG 3 Calculate, interpret, and evaluate the net present value (NPV) and economic value added (EVA).

LG 4 Calculate, interpret, and evaluate the internal rate of return (IRR).

LG 5 Use net present value profiles to compare NPV and IRR techniques.

LG 6 Discuss NPV and IRR in terms of conflicting rankings and the theoretical and practical strengths of each approach.

Why This Chapter Matters to You

In your *professional* life

ACCOUNTING You need to understand capital budgeting techniques to help determine the relevant cash flows associated with proposed capital expenditures.

INFORMATION SYSTEMS You need to understand capital budgeting techniques to design decision modules that help reduce the amount of work required to analyze proposed capital expenditures.

MANAGEMENT You need to understand capital budgeting techniques to correctly analyze the relevant cash flows of proposed projects and decide whether to accept or reject them.

MARKETING You need to understand capital budgeting techniques to grasp how proposals for new marketing programs, for new products, and for the expansion of existing product lines will be evaluated by the firm's decision makers.

OPERATIONS You need to understand capital budgeting techniques to know how proposals for the acquisition of new equipment and plants will be evaluated by the firm's decision makers.

In your *personal* life

You can use the capital budgeting techniques used by financial managers to measure either the value of a given asset purchase or its compound rate of return. The IRR technique is widely applied in personal finance to measure both actual and forecast rate of returns on investment securities, real estate, credit card debt, consumer loans, and leases.

Genco Resources

The Gold Standard for Evaluating Gold Mines

Genco Resources, a Canadian mining firm, announced the results of a feasibility study evaluating expansion of the firm's operations in Mexico. Specifically, the study examined the merits of opening a new cyanide leach plant that would allow the firm to increase its production by a factor of ten. Cost of the expansion included $149 million to build the plant, including $40 million in working capital and contingencies required to begin operations.

The study estimated cash flows from this investment over its 9-year projected life, assuming prices of silver and gold of $14 and $800 per ounce respectively. Based on those assumptions, the study claimed that the expansion project would pay back the initial cost in 3.6 years, would generate a 20 percent internal rate of return, and would produce a net present value of almost $75 million.

Payback, internal rate of return, and net present value are all methods that companies use to evaluate potential investment projects. Each of these techniques has advantages and disadvantages, but the net present value method has become the gold standard for analyzing investments. This chapter explains why.

LG 1

10.1 Overview of Capital Budgeting

capital budgeting
The process of evaluating and selecting long-term investments that are consistent with the firm's goal of maximizing owners' wealth.

Long-term investments represent sizable outlays of funds that commit a firm to some course of action. Consequently, the firm needs procedures to analyze and select its long-term investments. **Capital budgeting** is the process of evaluating and selecting long-term investments that are consistent with the firm's goal of maximizing owners' wealth. Firms typically make a variety of long-term investments, but the most common is in *fixed assets,* which include property (land), plant, and equipment. These assets, often referred to as *earning assets,* generally provide the basis for the firm's earning power and value.

Because firms treat capital budgeting (investment) and financing decisions *separately,* Chapters 10 through 12 concentrate on fixed-asset acquisition without regard to the specific method of financing used. We begin by discussing the motives for capital expenditure.

MOTIVES FOR CAPITAL EXPENDITURE

capital expenditure
An outlay of funds by the firm that is expected to produce benefits over a period of time *greater than* 1 year.

operating expenditure
An outlay of funds by the firm resulting in benefits received *within* 1 year.

A **capital expenditure** is an outlay of funds by the firm that is expected to produce benefits over a period of time *greater than* 1 year. An **operating expenditure** is an outlay resulting in benefits received *within* 1 year. Fixed-asset outlays are capital expenditures, but not all capital expenditures are classified as fixed assets. A $60,000 outlay for a new machine with a usable life of 15 years is a capital expenditure that would appear as a fixed asset on the firm's balance sheet. A $60,000 outlay for an advertising campaign that is expected to produce benefits over a long period is also a capital expenditure but would rarely be shown as a fixed asset.

Companies make capital expenditures for many reasons. The basic motives for capital expenditures are to expand operations, to replace or renew fixed assets, or to obtain some other, less tangible benefit over a long period.

STEPS IN THE PROCESS

capital budgeting process
Five distinct but interrelated steps: *proposal generation, review and analysis, decision making, implementation,* and *follow-up.*

The **capital budgeting process** consists of five distinct but interrelated steps:

1. *Proposal generation.* Proposals for new investment projects are made at all levels within a business organization and are reviewed by finance personnel. Proposals that require large outlays are more carefully scrutinized than less costly ones.
2. *Review and analysis.* Financial managers perform formal review and analysis to assess the merits of investment proposals.
3. *Decision making.* Firms typically delegate capital expenditure decision making on the basis of dollar limits. Generally, the board of directors must authorize expenditures beyond a certain amount. Often plant managers are given authority to make decisions necessary to keep the production line moving.
4. *Implementation.* Following approval, expenditures are made and projects implemented. Expenditures for a large project often occur in phases.
5. *Follow-up.* Results are monitored, and actual costs and benefits are compared with those that were expected. Action may be required if actual outcomes differ from projected ones.

Each step in the process is important. Review and analysis and decision making (Steps 2 and 3) consume the majority of time and effort, however. Follow-up (Step 5) is an important but often ignored step aimed at allowing the firm to improve the accuracy of its cash flow estimates continuously. Because of their fundamental importance, this and the following chapters give primary consideration to review and analysis and to decision making.

BASIC TERMINOLOGY

Before we develop the concepts, techniques, and practices related to the capital budgeting process, we need to explain some basic terminology. In addition, we will present some key assumptions that are used to simplify the discussion in the remainder of this chapter and in Chapters 11 and 12.

independent projects
Projects whose cash flows are unrelated to (or independent of) one another; the acceptance of one *does not eliminate* the others from further consideration.

mutually exclusive projects
Projects that compete with one another, so that the acceptance of one *eliminates* from further consideration all other projects that serve a similar function.

Independent versus Mutually Exclusive Projects

Most investments can be placed into one of two categories: (1) independent projects or (2) mutually exclusive projects. **Independent projects** are those whose cash flows are unrelated to (or independent of) one another; the acceptance of one project *does not eliminate* the others from further consideration. **Mutually exclusive projects** are those that have the same function and therefore compete with one another. The acceptance of one *eliminates* from further consideration all other projects that serve a similar function. For example, a firm in need of increased production capacity could obtain it by (1) expanding its plant, (2) acquiring another company, or (3) contracting with another company for production. Clearly, accepting any one option eliminates the immediate need for either of the others.

unlimited funds
The financial situation in which a firm is able to accept all independent projects that provide an acceptable return.

capital rationing
The financial situation in which a firm has only a fixed number of dollars available for capital expenditures, and numerous projects compete for these dollars.

Unlimited Funds versus Capital Rationing

The availability of funds for capital expenditures affects the firm's decisions. If a firm has **unlimited funds** for investment (or if it can raise as much money as it needs by borrowing or issuing stock), making capital budgeting decisions is quite simple: All independent projects that will provide an acceptable return can be accepted. Typically, though, firms operate under **capital rationing** instead. This means that they have only a fixed number of dollars available for capital expenditures and that numerous projects will compete for these dollars. Procedures for dealing with capital rationing are presented in Chapter 12. The discussions here and in the following chapter assume unlimited funds.

accept–reject approach
The evaluation of capital expenditure proposals to determine whether they meet the firm's minimum acceptance criterion.

ranking approach
The ranking of capital expenditure projects on the basis of some predetermined measure, such as the rate of return.

Accept–Reject versus Ranking Approaches

Two basic approaches to capital budgeting decisions are available. The **accept–reject approach** involves evaluating capital expenditure proposals to determine whether they meet the firm's minimum acceptance criterion. This approach can be used when the firm has unlimited funds, as a preliminary step when evaluating mutually exclusive projects, or in a situation in which capital must be rationed. In these cases, only acceptable projects should be considered.

The second method, the **ranking approach,** involves ranking projects on the basis of some predetermined measure, such as the rate of return. The project with the highest return is ranked first, and the project with the lowest return is ranked last. Only acceptable projects should be ranked. Ranking is useful in selecting the "best" of a group of mutually exclusive projects and in evaluating projects with a view of capital rationing.

TABLE 10.1 Capital Expenditure Data for Bennett Company

	Project A	Project B
Initial investment	**$42,000**	**$45,000**
Year	**Operating cash inflows**	
1	$14,000	$28,000
2	14,000	12,000
3	14,000	10,000
4	14,000	10,000
5	14,000	10,000

CAPITAL BUDGETING TECHNIQUES

Large firms evaluate dozens, perhaps even hundreds, of different ideas for new investments each year. To ensure that the investment projects selected have the best chance of increasing the value of the firm, financial managers need tools to help them evaluate the merits of individual projects and to rank competing investments. A number of techniques are available for performing such analyses. The preferred approaches integrate time value procedures, risk and return considerations, and valuation concepts to select capital expenditures that are consistent with the firm's goal of maximizing owners' wealth. This chapter focuses on the use of these techniques in an environment of certainty.

In more depth

To read about *The Accounting Rate of Return,* go to www.myfinancelab.com

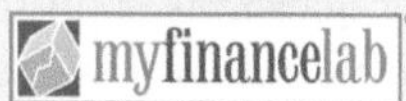

Bennett Company's Relevant Cash Flows

We will use one basic problem to illustrate all the techniques described in this chapter. The problem concerns Bennett Company, a medium-sized metal fabricator that is currently contemplating two projects: Project A requires an initial investment of $42,000; project B requires an initial investment of $45,000. The projected relevant cash flows for the two projects are presented in Table 10.1 and depicted on the time lines in Figure 10.1. Both projects involve one initial cash

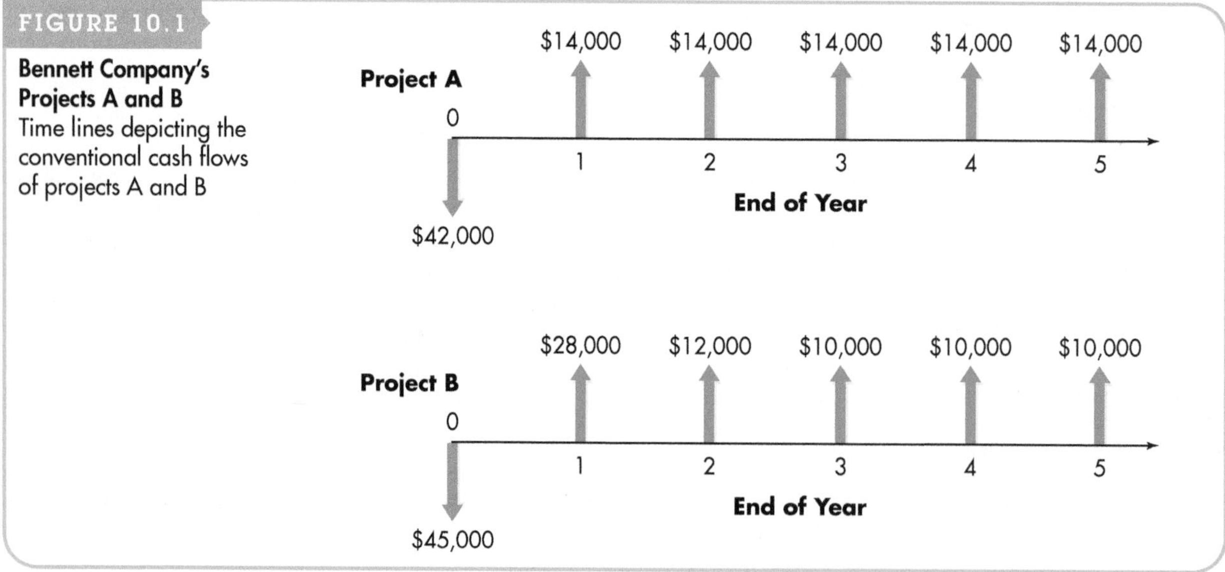

FIGURE 10.1

Bennett Company's Projects A and B
Time lines depicting the conventional cash flows of projects A and B

outlay followed by annual cash inflows, a fairly typical pattern for new investments. We begin with a look at the three most popular capital budgeting techniques: payback period, net present value, and internal rate of return.

→ REVIEW QUESTION

10–1 What is the financial manager's goal in selecting investment projects for the firm? Define the capital budgeting process and explain how it helps managers achieve their goal.

LG 2

10.2 Payback Period

payback period
The amount of time required for a firm to recover its initial investment in a project, as calculated from *cash inflows.*

Payback periods are commonly used to evaluate proposed investments. The **payback period** is the amount of time required for the firm to recover its initial investment in a project, as calculated from *cash inflows*. In the case of an *annuity* (such as the Bennett Company's project A), the payback period can be found by dividing the initial investment by the annual cash inflow. For a *mixed stream* of cash inflows (such as project B), the yearly cash inflows must be accumulated until the initial investment is recovered. Although popular, the payback period is generally viewed as an *unsophisticated capital budgeting technique,* because it does not *explicitly* consider the time value of money.

DECISION CRITERIA

When the payback period is used to make accept–reject decisions, the following decision criteria apply:

- If the payback period is *less than* the maximum acceptable payback period, *accept* the project.
- If the payback period is *greater than* the maximum acceptable payback period, *reject* the project.

The length of the maximum acceptable payback period is determined by management. This value is set *subjectively* on the basis of a number of factors, including the type of project (expansion, replacement or renewal, other), the perceived risk of the project, and the perceived relationship between the payback period and the share value. It is simply a value that management feels, on average, will result in value-creating investment decisions.

Example 10.1 ▶

We can calculate the payback period for Bennett Company's projects A and B using the data in Table 10.1. *For project A, which is an annuity, the payback period is 3.0 years ($42,000 initial investment ÷ $14,000 annual cash inflow).* Because project B generates a mixed stream of cash inflows, the calculation of its payback period is not as clear-cut. In year 1, the firm will recover $28,000 of its $45,000 initial investment. By the end of year 2, $40,000 ($28,000 from year 1 + $12,000 from year 2) will have been recovered. At the end of year 3, $50,000 will have been recovered. Only 50% of the year-3 cash inflow of $10,000 is needed to complete the payback of the initial $45,000. *The payback period for project B is therefore 2.5 years (2 years + 50% of year 3).*

If Bennett's maximum acceptable payback period were 2.75 years, project A would be rejected and project B would be accepted. If the maximum acceptable payback period were 2.25 years, both projects would be rejected. If the projects were being ranked, B would be preferred over A because it has a shorter payback period.

PROS AND CONS OF PAYBACK ANALYSIS

Large firms sometimes use the payback approach to evaluate small projects, and small firms use it to evaluate most projects. Its popularity results from its computational simplicity and intuitive appeal. By measuring how quickly the firm recovers its initial investment, the payback period also gives *implicit* consideration to the timing of cash flows and therefore to the time value of money. Because it can be viewed as a measure of *risk exposure,* many firms use the payback period as a decision criterion or as a supplement to other decision techniques. The longer the firm must wait to recover its invested funds, the greater the possibility of a calamity. Hence, the shorter the payback period the lower the firm's risk exposure.

The major weakness of the payback period is that the appropriate payback period is merely a subjectively determined number. It cannot be specified in light of the wealth maximization goal because it is not based on discounting cash flows to determine whether they add to the firm's value. Instead, the appropriate payback period is simply the maximum acceptable period of time over which management decides that a project's cash flows must break even (that is, just equal to the initial investment). The *Focus on Practice* box offers more information about these time limits in actual practice.

Personal Finance Example 10.2 ▸ Seema Mehdi is considering investing \$20,000 to obtain a 5% interest in a rental property. Her good friend and real estate agent, Akbar Ahmed, put the deal together and he conservatively estimates that Seema should receive between \$4,000 and \$6,000 per year in cash from her 5% interest in the property. The deal is structured in a way that forces all investors to maintain their investment in the property for at least 10 years. Seema expects to remain in the 25% income-tax bracket for quite a while. To be acceptable, Seema requires the investment to pay itself back in terms of after-tax cash flows in less than 7 years.

Seema's calculation of the payback period on this deal begins with calculation of the range of annual after-tax cash flow:

$$\begin{aligned} \text{After-tax cash flow} &= (1 - \text{tax rate}) \times \text{Pre-tax cash flow} \\ &= (1 - 0.25) \times \$4{,}000 = \$3{,}000 \\ &= (1 - 0.25) \times \$6{,}000 = \$4{,}500 \end{aligned}$$

The after-tax cash flow ranges from \$3,000 to \$4,500. Dividing the \$20,000 initial investment by each of the estimated after-tax cash flows, we get the payback period:

$$\begin{aligned} \text{Payback period} &= \text{Initial investment} \div \text{After-tax cash flow} \\ &= \$20{,}000 \div \$3{,}000 = 6.67 \text{ years} \\ &= \$20{,}000 \div \$4{,}500 = 4.44 \text{ years} \end{aligned}$$

Because Seema's proposed rental property investment will pay itself back between 4.44 and 6.67 years, which is a range below her maximum payback of 7 years, the investment is acceptable.

focus on PRACTICE

Limits on Payback Analysis

in practice In tough economic times, the standard for a payback period is often reduced. Chief information officers (CIOs) are apt to reject projects with payback periods of more than 2 years. "We start with payback period," says Ron Fijalkowski, CIO at Strategic Distribution, Inc., in Bensalem, Pennsylvania. "For sure, if the payback period is over 36 months, it's not going to get approved. But our rule of thumb is we'd like to see 24 months. And if it's close to 12, it's probably a no-brainer."

While easy to compute and easy to understand, the payback period's simplicity brings with it some drawbacks. "Payback gives you an answer that tells you a bit about the beginning stage of a project, but it doesn't tell you much about the full lifetime of the project," says Chris Gardner, a cofounder of iValue LLC, an IT valuation consultancy in Barrington, Illinois. "The simplicity of computing payback may encourage sloppiness, especially the failure to include all costs associated with an investment, such as training, maintenance, and hardware upgrade costs," says Douglas Emond, senior vice president and chief technology officer at Eastern Bank in Lynn, Massachusetts. For example, he says, "you may be bringing in a hot new technology, but uh-oh, after implementation you realize that you need a .Net guru in-house, and you don't have one."

But the payback method's emphasis on the short term has a special appeal for IT managers. "That's because the history of IT projects that take longer than 3 years is disastrous," says Gardner. Indeed, Ian Campbell, chief research officer at Nucleus Research, Inc., in Wellesley, Massachusetts, says payback period is an absolutely essential metric for evaluating IT projects—even more important than discounted cash flow (NPV and IRR)—because it spotlights the risks inherent in lengthy IT projects. "It should be a hard and fast rule to never take an IT project with a payback period greater than 3 years, unless it's an infrastructure project you can't do without," Campbell says.

Whatever the weaknesses of the payback period method of evaluating capital projects, the simplicity of the method does allow it to be used in conjunction with other, more sophisticated measures. It can be used to screen potential projects and winnow them down to the few that merit more careful scrutiny with, for example, net present value (NPV).

► ***In your view, if the payback period method is used in conjunction with the NPV method, should it be used before or after the NPV evaluation?***

Source: Gary Anthes, "ROI Guide: Payback Period," Computerworld.com (February 17, 2003), **www.computerworld.com/s/article/78529/ROI_Guide_Payback_Period?taxono.**

A second weakness is that this approach fails to take *fully* into account the time factor in the value of money.[1] This weakness can be illustrated by an example.

Example 10.3 ► DeYarman Enterprises, a small medical appliance manufacturer, is considering two mutually exclusive projects named Gold and Silver. The firm uses only the payback period to choose projects. The cash flows and payback period for each project are given in Table 10.2. Both projects have 3-year payback periods, which would suggest that they are equally desirable. But comparison of the pattern of cash inflows over the first 3 years shows that more of the $50,000 initial investment in project Silver is recovered sooner than is recovered for project Gold. For example, in year 1, $40,000 of the $50,000 invested in project Silver is recovered, whereas only $5,000 of the $50,000 investment in project Gold is recovered. Given the time value of money, project Silver would clearly be preferred over

1. To consider differences in timing explicitly in applying the payback method, the *discounted payback period* is sometimes used. It is found by first calculating the present value of the cash inflows at the appropriate discount rate and then finding the payback period by using the present value of the cash inflows.

TABLE 10.2 Relevant Cash Flows and Payback Periods for DeYarman Enterprises' Projects

	Project gold	Project silver
Initial investment	$50,000	$50,000
Year	Operating cash inflows	
1	$ 5,000	$40,000
2	5,000	2,000
3	40,000	8,000
4	10,000	10,000
5	10,000	10,000
Payback period	3 years	3 years

project Gold, in spite of the fact that both have identical 3-year payback periods. The payback approach does not fully account for the time value of money, which, if recognized, would cause project Silver to be preferred over project Gold.

A third weakness of payback is its failure to recognize cash flows that occur *after* the payback period.

Example 10.4 ▸ Rashid Company, a software developer, has two investment opportunities, X and Y. Data for X and Y are given in Table 10.3. The payback period for project X is 2 years; for project Y it is 3 years. Strict adherence to the payback approach suggests that project X is preferable to project Y. However, if we look beyond the payback period, we see that project X returns only an additional $1,200 ($1,000 in year 3 + $100 in year 4 + $100 in year 5), whereas project Y returns an additional $7,000 ($4,000 in year 4 + $3,000 in year 5). On the basis of this information, project Y appears preferable to X. The payback approach ignored the cash inflows occurring after the end of the payback period.

TABLE 10.3 Calculation of the Payback Period for Rashid Company's Two Alternative Investment Projects

	Project X	Project Y
Initial investment	$10,000	$10,000
Year	Operating cash inflows	
1	$5,000	$3,000
2	5,000	4,000
3	1,000	3,000
4	100	4,000
5	100	3,000
Payback period	2 years	3 years

→ **REVIEW QUESTIONS**

10–2 What is the *payback period?* How is it calculated?

10–3 What weaknesses are commonly associated with the use of the payback period to evaluate a proposed investment?

LG 3

10.3 Net Present Value (NPV)

The method used by most large companies to evaluate investment projects is called *net present value (NPV)*. The intuition behind the NPV method is simple. When firms make investments, they are spending money that they obtained, in one form or another, from investors. Investors expect a return on the money that they give to firms, so a firm should undertake an investment only if the present value of the cash flow that the investment generates is greater than the cost of making the investment in the first place. Because the *NPV* method takes into account the time value of investors' money, it is a more *sophisticated capital budgeting technique* than the payback rule. The NPV method discounts the firm's cash flows at the firm's cost of capital. This rate—as discussed in Chapter 9—is the minimum return that must be earned on a project to satisfy the firm's investors. Projects with lower returns fail to meet investors' expectations and therefore decrease firm value, and projects with higher returns increase firm value.

net present value (NPV)
A sophisticated capital budgeting technique; found by subtracting a project's initial investment from the present value of its cash inflows discounted at a rate equal to the firm's cost of capital.

The **net present value (NPV)** is found by subtracting a project's initial investment (CF_0) from the present value of its cash inflows (CF_t) discounted at a rate equal to the firm's cost of capital (r).

$$\text{NPV} = \text{Present value of cash inflows} - \text{Initial investment}$$

$$\text{NPV} = \sum_{t=1}^{n} \frac{CF_t}{(1+r)^t} - CF_0 \qquad (10.1)$$

When NPV is used, both inflows and outflows are measured in terms of present dollars. For a project that has cash outflows beyond the initial investment, the net present value of a project would be found by subtracting the present value of outflows from the present value of inflows.

DECISION CRITERIA

When NPV is used to make accept–reject decisions, the decision criteria are as follows:

- If the NPV is *greater than* \$0, *accept* the project.
- If the NPV is *less than* \$0, *reject* the project.

If the NPV is greater than \$0, the firm will earn a return greater than its cost of capital. Such action should increase the market value of the firm, and therefore the wealth of its owners by an amount equal to the NPV.

Example 10.5 ▸ We can illustrate the net present value (NPV) approach by using the Bennett Company data presented in Table 10.1. If the firm has a 10% cost of capital, the net present values for projects A (an annuity) and B (a mixed stream) can be

FIGURE 10.2

Calculation of NPVs for Bennett Company's Capital Expenditure Alternatives
Time lines depicting the cash flows and NPV calculations for projects A and B

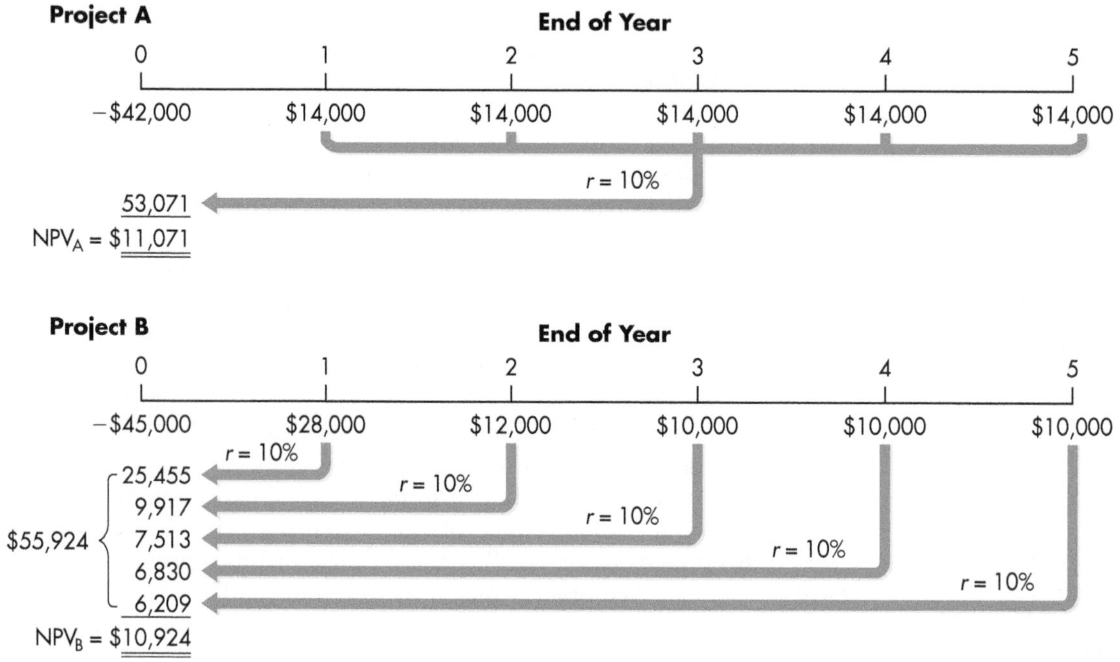

Project A
End of Year
0
1
2
3
4
5
−$42,000
$14,000
$14,000
$14,000
$14,000
$14,000
r = 10%
53,071
NPVA = $11,071
Project B
End of Year
0
1
2
3
4
5
−$45,000
$28,000
$12,000
$10,000
$10,000
$10,000
r = 10%
r = 10%
r = 10%
r = 10%
r = 10%
25,455
9,917
$55,924
7,513
6,830
6,209
NPVB = $10,924

calculated as shown on the time lines in Figure 10.2. These calculations result in net present values for projects A and B of $11,071 and $10,924, respectively. Both projects are acceptable, because the net present value of each is greater than $0. If the projects were being ranked, however, project A would be considered superior to B, because it has a higher net present value than that of B ($11,071 versus $10,924).

Project A

Input
Function
-42000
CF0
14000
CF1
5
N
10
I
NPV
Solution
11,071.01

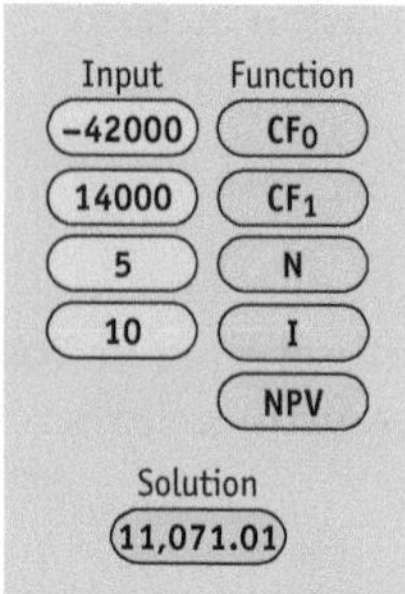

Calculator Use The preprogrammed NPV function in a financial calculator can be used to simplify the NPV calculation. The keystrokes for project A—the annuity—typically are as shown at left. Note that because project A is an annuity, only its first cash inflow, $CF_1 = 14000$, is input, followed by its frequency, $N = 5$.

The keystrokes for project B—the mixed stream—are as shown on page 397. Because the last three cash inflows for project B are the same ($CF_3 = CF_4 = CF_5 = 10{,}000$), after inputting the first of these cash inflows, CF_3, we merely input its frequency, $N = 3$.

The calculated NPVs for projects A and B of $11,071 and $10,924, respectively, agree with the NPVs already cited.

Spreadsheet Use The NPVs can be calculated as shown on the following Excel spreadsheet.

Project B

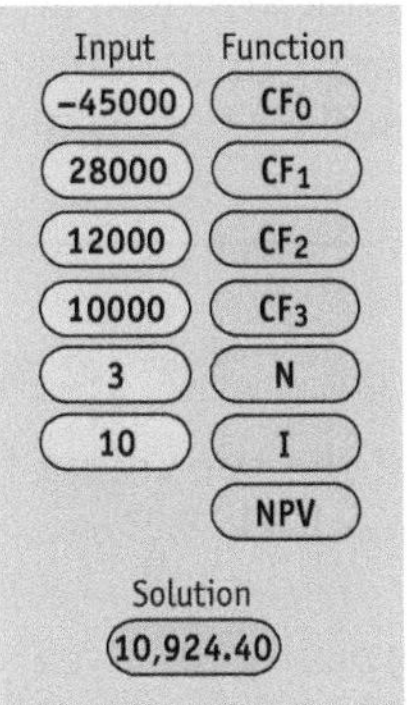

	A	B	C
1	DETERMINING THE NET PRESENT VALUE		
2	Firm's cost of capital		10%
3		Year-End Cash Flow	
4	Year	Project A	Project B
5	0	$ (42,000)	$ (45,000)
6	1	$ 14,000	$ 28,000
7	2	$ 14,000	$ 12,000
8	3	$ 14,000	$ 10,000
9	4	$ 14,000	$ 10,000
10	5	$ 14,000	$ 10,000
11	NPV	$ 11,071	$ 10,924
12	Choice of project		Project A

Entry in Cell B11 is
=NPV(C2,B6:B10)+B5
Copy the entry in Cell B11 to Cell C11.
Entry in Cell C12 is =IF(B11>C11,B4,C4).

NPV AND THE PROFITABILITY INDEX

A variation of the NPV rule is called the profitability index (PI). For a project that has an initial cash outflow followed by cash inflows, the profitability index (PI) is simply equal to the present value of cash inflows divided by the initial cash outflow:[2]

$$PI = \frac{\sum_{t=1}^{n} \frac{CF_t}{(1+r)^t}}{CF_0} \quad (10.2)$$

When companies evaluate investment opportunities using the PI, the decision rule they follow is to invest in the project when the index is greater than 1.0. When the PI is greater than one, that implies that the present value of cash inflows is greater than the (absolute value of the) initial cash outflow, so a profitability index greater than one corresponds to a net present value greater than zero. In other words, the NPV and PI methods will always come to the same conclusion regarding whether a particular investment is worth doing or not.

Example 10.6 ▸ We can refer back to Figure 10.2, which shows the present value of cash inflows for projects A and B, to calculate the PI for each of Bennett's investment options:

$$PI_A = \$53{,}071 \div \$42{,}000 = 1.26$$
$$PI_B = \$55{,}924 \div \$45{,}000 = 1.24$$

According to the profitability index, both projects are acceptable (because PI > 1.0 for both), which shouldn't be surprising because we already know that both projects

2. To be a bit more precise, the denominator in Equation 10.2 should be a positive number, so we are taking the absolute value of the initial cash outflow.

have positive NPVs. Furthermore, in this particular case, the NPV rule and the PI both indicate that project A is preferred over project B. It is not always true that the NPV and PI methods will rank projects in exactly the same order. Different rankings can occur when alternative projects require initial outlays that have very different magnitudes.

NPV AND ECONOMIC VALUE ADDED

Economic Value Added (or EVA), a registered trademark of the consulting firm Stern Stewart & Co., is another close cousin of the NPV method. Whereas the NPV approach calculates the value of an investment over its entire life, the EVA approach is typically used to measure an investment's performance on a year-by-year basis. The EVA method begins the same way that NPV does—by calculating a project's net cash flows. However, the EVA approach subtracts from those cash flows a charge that is designed to capture the return that the firm's investors demand on the project. That is, the EVA calculation asks whether a project generates positive cash flows *above and beyond what investors demand.* If so, then the project is worth undertaking.

pure economic profit
A profit above and beyond the normal competitive rate of return in a line of business.

The EVA method determines whether a project earns a *pure economic profit.* When accountants say that a firm has earned a profit, they mean that revenues are greater than expenses. But the term **pure economic profit** refers to a profit that is higher than expected given the competitive rate of return on a particular line of business. A firm that shows a positive profit on its income statement may or may not earn a pure economic profit, depending on how large the profit is relative to the capital invested in the business. For instance, in the first quarter of 2010, TomTom, the European maker of portable GPS devices, reported a net profit of €3 million. Does that seem like a large profit? Perhaps not when you consider that TomTom's balance sheet showed total assets of over €2.5 billion. In other words, TomTom's profit represented a return of just 0.0012 percent on the firm's assets. That return was below the rate offered on risk-free government securities in 2010, so it clearly fell below the expectations of TomTom's investors (who would have expected a higher return as compensation for the risks they were taking), so the company earned a *pure economic loss* that quarter. Stated differently, TomTom's EVA in the first quarter of 2010 was negative.

Example 10.7 ▸ Suppose a certain project costs $1,000,000 up front, but after that it will generate net cash inflows each year (in perpetuity) of $120,000. To calculate the NPV of this project, we would simply discount the cash flows and add them up. If the firm's cost of capital is 10%, then the project's NPV is:[3]

$$NPV = -\$1,000,000 + (\$120,000 \div 0.10) = \$200,000$$

To calculate the investment's economic value added in any particular year, we start with the annual $120,000 cash flow. Next, we assign a charge that accounts for the return that investors demand on the capital that the firm has invested in the project. In this case, the firm invested $1,000,000, and investors

3. We are using Equation 5.14 to calculate the present value of the perpetual stream of $120,000 cash flows.

expect a 10% return. That means that the project's annual capital charge is $100,000 ($1,000,000 × 10%), and its EVA is $20,000 per year:

$$\begin{aligned} \text{EVA} &= \text{project cash flow} - [(\text{cost of capital}) \times (\text{invested capital})] \\ &= \$120{,}000 - \$100{,}000 = \$20{,}000 \end{aligned}$$

In other words, this project earns more than its cost of capital each year, so the project is clearly worth doing. To calculate the EVA for the project over its entire life, we would simply discount the annual EVA figures using the firm's cost of capital. In this case, the project produces an annual EVA of $20,000 in perpetuity. Discounting this at 10% gives a project EVA of $200,000 ($20,000 ÷ 0.10), identical to the NPV. In this example, both the NPV and EVA methods reach the same conclusion, namely that the project creates $200,000 in value for shareholders. If the cash flows in our example had fluctuated through time rather than remaining fixed at $120,000 per year, an analyst would calculate the investment's EVA every year, then discount those figures to the present using the firm's cost of capital. If the resulting figure is positive, then the project generates a positive EVA and is worth doing.

→ REVIEW QUESTIONS

10–4 How is the *net present value (NPV)* calculated for a project with a *conventional cash flow pattern?*

10–5 What are the acceptance criteria for NPV? How are they related to the firm's market value?

10–6 Explain the similarities and differences between NPV, PI, and EVA.

LG 4

10.4 Internal Rate of Return (IRR)

internal rate of return (IRR) The discount rate that equates the NPV of an investment opportunity with $0 (because the present value of cash inflows equals the initial investment); it is the rate of return that the firm will earn if it invests in the project and receives the given cash inflows.

The *internal rate of return (IRR)* is one of the most widely used *capital budgeting techniques.* The **internal rate of return (IRR)** is the discount rate that equates the NPV of an investment opportunity with $0 (because the present value of cash inflows equals the initial investment). It is the rate of return that the firm will earn if it invests in the project and receives the given cash inflows. Mathematically, the IRR is the value of r in Equation 10.1 that causes NPV to equal $0.

$$\$0 = \sum_{t=1}^{n} \frac{CF_t}{(1 + IRR)^t} - CF_0 \qquad (10.3)$$

$$\sum_{t=1}^{n} \frac{CF_t}{(1 + IRR)^t} = CF_0 \qquad (10.3a)$$

DECISION CRITERIA

When IRR is used to make accept–reject decisions, the decision criteria are as follows:

- If the IRR is *greater than* the cost of capital, *accept* the project.
- If the IRR is *less than* the cost of capital, *reject* the project.

These criteria guarantee that the firm will earn at least its required return. Such an outcome should increase the market value of the firm and, therefore, the wealth of its owners.

CALCULATING THE IRR

Most financial calculators have a preprogrammed IRR function that can be used to simplify the IRR calculation. With these calculators, you merely punch in all cash flows just as if to calculate NPV and then depress IRR to find the internal rate of return. Computer software, including spreadsheets, is also available for simplifying these calculations. All NPV and IRR values presented in this and subsequent chapters are obtained by using these functions on a popular financial calculator.

Example 10.8 ▸ We can demonstrate the internal rate of return (IRR) approach by using the Bennett Company data presented in Table 10.1. Figure 10.3 uses time lines to depict the framework for finding the IRRs for Bennett's projects A and B. We can see in the figure that the IRR is the unknown discount rate that causes the NPV to equal $0.

Calculator Use To find the IRR using the preprogrammed function in a financial calculator, the keystrokes for each project are the same as those shown on pages 398 and 399 for the NPV calculation, except that the last two NPV keystrokes (punching **I** and then **NPV**) are replaced by a single **IRR** keystroke.

FIGURE 10.3

Calculation of IRRs for Bennett Company's Capital Expenditure Alternatives
Time lines depicting the cash flows and IRR calculations for projects A and B

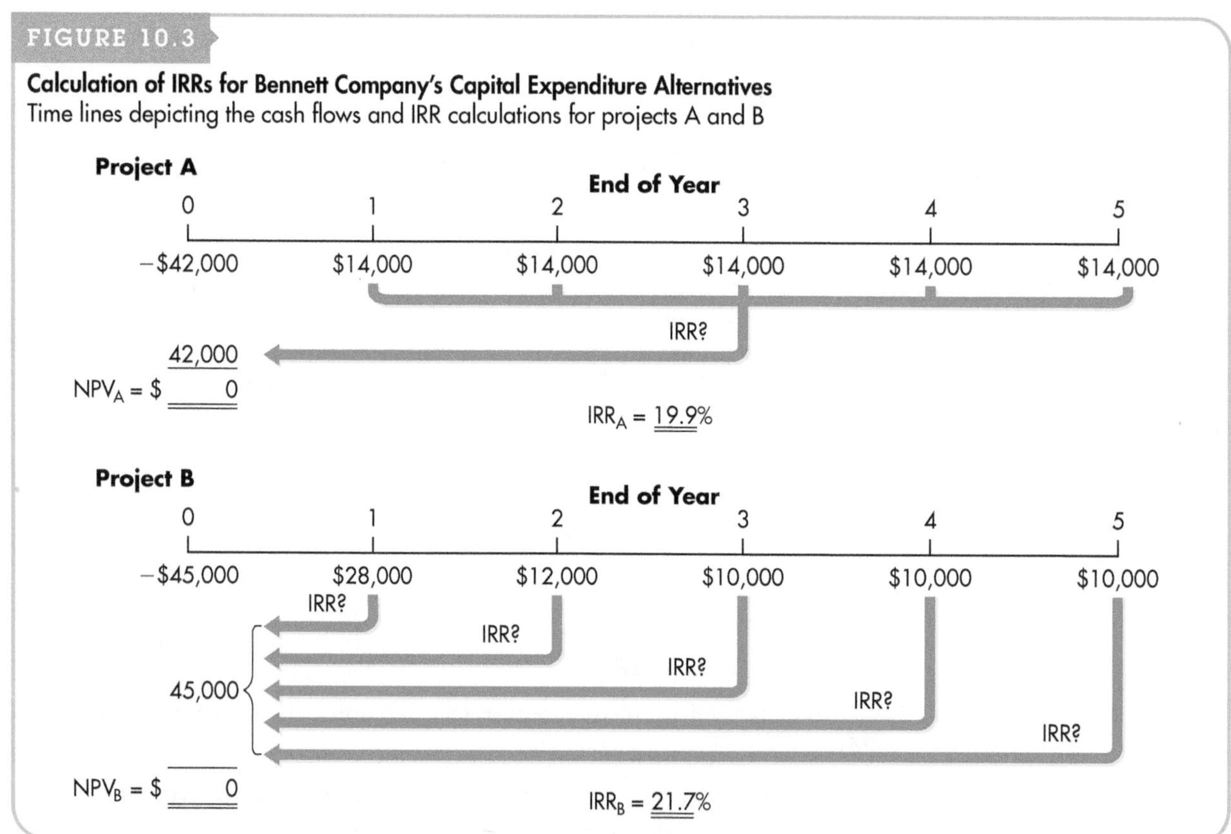

Comparing the IRRs of projects A and B given in Figure 10.3 to Bennett Company's 10% cost of capital, we can see that both projects are acceptable because

$$IRR_A = 19.9\% > 10.0\% \text{ cost of capital}$$
$$IRR_B = 21.7\% > 10.0\% \text{ cost of capital}$$

Comparing the two projects' IRRs, we would prefer project B over project A because $IRR_B = 21.7\% > IRR_A = 19.9\%$. If these projects are mutually exclusive, meaning that we can choose one project or the other but not both, the IRR decision technique would recommend project B.

Spreadsheet Use The internal rate of return also can be calculated as shown on the following Excel spreadsheet.

	A	B	C
1	DETERMINING THE INTERNAL RATE OF RETURN		
2		Year-End Cash Flow	
3	Year	Project A	Project B
4	0	$ (42,000)	$ (45,000)
5	1	$ 14,000	$ 28,000
6	2	$ 14,000	$ 12,000
7	3	$ 14,000	$ 10,000
8	4	$ 14,000	$ 10,000
9	5	$ 14,000	$ 10,000
10	IRR	19.9%	21.7%
11	Choice of project		Project B

Entry in Cell B10 is =IRR(B4:B9).
Copy the entry in Cell B10 to Cell C10.
Entry in Cell C11 is =IF(B10>C10,B3,C3).

It is interesting to note in the preceding Example 10.8 that the IRR suggests that project B, which has an IRR of 21.7%, is preferable to project A, which has an IRR of 19.9%. This conflicts with the NPV rankings obtained in an earlier example. Such conflicts are not unusual. *There is no guarantee that NPV and IRR will rank projects in the same order. However, both methods should reach the same conclusion about the acceptability or nonacceptability of projects.*

Personal Finance Example 10.9 ▸ Tony DiLorenzo is evaluating an investment opportunity. He is comfortable with the investment's level of risk. Based on competing investment opportunities, he feels that this investment must earn a minimum compound annual after-tax return of 9% to be acceptable. Tony's initial investment would be $7,500, and he expects to receive annual after-tax cash flows of $500 per year in each of the first 4 years, followed by $700 per year at the end of years 5 through 8. He plans to sell the investment at the end of year 8 and net $9,000, after taxes.

To calculate the investment's IRR (compound annual return), Tony first summarizes the after-tax cash flows as shown in the following table:

Year	Cash flow (− or +)
0	−$7,500 (Initial investment)
1	500
2	500
3	500
4	500
5	700
6	700
7	700
8	9,700 ($700 + $9,000)

Substituting the after-tax cash flows for years 0 through 8 into a financial calculator or spreadsheet, he finds the investment's IRR of 9.54%. Given that the expected IRR of 9.54% exceeds Tony's required minimum IRR of 9%, the investment is acceptable.

→ REVIEW QUESTIONS

10–7 What is the *internal rate of return (IRR)* on an investment? How is it determined?

10–8 What are the acceptance criteria for IRR? How are they related to the firm's market value?

10–9 Do the net present value (NPV) and internal rate of return (IRR) always agree with respect to accept–reject decisions? With respect to ranking decisions? Explain.

LG 5 LG 6 10.5 Comparing NPV and IRR Techniques

To understand the differences between the NPV and IRR techniques and decision makers' preferences in their use, we need to look at net present value profiles, conflicting rankings, and the question of which approach is better.

NET PRESENT VALUE PROFILES

net present value profile
Graph that depicts a project's NPVs for various discount rates.

Projects can be compared graphically by constructing **net present value profiles** that depict the project's NPVs for various discount rates. These profiles are useful in evaluating and comparing projects, especially when conflicting rankings exist. They are best demonstrated via an example.

Example 10.10 ▶

To prepare net present value profiles for Bennett Company's two projects, A and B, the first step is to develop a number of "discount rate–net present value" coordinates. Three coordinates can be easily obtained for each project; they are at discount

TABLE 10.4 Discount Rate–NPV Coordinates for Projects A and B

	Net present value	
Discount rate	Project A	Project B
0%	$28,000	$25,000
10	11,071	10,924
19.9	0	—
21.7	—	0

rates of 0%, 10% (the cost of capital, *r*), and the IRR. The net present value at a 0% discount rate is found by merely adding all the cash inflows and subtracting the initial investment. Using the data in Table 10.1 and Figure 10.1, we get

For project A:

($14,000 + $14,000 + $14,000 + $14,000 + $14,000) − $42,000 = $28,000

For project B:

($28,000 + $12,000 + $10,000 + $10,000 + $10,000) − $45,000 = $25,000

The net present values for projects A and B at the 10% cost of capital are $11,071 and $10,924, respectively (from Figure 10.2). Because the IRR is the discount rate for which net present value equals zero, the IRRs (from Figure 10.3) of 19.9% for project A and 21.7% for project B result in $0 NPVs. The three sets of coordinates for each of the projects are summarized in Table 10.4.

Plotting the data from Table 10.4 results in the net present value profiles for projects A and B shown in Figure 10.4. The figure reveals three important facts:

1. The IRR of project B is greater than the IRR of project A, so managers using the IRR method to rank projects will always choose B over A if both projects are acceptable.

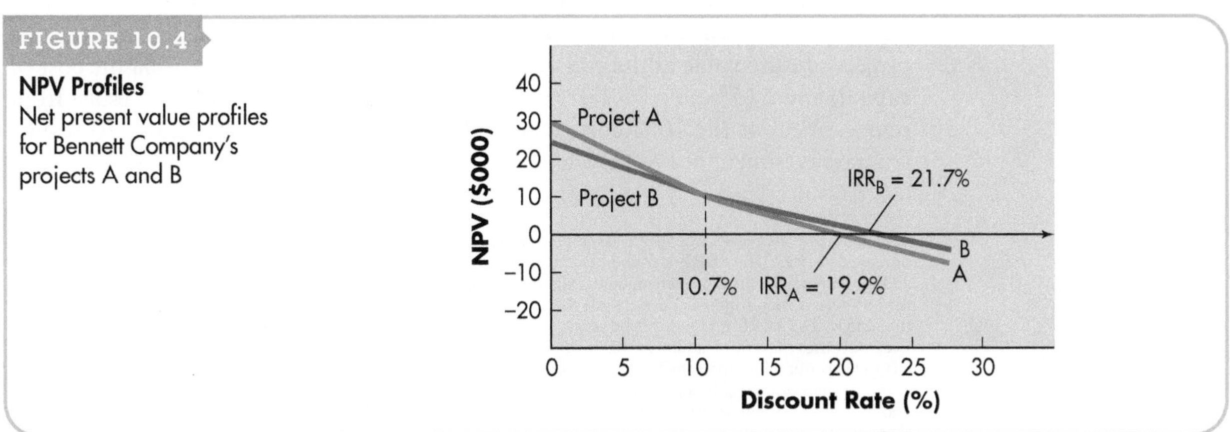

FIGURE 10.4

NPV Profiles

Net present value profiles for Bennett Company's projects A and B

2. The NPV of project A is sometimes higher and sometimes lower than the NPV of project B; thus, the NPV method will not consistently rank A above B or vice versa. The NPV ranking will depend on the firm's cost of capital.
3. When the cost of capital is approximately 10.7%, projects A and B have identical NPVs.

The cost of capital for Bennett Company is 10%, and at that rate project A has a higher NPV than project B (the red line is above the blue line in Figure 10.4 when the discount rate is 10%). Therefore, the NPV and IRR methods rank the two projects differently. If Bennett's cost of capital were a little higher, say 12%, the NPV method would rank project B over project A and there would be no conflict in the rankings provided by the NPV and IRR approaches.

CONFLICTING RANKINGS

Ranking different investment opportunities is an important consideration when projects are mutually exclusive or when capital rationing is necessary. When projects are mutually exclusive, ranking enables the firm to determine which project is best from a financial standpoint. When capital rationing is necessary, ranking projects will provide a logical starting point for determining which group of projects to accept. As we'll see, **conflicting rankings** using NPV and IRR result from *differences in the reinvestment rate assumption, the timing of each project's cash flows, and the magnitude of the initial investment.*

conflicting rankings
Conflicts in the ranking given a project by NPV and IRR, resulting from *differences in the magnitude and timing of cash flows.*

Reinvestment Assumption

One underlying cause of conflicting rankings is different implicit assumptions about the *reinvestment* of **intermediate cash inflows**—cash inflows received prior to the termination of a project. NPV assumes that intermediate cash inflows are reinvested at the cost of capital, whereas IRR assumes that intermediate cash inflows are reinvested at a rate equal to the project's IRR.[4] These differing assumptions can be demonstrated with an example.

intermediate cash inflows
Cash inflows received prior to the termination of a project.

Example 10.11 ▶ A project requiring a \$170,000 initial investment is expected to provide operating cash inflows of \$52,000, \$78,000, and \$100,000 at the end of each of the next 3 years. The NPV of the project (at the firm's 10% cost of capital) is \$16,867 and its IRR is 15%. Clearly, the project is acceptable (NPV = \$16,867 > \$0 and IRR = 15% > 10% cost of capital). Table 10.5 demonstrates calculation of the project's future value at the end of its 3-year life, assuming both a 10% (its cost of capital) and a 15% (its IRR) rate of return. A future value of \$248,720 results from reinvestment at the 10% cost of capital, and a future value of \$258,470 results from reinvestment at the 15% IRR.

4. To eliminate the reinvestment rate assumption of the IRR, some practitioners calculate the *modified internal rate of return (MIRR)*. The MIRR is found by converting each operating cash inflow to its future value measured at the end of the project's life and then summing the future values of all inflows to get the project's *terminal value*. Each future value is found by using the cost of capital, thereby eliminating the reinvestment rate criticism of the traditional IRR. The MIRR represents the discount rate that causes the terminal value just to equal the initial investment. Because it uses the cost of capital as the reinvestment rate the MIRR is generally viewed as a better measure of a project's true profitability than the IRR. Although this technique is frequently used in commercial real estate valuation and is a preprogrammed function on some financial calculators, its failure to resolve the issue of conflicting rankings and its theoretical inferiority to NPV have resulted in the MIRR receiving only limited attention and acceptance in the financial literature.

TABLE 10.5 Reinvestment Rate Comparisons for a Project[a]

Year	Operating cash inflows	Number of years earnings interest (t)	Reinvestment rate 10% Future value	Reinvestment rate 15% Future value
1	$ 52,000	2	$ 62,920	$ 68,770
2	78,000	1	85,800	89,700
3	100,000	0	100,000	100,000
		Future value end of year 3	$248,720	$258,470

NPV @ 10% = $16,867
IRR = 15%

[a]Initial investment in this project is $170,000.

If the future value in each case in Table 10.5 were viewed as the return received 3 years from today from the $170,000 initial investment, the cash flows would be those given in Table 10.6. The NPVs and IRRs in each case are shown below the cash flows in Table 10.6. You can see that at the 10% reinvestment rate, the NPV remains at $16,867; reinvestment at the 15% IRR produces an NPV of $24,418.

From this result, it should be clear that the NPV technique assumes reinvestment at the cost of capital (10% in this example). (Note that with reinvestment at 10%, the IRR would be 13.5%.) On the other hand, the IRR technique assumes an ability to reinvest intermediate cash inflows at the IRR. If reinvestment does not occur at this rate, the IRR will differ from 15%. Reinvestment at a rate lower than the IRR would result in an IRR lower than that calculated (at 13.5%, for example, if the reinvestment rate were only 10%). Reinvestment at a rate higher than the IRR would result in an IRR higher than that calculated.

In more depth

To read about *Modified Internal Rate of Return*, go to www.myfinancelab.com

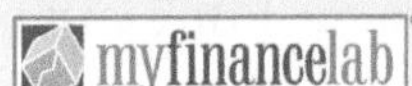

TABLE 10.6 Project Cash Flows after Reinvestment

	Reinvestment rate 10%	Reinvestment rate 15%
Initial investment	$170,000	
Year	Operating cash inflows	
1	$ 0	$ 0
2	0	0
3	248,720	258,470
NPV @ 10%	$ 16,867	$ 24,418
IRR	13.5%	15.0%

Timing of the Cash Flow

Another reason why the IRR and NPV methods may provide different rankings for investment options has to do with differences in the timing of cash flows. Go back to the timelines for investments A and B in Figure 10.1 on page 392. The up-front investment required by each investment is similar, but after that the timing of each project's cash flows is quite different. Project B has a large cash inflow almost immediately (in Year 1), whereas Project A provides cash flows that are distributed evenly across time. Because so much of Project B's cash flows arrive early in its life (especially compared to the timing for Project A), the NPV of Project B will not be particularly sensitive to changes in the discount rate. Project A's NPV, on the other hand, will fluctuate more as the discount rate changes. In essence, Project B is somewhat akin to a short-term bond, whose price doesn't change much when interest rates move, and Project A is more like a long-term bond whose price fluctuates a great deal when rates change.

You can see this pattern if you review the NPV profiles for projects A and B in Figure 10.4 on page 405. The red line representing project A is considerably steeper than the blue line representing project B. At very low discount rates, project A has a higher NPV, but as the discount rate increases, the NPV of project A declines rapidly. When the discount rate is high enough, the NPV of project B overtakes that of project A.

We can summarize this discussion as follows. Because project A's cash flows arrive later than project B's cash flows do, when the firm's cost of capital is relatively low (to be specific, below about 10.7 percent), the NPV method will rank project A ahead of project B. At a higher cost of capital, the early arrival of project B's cash flows becomes more advantageous, and the NPV method will rank project B over project A. The differences in the timing of cash flows between the two projects does not affect the ranking provided by the IRR method, which always puts project B ahead of project A. Table 10.7 illustrates how the conflict in rankings between the NPV and IRR approaches depends on the firm's cost of capital.

Magnitude of the Initial Investment

Suppose someone offered you the following two investment options. You could invest $2 today and receive $3 tomorrow, or you could invest $1,000 today and receive $1,100 tomorrow. The first investment provides a return (an IRR) of 50 percent in just one day, a return that surely would surpass any reasonable hurdle rate. But after making this investment, you're only better off by $1. On the

TABLE 10.7 Ranking Projects A and B Using IRR and NPV Methods

Method	Project A	Project B
IRR		✓
NPV		
if $r < 10.7\%$	✓	
if $r > 10.7\%$		✓

other hand, the second choice offers a return of 10 percent in a single day. That's far less than the first opportunity, but earning 10 percent in a single day is still a very high return. In addition, if you accept this investment, you will be $100 better off tomorrow than you were today.

Most people would choose the second option presented above, even though the rate of return on that option (10 percent) is far less than the rate offered by the first option (50 percent). They reason (correctly) that it is sometimes better to accept a lower return on a larger investment than to accept a very high return on a small investment. Said differently, most people know that they are better off taking the investment that pays them a $100 profit in just one day rather than the investment that generates just a $1 profit.[5]

The preceding example illustrates what is known as the scale (or magnitude) problem. The scale problem occurs when two projects are very different in terms of how much money is required to invest in each project. In these cases, the IRR and NPV methods may rank projects differently. The IRR approach (and the PI method) may favor small projects with high returns (like the $2 loan that turns into $3), whereas the NPV approach favors the investment that makes the investor the most money (like the $1,000 investment that yields $1,100 in one day). In the case of the Bennett Company's projects, the scale problem is not likely to be the cause of the conflict in project rankings because the initial investment required to fund each project is quite similar.

To summarize, it is important for financial managers to keep an eye out for conflicts in project rankings provided by the NPV and IRR methods, but differences in the magnitude and timing of cash inflows do not guarantee conflicts in ranking. In general, the greater the difference between the magnitude and timing of cash inflows, the greater the likelihood of conflicting rankings. Conflicts based on NPV and IRR can be reconciled computationally; to do so, one creates and analyzes an incremental project reflecting the difference in cash flows between the two mutually exclusive projects.

WHICH APPROACH IS BETTER?

Many companies use both the NPV and IRR techniques because current technology makes them easy to calculate. But it is difficult to choose one approach over the other because the theoretical and practical strengths of the approaches differ. Clearly, it is wise to evaluate NPV and IRR techniques from both theoretical and practical points of view.

Theoretical View

On a purely theoretical basis, NPV is the better approach to capital budgeting as a result of several factors. Most important, the NPV measures how much wealth a project creates (or destroys if the NPV is negative) for shareholders. Given that the financial manager's objective is to maximize shareholder wealth, the NPV approach has the clearest link to this objective and, therefore, is the "gold standard" for evaluating investment opportunities.

---

5. Note that the profitability index also provides an incorrect ranking in this example. The first option has a PI of 1.5 ($3 ÷ $2), and the second option's PI equals 1.1 ($1,100 ÷ $1,000). Just like the IRR, the PI suggests that the first option is better, but we know that the second option makes more money.

multiple IRRs
More than one IRR resulting from a capital budgeting project with a *nonconventional cash flow pattern;* the maximum number of IRRs for a project is equal to the number of sign changes in its cash flows.

In addition, certain mathematical properties may cause a project with a *nonconventional cash flow pattern* to have **multiple IRRs**—more than one IRR.[6] Mathematically, the maximum number of *real* roots to an equation is equal to its number of sign changes. Take an equation like $x^2 - 5x + 6 = 0$, which has two sign changes in its coefficients—from positive $(+x^2)$ to negative $(-5x)$ and then from negative $(-5x)$ to positive $(+6)$. If we factor the equation (remember factoring from high school math?), we get $(x - 2) \times (x - 3)$, which means that x can equal either 2 or 3—there are two correct values for x. Substitute them back into the equation, and you'll see that both values work.

This same outcome can occur when finding the IRR for projects with nonconventional cash flows, because they have more than one sign change. Clearly, when multiple IRRs occur for nonconventional cash flows, the analyst faces the time-consuming need to interpret their meanings so as to evaluate the project. The fact that such a challenge does not exist when using NPV enhances its theoretical superiority.

Practical View

Evidence suggests that in spite of the theoretical superiority of NPV, *financial managers use the IRR approach just as often as the NPV method.* The appeal of the IRR technique is due to the general disposition of business people to think in terms of *rates of return* rather than actual *dollar returns.* Because interest rates, profitability, and so on are most often expressed as annual rates of return, the use of IRR makes sense to financial decision makers. They tend to find NPV less intuitive because it does not measure benefits *relative to the amount invested.* Because a variety of techniques are available for avoiding the pitfalls of the IRR, its widespread use does not imply a lack of sophistication on the part of financial decision makers. Clearly, corporate financial analysts are responsible for identifying and resolving problems with the IRR before the decision makers use it as a decision technique.

Matter of fact

Which Methods Do Companies Actually Use?

A recent survey asked chief financial officers (CFOs) what methods they used to evaluate capital investment projects. One interesting finding was that many companies use more than one of the approaches we've covered in this chapter. The most popular approaches by far were IRR and NPV, used by 76 percent and 75 percent (respectively) of the CFOs responding to the survey. These techniques enjoy wider use in larger firms, with the payback approach being more common in smaller firms.[7]

6. A conventional cash flow pattern is one in which the up-front cash flow is negative and all subsequent cash flows are positive. A nonconventional pattern occurs if the up-front cash flow is positive and subsequent cash flows are negative (for example, when a firm sells extended warranties and pays benefits later) or when the cash flows oscillate between positive and negative (as might occur when firms have to reinvest in a project to extend its life).

7. John R. Graham and Campbell R. Harvey, "The Theory and Practice of Corporate Finance: Evidence from the Field," *Journal of Financial Economics* 60 (2001), pp. 187–243.

focus on ETHICS

Nonfinancial Considerations in Project Selection

in practice Corporate ethics codes are often faulted for being "window dressing"— that is, for having little or no effect on actual behavior. Financial ethics expert John Dobson says day-to-day behavior in the workplace "acculturates" employees—teaches them that the behavior they see is rational and acceptable in that environment. The good news is that professional ethics codes, such as those developed for chartered financial analysts, corporate treasury professionals, and certified financial planners, actually provide sound guidelines for behavior. These codes, notes Dobson, are based on economically rational concepts such as integrity and trustworthiness, which guide the decision maker in attempting to increase shareholder wealth. Financial executives insist that there should be no separation between an individual's personal ethics and his or her business ethics. "It's a jungle out there" and "Business is business" should not be excuses for engaging in unethical behavior.

How do ethics codes apply to project selection and capital budgeting? For most companies ethical considerations are primarily concerned with the reduction of potential risks associated with a project. For example, Gateway Computers clearly outlines in its corporate code of ethics the increased regulatory and procurement laws with which an employee must be familiar in order to sell to the government. The company points out that knowingly submitting a false claim or statement to a governmental agency could subject Gateway and its employees to significant monetary civil damages, penalties, and even criminal sanctions.

Another way to incorporate nonfinancial considerations into capital project evaluation is to take into account the likely effect of decisions on nonshareholder parties or stakeholders—employees, customers, the local community, and suppliers. Chipotle Mexican Grill's "Food with Integrity" mission is one example. Chipotle's philosophy is that the company "can always do better in terms of the food we buy. And when we say better, we mean better in every sense of the word—better tasting, coming from better sources, better for the environment, better for the animals, and better for the farmers who raise the animals and grow the produce."[a]

In support of their mission, Chipotle sources meat from animals that are raised humanely, fed a vegetarian diet, and never given antibiotics or hormones. The company favors locally grown produce, organically grown beans, and dairy products made from milk from cows raised in pastures and free of growth hormones. Chipotle's efforts have been rewarded, as sales increased by nearly 50 percent from 2007 to 2009. Investors have also profited, as shares that sold for $44 at the company's 2006 initial public offering were priced at over $150 in mid-2010.

▶ ***What are the potential risks to a company of unethical behaviors by employees? What are potential risks to the public and to stakeholders?***

[a]www.chipotle.com/html/fwi.aspx

In addition, decision makers should keep in mind that nonfinancial considerations may be important elements in project selection, as discussed in the *Focus on Ethics* box.

→ REVIEW QUESTIONS

10–10 How is a *net present value profile* used to compare projects? What causes conflicts in the ranking of projects via net present value and internal rate of return?

10–11 Does the assumption concerning the reinvestment of intermediate cash inflow tend to favor NPV or IRR? In practice, which technique is preferred and why?

Summary

FOCUS ON VALUE

The financial manager must apply appropriate decision techniques to assess whether proposed investment projects create value. Net present value (NPV) and internal rate of return (IRR) are the generally preferred capital budgeting techniques. Both use the cost of capital as the required return. The appeal of NPV and IRR stems from the fact that both indicate whether a proposed investment creates or destroys shareholder value.

NPV clearly indicates the expected dollar amount of wealth creation from a proposed project, whereas IRR only provides the same accept-or-reject decision as NPV. As a consequence of some fundamental differences, NPV and IRR do not necessarily rank projects in the same way. NPV is the theoretically preferred approach. In practice, however, IRR enjoys widespread use because of its intuitive appeal. Regardless, the application of NPV and IRR to good estimates of relevant cash flows should enable the financial manager to recommend projects that are consistent with the firm's goal of **maximizing shareholder wealth.**

REVIEW OF LEARNING GOALS

LG 1 **Understand the key elements of the capital budgeting process.** Capital budgeting techniques are the tools used to assess project acceptability and ranking. Applied to each project's relevant cash flows, they indicate which capital expenditures are consistent with the firm's goal of maximizing owners' wealth.

LG 2 **Calculate, interpret, and evaluate the payback period.** The payback period is the amount of time required for the firm to recover its initial investment, as calculated from cash inflows. Shorter payback periods are preferred. The payback period is relatively easy to calculate, has simple intuitive appeal, considers cash flows, and measures risk exposure. Its weaknesses include lack of linkage to the wealth maximization goal, failure to consider time value explicitly, and the fact that it ignores cash flows that occur after the payback period.

LG 3 **Calculate, interpret, and evaluate the net present value (NPV) and economic value added (EVA).** Because it gives explicit consideration to the time value of money, NPV is considered a sophisticated capital budgeting technique. NPV measures the amount of value created by a given project; only positive NPV projects are acceptable. The rate at which cash flows are discounted in calculating NPV is called the discount rate, required return, cost of capital, or opportunity cost. By whatever name, this rate represents the minimum return that must be earned on a project to leave the firm's market value unchanged. The EVA method begins the same way that NPV does—by calculating a project's net cash flows. However, the EVA approach subtracts from those cash flows a charge that is designed to capture the return that the firm's investors demand on the project. That is, the EVA calculation asks whether a project generates positive cash flows above and beyond what investors demand. If so, then the project is worth undertaking.

LG 4 **Calculate, interpret, and evaluate the internal rate of return (IRR).** Like NPV, IRR is a sophisticated capital budgeting technique. IRR is the compound annual rate of return that the firm will earn by investing in a project and receiving the given cash inflows. By accepting only those projects with IRRs in excess of the firm's cost of capital, the firm should enhance its market value and the wealth of its owners. Both NPV and IRR yield the same accept–reject decisions, but they often provide conflicting rankings.

LG 5 **Use net present value profiles to compare NPV and IRR techniques.** A net present value profile is a graph that depicts projects' NPVs for various discount rates. The NPV profile is prepared by developing a number of "discount rate–net present value" coordinates (including discount rates of 0 percent, the cost of capital, and the IRR for each project) and then plotting them on the same set of discount rate–NPV axes.

LG 6 **Discuss NPV and IRR in terms of conflicting rankings and the theoretical and practical strengths of each approach.** Conflicting rankings of projects frequently emerge from NPV and IRR as a result of differences in the reinvestment rate assumption, as well as the magnitude and timing of cash flows. NPV assumes reinvestment of intermediate cash inflows at the more conservative cost of capital; IRR assumes reinvestment at the project's IRR. On a purely theoretical basis, NPV is preferred over IRR because NPV assumes the more conservative reinvestment rate and does not exhibit the mathematical problem of multiple IRRs that often occurs when IRRs are calculated for nonconventional cash flows. In practice, the IRR is more commonly used because it is consistent with the general preference of business professionals for rates of return, and corporate financial analysts can identify and resolve problems with the IRR before decision makers use it.

Opener-in-Review

The chapter opener described a mining project that had a project NPV of $75 million and an IRR of 20%.

a. Based on the facts that the NPV is positive and the IRR is 20%, what can you infer about Genco's cost of capital? Is it more or less than 20%?

b. Expanding the firm's mining operations in Mexico takes $149 million. Suppose the expansion project will generate a level cash flow (an annuity) for 7 years. If the payback period is 3.6 years, what is the annual cash inflow produced by the expansion project?

c. Calculate the NPV and the IRR of the project given your answer to part **b** and a 9% cost of capital for Genco.

Self-Test Problem (Solutions in Appendix)

LG 2 LG 3 LG 4 LG 5 LG 6

ST10–1 **All techniques with NPV profile—Mutually exclusive projects** Fitch Industries is in the process of choosing the better of two equal-risk, mutually exclusive capital expenditure projects—M and N. The relevant cash flows for each project are shown in the following table. The firm's cost of capital is 14%.

	Project M	Project N
Initial investment (CF_0)	**$28,500**	**$27,000**
Year (t)	**Cash inflows (CF_t)**	
1	$10,000	$11,000
2	10,000	10,000
3	10,000	9,000
4	10,000	8,000

a. Calculate each project's *payback period.*
b. Calculate the *net present value (NPV)* for each project.
c. Calculate the *internal rate of return (IRR)* for each project.
d. Summarize the preferences dictated by each measure you calculated, and indicate which project you would recommend. Explain why.
e. Draw the *net present value profiles* for these projects on the same set of axes, and explain the circumstances under which a conflict in rankings might exist.

Warm-Up Exercises All problems are available in myfinancelab.

LG 2

E10–1 Elysian Fields, Inc., uses a maximum payback period of 6 years and currently must choose between two mutually exclusive projects. Project Hydrogen requires an initial outlay of $25,000; project Helium requires an initial outlay of $35,000. Using the expected cash inflows given for each project in the following table, calculate each project's *payback period.* Which project meets Elysian's standards?

	Expected cash inflows	
Year	**Hydrogen**	**Helium**
1	$6,000	$7,000
2	6,000	7,000
3	8,000	8,000
4	4,000	5,000
5	3,500	5,000
6	2,000	4,000

LG 3 **E10–2** Herky Foods is considering acquisition of a new wrapping machine. The initial investment is estimated at $1.25 million, and the machine will have a 5-year life with no salvage value. Using a 6% discount rate, determine the *net present value (NPV)* of the machine given its expected operating cash inflows shown in the following table. Based on the project's NPV, should Herky make this investment?

Year	Cash inflow
1	$400,000
2	375,000
3	300,000
4	350,000
5	200,000

LG 3 **E10–3** Axis Corp. is considering investment in the best of two mutually exclusive projects. Project Kelvin involves an overhaul of the existing system; it will cost $45,000 and generate cash inflows of $20,000 per year for the next 3 years. Project Thompson involves replacement of the existing system; it will cost $275,000 and generate cash inflows of $60,000 per year for 6 years. Using an 8% cost of capital, calculate each project's NPV, and make a recommendation based on your findings.

LG 4 **E10–4** Billabong Tech uses the *internal rate of return (IRR)* to select projects. Calculate the IRR for each of the following projects and recommend the best project based on this measure. Project T-Shirt requires an initial investment of $15,000 and generates cash inflows of $8,000 per year for 4 years. Project Board Shorts requires an initial investment of $25,000 and produces cash inflows of $12,000 per year for 5 years.

LG 4 LG 5 **E10–5** Cooper Electronics uses *NPV profiles* to visually evaluate competing projects. Key data for the two projects under consideration are given in the following table. Using these data, graph, on the same set of axes, the NPV profiles for each project using discount rates of 0%, 8%, and the IRR.

	Terra	Firma
Initial investment	**$30,000**	**$25,000**
Year	**Operating cash inflows**	
1	$ 7,000	$6,000
2	10,000	9,000
3	12,000	9,000
4	10,000	8,000

Problems

All problems are available in myfinancelab.

LG 2 **P10–1** **Payback period** Jordan Enterprises is considering a capital expenditure that requires an initial investment of $42,000 and returns after-tax cash inflows of $7,000 per year for 10 years. The firm has a maximum acceptable payback period of 8 years.

a. Determine the *payback period* for this project.

b. Should the company accept the project? Why or why not?

LG 2 **P10–2 Payback comparisons** Nova Products has a 5-year maximum acceptable payback period. The firm is considering the purchase of a new machine and must choose between two alternative ones. The first machine requires an initial investment of \$14,000 and generates annual after-tax cash inflows of \$3,000 for each of the next 7 years. The second machine requires an initial investment of \$21,000 and provides an annual cash inflow after taxes of \$4,000 for 20 years.

a. Determine the *payback period* for each machine.
b. Comment on the acceptability of the machines, assuming that they are independent projects.
c. Which machine should the firm accept? Why?
d. Do the machines in this problem illustrate any of the weaknesses of using payback? Discuss.

LG 2 **P10–3 Choosing between two projects with acceptable payback periods** Shell Camping Gear, Inc., is considering two mutually exclusive projects. Each requires an initial investment of \$100,000. John Shell, president of the company, has set a maximum payback period of 4 years. The after-tax cash inflows associated with each project are shown in the following table:

	Cash inflows (CF_t)	
Year	**Project A**	**Project B**
1	\$10,000	\$40,000
2	20,000	30,000
3	30,000	20,000
4	40,000	10,000
5	20,000	20,000

a. Determine the *payback period* of each project.
b. Because they are mutually exclusive, Shell must choose one. Which should the company invest in?
c. Explain why one of the projects is a better choice than the other.

Personal Finance Problem

LG 2 **P10–4 Long-term investment decision, payback method** Bill Williams has the opportunity to invest in project A that costs \$9,000 today and promises to pay annual end-of-year payments of \$2,200, \$2,500, \$2,500, \$2,000, and \$1,800 over the next 5 years. Or, Bill can invest \$9,000 in project B that promises to pay annual end-of-year payments of \$1,500, \$1,500, \$1,500, \$3,500, and \$4,000 over the next 5 years.

a. How long will it take for Bill to recoup his initial investment in project A?
b. How long will it take for Bill to recoup his initial investment in project B?
c. Using the *payback period,* which project should Bill choose?
d. Do you see any problems with his choice?

LG 3 **P10–5 NPV** Calculate the *net present value (NPV)* for the following 20-year projects. Comment on the acceptability of each. Assume that the firm has an opportunity cost of 14%.

a. Initial investment is \$10,000; cash inflows are \$2,000 per year.
b. Initial investment is \$25,000; cash inflows are \$3,000 per year.
c. Initial investment is \$30,000; cash inflows are \$5,000 per year.

LG 3 **P10–6 NPV for varying costs of capital** Dane Cosmetics is evaluating a new fragrance-mixing machine. The machine requires an initial investment of $24,000 and will generate after-tax cash inflows of $5,000 per year for 8 years. For each of the costs of capital listed, (1) calculate the *net present value (NPV)*, (2) indicate whether to accept or reject the machine, and (3) explain your decision.

a. The cost of capital is 10%.
b. The cost of capital is 12%.
c. The cost of capital is 14%.

LG 3 **P10–7 Net present value—Independent projects** Using a 14% cost of capital, calculate the *net present value* for each of the independent projects shown in the following table, and indicate whether each is acceptable.

	Project A	Project B	Project C	Project D	Project E
Initial investment (CF_0)	**$26,000**	**$500,000**	**$170,000**	**$950,000**	**$80,000**
Year (t)	**Cash inflows (CF_t)**				
1	$4,000	$100,000	$20,000	$230,000	$ 0
2	4,000	120,000	19,000	230,000	0
3	4,000	140,000	18,000	230,000	0
4	4,000	160,000	17,000	230,000	20,000
5	4,000	180,000	16,000	230,000	30,000
6	4,000	200,000	15,000	230,000	0
7	4,000		14,000	230,000	50,000
8	4,000		13,000	230,000	60,000
9	4,000		12,000		70,000
10	4,000		11,000		

LG 3 **P10–8 NPV** Simes Innovations, Inc., is negotiating to purchase exclusive rights to manufacture and market a solar-powered toy car. The car's inventor has offered Simes the choice of either a one-time payment of $1,500,000 today or a series of five year-end payments of $385,000.

a. If Simes has a cost of capital of 9%, which form of payment should it choose?
b. What yearly payment would make the two offers identical in value at a cost of capital of 9%?
c. Would your answer to part **a** of this problem be different if the yearly payments were made at the beginning of each year? Show what difference, if any, that change in timing would make to the present value calculation.
d. The after-tax cash inflows associated with this purchase are projected to amount to $250,000 per year for 15 years. Will this factor change the firm's decision about how to fund the initial investment?

LG 3 **P10–9 NPV and maximum return** A firm can purchase a fixed asset for a $13,000 initial investment. The asset generates an annual after-tax cash inflow of $4,000 for 4 years.

a. Determine the *net present value (NPV)* of the asset, assuming that the firm has a 10% cost of capital. Is the project acceptable?
b. Determine the maximum required rate of return (closest whole-percentage rate) that the firm can have and still accept the asset. Discuss this finding in light of your response in part **a.**

LG 3 **P10–10 NPV—Mutually exclusive projects** Hook Industries is considering the replacement of one of its old drill presses. Three alternative replacement presses are under consideration. The relevant cash flows associated with each are shown in the following table. The firm's cost of capital is 15%.

	Press A	Press B	Press C
Initial investment (CF_0)	$85,000	$60,000	$130,000
Year (t)		**Cash inflows (CF_t)**	
1	$18,000	$12,000	$50,000
2	18,000	14,000	30,000
3	18,000	16,000	20,000
4	18,000	18,000	20,000
5	18,000	20,000	20,000
6	18,000	25,000	30,000
7	18,000	—	40,000
8	18,000	—	50,000

a. Calculate the *net present value (NPV)* of each press.
b. Using NPV, evaluate the acceptability of each press.
c. Rank the presses from best to worst using NPV.
d. Calculate the *profitability index (PI)* for each press.
e. Rank the presses from best to worst using *PI*.

Personal Finance Problem

LG 3 **P10–11 Long-term investment decision, NPV method** Jenny Jenks has researched the financial pros and cons of entering into an elite MBA program at her state university. The tuition and needed books for a master's program will have an upfront cost of $100,000. On average, a person with an MBA degree earns an extra $20,000 per year over a business career of 40 years. Jenny feels that her opportunity cost of capital is 6%. Given her estimates, find the *net present value (NPV)* of entering this MBA program. Are the benefits of further education worth the associated costs?

LG 2 LG 3 **P10–12 Payback and NPV** Neil Corporation has three projects under consideration. The cash flows for each project are shown in the following table. The firm has a 16% cost of capital.

	Project A	Project B	Project C
Initial investment (CF_0)	$40,000	$40,000	$40,000
Year (t)		**Cash inflows (CF_t)**	
1	$13,000	$ 7,000	$19,000
2	13,000	10,000	16,000
3	13,000	13,000	13,000
4	13,000	16,000	10,000
5	13,000	19,000	7,000

a. Calculate each project's *payback period.* Which project is preferred according to this method?
b. Calculate each project's *net present value (NPV).* Which project is preferred according to this method?
c. Comment on your findings in parts **a** and **b,** and recommend the best project. Explain your recommendation.

LG 3 **P10–13 NPV and EVA** A project costs $2.5 million up front and will generate cash flows in perpetuity of $240,000. The firm's cost of capital is 9%.
a. Calculate the project's NPV.
b. Calculate the annual EVA in a typical year.
c. Calculate the overall project EVA and compare to your answer in part **a.**

LG 4 **P10–14 Internal rate of return** For each of the projects shown in the following table, calculate the *internal rate of return (IRR).* Then indicate, for each project, the maximum cost of capital that the firm could have and still find the IRR acceptable.

	Project A	Project B	Project C	Project D
Initial investment (CF_0)	**$90,000**	**$490,000**	**$20,000**	**$240,000**
Year (t)		**Cash inflows (CF_t)**		
1	$20,000	$150,000	$7,500	$120,000
2	25,000	150,000	7,500	100,000
3	30,000	150,000	7,500	80,000
4	35,000	150,000	7,500	60,000
5	40,000	—	7,500	—

LG 4 **P10–15 IRR—Mutually exclusive projects** Bell Manufacturing is attempting to choose the better of two mutually exclusive projects for expanding the firm's warehouse capacity. The relevant cash flows for the projects are shown in the following table. The firm's cost of capital is 15%.

	Project X	Project Y
Initial investment (CF_0)	**$500,000**	**$325,000**
Year (t)	**Cash inflows (CF_t)**	
1	$100,000	$140,000
2	120,000	120,000
3	150,000	95,000
4	190,000	70,000
5	250,000	50,000

a. Calculate the *IRR* to the nearest whole percent for each of the projects.
b. Assess the acceptability of each project on the basis of the IRRs found in part **a.**
c. Which project, on this basis, is preferred?

Personal Finance Problem

LG 4 **P10–16** **Long-term investment decision, IRR method** Billy and Mandy Jones have $25,000 to invest. On average, they do not make any investment that will not return at least 7.5% per year. They have been approached with an investment opportunity that requires $25,000 upfront and has a payout of $6,000 at the end of each of the next 5 years. Using the *internal rate of return (IRR)* method and their requirements, determine whether Billy and Mandy should undertake the investment.

LG 4 **P10–17** **IRR, investment life, and cash inflows** Oak Enterprises accepts projects earning more than the firm's 15% cost of capital. Oak is currently considering a 10-year project that provides annual cash inflows of $10,000 and requires an initial investment of $61,450. (*Note:* All amounts are after taxes.)

a. Determine the *IRR* of this project. Is it acceptable?

b. Assuming that the cash inflows continue to be $10,000 per year, how many *additional years* would the flows have to continue to make the project acceptable (that is, to make it have an IRR of 15%)?

c. With the given life, initial investment, and cost of capital, what is the minimum annual cash inflow that the firm should accept?

LG 3 LG 4 **P10–18** **NPV and IRR** Benson Designs has prepared the following estimates for a long-term project it is considering. The initial investment is $18,250, and the project is expected to yield after-tax cash inflows of $4,000 per year for 7 years. The firm has a 10% cost of capital.

a. Determine the *net present value (NPV)* for the project.

b. Determine the *internal rate of return (IRR)* for the project.

c. Would you recommend that the firm accept or reject the project? Explain your answer.

LG 3 LG 4 **P10–19** **NPV, with rankings** Botany Bay, Inc., a maker of casual clothing, is considering four projects. Because of past financial difficulties, the company has a high cost of capital at 15%. Which of these projects would be acceptable under those cost circumstances?

	Project A	Project B	Project C	Project D
Initial investment (CF_0)	$50,000	$100,000	$80,000	$180,000
Year (t)		Cash inflows (CF_t)		
1	$20,000	$35,000	$20,000	$100,000
2	20,000	50,000	40,000	80,000
3	20,000	50,000	60,000	60,000

a. Calculate the *NPV* of each project, using a cost of capital of 15%.

b. Rank acceptable projects by NPV.

c. Calculate the *IRR* of each project, and use it to determine the highest cost of capital at which all of the projects would be acceptable.

LG 2 LG 3 LG 4 **P10–20 All techniques, conflicting rankings** Nicholson Roofing Materials, Inc., is considering two mutually exclusive projects, each with an initial investment of $150,000. The company's board of directors has set a maximum 4-year payback requirement and has set its cost of capital at 9%. The cash inflows associated with the two projects are shown in the following table.

	Cash inflows (CF_t)	
Year	**Project A**	**Project B**
1	$45,000	$75,000
2	45,000	60,000
3	45,000	30,000
4	45,000	30,000
5	45,000	30,000
6	45,000	30,000

a. Calculate the *payback period* for each project.
b. Calculate the *NPV* of each project at 0%.
c. Calculate the *NPV* of each project at 9%.
d. Derive the *IRR* of each project.
e. Rank the projects by each of the techniques used. Make and justify a recommendation.

LG 2 LG 3 LG 4 **P10–21 Payback, NPV, and IRR** Rieger International is attempting to evaluate the feasibility of investing $95,000 in a piece of equipment that has a 5-year life. The firm has estimated the *cash inflows* associated with the proposal as shown in the following table. The firm has a 12% cost of capital.

Year (t)	**Cash inflows (CF_t)**
1	$20,000
2	25,000
3	30,000
4	35,000
5	40,000

a. Calculate the *payback period* for the proposed investment.
b. Calculate the *net present value (NPV)* for the proposed investment.
c. Calculate the *internal rate of return (IRR)*, rounded to the nearest whole percent, for the proposed investment.
d. Evaluate the acceptability of the proposed investment using NPV and IRR. What recommendation would you make relative to implementation of the project? Why?

LG 3 LG 4 LG 5 **P10–22 NPV, IRR, and NPV profiles** Thomas Company is considering two mutually exclusive projects. The firm, which has a 12% cost of capital, has estimated its cash flows as shown in the following table.

	Project A	Project B
Initial investment (CF_0)	**$130,000**	**$85,000**
Year (t)	**Cash inflows (CF_t)**	
1	$25,000	$40,000
2	35,000	35,000
3	45,000	30,000
4	50,000	10,000
5	55,000	5,000

a. Calculate the *NPV* of each project, and assess its acceptability.
b. Calculate the *IRR* for each project, and assess its acceptability.
c. Draw the *NPV profiles* for both projects on the same set of axes.
d. Evaluate and discuss the rankings of the two projects on the basis of your findings in parts **a, b,** and **c.**
e. Explain your findings in part **d** in light of the pattern of cash inflows associated with each project.

LG 2 LG 3 LG 4 LG 5 LG 6

P10–23 **All techniques—Decision among mutually exclusive investments** Pound Industries is attempting to select the best of three mutually exclusive projects. The initial investment and after-tax cash inflows associated with these projects are shown in the following table.

Cash flows	Project A	Project B	Project C
Initial investment (CF_0)	$60,000	$100,000	$110,000
Cash inflows (CF_t), t = 1 to 5	$20,000	$ 31,500	$ 32,500

a. Calculate the *payback period* for each project.
b. Calculate the *net present value (NPV)* of each project, assuming that the firm has a cost of capital equal to 13%.
c. Calculate the *internal rate of return (IRR)* for each project.
d. Draw the *net present value profiles* for both projects on the same set of axes, and discuss any conflict in ranking that may exist between NPV and IRR.
e. Summarize the preferences dictated by each measure, and indicate which project you would recommend. Explain why.

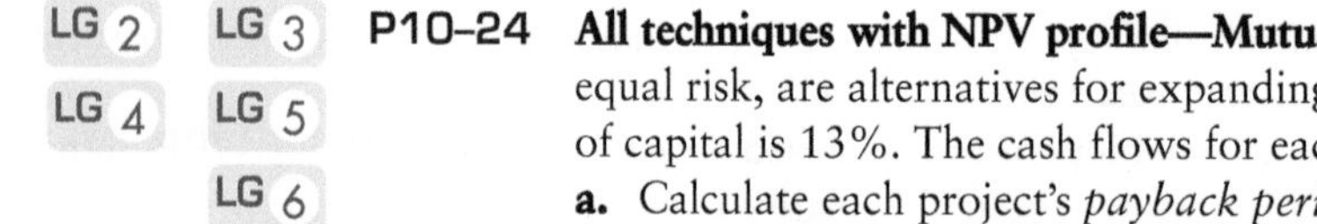

LG 2 LG 3 LG 4 LG 5 LG 6

P10–24 **All techniques with NPV profile—Mutually exclusive projects** Projects A and B, of equal risk, are alternatives for expanding Rosa Company's capacity. The firm's cost of capital is 13%. The cash flows for each project are shown in the following table.

a. Calculate each project's *payback period.*
b. Calculate the *net present value (NPV)* for each project.
c. Calculate the *internal rate of return (IRR)* for each project.
d. Draw the *net present value profiles* for both projects on the same set of axes, and discuss any conflict in ranking that may exist between NPV and IRR.
e. Summarize the preferences dictated by each measure, and indicate which project you would recommend. Explain why.

	Project A	Project B
Initial investment (CF_0)	$80,000	$50,000
Year (t)	Cash inflows (CF_t)	
1	$15,000	$15,000
2	20,000	15,000
3	25,000	15,000
4	30,000	15,000
5	35,000	15,000

LG 6 P10–25 **Integrative—Multiple IRRs** Froogle Enterprises is evaluating an unusual investment project. What makes the project unusual is the stream of cash inflows and outflows shown in the following table:

Year	Cash flow
0	$ 200,000
1	−920,000
2	1,582,000
3	−1,205,200
4	343,200

a. Why is it difficult to calculate the *payback period* for this project?
b. Calculate the investment's net present value at each of the following discount rates: 0%, 5%, 10%, 15%, 20%, 25%, 30%, 35%.
c. What does your answer to part **b** tell you about this project's *IRR?*
d. Should Froogle invest in this project if its cost of capital is 5%? What if the cost of capital is 15%?
e. In general, when faced with a project like this, how should a firm decide whether to invest in the project or reject it?

LG 3 LG 4 LG 5 P10–26 **Integrative—Conflicting Rankings** The High-Flying Growth Company (HFGC) has been growing very rapidly in recent years, making its shareholders rich in the process. The average annual rate of return on the stock in the last few years has been 20%, and HFGC managers believe that 20% is a reasonable figure for the firm's cost of capital. To sustain a high growth rate, the HFGC CEO argues that the company must continue to invest in projects that offer the highest rate of return possible. Two projects are currently under review. The first is an expansion of the firm's production capacity, and the second project involves introducing one of the firm's existing products into a new market. Cash flows from each project appear in the following table.
a. Calculate the NPV, IRR, and PI for both projects.
b. Rank the projects based on their NPVs, IRRs, and PIs.
c. Do the rankings in part **b** agree or not? If not, why not?
d. The firm can only afford to undertake one of these investments, and the CEO favors the product introduction because it offers a higher rate of return (that is, a higher IRR) than the plant expansion. What do you think the firm should do? Why?

Year	Plant expansion	Product introduction
0	−$3,500,000	−$500,000
1	1,500,000	250,000
2	2,000,000	350,000
3	2,500,000	375,000
4	2,750,000	425,000

LG 1 LG 6 **P10–27** **ETHICS PROBLEM** Gap, Inc., is trying to incorporate human resource and supplier considerations into its management decision making. Here is Gap's report of findings from a recent Social Responsibility Report:

> Because factory owners sometimes try to hide violations, Gap emphasizes training for factory managers. However, due to regional differences, the training varies from one site to another. The report notes that 10 to 25 percent of workers in China, Taiwan, and Saipan have been harassed and humiliated. Less than half of the factories in sub-Saharan Africa have adequate worker safety regulations and infrastructure. In Mexico, Latin America, and the Caribbean, 25 to 50 percent of the suppliers fail to pay even the minimum wage.

Calvert Group, Ltd., a mutual fund family that focuses on "socially responsible investing," had this to say about the impact of Gap's report:

> With revenues of $15.9 billion and over 300,000 employees worldwide, Gap leads the U.S. apparel sector and has contracts with over 3,000 factories globally. Calvert has been in dialogue with Gap for about five years, the last two as part of the Working Group.
>
> Gap's supplier monitoring program focuses on remediation, because its suppliers produce for multiple apparel companies and would likely move their capacity to different clients rather than adopt conditions deemed too demanding. About one-third of the factories Gap examined comfortably met Gap's criteria, another third had barely acceptable conditions, and the final third missed the minimum standards. Gap terminated contracts with 136 factories where it found conditions to be beyond remediation.
>
> Increased transparency and disclosure are crucial in measuring a company's commitment to raising human rights standards and improving the lives of workers. Gap's report is an important first step in the direction of a model format that other companies can adapt.[8]

If Gap were to aggressively pursue renegotiations with suppliers, based on this report, what is the likely effect on Gap's expenses in the next 5 years? In your opinion, what would be the impact on its stock price in the immediate future? After 10 years?

---

8. www.calvert.com/news_newsArticle.asp?article=4612&image=cn.gif&keepleftnav=Calvert+News

Spreadsheet Exercise

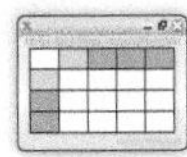

The Drillago Company is involved in searching for locations in which to drill for oil. The firm's current project requires an initial investment of $15 million and has an estimated life of 10 years. The expected future cash inflows for the project are as shown in the following table:

Year	Cash inflows
1	$ 600,000
2	1,000,000
3	1,000,000
4	2,000,000
5	3,000,000
6	3,500,000
7	4,000,000
8	6,000,000
9	8,000,000
10	12,000,000

The firm's current cost of capital is 13%.

TO DO

Create a spreadsheet to answer the following:

a. Calculate the project's *net present value (NPV)*. Is the project acceptable under the NPV technique? Explain.

b. Calculate the project's *internal rate of return (IRR)*. Is the project acceptable under the IRR technique? Explain.

c. In this case, did the two methods produce the same results? Generally, is there a preference between the NPV and IRR techniques? Explain.

d. Calculate the *payback period* for the project. If the firm usually accepts projects that have payback periods between 1 and 7 years, is this project acceptable?

Visit www.myfinancelab.com for **Chapter Case: *Making Norwich Tool's Lathe Investment Decision,*** Group Exercises, and numerous online resources.

11 Capital Budgeting Cash Flows

Learning Goals

LG 1 Discuss the three major cash flow components.

LG 2 Discuss relevant cash flows, expansion versus replacement decisions, sunk costs and opportunity costs, and international capital budgeting.

LG 3 Calculate the initial investment associated with a proposed capital expenditure.

LG 4 Discuss the tax implications associated with the sale of an old asset.

LG 5 Find the relevant operating cash inflows associated with a proposed capital expenditure.

LG 6 Determine the terminal cash flow associated with a proposed capital expenditure.

Why This Chapter Matters to You

In your *professional* life

ACCOUNTING You need to understand capital budgeting cash flows to provide revenue, cost, depreciation, and tax data for use both in monitoring existing projects and in developing cash flows for proposed projects.

INFORMATION SYSTEMS You need to understand capital budgeting cash flows to maintain and facilitate the retrieval of cash flow data for both completed and existing projects.

MANAGEMENT You need to understand capital budgeting cash flows so that you will understand which cash flows are relevant in making decisions about proposals for acquiring additional production facilities, for new marketing programs, for new products, and for the expansion of existing product lines.

MARKETING You need to understand capital budgeting cash flows so that you can make revenue and cost estimates for proposals for new marketing programs, for new products, and for the expansion of existing product lines.

OPERATIONS You need to understand capital budgeting cash flows so that you can make revenue and cost estimates for proposals for the acquisition of new equipment and production facilities.

In your *personal* life

You are not mandated to provide financial statements prepared using GAAP, so you naturally focus on cash flows. When considering a major outflow of funds (for example, purchase of a house, funding of a college education), you can project the associated cash flows and use these estimates to assess the value and affordability of the assets and any associated future outlays.

ExxonMobil

Maintaining Its Project Inventory

As the largest publicly traded oil company in the world, ExxonMobil's long-term investments are at the heart of its ability to generate shareholder wealth. Its 2009 earnings of more than $19 billion resulted in a 16 percent return on capital invested. Through dividends and share repurchases, ExxonMobil returned $26 billion to its shareholders in 2009 and more than $150 billion over the previous five years.

To maintain its petroleum reserves, ExxonMobil must continually add to its inventory of discovered oil and gas resources. It holds exploration rights to 109 million undeveloped acres in 37 countries. Each year, the company initiates a number of megaprojects that add to its exploration rights, locate and "prove" additional reserves, or increase the productivity of currently producing wells.

Total capital and exploration expenditures in 2009 amounted to a record $27 billion. Within the next 5 years, ExxonMobil anticipates investing more than $125 billion. ExxonMobil has partnered with Qatar Petroleum to develop a global-scale petrochemical complex in Ras Laffan Industrial City, Qatar. The plant is expected to start up in late 2015, and it will include two 650,000 ton-per-year polyethylene plants, a 1.6 million-ton-per-year steam cracker, and a 700,000 ton-per-year ethylene glycol facility.

While Exxon is often able to bring in projects on or under budget, increasing costs could cause some future development projects to go over budget. Drilling and exploration costs are expected to rise. Recent high oil prices have led to a surge in demand for exploration, and the cost of drilling equipment and workers has jumped at least 15 percent a year during the last several years. Further complicating oil production efforts in the future will be an increase in the use of less-than-suitable oil sources, such as shale oil and tar sands.

Like ExxonMobil, every firm must evaluate the costs and returns of projects for expansion, asset replacement or renewal, research and development, advertising, and other areas that require a long-term commitment of funds in expectation of future returns. Chapter 11 explains how to identify the relevant cash outflows and inflows that must be considered in making major investment decisions.

LG 1 LG 2

11.1 Relevant Cash Flows

relevant cash flows
The *incremental cash outflow (investment) and resulting subsequent inflows* associated with a proposed capital expenditure.

incremental cash flows
The *additional* cash flows—outflows or inflows—expected to result from a proposed capital expenditure.

Chapter 10 introduced the capital budgeting process and the techniques financial managers use for evaluating and selecting long-term investments. To evaluate investment opportunities, financial managers must determine the **relevant cash flows** associated with the project. These are the *incremental cash outflows (investment) and inflows (return)*. The **incremental cash flows** represent the *additional* cash flows—outflows or inflows—expected to result from a proposed capital expenditure. As noted in Chapter 4, cash flows rather than accounting figures are used because cash flows directly affect the firm's ability to pay bills and purchase assets. The nearby *Focus on Ethics* box discusses the accuracy of cash flow estimates and cites one reason that even well-estimated deals may not work out as planned.

The remainder of this chapter is devoted to the procedures for measuring the relevant cash flows associated with proposed capital expenditures.

MAJOR CASH FLOW COMPONENTS

The cash flows of any project may include three basic components: (1) an initial investment, (2) operating cash inflows, and (3) terminal cash flow. All projects—whether for expansion, replacement or renewal, or some other purpose—have the first two components. Some, however, lack the final component, terminal cash flow.

focus on ETHICS

A Question of Accuracy

in practice The process of capital budgeting based on projected cash flows has been a part of the investment decision process for more than 40 years. This procedure for evaluating investment opportunities works well when cash flows can be estimated with certainty, but in real-world corporate practice, many investment decisions involve a high degree of uncertainty. The decision is even more complicated when the project under consideration is the acquisition of another company or part of another company.

Because estimates of the cash flows from an investment project involve making assumptions about the future, they may be subject to considerable error. The problem becomes more complicated as the period of time under consideration becomes longer and when the project is unique in nature with no comparables. Other complications may arise involving accounting for additional (extraordinary) cash flows—for example, the cost of litigation, compliance with tougher environmental standards, or the costs of disposal or recycling of an asset at the completion of the project.

All too often, the initial champagne celebration gives way once the final cost of a deal is tallied. In fact, taken as a whole, mergers and acquisitions in recent years have produced a disheartening *negative* 12 percent return on investment. While the financial data necessary to generate discounted cash flow estimates are ever more readily available, these days more attention is being paid to the accuracy of the numbers. Inspired in part by post-Enron focus on governance and the threat of shareholder lawsuits, board members have been pushing corporate managers to make a stronger case for the deals they propose. Says Glenn Gurtcheff, managing director and co-head of middle market M&A for Piper Jaffray & Co., "They're not just taking the company's audited and unaudited financial statements at face value; they are really diving into the numbers and trying to understand not just their accuracy, but what they mean in terms of trends."

If valuation has improved so much, why do analyses show that companies often overpay? The answer lies in the imperial CEO. Improvements in valuation techniques can be negated when the process deteriorates into a game of tweaking the numbers to justify a deal the CEO wants to do, regardless of price. This "make it work" form of capital budgeting often results in building the empire under the CEO's control at the expense of the firm's shareholders.

► *What would your options be when faced with the demands of an imperial CEO who expects you to "make it work"? Brainstorm several options.*

FIGURE 11.1

Cash Flow Components
Time line for major cash flow components

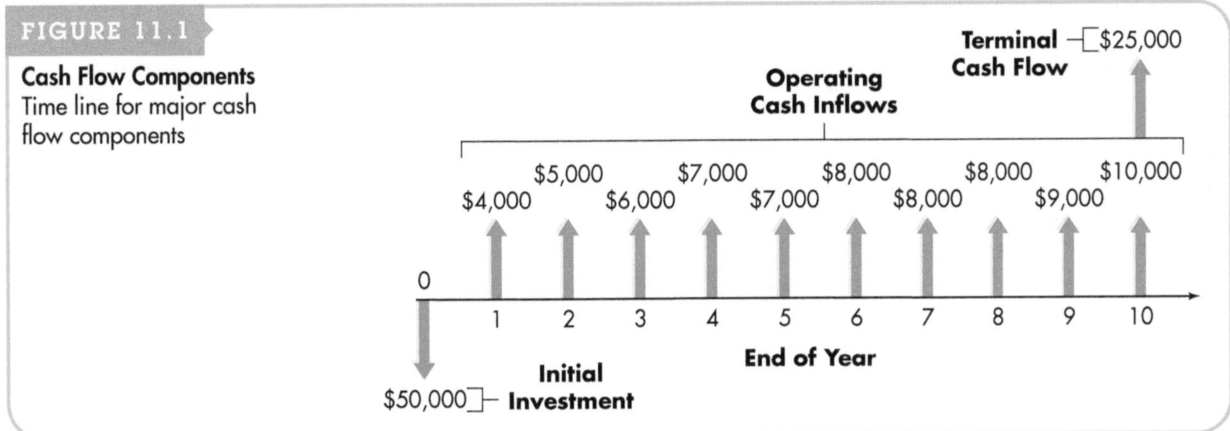

initial investment
The relevant cash outflow for a proposed project at time zero.

operating cash inflows
The incremental after-tax cash inflows resulting from implementation of a project during its life.

terminal cash flow
The after-tax nonoperating cash flow occurring in the final year of a project. It is usually attributable to liquidation of the project.

Figure 11.1 depicts on a time line the cash flows for a project. The **initial investment** for the proposed project is $50,000. This is the relevant cash outflow at time zero. The **operating cash inflows,** which are the incremental after-tax cash inflows resulting from implementation of the project during its life, gradually increase from $4,000 in its first year to $10,000 in its tenth and final year. The **terminal cash flow** is the after-tax nonoperating cash flow occurring in the final year of the project. It is usually attributable to liquidation of the project. In this case it is $25,000, received at the end of the project's 10-year life. Note that the terminal cash flow does *not* include the $10,000 operating cash inflow for year 10.

EXPANSION VERSUS REPLACEMENT DECISIONS

Developing relevant cash flow estimates is most straightforward in the case of *expansion decisions.* In this case, the initial investment, operating cash inflows, and terminal cash flow are merely the after-tax cash outflow and inflows associated with the proposed capital expenditure.

Identifying relevant cash flows for *replacement decisions* is more complicated, because the firm must identify the *incremental* cash outflow and inflows that would result from the proposed replacement. The initial investment in the case of replacement is the difference between the initial investment needed to acquire the new asset and any after-tax cash inflows expected from liquidation of the old asset. The operating cash inflows are the difference between the operating cash inflows from the new asset and those from the old asset. The terminal cash flow is the difference between the after-tax cash flows expected upon termination of the new and the old assets. These relationships are shown in Figure 11.2.

Actually, all capital budgeting decisions can be viewed as replacement decisions. *Expansion decisions are merely replacement decisions in which all cash flows from the old asset are zero.* In light of this fact, this chapter focuses primarily on replacement decisions.

SUNK COSTS AND OPPORTUNITY COSTS

When estimating the relevant cash flows associated with a proposed capital expenditure, the firm must recognize any sunk costs and opportunity costs. These costs are easy to mishandle or ignore, particularly when determining a project's

FIGURE 11.2

Relevant Cash Flows for Replacement Decisions
Calculation of the three components of relevant cash flows for a replacement decision

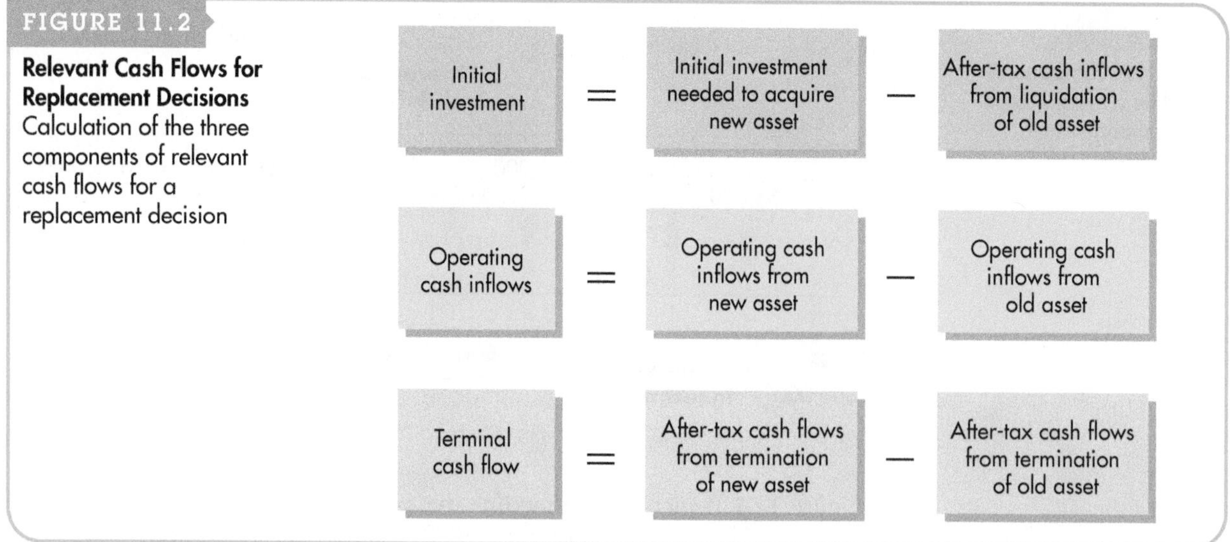

sunk costs
Cash outlays that have already been made (past outlays) and therefore have no effect on the cash flows relevant to a current decision.

opportunity costs
Cash flows that could be realized from the best alternative use of an owned asset.

incremental cash flows. **Sunk costs** are cash outlays that have already been made (past outlays) and therefore have no effect on the cash flows relevant to the current decision. As a result, *sunk costs should not be included in a project's incremental cash flows.*

Opportunity costs are cash flows that could be realized from the best alternative use of an owned asset. They therefore represent cash flows that *will not be realized* as a result of employing that asset in the proposed project. Because of this, any *opportunity costs should be included as cash outflows when one is determining a project's incremental cash flows.*

Example 11.1 ▸

Jankow Equipment is considering renewing its drill press X12, which it purchased 3 years earlier for $237,000, by retrofitting it with the computerized control system from an obsolete piece of equipment it owns. The obsolete equipment could be sold today for a high bid of $42,000, but without its computerized control system, it would be worth nothing. Jankow is in the process of estimating the labor and materials costs of retrofitting the system to drill press X12 and the benefits expected from the retrofit. The $237,000 cost of drill press X12 is a *sunk cost* because it represents an earlier cash outlay. It *would not be included* as a cash outflow when determining the cash flows relevant to the retrofit decision. Although Jankow owns the obsolete piece of equipment, the proposed use of its computerized control system represents an *opportunity cost* of $42,000—the highest price at which it could be sold today. This opportunity cost *would be included* as a cash outflow associated with using the computerized control system.

INTERNATIONAL CAPITAL BUDGETING AND LONG-TERM INVESTMENTS

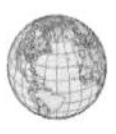

Although the same basic capital budgeting principles are used for domestic and international projects, several additional factors must be addressed in evaluating foreign investment opportunities. International capital budgeting differs from the domestic version because (1) cash outflows and inflows occur in a foreign currency, and (2) foreign investments entail potentially significant political risk. Both of these risks can be minimized through careful planning.

Companies face both long-term and short-term *currency risks* related to both the invested capital and the cash flows resulting from it. Long-term currency risk can be minimized by financing the foreign investment at least partly in the local capital markets. This step ensures that the project's revenues, operating costs, and financing costs will be in the local currency. Likewise, the dollar value of short-term, local-currency cash flows can be protected by using special securities and strategies such as futures, forwards, and options market instruments.

Political risks can be minimized by using both operating and financial strategies. For example, by structuring the investment as a joint venture and selecting a well-connected local partner, the U.S. company can minimize the risk of its operations being seized or harassed. Companies also can protect themselves from having their investment returns blocked by local governments by structuring the financing of such investments as debt rather than as equity. Debt-service payments are legally enforceable claims, whereas equity returns (such as dividends) are not. Even if local courts do not support the claims of the U.S. company, the company can threaten to pursue its case in U.S. courts.

foreign direct investment
The transfer of capital, managerial, and technical assets to a foreign country.

In spite of the preceding difficulties, **foreign direct investment (FDI)**, which involves the transfer of capital, managerial, and technical assets to a foreign country, has surged in recent years. This is evident in the growing market values of foreign assets owned by U.S.–based companies and of foreign direct investment in the United States, particularly by British, Canadian, Dutch, German, and Japanese companies. Furthermore, foreign direct investment by U.S. companies seems to be accelerating. See the *Global Focus* box on page 432 for a discussion of recent foreign direct investment in China.

Matter of fact

FDI in the United States

According to the U.S. Department of Commerce's Bureau of Economic Analysis (BEA), FDI plays an important role in the U.S. economy. BEA divides FDI into two categories: Greenfield Investment and Mergers and Acquisitions. Greenfield investments create new enterprises and develop or expand production facilities, while Mergers and Acquisitions involve the purchase of an existing enterprise.

In 2008 the United States was the world's largest recipient of FDI, receiving more than $325.3 billion in FDI. This amount was a 37 percent increase from the previous year. Further, the $2.1 trillion worth of FDI in the United States at the end of 2008 is the equivalent of approximately 16 percent of U.S. gross domestic product (GDP).

→ REVIEW QUESTIONS

11–1 Why is it important to evaluate capital budgeting projects on the basis of *incremental cash flows?*

11–2 What three components of cash flow may exist for a given project? How can expansion decisions be treated as replacement decisions? Explain.

GLOBAL focus

Changes May Influence Future Investments in China

in practice Foreign direct investment in China soared in 2009. Not including banks, insurance, and securities, foreign direct investment amounted to $90 billion. China's economy has surged more than tenfold since 1980, the first year it allowed foreign investments, when money began pouring into factories on China's east coast.

China's trade surplus in 2009 was $196 billion. With a strong foreign exchange surplus, China is no longer desperate for capital from overseas but is now primarily interested in foreign skills and technologies. Prime Minister Wen Jiabao wants to steer investments toward the manufacturing of higher-value products and toward less-developed regions. Wen is giving tax breaks and promising speedy approvals for investments away from areas in the east, such as Shanghai and the Pearl River Delta.

Typical of foreign investors in China is Intel Capital, a subsidiary of **Intel Corporation.** As of the middle of 2010, Intel Capital's portfolio had $200 million invested in 25 Chinese companies. Intel Capital is no beginner at foreign investment; it has invested more than $4 billion in more than 1,000 companies around the world.

China allows three types of foreign investments: a *wholly foreign-owned enterprise* (WFOE) in which the firm is entirely funded with foreign capital; a *joint venture* in which the foreign partner must provide at least 25 percent of initial capital; and a *representative office* (RO), the most common and easily established entity, which cannot perform business activities that directly result in profits. Generally an RO is the first step in establishing a China presence and includes mechanisms for upgrading to a WFOE or joint venture.

As with any foreign investment, investing in China is not without risk. One potential risk facing foreign investors in China is that the communist government could decide to nationalize private companies. Many public companies in China are firms that were once owned by the communist government, such as China Life Insurance Company, and it is always possible that the communist government may decide that it wishes to own and control these companies again. The list of governments similar to China's that have nationalized private companies is fairly long. While there is no evidence that this will happen in China, it should be considered one of the risks.

► ***Although China has been actively campaigning for foreign investment, how do you think having a communist government affects its foreign investment?***

11–3 What effect do *sunk costs* and *opportunity costs* have on a project's incremental cash flows?

11–4 How can *currency risk* and *political risk* be minimized when one is making *foreign direct investment?*

LG 3 LG 4

11.2 Finding the Initial Investment

The term *initial investment* as used here refers to the relevant cash outflows to be considered when evaluating a prospective capital expenditure. Our discussion of capital budgeting will focus on projects with initial investments that occur at *time zero*—the time at which the expenditure is made. The initial investment is calculated by subtracting all cash inflows occurring at time zero from all cash outflows occurring at time zero.

The basic format for determining the initial investment is given in Table 11.1. The cash flows that must be considered when determining the initial investment associated with a capital expenditure are the installed cost of the new asset, the after-tax proceeds (if any) from the sale of an old asset, and the change (if any) in

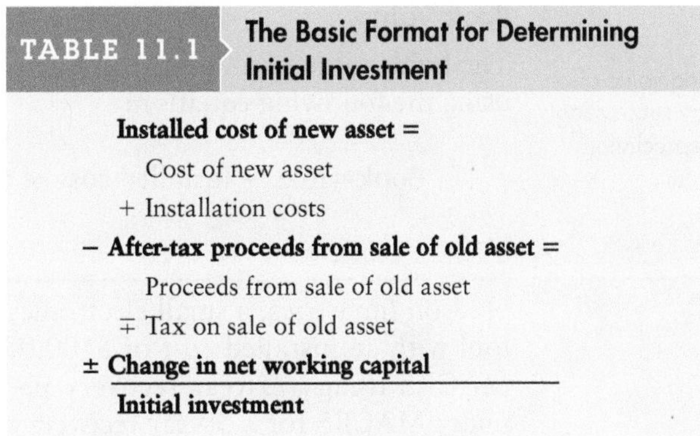

TABLE 11.1 The Basic Format for Determining Initial Investment

Installed cost of new asset =
Cost of new asset
+ Installation costs
− After-tax proceeds from sale of old asset =
Proceeds from sale of old asset
∓ Tax on sale of old asset
± Change in net working capital
Initial investment

net working capital. Note that if there are no installation costs and the firm is not replacing an existing asset, then the cost (purchase price) of the new asset, adjusted for any change in net working capital, is equal to the initial investment.

cost of new asset
The net outflow necessary to acquire a new asset.

installation costs
Any added costs that are necessary to place an asset into operation.

installed cost of new asset
The *cost of new asset* plus its *installation costs;* equals the asset's depreciable value.

after-tax proceeds from sale of old asset
The difference between the old asset's sale proceeds and any applicable taxes or tax refunds related to its sale.

proceeds from sale of old asset
The cash inflows, net of any *removal* or *cleanup costs,* resulting from the sale of an existing asset.

tax on sale of old asset
Tax that depends on the relationship between the old asset's sale price and *book value* and on existing government tax rules.

INSTALLED COST OF NEW ASSET

As shown in Table 11.1, the installed cost of the new asset is found by adding the cost of the new asset to its installation costs. The **cost of new asset** is the net outflow that its acquisition requires. Usually, we are concerned with the acquisition of a fixed asset for which a definite purchase price is paid. **Installation costs** are any added costs that are necessary to place an asset into operation. The Internal Revenue Service (IRS) requires the firm to add installation costs to the purchase price of an asset to determine its depreciable value, which is expensed over a period of years. The **installed cost of new asset,** calculated by adding the *cost of new asset* to its *installation costs,* equals its depreciable value.

AFTER-TAX PROCEEDS FROM SALE OF OLD ASSET

Table 11.1 shows that the **after-tax proceeds from sale of old asset** decrease the firm's initial investment in the new asset. These proceeds are the difference between the old asset's sale proceeds and any applicable taxes or tax refunds related to its sale. The **proceeds from sale of old asset** are the net cash inflows it provides. This amount is net of any costs incurred in the process of removing the asset. Included in these *removal costs* are *cleanup costs,* such as those related to removal and disposal of chemical and nuclear wastes. These costs may not be trivial.

The proceeds from the sale of an old asset are normally subject to some type of tax.[1] This **tax on sale of old asset** depends on the relationship between its sale price and *book value* and on existing government tax rules.

1. A brief discussion of the tax treatment of ordinary and capital gains income was presented in Chapter 2. Because corporate capital gains and ordinary income are taxed at the same rate, for convenience, we do not differentiate between them in the following discussions.

book value
The strict accounting value of an asset, calculated by subtracting its accumulated depreciation from its installed cost.

Book Value

The **book value** of an asset is its strict accounting value. It can be calculated by using the following equation:

$$\text{Book value} = \text{Installed cost of asset} - \text{Accumulated depreciation} \quad (11.1)$$

Example 11.2 ▶ Hudson Industries, a small electronics company, 2 years ago acquired a machine tool with an installed cost of $100,000. The asset was being depreciated under MACRS using a 5-year recovery period. Table 4.2 (on page 117) shows that under MACRS for a 5-year recovery period, 20% and 32% of the installed cost would be depreciated in years 1 and 2, respectively. In other words, 52% (20% + 32%) of the $100,000 cost, or $52,000 (0.52 × $100,000), would represent the accumulated depreciation at the end of year 2. Substituting into Equation 11.1, we get

$$\text{Book value} = \$100{,}000 - \$52{,}000 = \underline{\underline{\$48{,}000}}$$

The book value of Hudson's asset at the end of year 2 is therefore $48,000.

Basic Tax Rules

Three potential tax situations can occur when a firm sells an asset. These situations depend on the relationship between the asset's sale price and its book value. The two key forms of taxable income and their associated tax treatments are defined and summarized in Table 11.2. The assumed tax rates used throughout this text are noted in the final column. There are three possible tax situations. The asset may be sold (1) for more than its book value, (2) for its book value, or (3) for less than its book value. An example will illustrate.

Example 11.3 ▶ The old asset purchased 2 years ago for $100,000 by Hudson Industries has a current book value of $48,000. What will happen if the firm now decides to sell the asset and replace it? The tax consequences depend on the sale price. Figure 11.3 depicts the taxable income resulting from four possible sale prices in light of the asset's initial purchase price of $100,000 and its current book value of

TABLE 11.2 Tax Treatment on Sales of Assets

Form of taxable income	Definition	Tax treatment	Assumed tax rate
Gain on sale of asset	Portion of the sale price that is *greater than* book value.	All gains above book value are taxed as ordinary income.	40%
Loss on sale of asset	Amount by which sale price is *less than* book value.	If the asset is depreciable and used in business, loss is deducted from ordinary income.	40% of loss is a tax savings
		If the asset is *not* depreciable or is *not* used in business, loss is deductible only against capital gains.	40% of loss is a tax savings

FIGURE 11.3

Taxable Income from Sale of Asset
Taxable income from sale of asset at various sale prices for Hudson Industries

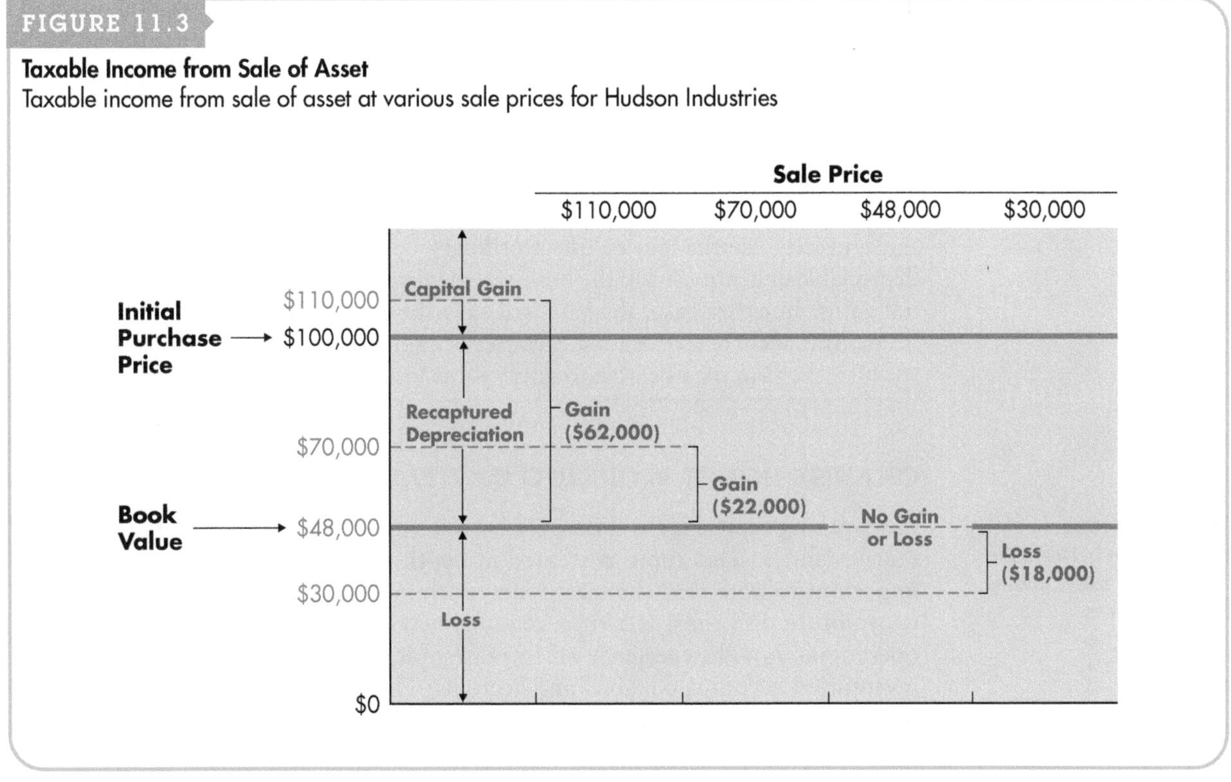

$48,000. The taxable consequences of each of these sale prices are described in the following paragraphs.

recaptured depreciation
The portion of an asset's sale price that is above its book value and below its initial purchase price.

The sale of the asset for more than its book value If Hudson sells the old asset for $110,000, it realizes a gain of $62,000 ($110,000 − $48,000). Technically this gain is made up of two parts—a capital gain and **recaptured depreciation,** which is the portion of the sale price that is above book value and below the initial purchase price. For Hudson, the capital gain is $10,000 ($110,000 sale price − $100,000 initial purchase price); recaptured depreciation is $52,000 (the $100,000 initial purchase price − $48,000 book value).

Both the $10,000 capital gain and the $52,000 recaptured depreciation are shown under the $110,000 sale price in Figure 11.3. The total gain above book value of $62,000 is taxed as ordinary income at the 40% rate, resulting in taxes of $24,800 (0.40 × $62,000). These taxes should be used in calculating the initial investment in the new asset, using the format in Table 11.1. In effect, the taxes raise the amount of the firm's initial investment in the new asset by reducing the proceeds from the sale of the old asset.

If Hudson instead sells the old asset for $70,000, it experiences a gain above book value (in the form of *recaptured depreciation*) of $22,000 ($70,000 − $48,000), as shown under the $70,000 sale price in Figure 11.3. This gain is taxed as ordinary income. Because the firm is assumed to be in the 40% tax bracket, the taxes on the $22,000 gain are $8,800 (0.40 × $22,000). This amount in taxes should be used in calculating the initial investment in the new asset.

The sale of the asset for its book value If the asset is sold for $48,000, its book value, the firm breaks even. There is no gain or loss, as shown under the $48,000 sale price in Figure 11.3. Because *no tax results from selling an asset for its book value,* there is no tax effect on the initial investment in the new asset.

The sale of the asset for less than its book value If Hudson sells the asset for $30,000, it experiences a loss of $18,000 ($48,000 − $30,000), as shown under the $30,000 sale price in Figure 11.3. If this is a depreciable asset used in the business, the firm may use the loss to offset ordinary operating income. If the asset is *not* depreciable or is *not* used in the business, the firm can use the loss only to offset capital gains. In either case, the loss will save the firm $7,200 (0.40 × $18,000) in taxes. And, if current operating earnings or capital gains are not sufficient to offset the loss, the firm may be able to apply these losses to prior or future years' taxes.

CHANGE IN NET WORKING CAPITAL

net working capital
The difference between the firm's current assets and its current liabilities.

Net working capital is the difference between the firm's current assets and its current liabilities. This topic is treated in depth in Chapter 15; at this point it is important to note that changes in net working capital often accompany capital expenditure decisions. If a firm acquires new machinery to expand its level of operations, it will experience an increase in levels of cash, accounts receivable, inventories, accounts payable, and accruals. These increases result from the need for more cash to support expanded operations, more accounts receivable and inventories to support increased sales, and more accounts payable and accruals to support increased outlays made to meet expanded product demand. As noted in Chapter 4, increases in cash, accounts receivable, and inventories are *outflows of cash,* whereas increases in accounts payable and accruals are *inflows of cash.*

change in net working capital
The difference between a change in current assets and a change in current liabilities.

The difference between the change in current assets and the change in current liabilities is the **change in net working capital.** Generally, current assets increase by more than current liabilities, resulting in an increased investment in net working capital. This increased investment is treated as an initial outflow.[2] If the change in net working capital were negative, it would be shown as an initial inflow. The change in net working capital—regardless of whether it is an increase or a decrease—*is not taxable* because it merely involves a net buildup or net reduction of current accounts.

Example 11.4 ▸ Danson Company, a metal products manufacturer, is contemplating expanding its operations. Financial analysts expect that the changes in current accounts summarized in Table 11.3 will occur and will be maintained over the life of the expansion. Current assets are expected to increase by $22,000, and current liabilities are expected to increase by $9,000, resulting in a $13,000 increase in net working capital. In this case, the change will represent an increased net working capital investment and will be treated as a cash outflow in calculating the initial investment.

2. When changes in net working capital apply to the initial investment associated with a proposed capital expenditure, they are for convenience assumed to be instantaneous and thereby occurring at time zero. In practice, the change in net working capital will frequently occur over a period of months as the capital expenditure is implemented.

TABLE 11.3 Calculation of Change in Net Working Capital for Danson Company

Current account	Change in balance	
Cash	+ $ 4,000	
Accounts receivable	+ 10,000	
Inventories	+ 8,000	
(1) Current assets		+$22,000
Accounts payable	+ $ 7,000	
Accruals	+ 2,000	
(2) Current liabilities		+ 9,000
Change in net working capital [(1) − (2)]		+$13,000

CALCULATING THE INITIAL INVESTMENT

A variety of tax and other considerations enter into the initial investment calculation. The following example illustrates calculation of the initial investment according to the format in Table 11.1.[3]

Example 11.5 ▶ Powell Corporation, a large, diversified manufacturer of aircraft components, is trying to determine the initial investment required to replace an old machine with a new, more sophisticated model. The proposed machine's purchase price is $380,000, and an additional $20,000 will be necessary to install it. It will be depreciated under MACRS using a 5-year recovery period. The present (old) machine was purchased 3 years ago at a cost of $240,000 and was being depreciated under MACRS using a 5-year recovery period. The firm has found a buyer willing to pay $280,000 for the present machine and to remove it at the buyer's expense. The firm expects that a $35,000 increase in current assets and an $18,000 increase in current liabilities will accompany the replacement; these changes will result in a $17,000 ($35,000 − $18,000) *increase* in net working capital. The firm pays taxes at a rate of 40%.

The only component of the initial investment calculation that is difficult to obtain is taxes. The book value of the present machine can be found by using the depreciation percentages from Table 4.2 (on page 117) of 20%, 32%, and 19% for years 1, 2, and 3, respectively. The resulting *book value* is $69,600 ($240,000 − [(0.20 + 0.32 + 0.19) × $240,000]). A *gain* of $210,400 ($280,000 − $69,600) is realized on the sale. The total taxes on the gain are $84,160 (0.40 × $210,400). These taxes must be subtracted from the $280,000 sale price of the present machine to calculate the after-tax proceeds from its sale.

3. Throughout the discussions of capital budgeting, all assets evaluated as candidates for replacement are assumed to be depreciable assets that are directly used in the business, so any losses on the sale of these assets can be applied against ordinary operating income. The decisions are also structured to ensure that the usable life remaining on the old asset is just equal to the life of the new asset; this assumption enables us to avoid the problem of unequal lives, which is discussed in Chapter 12.

Substituting the relevant amounts into the format in Table 11.1 results in an initial investment of $221,160, which represents the net cash outflow required at time zero.

Installed cost of proposed machine		
Cost of proposed machine	$380,000	
+ Installation costs	20,000	
Total installed cost—proposed (depreciable value)		$400,000
− After-tax proceeds from sale of present machine		
Proceeds from sale of present machine	$280,000	
− Tax on sale of present machine	84,160	
Total after-tax proceeds—present		195,840
+ Change in net working capital		17,000
Initial investment		$221,160

→ REVIEW QUESTIONS

11–5 Explain how each of the following inputs is used to calculate the *initial investment:* **(a)** cost of new asset, **(b)** installation costs, **(c)** proceeds from sale of old asset, **(d)** tax on sale of old asset, and **(e)** change in net working capital.

11–6 How is the *book value* of an asset calculated? What are the two key forms of taxable income?

11–7 What three tax situations may result from the sale of an asset that is being replaced?

11–8 Referring to the basic format for calculating initial investment, explain how a firm would determine the *depreciable value* of the new asset.

LG 5

11.3 Finding the Operating Cash Inflows

The benefits expected from a capital expenditure or "project" are embodied in its *operating cash inflows,* which are *incremental after-tax cash inflows.* In this section, we use the income statement format to develop clear definitions of the terms *after-tax, cash inflows,* and *incremental.*

INTERPRETING THE TERM *AFTER-TAX*

Benefits expected to result from proposed capital expenditures must be measured on an *after-tax basis* because the firm will not have the use of any benefits until it has satisfied the government's tax claims. These claims depend on the firm's taxable income, so deducting taxes *before* making comparisons between proposed investments is necessary for consistency when evaluating capital expenditure alternatives.

INTERPRETING THE TERM *CASH INFLOWS*

All benefits expected from a proposed project must be measured on a *cash flow basis*. Cash inflows represent dollars that can be spent, not merely "accounting profits." There is a simple technique for converting after-tax net profits into operating cash inflows. The basic calculation requires adding depreciation and any other *noncash charges* (amortization and depletion) deducted as expenses on the firm's income statement back to net profits after taxes. Because depreciation is commonly found on income statements, it is the only noncash charge we consider.

Example 11.6 ▸ Powell Corporation's estimates of its revenue and expenses (excluding depreciation and interest), with and without the proposed new machine described in Example 11.5, are given in Table 11.4. Note that both the expected usable life of the proposed machine and the remaining usable life of the present machine are 5 years. The amount to be depreciated with the proposed machine is calculated by summing the purchase price of $380,000 and the installation costs of $20,000. The proposed machine is to be depreciated under MACRS using a 5-year recovery period.[4] The resulting depreciation on this machine for each of the 6 years, as well as the remaining 3 years of depreciation (years 4, 5, and 6) on the present machine, are calculated in Table 11.5 (see page 440).[5]

The *operating cash inflows* each year can be calculated by using the income statement format shown in Table 11.6 (see page 440). Note that we exclude interest because we are focusing purely on the "investment decision." The interest is relevant to the "financing decision," which is separately considered. Because we exclude interest expense, "earnings before interest and taxes" (EBIT) is equivalent to "net profits before taxes," and the calculation of "operating cash inflow" in

TABLE 11.4 Powell Corporation's Revenue and Expenses (Excluding Depreciation and Interest) for Proposed and Present Machines

	With proposed machine			With present machine	
Year	Revenue (1)	Expenses (excl. depr. and int.) (2)	Year	Revenue (1)	Expenses (excl. depr. and int.) (2)
1	$2,520,000	$2,300,000	1	$2,200,000	$1,990,000
2	2,520,000	2,300,000	2	2,300,000	2,110,000
3	2,520,000	2,300,000	3	2,400,000	2,230,000
4	2,520,000	2,300,000	4	2,400,000	2,250,000
5	2,520,000	2,300,000	5	2,250,000	2,120,000

4. As noted in Chapter 4, it takes $n + 1$ years to depreciate an n-year class asset under current tax law. Therefore, MACRS percentages are given for each of 6 years for use in depreciating an asset with a 5-year recovery period.

5. It is important to recognize that, although both machines will provide 5 years of use, the proposed new machine will be depreciated over the 6-year period, whereas the present machine, as noted in the preceding example, has been depreciated over 3 years and therefore has remaining only its final 3 years (years 4, 5, and 6) of depreciation (12%, 12%, and 5%, respectively, under MACRS).

TABLE 11.5 Depreciation Expense for Proposed and Present Machines for Powell Corporation

Year	Cost (1)	Applicable MACRS depreciation percentages (from Table 4.2) (2)	Depreciation [(1) × (2)] (3)
With proposed machine			
1	$400,000	20%	$ 80,000
2	400,000	32	128,000
3	400,000	19	76,000
4	400,000	12	48,000
5	400,000	12	48,000
6	400,000	5	20,000
Totals		100%	$400,000
With present machine			
1	$240,000	12% (year-4 depreciation)	$28,800
2	240,000	12 (year-5 depreciation)	28,800
3	240,000	5 (year-6 depreciation)	12,000
4	Because the present machine is at the end of the third year of its cost recovery at the time the analysis is performed, it has only the final 3 years of depreciation (as noted above) still applicable.		0
5			0
6			0
Total			$69,600[a]

[a]The total $69,600 represents the book value of the present machine at the end of the third year, as calculated in Example 11.5.

Table 11.6 is equivalent to "operating cash flow (OCF)" (defined in Equation 4.3, on page 122). Simply stated, the income statement format calculates OCF.

Substituting the data from Tables 11.4 and 11.5 into this format and assuming a 40% tax rate, we get Table 11.7. It demonstrates the calculation of operating cash inflows for each year for both the proposed and the present machine. Because the proposed machine is depreciated over 6 years, the analysis must be performed

TABLE 11.6 Calculation of Operating Cash Inflows Using the Income Statement Format

Revenue
− Expenses (excluding depreciation and interest)
Earnings before depreciation, interest, and taxes (EBDIT)
− Depreciation
Earnings before interest and taxes (EBIT)
− Taxes (rate = T)
Net operating profit after taxes [NOPAT = EBIT × $(1 - T)$]
+ Depreciation
Operating cash inflows (same as OCF in Equation 4.3)

TABLE 11.7 **Calculation of Operating Cash Inflows for Powell Corporation's Proposed and Present Machines**

	Year 1	Year 2	Year 3	Year 4	Year 5	Year 6
With proposed machine						
Revenue[a]	$2,520,000	$2,520,000	$2,520,000	$2,520,000	$2,520,000	$ 0
− Expenses (excluding depreciation and interest)[b]	2,300,000	2,300,000	2,300,000	2,300,000	2,300,000	0
Earnings before depreciation, interest, and taxes	$ 220,000	$ 220,000	$ 220,000	$ 220,000	$ 220,000	$ 0
− Depreciation[c]	80,000	128,000	76,000	48,000	48,000	20,000
Earnings before interest and taxes	$ 140,000	$ 92,000	$ 144,000	$ 172,000	$ 172,000	−$20,000
− Taxes (rate, T = 40%)	56,000	36,800	57,600	68,800	68,800	− 8,000
Net operating profit after taxes	$ 84,000	$ 55,200	$ 86,400	$ 103,200	$ 103,200	−$12,000
+ Depreciation[c]	80,000	128,000	76,000	48,000	48,000	20,000
Operating cash inflows	$ 164,000	$ 183,200	$ 162,400	$ 151,200	$ 151,200	$ 8,000
With present machine						
Revenue[a]	$2,200,000	$2,300,000	$2,400,000	$2,400,000	$2,250,000	$ 0
− Expenses (excluding depreciation and interest)[b]	1,990,000	2,110,000	2,230,000	2,250,000	2,120,000	0
Earnings before depreciation, interest, and taxes	$ 210,000	$ 190,000	$ 170,000	$ 150,000	$ 130,000	$ 0
− Depreciation[c]	28,800	28,800	12,000	0	0	0
Earnings before interest and taxes	$ 181,200	$ 161,200	$ 158,000	$ 150,000	$ 130,000	$ 0
− Taxes (rate, T = 40%)	72,480	64,480	63,200	60,000	52,000	0
Net operating profit after taxes	$ 108,720	$ 96,720	$ 94,800	$ 90,000	$ 78,000	$ 0
+ Depreciation[c]	28,800	28,800	12,000	0	0	0
Operating cash inflows	$ 137,520	$ 125,520	$ 106,800	$ 90,000	$ 78,000	$ 0

[a]From column 1 of Table 11.4.
[b]From column 2 of Table 11.4.
[c]From column 3 of Table 11.5.

over the 6-year period to capture fully the tax effect of its year-6 depreciation. The resulting operating cash inflows are shown in the final row of Table 11.7 for each machine. The $8,000 year-6 operating cash inflow for the proposed machine results solely from the tax benefit of its year-6 depreciation deduction.[6]

INTERPRETING THE TERM *INCREMENTAL*

The final step in estimating the operating cash inflows for a proposed replacement project is to calculate the *incremental (relevant)* cash inflows. Incremental operating cash inflows are needed because our concern is *only* with the change in operating cash inflows that result from the proposed project. Clearly, if this were an expansion project, the project's cash flows would be the incremental cash flows.

6. Although here we have calculated the year-6 operating cash inflow for the proposed machine, this cash flow will later be eliminated as a result of the assumed sale of the machine at the end of year 5.

TABLE 11.8 Incremental (Relevant) Operating Cash Inflows for Powell Corporation

	Operating cash inflows		
Year	Proposed machine[a] (1)	Present machine[a] (2)	Incremental (relevant) [(1) − (2)] (3)
1	$164,000	$137,520	$26,480
2	183,200	125,520	57,680
3	162,400	106,800	55,600
4	151,200	90,000	61,200
5	151,200	78,000	73,200
6	8,000	0	8,000

[a]From final row for respective machine in Table 11.7.

Example 11.7 ▶ Table 11.8 demonstrates the calculation of Powell Corporation's *incremental (relevant) operating cash inflows* for each year. The estimates of operating cash inflows developed in Table 11.7 appear in columns 1 and 2. Column 2 values represent the amount of operating cash inflows that Powell Corporation will receive if it does not replace the present machine. If the proposed machine replaces the present machine, the firm's operating cash inflows for each year will be those shown in column 1. Subtracting the present machine's operating cash inflows from the proposed machine's operating cash inflows, we get the incremental operating cash inflows for each year, shown in column 3. These cash flows represent the amounts by which each respective year's cash inflows will increase as a result of the replacement. For example, in year 1, Powell Corporation's cash inflows would increase by $26,480 if the proposed project were undertaken. Clearly, these are the relevant inflows to be considered when evaluating the benefits of making a capital expenditure for the proposed machine.[7]

7. The following equation can be used to calculate more directly the incremental cash inflow in year t, ICI_t.

$$ICI_t = [\Delta EBDIT_t \times (1 - T)] + (\Delta D_t \times T)$$

where

$\Delta EBDIT_t$ = change in earnings before depreciation, interest, and taxes [revenues−expenses (excl. depr. and int.)] in year t

ΔD_t = change in depreciation expense in year t

T = firm's marginal tax rate

Applying this formula to the Powell Corporation data given in Tables 11.4 and 11.5 for year 3, we get the following values of variables:

$$\Delta EBDIT_3 = (\$2,520,000 - \$2,300,000) - (\$2,400,000 - \$2,230,000)$$
$$= \$220,000 - \$170,000 = \$50,000$$
$$\Delta D_3 = \$76,000 - \$12,000 = \$64,000$$
$$T = 0.40$$

Substituting into the equation yields

$$ICI_3 = [\$50,000 \times (1 - 0.40)] + (\$64,000 \times 0.40)$$
$$= \$30,000 + \$25,600 = \underline{\underline{\$55,600}}$$

The $55,600 of incremental cash inflow for year 3 is the same value as that calculated for year 3 in column 3 of Table 11.8.

→ **REVIEW QUESTIONS**

11–9 How does depreciation enter into the calculation of operating cash inflows? How does the income statement format in Table 11.6 relate to Equation 4.3 (on page 122) for finding operating cash flow (OCF)?

11–10 How are the *incremental (relevant) operating cash inflows* that are associated with a replacement decision calculated?

LG 6

11.4 Finding the Terminal Cash Flow

Terminal cash flow is the cash flow resulting from termination and liquidation of a project at the end of its economic life. It represents the after-tax cash flow, exclusive of operating cash inflows, that occurs in the final year of the project. When it applies, this flow can significantly affect the capital expenditure decision. Terminal cash flow can be calculated for replacement projects by using the basic format presented in Table 11.9.

PROCEEDS FROM SALE OF ASSETS

The proceeds from sale of the new and the old asset, often called "salvage value," represent the amount *net of any removal or cleanup costs* expected on termination of the project. For replacement projects, proceeds from both the new asset and the old asset must be considered. For expansion and renewal types of capital expenditures, the proceeds from the old asset are zero. Of course, it is not unusual for the value of an asset to be zero at the termination of a project.

TAXES ON SALE OF ASSETS

When the investment being analyzed involves replacing an old asset with a new one, there are two key elements in finding the terminal cash flow. First, at the end of the project's life, the firm will dispose of the new asset, so the after-tax proceeds from selling the new asset represent a cash inflow. However, remember that if the firm had not replaced the old asset, the firm would have received proceeds from disposal of the old asset at the end of the project (rather than counting those proceeds up front as part of the initial investment). Therefore, we must count as a cash outflow the after-tax proceeds that the firm would have received from disposal of the old asset. Taxes come into play whenever an asset is sold for a value different from its book value. If the net proceeds from the sale are expected to exceed

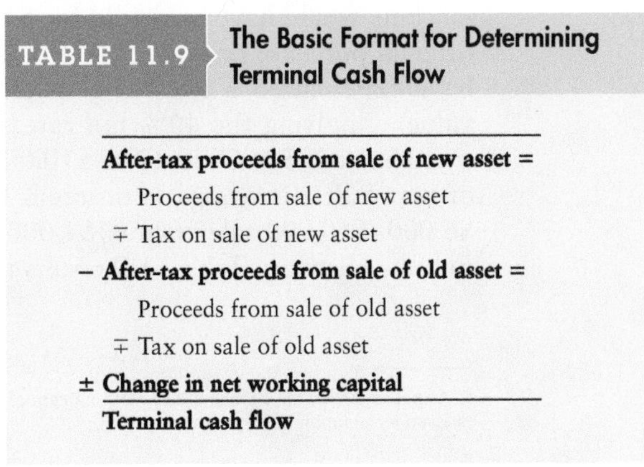

TABLE 11.9 The Basic Format for Determining Terminal Cash Flow

After-tax proceeds from sale of new asset =
Proceeds from sale of new asset
∓ Tax on sale of new asset
− **After-tax proceeds from sale of old asset =**
Proceeds from sale of old asset
∓ Tax on sale of old asset
± **Change in net working capital**
Terminal cash flow

book value, a tax payment shown as an *outflow* (deduction from sale proceeds) will occur. When the net proceeds from the sale are less than book value, a tax benefit shown as a cash *inflow* (addition to sale proceeds) will result. For assets sold to net exactly book value, no taxes will be due.

CHANGE IN NET WORKING CAPITAL

When we calculated the initial investment, we took into account any change in net working capital that is attributable to the new asset. Now, when we calculate the terminal cash flow, the change in net working capital represents the reversion of any initial net working capital investment. Most often, this will show up as a cash inflow due to the reduction in net working capital; with termination of the project, the need for the increased net working capital investment is assumed to end.[8] Because the net working capital investment is in no way consumed, the amount recovered at termination will equal the amount shown in the calculation of the initial investment. Tax considerations are not involved.

Calculating the terminal cash flow involves the same procedures as those used to find the initial investment. In the following example, the terminal cash flow is calculated for a replacement decision.

Example 11.8 ▶ Continuing with the Powell Corporation example, assume that the firm expects to be able to liquidate the new machine at the end of its 5-year usable life to net $50,000 after paying removal and cleanup costs. Had it not been replaced by the new machine, the old machine would have been liquidated at the end of the 5 years to net $10,000. The firm expects to recover its $17,000 net working capital investment upon termination of the project. The firm pays taxes at a rate of 40%.

From the analysis of the operating cash inflows presented earlier, we can see that the proposed (new) machine will have a book value of $20,000 (equal to the year-6 depreciation) at the end of 5 years. The present (old) machine would have been fully depreciated and therefore would have a book value of zero at the end of the 5 years. Because the sale price of $50,000 for the proposed (new) machine is below its initial installed cost of $400,000 but greater than its book value of $20,000, taxes will have to be paid only on the recaptured depreciation of $30,000 ($50,000 sale proceeds − $20,000 book value). Applying the ordinary tax rate of 40% to this $30,000 results in a tax of $12,000 (0.40 × $30,000) on the sale of the proposed machine. Its after-tax sale proceeds would therefore equal $38,000 ($50,000 sale proceeds − $12,000 taxes). Because the old machine would have been sold for $10,000 at termination, which is less than its original purchase price of $240,000 and above its book value of zero, it would have experienced a taxable gain of $10,000 ($10,000 sale price − $0 book value). Applying the 40% tax rate to the $10,000 gain, the firm would have owed a tax of $4,000 (0.40 × $10,000) on the sale of the old machine at the end of year 5. Its after-tax sale proceeds from the old machine would have equalled $6,000 ($10,000 sale price − $4,000 taxes). Substituting the appropriate values into the format in Table 11.9 results in the terminal cash inflow of $49,000.

8. As noted earlier, the change in net working capital is for convenience assumed to occur instantaneously—in this case, on termination of the project.

After-tax proceeds from sale of proposed machine		
Proceeds from sale of proposed machine	$50,000	
− Tax on sale of proposed machine	12,000	
Total after-tax proceeds—proposed		$38,000
− After-tax proceeds from sale of present machine		
Proceeds from sale of present machine	$10,000	
− Tax on sale of present machine	4,000	
Total after-tax proceeds—present		6,000
+ Change in net working capital		17,000
Terminal cash flow		$49,000

→ REVIEW QUESTION

11–11 Explain how the *terminal cash flow* is calculated for replacement projects.

LG 3 LG 5 LG 6

11.5 Summarizing the Relevant Cash Flows

The initial investment, operating cash inflows, and terminal cash flow together represent a project's *relevant cash flows*. These cash flows can be viewed as the incremental after-tax cash flows attributable to the proposed project. They represent, in a cash flow sense, how much better or worse off the firm will be if it chooses to implement the proposal.

Example 11.9 ▶ The relevant cash flows for Powell Corporation's proposed replacement expenditure can be shown graphically, on a time line. *Note that because the new asset is assumed to be sold at the end of its 5-year usable life, the year-6 incremental operating cash inflow calculated in Table 11.8 has no relevance; the terminal cash flow effectively replaces this value in the analysis.*

Time line for Powell Corporation's relevant cash flows with the proposed machine

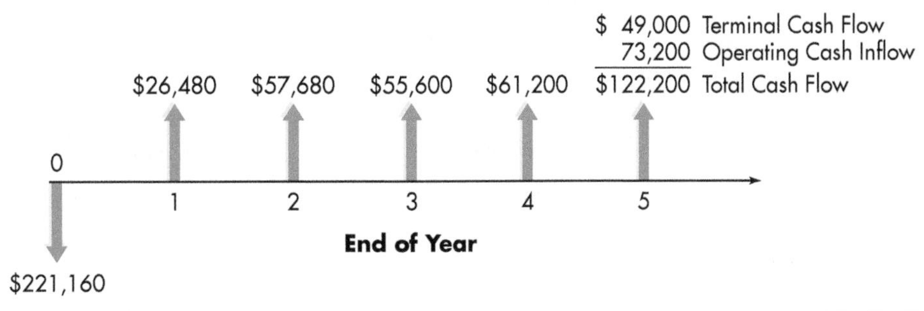

With these cash flow estimates in hand, a financial manager could then calculate the investment's NPV or IRR using the techniques covered in Chapter 10.

Personal Finance Example 11.10 ▶ After receiving a sizable bonus from her employer, Tina Talor is contemplating the purchase of a new car. She feels that by estimating and analyzing its cash flows she could make a more rational decision about whether to make this large purchase. Tina's cash flow estimates for the car purchase are as follows:

Negotiated price of new car	$23,500
Taxes and fees on new car purchase	$ 1,650
Proceeds from sale of old car	$ 9,750
Estimated value of new car in 3 years	$10,500
Estimated value of old car in 3 years	$ 5,700
Estimated annual repair costs on new car	0 (in warranty)
Estimated annual repair costs on old car	$ 400

Using the cash flow estimates, Tina calculates the initial investment, operating cash inflows, terminal cash flow, and a summary of all cash flows for the car purchase.

Initial Investment

Total cost of new car		
Cost of car	$23,500	
+ Taxes and fees	1,650	$25,150
− Proceeds from sale of old car		9,750
Initial investment		$15,400

Operating Cash Inflows	**Year 1**	**Year 2**	**Year 3**
Cost of repairs on new car	$ 0	$ 0	$ 0
− Cost of repairs on old car	400	400	400
Operating cash inflows (savings)	$400	$400	$400

Terminal Cash Flow—End of Year 3

Proceeds from sale of new car	$10,500
− Proceeds from sale of old car	5,700
Terminal cash flow	$ 4,800

Summary of Cash Flows

End of Year	**Cash Flow**
0	−$15,400
1	+ 400
2	+ 400
3	+ 5,200 ($400 + $4,800)

The cash flows associated with Tina's car purchase decision reflect her net costs of the new car over the assumed 3-year ownership period, but they ignore the many intangible benefits of owning a car. Whereas the fuel cost and basic transportation service provided are assumed to be the same with the new car as with the old car, Tina will have to decide if the cost of moving up to a new car can be justified in terms of intangibles, such as luxury and prestige.

→ REVIEW QUESTION

11–12 Diagram and describe the three components of the relevant cash flows for a capital budgeting project.

Summary

FOCUS ON VALUE

A key responsibility of financial managers is to review and analyze proposed investment decisions to make sure that the firm undertakes only those that contribute positively to the value of the firm. Utilizing a variety of tools and techniques, financial managers estimate the cash flows that a proposed investment will generate and then apply decision techniques to assess the investment's impact on the firm's value. The most difficult and important aspect of this capital budgeting process is developing good estimates of the relevant cash flows.

The relevant cash flows are the incremental after-tax cash flows resulting from a proposed investment. These estimates represent the cash flow benefits that are likely to accrue to the firm as a result of implementing the investment. By applying to the cash flows decision techniques that capture the time value of money and risk factors, the financial manager can estimate how the investment will affect the firm's share price. Consistent application of capital budgeting procedures to proposed long-term investments should therefore allow the firm to **maximize its stock price.**

REVIEW OF LEARNING GOALS

LG 1 **Discuss the three major cash flow components.** The three major cash flow components of any project can include: (1) an initial investment, (2) operating cash inflows, and (3) terminal cash flow. The initial investment occurs at *time zero,* the operating cash inflows occur during the project life, and the terminal cash flow occurs at the end of the project.

LG 2 **Discuss relevant cash flows, expansion versus replacement decisions, sunk costs and opportunity costs, and international capital budgeting.** The relevant cash flows for capital budgeting decisions are the initial investment, the operating cash inflows, and the terminal cash flow. For replacement decisions, these flows are the difference between the cash flows of the new asset and the old asset. Expansion decisions are viewed as replacement decisions in which all cash flows from the old asset are zero. When estimating relevant cash flows, ignore sunk costs and include opportunity costs as cash outflows. In international capital budgeting, currency risks and political risks can be minimized through careful planning.

LG 3 **Calculate the initial investment associated with a proposed capital expenditure.** The initial investment is the initial outflow required, taking into account the installed cost of the new asset, the after-tax proceeds from the sale of the old asset, and any change in net working capital. The initial investment is reduced by finding the after-tax proceeds from sale of the old asset. The book value of an asset is used to determine the taxes owed as a result of its sale. Either of two forms of taxable income—a gain or a loss—can result from sale of an asset, depending on whether the asset is sold for (1) more than book value, (2) book value, or (3) less than book value. The change in net working capital is the difference between the change in current assets and the change in current liabilities expected to accompany a given capital expenditure.

LG 4 **Discuss the tax implications associated with the sale of an old asset.** There is typically a tax implication from the sale of an old asset. The tax implication depends on the relationship between its sale price and book value and on existing government tax rules. Generally, if the old asset is sold for an amount greater than its book value, then the difference is subject to a capital gains tax, and if the old asset is sold for an amount less than its book value, then the company is entitled to tax deduction equal to the difference.

LG 5 **Find the relevant operating cash inflows associated with a proposed capital expenditure.** The operating cash inflows are the incremental after-tax cash inflows expected to result from a project. The income statement format involves adding depreciation back to net operating profit after taxes and gives the operating cash inflows, which are the same as operating cash flows (OCF), associated with the proposed and present projects. The relevant (incremental) cash inflows for a replacement project are the difference between the operating cash inflows of the proposed project and those of the present project.

LG 6 **Determine the terminal cash flow associated with a proposed capital expenditure.** The terminal cash flow represents the after-tax cash flow (exclusive of operating cash inflows) that is expected from liquidation of a project. It is calculated for replacement projects by finding the difference between the after-tax proceeds from sale of the new and the old asset at termination and then adjusting this difference for any change in net working capital. Sale price and depreciation data are used to find the taxes and the after-tax sale proceeds on the new and old assets. The change in net working capital typically represents the reversion of any initial net working capital investment.

Opener-in-Review

The chapter opener talked about ExxonMobil's considerable investment in long-term projects and the sometimes difficult task of having projects come in on budget. How are project cash flows affected by budget overruns? In the capital budgeting process, how should financial managers account for the potential of budget overruns?

Self-Test Problems (Solutions in Appendix)

LG 3 LG 4 **ST11–1** **Book value, taxes, and initial investment** Irvin Enterprises is considering the purchase of a new piece of equipment to replace the current equipment. The new equipment costs $75,000 and requires $5,000 in installation costs. It will be depreciated under MACRS using a 5-year recovery period. The old piece of equipment was purchased 4 years ago for an installed cost of $50,000; it was being depreciated under MACRS using a 5-year recovery period. The old equipment can be sold today for $55,000 net of any removal or cleanup costs. As a result of the proposed replacement, the firm's investment in net working capital is expected to increase by $15,000. The firm pays taxes at a rate of 40%. (Table 4.2 on page 117 contains the applicable MACRS depreciation percentages.)

a. Calculate the book value of the old piece of equipment.

b. Determine the taxes, if any, attributable to the sale of the old equipment.

c. Find the *initial investment* associated with the proposed equipment replacement.

LG 3 LG 4 LG 5 LG 6 **ST11–2** **Determining relevant cash flows** A machine currently in use was originally purchased 2 years ago for $40,000. The machine is being depreciated under MACRS using a 5-year recovery period; it has 3 years of usable life remaining. The current machine can be sold today to net $42,000 after removal and cleanup costs. A new machine, using a 3-year MACRS recovery period, can be purchased at a price of $140,000. It requires $10,000 to install and has a 3-year usable life. If the new machine is acquired, the investment in accounts receivable will be expected to rise by $10,000, the inventory investment will increase by $25,000, and accounts payable will increase by $15,000. *Earnings before depreciation, interest, and taxes* are expected to be $70,000 for each of the next 3 years with the old machine and to be $120,000 in the first year and $130,000 in the second and third years with the new machine. At the end of 3 years, the market value of the old machine will equal zero, but the new machine could be sold to net $35,000 before taxes. The firm is subject to a 40% tax rate. (Table 4.2 on page 117 contains the applicable MACRS depreciation percentages.)

a. Determine the *initial investment* associated with the proposed replacement decision.

b. Calculate the *incremental operating cash inflows* for years 1 to 4 associated with the proposed replacement. (*Note:* Only depreciation cash flows must be considered in year 4.)

c. Calculate the *terminal cash flow* associated with the proposed replacement decision. (*Note:* This is at the end of year 3.)

d. Depict on a time line the relevant cash flows found in parts **a, b,** and **c** that are associated with the proposed replacement decision, assuming that it is terminated at the end of year 3.

Warm-Up Exercises

All problems are available in myfinancelab.

LG 2 **E11–1** If Halley Industries reimburses employees who earn master's degrees and who agree to remain with the firm for an additional 3 years, should the expense of the tuition reimbursement be categorized as a *capital expenditure* or an *operating expenditure?*

LG 2 **E11–2** Iridium Corp. has spent $3.5 billion over the past decade developing a satellite-based telecommunication system. It is currently trying to decide whether to spend an additional $350 million on the project. The firm expects that this outlay will finish the project and will generate cash flow of $15 million per year over the next 5 years. A competitor has offered $450 million for the satellites already in orbit. Classify the firm's outlays as *sunk costs* or *opportunity costs,* and specify the *relevant cash flows.*

LG 3 LG 4 **E11–3** Canvas Reproductions, Inc., has spent $4,500 dollars researching a new project. The project requires $20,000 worth of new machinery, which would cost $3,000 to install. The company would realize $4,500 in after-tax proceeds from the sale of old machinery. If Canvas's working capital is unaffected by this project, what is the initial investment amount for this project?

LG 3 LG 4 **E11–4** A few years ago, Largo Industries implemented an inventory auditing system at an installed cost of $175,000. Since then, it has taken depreciation deductions totaling $124,250. What is the system's current *book value?* If Largo sold the system for $110,000, how much *recaptured depreciation* would result?

LG 5 **E11–5** Bryson Sciences is planning to purchase a high-powered microscopy machine for $55,000 and incur an additional $7,500 in installation expenses. It is replacing similar microscopy equipment that can be sold to net $35,000, resulting in taxes from a gain on the sale of $11,250. Because of this transaction, current assets will increase by $6,000 and current liabilities will increase by $4,000. Calculate the *initial investment* in the high-powered microscopy machine.

Problems

All problems are available in myfinancelab.

LG 2 **P11–1** **Classification of expenditures** Given the following list of outlays, indicate whether each is normally considered a *capital expenditure* or an *operating expenditure.* Explain your answers.

a. An initial lease payment of $5,000 for electronic point-of-sale cash register systems.
b. An outlay of $20,000 to purchase patent rights from an inventor.
c. An outlay of $80,000 for a major research and development program.
d. An $80,000 investment in a portfolio of marketable securities.
e. A $300 outlay for an office machine.
f. An outlay of $2,000 for a new machine tool.
g. An outlay of $240,000 for a new building.
h. An outlay of $1,000 for a marketing research report.

LG 1 LG 2 **P11–2** **Relevant cash flow and timeline depiction** For each of the following projects, determine the *relevant cash flows,* and depict the cash flows on a time line.

a. A project that requires an initial investment of $120,000 and will generate annual operating cash inflows of $25,000 for the next 18 years. In each of the 18 years, maintenance of the project will require a $5,000 cash outflow.
b. A new machine with an installed cost of $85,000. Sale of the old machine will yield $30,000 after taxes. Operating cash inflows generated by the replacement will exceed the operating cash inflows of the old machine by $20,000 in each

year of a 6-year period. At the end of year 6, liquidation of the new machine will yield $20,000 after taxes, which is $10,000 greater than the after-tax proceeds expected from the old machine had it been retained and liquidated at the end of year 6.

c. An asset that requires an initial investment of $2 million and will yield annual operating cash inflows of $300,000 for each of the next 10 years. Operating cash outlays will be $20,000 for each year except year 6, when an overhaul requiring an additional cash outlay of $500,000 will be required. The asset's liquidation value at the end of year 10 is expected to be zero.

LG 3 **P11–3** **Expansion versus replacement cash flows** Edison Systems has estimated the cash flows over the 5-year lives for two projects, A and B. These cash flows are summarized in the table below.

a. If project A were actually a *replacement* for project B and if the $12,000 initial investment shown for project B were the after-tax cash inflow expected from liquidating it, what would be the *relevant cash flows* for this replacement decision?

b. How can an *expansion decision* such as project A be viewed as a special form of a replacement decision? Explain.

	Project A	Project B
Initial investment	**$40,000**	**$12,000[a]**
Year	**Operating cash inflows**	
1	$10,000	$ 6,000
2	12,000	6,000
3	14,000	6,000
4	16,000	6,000
5	10,000	6,000

[a]After-tax cash inflow expected from liquidation.

LG 2 **P11–4** **Sunk costs and opportunity costs** Masters Golf Products, Inc., spent 3 years and $1,000,000 to develop its new line of club heads to replace a line that is becoming obsolete. To begin manufacturing them, the company will have to invest $1,800,000 in new equipment. The new clubs are expected to generate an increase in operating cash inflows of $750,000 per year for the next 10 years. The company has determined that the existing line could be sold to a competitor for $250,000.

a. How should the $1,000,000 in development costs be classified?

b. How should the $250,000 sale price for the existing line be classified?

c. Depict all of the known relevant cash flows on a time line.

LG 2 **P11–5** **Sunk costs and opportunity costs** Covol Industries is developing the relevant cash flows associated with the proposed replacement of an existing machine tool with a new, technologically advanced one. Given the following costs related to the proposed project, explain whether each would be treated as a *sunk cost* or an *opportunity cost* in developing the relevant cash flows associated with the proposed replacement decision.

a. Covol would be able to use the same tooling, which had a book value of $40,000, on the new machine tool as it had used on the old one.

b. Covol would be able to use its existing computer system to develop programs for operating the new machine tool. The old machine tool did not require these programs. Although the firm's computer has excess capacity available, the capacity could be leased to another firm for an annual fee of $17,000.

c. Covol would have to obtain additional floor space to accommodate the larger new machine tool. The space that would be used is currently being leased to another company for $10,000 per year.

d. Covol would use a small storage facility to store the increased output of the new machine tool. The storage facility was built by Covol 3 years earlier at a cost of $120,000. Because of its unique configuration and location, it is currently of no use to either Covol or any other firm.

e. Covol would retain an existing overhead crane, which it had planned to sell for its $180,000 market value. Although the crane was not needed with the old machine tool, it would be used to position raw materials on the new machine tool.

Personal Finance Problem

LG 2 **P11–6 Sunk and opportunity cash flows** Dave and Ann Stone have been living at their present home for the past 6 years. During that time, they have replaced the water heater for $375, have replaced the dishwasher for $599, and have had to make miscellaneous repair and maintenance expenditures of approximately $1,500. They have decided to move out and rent the house for $975 per month. Newspaper advertising will cost $75. Dave and Ann intend to paint the interior of the home and power-wash the exterior. They estimate that that will run about $900.

The house should be ready to rent after that. In reviewing the financial situation, Dave views all the expenditures as being relevant, and so he plans to net out the estimated expenditures discussed above from the rental income.

a. Do Dave and Ann understand the difference between *sunk costs* and *opportunity costs?* Explain the two concepts to them.

b. Which of the expenditures should be classified as sunk cash flows and which should be viewed as opportunity cash flows?

LG 3 **P11–7 Book value** Find the book value for each of the assets shown in the accompanying table, assuming that MACRS depreciation is being used. (*Note:* See Table 4.2 on page 117 for the applicable depreciation percentages.)

Asset	Installed cost	Recovery period (years)	Elapsed time since purchase (years)
A	$ 950,000	5	3
B	40,000	3	1
C	96,000	5	4
D	350,000	5	1
E	1,500,000	7	5

LG 3 LG 4 **P11–8 Book value and taxes on sale of assets** Troy Industries purchased a new machine 3 years ago for $80,000. It is being depreciated under MACRS with a 5-year recovery period using the percentages given in Table 4.2 on page 117. Assume a 40% tax rate.

a. What is the *book value* of the machine?

b. Calculate the firm's tax liability if it sold the machine for each of the following amounts: $100,000; $56,000; $23,200; and $15,000.

LG 3 LG 4 **P11-9 Tax calculations** For each of the following cases, determine the total taxes resulting from the transaction. Assume a 40% tax rate. The asset was purchased 2 years ago for $200,000 and is being depreciated under MACRS using a 5-year recovery period. (See Table 4.2 on page 117 for the applicable depreciation percentages.)

a. The asset is sold for $220,000.
b. The asset is sold for $150,000.
c. The asset is sold for $96,000.
d. The asset is sold for $80,000.

LG 3 **P11-10 Change in net working capital calculation** Samuels Manufacturing is considering the purchase of a new machine to replace one it believes is obsolete. The firm has total current assets of $920,000 and total current liabilities of $640,000. As a result of the proposed replacement, the following *changes* are anticipated in the levels of the current asset and current liability accounts noted.

Account	Change
Accruals	+$ 40,000
Marketable securities	0
Inventories	− 10,000
Accounts payable	+ 90,000
Notes payable	0
Accounts receivable	+ 150,000
Cash	+ 15,000

a. Using the information given, calculate any *change in net working capital* that is expected to result from the proposed replacement action.
b. Explain why a change in these current accounts would be relevant in determining the *initial investment* for the proposed capital expenditure.
c. Would the change in net working capital enter into any of the other cash flow components that make up the relevant cash flows? Explain.

LG 3 LG 4 **P11-11 Calculating initial investment** Vastine Medical, Inc., is considering replacing its existing computer system, which was purchased 2 years ago at a cost of $325,000. The system can be sold today for $200,000. It is being depreciated using MACRS and a 5-year recovery period (see Table 4.2, page 117). A new computer system will cost $500,000 to purchase and install. Replacement of the computer system would not involve any change in net working capital. Assume a 40% tax rate.

a. Calculate the *book value* of the existing computer system.
b. Calculate the after-tax proceeds of its sale for $200,000.
c. Calculate the *initial investment* associated with the replacement project.

LG 3 LG 4 **P11-12 Initial investment—Basic calculation** Cushing Corporation is considering the purchase of a new grading machine to replace the existing one. The existing machine was purchased 3 years ago at an installed cost of $20,000; it was being depreciated under MACRS using a 5-year recovery period. (See Table 4.2 on page 117 for the applicable depreciation percentages.) The existing machine is expected to have a usable life of at least 5 more years. The new machine costs $35,000 and requires $5,000 in installation costs; it will be depreciated using a 5-year recovery period under MACRS. The existing machine can currently be sold for $25,000 without incurring any removal or cleanup costs. The firm is subject to a 40% tax rate. Calculate the *initial investment* associated with the proposed purchase of a new grading machine.

LG 3 LG 4 **P11–13 Initial investment at various sale prices** Edwards Manufacturing Company (EMC) is considering replacing one machine with another. The old machine was purchased 3 years ago for an installed cost of $10,000. The firm is depreciating the machine under MACRS, using a 5-year recovery period. (See Table 4.2 on page 117 for the applicable depreciation percentages.) The new machine costs $24,000 and requires $2,000 in installation costs. The firm is subject to a 40% tax rate. In each of the following cases, calculate the *initial investment* for the replacement.

a. EMC sells the old machine for $11,000.
b. EMC sells the old machine for $7,000.
c. EMC sells the old machine for $2,900.
d. EMC sells the old machine for $1,500.

LG 3 LG 4 **P11–14 Calculating initial investment** DuPree Coffee Roasters, Inc., wishes to expand and modernize its facilities. The installed cost of a proposed computer-controlled automatic-feed roaster will be $130,000. The firm has a chance to sell its 4-year-old roaster for $35,000. The existing roaster originally cost $60,000 and was being depreciated using MACRS and a 7-year recovery period (see Table 4.2 on page 117). DuPree is subject to a 40% tax rate.

a. What is the *book value* of the existing roaster?
b. Calculate the after-tax proceeds of the sale of the existing roaster.
c. Calculate the *change in net working capital* using the following figures:

Anticipated Changes in Current Assets and Current Liabilities	
Accruals	−$20,000
Inventory	+ 50,000
Accounts payable	+ 40,000
Accounts receivable	+ 70,000
Cash	0
Notes payable	+ 15,000

d. Calculate the *initial investment* associated with the proposed new roaster.

LG 5 **P11–15 Depreciation** A firm is evaluating the acquisition of an asset that costs $64,000 and requires $4,000 in installation costs. If the firm depreciates the asset under MACRS, using a 5-year recovery period (see Table 4.2 on page 117 for the applicable depreciation percentages), determine the depreciation charge for each year.

LG 5 **P11–16 Incremental operating cash inflows** A firm is considering renewing its equipment to meet increased demand for its product. The cost of equipment modifications is $1.9 million plus $100,000 in installation costs. The firm will depreciate the equipment modifications under MACRS, using a 5-year recovery period. (See Table 4.2 on page 117 for the applicable depreciation percentages.) Additional sales revenue from the renewal should amount to $1.2 million per year, and additional operating expenses and other costs (excluding depreciation and interest) will amount to 40% of the additional sales. The firm is subject to a tax rate of 40%. (*Note:* Answer the following questions for each of the next *6 years.*)

a. What incremental earnings before depreciation, interest, and taxes will result from the renewal?

b. What incremental net operating profits after taxes will result from the renewal?

c. What *incremental operating cash inflows* will result from the renewal?

Personal Finance Problem

LG 5 **P11–17** **Incremental operating cash flows** Richard and Linda Thomson operate a local lawn maintenance service for commercial and residential property. They have been using a John Deere riding mower for the past several years and feel it is time to buy a new one. They would like to know the incremental (relevant) cash flows associated with the replacement of the old riding mower. The following data are available.

There are 5 years of remaining useful life on the old mower.

The old mower has a zero book value.

The new mower is expected to last 5 years.

The Thomsons will follow a 5-year MACRS recovery period for the new mower.

Depreciable value of the new mower is $1,800.

They are subject to a 40% tax rate.

The new mower is expected to be more fuel efficient, maneuverable, and durable than previous models and can result in reduced operating expenses of $500 per year.

The Thomsons will buy a maintenance contract that calls for annual payments of $120.

Create an *incremental operating cash flow* statement for the replacement of Richard and Linda's John Deere riding mower. Show the incremental operating cash flow for the next 6 years.

LG 5 **P11–18** **Incremental operating cash inflows—Expense reduction** Miller Corporation is considering replacing a machine. The replacement will reduce operating expenses (that is, increase earnings before depreciation, interest, and taxes) by $16,000 per year for each of the 5 years the new machine is expected to last. Although the old machine has zero book value, it can be used for 5 more years. The depreciable value of the new machine is $48,000. The firm will depreciate the machine under MACRS using a 5-year recovery period (see Table 4.2 on page 117 for the applicable depreciation percentages) and is subject to a 40% tax rate. Estimate the *incremental operating cash inflows* generated by the replacement. (*Note:* Be sure to consider the depreciation in year 6.)

LG 5 **P11–19** **Incremental operating cash inflows** Strong Tool Company has been considering purchasing a new lathe to replace a fully depreciated lathe that will last 5 more years. The new lathe is expected to have a 5-year life and depreciation charges of $2,000 in year 1; $3,200 in year 2; $1,900 in year 3; $1,200 in both year 4 and year 5; and $500 in year 6. The firm estimates the revenues and expenses (excluding depreciation and interest) for the new and the old lathes to be as shown in the table at the top of page 456. The firm is subject to a 40% tax rate.

	New lathe		Old lathe	
Year	Revenue	Expenses (excluding depreciation and interest)	Revenue	Expenses (excluding depreciation and interest)
1	$40,000	$30,000	$35,000	$25,000
2	41,000	30,000	35,000	25,000
3	42,000	30,000	35,000	25,000
4	43,000	30,000	35,000	25,000
5	44,000	30,000	35,000	25,000

a. Calculate the *operating cash inflows* associated with each lathe. (*Note:* Be sure to consider the depreciation in year 6.)

b. Calculate the *incremental (relevant) operating cash inflows* resulting from the proposed lathe replacement.

c. Depict on a time line the incremental operating cash inflows calculated in part **b.**

LG 5 **P11–20** **Determining incremental operating cash inflows** Scenic Tours, Inc., is a provider of bus tours throughout the New England area. The corporation is considering the replacement of 10 of its older buses. The existing buses were purchased 4 years ago at a total cost of $2,700,000 and are being depreciated using MACRS and a 5-year recovery period (see Table 4.2, page 117). The new buses would have larger passenger capacity and better fuel efficiency as well as lower maintenance costs. The total cost for 10 new buses is $3,000,000. Like the older buses, the new ones would be depreciated using MACRS and a 5-year recovery period. Scenic is subject to a tax rate of 40%. The accompanying table presents revenues and cash expenses (excluding depreciation and interest) for the proposed purchase as well as the present fleet. Use all of the information given to calculate *incremental (relevant) operating cash inflows* for the proposed bus replacement.

	Year					
	1	2	3	4	5	6
With the proposed new buses						
Revenue	$1,850,000	$1,850,000	$1,830,000	$1,825,000	$1,815,000	$1,800,000
Expenses (excluding depreciation and interest)	460,000	460,000	468,000	472,000	485,000	500,000
With the present buses						
Revenue	$1,800,000	$1,800,000	$1,790,000	$1,785,000	$1,775,000	$1,750,000
Expenses (excluding depreciation and interest)	500,000	510,000	520,000	520,000	530,000	535,000

LG 6 **P11–21** **Terminal cash flow—Various lives and sale prices** Looner Industries is currently analyzing the purchase of a new machine that costs $160,000 and requires $20,000 in installation costs. Purchase of this machine is expected to result in an increase in net working capital of $30,000 to support the expanded level of operations. The firm plans to depreciate the machine under MACRS using a 5-year recovery period

(see Table 4.2 on page 117 for the applicable depreciation percentages) and expects to sell the machine to net $10,000 before taxes at the end of its usable life. The firm is subject to a 40% tax rate.

a. Calculate the *terminal cash flow* for a usable life of (1) 3 years, (2) 5 years, and (3) 7 years.

b. Discuss the effect of usable life on terminal cash flows using your findings in part **a.**

c. Assuming a 5-year usable life, calculate the terminal cash flow if the machine were sold to net (1) $9,000 or (2) $170,000 (before taxes) at the end of 5 years.

d. Discuss the effect of sale price on terminal cash flow using your findings in part **c.**

LG 6 **P11–22 Terminal cash flow—Replacement decision** Russell Industries is considering replacing a fully depreciated machine that has a remaining useful life of 10 years with a newer, more sophisticated machine. The new machine will cost $200,000 and will require $30,000 in installation costs. It will be depreciated under MACRS using a 5-year recovery period (see Table 4.2 on page 117 for the applicable depreciation percentages). A $25,000 increase in net working capital will be required to support the new machine. The firm's managers plan to evaluate the potential replacement over a 4-year period. They estimate that the old machine could be sold at the end of 4 years to net $15,000 before taxes; the new machine at the end of 4 years will be worth $75,000 before taxes. Calculate the *terminal cash flow* at the end of year 4 that is relevant to the proposed purchase of the new machine. The firm is subject to a 40% tax rate.

LG 3 LG 4 LG 5 LG 6 **P11–23 Relevant cash flows for a marketing campaign** Marcus Tube, a manufacturer of high-quality aluminum tubing, has maintained stable sales and profits over the past 10 years. Although the market for aluminum tubing has been expanding by 3% per year, Marcus has been unsuccessful in sharing this growth. To increase its sales, the firm is considering an aggressive marketing campaign that centers on regularly running ads in all relevant trade journals and exhibiting products at all major regional and national trade shows. The campaign is expected to require an *annual* tax-deductible expenditure of $150,000 over the next 5 years. Sales revenue, as shown in the accompanying income statement for 2012, totaled $20,000,000. If the proposed marketing campaign is not initiated, sales are expected to remain at this level in each of the next 5 years, 2013 through 2017. With the marketing campaign, sales

Marcus Tube Income Statement for the Year Ended December 31, 2012

Sales revenue		$20,000,000
Less: Cost of goods sold (80%)		16,000,000
Gross profits		$ 4,000,000
Less: Operating expenses		
General and administrative expense (10%)	$2,000,000	
Depreciation expense	500,000	
Total operating expense		$ 2,500,000
Earnings before interest and taxes		$ 1,500,000
Less: Taxes (rate = 40%)		600,000
Net operating profit after taxes		$ 900,000

Marcus Tube Sales Forecast

Year	Sales revenue
2013	$20,500,000
2014	21,000,000
2015	21,500,000
2016	22,500,000
2017	23,500,000

are expected to rise to the levels shown in the accompanying table for each of the next 5 years; cost of goods sold is expected to remain at 80% of sales; general and administrative expense (exclusive of any marketing campaign outlays) is expected to remain at 10% of sales; and annual depreciation expense is expected to remain at $500,000. Assuming a 40% tax rate, find the *relevant cash flows* over the next 5 years associated with the proposed marketing campaign.

LG 3 LG 4 LG 5

P11–24 Relevant cash flows—No terminal value Central Laundry and Cleaners is considering replacing an existing piece of machinery with a more sophisticated machine. The old machine was purchased 3 years ago at a cost of $50,000, and this amount was being depreciated under MACRS using a 5-year recovery period. The machine has 5 years of usable life remaining. The new machine that is being considered costs $76,000 and requires $4,000 in installation costs. The new machine would be depreciated under MACRS using a 5-year recovery period. The firm can currently sell the old machine for $55,000 without incurring any removal or cleanup costs. The firm is subject to a tax rate of 40%. The revenues and expenses (excluding depreciation and interest) associated with the new and the old machines for the next 5 years are given in the table below. (Table 4.2 on page 117 contains the applicable MACRS depreciation percentages.)

	New machine		Old machine	
Year	Revenue	Expenses (excl. depr. and int.)	Revenue	Expenses (excl. depr. and int.)
1	$750,000	$720,000	$674,000	$660,000
2	750,000	720,000	676,000	660,000
3	750,000	720,000	680,000	660,000
4	750,000	720,000	678,000	660,000
5	750,000	720,000	674,000	660,000

a. Calculate the *initial investment* associated with replacement of the old machine by the new one.

b. Determine the *incremental operating cash inflows* associated with the proposed replacement. (*Note:* Be sure to consider the depreciation in year 6.)

c. Depict on a time line the *relevant cash flows* found in parts **a** and **b** associated with the proposed replacement decision.

LG 3 LG 4 LG 5 LG 6

P11–25 Integrative—Determining relevant cash flows Lombard Company is contemplating the purchase of a new high-speed widget grinder to replace the existing grinder. The existing grinder was purchased 2 years ago at an installed cost of $60,000; it was being depreciated under MACRS using a 5-year recovery period. The existing grinder is expected to have a usable life of 5 more years. The new grinder costs $105,000 and requires $5,000 in installation costs; it has a 5-year usable life and would be depreciated under MACRS using a 5-year recovery period. Lombard can currently sell the existing grinder for $70,000 without incurring any removal or cleanup costs. To support the increased business resulting from purchase of the new grinder, accounts receivable would increase by $40,000, inventories by $30,000, and accounts payable by $58,000. At the end of 5 years, the existing grinder would have a market value of zero; the new grinder would be sold to net $29,000 after removal and cleanup costs and before taxes. The firm is subject a 40% tax rate. The estimated *earnings before depreciation, interest, and taxes* over the 5 years for both the new and the existing grinder are shown in the following table. (Table 4.2 on page 117 contains the applicable MACRS depreciation percentages.)

	Earnings before depreciation, interest, and taxes	
Year	**New grinder**	**Existing grinder**
1	$43,000	$26,000
2	43,000	24,000
3	43,000	22,000
4	43,000	20,000
5	43,000	18,000

a. Calculate the *initial investment* associated with the replacement of the existing grinder by the new one.
b. Determine the *incremental operating cash inflows* associated with the proposed grinder replacement. (*Note:* Be sure to consider the depreciation in year 6.)
c. Determine the *terminal cash flow* expected at the end of year 5 from the proposed grinder replacement.
d. Depict on a time line the *relevant cash flows* associated with the proposed grinder replacement decision.

Personal Finance Problem

LG 3 LG 4 LG 5 LG 6

P11–26 Determining relevant cash flows for a new boat Jan and Deana have been dreaming about owning a boat for some time and have decided that estimating its cash flows will help them in their decision process. They expect to have a disposable annual income of $24,000. Their cash flow estimates for the boat purchase are as follows:

Negotiated price of the new boat	$70,000
Sales tax rate (applicable to purchase price)	6.5%
Boat trade-in	0
Estimated value of new boat in 4 years	$40,000
Estimated monthly repair and maintenance	$800
Estimated monthly docking fee	$500

Using these cash flow estimates, calculate the following:
a. The initial investment
b. Operating cash flow
c. Terminal cash flow
d. Summary of annual cash flow
e. Based on their disposable annual income, what advice would you give Jan and Deana regarding the proposed boat purchase?

LG 3 LG 4 LG 5 LG 6

P11–27 Integrative—Determining relevant cash flows Atlantic Drydock is considering replacing an existing hoist with one of two newer, more efficient pieces of equipment. The existing hoist is 3 years old, cost $32,000, and is being depreciated under MACRS using a 5-year recovery period. Although the existing hoist has only 3 years (years 4, 5, and 6) of depreciation remaining under MACRS, it has a remaining usable life of 5 years. Hoist A, one of the two possible replacement hoists, costs $40,000 to purchase and $8,000 to install. It has a 5-year usable life and will be depreciated under MACRS using a 5-year recovery period. Hoist B costs $54,000 to purchase and $6,000 to install. It also has a 5-year usable life and will be depreciated under MACRS using a 5-year recovery period.

Increased investments in net working capital will accompany the decision to acquire hoist A or hoist B. Purchase of hoist A would result in a $4,000 increase in net working capital; hoist B would result in a $6,000 increase in net working capital. The projected *earnings before depreciation, interest, and taxes* with each alternative hoist and the existing hoist are given in the following table.

	Earnings before depreciation, interest, and taxes		
Year	With hoist A	With hoist B	With existing hoist
1	$21,000	$22,000	$14,000
2	21,000	24,000	14,000
3	21,000	26,000	14,000
4	21,000	26,000	14,000
5	21,000	26,000	14,000

The existing hoist can currently be sold for $18,000 and will not incur any removal or cleanup costs. At the end of 5 years, the existing hoist can be sold to net $1,000 before taxes. Hoists A and B can be sold to net $12,000 and $20,000 before taxes, respectively, at the end of the 5-year period. The firm is subject to a 40% tax rate. (Table 4.2 on page 117 contains the applicable MACRS depreciation percentages.)

a. Calculate the *initial investment* associated with each alternative.

b. Calculate the *incremental operating cash inflows* associated with each alternative. (*Note:* Be sure to consider the depreciation in year 6.)

c. Calculate the *terminal cash flow* at the end of year 5 associated with each alternative.

d. Depict on a time line the *relevant cash flows* associated with each alternative.

LG 1 LG 2 LG 3 LG 4 LG 5 LG 6

P11–28 Integrative—Complete investment decision Wells Printing is considering the purchase of a new printing press. The total installed cost of the press is $2.2 million. This outlay would be partially offset by the sale of an existing press. The old press has zero book value, cost $1 million 10 years ago, and can be sold currently for $1.2 million before taxes. As a result of acquisition of the new press, sales in each of the next 5 years are expected to be $1.6 million higher than with the existing press, but product costs (excluding depreciation) will represent 50% of sales. The new press will not affect the firm's net working capital requirements. The new press will be depreciated under MACRS using a 5-year recovery period. The firm is subject to a

40% tax rate. Wells Printing's cost of capital is 11%. (*Note:* Assume that the old and the new presses will each have a terminal value of $0 at the end of year 6.)

a. Determine the *initial investment* required by the new press.

b. Determine the *operating cash inflows* attributable to the new press. (*Note:* Be sure to consider the depreciation in year 6.)

c. Determine the *payback period.*

d. Determine the *net present value (NPV)* and the *internal rate of return (IRR)* related to the proposed new press.

e. Make a recommendation to accept or reject the new press, and justify your answer.

LG 1 LG 2 LG 3 LG 4 LG 5 LG 6

P11–29 Integrative—Investment decision Holliday Manufacturing is considering the replacement of an existing machine. The new machine costs $1.2 million and requires installation costs of $150,000. The existing machine can be sold currently for $185,000 before taxes. It is 2 years old, cost $800,000 new, and has a $384,000 book value and a remaining useful life of 5 years. It was being depreciated under MACRS using a 5-year recovery period (see Table 4.2 on page 117) and therefore has the final 4 years of depreciation remaining. If it is held for 5 more years, the machine's market value at the end of year 5 will be $0. Over its 5-year life, the new machine should reduce operating costs by $350,000 per year. The new machine will be depreciated under MACRS using a 5-year recovery period. The new machine can be sold for $200,000 net of removal and cleanup costs at the end of 5 years. An increased investment in net working capital of $25,000 will be needed to support operations if the new machine is acquired. Assume that the firm has adequate operating income against which to deduct any loss experienced on the sale of the existing machine. The firm has a 9% cost of capital and is subject to a 40% tax rate.

a. Develop the *relevant cash flows* needed to analyze the proposed replacement.

b. Determine the *net present value (NPV)* of the proposal.

c. Determine the *internal rate of return (IRR)* of the proposal.

d. Make a recommendation to accept or reject the replacement proposal, and justify your answer.

e. What is the highest cost of capital that the firm could have and still accept the proposal? Explain.

LG 2

P11–30 ETHICS PROBLEM Cash flow projections are a central component to the analysis of new investment ideas. In most firms, the person responsible for making these projections is not the same person who generated the investment idea in the first place. Why?

Spreadsheet Exercise

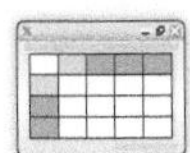

Damon Corporation, a sports equipment manufacturer, has a machine currently in use that was originally purchased 3 years ago for $120,000. The firm depreciates the machine under MACRS using a 5-year recovery period. Once removal and cleanup costs are taken into consideration, the expected net selling price for the present machine will be $70,000.

Damon can buy a new machine for a net price of $160,000 (including installation costs of $15,000). The proposed machine will be depreciated under MACRS using a 5-year recovery period. If the firm acquires the new machine, its working capital needs will change—accounts receivable will increase $15,000, inventory will increase $19,000, and accounts payable will increase $16,000.

Earnings before depreciation, interest, and taxes (EBDIT) for the present machine are expected to be $95,000 for each of the successive 5 years. For the proposed machine, the expected EBDIT for each of the next 5 years are $105,000, $110,000, $120,000, $120,000, and $120,000, respectively. The corporate tax rate (T) for the firm is 40%. (Table 4.2 on page 117 contains the applicable MACRS depreciation percentages.)

Damon expects to be able to liquidate the proposed machine at the end of its 5-year usable life for $24,000 (after paying removal and cleanup costs). The present machine is expected to net $8,000 upon liquidation at the end of the same period. Damon expects to recover its net working capital investment upon termination of the project. The firm is subject to a tax rate of 40%.

TO DO

Create a spreadsheet similar to Tables 11.1, 11.5, 11.7, and 11.9 to answer the following:

a. Create a spreadsheet to calculate the *initial investment.*

b. Create a spreadsheet to prepare a *depreciation schedule* for both the proposed and the present machine. Both machines are depreciated under MACRS using a 5-year recovery period. Remember, the present machine has only 3 years of depreciation remaining.

c. Create a spreadsheet to calculate the *operating cash inflows* for Damon Corporation for both the proposed and the present machine.

d. Create a spreadsheet to calculate the *terminal cash flow* associated with the project.

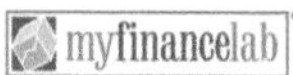

Visit www.myfinancelab.com for **Chapter Case: *Developing Relevant Cash Flows for Clark Upholstery Company's Machine Renewal or Replacement Decision,*** Group Exercises, and numerous online resources.

12 Risk and Refinements in Capital Budgeting

Learning Goals

LG 1 Understand the importance of recognizing risk in the analysis of capital budgeting projects.

LG 2 Discuss risk and cash inflows, scenario analysis, and simulation as behavioral approaches for dealing with risk.

LG 3 Review the unique risks that multinational companies face.

LG 4 Describe the determination and use of risk-adjusted discount rates (RADRs), portfolio effects, and the practical aspects of RADRs.

LG 5 Select the best of a group of unequal-lived, mutually exclusive projects using annualized net present values (ANPVs).

LG 6 Explain the role of real options and the objective and procedures for selecting projects under capital rationing.

Why This Chapter Matters to You

In your *professional* life

ACCOUNTING You need to understand the risk caused by the variability of cash flows, how to compare projects with unequal lives, and how to measure project returns when capital is being rationed.

INFORMATION SYSTEMS You need to understand how risk is incorporated into capital budgeting techniques and how those techniques may be refined in the face of special circumstances, so as to design decision modules for use in analyzing proposed capital projects.

MANAGEMENT You need to understand behavioral approaches for dealing with risk, including international risk, in capital budgeting decisions; how to risk-adjust discount rates; how to refine capital budgeting techniques when projects have unequal lives or when capital must be rationed; and how to recognize real options embedded in capital projects.

MARKETING You need to understand how the risk of proposed projects is measured in capital budgeting, how projects with unequal lives will be evaluated, how to recognize and treat real options embedded in proposed projects, and how projects will be evaluated when capital must be rationed.

OPERATIONS You need to understand how proposals for the acquisition of new equipment and plants will be evaluated by the firm's decision makers, especially projects that are risky, have unequal lives, or may need to be abandoned or slowed, or when capital is limited.

In your *personal* life

Risk is present in all long-term decisions. When making personal financial decisions, you should consider risk in the decision-making process. Simply put, you should demand higher returns for greater risk. Failing to incorporate risk into your financial decision-making process will likely result in poor decisions and reduced wealth.

BP

Worst Case Scenario

On April 20, 2010, an explosion destroyed BP's Deepwater Horizon offshore oil rig, resulting in the largest oil spill in U.S. history. As much as 2.5 million gallons of oil spewed into the Gulf of Mexico each day, eventually reaching the shoreline in several states and causing serious harm to the environment. Under pressure from the Obama administration, BP agreed to establish a $20 billion fund to pay for spill-related expenses such as clean-up costs and compensation for lost income for individuals and businesses directly harmed by the accident.

When managers undertake large investments, they often invest a tremendous amount of time and money trying to understand the risks associated with these investments. In the case of BP, an accident at a rig that cost $500 million to build cost the company more than $20 billion. As news of the accident and subsequent spill evolved, BP's stock price plunged, falling from $60 to less than $30 in just 7 weeks, wiping out more than $90 billion of the firm's market capitalization.

This chapter focuses on the tools available to managers that help them better understand the risks of major investments.

LG 1

12.1 Introduction to Risk in Capital Budgeting

In our discussion of capital budgeting thus far, we have assumed that all investment projects have the same level of risk for the firm. In other words, we assumed that all projects are equally risky, and the acceptance of any project would not change the firm's overall risk. In actuality, these situations are rare—projects are not equally risky, and the acceptance of a project can affect the firm's overall risk. We begin this chapter by relaxing these assumptions and focusing on how managers evaluate the risks of different projects. Naturally, we will utilize many of the risk concepts developed in Chapter 8.

We continue the Bennett Company example from Chapter 10. The relevant cash flows and NPVs for Bennett Company's two mutually exclusive projects—A and B—appear in Table 12.1.

In the following three sections, we use the basic risk concepts presented in Chapter 8 to demonstrate behavioral approaches for dealing with risk, international risk considerations, and the use of risk-adjusted discount rates to explicitly recognize risk in the analysis of capital budgeting projects.

→ REVIEW QUESTION

12–1 Are most mutually exclusive capital budgeting projects equally risky? If you think about a firm as a portfolio of many different kinds of investments, how can the acceptance of a project change a firm's overall risk?

TABLE 12.1 Relevant Cash Flows and NPVs for Bennett Company's Projects

	Project A	Project B
A. Relevant cash flows		
Initial investment	**$42,000**	**$45,000**
Year	**Operating cash inflows**	
1	$14,000	$28,000
2	14,000	12,000
3	14,000	10,000
4	14,000	10,000
5	14,000	10,000
B. Decision technique		
NPV @ 10% cost of capital[a]	$11,071	$10,924

[a]From Figure 10.2 on page 396; calculated using a financial calculator.

LG 2

12.2 Behavioral Approaches for Dealing with Risk

Behavioral approaches can be used to get a "feel" for the level of project risk, whereas other approaches try to quantify and measure project risk. Here we present a few behavioral approaches for dealing with risk in capital budgeting: risk and cash inflows, scenario analysis, and simulation.

RISK AND CASH INFLOWS

risk (in capital budgeting) The uncertainty surrounding the cash flows that a project will generate or, more formally, the degree of variability of cash flows.

In the context of capital budgeting, the term **risk** refers to the uncertainty surrounding the cash flows that a project will generate. More formally, risk in capital budgeting is the degree of variability of cash flows. Projects with a broad range of possible cash flows are more risky than projects that have a narrow range of possible cash flows.

In many projects, risk stems almost entirely from the *cash flows* that a project will generate several years in the future because the initial investment is generally known with relative certainty. These cash flows, of course, derive from a number of variables related to revenues, expenditures, and taxes. Examples include the level of sales, the cost of raw materials, labor rates, utility costs, and tax rates. We will concentrate on the risk in the cash flows, but remember that this risk actually results from the interaction of these underlying variables. Therefore, to assess the risk of a proposed capital expenditure, the analyst needs to evaluate the probability that the cash inflows will be large enough to produce a positive NPV.

Example 12.1 ▶

Treadwell Tire Company, a tire retailer with a 10% cost of capital, is considering investing in either of two mutually exclusive projects, A and B. Each requires a \$10,000 initial investment, and both are expected to provide constant annual cash inflows over their 15-year lives. For either project to be acceptable, its NPV must be greater than zero. Another way to say this is that the present value of the annuity (that is, the project's cash inflows) must be greater than the initial cash outflow. If we let *CF* equal the annual cash inflow and let CF_0 equal the initial investment, the following condition must be met for projects with annuity cash inflows, such as A and B, to be acceptable:[1]

breakeven cash inflow The minimum level of cash inflow necessary for a project to be acceptable, that is, NPV > \$0.

$$\text{NPV} = \left(\frac{CF}{i}\right) \times \left[1 - \frac{1}{(1+i)^n}\right] - CF_0 > \$0 \tag{12.1}$$

By substituting $i = 10\%$, $n = 15$ years, and $CF_0 = \$10,000$, we can find the **breakeven cash inflow**—the minimum level of cash inflow necessary for Treadwell's projects to be acceptable.

Calculator Use Recognizing that the initial investment (CF_0) is the present value (PV), we can use the calculator inputs shown at the left to find the breakeven cash inflow (CF), which is an ordinary annuity (PMT).

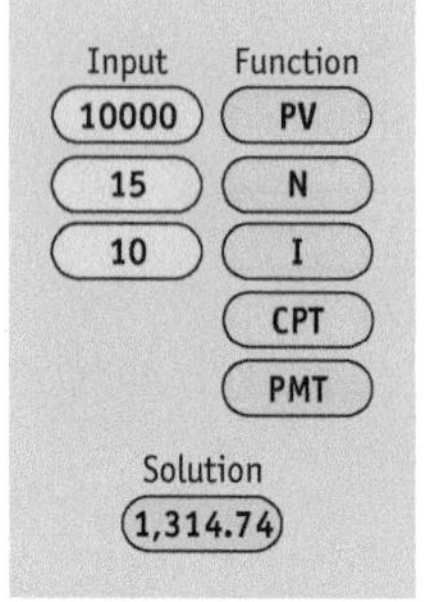

1. This equation makes use of the algebraic shortcut for the present value of an annuity, introduced as Equation 5.11 on page 173.

Spreadsheet Use The breakeven cash inflow also can be calculated as shown on the following Excel spreadsheet.

	A	B
1	BREAKEVEN CASH INFLOW	
2	Cost of capital	10%
3	Number of years	15
4	Initial investment	$10,000
5	Breakeven cash inflow	$1,314.74

Entry in Cell B5 is =PMT(B2,B3,–B4).
The minus sign appears before B4 because the initial investment is a cash outflow.

The calculator and spreadsheet values indicate that, for the projects to be acceptable, they must have annual cash inflows of at least $1,315. Given this breakeven level of cash inflows, the risk of each project can be assessed by determining the probability that the project's cash inflows will equal or exceed this breakeven level. The various statistical techniques that would determine that probability are covered in more advanced courses.[2] For now, we can simply assume that such a statistical analysis results in the following:

$$\text{Probability of } CF_A > \$1{,}315 \rightarrow 100\%$$
$$\text{Probability of } CF_B > \$1{,}315 \rightarrow 65\%$$

Because project A is certain (100% probability) to have a positive net present value, whereas there is only a 65% chance that project B will have a positive NPV, project A seems less risky than project B. Of course, the expected level of annual cash inflow and NPV associated with each project must be evaluated in view of the firm's risk preference before the preferred project is selected.

The example clearly identifies risk as it is related to the chance that a project is acceptable, but it does not address the issue of cash flow variability. Even though project B has a greater chance of loss than project A, it might result in higher potential NPVs. Recall that it is the *combination* of risk and return that determines value. Similarly, the worth of a capital expenditure and its impact on the firm's value must be viewed in light of both risk and return. The analyst must therefore consider the *variability* of cash inflows and NPVs to assess project risk and return fully.

SCENARIO ANALYSIS

Scenario analysis can be used to deal with project risk to capture the variability of cash inflows and NPVs. *Scenario analysis* is a behavioral approach that uses several possible alternative outcomes (scenarios), to obtain a sense of the variability of returns, measured here by NPV. This technique is often useful in getting a feel for the variability of return in response to changes in a key outcome. In capital

2. Normal distributions are commonly used to develop the concept of the *probability of success*—that is, of a project having a positive NPV. The reader interested in learning more about this technique should see any second- or MBA-level managerial finance text.

TABLE 12.2 Scenario Analysis of Treadwell's Projects A and B

	Project A	Project B
Initial investment	**$10,000**	**$10,000**
	Annual cash inflows	
Outcome		
Pessimistic	$1,500	$ 0
Most likely	2,000	2,000
Optimistic	2,500	4,000
Range	1,000	4,000
	Net present values[a]	
Outcome		
Pessimistic	$1,409	$10,000
Most likely	5,212	5,212
Optimistic	9,015	20,424
Range	7,606	30,424

[a]These values were calculated by using the corresponding annual cash inflows. A 10% cost of capital and a 15-year life for the annual cash inflows were used.

budgeting, one of the most common scenario approaches is to estimate the NPVs associated with pessimistic (worst), most likely (expected), and optimistic (best) estimates of cash inflow. The *range* can be determined by subtracting the pessimistic-outcome NPV from the optimistic-outcome NPV.

Example 12.2 ▸

Continuing with Treadwell Tire Company, assume that the financial manager created three scenarios for each project: pessimistic, most likely, and optimistic. The cash inflows and resulting NPVs in each case are summarized in Table 12.2. Comparing the ranges of cash inflows ($1,000 for project A and $4,000 for B) and, more important, the ranges of NPVs ($7,606 for project A and $30,424 for B) makes it clear that project A is less risky than project B. Given that both projects have the same most likely NPV of $5,212, the assumed risk-averse decision maker will take project A because it has less risk (smaller NPV range) and no possibility of loss (all NPVs > $0).

The widespread availability of computers and spreadsheets has greatly enhanced the use of scenario analysis because technology allows analysts to quickly create a wide range of different scenarios.

simulation
A statistics-based behavioral approach that applies predetermined probability distributions and random numbers to estimate risky outcomes.

SIMULATION

Simulation is a statistics-based behavioral approach that applies predetermined probability distributions and random numbers to estimate risky outcomes. By tying the various cash flow components together in a mathematical model and

FIGURE 12.1

NPV Simulation
Flowchart of a net present value simulation

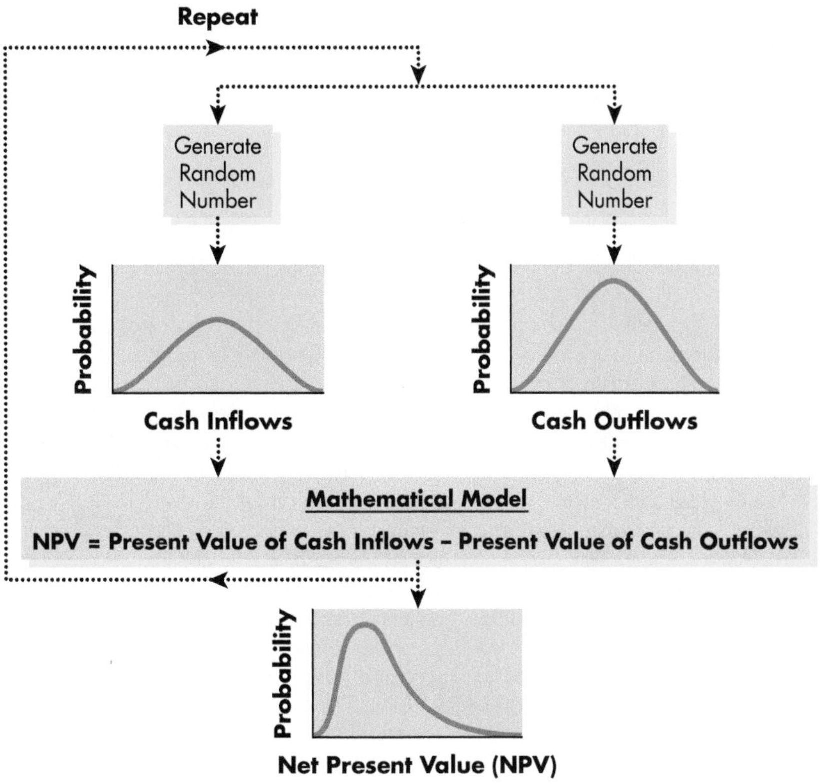

repeating the process numerous times, the financial manager can develop a probability distribution of project returns.

Figure 12.1 presents a flowchart of the simulation of the net present value of a project. The process of generating random numbers and using the probability distributions for cash inflows and cash outflows enables the financial manager to determine values for each of these variables. Substituting these values into the mathematical model results in an NPV. By repeating this process perhaps a thousand times, managers can create a probability distribution of net present values.

In more depth

To read about *Monte Carlo Simulations,* go to www.myfinancelab.com

Although Figure 12.1 simulates only gross cash inflows and cash outflows, more sophisticated simulations using individual inflow and outflow components, such as sales volume, sale price, raw material cost, labor cost, or maintenance expense, are quite common. From the distribution of returns, the decision maker can determine not only the expected value of the return but also the probability of achieving or surpassing a given return. The use of computers has made the simulation approach feasible. Monte Carlo simulation programs, made popular by widespread use of personal computers, are described in the nearby *Focus on Practice* box.

The output of simulation provides an excellent basis for decision making, because it enables the decision maker to view a continuum of risk–return tradeoffs rather than a single-point estimate.

focus on **PRACTICE**

The Monte Carlo Method: The Forecast Is for Less Uncertainty

in practice Most capital budgeting decisions involve some degree of uncertainty. For example, a company faces some degree of uncertainty associated with the demand for a new product. One method of accounting for this uncertainty is to average the highest and the lowest prediction of sales. However, such a method is flawed. Producing the average of the expected possible demand can lead to gross overproduction or gross underproduction, neither of which is as profitable as having the right volume of production.

To combat uncertainty in the decision-making process, some companies use a Monte Carlo simulation program to model possible outcomes. Developed by mathematicians in World War II while working on the atomic bomb, the *Monte Carlo method* was not widely used until the advent of the personal computer. A Monte Carlo simulation program randomly generates values for uncertain variables over and over to simulate a model. The simulation then requires project practitioners to develop low, high, and most likely cost estimates along with correlation coefficients. Once these inputs are derived, the Monte Carlo program can be run through just a few simulations, or thousands, in just a few seconds.

A Monte Carlo program usually builds a histogram of the results, referred to as a *frequency chart,* for each forecast or output cell that the user wants to analyze. The program then delivers a percentage *certainty* that a particular forecast will fall within a specified range, much like a weather forecast. The program also has an optimization feature that allows a project manager with budget constraints to figure out which combination of possible projects will result in the highest profit.

One of the problems with using a Monte Carlo program is the difficulty of establishing the correct input ranges for the variables and determining the correlation coefficients for those variables. However, the work put into developing the input for the program can often clarify some uncertainty in a proposed project. Although Monte Carlo simulation is not the perfect answer to capital budgeting problems, it is another tool that corporations, including ALCOA, Motorola, RJR Nabisco, and Walt Disney, use to manage risk and make more informed business and strategic decisions.

► ***A Monte Carlo simulation program requires the user to first build an Excel spreadsheet model that captures the input variables for the proposed project. What issues and what benefits can the user derive from this process?***

→ **REVIEW QUESTIONS**

12–2 Define *risk* in terms of the cash flows from a capital budgeting project. How can determination of the *breakeven cash inflow* be used to gauge project risk?

12–3 Describe how each of the following behavioral approaches can be used to deal with project risk: (**a**) scenario analysis and (**b**) simulation.

LG 3 12.3 International Risk Considerations

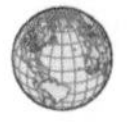

exchange rate risk
The danger that an unexpected change in the exchange rate between the dollar and the currency in which a project's cash flows are denominated will reduce the market value of that project's cash flow.

Although the basic techniques of capital budgeting are the same for multinational companies (MNCs) as for purely domestic firms, firms that operate in several countries face risks that are unique to the international arena. Two types of risk are particularly important, exchange rate risk and political risk.

Exchange rate risk reflects the danger that an unexpected change in the exchange rate between the dollar and the currency in which a project's cash flows are denominated will reduce the market value of that project's cash flow. The dollar value of future cash inflows can be dramatically altered if the local currency depreciates against the dollar. In the short term, specific cash flows can be hedged

Matter of fact

Adjusting for Currency Risk

A survey of chief financial officers (CFOs) found that more than 40 percent of the CFOs felt that it was important to adjust an investment project's cash flows or discount rates to account for foreign exchange risk.

by using financial instruments such as currency futures and options. Long-term exchange rate risk can best be minimized by financing the project, in whole or in part, in local currency.

Political risk is much harder to protect against. Firms that make investments abroad may find that the host-country government can limit the firm's ability to return profits back home. Governments can seize the firm's assets or otherwise interfere with a project's operation. The difficulties of managing political risk after the fact make it even more important that managers account for political risks *before* making an investment. They can do so either by adjusting a project's expected cash inflows to account for the probability of political interference or by using *risk-adjusted discount rates* (discussed later in this chapter) in capital budgeting formulas. In general, it is much better to adjust individual project cash flows for political risk subjectively than to use a blanket adjustment for all projects.

In addition to unique risks that MNCs must face, several other special issues are relevant only for international capital budgeting. One of these special issues is *taxes*. Because only after-tax cash flows are relevant for capital budgeting, financial managers must carefully account for taxes paid to foreign governments on profits earned within their borders. They must also assess the impact of these tax payments on the parent company's U.S. tax liability.

Another special issue in international capital budgeting is *transfer pricing*. Much of the international trade involving MNCs is, in reality, simply the shipment of goods and services from one of a parent company's subsidiaries to another subsidiary located abroad. The parent company therefore has great discretion in setting **transfer prices,** the prices that subsidiaries charge each other for the goods and services traded between them. The widespread use of transfer pricing in international trade makes capital budgeting in MNCs very difficult unless the transfer prices that are used accurately reflect actual costs and incremental cash flows.

transfer prices
Prices that subsidiaries charge each other for the goods and services traded between them.

Finally, MNCs often must approach international capital projects from a *strategic point of view,* rather than from a strictly financial perspective. For example, an MNC may feel compelled to invest in a country to ensure continued access, even if the project itself may not have a positive net present value. This motivation was important for Japanese automakers that set up assembly plants in the United States in the early 1980s. For much the same reason, U.S. investment in Europe surged during the years before the market integration of the European Community in 1992. MNCs often invest in production facilities in the home country of major rivals to deny these competitors an uncontested home market. MNCs also may feel compelled to invest in certain industries or countries to achieve a broad corporate objective such as completing a product line or diversifying raw material sources, even when the project's cash flows may not be sufficiently profitable.

→ REVIEW QUESTION

12–4 Briefly explain how the following items affect the capital budgeting decisions of multinational companies: **(a)** exchange rate risk; **(b)** political risk; **(c)** tax law differences; **(d)** transfer pricing; and **(e)** a strategic, rather than a strict, financial viewpoint.

LG 4

12.4 Risk-Adjusted Discount Rates

The approaches for dealing with risk that have been presented so far enable the financial manager to get a "feel" for project risk. Unfortunately, they do not explicitly recognize project risk. We will now illustrate the most popular risk-adjustment technique that employs the net present value (NPV) decision method. The NPV decision rule of accepting only those projects with NPVs > $0 will continue to hold. Close examination of the basic equation for NPV, Equation 10.1, should make it clear that because the initial investment (CF_0) is known with certainty, a project's risk is embodied in the present value of its cash inflows:

$$NPV = \sum_{t=1}^{n} \frac{CF_t}{(1 + r)^t} - CF_0$$

Two opportunities to adjust the present value of cash inflows for risk exist: (1) The cash inflows (CF_t) can be adjusted, or (2) the discount rate (r) can be adjusted. Adjusting the cash inflows is highly subjective, so here we describe the more popular process of adjusting the discount rate. In addition, we consider the portfolio effects of project analysis as well as the practical aspects of the risk-adjusted discount rate.

DETERMINING RISK-ADJUSTED DISCOUNT RATES (RADRS)

A popular approach for risk adjustment involves the use of risk-adjusted discount rates (RADRs). This approach uses Equation 10.1 but employs a risk-adjusted discount rate, as noted in the following expression:[3]

$$NPV = \sum_{t=1}^{n} \frac{CF_t}{(1 + RADR)^t} - CF_0 \tag{12.2}$$

risk-adjusted discount rate (RADR)
The rate of return that must be earned on a given project to compensate the firm's owners adequately—that is, to maintain or improve the firm's share price.

The **risk-adjusted discount rate (RADR)** is the rate of return that must be earned on a given project to compensate the firm's owners adequately—that is, to maintain or improve the firm's share price. The higher the risk of a project, the higher the RADR, and therefore the lower the net present value for a given stream of cash inflows.

Personal Finance Example 12.3 ▶ Talor Namtig is considering investing $1,000 in either of two stocks—A or B. She plans to hold the stock for exactly 5 years and expects both stocks to pay $80 in annual end-of-year cash dividends. At the end of year 5 she estimates that stock A can be sold to net $1,200 and stock B can be sold to net $1,500. Talor has carefully researched the two stocks and feels that although stock A has average risk, stock B is considerably riskier. Her research indicates that she should earn an annual return on an average-risk stock of 11%. Because stock B is considerably riskier, she will require a 14% return from it.

3. The risk-adjusted discount rate approach can be applied in using the internal rate of return as well as the net present value. When the IRR is used, the risk-adjusted discount rate becomes the cutoff rate that must be exceeded by the IRR for the project to be accepted. When NPV is used, the projected cash inflows are merely discounted at the risk-adjusted discount rate.

Talor makes the following calculations to find the risk-adjusted net present values (NPVs) for the two stocks:

$$NPV_A = \frac{\$80}{(1+0.11)^1} + \frac{\$80}{(1+0.11)^2} + \frac{\$80}{(1+0.11)^3} + \frac{\$80}{(1+0.11)^4} + \frac{\$80}{(1+0.11)^5} + \frac{\$1{,}200}{(1+0.11)^5} - \$1{,}000 = \$7.81$$

$$NPV_B = \frac{\$80}{(1+0.14)^1} + \frac{\$80}{(1+0.14)^2} + \frac{\$80}{(1+0.14)^3} + \frac{\$80}{(1+0.14)^4} + \frac{\$80}{(1+0.14)^5} + \frac{\$1{,}500}{(1+0.14)^5} - \$1{,}000 = \$53.70$$

Although Talor's calculations indicate that both stock investments are acceptable (NPVs > \$0), on a risk-adjusted basis, she should invest in Stock B because it has a higher NPV.

Because the logic underlying the use of RADRs is closely linked to the capital asset pricing model (CAPM) developed in Chapter 8, here we review CAPM and discuss its use in finding RADRs.

Review of CAPM

In Chapter 8, we used the *capital asset pricing model (CAPM)* to link the *relevant* risk and return for all assets traded in *efficient markets.* In the development of the CAPM, the *total risk* of an asset was defined as

$$\text{Total risk} = \text{Nondiversifiable risk} + \text{Diversifiable risk} \quad (12.3)$$

For assets traded in an efficient market, the *diversifiable risk,* which results from uncontrollable or random events, can be eliminated through diversification. The relevant risk is therefore the *nondiversifiable risk*—the risk for which owners of these assets are rewarded. Nondiversifiable risk for securities is commonly measured by using *beta,* which is an index of the degree of movement of an asset's return in response to a change in the market return.

Using beta, b_j, to measure the relevant risk of any asset *j*, the CAPM is

$$r_j = R_F + [b_j \times (r_m - R_F)] \quad (12.4)$$

where

r_j = required return on asset *j*
R_F = risk-free rate of return
b_j = beta coefficient for asset *j*
r_m = return on the market portfolio of assets

In Chapter 8, we demonstrated that the required return on any asset could be determined by substituting values of R_F, b_j, and r_m into the CAPM—Equation 12.4. Any security that is expected to earn in excess of its required return would be acceptable, and those that are expected to earn an inferior return would be rejected.

FIGURE 12.2

CAPM and SML
CAPM and SML in capital budgeting decision making

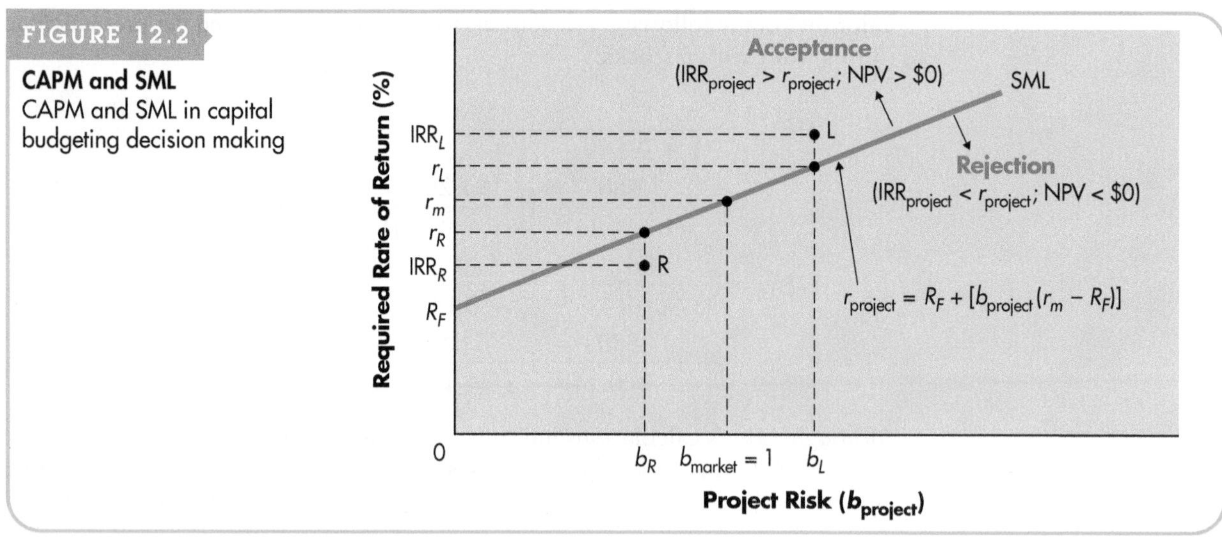

Using CAPM to Find RADRs

If we assume for a moment that real corporate assets such as computers, machine tools, and special-purpose machinery are traded in efficient markets, the CAPM can be redefined as noted in Equation 12.5:

$$r_{\text{project } j} = R_F + [b_{\text{project } j} \times (r_m - R_F)] \quad (12.5)$$

The *security market line* (SML)—the graphical depiction of the CAPM—is shown for Equation 12.5 in Figure 12.2. Any project having an IRR above the SML would be acceptable, because its IRR would exceed the required return, r_{project}; any project with an IRR below r_{project} would be rejected. In terms of NPV, any project falling above the SML would have a positive NPV, and any project falling below the SML would have a negative NPV.[4]

Example 12.4 ▶ Figure 12.2 shows two projects, L and R. Project L has a beta, b_L, and generates an internal rate of return, IRR_L. The required return for a project with risk b_L is r_L. Because project L generates a return greater than that required ($IRR_L > r_L$), project L is acceptable. Project L will have a positive NPV when its cash inflows are discounted at its required return, r_L. Project R, on the other hand, generates an IRR below that required for its risk, b_R ($IRR_R < r_R$). This project will have a negative NPV when its cash inflows are discounted at its required return, r_R. Project R should be rejected.

4. As noted earlier, whenever the IRR is above the cost of capital or required return ($IRR > r$), the NPV is positive, and whenever the IRR is below the cost of capital or required return ($IRR < r$), the NPV is negative. Because by definition the IRR is the discount rate that causes NPV to equal zero and the IRR and NPV always agree on accept–reject decisions, the relationship noted in Figure 12.2 logically follows.

focus on ETHICS

Ethics and the Cost of Capital

in practice At the dawn of the new millennium, the company formerly known as British Petroleum was trying to reinvent itself. BP introduced a new corporate logo, a green, yellow, and white sunburst, which "symbolized energy in all its dynamic forms." In their 2009 sustainability review, BP defined sustainability as "the capacity to endure as a group: by renewing assets; creating and delivering better products and services that meet the evolving needs of society; attracting successive generations of employees; contributing to a sustainable environment; and retaining the trust and support of our customers, shareholders and the communities in which we operate."[a]

However, BP's environmental track record didn't always support the image the company was trying to portray. In 2005, a fire at BP's Texas City Refinery killed fifteen workers and injured many more. The following year, BP shut down their Prudhoe Bay oil field due to corrosion in an oil transit line that resulted in an oil spill. BP was widely criticized for these events, but that did not stop BP from causing the largest oil spill in U.S. history.

The Deepwater Horizon accident and subsequent oil spill had a significant impact on BP's cost of capital. By June 2010, BP's stock price was 50 percent below precrisis levels, and the company's bonds traded at levels comparable to junk-rated companies. Over the course of a single week, when BP's "top kill" attempt to stop the leak proved unsuccessful, the yield on the company's main 5-year dollar bond jumped by 2 percent. The bond rating agencies downgraded BP, although the firm continued to possess one of the highest investment grade credit ratings. However, the rating agencies warned that further downgrades could follow if the crisis, and the expected costs, continued to escalate.

▶ *Is the ultimate goal of the firm, to maximize the wealth of the owners for whom the firm is being operated, ethical?*

▶ *Why might ethical companies benefit from a lower cost of capital than less ethical companies?*

[a]www.bp.com/liveassets/bp_internet/globalbp/STAGING/global_assets/e_s_assets/e_s_assets_2009/downloads_pdfs/bp_sustainability_review_2009.pdf

APPLYING RADRS

Because the CAPM is based on an assumed efficient market, which does *not* always exist for real corporate (nonfinancial) assets such as plant and equipment, managers sometimes argue that the CAPM is not directly applicable in calculating RADRs. Instead, financial managers sometimes assess the *total risk* of a project and use it to determine the risk-adjusted discount rate (RADR), which can be used in Equation 12.2 to find the NPV.

To avoid damaging its market value, the firm must use the correct discount rate to evaluate a project. The nearby *Focus on Ethics* box describes a real example of a company that failed to recognize (or that ignored) certain risks associated with their business operations. As a result, the firm experienced monetary sanctions. If a firm fails to incorporate all relevant risks in its decision-making process, it may discount a risky project's cash inflows at too low a rate and accept the project. The firm's market price may drop later as investors recognize that the firm itself has become more risky. Conversely, if the firm discounts a project's cash inflows at too high a rate, it will reject acceptable projects. Eventually the firm's market price may drop because investors who believe that the firm is being overly conservative will sell their stock, putting downward pressure on the firm's market value.

Unfortunately, there is no formal mechanism for linking *total project risk* to the level of required return. As a result, most firms subjectively determine the RADR by adjusting their existing required return. They adjust it up or down depending on whether the proposed project is more or less risky, respectively, than the average risk of the firm. This CAPM-type of approach provides a "rough estimate" of the project risk and required return because both the project risk measure and the linkage between risk and required return are estimates.

Example 12.5 ▶

Bennett Company wishes to use the risk-adjusted discount rate approach to determine, according to NPV, whether to implement project A or project B. In addition to the data presented in part A of Table 12.1, Bennett's management after much analysis subjectively assigned "risk indexes" of 1.6 to project A and 1.0 to project B. The risk index is merely a numerical scale used to classify project risk: Higher index values are assigned to higher-risk projects, and vice versa. The CAPM-type relationship used by the firm to link risk (measured by the risk index) and the required return (RADR) is shown in the following table. Management developed this relationship after analyzing CAPM and the risk–return relationships of the projects that they considered and implemented during the past few years.

	Risk index	**Required return (RADR)**
	0.0	6% (risk-free rate, R_F)
	0.2	7
	0.4	8
	0.6	9
	0.8	10
Project B →	1.0	11
	1.2	12
	1.4	13
Project A →	1.6	14
	1.8	16
	2.0	18

Project A

Input	Function
–42000	CF_0
14000	CF_1
5	N
14	I
	NPV

Solution
6,063.13

Project B

Input	Function
–45000	CF_0
28000	CF_1
12000	CF_2
10000	CF_3
3	N
11	I
	NPV

Solution
9,798.43

Because project A is riskier than project B, its RADR of 14% is greater than project B's 11%. The net present value of each project, calculated using its RADR, is found as shown on the time lines in Figure 12.3. The results clearly show that project B is preferable, because its risk-adjusted NPV of $9,798 is greater than the $6,063 risk-adjusted NPV for project A. As reflected by the NPVs in part B of Table 12.1, if the discount rates were not adjusted for risk, project A would be preferred to project B.

Calculator Use We can again use the preprogrammed NPV function in a financial calculator to simplify the NPV calculation. The keystrokes for project A—the annuity—typically are as shown at the left. The keystrokes for project B—the mixed stream—are also shown at the left. The calculated NPVs for projects A and B of $6,063 and $9,798, respectively, agree with those shown in Figure 12.3.

Spreadsheet Use Analysis of projects using risk-adjusted discount rates (RADRs) also can be performed as shown on the following Excel spreadsheet.

	A	B	C	D
1	ANALYSIS OF PROJECTS USING RISK-ADJUSTED DISCOUNT RATES			
2	Year	Cash Inflow	Present Value	Formulas for Calculated Values in Column C
3	Project A			
4	1-5	$ 14,000	$48,063	–PV(C7,5,B4,0)
5	Initial Investment		$42,000	
6	Net Present Value		$ 6,063	C4–C5
7	Required Return (RADAR)		14%	
8	Project B			
9	1	$ 28,000	$25,225	–PV(C17,A9,0,B9,0)
10	2	12,000	9,739	–PV(C17,A10,0,B10,0)
11	3	10,000	7,312	–PV(C17,A11,0,B11,0)
12	4	10,000	6,587	–PV(C17,A12,0,B12,0)
13	5	10,000	5,935	–PV(C17,A13,0,B13,0)
14	Present value		$54,798	SUM(C9:C13) or NPV(C17,B9:B13)
15	Initial Investment		$45,000	
16	Net Present Value		$ 9,798	C14–C15
17	Required Return (RADAR)		11%	
18	Choice of project		B	IF(C6>=C16,"A","B")

The minus signs appear before the entries in Cells D4 and D9:D13 to convert the results to positive values.

FIGURE 12.3

Calculation of NPVS for Bennett Company's Capital Expenditure Alternatives Using RADRs

Time lines depicting the cash flows and NPV calculations using RADRs for projects A and B

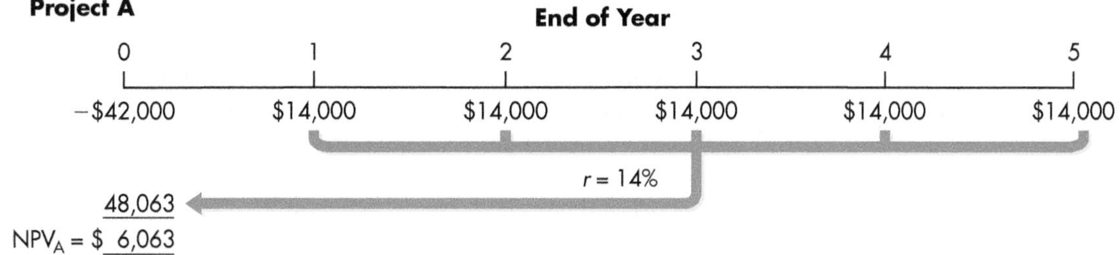

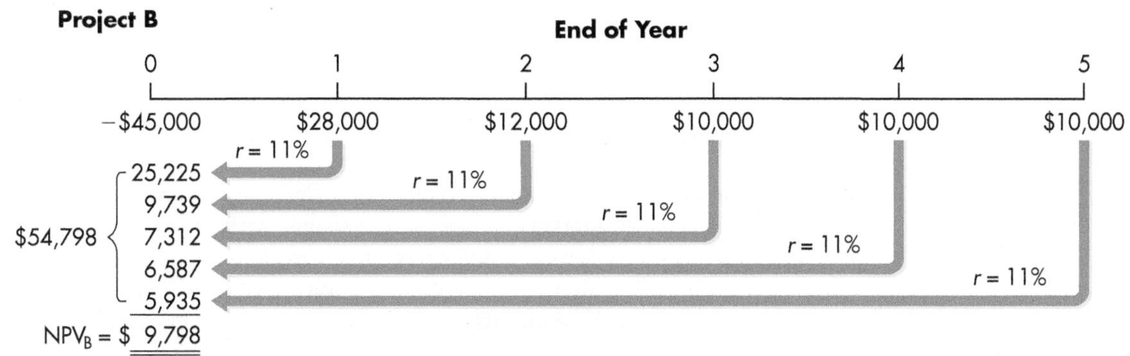

Note: When we use the risk indexes of 1.6 and 1.0 for projects A and B, respectively, along with the table above, a risk-adjusted discount rate (RADR) of 14% results for project A and an RADR of 11% results for project B.

The usefulness of risk-adjusted discount rates should now be clear. The real difficulty lies in estimating project risk and linking it to the required return (RADR).

PORTFOLIO EFFECTS

As noted in Chapter 8, because investors are not rewarded for taking diversifiable risk, they should hold a diversified portfolio of securities. Because a business firm can be viewed as a portfolio of assets, is it similarly important that the firm maintain a diversified portfolio of assets?

It seems logical that by holding a diversified portfolio the firm could reduce the variability of its cash flows. By combining two projects with negatively correlated cash inflows, the firm could reduce the combined cash inflow variability—and therefore the risk.

Are firms rewarded for diversifying risk in this fashion? If they are, the value of the firm could be enhanced through diversification into other lines of business. Surprisingly, the value of the stock of firms whose shares are traded publicly in an efficient marketplace is generally *not* affected by diversification. In other words, diversification is not normally rewarded and therefore is generally not necessary.

Why are firms not rewarded for diversification? Because investors themselves can diversify by holding securities in a variety of firms; they do not need the firm to do it for them. And investors can diversify more readily—they can make transactions more easily and at a lower cost because of the greater availability of information and trading mechanisms.

Of course, if a firm acquires a new line of business and its cash flows tend to respond more to changing economic conditions (that is, greater nondiversifiable risk), greater returns would be expected. If, for the additional risk, the firm earned a return in excess of that required (IRR $> r$), the value of the firm could be enhanced. Also, other benefits, such as increased cash, greater borrowing capacity, guaranteed availability of raw materials, and so forth, could result from and therefore justify diversification, in spite of any immediate impact on cash flow.

Although a strict theoretical view supports the use of a technique that relies on the CAPM framework, the presence of market imperfections causes the market for real corporate assets to be inefficient at least some of the time. The relative inefficiency of this market, coupled with difficulties associated with measurement of nondiversifiable project risk and its relationship to return, tend to favor the use of total risk to evaluate capital budgeting projects. Therefore, the use of *total risk* as an approximation for the relevant risk does have widespread practical appeal.

RADRS IN PRACTICE

In spite of the appeal of total risk, *RADRs are often used in practice.* Their popularity stems from two facts: (1) They are consistent with the general disposition of financial decision makers toward rates of return, and (2) they are easily estimated and applied. The first reason is clearly a matter of personal preference, but the second is based on the computational convenience and well-developed procedures involved in the use of RADRs.

In practice, firms often establish a number of *risk classes,* with an RADR assigned to each. Like the CAPM-type risk–return relationship described earlier,

TABLE 12.3 Bennett Company's Risk Classes and RADRs

Risk class	Description	Risk-adjusted discount rate, RADR
I	*Below-average risk:* Projects with low risk. Typically involve routine replacement without renewal of existing activities.	8%
II	*Average risk:* Projects similar to those currently implemented. Typically involve replacement or renewal of existing activities.	10% [a]
III	*Above-average risk:* Projects with higher than normal, but not excessive, risk. Typically involve expansion of existing or similar activities.	14%
IV	*Highest risk:* Projects with very high risk. Typically involve expansion into new or unfamiliar activities.	20%

[a]This RADR is actually the firm's cost of capital, which is discussed in detail in Chapter 9. It represents the firm's required return on its existing portfolio of projects, which is assumed to be unchanged with acceptance of the "average-risk" project.

management develops the risk classes and RADRs based on both CAPM and the risk–return behaviors of past projects. Each new project is then subjectively placed in the appropriate risk class, and the corresponding RADR is used to evaluate it. This is sometimes done on a division-by-division basis, in which case each division has its own set of risk classes and associated RADRs, similar to those for Bennett Company in Table 12.3. The use of *divisional costs of capital* and associated risk classes enables a large multidivisional firm to incorporate differing levels of divisional risk into the capital budgeting process and still recognize differences in the levels of individual project risk.

Example 12.6 ▸ Assume that the management of Bennett Company decided to use risk classes to analyze projects and so placed each project in one of four risk classes according to its perceived risk. The classes ranged from I for the lowest-risk projects to IV for the highest-risk projects. Associated with each class was an RADR appropriate to the level of risk of projects in the class, as given in Table 12.3. Bennett classified as lower-risk those projects that tend to involve routine replacement or renewal activities; higher-risk projects involve expansion, often into new or unfamiliar activities.

The financial manager of Bennett has assigned project A to class III and project B to class II. The cash flows for project A would be evaluated using a 14% RADR, and project B's would be evaluated using a 10% RADR.[5] The NPV of project A at 14% was calculated in Figure 12.3 to be $6,063, and the NPV for project B at a 10% RADR was shown in Table 12.1 to be $10,924. Clearly, with RADRs based on the use of risk classes, project B is preferred over project A.

5. Note that the 10 percent RADR for project B using the risk classes in Table 12.3 differs from the 11 percent RADR used in the preceding example for project B. This difference is attributable to the less precise nature of the use of risk classes.

As noted earlier, this result is contrary to the preferences shown in Table 12.1, where differing risks of projects A and B were not taken into account.

→ REVIEW QUESTIONS

12–5 Describe the basic procedures involved in using *risk-adjusted discount rates (RADRs)*. How is this approach related to the *capital asset pricing model (CAPM)*?

12–6 Explain why a firm whose stock is actively traded in the securities markets need not concern itself with diversification. In spite of this, how is the risk of capital budgeting projects frequently measured? Why?

12–7 How are *risk classes* often used to apply RADRs?

LG 5 LG 6

12.5 Capital Budgeting Refinements

Refinements must often be made in the analysis of capital budgeting projects to accommodate special circumstances. These adjustments permit the relaxation of certain simplifying assumptions presented earlier. Three areas in which special forms of analysis are frequently needed are (1) comparison of mutually exclusive projects having unequal lives, (2) recognition of real options, and (3) capital rationing caused by a binding budget constraint.

COMPARING PROJECTS WITH UNEQUAL LIVES

The financial manager must often select the best of a group of unequal-lived projects. If the projects are independent, the length of the project lives is not critical. But when unequal-lived projects are mutually exclusive, the impact of differing lives must be considered because the projects do not provide service over comparable time periods. This is especially important when continuing service is needed from the project under consideration. The discussions that follow assume that the unequal-lived, mutually exclusive projects being compared *are ongoing*. If they were not, the project with the highest NPV would be selected.

The Problem

A simple example will demonstrate the basic problem of noncomparability caused by the need to select the best of a group of mutually exclusive projects with differing usable lives.

Example 12.7 ► The AT Company, a regional cable television company, is evaluating two projects, X and Y. The relevant cash flows for each project are given in the following table. The applicable cost of capital for use in evaluating these equally risky projects is 10%.

	Project X	Project Y
Initial investment	**$70,000**	**$85,000**
Year	**Annual cash inflows**	
1	$28,000	$35,000
2	33,000	30,000
3	38,000	25,000
4	—	20,000
5	—	15,000
6	—	10,000

Project X

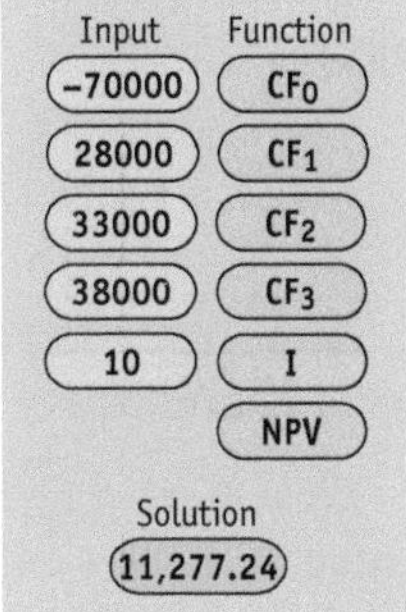

Project Y

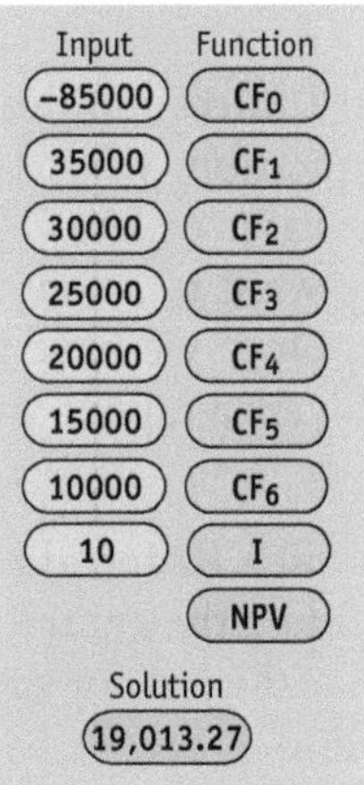

Calculator Use Employing the preprogrammed NPV function in a financial calculator, we use the keystrokes shown at the left for project X and for project Y to find their respective NPVs of $11,277.24 and $19,013.27.

Spreadsheet Use The net present values of two projects with unequal lives also can be compared as shown on the following Excel spreadsheet.

	A	B	C
1	COMPARISON OF NET PRESENT VALUES OF TWO PROJECTS WITH UNEQUAL LIVES		
2		Cost of Capital	10%
3		Year-End Cash Flows	
4	Year	Project X	Project Y
5	0	$ (70,000)	$ (85,000)
6	1	$ 28,000	$ 35,000
7	2	$ 33,000	$ 30,000
8	3	$ 38,000	$ 25,000
9	4		$ 20,000
10	5		$ 15,000
11	6		$ 10,000
12	NPV	$ 11,277.24	$ 19,013.27
13	Choice of project		Project Y

Entry in Cell B12 is =NPV(C2,B6:B11)+B5.
Copy the entry in Cell B12 to Cell C12.
Entry in Cell C13 is =IF(B12>=C12,B4,C4).

Ignoring the differences in project lives, we can see that both projects are acceptable (both NPVs are greater than zero) and that project Y is preferred over project X. If the projects were independent and only one could be accepted, project Y—with the larger NPV—would be preferred. If the projects were mutually exclusive, their differing lives would have to be considered. Project Y provides 3 more years of service than project X.

The analysis in the preceding example is incomplete if the projects are mutually exclusive (which will be our assumption throughout the remaining discussions). To compare these unequal-lived, mutually exclusive projects correctly, we must consider the differing lives in the analysis; an incorrect decision could result from simply using NPV to select the better project. Although a number of approaches are available for dealing with unequal lives, here we present the most efficient technique—the *annualized net present value (ANPV) approach.*

Annualized Net Present Value (ANPV) Approach

annualized net present value (ANPV) approach
An approach to evaluating unequal-lived projects that converts the net present value of unequal-lived, mutually exclusive projects into an equivalent annual amount (in NPV terms).

The **annualized net present value (ANPV) approach**[6] converts the net present value of unequal-lived, mutually exclusive projects into an equivalent annual amount (in NPV terms) that can be used to select the best project.[7] This net present value based approach can be applied to unequal-lived, mutually exclusive projects by using the following steps:

Step 1 Calculate the net present value of each project j, NPV_j, over its life, n_j, using the appropriate cost of capital, r.

Step 2 Convert the NPV_j into an annuity having life n_j. That is, find an annuity that has the same life and the same NPV as the project.

Step 3 Select the project that has the highest ANPV.

Example 12.8 ▶

Project X

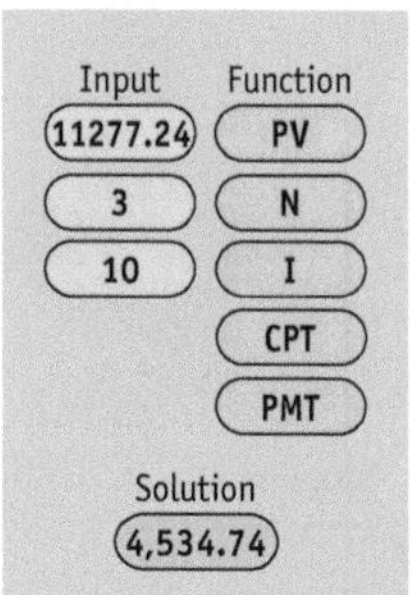

Project Y

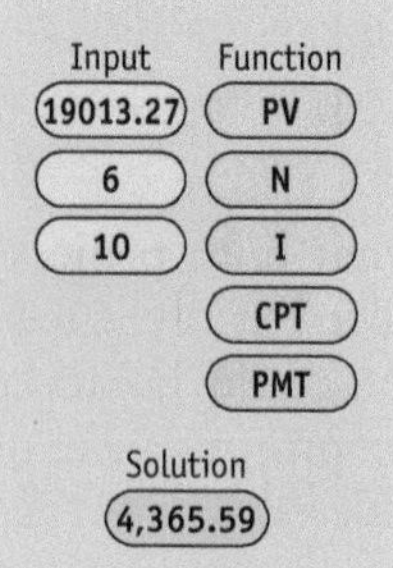

By using the AT Company data presented earlier for projects X and Y, we can apply the three-step ANPV approach as follows:

Step 1 The net present values of projects X and Y discounted at 10%—as calculated in the preceding example for a single purchase of each asset—are

$$NPV_X = \$11{,}277.24$$
$$NPV_Y = \$19{,}013.27$$

Step 2 In this step, we want to convert the NPVs from Step 1 into annuities. For project X, we are trying to find the answer to the question, what 3-year annuity (equal to the life of project X) has a present value of $11,277.24 (the NPV of project X)? Likewise, for project Y we want to know what 6-year annuity has a present value of $19,013.27. Once we have these values, we can determine which project, X or Y, delivers a higher annual cash flow on a present value basis.

Calculator Use The keystrokes required to find the ANPV on a financial calculator are identical to those demonstrated in Chapter 5 for finding the annual payments on an installment loan. These keystrokes are shown at the left for project X and for project Y. The resulting ANPVs for projects X and Y are $4,534.74 and $4,365.59, respectively.

Spreadsheet Use The annualized net present values of two projects with unequal lives also can be compared as shown on the following Excel spreadsheet.

---

6. This approach is also called the "equivalent annual annuity (EAA)" or the "equivalent annual cost." The term *annualized net present value (ANPV)* is used here due to its descriptive clarity.

7. The theory underlying this as well as other approaches for comparing projects with unequal lives assumes that each project can be replaced in the future for the same initial investment and that each will provide the same expected future cash inflows. Although changing technology and inflation will affect the initial investment and expected cash inflows, the lack of specific attention to them does not detract from the usefulness of this technique.

	A	B	C
1	COMPARISON OF ANNUALIZED NET PRESENT VALUES OF TWO PROJECTS WITH UNEQUAL LIVES		
2		Cost of Capital	10%
3		Year-End Cash Flows	
4	Year	Project X	Project Y
5	0	$ (70,000)	$ (85,000)
6	1	$ 28,000	$ 35,000
7	2	$ 33,000	$ 30,000
8	3	$ 38,000	$ 25,000
9	4		$ 20,000
10	5		$ 15,000
11	6		$ 10,000
12	NPV	$ 11,277.24	$ 19,013.27
13	ANPV	$ 4,534.74	$ 4,365.59
14	Choice of project		Project X

Entry in Cell B12 is =NPV(C2,B6:B11)+B5.
Copy the entry in Cell B12 to Cell C12.
Entry in Cell B13 is =B12/PV(C2,3,–1).
Entry in Cell C13 is =C12/PV(C2,6,–1).
Entry in Cell C14 is =IF(B13>=C13,B4,C4).

Step 3 Reviewing the ANPVs calculated in Step 2, we can see that project X would be preferred over project Y. Given that projects X and Y are mutually exclusive, project X would be the recommended project because it provides the higher annualized net present value.

RECOGNIZING REAL OPTIONS

The procedures described in Chapters 10 and 11 and thus far in this chapter suggest that to make capital budgeting decisions, we must (1) estimate relevant cash flows, (2) apply an appropriate decision technique such as NPV or IRR to those cash flows, and (3) recognize and adjust the decision technique for project risk. Although this traditional procedure is believed to yield good decisions, a more *strategic approach* to these decisions has emerged in recent years. This more modern view considers any **real options**—opportunities that are embedded in capital projects ("real," rather than financial, asset investments) that enable managers to alter their cash flows and risk in a way that affects project acceptability (NPV). Because these opportunities are more likely to exist in, and be more important to, large "strategic" capital budgeting projects, they are sometimes called *strategic options.*

real options
Opportunities that are embedded in capital projects that enable managers to alter their cash flows and risk in a way that affects project acceptability (NPV). Also called *strategic options.*

Table 12.4 briefly describes some of the more common types of real options—abandonment, flexibility, growth, and timing. It should be clear from their descriptions that each of these types of options could be embedded in a capital budgeting decision and that explicit recognition of them would probably alter the cash flow and risk of a project and change its NPV.

By explicitly recognizing these options when making capital budgeting decisions, managers can make improved, more strategic decisions that consider in advance the economic impact of certain contingent actions on project cash flow

TABLE 12.4 Major Types of Real Options

Option type	Description
Abandonment option	The option to abandon or terminate a project prior to the end of its planned life. This option allows management to avoid or minimize losses on projects that turn bad. Explicitly recognizing the abandonment option when evaluating a project often increases its NPV.
Flexibility option	The option to incorporate flexibility into the firm's operations, particularly production. It generally includes the opportunity to design the production process to accept multiple inputs, use flexible production technology to create a variety of outputs by reconfiguring the same plant and equipment, and to purchase and retain excess capacity in capital-intensive industries subject to wide swings in output demand and long lead time in building new capacity from scratch. Recognition of this option embedded in a capital expenditure should increase the NPV of the project.
Growth option	The option to develop follow-on projects, expand markets, expand or retool plants, and so on, that would not be possible without implementation of the project that is being evaluated. If a project being considered has the measurable potential to open new doors if successful, then recognition of the cash flows from such opportunities should be included in the initial decision process. Growth opportunities embedded in a project often increase the NPV of the project in which they are embedded.
Timing option	The option to determine when various actions with respect to a given project are taken. This option recognizes the firm's opportunity to delay acceptance of a project for one or more periods, to accelerate or slow the process of implementing a project in response to new information, or to shut down a project temporarily in response to changing product market conditions or competition. As in the case of the other types of options, the explicit recognition of timing opportunities can improve the NPV of a project that fails to recognize this option in an investment decision.

and risk. The explicit recognition of real options embedded in capital budgeting projects will cause the project's *strategic NPV* to differ from its *traditional NPV*, as indicated by Equation 12.7.

$$\text{NPV}_{\text{strategic}} = \text{NPV}_{\text{traditional}} + \text{Value of real options} \qquad (12.7)$$

Application of this relationship is illustrated in the following example.

Example 12.9 ▸ Assume that a strategic analysis of Bennett Company's projects A and B (see cash flows and NPVs in Table 12.1) finds no real options embedded in project A and two real options embedded in project B. The two real options in project B are as follows: (1) The project would have, during the first two years, some downtime that would result in unused production capacity that could be used to perform contract manufacturing for another firm, and (2) the project's computerized control system could, with some modification, control two other machines, thereby reducing labor cost, without affecting operation of the new project.

Bennett's management estimated the NPV of the contract manufacturing over the two years following implementation of project B to be \$1,500 and the NPV of the computer control sharing to be \$2,000. Management felt there was a 60% chance that the contract manufacturing option would be exercised and only a 30% chance that the computer control sharing option would be exercised. The combined value of these two real options would be the sum of their expected values:

$$\text{Value of real options for project B} = (0.60 \times \$1{,}500) + (0.30 \times \$2{,}000)$$
$$= \$900 + \$600 = \$1{,}500$$

Substituting the \$1,500 real options value along with the traditional NPV of \$10,924 for project B (from Table 12.1) into Equation 12.7, we get the strategic NPV for project B:

$$NPV_{strategic} = \$10{,}924 + \$1{,}500 = \underline{\underline{\$12{,}424}}$$

Bennett Company's project B therefore has a strategic NPV of \$12,424, which is above its traditional NPV and now exceeds project A's NPV of \$11,071. Clearly, recognition of project B's real options improved its NPV (from \$10,924 to \$12,424) and causes it to be preferred over project A (NPV of \$12,424 for B $>$ NPV of \$11,071 for A), which has no real options embedded in it.

It is important to realize that the recognition of attractive real options when determining NPV could cause an otherwise unacceptable project ($NPV_{traditional} < \$0$) to become acceptable ($NPV_{strategic} > \$0$). The failure to recognize the value of real options could therefore cause management to reject projects that are acceptable. Although doing so requires more strategic thinking and analysis, it is important for the financial manager to identify and incorporate real options in the NPV process. The procedures for doing this efficiently are emerging, and the use of the strategic NPV that incorporates real options is expected to become more commonplace in the future.

CAPITAL RATIONING

Firms commonly operate under *capital rationing*—they have more acceptable independent projects than they can fund. In theory, capital rationing should not exist. Firms should accept all projects that have positive NPVs (or IRRs $>$ the cost of capital). However, in practice, most firms operate under capital rationing. Generally, firms attempt to isolate and select the best acceptable projects subject to a capital expenditure budget set by management. Research has found that management internally imposes capital expenditure constraints to avoid what it deems to be "excessive" levels of new financing, particularly debt. Although failing to fund all acceptable independent projects is theoretically inconsistent with the goal of maximizing owner wealth, here we will discuss capital rationing procedures because they are widely used in practice.

The objective of *capital rationing* is to select the group of projects that provides the *highest overall net present value* and does not require more dollars than are budgeted. As a prerequisite to capital rationing, the best of any mutually exclusive projects must be chosen and placed in the group of independent projects. Two basic approaches to project selection under capital rationing are discussed here.

internal rate of return approach
An approach to capital rationing that involves graphing project IRRs in descending order against the total dollar investment to determine the group of acceptable projects.

investment opportunities schedule (IOS)
The graph that plots project IRRs in descending order against the total dollar investment.

Internal Rate of Return Approach

The **internal rate of return approach** involves graphing project IRRs in descending order against the total dollar investment. This graph is called the **investment opportunities schedule (IOS).** By drawing the cost-of-capital line and then imposing a budget constraint, the financial manager can determine the group of acceptable projects. The problem with this technique is that it does not guarantee the maximum dollar return to the firm. It merely provides a satisfactory solution to capital-rationing problems.

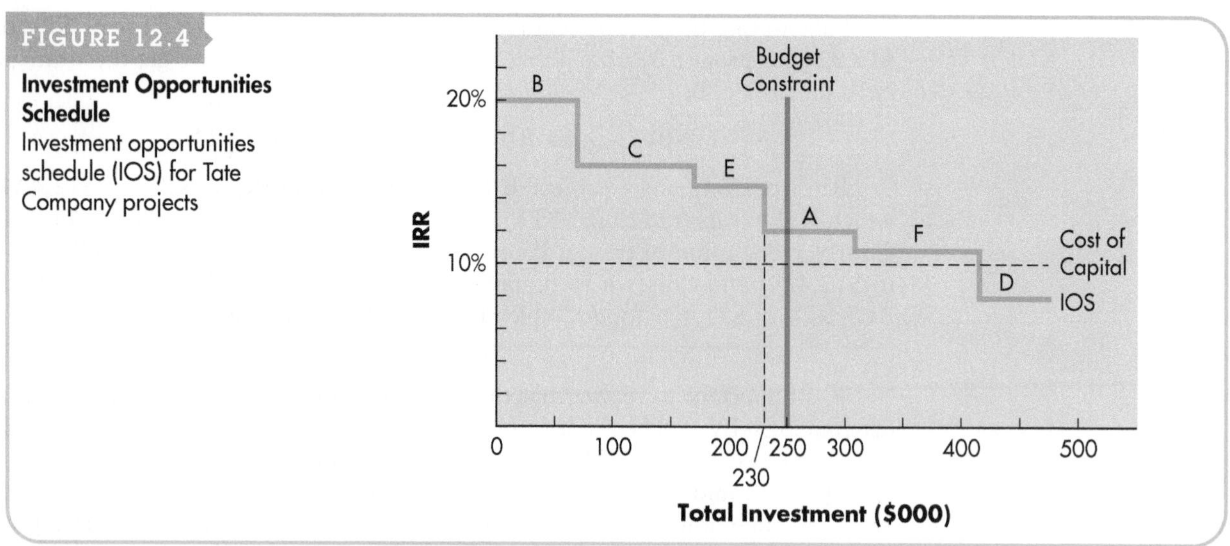

FIGURE 12.4

Investment Opportunities Schedule

Investment opportunities schedule (IOS) for Tate Company projects

Example 12.10 ▶

Tate Company, a fast-growing plastics company, is confronted with six projects competing for its fixed budget of $250,000. The initial investment and IRR for each project are shown in the following table:

Project	Initial investment	IRR
A	$ 80,000	12%
B	70,000	20
C	100,000	16
D	40,000	8
E	60,000	15
F	110,000	11

The firm has a cost of capital of 10%. Figure 12.4 presents the IOS that results from ranking the six projects in descending order on the basis of their IRRs. According to the schedule, only projects B, C, and E should be accepted. Together they will absorb $230,000 of the $250,000 budget. Projects A and F are acceptable but cannot be chosen because of the budget constraint. Project D is not worthy of consideration; its IRR is less than the firm's 10% cost of capital.

The drawback of this approach is that there is no guarantee that the acceptance of projects B, C, and E will maximize *total dollar returns* and therefore owners' wealth.

net present value approach An approach to capital rationing that is based on the use of present values to determine the group of projects that will maximize owners' wealth.

Net Present Value Approach

The **net present value approach** is based on the use of present values to determine the group of projects that will maximize owners' wealth. It is implemented by ranking projects on the basis of IRRs and then evaluating the present value of the benefits from each potential project to determine *the combination of projects*

TABLE 12.5 Rankings for Tate Company Projects

Project	Initial investment	IRR	Present value of inflows at 10%	
B	$ 70,000	20%	$112,000	
C	100,000	16	145,000	
E	60,000	15	79,000	
A	80,000	12	100,000	
F	110,000	11	126,500	Cutoff point
D	40,000	8	36,000	(IRR < 10%)

with the highest overall present value. This is the same as maximizing net present value because the entire budget is viewed as the total initial investment. Any portion of the firm's budget that is not used does not increase the firm's value. At best, the unused money can be invested in marketable securities or returned to the owners in the form of cash dividends. In either case, the wealth of the owners is not likely to be enhanced.

Example 12.11 ▶ The projects described in the preceding example are ranked in Table 12.5 on the basis of IRRs. The present value of the cash inflows associated with the projects is also included in the table. Projects B, C, and E, which together require $230,000, yield a present value of $336,000. However, if projects B, C, and A were implemented, the total budget of $250,000 would be used, and the present value of the cash inflows would be $357,000. This is greater than the return expected from selecting the projects on the basis of the highest IRRs. Implementing B, C, and A is preferable because they maximize the present value for the given budget. *The firm's objective is to use its budget to generate the highest present value of inflows.* Assuming that any unused portion of the budget does not gain or lose money, the total NPV for projects B, C, and E would be $106,000 ($336,000 − $230,000), whereas the total NPV for projects B, C, and A would be $107,000 ($357,000 − $250,000). Selection of projects B, C, and A will therefore maximize NPV.

→ REVIEW QUESTIONS

12–8 Explain why a mere comparison of the NPVs of unequal-lived, ongoing, mutually exclusive projects is inappropriate. Describe the *annualized net present value (ANPV) approach* for comparing unequal-lived, mutually exclusive projects.

12–9 What are *real options?* What are some major types of real options?

12–10 What is the difference between the *strategic NPV* and the *traditional NPV?* Do they always result in the same accept–reject decisions?

12–11 What is *capital rationing?* In theory, should capital rationing exist? Why does it frequently occur in practice?

12–12 Compare and contrast the *internal rate of return approach* and the *net present value approach* to capital rationing. Which is better? Why?

Summary

FOCUS ON VALUE

Not all capital budgeting projects have the same level of risk as the firm's existing portfolio of projects. The financial manager must adjust projects for differences in risk when evaluating their acceptability. Without such an adjustment, management could mistakenly accept projects that destroy shareholder value or could reject projects that create shareholder value. To ensure that neither of these outcomes occurs, the financial manager must make sure that only those projects that create shareholder value are recommended.

Risk-adjusted discount rates (RADRs) provide a mechanism for adjusting the discount rate so that it is consistent with the risk–return preferences of market participants. Procedures for comparing projects with unequal lives, for explicitly recognizing real options embedded in capital projects, and for selecting projects under capital rationing enable the financial manager to refine the capital budgeting process further. These procedures, along with risk-adjustment techniques, should enable the financial manager to make capital budgeting decisions that are consistent with the firm's goal of **maximizing stock price.**

REVIEW OF LEARNING GOALS

LG 1 **Understand the importance of recognizing risk in the analysis of capital budgeting projects.** The cash flows associated with capital budgeting projects typically have different levels of risk, and the acceptance of a project generally affects the firm's overall risk. Thus it is important to incorporate risk considerations in capital budgeting. Various behavioral approaches can be used to get a "feel" for the level of project risk. Other approaches explicitly recognize project risk in the analysis of capital budgeting projects.

LG 2 **Discuss risk and cash inflows, scenario analysis, and simulation as behavioral approaches for dealing with risk.** Risk in capital budgeting is the degree of variability of cash flows, which for conventional capital budgeting projects stems almost entirely from net *cash flows*. Finding the breakeven cash inflow and estimating the probability that it will be realized make up one behavioral approach for assessing capital budgeting risk. Scenario analysis is another behavioral approach for capturing the variability of cash inflows and NPVs. Simulation is a statistically based approach that results in a probability distribution of project returns.

LG 3 **Review the unique risks that multinational companies face.** Although the basic capital budgeting techniques are the same for multinational and purely domestic companies, firms that operate in several countries must also deal with exchange rate and political risks, tax law differences, transfer pricing, and strategic issues.

LG 4 **Describe the determination and use of risk-adjusted discount rates (RADRs), portfolio effects, and the practical aspects of RADRs.** The risk of a project whose initial investment is known with certainty is embodied in the present value of its cash inflows, using NPV. Two opportunities to adjust the present value of cash inflows for risk exist—adjust the cash inflows or adjust the discount rate.

Because adjusting the cash inflows is highly subjective, adjusting discount rates is more popular. RADRs use a market-based adjustment of the discount rate to calculate NPV. The RADR is closely linked to CAPM, but because real corporate assets are generally not traded in an efficient market the CAPM cannot be applied directly to capital budgeting. Instead, firms develop some CAPM-type relationship to link a project's risk to its required return, which is used as the discount rate. Often, for convenience, firms will rely on total risk as an approximation for relevant risk when estimating required project returns. RADRs are commonly used in practice because decision makers find rates of return easy to estimate and apply.

LG 5 **Select the best of a group of unequal-lived, mutually exclusive projects using annualized net present values (ANPVs).** The ANPV approach is the most efficient method of comparing ongoing, mutually exclusive projects that have unequal usable lives. It converts the NPV of each unequal-lived project into an equivalent annual amount—its ANPV. The ANPV can be calculated using equations, a financial calculator, or a spreadsheet. The project with the highest ANPV is best.

LG 6 **Explain the role of real options and the objective and procedures for selecting projects under capital rationing.** Real options are opportunities that are embedded in capital projects and that allow managers to alter their cash flow and risk in a way that affects project acceptability (NPV). By explicitly recognizing real options, the financial manager can find a project's strategic NPV. Some of the more common types of real options are abandonment, flexibility, growth, and timing options. The strategic NPV improves the quality of the capital budgeting decision.

Capital rationing exists when firms have more acceptable independent projects than they can fund. Capital rationing commonly occurs in practice. Its objective is to select from all acceptable projects the group that provides the highest overall net present value and does not require more dollars than are budgeted. The two basic approaches for choosing projects under capital rationing are the internal rate of return approach and the net present value approach. The NPV approach better achieves the objective of using the budget to generate the highest present value of inflows.

Opener-in-Review

The chapter opener and the *Focus on Ethics* box on page 475 described some of the consequences of the accident at BP's Deepwater Horizon oil rig. The company put up $20 billion to help pay for damages related to the oil spill, yet BP's market value declined by more than $90 billion. That means that the market assessed BP an additional penalty of roughly $70 billion, above and beyond the direct costs associated with the spill. Describe the effects that an increase in BP's cost of capital could have on the market value of BP. Oil spills have happened before, so it is plausible that engineers and analysts at BP could have imagined a worst-case scenario in which a major spill occurred at one of the firm's offshore rigs. How might a thorough scenario analysis have influenced BP's offshore drilling activities?

Self-Test Problems (Solutions in Appendix)

LG 4 **ST12–1** **Risk-adjusted discount rates** CBA Company is considering two mutually exclusive projects, A and B. The following table shows the CAPM-type relationship between a risk index and the required return (RADR) applicable to CBA Company.

Risk index	Required return (RADR)
0.0	7.0% (risk-free rate, R_F)
0.2	8.0
0.4	9.0
0.6	10.0
0.8	11.0
1.0	12.0
1.2	13.0
1.4	14.0
1.6	15.0
1.8	16.0
2.0	17.0

Project data are shown as follows:

	Project A	Project B
Initial investment (CF_0)	$15,000	$20,000
Project life	3 years	3 years
Annual cash inflow (CF)	$7,000	$10,000
Risk index	0.4	1.8

a. Ignoring any differences in risk and assuming that the firm's cost of capital is 10%, calculate the *net present value (NPV)* of each project.
b. Use NPV to evaluate the projects, using *risk-adjusted discount rates (RADRs)* to account for risk.
c. Compare, contrast, and explain your findings in parts **a** and **b.**

Warm-Up Exercises All problems are available in myfinancelab.

LG 2 **E12–1** Birkenstock is considering an investment in a nylon-knitting machine. The machine requires an initial investment of $25,000, has a 5-year life, and has no residual value at the end of the 5 years. The company's cost of capital is 12%. Known with less certainty are the actual after-tax cash inflows for each of the 5 years. The company has estimated expected cash inflows for three scenarios: pessimistic, most likely, and optimistic. These expected cash inflows are listed in the following table. Calculate the range for the NPV given each scenario.

Year	Expected cash inflows		
	Pessimistic	Most likely	Optimistic
1	$5,500	$ 8,000	$10,500
2	6,000	9,000	12,000
3	7,500	10,500	14,500
4	6,500	9,500	11,500
5	4,500	6,500	7,500

LG 2 **E12–2** You wish to evaluate a project requiring an initial investment of $45,000 and having a useful life of 5 years. What minimum amount of annual cash inflow do you need if your firm has an 8% cost of capital? If the project is forecast to earn $12,500 per year over the 5 years, what is its IRR? Is the project acceptable?

LG 4 **E12–3** Like most firms in its industry, Yeastime Bakeries uses a subjective risk assessment tool of its own design. The tool is a simple index by which projects are ranked by level of perceived risk on a scale of 0–10. The scale is recreated in the following table.

Risk index	Required return
0	4.0% (current risk-free rate)
1	4.5
2	5.0
3	5.5
4	6.0
5	6.5 (current IRR)
6	7.0
7	7.5
8	8.0
9	8.5
10	9.0

The firm is analyzing two projects based on their RADRs. Project Sourdough requires an initial investment of $12,500 and is assigned a risk index of 6. Project Greek Salad requires an initial investment of $7,500 and is assigned a risk index of 8. The two projects have 7-year lives. Sourdough is projected to generate cash inflows of $5,500 per year. Greek Salad is projected to generate cash inflows of $4,000 per year. Use each project's RADR to select the better project.

LG 5 **E12–4** Outcast, Inc., has hired you to advise the firm on a capital budgeting issue involving two unequal-lived, mutually exclusive projects, M and N. The cash flows for each project are presented in the following table. Calculate the NPV and the *annualized net present value (ANPV)* for each project using the firm's cost of capital of 8%. Which project would you recommend?

	Project M	Project N
Initial investment	**$35,000**	**$55,000**
Year	**Cash inflows**	
1	$12,000	$18,000
2	25,000	15,000
3	30,000	25,000
4	—	10,000
5	—	8,000
6	—	5,000
7	—	5,000

LG 6 **E12–5** Longchamps Electric is faced with a capital budget of $150,000 for the coming year. It is considering six investment projects and has a cost of capital of 7%. The six projects are listed in the following table, along with their initial investments and their IRRs. Using the data given, prepare an *investment opportunities schedule (IOS)*. Which projects does the IOS suggest should be funded? Does this group of projects maximize NPV? Explain.

Project	Initial investment	IRR
1	$75,000	8%
2	40,000	10
3	35,000	7
4	50,000	11
5	45,000	9
6	20,000	6

Problems

All problems are available in myfinancelab.

LG 1 **P12–1** **Recognizing risk** Caradine Corp., a media services firm with net earnings of $3,200,000 in the last year, is considering the following projects.

Project	Initial investment	Details
A	$ 35,000	Replace existing office furnishings.
B	500,000	Purchase digital film-editing equipment for use with several existing accounts.
C	450,000	Develop proposal to bid for a $2,000,000 per year 10-year contract with the U.S. Navy, not now an account.
D	685,000	Purchase the exclusive rights to market a quality educational television program in syndication to local markets in the European Union, a part of the firm's existing business activities.

The media services business is cyclical and highly competitive. The board of directors has asked you, as chief financial officer, to do the following:

a. Evaluate the risk of each proposed project and rank it "low," "medium," or "high."

b. Comment on why you chose each ranking.

LG 2 **P12–2** **Breakeven cash inflows** Etsitty Arts, Inc., a leading producer of fine cast silver jewelry, is considering the purchase of new casting equipment that will allow it to expand the product line into award plaques. The proposed initial investment is \$35,000. The company expects that the equipment will produce steady income throughout its 12-year life.

a. If Etsitty requires a 14% return on its investment, what minimum yearly cash inflow will be necessary for the company to go forward with this project?

b. How would the minimum yearly cash inflow change if the company required a 10% return on its investment?

LG 2 **P12–3** **Breakeven cash inflows and risk** Pueblo Enterprises is considering investing in either of two mutually exclusive projects, X and Y. Project X requires an initial investment of \$30,000; project Y requires \$40,000. Each project's cash inflows are 5-year annuities: Project X's inflows are \$10,000 per year; project Y's are \$15,000. The firm has unlimited funds and, in the absence of risk differences, accepts the project with the highest NPV. The cost of capital is 15%.

a. Find the NPV for each project. Are the projects acceptable?

b. Find the *breakeven cash inflow* for each project.

c. The firm has estimated the probabilities of achieving various ranges of cash inflows for the two projects, as shown in the following table. What is the probability that each project will achieve the breakeven cash inflow found in part **b?**

	Probability of achieving cash inflow in given range	
Range of cash inflow	**Project X**	**Project Y**
\$0 to \$5,000	0%	5%
\$5,000 to \$7,500	10	10
\$7,500 to \$10,000	60	15
\$10,000 to \$12,500	25	25
\$12,500 to \$15,000	5	20
\$15,000 to \$20,000	0	15
Above \$20,000	0	10

d. Which project is more risky? Which project has the potentially higher NPV? Discuss the risk–return tradeoffs of the two projects.

e. If the firm wished to minimize losses (that is, NPV < \$0), which project would you recommend? Which would you recommend if the goal was achieving a higher NPV?

LG 2 **P12–4** **Basic scenario analysis** Murdock Paints is in the process of evaluating two mutually exclusive additions to its processing capacity. The firm's financial analysts have developed pessimistic, most likely, and optimistic estimates of the annual cash inflows associated with each project. These estimates are shown in the following table.

	Project A	Project B
Initial investment (CF_0)	**\$8,000**	**\$8,000**
Outcome	**Annual cash inflows (CF)**	
Pessimistic	\$ 200	\$ 900
Most likely	1,000	1,000
Optimistic	1,800	1,100

a. Determine the *range* of annual cash inflows for each of the two projects.
b. Assume that the firm's cost of capital is 10% and that both projects have 20-year lives. Construct a table similar to this for the NPVs for each project. Include the *range* of NPVs for each project.
c. Do parts **a** and **b** provide consistent views of the two projects? Explain.
d. Which project do you recommend? Why?

LG 2 P12-5 **Scenario analysis** James Secretarial Services is considering the purchase of one of two new personal computers, P and Q. The company expects both to provide benefits over a 10-year period, and each has a required investment of \$3,000. The firm uses a 10% cost of capital. Management has constructed the following table of estimates of annual cash inflows for pessimistic, most likely, and optimistic results.

	Computer P	Computer Q
Initial investment (CF_0)	**\$3,000**	**\$3,000**
Outcome	**Annual cash inflows (CF)**	
Pessimistic	\$ 500	\$ 400
Most likely	750	750
Optimistic	1,000	1,200

a. Determine the *range* of annual cash inflows for each of the two computers.
b. Construct a table similar to this for the NPVs associated with each outcome for both computers.
c. Find the *range* of NPVs, and subjectively compare the risks associated with purchasing these computers.

Personal Finance Problem

LG 2 P12-6 **Impact of inflation on investments** You are interested in an investment project that costs \$7,500 initially. The investment has a 5-year horizon and promises future end-of-year cash inflows of \$2,000, \$2,000, \$2,000, \$1,500, and \$1,500, respectively. Your current opportunity cost is 6.5% per year. However, the Fed has stated that inflation may rise by 1% or may fall by the same amount over the next 5 years.

Assume a direct positive impact of inflation on the prevailing rates (Fisher effect) and answer the following questions.

a. What is the *net present value (NPV)* of the investment under the current required rate of return?

b. What is the *net present value (NPV)* of the investment under a period of rising inflation?

c. What is the *net present value (NPV)* of the investment under a period of falling inflation?

d. From your answers in **a, b,** and **c,** what relationship do you see emerge between changes in inflation and asset valuation?

LG 2 **P12-7 Simulation** Ogden Corporation has compiled the following information on a capital expenditure proposal:

(1) The projected cash *inflows* are normally distributed with a mean of $36,000 and a standard deviation of $9,000.

(2) The projected cash *outflows* are normally distributed with a mean of $30,000 and a standard deviation of $6,000.

(3) The firm has an 11% cost of capital.

(4) The probability distributions of cash inflows and cash outflows are not expected to change over the project's 10-year life.

a. Describe how the foregoing data can be used to develop a simulation model for finding the net present value of the project.

b. Discuss the advantages of using a simulation to evaluate the proposed project.

LG 4 **P12-8 Risk-adjusted discount rates—Basic** Country Wallpapers is considering investing in one of three mutually exclusive projects, E, F, and G. The firm's cost of capital, r, is 15%, and the risk-free rate, R_F, is 10%. The firm has gathered the basic cash flow and risk index data for each project, as shown in the following table.

	Project (j)		
	E	**F**	**G**
Initial investment (CF_0)	**$15,000**	**$11,000**	**$19,000**
Year (t)	**Cash inflows (CF_t)**		
1	$6,000	$6,000	$ 4,000
2	6,000	4,000	6,000
3	6,000	5,000	8,000
4	6,000	2,000	12,000
Risk index (RI_j)	1.80	1.00	0.60

a. Find the *net present value (NPV)* of each project using the firm's cost of capital. Which project is preferred in this situation?

b. The firm uses the following equation to determine the risk-adjusted discount rate, $RADR_j$, for each project j:

$$RADR_j = R_F + [RI_j \times (r - R_F)]$$

where

$$R_F = \text{risk-free rate of return}$$
$$RI_j = \text{risk index for project } j$$
$$r = \text{cost of capital}$$

Substitute each project's risk index into this equation to determine its RADR.

c. Use the RADR for each project to determine its *risk-adjusted NPV.* Which project is preferable in this situation?

d. Compare and discuss your findings in parts **a** and **c.** Which project do you recommend that the firm accept?

LG 4 **P12–9** **Risk-adjusted discount rates—Tabular** After a careful evaluation of investment alternatives and opportunities, Masters School Supplies has developed a CAPM-type relationship linking a risk index to the required return (RADR), as shown in the following table.

Risk index	Required return (RADR)
0.0	7.0% (risk-free rate, R_F)
0.2	8.0
0.4	9.0
0.6	10.0
0.8	11.0
1.0	12.0
1.2	13.0
1.4	14.0
1.6	15.0
1.8	16.0
2.0	17.0

The firm is considering two mutually exclusive projects, A and B. Following are the data the firm has been able to gather about the projects.

	Project A	Project B
Initial investment (CF_0)	$20,000	$30,000
Project life	5 years	5 years
Annual cash inflow (CF)	$7,000	$10,000
Risk index	0.2	1.4

All the firm's cash inflows have already been adjusted for taxes.

a. Evaluate the projects using *risk-adjusted discount rates.*

b. Discuss your findings in part **a,** and recommend the preferred project.

Personal Finance Problem

LG 4 **P12–10** **Mutually exclusive investments and risk** Lara Fredericks is interested in two mutually exclusive investments. Both investments cover the same time horizon of 6 years. The cost of the first investment is $10,000, and Lara expects equal and consecutive year-end payments of $3,000. The second investment promises equal and consecutive payments of $3,800 with an initial outlay of $12,000 required. The current required return on the first investment is 8.5%, and the second carries a required return of 10.5%.

a. What is the *net present value* of the first investment?
b. What is the *net present value* of the second investment?
c. Being mutually exclusive, which investment should Lara choose? Explain.
d. Which investment was relatively more risky? Explain.

LG 4 **P12–11** **Risk-adjusted rates of return using CAPM** Centennial Catering, Inc., is considering two mutually exclusive investments. The company wishes to use a CAPM-type risk-adjusted discount rate (RADR) in its analysis. Centennial's managers believe that the appropriate market rate of return is 12%, and they observe that the current risk-free rate of return is 7%. Cash flows associated with the two projects are shown in the following table.

	Project X	Project Y
Initial investment (CF_0)	**$70,000**	**$78,000**
Year (t)	**Cash inflows (CF_t)**	
1	$30,000	$22,000
2	30,000	32,000
3	30,000	38,000
4	30,000	46,000

a. Use a *risk-adjusted discount rate* approach to calculate the net present value of each project, given that project X has an RADR factor of 1.20 and project Y has an RADR factor of 1.40. The RADR factors are similar to project betas. (Use Equation 12.5 to calculate the required project return for each.)
b. Discuss your findings in part **a,** and recommend the preferred project.

LG 4 **P12–12** **Risk classes and RADR** Moses Manufacturing is attempting to select the best of three mutually exclusive projects, X, Y, and Z. Although all the projects have 5-year lives, they possess differing degrees of risk. Project X is in class V, the highest-risk class; project Y is in class II, the below-average-risk class; and project Z is in class III, the average-risk class. The basic cash flow data for each project and the risk classes and risk-adjusted discount rates (RADRs) used by the firm are shown in the following tables.

	Project X	Project Y	Project Z
Initial investment (CF_0)	**$180,000**	**$235,000**	**$310,000**
Year (t)		**Cash inflows (CF_t)**	
1	$80,000	$50,000	$90,000
2	70,000	60,000	90,000
3	60,000	70,000	90,000
4	60,000	80,000	90,000
5	60,000	90,000	90,000

Risk Classes and RADRs		
Risk class	**Description**	**Risk-adjusted discount rate (RADR)**
I	Lowest risk	10%
II	Below-average risk	13
III	Average risk	15
IV	Above-average risk	19
V	Highest risk	22

a. Find the *risk-adjusted NPV* for each project.
b. Which project, if any, would you recommend that the firm undertake?

LG 5 **P12–13 Unequal lives—ANPV approach** Evans Industries wishes to select the best of three possible machines, each of which is expected to satisfy the firm's ongoing need for additional aluminum-extrusion capacity. The three machines—A, B, and C—are equally risky. The firm plans to use a 12% cost of capital to evaluate each of them. The initial investment and annual cash inflows over the life of each machine are shown in the following table.

	Machine A	**Machine B**	**Machine C**
Initial investment (CF_0)	**$92,000**	**$65,000**	**$100,500**
Year (t)		**Cash inflows (CF_t)**	
1	$12,000	$10,000	$30,000
2	12,000	20,000	30,000
3	12,000	30,000	30,000
4	12,000	40,000	30,000
5	12,000	—	30,000
6	12,000	—	—

a. Calculate the *NPV* for each machine over its life. Rank the machines in descending order on the basis of NPV.
b. Use the *annualized net present value (ANPV)* approach to evaluate and rank the machines in descending order on the basis of ANPV.
c. Compare and contrast your findings in parts **a** and **b.** Which machine would you recommend that the firm acquire? Why?

LG 5 **P12–14 Unequal lives—ANPV approach** Portland Products is considering the purchase of one of three mutually exclusive projects for increasing production efficiency. The firm plans to use a 14% cost of capital to evaluate these equal-risk projects. The initial investment and annual cash inflows over the life of each project are shown in the following table.

	Project X	Project Y	Project Z
Initial investment (CF_0)	**$78,000**	**$52,000**	**$66,000**
Year (t)		**Cash inflows (CF_t)**	
1	$17,000	$28,000	$15,000
2	25,000	38,000	15,000
3	33,000	—	15,000
4	41,000	—	15,000
5	—	—	15,000
6	—	—	15,000
7	—	—	15,000
8	—	—	15,000

a. Calculate the *NPV* for each project over its life. Rank the projects in descending order on the basis of NPV.
b. Use the *annualized net present value (ANPV)* approach to evaluate and rank the projects in descending order on the basis of ANPV.
c. Compare and contrast your findings in parts **a** and **b.** Which project would you recommend that the firm purchase? Why?

LG 5 **P12–15 Unequal lives—ANPV approach** JBL Co. has designed a new conveyor system. Management must choose among three alternative courses of action: (1) The firm can sell the design outright to another corporation with payment over 2 years. (2) It can license the design to another manufacturer for a period of 5 years, its likely product life. (3) It can manufacture and market the system itself; this alternative will result in 6 years of cash inflows. The company has a cost of capital of 12%. Cash flows associated with each alternative are as shown in the following table.

Alternative	Sell	License	Manufacture
Initial investment (CF_0)	**$200,000**	**$200,000**	**$450,000**
Year (t)		**Cash inflows (CF_t)**	
1	$200,000	$250,000	$200,000
2	250,000	100,000	250,000
3	—	80,000	200,000
4	—	60,000	200,000
5	—	40,000	200,000
6	—	—	200,000

a. Calculate the *net present value* of each alternative and rank the alternatives on the basis of NPV.
b. Calculate the *annualized net present value (ANPV)* of each alternative and rank them accordingly.
c. Why is ANPV preferred over NPV when ranking projects with unequal lives?

Personal Finance Problem

LG 5 **P12–16 NPV and ANPV decisions** Richard and Linda Butler decide that it is time to purchase a high-definition (HD) television because the technology has improved and prices have fallen over the past 3 years. From their research, they narrow their choices to two sets, the Samsung 42-inch LCD with 1080p capability and the Sony 42-inch LCD with 1080p features. The price of the Samsung is \$2,350 and the Sony will cost \$2,700. They expect to keep the Samsung for 3 years; if they buy the more expensive Sony unit, they will keep the Sony for 4 years. They expect to be able to sell the Samsung for \$400 by the end of 3 years; they expect they could sell the Sony for \$350 at the end of year 4. Richard and Linda estimate the end-of-year entertainment benefits (that is, not going to movies or events and watching at home) from the Samsung to be \$900 and for the Sony to be \$1,000. Both sets can be viewed as quality units and are equally risky purchases. They estimate their opportunity cost to be 9%.

The Butlers wish to choose the better alternative from a purely financial perspective. To perform this analysis they wish to do the following:

a. Determine the *NPV* of the Samsung HD LCD.
b. Determine the *ANPV* of the Samsung HD LCD.
c. Determine the *NPV* of the Sony HD LCD.
d. Determine the *ANPV* of the Sony HD LCD.
e. Which set should the Butlers purchase and why?

LG 6 **P12–17 Real options and the strategic NPV** Jenny Rene, the CFO of Asor Products, Inc., has just completed an evaluation of a proposed capital expenditure for equipment that would expand the firm's manufacturing capacity. Using the traditional NPV methodology, she found the project unacceptable because

$$\text{NPV}_{\text{traditional}} = -\$1,700 < \$0$$

Before recommending rejection of the proposed project, she has decided to assess whether there might be real options embedded in the firm's cash flows. Her evaluation uncovered three options:

Option 1: Abandonment—The project could be abandoned at the end of 3 years, resulting in an addition to NPV of \$1,200.

Option 2: Growth—If the projected outcomes occurred, an opportunity to expand the firm's product offerings further would become available at the end of 4 years. Exercise of this option is estimated to add \$3,000 to the project's NPV.

Option 3: Timing—Certain phases of the proposed project could be delayed if market and competitive conditions caused the firm's forecast revenues to develop more slowly than planned. Such a delay in implementation at that point has an NPV of \$10,000.

Jenny estimated that there was a 25% chance that the abandonment option would need to be exercised, a 30% chance that the growth option would be exercised, and only a 10% chance that the implementation of certain phases of the project would affect timing.

a. Use the information provided to calculate the *strategic NPV*, $\text{NPV}_{\text{strategic}}$, for Asor Products' proposed equipment expenditure.
b. Judging on the basis of your findings in part **a,** what action should Jenny recommend to management with regard to the proposed equipment expenditure?
c. In general, how does this problem demonstrate the importance of considering real options when making capital budgeting decisions?

LG 6 **P12–18 Capital rationing—IRR and NPV approaches** Valley Corporation is attempting to select the best of a group of independent projects competing for the firm's fixed capital budget of $4.5 million. The firm recognizes that any unused portion of this budget will earn less than its 15% cost of capital, thereby resulting in a present value of inflows that is less than the initial investment. The firm has summarized, in the following table, the key data to be used in selecting the best group of projects.

Project	Initial investment	IRR	Present value of inflows at 15%
A	$5,000,000	17%	$5,400,000
B	800,000	18	1,100,000
C	2,000,000	19	2,300,000
D	1,500,000	16	1,600,000
E	800,000	22	900,000
F	2,500,000	23	3,000,000
G	1,200,000	20	1,300,000

a. Use the *internal rate of return (IRR) approach* to select the best group of projects.
b. Use the *net present value (NPV) approach* to select the best group of projects.
c. Compare, contrast, and discuss your findings in parts **a** and **b.**
d. Which projects should the firm implement? Why?

LG 6 **P12–19 Capital rationing—NPV approach** A firm with a 13% cost of capital must select the optimal group of projects from those shown in the following table, given its capital budget of $1 million.

Project	Initial investment	NPV at 13% cost of capital
A	$300,000	$ 84,000
B	200,000	10,000
C	100,000	25,000
D	900,000	90,000
E	500,000	70,000
F	100,000	50,000
G	800,000	160,000

a. Calculate the *present value of cash inflows* associated with each project.
b. Select the optimal group of projects, keeping in mind that unused funds are costly.

LG 4 **P12–20 ETHICS PROBLEM** The Environmental Protection Agency sometimes imposes penalties on firms that pollute the environment (see the *Focus on Ethics* box on page 475). But did you know that there is a legal market for pollution? A mechanism that has been developed to limit excessive air pollution is to use carbon credits. Carbon credits are a tradable permit scheme that allows businesses that cannot meet their greenhouse-gas-emissions limits to purchase carbon credits from businesses that are below their quota. By allowing credits to be bought and sold, a business for which reducing its emissions would be expensive or prohibitive can pay another business to make the reduction for it. Do you agree with this arrangement? How would you feel as an investor in a company that utilizes carbon credits to legally exceed its pollution limits?

Spreadsheet Exercise

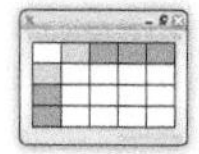

Isis Corporation has two projects that it would like to undertake. However, due to capital restraints, the two projects—Alpha and Beta—must be treated as mutually exclusive. Both projects are equally risky, and the firm plans to use a 10% cost of capital to evaluate each. Project Alpha has an estimated life of 12 years, and project Beta has an estimated life of 9 years. The cash flow data have been prepared as shown in the following table.

	Cash flows	
	Project alpha	**Project beta**
CF_0	−\$5,500,000	−\$6,500,000
CF_1	300,000	400,000
CF_2	500,000	600,000
CF_3	500,000	800,000
CF_4	550,000	1,100,000
CF_5	700,000	1,400,000
CF_6	800,000	2,000,000
CF_7	950,000	2,500,000
CF_8	1,000,000	2,000,000
CF_9	1,250,000	1,000,000
CF_{10}	1,500,000	
CF_{11}	2,000,000	
CF_{12}	2,500,000	

TO DO

Create a spreadsheet to answer the following questions.

a. Calculate the *NPV* for each project over its respective life. Rank the projects in descending order on the basis of NPV. Which one would you choose?

b. Use the *annualized net present value (ANPV) approach* to evaluate and rank the projects in descending order on the basis of ANPV. Which one would you choose?

c. Compare and contrast your findings in parts **a** and **b.** Which project would you recommend that the firm choose? Explain.

Visit www.myfinancelab.com for **Chapter Case: *Evaluating Cherone Equipment's Risky Plans for Increasing Its Production Capacity,*** Group Exercises, and numerous online resources.

Integrative Case 5

Lasting Impressions Company

Lasting Impressions (LI) Company is a medium-sized commercial printer of promotional advertising brochures, booklets, and other direct-mail pieces. The firm's major clients are ad agencies based in New York and Chicago. The typical job is characterized by high quality and production runs of more than 50,000 units. LI has not been able to compete effectively with larger printers because of its existing older, inefficient presses. The firm is currently having problems cost-effectively meeting run length requirements as well as meeting quality standards.

The general manager has proposed the purchase of one of two large, six-color presses designed for long, high-quality runs. The purchase of a new press would enable LI to reduce its cost of labor and therefore the price to the client, putting the firm in a more competitive position. The key financial characteristics of the old press and of the two proposed presses are summarized in what follows.

Old press Originally purchased 3 years ago at an installed cost of \$400,000, it is being depreciated under MACRS using a 5-year recovery period. The old press has a remaining economic life of 5 years. It can be sold today to net \$420,000 before taxes; if it is retained, it can be sold to net \$150,000 before taxes at the end of 5 years.

Press A This highly automated press can be purchased for \$830,000 and will require \$40,000 in installation costs. It will be depreciated under MACRS using a 5-year recovery period. At the end of the 5 years, the machine could be sold to net \$400,000 before taxes. If this machine is acquired, it is anticipated that the current account changes shown in the following table would result.

Cash	+ \$ 25,400
Accounts receivable	+ 120,000
Inventories	− 20,000
Accounts payable	+ 35,000

Press B This press is not as sophisticated as press A. It costs \$640,000 and requires \$20,000 in installation costs. It will be depreciated under MACRS using a 5-year recovery period. At the end of 5 years, it can be sold to net \$330,000 before taxes. Acquisition of this press will have no effect on the firm's net working capital investment.

The firm estimates that its earnings before depreciation, interest, and taxes with the old press and with press A or press B for each of the 5 years would be as shown in Table 1 (see page 504). The firm is subject to a 40% tax rate. The firm's cost of capital, r, applicable to the proposed replacement is 14%.

TABLE 1

Earnings before Depreciation, Interest, and Taxes for Lasting Impressions Company's Presses			
Year	**Old press**	**Press A**	**Press B**
1	$120,000	$250,000	$210,000
2	120,000	270,000	210,000
3	120,000	300,000	210,000
4	120,000	330,000	210,000
5	120,000	370,000	210,000

TO DO

a. For each of the two proposed replacement presses, determine:
(1) Initial investment.
(2) Operating cash inflows. (*Note:* Be sure to consider the depreciation in year 6.)
(3) Terminal cash flow. (*Note:* This is at the end of year 5.)

b. Using the data developed in part **a,** find and depict on a time line the relevant cash flow stream associated with each of the two proposed replacement presses, assuming that each is terminated at the end of 5 years.

c. Using the data developed in part **b,** apply each of the following decision techniques:
(1) Payback period. (*Note:* For year 5, use only the operating cash inflows—that is, exclude terminal cash flow—when making this calculation.)
(2) Net present value (NPV).
(3) Internal rate of return (IRR).

d. Draw *net present value profiles* for the two replacement presses on the same set of axes, and discuss conflicting rankings of the two presses, if any, resulting from use of NPV and IRR decision techniques.

e. Recommend which, if either, of the presses the firm should acquire if the firm has (1) unlimited funds or (2) capital rationing.

f. What is the impact on your recommendation of the fact that the operating cash inflows associated with press A are characterized as very risky in contrast to the low-risk operating cash inflows of press B?

Appendix Solutions to Self-Test Problems

Chapter 1

ST1–1

Accounting view (accrual basis)		Financial view (cash basis)	
Worldwide Rugs income statement for the year ended 12/31		**Worldwide Rugs cash flow statement for the year ended 12/31**	
Sales revenue	$3,000,000	Cash inflow	$2,550,000
Less: Costs	2,500,000	Less: Cash outflow	2,500,000
Net profit	$ 500,000	Net cash flow	$ 50,000

a. $3,000,000 − $2,500,000 = $500,000

b. Yes, from an accounting perspective Worldwide Rug was profitable. It generated a 20% profit ($500,000/$2,500,000 = 0.20) on its investment.

c. $2,550,000 − $2,500,000 = $50,000

d. It generated a positive cash flow, but it only represents a 2% return on investment ($50,000/$2,500,000 = 0.02), and it may not be enough to cover operating costs.

e. Given the risk associated with importing and Worldwide Rug's ability to collect on its accounts receivables, a 2% return on investment seems unlikely to lead to long-term success. Without adequate cash inflows to meet its obligations, the firm will not survive, regardless of its level of profits.

Chapter 2

ST2–1 **a.** Capital gains = $180,000 sale price − $150,000 original purchase price = $30,000

b. Total taxable income = $280,000 operating earnings + $30,000 capital gain = $310,000

c. Firm's tax liability:

Using Table 2.1:

$$\begin{aligned}\text{Total taxes due} &= \$22{,}250 + [0.39 \times (\$310{,}000 - \$100{,}000)] \\ &= \$22{,}250 + (0.39 \times \$210{,}000) = \$22{,}250 + \$81{,}900 \\ &= \underline{\underline{\$104{,}150}}\end{aligned}$$

d. $\text{Average tax rate} = \dfrac{\$104{,}150}{\$310{,}000} = \underline{\underline{33.6\%}}$

$\text{Marginal tax rate} = \underline{\underline{39}}\%$

Chapter 3

ST3–1

Ratio	**Too high**	**Too low**
Current ratio = current assets/ current liabilities	May indicate that the firm is holding excessive cash, accounts receivable, or inventory.	May indicate poor ability to satisfy short-term obligations.
Inventory turnover = CGS/inventory	May indicate lower level of inventory, which may cause stockouts and lost sales.	May indicate poor inventory management, excessive inventory, or obsolete inventory.
Times interest earned = earnings before interest and taxes/interest		May indicate poor ability to pay contractual interest payments.
Gross profit margin = gross profits/sales	Indicates the low cost of merchandise sold relative to the sales price; may indicate noncompetitive pricing and potential lost sales.	Indicates the high cost of the merchandise sold relative to the sales price; may indicate either a low sales price or a high cost of goods sold.
Return on total assets = net profits after taxes/ total assets		Indicates ineffective management in generating profits with the available assets.
Price/earnings (P/E) ratio = market price per share of common stock/earnings per share	Investors may have an excessive degree of confidence in the firm's future and underestimate its risk.	Investors lack confidence in the firm's future outcomes and feel that the firm has an excessive level of risk.

ST3–2

O'Keefe Industries
Balance Sheet
December 31, 2012

Assets		Liabilities and Stockholders' Equity	
Cash	$ 32,720	Accounts payable	$ 120,000
Marketable securities	25,000	Notes payable	160,000[e]
Accounts receivable	197,280[a]	Accruals	20,000
Inventories	225,000[b]	Total current liabilities	$ 300,000[d]
Total current assets	$ 480,000	Long-term debt	$ 600,000[f]
Net fixed assets	$1,020,000[c]	Stockholders' equity	$ 600,000
Total assets	$1,500,000	Total liabilities and stockholders' equity	$1,500,000

[a]Average collection period (ACP) = 40 days
ACP = Accounts receivable/Average sales per day
40 = Accounts receivable/($1,800,000/365)
40 = Accounts receivable/$4,932
$197,280 = Accounts receivable

[b]Inventory turnover = 6.0
Inventory turnover = Cost of goods sold/Inventory
6.0 = [Sales × (1 − Gross profit margin)]/Inventory
6.0 = [$1,800,000 × (1 − 0.25)]/Inventory
$225,000 = Inventory

[c]Total asset turnover = 1.20
Total asset turnover = Sales/Total assets
1.20 = $1,800,000/Total assets
$1,500,000 = Total assets
Total assets = Current assets + Net fixed assets
$1,500,000 = $480,000 + Net fixed assets
$1,020,000 = Net fixed assets

[d]Current ratio = 1.60
Current ratio = Current assets/Current liabilities
1.60 = $480,000/Current liabilities
$300,000 = Current liabilities

[e] Notes payable = Total current liabilities − Accounts payable − Accruals
= $300,000 − $120,000 − $20,000
= $160,000

[f]Debt ratio = 0.60
Debt ratio = Total liabilities/Total assets
0.60 = Total liabilities/$1,500,000
$900,000 = Total liabilities
Total liabilities = Current liabilities + Long-term debt
$900,000 = $300,000 + Long-term debt
$600,000 = Long-term debt

Chapter 4

ST4–1 **a.** Depreciation Schedule

Year	Cost[a] (1)	Percentages (from Table 4.2) (2)	Depreciation [(1) × (2)] (3)
1	$150,000	20%	$ 30,000
2	150,000	32	48,000
3	150,000	19	28,500
4	150,000	12	18,000
5	150,000	12	18,000
6	150,000	5	7,500
	Totals	100%	$150,000

[a]$140,000 asset cost + $10,000 installation cost.

b. Operating cash flow:

Year	EBIT (1)	NOPAT [(1) × (1 − 0.40)] (2)	Depreciation (3)	Operating cash flows [(2) + (3)] (4)
1	$160,000	$96,000	$30,000	$126,000
2	160,000	96,000	48,000	144,000
3	160,000	96,000	28,500	124,500
4	160,000	96,000	18,000	114,000
5	160,000	96,000	18,000	114,000
6	160,000	96,000	7,500	103,500

c. Change in net fixed assets in year 6 = $0 − $7,500 = −$7,500

NFAI in year 6 = −$7,500 + $7,500 = $0

Change in current assets in year 6 = $110,000 − $90,000 = $20,000

Change in (Accounts payable + Accruals) in year 6 = ($45,000 + $7,000) − ($40,000 + $8,000) = $52,000 − $48,000 = $4,000

NCAI in year 6 = $20,000 − $4,000 = $16,000

For year 6

FCF = OCF − NFAI − NCAI

= $103,500* − $0 − $16,000 = $87,500

*From part **b**, column 4 value for year 6.

d. In part **b** we can see that, in each of the six years, the operating cash flow is positive, which means that the firm is generating cash that it could use to invest in fixed assets or working capital, or it could distribute some of the cash flow to investors by paying interest or dividends. The free cash flow (FCF) calculated in part **c** for year 6 represents the cash flow available to investors—providers of debt and equity—after covering all operating needs and paying for net fixed asset investment (NFAI) and net current asset investment (NCAI) that occurred during the year.

ST4–2 a.

Carroll Company Cash Budget April–June						Accounts receivable at end of June	
	February	**March**	**April**	**May**	**June**	**July**	**August**
Forecast sales	**$500**	**$600**	**$400**	**$200**	**$200**		
Cash sales (0.30)	$150	$180	$120	$ 60	$ 60		
Collections of A/R							
Lagged 1 month [(0.7 × 0.7) = 0.49]		245	294	196	98	$ 98	
Lagged 2 months [(0.3 × 0.7) = 0.21]			105	126	84	42	$42
						$140 + $42 = $182	
Total cash receipts			$519	$382	$242		
Less: Total cash disbursements			600	500	200		
Net cash flow			($ 81)	($118)	$ 42		
Add: Beginning cash			115	34	(84)		
Ending cash			$ 34	($ 84)	($ 42)		
Less: Minimum cash balance			25	25	25		
Required total financing (notes payable)			—	$109	$ 67		
Excess cash balance (marketable securities)			$ 9	—	—		

b. Carroll Company would need a maximum of $109 in financing over the 3-month period.

c.

Account	Amount	Source of amount
Cash	$ 25	Minimum cash balance—June
Notes payable	67	Required total financing—June
Marketable securities	0	Excess cash balance—June
Accounts receivable	182	Calculation at right of cash budget statement

ST4–3 a.

Euro Designs, Inc.,
Pro Forma Income Statement
for the Year Ended December 31, 2013

Sales revenue (given)	$3,900,000
Less: Cost of goods sold (0.55)[a]	2,145,000
Gross profits	$1,755,000
Less: Operating expenses (0.12)[b]	468,000
Operating profits	$1,287,000
Less: Interest expense (given)	325,000
Net profits before taxes	$ 962,000
Less: Taxes (0.40 × $962,000)	384,800
Net profits after taxes	$ 577,200
Less: Cash dividends (given)	320,000
To retained earnings	$ 257,200

[a]From 2009: CGS/Sales = $1,925,000/$3,500,000 = 0.55.
[b]From 2009: Oper. Exp./Sales = $420,000/$3,500,000 = 0.12.

b. The percent-of-sales method may underestimate actual 2013 pro forma income by assuming that all costs are variable. If the firm has fixed costs, which by definition would not increase with increasing sales, the 2013 pro forma income would probably be underestimated.

Chapter 5

ST5–1 **a.** *Bank A:*

$FV_3 = \$10{,}000 \times (1 + 0.04)^3 = \$10{,}000 \times 1.125 = \underline{\underline{\$11{,}250}}$

(Calculator solution = $11,248.64)

Bank B:

$FV_3 = \$10{,}000 \times (1 + 0.04/2)^6 = \$10{,}000 \times 1.126 = \underline{\underline{\$11{,}260}}$

(Calculator solution = $11,261.62)

Bank C:

$FV_3 = \$10{,}000 \times (1 + 0.04/4)^{12} = \$10{,}000 \times 1.127 = \underline{\underline{\$11{,}270}}$

(Calculator solution = $11,268.25)

b. *Bank A:*

$\text{EAR} = (1 + 0.04/1)^1 - 1 = (1 + 0.04)^1 - 1 = 1.04 - 1 = 0.04 = \underline{\underline{4}}\%$

Bank B:

$\text{EAR} = (1 + 0.04/2)^2 - 1 = (1 + 0.02)^2 - 1$

$= 1.0404 - 1 = 0.0404 = \underline{\underline{4.04}}\%$

Bank C:

$\text{EAR} = (1 + 0.04/4)^4 - 1 = (1 + 0.01)^4 - 1 = 1.0406 - 1$

$= 0.0406 = \underline{\underline{4.06}}\%$

c. Ms. Martin should deal with Bank C: The quarterly compounding of interest at the given 4% rate results in the highest future value as a result of the corresponding highest effective annual rate.

d. *Bank D:*

$FV_3 = \$10{,}000 \times e^{0.04 \times 3} = \$10{,}000 \times e^{0.12}$

$= \$10{,}000 \times 1.127497 = \underline{\underline{\$11{,}274.97}}$

This alternative is better than Bank C; it results in a higher future value because of the use of continuous compounding, which with otherwise identical cash flows always results in the highest future value of any compounding period.

ST5–2 **a.** On the surface, annuity Y looks more attractive than annuity X because it provides $1,000 more each year than does annuity X. Of course, the fact that X is an annuity due means that the $9,000 would be received at the beginning each year, unlike the $10,000 at the end of each year, and this makes annuity X more appealing than it otherwise would be.

b. *Annuity X:*

$FV_6 = \$9{,}000 \times \{[(1 + 0.15)^6 - 1]/0.15\} \times (1 + 0.15)$

$= \$9{,}000 \times 8.754 \times 1.15 = \underline{\underline{\$90{,}603.90}}$

(Calculator solution = $90,601.19)

Annuity Y:

$FV_6 = \$10{,}000 \times \{[(1 + 0.15)^6 - 1]/0.15\}$

$= \$10{,}000 \times 8.754 = \underline{\underline{\$87{,}540.00}}$

(Calculator solution = \$87,537.38)

c. Annuity X is more attractive because its future value at the end of year 6, FV_6, of \$90,603.90 is greater than annuity Y's end-of-year-6 future value, FV_6, of \$87,540.00. The subjective assessment in part **a** was incorrect. The benefit of receiving annuity X's cash inflows at the beginning of each year appears to have outweighed the fact that annuity Y's annual cash inflow, which occurs at the end of each year, is \$1,000 larger (\$10,000 vs. \$9,000) than annuity X's.

ST5–3 *Alternative A:*

Cash flow stream:

$PV_5 = \$700/0.09 \times [1 - 1/(1 + 0.09)^5]$

$= \$700/0.09 \times 0.350 = \underline{\underline{\$2{,}723}}$

(Calculator solution = \$2,722.76)

Single amount: $\underline{\underline{\$2{,}825}}$

Alternative B:

Cash flow stream:

Year (n)	Present value calculation	Present value
1	$\$1{,}100/(1 + 0.09) =$	\$1,009.17
2	$900/(1 + 0.09)^2 =$	757.51
3	$700/(1 + 0.09)^3 =$	540.53
4	$500/(1 + 0.09)^4 =$	354.21
5	$300/(1 + 0.09)^5 =$	194.98
	Present value	\$2,856.40

(Calculator solution = \$2,856.41)

Single amount: $\underline{\underline{\$2{,}800}}$

Conclusion: Alternative B in the form of a cash flow stream is preferred because its present value of \$2,856.40 is greater than the other three values.

ST5–4 $CF = \$8{,}000/\{[(1 + 0.07)^5 - 1]/0.07\}$

$CF = \$8{,}000/5.751$

$CF = \$1{,}391.06$

(Calculator solution = \$1,391.13)

Judi should deposit \$1,391.06 at the end of each of the 5 years to meet her goal of accumulating \$8,000 at the end of the fifth year.

Chapter 6

ST6–1 **a.** $B_0 = I/r_d \times [1 - 1/(1 + r_d)^n] + M \times 1/(1 + r_d)^n$

$I = 0.08 \times \$1{,}000 = \$80$

$M = \$1{,}000$

$n = 12$ yrs

1. $r_d = 7\%$

$B_0 = \$80/0.07 \times [1 - 1/(1 + 0.07)^{12}] + \$1{,}000 \times 1/(1 + 0.07)^{12}$

$= (\$1{,}142.86 \times 0.556) + (\$1{,}000 \times 0.444)$

$= \$635.43 + \$444.00 = \underline{\underline{\$1{,}079.43}}$

(Calculator solution = \$1,079.43)

2. $r_d = 8\%$

$B_0 = \$80/0.08 \times [1 - 1/(1 + 0.08)^{12}] + \$1{,}000 \times 1/(1 + 0.08)^{12}$

$= (\$1{,}000 \times 0.603) + (\$1{,}000 \times 0.397)$

$= \$603.00 + \$397.00 = \underline{\underline{\$1{,}000.00}}$

(Calculator solution = \$1,000.00)

3. $r_d = 10\%$

$B_0 = \$80/0.10 \times [1 - 1/(1 + 0.10)^{12}] + \$1{,}000 \times 1/(1 + 0.10)^{12}$

$= (\$800 \times 0.681) + (\$1{,}000 \times 0.319)$

$= \$544.80 + \$319.00 = \underline{\underline{\$863.80}}$

(Calculator solution = \$863.73)

b. **1.** $r_d = 7\%$, $B_0 = \$1{,}079.43$; sells at a *premium*

2. $r_d = 8\%$, $B_0 = \$1{,}000.00$; sells at its *par value*

3. $r_d = 10\%$, $B_0 = \$863.80$; sells at a *discount*

c. $B_0 = (I/2)/r_d \times [1 - 1/(1 + r_d/2)^{2n}] + M \times 1/(1 + r_d/2)^{2n}$

$= (\$80/2)/(0.10/2) \times [1 - 1/(1 + 0.10/2)^{24}]$

$+ \$1{,}000 \times 1/(1 + 0.10/2)^{24}$

$= \$800 \times 0.690 + \$1{,}000 \times 0.310$

$= \$552.00 + \$310.00 = \underline{\underline{\$862.00}}$

(Calculator solution = \$862.01)

ST6–2 **a.** $B_0 = \$1{,}150$

$I = 0.11 \times \$1{,}000 = \$110$ Current yield $= \dfrac{\text{annual interest}}{\text{current price}}$

$M = \$1{,}000$

$n = 18$ yrs $\qquad = \dfrac{\$110}{\$1{,}150} = 9.57\%$

b. $\$1{,}150 = \$110/r_d \times [1 - 1/(1 + r_d)^{18}] + \$1{,}000 \times 1/(1 + r_d)^{18}$

Because if $r_d = 11\%$, $B_0 = \$1{,}000 = M$, try $r_d = 10\%$.

$$\begin{aligned} B_0 &= \$110/0.10 \times [1 - 1/(1 + 0.10)^{18}] + \$1{,}000 \times 1/(1 + 0.10)^{18} \\ &= (\$1{,}100 \times 0.820) + (\$1{,}000 \times 0.180) \\ &= \$902.00 + \$180.00 = \$1{,}082.00 \end{aligned}$$

Because $\$1{,}082.00 < \$1{,}150$, try $r_d = 9\%$.

$$\begin{aligned} B_0 &= \$110/0.09 \times [1 - 1/(1 + 0.09)^{18}] + \$1{,}000 \times 1/(1 + 0.09)^{18} \\ &= (\$1{,}222.22 \times 0.788) + (\$1{,}000 \times 0.212) \\ &= \$963.11 + \$212.00 = \$1{,}175.11 \end{aligned}$$

Because the $1,175.11 value at 9% is higher than $1,150, and the $1,082.00 value at 10% rate is lower than $1,150, the bond's yield to maturity must be between 9% and 10%. Because the $1,175.11 value is closer to $1,150, rounding to the nearest whole percent, the YTM is 9%. (By using interpolation, the more precise YTM value is 9.27%.)

(Calculator solution = 9.26%)

c. The YTM of 9.27% is below both the bond's 11% coupon interest rate and its current yield of 9.57% calculated in part **a**, because the bond's market value of $1,150 is above its $1,000 par value. Whenever a bond's market value is above its par value (it sells at a *premium*), its YTM and current yield will be below its coupon interest rate; when a bond sells at *par,* the YTM and current yield will equal its coupon interest rate; and when the bond sells for less than par (at a *discount*), its YTM and current yield will be greater than its coupon interest rate. Observe also that the current yield measures the bond's coupon payment relative to its current price. When the bond sells at a premium, its YTM will be below its current yield because the YTM also takes into account that the bondholder will receive just $1,000 back at maturity, which represents a loss relative to the bond's current market price. In other words, the YTM is measuring both the value of the coupon payment that the investor receives (just like the current yield does) and the "loss" that the bondholder endures when the bond matures.

Chapter 7

ST7–1 $D_0 = \$1.80/\text{share}$

$r_s = 12\%$

a. *Zero growth:*

$$P_0 = \frac{D_1}{r_s} = \frac{D_1 = D_0 = \$1.80}{0.12} = \underline{\underline{\$15}}/\text{share}$$

b. *Constant growth, g = 5%:*

$$D_1 = D_0 \times (1 + g) = \$1.80 = (1 + 0.05) = \$1.89/\text{share}$$

$$P_0 = \frac{D_1}{r_s - g} = \frac{\$1.89}{0.12 - 0.05} = \frac{\$1.89}{0.07} = \underline{\underline{\$27}}/\text{share}$$

c. *Variable growth*, $N = 3$, $g_1 = 5\%$ for years 1 to 3 and $g_2 = 4\%$ for years 4 to ∞:

$D_1 = D_0 \times (1 + g_1)^1 = \$1.80 \times (1 + 0.05)^1 = \$1.89\text{/share}$
$D_2 = D_0 \times (1 + g_1)^2 = \$1.80 \times (1 + 0.05)^2 = \$1.98\text{/share}$
$D_3 = D_0 \times (1 + g_1)^3 = \$1.80 \times (1 + 0.05)^3 = \$2.08\text{/share}$
$D_4 = D_3 \times (1 + g_2) = \$2.08 \times (1 + 0.04) = \$2.16\text{/share}$

$$P_0 = \sum_{t=1}^{N} \frac{D_0 \times (1 + g_1)^t}{(1 + r_s)^t} + \left(\frac{1}{(1 + r_s)^N} \times \frac{D_{N+1}}{r_s - g_2}\right)$$

$$\sum_{t=1}^{N} \frac{D_0 \times (1 + g_1)^t}{(1 + r_s)^t} = \frac{1.89}{(1 + 0.12)^1} + \frac{1.98}{(1 + 0.12)^2} + \frac{2.08}{(1 + 0.12)^3}$$

$$= \$1.69 + \$1.58 + \$1.48 = \$4.75$$

$$\left[\frac{1}{(1 + r_s)^N} \times \frac{D_{N+1}}{r_s - g_2}\right] = \frac{1}{(1 + 0.12)^3} \times \frac{D_4 = \$2.16}{0.12 - 0.04}$$

$$= 0.712 \times \$27.00 = \$19.22$$

$$P_0 = \sum_{t=1}^{N} \frac{D_0 \times (1 + g_1)^t}{(1 + r_s)^t} + \left[\frac{1}{(1 + r_s)^N} \times \frac{D_{N+1}}{r_s - g_2}\right] = \$4.75 + \$19.22$$

$$= \underline{\underline{\$23.97\text{/share}}}$$

ST7–2 a. Step 1: Present value of free cash flow from end of 2017 to infinity measured at the end of 2016:

$$FCF_{2017} = \$1{,}500{,}000 \times (1 + 0.04) = \$1{,}560{,}000$$

$$\text{Value of } FCF_{2017 \to \infty} = \frac{\$1{,}560{,}000}{0.10 - 0.04} = \frac{\$1{,}560{,}000}{0.06} = \underline{\underline{\$26{,}000{,}000}}$$

Step 2: Add the value found in Step 1 to the 2016 FCF.

Total $FCF_{2016} = \$1{,}500{,}000 + \$26{,}000{,}000 = \underline{\underline{\$27{,}500{,}000}}$

Step 3: Find the sum of the present values of the FCFs for 2013 through 2016 to determine company value, V_C.

Year (t)	Present value calculation	Present value of FCF_t
2013	\$ 800,000/(1 + 0.10) =	\$ 727,272.73
2014	1,200,000/(1 + 0.10)^2 =	991,735.54
2015	1,400,000/(1 + 0.10)^3 =	1,051,840.72
2016	27,500,000/(1 + 0.10)^4 =	18,782,870.02
	Value of entire company, V_C =	\$21,553,719.01

(Calculator solution = \$21,553,719.01)

b. Common Stock value, $V_S = V_C - V_D - V_P$

$V_C = \$21{,}553{,}719.01$ (calculated in part **a**)
$V_D = \$12{,}500{,}000$ (given)
$V_P = \$0$ (given)
$V_S = \$21{,}553{,}719.01 - \$12{,}500{,}000 - \$0 = \underline{\underline{\$9{,}053{,}719.01}}$
(Calculator solution = \$9,053,719.01)

c. Price per share $= \dfrac{\$9{,}053{,}719.01}{500{,}000} = \underline{\underline{\$18.11}}\text{/share}$

(Calculator solution = \$18.11/share)

Chapter 8

ST8–1 **a.** Expected return, $\bar{r} = \dfrac{\sum \text{Returns}}{3}$

$$\bar{r}_A = \frac{12\% + 14\% + 16\%}{3} = \frac{42\%}{3} = \underline{\underline{14\%}}$$

$$\bar{r}_B = \frac{16\% + 14\% + 12\%}{3} = \frac{42\%}{3} = \underline{\underline{14\%}}$$

$$\bar{r}_C = \frac{12\% + 14\% + 16\%}{3} = \frac{42\%}{3} = \underline{\underline{14\%}}$$

b. Standard deviation, $\sigma_r = \sqrt{\dfrac{\sum_{j=1}^{n}(r_i - \bar{r})^2}{n-1}}$

$$\sigma_{r_A} = \sqrt{\frac{(12\% - 14\%)^2 + (14\% - 14\%)^2 + (16\% - 14\%)^2}{3-1}}$$

$$= \sqrt{\frac{4\% + 0\% + 4\%}{2}} = \sqrt{\frac{8\%}{2}} = \underline{\underline{2\%}}$$

$$\sigma_{r_B} = \sqrt{\frac{(16\% - 14\%)^2 + (14\% - 14\%)^2 + (12\% - 14\%)^2}{3-1}}$$

$$= \sqrt{\frac{4\% + 0\% + 4\%}{2}} = \sqrt{\frac{8\%}{2}} = \underline{\underline{2\%}}$$

$$\sigma_{r_C} = \sqrt{\frac{(12\% - 14\%)^2 + (14\% - 14\%)^2 + (16\% - 14\%)^2}{3-1}}$$

$$= \sqrt{\frac{4\% + 0\% + 4\%}{2}} = \sqrt{\frac{8\%}{2}} = \underline{\underline{2\%}}$$

c.

Annual expected returns

Year	Portfolio AB	Portfolio AC
2010	(0.50 × 12%) + (0.50 × 16%) = 14%	(0.50 × 12%) + (0.50 × 12%) = 12%
2011	(0.50 × 14%) + (0.50 × 14%) = 14%	(0.50 × 14%) + (0.50 × 14%) = 14%
2012	(0.50 × 16%) + (0.50 × 12%) = 14%	(0.50 × 16%) + (0.50 × 16%) = 16%

Over the 3-year period:

$$\bar{r}_{AB} = \frac{14\% + 14\% + 14\%}{3} = \frac{42\%}{3} = \underline{\underline{14\%}}$$

$$\bar{r}_{AC} = \frac{12\% + 14\% + 16\%}{3} = \frac{42\%}{3} = \underline{\underline{14\%}}$$

d. AB is perfectly negatively correlated.
AC is perfectly positively correlated.

e. Standard deviation of the portfolios

$$\sigma_{r_{AB}} = \sqrt{\frac{(14\% - 14\%)^2 + (14\% - 14\%)^2 + (14\% - 14\%)^2}{3 - 1}}$$

$$= \sqrt{\frac{(0\% + 0\% + 0\%)}{2}} = \sqrt{\frac{0\%}{2}} = \underline{\underline{0\%}}$$

$$\sigma_{r_{AC}} = \sqrt{\frac{(12\% - 14\%)^2 + (14\% - 14\%)^2 + (16\% - 14\%)^2}{3 - 1}}$$

$$= \sqrt{\frac{4\% + 0\% + 4\%}{2}} = \sqrt{\frac{8\%}{2}} = \underline{\underline{2\%}}$$

f. Portfolio AB is preferred because it provides the same return (14%) as AC but with less risk $[(\sigma_{r_{AB}} = 0\%) < (\sigma_{r_{AC}} = 2\%)]$.

ST8–2 **a.** When the market return increases by 10%, the investment's return would be expected to increase by 15% (1.50 × 10%). When the market return decreases by 10%, the investment's return would be expected to decrease by 15% [1.50 × (−10%)].

b. $r_j = R_F + [b_j \times (r_m - R_F)]$
$= 7\% + [1.50 \times (10\% - 7\%)]$
$= 7\% + 4.5\% = \underline{\underline{11.5\%}}$

c. No, the investment should be rejected because its *expected* return of 11% is less than the 11.5% return *required* from the investment.

d. $r_j = 7\% + [1.50 \times (9\% - 7\%)]$
$= 7\% + 3\% = \underline{\underline{10\%}}$

The investment would now be acceptable because its *expected* return of 11% is now in excess of the *required* return, which has declined to 10% as a result of investors in the marketplace becoming less risk averse.

Chapter 9

ST9–1 **a.** Cost of debt, r_i (using approximation formula)

$$r_d = \frac{I + \dfrac{\$1{,}000 - N_d}{n}}{\dfrac{N_d + \$1{,}000}{2}}$$

$I = 0.10 \times \$1{,}000 = \$100$
$N_d = \$1{,}000 - \$30 \text{ discount} - \$20 \text{ flotation cost} = \$950$
$n = 10 \text{ years}$

$$r_d = \frac{\$100 + \dfrac{\$1{,}000 - \$950}{10}}{\dfrac{\$950 + \$1{,}000}{2}} = \frac{\$100 + \$5}{\$975} = 10.8\%$$

(Calculator solution = 10.8%)

$r_i = r_d \times (1 - T)$

$T = 0.40$

$r_i = 10.8\% \times (1 - 0.40) = \underline{\underline{6.5\%}}$

Cost of preferred stock, r_p

$$r_p = \frac{D_p}{N_p}$$

$D_p = 0.11 \times \$100 = \$11$

$N_p = \$100 - \$4 \text{ flotation cost} = \$96$

$$r_p = \frac{\$11}{\$96} = \underline{\underline{11.5\%}}$$

Cost of retained earnings, r_r

$$r_r = r_s = \frac{D_1}{P_0} + g$$

$$= \frac{\$6}{\$80} + 6.0\% = 7.5\% + 6.0\% = \underline{\underline{13.5\%}}$$

Cost of new common stock, r_n

$$r_n = \frac{D_1}{N_n} + g$$

$D_1 = \$6$

$N_n = \$80 - \$4 \text{ underpricing} - \$4 \text{ flotation cost} = \$72$

$g = 6.0\%$

$$r_n = \frac{\$6}{\$72} + 6.0\% = 8.3\% + 6.0\% = \underline{\underline{14.3\%}}$$

b. WACC for total new financing < $500,000. This level of new financing is obtained by using retained earning so the cost of common equity is equal to the cost of retained earnings.

Source of capital	Weight (1)	Cost (2)	Weighted cost [(1) × (2)] (3)
Long-term debt	.40	6.5%	2.6%
Preferred stock	.15	11.5	1.7
Common stock equity	.45	13.5	6.1
Totals	1.00		10.4%

Weighted average cost of capital = 10.4%

WACC for total new financing > $500,000. This level of new financing requires the use of new common stock so the cost of common equity is equal to the cost of new common stock.

Source of capital	Weight (1)	Cost (2)	Weighted cost [(1) × (2)] (3)
Long-term debt	.40	6.5%	2.6%
Preferred stock	.15	11.5	1.7
Common stock equity	.45	14.3	6.4
Totals	1.00		10.7%

Weighted average cost of capital = 10.7%

c.

Investment opportunity	Internal rate of return (IRR)	Initial investment	Cumulative investment
D	16.5%	$200,000	$ 200,000
C	12.9	150,000	350,000
E	11.8	450,000	800,000
A	11.2	100,000	900,000
G	10.5	300,000	1,200,000
F	10.1	600,000	1,800,000
B	9.7	500,000	2,300,000

Projects D, C, E, and A should be accepted because their respective IRRs exceed the WMCC. They will require $900,000 of total new financing.

Chapter 10

ST10–1 **a.** Payback period:

Project M: $= \dfrac{\$28{,}500}{\$10{,}000} = \underline{\underline{2.85}}$ years

Project N:

Year (t)	Cash inflows (CF_t)	Cumulative cash inflows
1	$11,000	$11,000
2	10,000	21,000 ←
3	9,000	30,000
4	8,000	38,000

$$2 + \frac{\$27{,}000 - \$21{,}000}{\$9{,}000} \text{ years}$$

$$2 + \frac{\$6{,}000}{\$9{,}000} \text{ years} = \underline{\underline{2.67}} \text{ years}$$

b. Net present value (NPV):

Project M: $NPV = \$10{,}000/0.14 \times [1 - 1/(1 + 0.14)^4] - \$28{,}500$

$= (\$71{,}428.57 \times 0.408) - \$28{,}500$

$= \$29{,}142.86 - \$28{,}500 = \underline{\underline{\$642.86}}$

(Calculator solution = $637.12)

Project N:

Year (t)	Present value	Present values
1	$11,000/(1 + 0.14) =	$ 9,649.12
2	$10{,}000/(1 + 0.14)^2 =$	7,694.68
3	$9{,}000/(1 + 0.14)^3 =$	6,074.74
4	$8{,}000/(1 + 0.14)^4 =$	4,736.64
	Present value of cash inflows	28,155.18
	– Initial investment	27,000.00
	Net present value (NPV)	$ 1,155.18

(Calculator solution = $1,155.18)

c. Internal rate of return (IRR):

Project M: $NPV = 0 = \$10{,}000/IRR \times [1 - 1/(1 + IRR)^4] - \$28{,}500$

Since a 14% discount rate results in a positive NPV of $637.12 the IRR must be greater than 14%, but not a lot greater. Guess 15%.

Project M: $NPV = \$10{,}000/0.15 \times [1 - 1/(1 + 0.15)^4] - \$28{,}500$

$= (\$66{,}666.67 \times 0.428) - \$28{,}500$

$= \$8{,}533.34 - \$28{,}500 = \underline{\underline{\$33.34}}$

$IRR \approx \underline{\underline{15\%}}$

(Calculator solution = 15.09%)

Project N:

$NPV = 0 = 11{,}000/(1 + IRR) + 10{,}000/(1 + IRR)^2 +$
$9{,}000/(1 + IRR)^3 + 8{,}000/(1 + IRR)^4 - 27{,}000$

Because a 14% discount rate results in a positive NPV of $1,155.18 the IRR must be greater than 14%. Guess 15%.

Project N:

$NPV = 11{,}000/(1 + 0.15) + 10{,}000/(1 + 0.15)^2$
$+ 9{,}000/(1 + 0.15)^3 + 8{,}000/(1 + 0.15)^4 - 27{,}000$
$= 9{,}565.22 + 7{,}561.44 + 5{,}917.65 + 4{,}574.03 - 27{,}000$
$= \$618.34$

Because a 15% discount rate results in a positive NPV of $618.34 the IRR must be greater than 15%. Guess 16%

Project N:

$$\begin{aligned}\text{NPV} &= 11{,}000/(1 + 0.16) + 10{,}000/(1 + 0.16)^2 \\ &\quad + 9{,}000/(1 + 0.16)^3 + 8{,}000/(1 + 0.16)^4 - 27{,}000 \\ &= 9{,}482.76 + 7{,}431.63 + 5{,}765.92 + 4{,}418.33 - 27{,}000 \\ &= \$98.64\end{aligned}$$

So IRR $\approx$ 16%

(Calculator solution = 16.19%)

d.

	Project	
	M	**N**
Payback period	2.85 years	2.67 years[a]
NPV	$642.86	$1,155.18[a]
IRR	15%	16%[a]

[a]Preferred project.

Project N is recommended because it has the shorter payback period and the higher NPV, which is greater than zero, and the larger IRR, which is greater than the 14% cost of capital.

e. Net present value profiles:

Data

	NPV	
Discount rate	**Project M**	**Project N**
0%	$11,500[a]	$11,000[b]
14	642.86	1,155.18
15	0	—
16	—	0

[a]($10,000 + $10,000 + $10,000 + $10,000) − $28,500
= $40,000 − $28,500
= $11,500

[b]($11,000 + $10,000 + $9,000 + $8,000) − $27,000
= $38,000 − $27,000
= $11,000

From the NPV profile that follows, it can be seen that if the firm has a cost of capital below approximately 6% (exact value is 5.75%), conflicting rankings of the projects would exist using the NPV and IRR decision techniques. Because the firm's cost of capital is 14%, it can be seen in part **d** that no conflict exists.

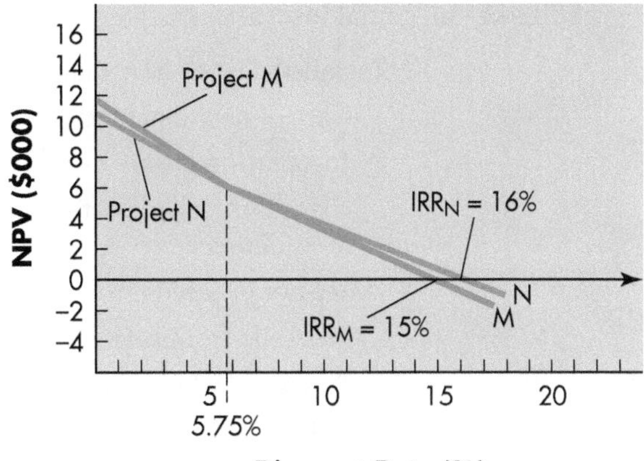

Chapter 11

ST11–1 a.

$$\text{Book value} = \text{Installed cost} - \text{Accumulated depreciation}$$

$$\text{Installed cost} = \$50{,}000$$

$$\text{Accumulated depreciation} = \$50{,}000 \times (0.20 + 0.32 + 0.19 + 0.12)$$

$$= \$50{,}000 \times 0.83 = \$41{,}500$$

$$\text{Book value} = \$50{,}000 - \$41{,}500 = \underline{\underline{\$8{,}500}}$$

b. Taxes on sale of old equipment:

$$\text{Gain on sale} = \text{Sale price} - \text{Book value}$$

$$= \$55{,}000 - \$8{,}500 = \$46{,}500$$

$$\text{Taxes} = 0.40 \times \$46{,}500 = \underline{\underline{\$18{,}600}}$$

c. Initial investment:

Installed cost of new equipment	
Cost of new equipment	$75,000
+ Installation costs	5,000
Total installed cost—new	$80,000
– After-tax proceeds from sale of old equipment	
Proceeds from sale of old equipment	55,000
– Taxes on sale of old equipment	18,600
Total after-tax proceeds—old	$36,400
+ Change in net working capital	15,000
Initial investment	$58,600

ST11–2 **a.** Initial investment:

Installed cost of new machine	
Cost of new machine	$140,000
+ Installation costs	10,000
Total installed cost—new (depreciable value)	$150,000
− After-tax proceeds from sale of old machine	
Proceeds from sale of old machine	42,000
− Taxes on sale of old machine[1]	9,120
Total after-tax proceeds—old	$ 32,880
+ Change in net working capital[2]	20,000
Initial investment	$137,120

[1]Book value of old machine = $40,000 − [(0.20 + 0.32) × $40,000]
= $40,000 − (0.52 × $40,000)
= $40,000 − $20,800 = $19,200

Gain on sale = $42,000 − $19,200 = $22,800

Taxes = 0.40 × $22,800 = $9,120

[2]Change in net working capital = +$10,000 + $25,000 − $15,000
= $35,000 − $15,000 = $20,000

b. Incremental operating cash inflows:

Calculation of Depreciation Expense

Year	Cost (1)	Applicable MACRS depreciation percentages (from Table 4.2) (2)	Depreciation [(1) × (2)] (3)
With new machine			
1	$150,000	33%	$ 49,500
2	150,000	45	67,500
3	150,000	15	22,500
4	150,000	7	10,500
		Totals 100%	$150,000
With old machine			
1	$ 40,000	19% (year-3 depreciation)	$ 7,600
2	40,000	12 (year-4 depreciation)	4,800
3	40,000	12 (year-5 depreciation)	4,800
4	40,000	5 (year-6 depreciation)	2,000
		Total	$19,200[a]

[a]The total of $19,200 represents the book value of the old machine at the end of the second year, which was calculated in part **a.**

Calculation of Operating Cash Inflows

	Year 1	Year 2	Year 3	Year 4
With new machine				
Earnings before depr., int., and taxes[a]	$120,000	$130,000	$130,000	$ 0
− Depreciation[b]	49,500	67,500	22,500	10,500
Earnings before int. and taxes	$ 70,500	$ 62,500	$107,500	−$10,500
− Taxes (rate, T = 40%)	28,200	25,000	43,000	− 4,200
Net operating profit after taxes	$ 42,300	$ 37,500	$ 64,500	−$ 6,300
+ Depreciation[b]	49,500	67,500	22,500	10,500
Operating cash inflows	91,800	$105,000	$ 87,000	$ 4,200
With old machine				
Earnings before depr., int., and taxes[a]	$ 70,000	$ 70,000	$ 70,000	$ 0
− Depreciation[c]	7,600	4,800	4,800	2,000
Earnings before int. and taxes	$ 62,400	$ 65,200	$ 65,200	−$ 2,000
− Taxes (rate, T = 40%)	24,960	26,080	26,080	− 800
Net operating profit after taxes	$ 37,440	$ 39,120	$ 39,120	−$ 1,200
+ Depreciation	7,600	4,800	4,800	2,000
Operating cash inflows	$ 45,040	$ 43,920	$ 43,920	$ 800

[a]Given in the problem.

[b]From column 3 of the preceding table, top.

[c]From column 3 of the preceding table, bottom.

Calculation of Incremental Operating Cash Inflows

Year	Operating cash inflows: New machine[a] (1)	Old machine[a] (2)	Incremental (relevant) [(1) − (2)] (3)
1	$ 91,800	$45,040	$46,760
2	105,000	43,920	61,080
3	87,000	43,920	43,080
4	4,200	800	3,400

[a]From the final row for the respective machine in the preceding table.

c. Terminal cash flow (end of year 3):

After-tax proceeds from sale of new machine	
Proceeds from sale of new machine	$35,000
Taxes on sale of new machine[3]	9,800
Total after-tax proceeds—new	$25,200
− After-tax proceeds from sale of old machine	
Proceeds from sale of old machine	0
− Tax on sale of old machine[4]	−800
Total after-tax proceeds—old	$ 800
+ Change in net working capital	20,000
Terminal cash flow	$44,400

[3]Book value of new machine at end of year 3
= $150,000 − [(0.33 + 0.45 + 0.15) × $150,000] = $150,000 − (0.93 × $150,000)
= $15,000 − $139,500 = $10,500
Tax on sale = 0.40 × ($35,000 sale price − $10,500 book value)
= 0.40 × $24,500 = $9,800

[4]Book value of old machine at end of year 3
= $40,000 − [(0.20 + 0.32 + 0.19 + 0.12 + 0.12) × $40,000] = $40,000 − (0.95 × $40,000)
= $40,000 − $38,000 = $2,000
Tax on sale = 0.40 × ($0 sale price − $2,000 book value)
= 0.40 × −$2,000 = −$800 (i.e., $800 tax saving)

d.

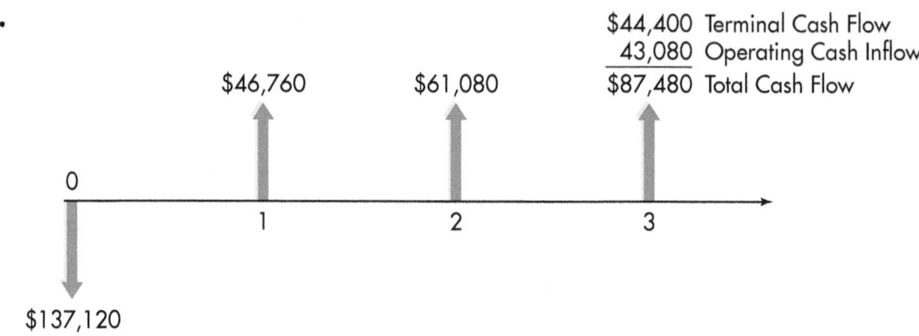

Note: The year-4 incremental operating cash inflow of $3,400 is not directly included; it is instead reflected in the book values used to calculate the taxes on sale of the machines at the end of year 3 and is therefore part of the terminal cash flow.

Chapter 12

ST12–1 a. Net present value (NPV) using a 10% cost of capital:

Project A: NPV = $7,000/0.10 × [1 − 1/(1 + 0.10)^3] − $15,000
= ($70,000.00 × 0.249) − $15,000
= $17,430.00 − $15,000 = $2,430

(Calculator solution = $2,407.96)

Project B:

$$\begin{aligned} NPV &= \$10{,}000/0.10 \times [1 - 1/(1 + 0.10)^3] - \$20{,}000 \\ &= (\$100{,}000.00 \times 0.249) - \$20{,}000 \\ &= \$24{,}900.00 - \$20{,}000 = \underline{\underline{\$4{,}900}}^* \end{aligned}$$

(Calculator solution = $4,868.52)

---

*Preferred project, because higher NPV.

b. Net present value (NPV) using the risk-adjusted discount rate (*RADR*) for project A of 9% and for project B of 16%.

Project A:

$$\begin{aligned} NPV &= \$7{,}000/0.09 \times [1 - 1/(1 + 0.09)^3] - \$15{,}000 \\ &= (\$77{,}777.78 \times 0.228) - \$15{,}000 \\ &= \$17{,}733.33 - \$15{,}000 = \underline{\underline{\$2{,}733.33}}^* \end{aligned}$$

(Calculator solution = $2,719.06)

Project B:

$$\begin{aligned} NPV &= \$10{,}000/0.16 \times [1 - 1/(1 + 0.16)^3] - \$20{,}000 \\ &= (\$62{,}500.00 \times 0.359) - \$20{,}000 \\ &= \$22{,}437.50 - \$20{,}000 = \underline{\underline{\$2{,}437.50}} \end{aligned}$$

(Calculator solution = $2,458.90)

---

*Preferred project, because higher NPV.

c. When the differences in risk were ignored in part **a,** project B was preferred over project A; but when the higher risk of project B is incorporated into the analysis using risk-adjusted discount rates in part **b,** *project A is preferred over project B*. Clearly, project A should be implemented.

Chapter 13

ST13–1 **a.**

$$\begin{aligned} Q &= \frac{FC}{P - VC} \\ &= \frac{\$250{,}000}{\$7.50 - \$3.00} = \frac{\$250{,}000}{\$4.50} = \underline{\underline{55{,}556}} \text{ units} \end{aligned}$$

b.

		+20%	
Sales (in units)	100,000		120,000
Sales revenue (units × $7.50/unit)	$750,000		$900,000
Less: Variable operating costs (units × $3.00/unit)	300,000		360,000
Less: Fixed operating costs	250,000		250,000
Earnings before interest and taxes (EBIT)	$200,000		$290,000
		+45%	
Less: Interest	80,000		80,000
Net profits before taxes	$120,000		$210,000
Less: Taxes (T = 0.40)	48,000		84,000
Net profits after taxes	$ 72,000		$126,000
Less: Preferred dividends (8,000 shares × $5.00/share)	40,000		40,000
Earnings available for common	$132,000		$ 86,000
Earnings per share (EPS)	$32,000/20,000 = $1.60/share		$86,000/20,000 = $4.30/share
		+169%	

c. $$\text{DOL} = \frac{\%\text{ change in EBIT}}{\%\text{ change in sales}} = \frac{+45\%}{+20\%} = \underline{\underline{2.25}}$$

d. $$\text{DFL} = \frac{\%\text{ change in EPS}}{\%\text{ change in EBIT}} = \frac{+169\%}{+45} = \underline{\underline{3.76}}$$

e. $$\text{DTL} = \text{DOL} \times \text{DFL}$$
$$= 2.25 \times 3.76 = \underline{\underline{8.46}}$$

Using the other DTL formula:

$$\text{DTL} = \frac{\%\text{ change in EPS}}{\%\text{ change in sales}}$$

$$8.46 = \frac{\%\text{ change in EPS}}{+50\%}$$

$$\%\text{ change in EPS} = 8.46 \times 0.50 = 4.23 = \underline{\underline{+423}}\%$$

ST13–2

Data summary for alternative plans

Source of capital	Plan A (bond)	Plan B (stock)
Long-term debt	$60,000 at 12% annual interest	$50,000 at 12% annual interest
Annual interest =	0.12 × $60,000 = $7,200	0.12 × $50,000 = $6,000
Common stock	10,000 shares	11,000 shares

a.

	Plan A (bond)		Plan B (stock)	
EBIT[a]	$30,000	$40,000	$30,000	$40,000
Less: Interest	7,200	7,200	6,000	6,000
Net profits before taxes	$22,800	$32,800	$24,000	$34,000
Less: Taxes (T = 0.40)	9,120	13,120	9,600	13,600
Net profits after taxes	$13,680	$19,680	$14,400	$20,400
EPS (10,000 shares)	$1.37	$1.97		
(11,000 shares)			$1.31	$1.85

[a]Values were arbitrarily selected; other values could have been used.

Coordinates

	EBIT	
	$30,000	**$40,000**
Financing plan	**Earnings per share (EPS)**	
A (Bond)	$1.37	$1.97
B (Stock)	1.31	1.85

b.

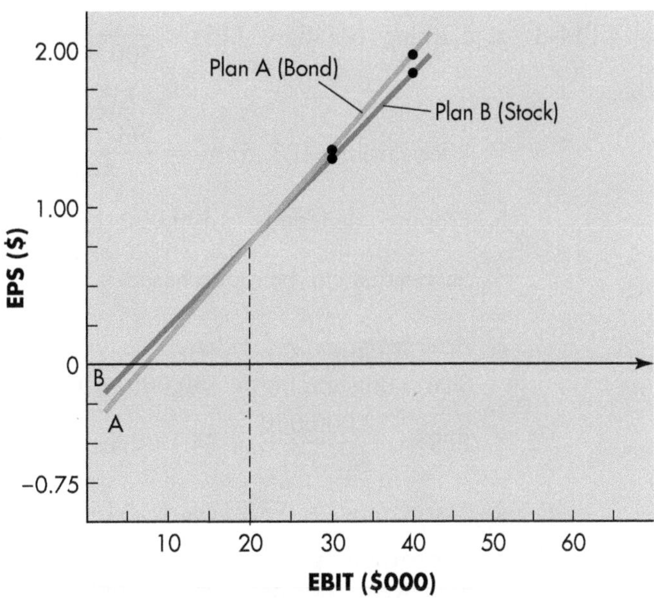

c. The bond plan (Plan A) becomes superior to the stock plan (Plan B) at *around $20,000* of EBIT, as represented by the dashed vertical line in the figure in part **b.** (*Note:* The actual point is $19,200, which was determined algebraically by using the technique described in footnote 18.)

ST13–3 **a.**

Capital structure debt ratio	Expected EPS (1)	Required return, r_s (2)	Estimated share value [(1) ÷ (2)] (3)
0%	$3.12	.13	$24.00
10	3.90	.15	26.00
20	4.80	.16	30.00
30	5.44	.17	32.00
40	5.51	.19	29.00
50	5.00	.20	25.00
60	4.40	.22	20.00

b. Using the table in part **a:**

1. Maximization of EPS: *40% debt ratio,* EPS = $5.51/share (see column 1).

2. Maximization of share value: *30% debt ratio,* share value = $32.00 (see column 3).

c. Recommend *30% debt ratio* because it results in the maximum share value and is therefore consistent with the firm's goal of owner wealth maximization.

Chapter 14

ST14–1 **a.** Earnings per share (EPS) $= \dfrac{\$2{,}000{,}000 \text{ earnings available}}{500{,}000 \text{ shares of common outstanding}}$

$= \underline{\underline{\$4.00}}\text{/share}$

Price/earnings (P/E) ratio $= \dfrac{\$60 \text{ market price}}{\$4.00 \text{ EPS}} = \underline{\underline{15}}$

b. Proposed dividends = 500,000 shares × $2 per share = $1,000,000

Shares that can be repurchased $= \dfrac{\$1{,}000{,}000}{\$62} = \underline{\underline{16{,}129}}$ shares

c. *After proposed repurchase:*

Shares outstanding = 500,000 − 16,129 = 483,871

$\text{EPS} = \dfrac{\$2{,}000{,}000}{483{,}871} = \underline{\underline{\$4.13}}\text{/share}$

d. Market price = $4.13/share × 15 = $\underline{\underline{\$61.95}}$/share

e. The earnings per share (EPS) are higher after the repurchase because there are fewer shares of stock outstanding (483,871 shares versus 500,000 shares) to divide up the firm's $2,000,000 of available earnings.

f. In both cases, the stockholders would receive $2 per share—a $2 cash dividend in the dividend case or an approximately $2 increase in share price ($60.00 per share to $61.95 per share) in the repurchase case. (*Note:* The difference of $0.05 per share ($2.00 − $1.95) is due to rounding.)

Chapter 15

ST15–1

Basic data

Time component	Current	Proposed
Average payment period (APP)	10 days	30 days
Average collection period (ACP)	30 days	30 days
Average age of inventory (AAI)	40 days	40 days

Cash conversion cycle (CCC) = AAI + ACP − APP

$CCC_{current}$ = 40 days + 30 days − 10 days = 60 days

$CCC_{proposed}$ = 40 days + 30 days − 30 days = $\underline{40}$ days

Reduction in CCC $\underline{\underline{20}}$ days

Old accounts payable = 10 days × (\$14,000,000 ÷ 360 days) = \$388,889

New accounts payable = 30 days × (\$14,000,000 ÷ 360 days) = \$1,166,667

Change in accounts payable = \$1,166,667 − \$388,889 = \$777,778

Since accounts payable has increased the amount represents a decrease in net working capital.

Reduction in resource investment = \$777,778

Annual profit increase = 0.12 × \$777,778 = $\underline{\underline{\$93,333}}$

ST15–2 **a.** *Data:*

S = 60,000 gallons

O = \$200 per order

C = \$1 per gallon per year

Calculation:

$$EOQ = \sqrt{\frac{2 \times S \times O}{C}}$$

$$= \sqrt{\frac{2 \times 60{,}000 \times \$200}{\$1}}$$

$$= \sqrt{24{,}000{,}000}$$

$$= \underline{\underline{4{,}899}} \text{ gallons}$$

b. *Data:*

Lead time = 20 days

Daily usage = 60,000 gallons/365 days
= 164.38 gallons/day

Calculation:

Reorder point = lead time in days × daily usage
= 20 days × 164.38 gallons/day
= $\underline{\underline{3{,}287.6}}$ gallons

ST15–3 Tabular Calculation of the Effects of Relaxing Credit Standards on Regency Rug Repair Company:

Additional profit contribution from sales		
[4,000 rugs × ($32 avg. sale price − $28 var. cost)]		$16,000
Cost of marginal investment in accounts receivable		
Average investment under proposed plan:		
$\frac{(\$28 \times 76{,}000 \text{ rugs})}{365/48} = \frac{\$2{,}128{,}000}{7.6}$	$280,000	
Average investment under present plan:		
$\frac{(\$28 \times 72{,}000 \text{ rugs})}{365/40} = \frac{\$2{,}016{,}000}{9.1}$	221,538	
Marginal investment in A/R	$ 58,462	
Cost of marginal investment in A/R (0.14 × $58,462)		($ 8,185)
Cost of marginal bad debts		
Bad debts under proposed plan (0.015 × $32 × 76,000 rugs)	$ 36,480	
Bad debts under present plan (0.010 × $32 × 72,000 rugs)	23,040	
Cost of marginal bad debts		($13,440)
Net loss from implementation of proposed plan		($ 5,625)

Recommendation: Because a net loss of $5,625 is expected to result from relaxing credit standards, *the proposed plan should not be implemented.*

Chapter 16

ST16–1 **a.**

Supplier	Approximate cost of giving up cash discount
X	1% × [365/(55 − 10)] = 1% × 365/45 = 1% × 8.1 = 8.1%
Y	2% × [365/(30 − 10)] = 2% × 365/20 = 2% × 18.25 = 36.5%
Z	2% × [365/(60 − 20)] = 2% × 365/40 = 2% × 9.125 = 18.25%

b.

Supplier	Recommendation
X	8.1% cost of giving up discount < 15% interest cost from bank; therefore, *give up discount.*
Y	36.5% cost of giving up discount > 15% interest cost from bank; therefore, *take discount and borrow from bank.*
Z	18.25% cost of giving up discount > 15% interest cost from bank; therefore, *take discount and borrow from bank.*

c. Stretching accounts payable for supplier Z would change the cost of giving up the cash discount to

$2\% \times [365/[(60 + 20) - 20]) = 2\% \times 365/60 = 2\% \times 6.1 = \underline{\underline{12.2\%}}$

In this case, in light of the 15% interest cost from the bank, the recommended strategy in part **b** would be to *give up the discount* because the 12.2% cost of giving up the discount would be less than the 15% interest cost from the bank.

Chapter 17

ST17–1 **a.** (1) and (2). In tabular form—after-tax cash outflows in column 3 and present value of the cash outflows in column 5.

End of year	Lease payment (1)	Tax adjustment [(1 − 0.40) = 0.60] (2)	After-tax cash outflows [(1) × (2)] (3)	Present value calculation (4)	Present value of outflows
1	$5,000	0.60	$3,000	$ 3,000/(1 + 0.09) =	$ 2,752.29
2	5,000	0.60	3,000	$3,000/(1 + 0.09)^2$ =	2,525.04
3	5,000	0.60	3,000	$3,000/(1 + 0.09)^3$ =	2,316.55
4	5,000	0.60	3,000	$3,000/(1 + 0.09)^4$ =	2,125.28
5	5,000	0.60	7,000[a]	$7,000/(1 + 0.09)^5$ =	4,549.52
				Present value of cash outflows	$14,268.68

[a]After-tax lease payment outflow of $3,000 plus the $4,000 cost of exercising the purchase option.

(Calculator solution = $14,268.68)

b. (1) In tabular form—annual interest expense in column 3.

End of year	Loan payments (1)	Beginning-of-year principal (2)	Payments: Interest [0.15 × (2)] (3)	Payments: principal [(1) − (3)] (4)	End-of-year principal [(2) − (4)] (5)
1	$5,967	$20,000	$3,000	$2,967	$17,033
2	5,967	17,033	2,555	3,412	13,621
3	5,967	13,621	2,043	3,924	9,697
4	5,967	9,697	1,455	4,512	5,185
5	5,967	5,185	778	5,189	—[a]

[a]The values in this table have been rounded to the nearest dollar, which results in a slight difference ($4) between the beginning-of-year-5 principal (in column 2) and the year-5 principal payment (in column 4).

(2) In tabular form—after-tax cash outflows in column 9.

End of year	Loan payments (1)	Maintenance costs (2)	Cost of oven (3)	Depreciation percentages[a] (4)	Depreciation [(3) × (4)] (5)	Interest[b] (6)	Total deductions [(2) + (5) + (6)] (7)	Tax shields [0.40 × (7)] (8)	After-tax cash outflows [(1) + (2) − (8)] (9)
1	$5,967	$1,000	$20,000	.20	$4,000	$3,000	$8,000	$3,200	$3,767
2	5,967	1,000	20,000	.32	6,400	2,555	9,955	3,982	2,985
3	5,967	1,000	20,000	.19	3,800	2,043	6,843	2,737	4,230
4	5,967	1,000	20,000	.12	2,400	1,455	4,855	1,942	5,025
5	5,967	1,000	20,000	.12	2,400	778	4,178	1,671	5,296

[a]From Table 4.2 on page 108.
[b]From column 3 of table in part **b**(1).

(3) In tabular form—present value of the cash outflows in column 3.

End of year	After-tax cash outflows[a] (1)	Present value calculation (2)	Present value of outflows (3)
1	$3,767	$\$3,767/(1 + 0.09)$ =	$ 3,455.96
2	2,985	$2,985/(1 + 0.09)^2$ =	2,512.41
3	4,230	$4,230/(1 + 0.09)^3$ =	3,266.34
4	5,025	$5,025/(1 + 0.09)^4$ =	3,559.84
5	5,296	$5,296/(1 + 0.09)^5$ =	3,442.04
		Present value of cash outflows	$16,236.59

[a]From column 9 of table in part **b**(2).

(Calculator solution = $16,236.59)

c. Because the present value of the lease outflows of $14,268.68 is well below the present value of the purchase outflows of $16,236.59, *the lease is preferred.* Leasing rather than purchasing the oven should result in an incremental savings of $1,967.91 ($16,236.59 purchase cost − $14,268.68 lease cost).

ST17–2 **a.** Straight bond value:

$$B_0 = I/r_d \times [1 - 1/(1 + r_d)^n] + M \times 1/(1 + r_d)^n$$

$$I = 0.11 \times \$1{,}000 = \$110$$

$$M = \$1{,}000$$

$$n = 25 \text{ yrs}$$

(1) $r_d = 13\%$

$$B_0 = \$110/0.13 \times [1 - 1/(1 + 0.13)^{25}] + \$1{,}000 \times 1/(1 + 0.13)^{25}$$

$$= (\$846.15 \times 0.953) + (\$1{,}000 \times 0.047)$$

$$= \$806.38 + \$47.00 = \underline{\underline{\$853.38}}$$

(Calculator solution = $853.40)

b. In tabular form:

Market price of stock (1)	Conversion ratio (2)	Conversion value [(1) × (2)] (3)
$20	40	$ 800
25 (conversion price)	40	1,000 (par value)
28	40	1,120
35	40	1,400
50	40	2,000

c. The bond would be expected to sell at the higher of the conversion value and the straight value. In no case would it be expected to sell for less than the straight value of $853.38. Therefore, at a price of $20, the bond would sell for its straight value of $853.38; at prices of $25, $28, $35, and $50, the bond would be expected to sell at the associated conversion values (calculated in part **b**) of $1,000, $1,120, $1,400, and $2,000, respectively.

d. The straight bond value of $853.38.

Chapter 18

ST18–1 **a.** Net present value at 11%:

Year(s)	Cash inflow (1)	Present value calculation at 11% (2)	Present value (3)
1–3	$20,000	$\$20{,}000/0.11 \times [1 - 1/(1 + 0.11)^3] =$	$ 48,874.29
4–15	30,000	$30{,}000/0.11 \times [1 - 1/(1 + 0.11)^{12}] \times 1/(1 + 0.11)^3 =$	142,414.65
		Present value of inflows	$191,288.94
		Less: Cash purchase price	180,000.00
		Net present value (NPV)	$ 11,288.94

(Calculator solution = 11,288.94)

Because the NPV of $11,288.94 is greater than zero, *Luxe Foods should acquire Valley Canning.*

b. In this case, the 14% cost of capital must be used. Net present value at 14%:

Year(s)	Cash inflow (1)	Present value calculation at 14% (2)	Present value (3)
1–3	$20,000	$\$20{,}000/0.14 \times [1 - 1/(1 + 0.14)^3] =$	$ 46,432.64
4–15	30,000	$30{,}000/0.14 \times [1 - 1/(1 + 0.14)^{12}] \times 1/(1 + 0.14)^3 =$	114,616.08
		Present value of inflows	$161,048.72
		Less: Cash purchase price	180,000.00
		Net present value (NPV)	($ 18,951.28)

(Calculator solution = −$18,951.28)

At the higher cost of capital, the *acquisition of Valley by Luxe cannot be justified.*

ST18–2 **a.** Lake Industries' EPS without merger:

	Earnings available for common				
Year	**Initial value (1)**	**Future value calculation at 5% (2)**	**End-of-year value (3)**	**Number of shares outstanding (4)**	**EPS [(3) ÷ (4)] (5)**
2012	$160,000	$\$160{,}000 \times (1 + 0.05)^0 =$	$160,000	80,000	$2.00
2013	160,000	$160{,}000 \times (1 + 0.05)^1 =$	168,000	80,000	2.10
2014	160,000	$160{,}000 \times (1 + 0.05)^2 =$	176,400	80,000	2.21
2015	160,000	$160{,}000 \times (1 + 0.05)^3 =$	185,220	80,000	2.32
2016	160,000	$160{,}000 \times (1 + 0.05)^4 =$	194,481	80,000	2.43
2017	160,000	$160{,}000 \times (1 + 0.05)^5 =$	204,205	80,000	2.55

b. Number of postmerger shares outstanding for Lake Industries:

$$\text{Number of new shares issued} = \text{Initial number of Butler Company shares} \times \text{Ratio of exchange}$$

$$= 10{,}000 \times 1.1 = 11{,}000 \text{ shares}$$

Plus: Lake's premerger shares 80,000

Lake's postmerger shares 91,000 shares

	Earnings available for common						
	Butler Company			Lake Industries			
				Without merger	With merger		
Year	**Initial value (1)**	**Future value calculation at 10% (2)**	**End-of-year value (3)**	**End-of-year value[a] (4)**	**End-of-year value [(3) + (4)] (5)**	**Number of shares outstanding[b] (6)**	**EPS [(5) ÷ (6)] (7)**
2009	$20,000	$\$20{,}000 \times (1 + 0.10)^0 =$	$20,000	$160,000	$180,000	91,000	$1.98
2010	20,000	$20{,}000 \times (1 + 0.10)^1 =$	22,000	168,000	190,000	91,000	2.09
2011	20,000	$20{,}000 \times (1 + 0.10)^2 =$	24,200	176,400	200,600	91,000	2.20
2012	20,000	$20{,}000 \times (1 + 0.10)^3 =$	26,620	185,220	211,840	91,000	2.33
2013	20,000	$20{,}000 \times (1 + 0.10)^4 =$	29,280	194,481	223,761	91,000	2.46
2014	20,000	$20{,}000 \times (1 + 0.10)^5 =$	32,210	204,205	236,415	91,000	2.60

[a] From column 3 of table in part **a.**

[b] Calculated at beginning of this part.

c. Comparing the EPS without the proposed merger calculated in part **a** (see column 5 of table in part **a**) with the EPS with the proposed merger calculated in part **b** (see column 7 of table in part **b**), we can see that after 2014, the EPS *with* the merger rises above the EPS *without* the merger. Clearly, over the long run, the EPS with the merger will exceed those without the merger. This outcome is attributed to the higher rate of growth associated with Butler's earnings (10% versus 5% for Lake).

Chapter 19

ST19–1 MNC's receipt of dividends can be calculated as follows:

Subsidiary income before local taxes	$150,000
Foreign income tax at 32%	− 48,000
Dividend available to be declared	$102,000
Foreign dividend withholding tax at 8%	− 8,160
MNC's receipt of dividends	$ 93,840

a. If tax credits are allowed, then the so-called grossing up procedure will be applicable:

Additional MNC income		$150,000
U.S. tax liability at 34%	$51,000	
Total foreign taxes paid to be used as a credit ($48,000 + $8,160)	− 56,160	− 56,160
U.S. taxes due		− 0
Net funds available to the MNC		$ 93,840

b. If no tax credits are permitted, then:

MNC's receipt of dividends	$93,840
U.S. tax liability at 34%	− 31,906
Net funds available to the parent MNC	$61,934

Glossary

ABC inventory system
Inventory management technique that divides inventory into three groups—A, B, and C, in descending order of importance and level of monitoring, on the basis of the dollar investment in each. (Chapter 15)

ability to service debts
The ability of a firm to make the payments required on a scheduled basis over the life of a debt. (Chapter 3)

accept–reject approach
The evaluation of capital expenditure proposals to determine whether they meet the firm's minimum acceptance criterion. (Chapter 10)

accounting exposure
The risk resulting from the effects of changes in foreign exchange rates on the translated value of a firm's financial statement accounts denominated in a given foreign currency. (Chapter 19)

accounts payable management
Management by the firm of the time that elapses between its purchase of raw materials and its mailing payment to the supplier. (Chapter 16)

accrual basis
In preparation of financial statements, recognizes revenue at the time of sale and recognizes expenses when they are incurred. (Chapter 1)

accruals
Liabilities for services received for which payment has yet to be made. (Chapter 16)

ACH (automated clearinghouse) transfer
Preauthorized electronic withdrawal from the payer's account and deposit into the payee's account via a settlement among banks by the *automated clearinghouse,* or *ACH.* (Chapter 15)

acquiring company
The firm in a merger transaction that attempts to acquire another firm. (Chapter 18)

activity ratios
Measure the speed with which various accounts are converted into sales or cash—inflows or outflows. (Chapter 3)

after-tax proceeds from sale of old asset
The difference between the old asset's sale proceeds and any applicable taxes or tax refunds related to its sale. (Chapter 11)

agency costs
Costs arising from agency problems that are borne by shareholders and represent a loss of shareholder wealth. (Chapter 1)

agency problems
Problems that arise when managers place personal goals ahead of the goals of shareholders. (Chapter 1)

aggressive funding strategy
A funding strategy under which the firm funds its seasonal requirements with short-term debt and its permanent requirements with long-term debt. (Chapter 15)

aging schedule
A credit-monitoring technique that breaks down accounts receivable into groups on the basis of their time of origin; it indicates the percentages of the total accounts receivable balance that have been outstanding for specified periods of time. (Chapter 15)

all-current-rate method
The method by which the *functional-currency-denominated* financial statements of an MNC's subsidiary are translated into the parent company's currency. (Chapter 19)

American depositary receipts (ADRs)
Securities, backed by *American depositary shares (ADSs),* that permit U.S. investors to hold shares of non-U.S. companies and trade them in U.S. markets. (Chapter 7)

American depositary shares (ADSs)
Dollar-denominated receipts for the stocks of foreign companies that are held by a U.S. financial institution overseas. (Chapter 7)

angel capitalists (angels)
Wealthy individual investors who do not operate as a business but invest in promising early-stage companies in exchange for a portion of the firm's equity. (Chapter 7)

annual cleanup
The requirement that for a certain number of days during the year borrowers under a line of credit carry a zero loan balance (that is, owe the bank nothing). (Chapter 16)

annual percentage rate (APR)
The *nominal annual rate* of interest, found by multiplying the periodic rate by the number of periods in one year, that must be disclosed to consumers on credit cards and loans as a result of "truth-in-lending laws." (Chapter 5)

annual percentage yield (APY)
The *effective annual rate* of interest that must be disclosed to consumers by banks on their savings products as a result of "truth-in-savings laws." (Chapter 5)

annualized net present value (ANPV) approach
An approach to evaluating unequal-lived projects that converts the net present value of unequal-lived, mutually exclusive projects into an equivalent annual amount (in NPV terms). (Chapter 12)

annuity
A stream of equal periodic cash flows over a specified time period. These cash flows can be *inflows* of returns earned on investments or *outflows* of funds invested to earn future returns. (Chapter 5)

annuity due
An annuity for which the cash flow occurs at the *beginning* of each period. (Chapter 5)

articles of partnership
The written contract used to formally establish a business partnership. (Chapter 1)

ASEAN
A large trading bloc that comprises ten member nations, all in Southeast Asia. China is expected to join this bloc in 2010. Also called the *Association of Southeast Asian Nations.* (Chapter 19)

ask price
The lowest price at which a security is offered for sale. (Chapter 2)

assignment
A voluntary liquidation procedure by which a firm's creditors pass the power to liquidate the firm's assets to an adjustment bureau, a trade association, or a third party, which is designated the *assignee.* (Chapter 18)

asymmetric information
The situation in which managers of a firm have more information about operations and future prospects than do investors. (Chapter 13)

authorized shares
Shares of common stock that a firm's corporate charter allows it to issue. (Chapter 7)

average age of inventory
Average number of days' sales in inventory. (Chapter 3)

average collection period
The average amount of time needed to collect accounts receivable. (Chapter 3)

average payment period
The average amount of time needed to pay accounts payable. (Chapter 3)

average tax rate
A firm's taxes divided by its taxable income. (Chapter 2)

balance sheet
Summary statement of the firm's financial position at a given point in time. (Chapter 3)

bankruptcy
Business failure that occurs when the stated value of a firm's liabilities exceeds the fair market value of its assets. (Chapter 18)

Bankruptcy Reform Act of 1978
The governing bankruptcy legislation in the United States today. (Chapter 18)

bar chart
The simplest type of probability distribution; shows only a limited number of outcomes and associated probabilities for a given event. (Chapter 8)

basic EPS
Earnings per share (EPS) calculated without regard to any contingent securities. (Chapter 17)

behavioral finance
A growing body of research that focuses on investor behavior and its impact on investment decisions and stock prices. Advocates are commonly referred to as "behaviorists." (Chapter 7)

benchmarking
A type of *cross-sectional analysis* in which the firm's ratio values are compared to those of a key competitor or group of competitors that it wishes to emulate. (Chapter 3)

beta coefficient (*b*)
A relative measure of nondiversifiable risk. An index of the degree of movement of an asset's return in response to a change in the *market return*. (Chapter 8)

bid price
The highest price offered to purchase a security. (Chapter 2)

bird-in-the-hand argument
The belief, in support of *dividend relevance theory*, that investors see current dividends as less risky than future dividends or capital gains. (Chapter 14)

board of directors
Group elected by the firm's stockholders and typically responsible for approving strategic goals and plans, setting general policy, guiding corporate affairs, and approving major expenditures. (Chapter 1)

bond
Long-term debt instrument used by business and government to raise large sums of money, generally from a diverse group of lenders. (Chapter 2)

bond indenture
A legal document that specifies both the rights of the bondholders and the duties of the issuing corporation. (Chapter 6)

book value
The strict accounting value of an asset, calculated by subtracting its accumulated depreciation from its installed cost. (Chapter 11)

book value per share
The amount per share of common stock that would be received if all of the firm's assets were sold for their exact book *(accounting)* value and the proceeds remaining after paying all liabilities (including preferred stock) were divided among the common stockholders. (Chapter 7)

book value weights
Weights that use accounting values to measure the proportion of each type of capital in the firm's financial structure. (Chapter 9)

breakeven analysis
Used to indicate the level of operations necessary to cover all costs and to evaluate the profitability associated with various levels of sales; also called *cost-volume-profit analysis*. (Chapter 13)

breakeven cash inflow
The minimum level of cash inflow necessary for a project to be acceptable, that is, NPV > \$0. (Chapter 12)

breakup value
The value of a firm measured as the sum of the values of its operating units if each were sold separately. (Chapter 18)

broker market
The securities exchanges on which the two sides of a transaction, the buyer and seller, are brought together to trade securities. (Chapter 2)

business ethics
Standards of conduct or moral judgment that apply to persons engaged in commerce. (Chapter 1)

call feature
A feature included in nearly all corporate bond issues that gives the issuer the opportunity to repurchase bonds at a stated call price prior to maturity. (Chapter 6)

call option
An option to *purchase* a specified number of shares of a stock (typically 100) on or before a specified future date at a stated price. (Chapter 17)

call premium
The amount by which a bond's *call price* exceeds its par value. (Chapter 6)

call price
The stated price at which a bond may be repurchased, by use of *a call feature,* prior to maturity. (Chapter 6)

callable feature (preferred stock)
A feature of *callable preferred stock* that allows the issuer to retire the shares within a certain period of time and at a specified price. (Chapter 7)

capital asset pricing model (CAPM)
Describes the relationship between the required return, r_s, and the nondiversifiable risk of the firm as measured by the beta coefficient, b. (Chapter 8)

capital asset pricing model (CAPM)
The basic theory that links risk and return for all assets. (Chapter 9)

capital budgeting
The process of evaluating and selecting long-term investments that are consistent with the firm's goal of maximizing owners' wealth. (Chapter 10)

capital budgeting process
Five distinct but interrelated steps: *proposal generation, review and analysis, decision making, implementation,* and *follow-up*. (Chapter 10)

capital expenditure
An outlay of funds by the firm that is expected to produce benefits over a period of time greater than 1 year. (Chapter 10)

capital gain
The amount by which the sale price of an asset exceeds the asset's purchase price. (Chapter 2)

capital market
A market that enables suppliers and demanders of *long-term funds* to make transactions. (Chapter 2)

capital rationing
The financial situation in which a firm has only a fixed number of dollars available for capital expenditures, and numerous projects compete for these dollars. (Chapter 10)

capital structure
The mix of long-term debt and equity maintained by the firm. (Chapter 13)

capitalized lease
A *financial (capital) lease* that has the present value of all its payments included as an asset and corresponding liability on the firm's balance sheet, as required by the Financial Accounting Standards Board (FASB) in *FASB Statement No. 13*. (Chapter 17)

carrying costs
The variable costs per unit of holding an item in inventory for a specific period of time. (Chapter 15)

cash basis
Recognizes revenues and expenses only with respect to actual inflows and outflows of cash. (Chapter 1)

cash bonuses
Cash paid to management for achieving certain performance goals. (Chapter 1)

cash budget (cash forecast)
A statement of the firm's planned inflows and outflows of cash that is used to estimate its short-term cash requirements. (Chapter 4)

cash concentration
The process used by the firm to bring lockbox and other deposits together into one bank, often called the *concentration bank*. (Chapter 15)

cash conversion cycle (CCC)
The length of time required for a company to convert cash invested in its operations to cash received as a result of its operations. (Chapter 15)

cash disbursements
All outlays of cash by the firm during a given financial period. (Chapter 4)

cash discount
A percentage deduction from the purchase price; available to the credit customer who pays its account within a specified time. (Chapter 15)

cash discount period
The number of days after the beginning of the credit period during which the cash discount is available. (Chapter 15)

cash receipts
All of a firm's inflows of cash during a given financial period. (Chapter 4)

catering theory
A theory that says firms cater to the preferences of investors, initiating or increasing dividend payments during periods in which high-dividend stocks are particularly appealing to investors. (Chapter 14)

Central American Free Trade Agreement (CAFTA)
A trade agreement signed in 2003–2004 by the United States, the Dominican Republic, and five Central American countries (Costa Rica, El Salvador, Guatemala, Honduras, and Nicaragua). (Chapter 19)

change in net working capital
The difference between a change in current assets and a change in current liabilities. (Chapter 11)

Chapter 7
The portion of the *Bankruptcy Reform Act of 1978* that details the procedures to be followed when liquidating a failed firm. (Chapter 18)

Chapter 11
The portion of the *Bankruptcy Reform Act of 1978* that outlines the procedures for reorganizing a failed (or failing) firm, whether its petition is filed voluntarily or involuntarily. (Chapter 18)

clearing float
The time between deposit of a payment and when spendable funds become available to the firm. (Chapter 15)

clientele effect
The argument that different payout policies attract different types of investors but still do not change the value of the firm. (Chapter 14)

closely owned (stock)
The common stock of a firm is owned by an individual or a small group of investors (such as a family); these are usually privately owned companies. (Chapter 7)

coefficient of variation (*CV*)
A measure of relative dispersion that is useful in comparing the risks of assets with differing expected returns. (Chapter 8)

collateral trust bonds
See Table 6.4.

commercial banks
Institutions that provide savers with a secure place to invest their funds and that offer loans to individual and business borrowers. (Chapter 2)

commercial finance companies
Lending institutions that make only secured loans—both short-term and long-term—to businesses. (Chapter 16)

commercial paper
A form of financing consisting of short-term, unsecured promissory notes issued by firms with a high credit standing. (Chapter 16)

commitment fee
The fee that is normally charged on a *revolving credit agreement;* it often applies to the *average unused portion* of the borrower's credit line. (Chapter 16)

common-size income statement
An income statement in which each item is expressed as a percentage of sales. (Chapter 3)

common stock
The purest and most basic form of corporate ownership. (Chapter 1)

compensating balance
A required checking account balance equal to a certain percentage of the amount borrowed from a bank under a line-of-credit or revolving credit agreement. (Chapter 16)

composition
A pro rata cash settlement of creditor claims by the debtor firm; a uniform percentage of each dollar owed is paid. (Chapter 18)

compound interest
Interest that is earned on a given deposit and has become part of the *principal* at the end of a specified period. (Chapter 5)

conflicting rankings
Conflicts in the ranking given a project by NPV and IRR, resulting from *differences in the magnitude and timing of cash flows*. (Chapter 10)

congeneric merger
A merger in which one firm acquires another firm that is *in the same general industry* but is neither in the same line of business nor a supplier or customer. (Chapter 18)

conglomerate merger
A merger combining firms in *unrelated businesses*. (Chapter 18)

conservative funding strategy
A funding strategy under which the firm funds both its seasonal and its permanent requirements with long-term debt. (Chapter 15)

consolidation
The combination of two or more firms to form a completely new corporation. (Chapter 18)

constant-growth model
A widely cited dividend valuation approach that assumes that dividends will grow at a constant rate, but a rate that is less than the required return. (Chapter 7)

constant-growth valuation (Gordon growth) model
Assumes that the value of a share of stock equals the present value of all future dividends (assumed to grow at a constant rate) that it is expected to provide over an infinite time horizon. (Chapter 9)

constant-payout-ratio dividend policy
A dividend policy based on the payment of a certain percentage of earnings to owners in each dividend period. (Chapter 14)

contingent securities
Convertibles, warrants, and stock options. Their presence affects the reporting of a firm's earnings per share (EPS). (Chapter 17)

continuous compounding
Compounding of interest an infinite number of times per year at intervals of microseconds. (Chapter 5)

continuous probability distribution
A probability distribution showing all the possible outcomes and associated probabilities for a given event. (Chapter 8)

controlled disbursing
The strategic use of mailing points and bank accounts to lengthen mail float and clearing float, respectively. (Chapter 15)

controller
The firm's chief accountant, who is responsible for the firm's accounting activities, such as corporate accounting, tax management, financial accounting, and cost accounting. (Chapter 1)

conversion feature
A feature of convertible bonds that allows bondholders to change each bond into a stated number of shares of common stock. (Chapter 6)

conversion feature
An option that is included as part of a bond or a preferred stock issue and allows its holder to change the security into a stated number of shares of common stock. (Chapters 6 and 17)

conversion feature (preferred stock)
A feature of *convertible preferred stock* that allows holders to change each share into a stated number of shares of common stock. (Chapter 7)

conversion (or stock) value
The value of a convertible security measured in terms of the market price of the common stock into which it can be converted. (Chapter 17)

conversion price
The per-share price that is effectively paid for common stock as the result of conversion of a convertible security. (Chapter 17)

conversion ratio
The ratio at which a convertible security can be exchanged for common stock. (Chapter 17)

convertible bond
A bond that can be changed into a specified number of shares of common stock. (Chapter 17)

convertible preferred stock
Preferred stock that can be changed into a specified number of shares of common stock. (Chapter 17)

corporate bond
A long-term debt instrument indicating that a corporation has borrowed a certain amount of money and promises to repay it in the future under clearly defined terms (Chapter 6).

corporate governance
The rules, processes, and laws by which companies are operated, controlled, and regulated. (Chapter 1)

corporate restructuring
The activities involving expansion or contraction of a firm's operations or changes in its asset or financial (ownership) structure. (Chapter 18)

corporation
An entity created by law. (Chapter 1)

correlation
A statistical measure of the relationship between any two series of numbers. (Chapter 8)

correlation coefficient
A measure of the degree of correlation between two series. (Chapter 8)

cost of a new issue of common stock, r_n
The cost of common stock, net of underpricing and associated flotation costs. (Chapter 9)

cost of capital
Represents the firm's cost of financing and is the minimum rate of return that a project must earn to increase firm value. (Chapter 9)

cost of common stock equity, r_s
The rate at which investors discount the expected dividends of the firm to determine its share value. (Chapter 9)

cost of giving up a cash discount
The implied rate of interest paid to delay payment of an account payable for an additional number of days. (Chapter 16)

cost of long-term debt
The financing cost associated with new funds raised through long-term borrowing. (Chapter 9)

cost of new asset
The net outflow necessary to acquire a new asset. (Chapters 9 and 11)

cost of preferred stock, r_p
The ratio of the preferred stock dividend to the firm's net proceeds from the sale of preferred stock. (Chapter 9)

cost of retained earnings, r_r
The same as the cost of an *equivalent fully subscribed issue of additional common stock,* which is equal to the cost of common stock equity, r_s. (Chapter 9)

coupon interest rate
The percentage of a bond's par value that will be paid annually, typically in two equal semiannual payments, as interest. (Chapter 6)

coverage ratios
Ratios that measure the firm's ability to pay certain fixed charges. (Chapter 3)

credit monitoring
The ongoing review of a firm's accounts receivable to determine whether customers are paying according to the stated credit terms. (Chapter 15)

creditor control
An arrangement in which the creditor committee replaces the firm's operating management and operates the firm until all claims have been settled. (Chapter 18)

credit period
The number of days after the beginning of the credit period until full payment of the account is due. (Chapter 15)

credit scoring
A credit selection method commonly used with high-volume/small-dollar credit requests; relies on a credit score determined by applying statistically derived weights to a credit applicant's scores on key financial and credit characteristics. (Chapter 15)

credit standards
The firm's minimum requirements for extending credit to a customer. (Chapter 15)

credit terms
The terms of sale for customers who have been extended credit by the firm. (Chapter 15)

cross-sectional analysis
Comparison of different firms' financial ratios at the same point in time; involves comparing the firm's ratios to those of other firms in its industry or to industry averages. (Chapter 3)

cumulative (preferred stock)
Preferred stock for which all passed (unpaid) dividends in arrears, along with the current dividend, must be paid before dividends can be paid to common stockholders. (Chapter 7)

current assets
Short-term assets, expected to be converted into cash within 1 year or less. (Chapter 3)

current liabilities
Short-term liabilities, expected to be paid within 1 year or less. (Chapter 3)

current rate (translation) method
Technique used by U.S.–based companies to translate their foreign-currency-denominated assets and liabilities into dollars, for consolidation with the parent company's financial statements, using the year-end (current) exchange rate. (Chapter 3)

current ratio
A measure of liquidity calculated by dividing the firm's current assets by its current liabilities. (Chapter 3)

current yield
A measure of a bond's cash return for the year; calculated by dividing the bond's annual interest payment by its current price. (Chapter 6)

date of record (dividends)
Set by the firm's directors, the date on which all persons whose names are recorded as stockholders receive a declared dividend at a specified future time. (Chapter 14)

dealer market
The market in which the buyer and seller are not brought together directly but instead have their orders executed by securities dealers that "make markets" in the given security. (Chapter 2)

debentures
See Table 6.4.

debt
Includes borrowing incurred by a firm, including bonds, and is repaid according to a fixed schedule of payments. (Chapter 7)

debtor in possession (DIP)
The term for a firm that files a reorganization petition under Chapter 11 and then develops, if feasible, a reorganization plan. (Chapter 18)

debt ratio
Measures the proportion of total assets financed by the firm's creditors. (Chapter 3)

deflation
A general trend of falling prices. (Chapter 6)

degree of financial leverage (DFL)
The numerical measure of the firm's financial leverage. (Chapter 13)

degree of indebtedness
Measures the amount of debt relative to other significant balance sheet amounts. (Chapter 3)

degree of operating leverage (DOL)
The numerical measure of the firm's operating leverage. (Chapter 13)

degree of total leverage (DTL)
The numerical measure of the firm's total leverage. (Chapter 13)

depository transfer check (DTC)
An unsigned check drawn on one of a firm's bank accounts and deposited in another. (Chapter 15)

depreciable life
Time period over which an asset is depreciated. (Chapter 4)

depreciation
A portion of the costs of fixed assets charged against annual revenues over time. (Chapter 4)

derivative security
A security that is neither debt nor equity but derives its value from an underlying asset that is often another security; called "derivatives," for short. (Chapter 17)

diluted EPS
Earnings per share (EPS) calculated under the assumption that *all* contingent securities that would have dilutive effects are converted and exercised and are therefore common stock. (Chapter 17)

dilution of earnings
A reduction in each previous shareholder's fractional claim on the firm's earnings resulting from the issuance of additional shares of common stock. (Chapter 7)

dilution of ownership
A reduction in each previous shareholder's fractional ownership resulting from the issuance of additional shares of common stock. (Chapter 7)

direct lease
A lease under which a lessor owns or acquires the assets that are leased to a given lessee. (Chapter 17)

discount
The amount by which a bond sells at a value that is less than its par value. (Chapter 6)

discounting cash flows
The process of finding present values; the inverse of compounding interest. (Chapter 5)

discount loan
Loan on which interest is paid in advance by being deducted from the amount borrowed. (Chapter 16)

diversifiable risk
The portion of an asset's risk that is attributable to firm-specific, random causes; can be eliminated through diversification. Also called *unsystematic risk*. (Chapter 8)

divestiture
The selling of some of a firm's assets for various strategic reasons. (Chapters 8 and 18)

dividend irrelevance theory
Miller and Modigliani's theory that in a perfect world, the firm's value is determined solely by the earning power and risk of its assets (investments) and that the manner in which it splits its earnings stream between dividends and internally retained (and reinvested) funds does not affect this value. (Chapter 14)

dividend payout ratio
Indicates the percentage of each dollar earned that a firm distributes to the owners in the form of cash. It is calculated by dividing the firm's cash dividend per share by its earnings per share. (Chapter 14)

dividend per share (DPS)
The dollar amount of cash distributed during the period on behalf of each outstanding share of common stock. (Chapter 3)

dividend policy
The firm's plan of action to be followed whenever it makes a dividend decision. (Chapter 14)

dividend reinvestment plans (DRIPs)
Plans that enable stockholders to use dividends received on the firm's stock to acquire additional shares—even fractional shares—at little or no transaction cost. (Chapter 14)

dividend relevance theory
The theory, advanced by Gordon and Lintner, that there is a direct relationship between a firm's dividend policy and its market value. (Chapter 14)

dividends
Periodic distributions of cash to the stockholders of a firm. (Chapter 1)

double taxation
Situation that occurs when after-tax corporate earnings are distributed as cash dividends to stockholders, who then must pay personal taxes on the dividend amount. (Chapter 2)

DuPont formula
Multiplies the firm's *net profit margin* by its *total asset turnover* to calculate the firm's *return on total assets (ROA)*. (Chapter 3)

DuPont system of analysis
System used to dissect the firm's financial statements and to assess its financial condition. (Chapter 3)

Dutch auction repurchase
A repurchase method in which the firm specifies how many shares it wants to buy back and a range of prices at which it is willing to repurchase shares. Investors specify how many shares they will sell at each price in the range, and the firm determines the minimum price required to repurchase its target number of shares. All investors who tender receive the same price. (Chapter 14)

earnings per share (EPS)
The amount earned during the period on behalf of each outstanding share of common stock, calculated by dividing the period's total earnings available for

the firm's common stockholders by the number of shares of common stock outstanding. (Chapter 1)

EBIT–EPS approach
An approach for selecting the capital structure that maximizes earnings per share (EPS) over the expected range of earnings before interest and taxes (EBIT). (Chapter 13)

economic exposure
The risk resulting from the effects of changes in foreign exchange rates on the firm's value. (Chapter 19)

economic order quantity (EOQ) model
Inventory management technique for determining an item's optimal order size, which is the size that minimizes the total of its *order costs* and *carrying costs.* (Chapter 15)

effective interest rate
In the international context, the rate equal to the nominal rate plus (or minus) any forecast appreciation (or depreciation) of a foreign currency relative to the currency of the MNC parent. (Chapter 19)

effective (true) annual rate (EAR)
The annual rate of interest actually paid or earned. (Chapter 5)

efficient market
A market that allocates funds to their most productive uses as a result of competition among wealth-maximizing investors and that determines and publicizes prices that are believed to be close to their true value. (Chapter 2)

efficient-market hypothesis (EMH)
Theory describing the behavior of an assumed "perfect" market in which (1) securities are in equilibrium, (2) security prices fully reflect all available information and react swiftly to new information, and (3), because stocks are fully and fairly priced, investors need not waste time looking for mispriced securities. (Chapter 7)

efficient portfolio
A portfolio that maximizes return for a given level of risk. (Chapter 8)

ending cash
The sum of the firm's beginning cash and its net cash flow for the period. (Chapter 4)

enterprise resource planning (ERP)
A computerized system that electronically integrates external information about the firm's suppliers and customers with the firm's departmental data so that information on all available resources—human and material—can be instantly obtained in a fashion that eliminates production delays and controls costs. (Chapter 15)

equipment trust certificates
See Table 6.4.

equity
Funds provided by the firm's owners (investors or stockholders) that are repaid subject to the firm's performance. (Chapter 7)

euro
A single currency adopted on January 1, 1999, by 12 EU nations, which switched to a single set of euro bills and coins on January 1, 2002. (Chapter 19)

Eurobond
A bond issued by an international borrower and sold to investors in countries with currencies other than the currency in which the bond is denominated. (Chapters 6 and 19)

Eurobond market
The market in which corporations and governments typically issue bonds denominated in dollars and sell them to investors located outside the United States. (Chapters 2 and 19)

Eurocurrency market
International equivalent of the domestic money market. (Chapter 2)

Eurocurrency markets
The portion of the Euromarket that provides short-term, foreign-currency financing to subsidiaries of MNCs. (Chapter 19)

Euromarket
The international financial market that provides for borrowing and lending currencies outside their country of origin. (Chapter 19)

European Open Market
The transformation of the European Union into a *single* market at year-end 1992. (Chapter 19)

European Union (EU)
A significant economic force currently made up of 27 nations that permit free trade within the union. (Chapter 19)

ex dividend
A period beginning 2 *business days* prior to the date of record, during which a stock is sold without the right to receive the current dividend. (Chapter 14)

excess cash balance
The (excess) amount available for investment by the firm if the period's ending cash is greater than the desired minimum cash balance; assumed to be invested in marketable securities. (Chapter 4)

excess earnings accumulation tax
The tax the IRS levies on retained earnings above $250,000 for most businesses when it determines that the firm has accumulated an excess of earnings to allow owners to delay paying ordinary income taxes on dividends received. (Chapter 14)

exchange rate risk
The danger that an unexpected change in the exchange rate between the dollar and the currency in which a project's cash flows are denominated will reduce the market value of that project's cash flow. (Chapter 12)

exchange rate risk
The risk caused by varying exchange rates between two currencies. (Chapter 19)

exercise (or option) price
The price at which holders of warrants can purchase a specified number of shares of common stock. (Chapter 17)

expectations theory
The theory that the yield curve reflects investor expectations about future interest rates; an expectation of rising interest rates results in an upward-sloping yield curve, and an expectation of declining rates results in a downward-sloping yield curve. (Chapter 6)

expected value of a return ($\bar{r}$)
The average return that an investment is expected to produce over time. (Chapter 8)

extendible notes
See Table 6.5.

extension
An arrangement whereby the firm's creditors receive payment in full, although not immediately. (Chapter 18)

external financing required ("plug" figure)
Under the judgmental approach for developing a pro forma balance sheet, the amount of external financing needed to bring the statement into balance. It can be either a positive or a negative value. (Chapter 4)

external forecast
A sales forecast based on the relationships observed between the firm's sales and certain key external economic indicators. (Chapter 4)

extra dividend
An additional dividend optionally paid by the firm when earnings are higher than normal in a given period. (Chapter 14)

factor
A financial institution that specializes in purchasing accounts receivable from businesses. (Chapter 16)

factoring accounts receivable
The outright sale of accounts receivable at a discount to a *factor* or other financial institution. (Chapter 16)

FASB No. 52
Statement issued by the FASB requiring U.S. multinationals first to convert the financial statement accounts of foreign subsidiaries into the *functional currency* and then to translate the accounts into the parent firm's currency using the *all-current-rate method.* (Chapter 19)

Federal Deposit Insurance Corporation (FDIC)
An agency created by the Glass-Steagall Act that provides insurance for deposits at banks and monitors banks to ensure their safety and soundness. (Chapter 2)

finance
The science and art of managing money. (Chapter 1)

Financial Accounting Standards Board (FASB)
The accounting profession's rule-setting body, which authorizes *generally accepted accounting principles (GAAP).* (Chapter 3)

Financial Accounting Standards Board (FASB) Standard No. 52
Mandates that U.S.–based companies translate their foreign-currency-denominated assets and liabilities into dollars, for consolidation with the parent com-

pany's financial statements. This is done by using the *current rate (translation) method.* (Chapters 3 and 19)

financial breakeven point
The level of EBIT necessary to just cover all *fixed financial costs;* the level of EBIT for which EPS = $0. (Chapter 13)

financial institution
An intermediary that channels the savings of individuals, businesses, and governments into loans or investments. (Chapter 2)

financial (or capital) lease
A *longer-term lease* than an operating lease that is noncancelable and obligates the lessee to make payments for the use of an asset over a predefined period of time; the total payments over the term of the lease are *greater* than the lessor's initial cost of the leased asset. (Chapter 17)

financial leverage
The magnification of risk and return through the use of fixed-cost financing, such as debt and preferred stock. (Chapter 3)

financial leverage
The use of *fixed financial costs* to magnify the effects of changes in earnings before interest and taxes on the firm's earnings per share. (Chapter 13)

financial leverage multiplier (FLM)
The ratio of the firm's total assets to its common stock equity. (Chapter 3)

financial manager
Actively manages the financial affairs of all types of businesses, whether private or public, large or small, profit seeking or not for profit. (Chapter 1)

financial markets
Forums in which suppliers of funds and demanders of funds can transact business directly. (Chapter 2)

financial merger
A merger transaction undertaken with the goal of restructuring the acquired company to improve its cash flow and unlock its unrealized value. (Chapter 18)

financial planning process
Planning that begins with long-term, or *strategic,* financial plans that in turn guide the formulation of short-term, or *operating,* plans and budgets. (Chapter 4)

financial services
The area of finance concerned with the design and delivery of advice and financial products to individuals, businesses, and governments. (Chapter 1)

financing flows
Cash flows that result from debt and equity financing transactions; include incurrence and repayment of debt, cash inflow from the sale of stock, and cash outflows to repurchase stock or pay cash dividends. (Chapter 4)

five C's of credit
The five key dimensions—character, capacity, capital, collateral, and conditions—used by credit analysts to provide a framework for in-depth credit analysis. (Chapter 15)

fixed (or semifixed) relationship
The constant (or relatively constant) relationship of a currency to one of the major currencies, a combination (basket) of major currencies, or some type of international foreign exchange standard. (Chapter 19)

fixed-payment coverage ratio
Measures the firm's ability to meet all fixed-payment obligations. (Chapter 3)

fixed-rate loan
A loan with a rate of interest that is determined at a set increment above the prime rate and remains unvarying until maturity. (Chapter 16)

flat yield curve
A yield curve that indicates that interest rates do not vary much at different maturities. (Chapter 6)

float
Funds that have been sent by the payer but are not yet usable funds to the payee. (Chapter 15)

floating inventory lien
A secured short-term loan against inventory under which the lender's claim is on the borrower's inventory in general. (Chapter 16)

floating-rate bonds
See Table 6.5.

floating-rate loan
A loan with a rate of interest initially set at an increment above the prime rate and allowed to "float," or vary, above prime *as the prime rate varies* until maturity. (Chapter 16)

floating relationship
The fluctuating relationship of the values of two currencies with respect to each other. (Chapter 19)

flotation costs
The total costs of issuing and selling a security. (Chapter 9)

foreign bond
A bond that is issued by a foreign corporation or government and is denominated in the investor's home currency and sold in the investor's home market. (Chapters 2, 6, and 19)

foreign direct investment
The transfer of capital, managerial, and technical assets to a foreign country. (Chapters 11 and 19)

foreign exchange manager
The manager responsible for managing and monitoring the firm's exposure to loss from currency fluctuations. (Chapter 1)

forward exchange rate
The rate of exchange between two currencies at some specified future date. (Chapter 19)

foreign exchange rate
The value of two currencies with respect to each other. (Chapter 19)

free cash flow (FCF)
The amount of cash flow available to investors (creditors and owners) after the firm has met all operating needs and paid for investments in net fixed assets and net current assets. (Chapter 4)

free cash flow valuation model
A model that determines the value of an entire company as the present value of its expected *free cash flows* discounted at the firm's *weighted average cost of capital,* which is its expected average future cost of funds over the long run. (Chapter 7)

friendly merger
A merger transaction endorsed by the target firm's management, approved by its stockholders, and easily consummated. (Chapter 18)

functional currency
The currency in which a subsidiary primarily generates and expends cash and in which its accounts are maintained. (Chapter 19)

future value
The value at a given future date of an amount placed on deposit today and earning interest at a specified rate. Found by applying *compound interest* over a specified period of time. (Chapter 5)

General Agreement on Tariffs and Trade (GATT)
A treaty that has governed world trade throughout most of the postwar era; it extends free-trading rules to broad areas of economic activity and is policed by the *World Trade Organization (WTO).* (Chapters 3 and 19)

generally accepted accounting principles (GAAP)
The practice and procedure guidelines used to prepare and maintain financial records and reports; authorized by the *Financial Accounting Standards Board (FASB).* (Chapter 3)

Glass-Steagall Act
An act of Congress in 1933 that created the federal deposit insurance program and separated the activities of commercial and investment banks. (Chapter 2)

golden parachutes
Provisions in the employment contracts of key executives that provide them with sizable compensation if the firm is taken over; deters hostile takeovers to the extent that the cash outflows required are large enough to make the takeover unattractive. (Chapter 18)

Gordon growth model
A common name for the *constant-growth model* that is widely cited in dividend valuation. (Chapter 7)

Gramm-Leach-Bliley Act
An act that allows business combinations (that is, mergers) between commercial banks, investment banks, and insurance companies, and thus permits these institutions to compete in markets that prior regulations prohibited them from entering. (Chapter 2)

greenmail
A takeover defense under which a target firm repurchases, through private negotiation, a large block of stock at a premium from one or more shareholders to end a hostile takeover attempt by those shareholders. (Chapter 18)

gross profit margin
Measures the percentage of each sales dollar remaining after the firm has paid for its goods. (Chapter 3)

hedging
Offsetting or protecting against the risk of adverse price movements. (Chapter 17)

hedging strategies
Techniques used to offset or protect against risk; in the international context, these include borrowing or lending in different currencies; undertaking contracts in the forward, futures, and/or options markets; and swapping assets/liabilities with other parties. (Chapter 19)

historical weights
Either book or market value weights based on *actual* capital structure proportions. (Chapter 9)

holding company
A corporation that has voting control of one or more other corporations. (Chapter 18)

horizontal merger
A merger of two firms *in the same line of business*. (Chapter 18)

hostile merger
A merger transaction that the target firm's management does not support, forcing the acquiring company to try to gain control of the firm by buying shares in the marketplace. (Chapter 18)

hybrid security
A form of debt or equity financing that possesses characteristics of *both* debt and equity financing. (Chapter 17)

implied price of a warrant
The price effectively paid for each warrant attached to a bond. (Chapter 17)

incentive plans
Management compensation plans that tie management compensation to share price; one example involves the granting of *stock options*. (Chapter 1)

income bonds
See Table 6.4.

income statement
Provides a financial summary of the firm's operating results during a specified period. (Chapter 3)

incremental cash flows
The *additional* cash flows—outflows or inflows—expected to result from a proposed capital expenditure. (Chapter 11)

independent projects
Projects whose cash flows are unrelated to (or independent of) one another; the acceptance of one does not *eliminate* the others from further consideration. (Chapter 10)

individual investors
Investors who own relatively small quantities of shares so as to meet personal investment goals. (Chapter 1)

inflation
A rising trend in the prices of most goods and services. (Chapter 6)

informational content
The information provided by the dividends of a firm with respect to future earnings, which causes owners to bid up or down the price of the firm's stock. (Chapter 14)

initial investment
The relevant cash outflow for a proposed project at time zero. (Chapter 11)

initial public offering (IPO)
The first public sale of a firm's stock. (Chapter 7)

insolvency
Business failure that occurs when a firm is unable to pay its liabilities as they come due. (Chapter 18)

insolvent
Describes a firm that is unable to pay its bills as they come due. (Chapter 15)

installation costs
Any added costs that are necessary to place an asset into operation. (Chapter 11)

installed cost of new asset
The *cost of new asset* plus its *installation costs;* equals the asset's depreciable value. (Chapter 11)

institutional investors
Investment professionals, such as banks, insurance companies, mutual funds, and pension funds, that are paid to manage and hold large quantities of securities on behalf of others. (Chapter 1)

interest rate
Usually applied to debt instruments such as bank loans or bonds; the compensation paid by the borrower of funds to the lender; from the borrower's point of view, the cost of borrowing funds. (Chapter 6)

interest rate risk
The chance that interest rates will change and thereby change the required return and bond value. Rising rates, which result in decreasing bond values, are of greatest concern. (Chapter 6)

intermediate cash inflows
Cash inflows received prior to the termination of a project. (Chapter 10)

internal forecast
A sales forecast based on a buildup, or consensus, of sales forecasts through the firm's own sales channels. (Chapter 4)

internal rate of return (IRR)
The discount rate that equates the NPV of an investment opportunity with $0 (because the present value of cash inflows equals the initial investment); it is the rate of return that the firm will earn if it invests in the project and receives the given cash inflows. (Chapter 10)

internal rate of return approach
An approach to capital rationing that involves graphing project IRRs in descending order against the total dollar investment to determine the group of acceptable projects. (Chapter 12)

international bond
A bond that is initially sold outside the country of the borrower and is often distributed in several countries. (Chapter 19)

international equity market
A market that allows corporations to sell blocks of shares to investors in a number of different countries simultaneously. (Chapter 2)

international stock market
A market with uniform rules and regulations governing major stock exchanges. MNCs would benefit greatly from such a market, which has yet to evolve. (Chapter 19)

inventory turnover
Measures the activity, or liquidity, of a firm's inventory. (Chapter 3)

inverted yield curve
A *downward-sloping* yield curve indicates that short-term interest rates are generally higher than long-term interest rates. (Chapter 6)

investment banker
Financial intermediary that specializes in selling new security issues and advising firms with regard to major financial transactions. (Chapter 7)

investment bankers
Financial intermediaries who, in addition to their role in selling new security issues, can be hired by acquirers in mergers to find suitable target companies and assist in negotiations. (Chapter 18)

investment banks
Institutions that assist companies in raising capital, advise firms on major transactions such as mergers or financial restructurings, and engage in trading and market making activities. (Chapter 2)

investment flows
Cash flows associated with purchase and sale of both fixed assets and equity investments in other firms. (Chapter 4)

investment opportunities schedule (IOS)
The graph that plots project IRRs in descending order against the total dollar investment. (Chapter 12)

involuntary reorganization
A petition initiated by an outside party, usually a creditor, for the reorganization and payment of creditors of a failed firm. (Chapter 18)

issued shares
Shares of common stock that have been put into circulation; the sum of *outstanding shares* and *treasury stock*. (Chapter 7)

joint venture
A partnership under which the participants have contractually agreed to contribute specified amounts of money and expertise in exchange for stated proportions of ownership and profit. (Chapter 19)

judgmental approach
A simplified approach for preparing the pro forma balance sheet under which the firm estimates the values of certain balance sheet accounts and uses its external financing as a balancing, or "plug," figure. (Chapter 4)

junk bonds
See Table 6.5.

just-in-time (JIT) system
Inventory management technique that minimizes inventory investment by having materials arrive at exactly the time they are needed for production. (Chapter 15)

lease-versus-purchase (or lease-versus-buy) decision
The decision facing firms needing to acquire new fixed assets: whether to lease the assets or to purchase them, using borrowed funds or available liquid resources. (Chapter 17)

leasing
The process by which a firm can obtain the use of certain fixed assets for which it must make a series of contractual, periodic, tax-deductible payments. (Chapter 17)

lessee
The receiver of the services of the assets under a lease contract. (Chapter 17)

lessor
The owner of assets that are being leased. (Chapter 17)

letter of credit
A letter written by a company's bank to the company's foreign supplier, stating that the bank guarantees payment of an invoiced amount if all the underlying agreements are met. (Chapter 16)

letter to stockholders
Typically, the first element of the annual stockholders' report and the primary communication from management. (Chapter 3)

leverage
Refers to the effects that fixed costs have on the returns that shareholders earn; higher leverage generally results in higher but more volatile returns. (Chapter 13)

leveraged buyout (LBO)
An acquisition technique involving the use of a large amount of debt to purchase a firm; an example of a *financial merger*. (Chapter 18)

leveraged lease
A lease under which the lessor acts as an equity participant, supplying only about 20 percent of the cost of the asset, while a lender supplies the balance. (Chapter 17)

leveraged recapitalization
A takeover defense in which the target firm pays a large debt-financed cash dividend, increasing the firm's financial leverage and thereby deterring the takeover attempt. (Chapter 18)

lien
A publicly disclosed legal claim on loan collateral. (Chapter 16)

limited liability
A legal provision that limits stockholders' liability for a corporation's debt to the amount they initially invested in the firm by purchasing stock. (Chapter 1)

limited liability company (LLC)
See Chapter 1 "In More Depth" feature. (Chapter 1)

limited liability partnership (LLP)
See Chapter 1 "In More Depth" feature. (Chapter 1)

limited partnership (LP)
See Chapter 1 "In More Depth" feature. (Chapter 1)

line of credit
An agreement between a commercial bank and a business specifying the amount of unsecured short-term borrowing the bank will make available to the firm over a given period of time. (Chapter 16)

liquidation value per share
The *actual amount* per share of common stock that would be received if all of the firm's assets were sold for their market value, liabilities (including preferred stock) were paid, and any remaining money were divided among the common stockholders. (Chapter 7)

liquidity
A firm's ability to satisfy its short-term obligations *as they come due.* (Chapter 3)

liquidity preference
A general tendency for investors to prefer short-term (that is, more liquid) securities. (Chapter 6)

liquidity preference theory
Theory suggesting that long-term rates are generally higher than short-term rates (hence, the yield curve is upward sloping) because investors perceive short-term investments to be more liquid and less risky than long-term investments. Borrowers must offer higher rates on long-term bonds to entice investors away from their preferred short-term securities. (Chapter 6)

loan amortization
The determination of the equal periodic loan payments necessary to provide a lender with a specified interest return and to repay the loan principal over a specified period. (Chapter 5)

loan amortization schedule
A schedule of equal payments to repay a loan. It shows the allocation of each loan payment to interest and principal. (Chapter 5)

lockbox system
A collection procedure in which customers mail payments to a post office box that is emptied regularly by the firm's bank, which processes the payments and deposits them in the firm's account. This system speeds up collection time by reducing processing time as well as mail and clearing time. (Chapter 15)

long-term debt
Debt for which payment is not due in the current year. (Chapter 3)

long-term (strategic) financial plans
Plans that lay out a company's planned financial actions and the anticipated impact of those actions over periods ranging from 2 to 10 years. (Chapter 4)

low-regular-and-extra dividend policy
A dividend policy based on paying a low regular dividend, supplemented by an additional ("extra") dividend when earnings are higher than normal in a given period. (Chapter 14)

macro political risk
The subjection of all foreign firms to *political risk* (takeover) by a host country because of political change, revolution, or the adoption of new policies. (Chapter 19)

mail float
The time delay between when payment is placed in the mail and when it is received. (Chapter 15)

maintenance clauses
Provisions normally included in an operating lease that require the lessor to maintain the assets and to make insurance and tax payments. (Chapter 17)

managerial finance
Concerns the duties of the *financial manager* in a business. (Chapter 1)

manufacturing resource planning II (MRP II)
A sophisticated computerized system that integrates data from numerous areas such as finance, accounting, marketing, engineering, and manufacturing and generates production plans as well as numerous financial and management reports. (Chapter 15)

marginal cost–benefit analysis
Economic principle that states that financial decisions should be made and actions taken only when the added benefits exceed the added costs. (Chapter 1)

marginal tax rate
The rate at which *additional income* is taxed. (Chapter 2)

marketable securities
Short-term debt instruments, such as U.S. Treasury bills, commercial paper, and negotiable certificates of deposit issued by government, business, and financial institutions, respectively. (Chapter 2)

market/book (M/B) ratio
Provides an assessment of how investors view the firm's performance. Firms expected to earn high returns relative to their risk typically sell at higher M/B multiples. (Chapter 3)

market makers
Securities dealers who "make markets" by offering to buy or sell certain securities at stated prices. (Chapter 2)

market premium
The amount by which the market value exceeds the straight or conversion value of a convertible security. (Chapter 17)

market ratios
Relate a firm's market value, as measured by its current share price, to certain accounting values. (Chapter 3)

market return
The return on the market portfolio of all traded securities. (Chapter 8)

market segmentation theory
Theory suggesting that the market for loans is segmented on the basis of maturity and that the supply of and demand for loans within each segment determine its prevailing interest rate; the slope of the yield curve is determined by the general relationship between the prevailing rates in each market segment. (Chapter 6)

market value weights
Weights that use market values to measure the proportion of each type of capital in the firm's financial structure (Chapter 9).

materials requirement planning (MRP) system
Inventory management technique that applies EOQ concepts and a computer to compare production needs to available inventory balances and determine when orders should be placed for various items on a product's *bill of materials*. (Chapter 15)

Mercosur
A major South American trading bloc that includes countries that account for more than half of total Latin American GDP. (Chapter 19)

merger
The combination of two or more firms, in which the resulting firm maintains the identity of one of the firms, usually the larger. (Chapter 18)

micro political risk
The subjection of an individual firm, a specific industry, or companies from a particular foreign country to *political risk* (takeover) by a host country. (Chapter 19)

mixed stream
A stream of unequal periodic cash flows that reflect no particular pattern. (Chapter 5)

modified accelerated cost recovery system (MACRS)
System used to determine the depreciation of assets for tax purposes. (Chapter 4)

modified DuPont formula
Relates the firm's *return on total assets (ROA)* to its *return on common equity (ROE)* using the *financial leverage multiplier (FLM)*. (Chapter 3)

monetary union
The official melding of the national currencies of the EU nations into one currency, the *euro,* on January 1, 2002. (Chapter 19)

money market
A financial relationship created between suppliers and demanders of *short-term funds*. (Chapter 2)

mortgage-backed securities
Securities that represent claims on the cash flows generated by a pool of mortgages. (Chapter 2)

mortgage bonds
See Table 6.4.

multinational companies (MNCs)
Firms that have international assets and operations in foreign markets and draw part of their total revenue and profits from such markets. (Chapter 19)

multiple IRRs
More than one IRR resulting from a capital budgeting project with a *nonconventional cash flow pattern;* the maximum number of IRRs for a project is equal to the number of sign changes in its cash flows. (Chapter 10)

mutually exclusive projects
Projects that compete with one another, so that the acceptance of one *eliminates* from further consideration all other projects that serve a similar function. (Chapter 10)

Nasdaq market
An all-electronic trading platform used to execute securities trades. (Chapter 2)

national entry control systems
Comprehensive rules, regulations, and incentives introduced by host governments to regulate inflows of *foreign direct investments* from MNCs and at the same time extract more benefits from their presence. (Chapter 19)

negatively correlated
Describes two series that move in opposite directions. (Chapter 8)

net cash flow
The mathematical difference between the firm's cash receipts and its cash disbursements in each period. (Chapter 4)

net operating profits after taxes (NOPAT)
A firm's earnings before interest and after taxes, EBIT $\times$ $(1 - T)$. (Chapter 4)

net present value (NPV)
A sophisticated capital budgeting technique; found by subtracting a project's initial investment from the present value of its cash inflows discounted at a rate equal to the firm's cost of capital. (Chapter 10)

net present value approach
An approach to capital rationing that is based on the use of present values to determine the group of projects that will maximize owners' wealth. (Chapter 12)

net present value profile
Graph that depicts a project's NPVs for various discount rates. (Chapter 10)

net proceeds
Funds actually received by the firm from the sale of a security. (Chapter 9)

net profit margin
Measures the percentage of each sales dollar remaining after all costs and expenses, *including* interest, taxes, and preferred stock dividends, have been deducted. (Chapter 3)

net working capital
The difference between the firm's current assets and its current liabilities. (Chapters 11 and 15)

no-par preferred stock
Preferred stock with no stated face value but with a stated annual dollar dividend. (Chapter 7)

nominal (stated) annual rate
Contractual annual rate of interest charged by a lender or promised by a borrower. (Chapter 5)

nominal interest rate
In the international context, the stated interest rate charged on financing when only the MNC parent's currency is involved. (Chapter 19)

nominal rate of interest
The actual rate of interest charged by the supplier of funds and paid by the demander. (Chapter 6)

noncash charge
An expense that is deducted on the income statement but does not involve the actual outlay of cash during the period; includes depreciation, amortization, and depletion. (Chapter 4)

noncumulative (preferred stock)
Preferred stock for which passed (unpaid) dividends do not accumulate. (Chapter 7)

nondiversifiable risk
The relevant portion of an asset's risk attributable to market factors that affect all firms; cannot be eliminated through diversification. Also called *systematic risk*. (Chapter 8)

nonnotification basis
The basis on which a borrower, having pledged an account receivable, continues to collect the account payments without notifying the account customer. (Chapter 16)

nonrecourse basis
The basis on which accounts receivable are sold to a factor with the understanding that the factor accepts all credit risks on the purchased accounts. (Chapter 16)

nonvoting common stock
Common stock that carries no voting rights; issued when the firm wishes to raise capital through the sale of common stock but does not want to give up its voting control. (Chapter 7)

normal probability distribution
A symmetrical probability distribution whose shape resembles a "bell-shaped" curve. (Chapter 8)

normal yield curve
An *upward-sloping* yield curve indicates that long-term interest rates are generally higher than short-term interest rates. (Chapter 6)

North American Free Trade Agreement (NAFTA)
The treaty establishing free trade and open markets among Canada, Mexico, and the United States. (Chapter 19)

notes to the financial statements
Explanatory notes keyed to relevant accounts in the statements; they provide detailed information on the accounting policies, procedures, calculations, and transactions underlying entries in the financial statements. (Chapter 3)

notification basis
The basis on which an account customer whose account has been pledged (or factored) is notified to remit payment directly to the lender (or factor). (Chapter 16)

offshore centers
Certain cities or states (including London, Singapore, Bahrain, Nassau, Hong Kong, and Luxembourg) that have achieved prominence as major centers for Euromarket business. (Chapter 19)

open-market share repurchase
A share repurchase program in which firms simply buy back some of their outstanding shares on the open market. (Chapter 14)

operating breakeven point
The level of sales necessary to cover all *operating costs;* the point at which EBIT = $0. (Chapter 13)

operating cash flow (OCF)
The cash flow a firm generates from its normal operations; calculated as *net operating profits after taxes (NOPAT)* plus depreciation. (Chapter 4)

operating cash inflows
The incremental after-tax cash inflows resulting from implementation of a project during its life. (Chapter 11)

operating-change restrictions
Contractual restrictions that a bank may impose on a firm's financial condition or operations as part of a line-of-credit agreement. (Chapter 16)

operating cycle (OC)
The time from the beginning of the production process to collection of cash from the sale of the finished product. (Chapter 15)

operating expenditure
An outlay of funds by the firm resulting in benefits received *within* 1 year. (Chapter 10)

operating flows
Cash flows directly related to sale and production of the firm's products and services. (Chapter 4)

operating lease
A cancelable contractual arrangement whereby the lessee agrees to make periodic payments to the lessor, often for 5 or fewer years, to obtain an asset's services; generally, the total payments over the term of the lease are *less* than the lessor's initial cost of the leased asset. (Chapter 17)

operating leverage
The use of *fixed operating costs* to magnify the effects of changes in sales on the firm's earnings before interest and taxes. (Chapter 13)

operating profit margin
Measures the percentage of each sales dollar remaining after all costs and expenses *other than* interest, taxes, and preferred stock dividends are deducted; the "pure profits" earned on each sales dollar. (Chapter 3)

operating unit
A part of a business, such as a plant, division, product line, or subsidiary, that contributes to the actual operations of the firm. (Chapter 18)

opportunity costs
Cash flows that could be realized from the best alternative use of an owned asset. (Chapter 11)

optimal capital structure
The capital structure at which the weighted average cost of capital is minimized, thereby maximizing the firm's value. (Chapter 13)

option
An instrument that provides its holder with an opportunity to purchase or sell a specified asset at a stated price on or before a set *expiration date*. (Chapter 17)

order costs
The fixed clerical costs of placing and receiving an inventory order. (Chapter 15)

ordinary annuity
An annuity for which the cash flow occurs at the *end* of each period. (Chapter 5)

ordinary income
Income earned through the sale of a firm's goods or services. (Chapter 2)

outstanding shares
Issued shares of common stock held by investors, including both private and public investors. (Chapter 7)

overhanging issue
A convertible security that cannot be forced into conversion by using the call feature. (Chapter 17)

over-the-counter (OTC) market
Market where smaller, unlisted securities are traded. (Chapter 2)

paid-in capital in excess of par
The amount of proceeds in excess of the par value received from the original sale of common stock. (Chapter 3)

partnership
A business owned by two or more people and operated for profit. (Chapter 1)

par-value common stock
An arbitrary value established for legal purposes in the firm's corporate charter and which can be used to find the total number of shares outstanding by dividing it into the book value of common stock. (Chapter 7)

par-value preferred stock
Preferred stock with a stated face value that is used with the specified dividend percentage to determine the annual dollar dividend. (Chapter 7)

payback period
The amount of time required for a firm to recover its initial investment in a project, as calculated from cash *inflows*. (Chapter 10)

payment date
Set by the firm's directors, the actual date on which the firm mails the dividend payment to the holders of record. (Chapter 14)

payout policy
Decisions that a firm makes regarding whether to distribute cash to shareholders, how much cash to distribute, and the means by which cash should be distributed. (Chapter 14)

pecking order
A hierarchy of financing that begins with retained earnings, which is followed by debt financing and finally external equity financing. (Chapter 13)

percentage advance
The percentage of the book value of the collateral that constitutes the principal of a secured loan. (Chapter 16)

percent-of-sales method
A simple method for developing the pro forma income statement; it forecasts sales and then expresses the various income statement items as percentages of projected sales. (Chapter 4)

perfectly negatively correlated
Describes two *negatively correlated* series that have a *correlation coefficient* of −1. (Chapter 8)

perfectly positively correlated
Describes two *positively correlated* series that have a *correlation coefficient* of +1. (Chapter 8)

performance plans
Plans that tie management compensation to measures such as EPS or growth in EPS. *Performance shares* and/or *cash bonuses* are used as compensation under these plans. (Chapter 1)

performance shares
Shares of stock given to management for meeting stated performance goals. (Chapter 1)

permanent funding requirement
A constant investment in operating assets resulting from constant sales over time. (Chapter 15)

perpetuity
An annuity with an infinite life, providing continual annual cash flow. (Chapter 5)

pledge of accounts receivable
The use of a firm's accounts receivable as security, or collateral, to obtain a short-term loan. (Chapter 16)

poison pill
A takeover defense in which a firm issues securities that give their holders certain rights that become effective when a takeover is attempted; these rights make the target firm less desirable to a hostile acquirer. (Chapter 18)

political risk
Risk that arises from the possibility that a host government will take actions harmful to foreign investors or that political turmoil will endanger investments. (Chapter 8)

political risk
The potential discontinuity or seizure of an MNC's operations in a host country via the host's implementation of specific rules and regulations. (Chapter 19)

portfolio
A collection, or group, of assets. (Chapter 8)

positively correlated
Describes two series that move in the same direction. (Chapter 8)

preemptive right
Allows common stockholders to maintain their proportionate ownership in the corporation when new shares are issued, thus protecting them from dilution of their ownership. (Chapter 7)

preferred stock
A special form of ownership having a fixed periodic dividend that must be paid prior to payment of any dividends to common stockholders. (Chapter 2)

premium
The amount by which a bond sells at a value that is greater than its par value. (Chapter 6)

present value
The current dollar value of a future amount—the amount of money that would have to be invested today at a given interest rate over a specified period to equal the future amount. (Chapter 5)

president or chief executive officer (CEO)
Corporate official responsible for managing the firm's day-to-day operations and carrying out the policies established by the board of directors. (Chapter 1)

price/earnings multiple approach
A popular technique used to estimate the firm's share value; calculated by multiplying the firm's expected earnings per share (EPS) by the average price/earnings (P/E) ratio for the industry. (Chapter 7)

price/earnings (P/E) ratio
Measures the amount that investors are willing to pay for each dollar of a firm's earnings; the higher the P/E ratio, the greater the investor confidence. (Chapter 3)

primary market
Financial market in which securities are initially issued; the only market in which the issuer is directly involved in the transaction. (Chapter 2)

prime rate of interest (prime rate)
The lowest rate of interest charged by leading banks on business loans to their most important business borrowers. (Chapter 16)

principal
The amount of money on which interest is paid. (Chapter 5)

principal–agent relationship
An arrangement in which an agent acts on the behalf of a principal. For example, shareholders of a company (principals) elect management (agents) to act on their behalf. (Chapter 1)

privately owned (stock)
The common stock of a firm is owned by private investors; this stock is not publicly traded. (Chapter 7)

private placement
The sale of a new security directly to an investor or group of investors. (Chapter 2)

probability
The *chance* that a given outcome will occur. (Chapter 8)

probability distribution
A model that relates probabilities to the associated outcomes. (Chapter 8)

proceeds from sale of old asset
The cash inflows, net of any removal or cleanup costs, resulting from the sale of an existing asset. (Chapter 11)

processing float
The time between receipt of a payment and its deposit into the firm's account. (Chapter 15)

profitability
The relationship between revenues and costs generated by using the firm's assets—both current and fixed—in productive activities. (Chapter 15)

pro forma statements
Projected, or forecast, income statements and balance sheets. (Chapter 4)

prospectus
A portion of a security registration statement that describes the key aspects of the issue, the issuer, and its management and financial position. (Chapter 7)

proxy battle
The attempt by a nonmanagement group to gain control of the management of a firm by soliciting a sufficient number of proxy votes. (Chapter 7)

proxy statement
A statement transferring the votes of a stockholder to another party. (Chapter 7)

Public Company Accounting Oversight Board (PCAOB)
A not-for-profit corporation established by the *Sarbanes-Oxley Act of 2002* to protect the interests of investors and further the public interest in the preparation of informative, fair, and independent audit reports. (Chapter 3)

publicly owned (stock)
The common stock of a firm is owned by public investors; this stock is publicly traded. (Chapter 7)

public offering
The sale of either bonds or stocks to the general public. (Chapter 2)

purchase options
Provisions frequently included in both operating and financial leases that allow the lessee to purchase the leased asset at maturity, typically for a prespecified price. (Chapter 17)

pure economic profit
A profit above and beyond the normal competitive rate of return in a line of business. (Chapter 10)

putable bonds
See Table 6.5.

put option
An option to *sell* a specified number of shares of a stock (typically 100) on or before a specified future date at a stated price. (Chapter 17)

pyramiding
An arrangement among holding companies wherein one holding company controls other holding companies, thereby causing an even greater magnification of earnings and losses. (Chapter 18)

quarterly compounding
Compounding of interest over four periods within the year. (Chapter 5)

quick (acid-test) ratio
A measure of liquidity calculated by dividing the firm's current assets minus inventory by its current liabilities. (Chapter 3)

range
A measure of an asset's risk, which is found by subtracting the return associated with the pessimistic (worst) outcome from the return associated with the optimistic (best) outcome. (Chapter 8)

ranking approach
The ranking of capital expenditure projects on the basis of some predetermined measure, such as the rate of return. (Chapter 10)

ratio analysis
Involves methods of calculating and interpreting financial ratios to analyze and monitor the firm's performance. (Chapter 3)

ratio of exchange
The ratio of the amount *paid* per share of the target company to the market price per share of the acquiring firm. (Chapter 18)

ratio of exchange in market price
Indicates the market price per share of the acquiring firm paid for each dollar of market price per share of the target firm. (Chapter 18)

real options
Opportunities that are embedded in capital projects that enable managers to alter their cash flows and risk in a way that affects project acceptability (NPV). Also called *strategic options*. (Chapter 12)

real rate of interest
The rate that creates equilibrium between the supply of savings and the demand for investment funds in a perfect world, without inflation, where suppliers and demanders of funds have no liquidity preferences and there is no risk. (Chapter 6)

recapitalization
The reorganization procedure under which a failed firm's debts are generally exchanged for equity or the maturities of existing debts are extended. (Chapter 18)

recaptured depreciation
The portion of an asset's sale price that is above its book value and below its initial purchase price. (Chapter 11)

recovery period
The appropriate depreciable life of a particular asset as determined by MACRS. (Chapter 4)

red herring
A preliminary prospectus made available to prospective investors during the waiting period between the registration statement's filing with the SEC and its approval. (Chapter 7)

regular dividend policy
A dividend policy based on the payment of a fixed-dollar dividend in each period. (Chapter 14)

relevant cash flows
The *incremental cash outflow (investment) and resulting subsequent inflows* associated with a proposed capital expenditure. (Chapter 11)

renewal options
Provisions especially common in operating leases that grant the lessee the right to re-lease assets at the expiration of the lease. (Chapter 17)

reorder point
The point at which to reorder inventory, expressed as days of lead time × daily usage. (Chapter 15)

required return
Usually applied to equity instruments such as common stock; the cost of funds obtained by selling an ownership interest. (Chapter 6)

required total financing
Amount of funds needed by the firm if the ending cash for the period is less than the desired minimum cash balance; typically represented by notes payable. (Chapter 4)

residual theory of dividends
A school of thought that suggests that the dividend paid by a firm should be viewed as a *residual*—the amount left over after all acceptable investment opportunities have been undertaken. (Chapter 14)

restrictive covenants
Provisions in a bond indenture that place operating and financial constraints on the borrower. (Chapter 6)

retained earnings
The cumulative total of all earnings, net of dividends, that have been retained and reinvested in the firm since its inception. (Chapter 3)

return on common equity (ROE)
Measures the return earned on the common stockholders' investment in the firm. (Chapter 3)

return on total assets (ROA)
Measures the overall effectiveness of management in generating profits with its available assets; also called the *return on investment (ROI)*. (Chapter 3)

reverse stock split
A method used to raise the market price of a firm's stock by exchanging a certain number of outstanding shares for one new share. (Chapter 14)

revolving credit agreement
A line of credit *guaranteed* to a borrower by a commercial bank regardless of the scarcity of money. (Chapter 16)

rights
Financial instruments that allow stockholders to purchase additional shares at a price below the market price, in direct proportion to their number of owned shares. (Chapter 7)

risk
A measure of the uncertainty surrounding the return that an investment will earn or, more formally, *the variability of returns associated with a given asset*. (Chapter 8)

risk
The chance that actual outcomes may differ from those expected. (Chapter 1)

risk (in capital budgeting)
The uncertainty surrounding the cash flows that a project will generate or, more formally, the degree of variability of cash flows. (Chapter 12)

risk (of insolvency)
The probability that a firm will be unable to pay its bills as they come due. (Chapter 15)

risk-adjusted discount rate (RADR)
The rate of return that must be earned on a given project to compensate the firm's owners adequately—that is, to maintain or improve the firm's share price. (Chapter 12)

risk averse
Requiring compensation to bear risk. (Chapter 1)

risk averse
The attitude toward risk in which investors would require an increased return as compensation for an increase in risk. (Chapter 8)

risk-free rate of return, (R_F)
The required return on a *risk-free asset,* typically a 3-month *U.S. Treasury bill.* (Chapter 8)

risk neutral
The attitude toward risk in which investors choose the investment with the higher return regardless of its risk. (Chapter 8)

risk seeking
The attitude toward risk in which investors prefer investments with greater risk even if they have lower expected returns. (Chapter 8)

S corporation (S corp)
See Chapter 1 "In More Depth" feature.

safety stock
Extra inventory that is held to prevent stockouts of important items. (Chapter 15)

sale-leaseback arrangement
A lease under which the lessee sells an asset to a prospective lessor and then *leases back* the same asset, making fixed periodic payments for its use. (Chapter 17)

sales forecast
The prediction of the firm's sales over a given period, based on external and/or internal data; used as the key input to the short-term financial planning process. (Chapter 4)

Sarbanes-Oxley Act of 2002 (SOX)
An act aimed at eliminating corporate disclosure and conflict of interest problems. Contains provisions about corporate financial disclosures and the relationships among corporations, analysts, auditors, attorneys, directors, officers, and shareholders. (Chapter 1)

scenario analysis
An approach for assessing risk that uses several possible alternative outcomes (scenarios) to obtain a sense of the variability among returns. (Chapter 8)

seasonal funding requirement
An investment in operating assets that varies over time as a result of cyclic sales. (Chapter 15)

secondary market
Financial market in which preowned securities (those that are not new issues) are traded. (Chapter 2)

secured creditors
Creditors who have specific assets pledged as collateral and, in liquidation of the failed firm, receive proceeds from the sale of those assets. (Chapter 18)

secured short-term financing
Short-term financing (loan) that has specific assets pledged as collateral. (Chapter 16)

Securities Act of 1933
An act that regulates the sale of securities to the public via the primary market. (Chapter 2)

Securities and Exchange Commission (SEC)
The primary government agency responsible for enforcing federal securities laws. (Chapter 2)

Securities Exchange Act of 1934
An act that regulates the trading of securities such as stocks and bonds in the secondary market. (Chapter 2)

securities exchanges
Organizations that provide the marketplace in which firms can raise funds through the sale of new securities and purchasers can resell securities. (Chapter 2)

securitization
The process of pooling mortgages or other types of loans and then selling claims or securities against that pool in the secondary market. (Chapter 2)

security agreement
The agreement between the borrower and the lender that specifies the collateral held against a secured loan. (Chapter 16)

security market line (SML)
The depiction of the *capital asset pricing model (CAPM)* as a graph that reflects the required return in the marketplace for each level of nondiversifiable risk (beta). (Chapter 8)

selling group
A large number of brokerage firms that join the originating investment banker(s); each accepts responsibility for selling a certain portion of a new security issue on a commission basis. (Chapter 7)

semiannual compounding
Compounding of interest over two periods within the year. (Chapter 5)

shadow banking system
A group of institutions that engage in lending activities, much like traditional banks, but do not accept deposits and therefore are not subject to the same regulations as traditional banks. (Chapter 2)

shark repellents
Antitakeover amendments to a corporate charter that constrain the firm's ability to transfer managerial control of the firm as a result of a merger. (Chapter 18)

short-term (operating) financial plans
Specify short-term financial actions and the anticipated impact of those actions. (Chapter 4)

short-term, self-liquidating loan
An unsecured short-term loan in which the use to which the borrowed money is put provides the mechanism through which the loan is repaid. (Chapter 16)

signal
A financing action by management that is believed to reflect its view of the firm's stock value; generally, debt financing is viewed as a *positive signal* that management believes the stock is "undervalued," and a stock issue is viewed as a *negative signal* that management believes the stock is "overvalued." (Chapter 13)

simulation
A statistics-based behavioral approach that applies predetermined probability distributions and random numbers to estimate risky outcomes. (Chapter 12)

single-payment note
A short-term, one-time loan made to a borrower who needs funds for a specific purpose for a short period. (Chapter 16)

sinking-fund requirement
A restrictive provision often included in a bond indenture, providing for the systematic retirement of bonds prior to their maturity. (Chapter 6)

small (ordinary) stock dividend
A stock dividend representing less than 20 percent to 25 percent of the common stock outstanding when the dividend is declared. (Chapter 14)

sole proprietorship
A business owned by one person and operated for his or her own profit. (Chapter 1)

spin-off
A form of divestiture in which an operating unit becomes an independent company through the issuance of shares in it, on a pro rata basis, to the parent company's shareholders. (Chapter 18)

spontaneous liabilities
Financing that arises from the normal course of business; the two major short-term sources of such liabilities are accounts payable and accruals. (Chapter 16)

spot exchange rate
The rate of exchange between two currencies on any given day. (Chapter 19)

stakeholders
Groups such as employees, customers, suppliers, creditors, owners, and others who have a direct economic link to the firm. (Chapter 1)

standard debt provisions
Provisions in a *bond indenture* specifying certain record-keeping and general business practices that the bond issuer must follow; normally, they do not place a burden on a financially sound business. (Chapter 6)

standard deviation (σ_r)
The most common statistical indicator of an asset's risk; it measures the dispersion around the expected value. (Chapter 8)

statement of cash flows
Provides a summary of the firm's operating, investment, and financing cash flows and reconciles them with changes in its cash and marketable securities during the period. (Chapter 3)

statement of retained earnings
Reconciles the net income earned during a given year, and any cash dividends paid, with the change in retained earnings between the start and the end of that year. An abbreviated form of the *statement of stockholders' equity*. (Chapter 3)

statement of stockholders' equity
Shows all equity account transactions that occurred during a given year. (Chapter 3)

stock dividend
The payment, to existing owners, of a dividend in the form of stock. (Chapter 14)

stockholders
The owners of a corporation, whose ownership, or equity, takes the form of either common stock or preferred stock. (Chapter 1)

stockholders' report
Annual report that publicly owned corporations must provide to stockholders; it summarizes and documents the firm's financial activities during the past year. (Chapter 3)

stock options
Options extended by the firm that allow management to benefit from increases in stock prices over time. (Chapter 1)

stock purchase warrants
Instruments that give their holders the right to purchase a certain number of shares of the issuer's common stock at a specified price over a certain period of time. (Chapters 6 and 17)

stock split
A method commonly used to lower the market price of a firm's stock by increasing the number of shares belonging to each shareholder. (Chapter 14)

stock swap transaction
An acquisition method in which the acquiring firm exchanges its shares for shares of the target company according to a predetermined ratio. (Chapter 18)

straight bond
A bond that is nonconvertible, having no conversion feature. (Chapter 17)

straight bond value
The price at which a convertible bond would sell in the market without the conversion feature. (Chapter 17)

straight preferred stock
Preferred stock that is nonconvertible, having no conversion feature. (Chapter 17)

strategic merger
A merger transaction undertaken to achieve economies of scale. (Chapter 18)

stretching accounts payable
Paying bills as late as possible without damaging the firm's credit rating. (Chapter 16)

strike price
The price at which the holder of a call option can buy (or the holder of a put option can sell) a specified amount of stock at any time prior to the option's expiration date. (Chapter 17)

subordinated debentures
See Table 6.4.

subordination
In a bond indenture, the stipulation that subsequent creditors agree to wait until all claims of the *senior debt* are satisfied. (Chapter 6)

subsidiaries
The companies controlled by a holding company. (Chapter 18)

sunk costs
Cash outlays that have already been made (past outlays) and therefore have no effect on the cash flows relevant to a current decision. (Chapter 11)

supervoting shares
Stock that carries with it multiple votes per share rather than the single vote per share typically given on regular shares of common stock. (Chapter 7)

takeover defenses
Strategies for fighting hostile takeovers. (Chapter 18)

target company
The firm in a merger transaction that the acquiring company is pursuing. (Chapter 18)

target dividend-payout ratio
A dividend policy under which the firm attempts to pay out a certain percentage of earnings as a stated dollar dividend and adjusts that dividend toward a target payout as proven earnings increases occur. (Chapter 14)

target weights
Either book or market value weights based on *desired* capital structure proportions. (Chapter 9)

tax loss carryforward
In a merger, the tax loss of one of the firms that can be applied against a limited amount of future income of the merged firm over 20 years or until the total tax loss has been fully recovered, whichever comes first. (Chapter 18)

tax on sale of old asset
Tax that depends on the relationship between the old asset's sale price and book value and on existing government tax rules. (Chapter 11)

temporal method
A method that requires specific assets and liabilities to be translated at so-called historical exchange rates and foreign-exchange translation gains or losses to be reflected in the current year's income. (Chapter 19)

tender offer repurchase
A repurchase program in which a firm offers to repurchase a fixed number of shares, usually at a premium relative to the market value, and shareholders decide whether or not they want to sell back their shares at that price. (Chapter 14)

term structure of interest rates
The relationship between the maturity and rate of return for bonds with similar levels of risk. (Chapter 6)

terminal cash flow
The after-tax nonoperating cash flow occurring in the final year of a project. It is usually attributable to liquidation of the project. (Chapter 11)

time line
A horizontal line on which time zero appears at the leftmost end and future periods are marked from left to right; can be used to depict investment cash flows. (Chapter 5)

time-series analysis
Evaluation of the firm's financial performance over time using financial ratio analysis. (Chapter 3)

times interest earned ratio
Measures the firm's ability to make contractual interest payments; sometimes called the *interest coverage ratio*. (Chapter 3)

total asset turnover
Indicates the efficiency with which the firm uses its assets to generate sales. (Chapter 3)

total cost of inventory
The sum of order costs and carrying costs of inventory. (Chapter 15)

total leverage
The use of *fixed costs, both operating and financial,* to magnify the effects of changes in sales on the firm's earnings per share. (Chapter 13)

total rate of return
The total gain or loss experienced on an investment over a given period of time; calculated by dividing the asset's cash distributions during the period, plus change in value, by its beginning-of-period investment value. (Chapter 8)

total risk
The combination of a security's *nondiversifiable risk* and *diversifiable risk.* (Chapter 8)

transfer prices
Prices that subsidiaries charge each other for the goods and services traded between them. (Chapter 12)

treasurer
The firm's chief financial manager, who manages the firm's cash, oversees its pension plans, and manages key risks. (Chapter 1)

treasury stock
Issued shares of common stock held by the firm; often these shares have been repurchased by the firm. (Chapter 7)

trust receipt inventory loan
A secured short-term loan against inventory under which the lender advances 80 to 100 percent of the cost of the borrower's relatively expensive inventory items in exchange for the borrower's promise to repay the lender, with accrued interest, immediately after the sale of each item of collateral. (Chapter 16)

trustee
A paid individual, corporation, or commercial bank trust department that acts as the third party to a *bond indenture* and can take specified actions on behalf of the bondholders if the terms of the indenture are violated. (Chapter 6)

two-bin method
Unsophisticated inventory-monitoring technique that is typically applied to C group items and involves reordering inventory when one of two bins is empty. (Chapter 15)

two-tier offer
A *tender offer* in which the terms offered are more attractive to those who tender shares early. (Chapter 18)

U.S. Treasury bills (T-bills)
Short-term IOUs issued by the U.S. Treasury; considered the *risk-free asset.* (Chapter 8)

uncorrelated
Describes two series that lack any interaction and therefore have a *correlation coefficient* close to zero. (Chapter 8)

underpriced
Stock sold at a price below its current market price, P_0. (Chapter 9)

underwriting
The role of the investment banker in bearing the risk of reselling, at a profit, the securities purchased from an issuing corporation at an agreed-on price. (Chapter 7)

underwriting syndicate
A group of other bankers formed by an *investment banker* to share the financial risk associated with underwriting new securities. (Chapter 7)

unlimited funds
The financial situation in which a firm is able to accept all independent projects that provide an acceptable return. (Chapter 10)

unlimited liability
The condition of a sole proprietorship (or general partnership), giving creditors the right to make claims against the owner's personal assets to recover debts owed by the business. (Chapter 1)

unsecured short-term financing
Short-term financing obtained without pledging specific assets as collateral. (Chapter 16)

unsecured, or general, creditors
Creditors who have a general claim against all the firm's assets other than those specifically pledged as collateral. (Chapter 18)

valuation
The process that links risk and return to determine the worth of an asset. (Chapter 6)

variable-growth model
A dividend valuation approach that allows for a change in the dividend growth rate. (Chapter 7)

venture capital
Privately raised external equity capital used to fund early-stage firms with attractive growth prospects. (Chapter 7)

venture capitalists (VCs)
Providers of venture capital; typically, formal businesses that maintain strong oversight over the firms they invest in and that have clearly defined exit strategies. (Chapter 7)

vertical merger
A merger in which a firm acquires *a supplier or a customer*. (Chapter 18)

voluntary reorganization
A petition filed by a failed firm on its own behalf for reorganizing its structure and paying its creditors. (Chapter 18)

voluntary settlement
An arrangement between an insolvent or bankrupt firm and its creditors enabling it to bypass many of the costs involved in legal bankruptcy proceedings. (Chapter 18)

warehouse receipt loan
A secured short-term loan against inventory under which the lender receives control of the pledged inventory collateral, which is stored by a designated warehousing company on the lender's behalf. (Chapter 16)

warrant premium
The difference between the market value and the theoretical value of a warrant. (Chapter 17)

weighted average cost of capital (WACC), r_a
Reflects the expected average future cost of capital over the long run; found by weighting the cost of each specific type of capital by its proportion in the firm's capital structure. (Chapter 9)

white knight
A takeover defense in which the target firm finds an acquirer more to its liking than the initial hostile acquirer and prompts the two to compete to take over the firm. (Chapter 18)

widely owned (stock)
The common stock of a firm is owned by many unrelated individual or institutional investors. (Chapter 7)

wire transfer
An electronic communication that, via bookkeeping entries, removes funds from the payer's bank and deposits them in the payee's bank. (Chapter 15)

working capital
Current assets, which represent the portion of investment that circulates from one form to another in the ordinary conduct of business. (Chapter 15)

working capital (or short-term financial) management
Management of current assets and current liabilities. (Chapter 15)

World Trade Organization (WTO)
International body that polices world trading practices and mediates disputes among member countries. (Chapter 19)

yield curve
A graphic depiction of the term structure of interest rates. (Chapter 6)

yield to maturity
Compound annual rate of return earned on a debt security purchased on a given day and held to maturity. (Chapter 6)

zero-balance account (ZBA)
A disbursement account that always has an end-of-day balance of zero because the firm deposits money to cover checks drawn on the account only as they are presented for payment each day. (Chapter 15)

zero- (or low-) coupon bonds
See Table 6.5.

zero-growth model
An approach to dividend valuation that assumes a constant, nongrowing dividend stream. (Chapter 7)

Credits

p. 3: Archivo particular/GDA Photo Service/Newscom

p. 31: Richard B. Levine/Levine Roberts Photography/Newscom

p. 57: Kimimasa Mayama/Bloomberg/Getty Images

p. 114: Zuma Press/Newscom

p. 160: John A. Rizzo/PhotoDisc/Getty Images

p. 221: Sara Piaseczynski

p. 265: Reprinted with permission by A123 Systems.

p. 309: © 2010 Morningstar, Inc. All Rights Reserved. The information contained herein: (1) is proprietary to Morningstar and/or its content providers; (2) may not be copied or distributed; (3) does not constitute investment advice offered by Morningstar; and (4) is not warranted to be accurate, complete or timely. Neither Morningstar nor its content providers are responsible for any damages or losses arising from any use of this information. Past performance is no guarantee of future results. Use of information from Morningstar does not necessarily constitute agreement by Morningstar, Inc. of any investment philosophy or strategy presented in this publication.

p. 357: Bloomberg/Getty Images

p. 389: Jenny Matthews/Alamy

p. 427: Digital Vision/Getty Images

p. 464: US Coast Guard/Sipa Press/Newscom

p. 507: Blickwinkel/Alamy

p. 560: Richard Levine/Alamy

p. 599: James Steidl/Dreamstime

p. 641: AP Images

p. 677: © Robert Sorbo/Reuters/Corbis

p. 715: Douglas Healey/AP Images

p. 758: Bruce Connolly/Corbis

Index

Note: Boldface page numbers indicate pages where terms are defined.

J

K

L

M

N

Q

R

S